REGIMENTAL RECORDS
OF THE
ROYAL WELCH FUSILIERS

REGIMENTAL RECORDS
OF THE
ROYAL WELCH FUSILIERS
(LATE THE 23RD FOOT)

COMPILED BY

A. D. L. CARY, O.B.E., & STOUPPE McCANCE
LIBRARIAN, R.U.S.I. CAPTAIN (LATE R.A.S.C.)

WITH ILLUSTRATIONS BY
GERALD C. HUDSON
CAPTAIN (LATE DURHAM L.I.)

VOL. II
1816—1914 (JULY)

The Naval & Military Press Ltd

❖

Reproduced by kind permission of the Regimental Trustees

Published by
The Naval & Military Press Ltd
Unit 10, Ridgewood Industrial Park,
Uckfield, East Sussex,
TN22 5QE England
Tel: +44 (0) 1825 749494
Fax: +44 (0) 1825 765701
www.naval-military-press.com
© The Naval & Military Press Ltd 2005

In reprinting in facsimile from the original, any imperfections are inevitably reproduced and the quality may fall short of modern type and cartographic standards.

Printed and bound by Antony Rowe Ltd, Eastbourne

INTRODUCTION

THE compilers have again, in this the second volume of the Regimental Records, to acknowledge the continued help and support rendered to them in every way by Major G. F. Barttelot. They also wish to express their thanks to Colonel R. Broughton Mainwaring, C.M.G., for permission to use his account of the doings of the various detachments of the 1st Battalion during the Burmese War of 1885–87. The Journal and Diaries of the 2nd Battalion in the Expedition to Pekin, kindly lent by Colonel the Hon. R. H. Bertie, C.B., have been of the utmost assistance in supplying interesting regimental and other details which were unobtainable from the ordinary official sources. To General Sir Robert Colleton, Bart., C.B., the compilers are greatly indebted for permission to use *in extenso* his narrative of the part taken by the 1st Battalion in the South African War, and also for the use of his Diary of the Black Mountain Expedition, and to Captain Henry McCance (late The Royal Scots) for again most kindly perusing the proofs.

Notes on " Clothing," " Medals," and " Colours " contributed by the late D. Hastings Irwin have been extensively used in compiling the Appendices on those subjects.

CHRONOLOGICAL SUMMARY

1816.			Stationed at Hamelincourt.
	April	1.	Depôt moved to Deal.
1817.	,,	14.	Moved to Valenciennes.
			Depôt stationed at Deal.
1818.	Aug.	17.	Moved to Cambrai.
	Oct.	26.	Marched to Calais.
	Nov.	2.	Landed at Dover.
	,,	19.	Moved to Deal and embarked for Cork.
	,,	27.	Landed at Cork and moved to Limerick.
	,,		Depôt joined headquarters.
1819.			Stationed at Limerick.
1820.	Dec.		Moved to Dublin.
1821.	Sept.	6.	,, ,, Londonderry.
1822.	April	8.	,, ,, Boyle, co. Roscommon.
1823.	,,	23.	Major-General Sir James Willoughby Gordon, Bart., K.C.B., was appointed Colonel in succession to General Sir Richard Grenville, deceased.
	May.		Moved to Dublin.
	Dec.		Embarked for Gibraltar.
	,,	21, etc.	Arrived at Gibraltar.
	,,		Depôt at Fermoy.
1824.			Stationed at Gibraltar.
	Feb.	25.	Depôt moved to Isle of Wight.
1825.			Stationed at Gibraltar.
	April	26.	Depôt arrived at Plymouth.
	July	20.	,, ,, ,, Brecon.
1826.			Stationed at Gibraltar.
	Dec.	1.	New colours were presented by Lieutenant-General Sir J. W. Gordon.
	May	12.	Depôt arrived in Guernsey.
	Sept.	22.	,, ,, ,, Brecon.
1827.	Jan.	8.	Embarked for Portugal.
	,,	20.	Disembarked at Lisbon.
	Feb.	18.	Arrived at Coimbra.
	Aug.	27.	,, ,, Mafra.
1828.	Mar.	11.	Left Mafra.
	,,	12.	Embarked at Lisbon.
	,,	22.	Disembarked at Gibraltar.

CHRONOLOGICAL SUMMARY

1829.		Stationed at Gibraltar.
1830.		,, ,, ,,
	June.	Depôt moved to Plymouth.
	Nov.	,, ,, ,, Drogheda.
1831.		Stationed at Gibraltar.
	Oct. 10.	Depôt moved to Dublin.
1832.		Stationed at Gibraltar.
	April 19.	Depôt arrived in Belfast
	July 24.	,, ,, ,, Naas.
1833.		Stationed at Gibraltar.
	Feb. 23.	Depôt arrived at Fermoy.
	Mar. 13.	,, ,, ,, Clonmel.
1834.	Oct. 28.	Embarked for Portsmouth.
	Nov. 10.	Disembarked at Portsmouth.
	,, 15.	Arrived at Winchester.
	Aug. 19.	Depôt arrived at Cork, embarked for Portsmouth.
	Nov. 15.	,, ,, ,, Winchester.
1835.	May 18.	Proceeded to Weedon.
	Nov. 19.	,, ,, Manchester.
1836.	Sept. 13.	,, ,, Liverpool and embarked for Dublin.
	,, 21.	Arrived at Kilkenny, etc.
1837.	May 25.	,, ,, Dublin.
1838.	Mar. 17.	Service companies proceeded to Cork, and sailed on 25th for Canada.
	June 12.	,, ,, arrived at Halifax.
	April 1.	Depôt companies formed at Dublin.
	May 14.	,, ,, arrived at Armagh.
1839.		Service companies at Halifax.
	April 26.	Depôt companies at Castlebar.
1840.	Oct. 3.	Service companies embarked at Halifax, landed Montreal on 9th.
	May 1.	Depôt companies moved to Newbridge.
	June 12.	,, ,, left Kingstown, arrived at Chester on 14th.
1841.		Service companies at Montreal.
	May 8.	Depôt companies embarked at Birkenhead, arrived Carlisle 9th.
1842.	July 5.	First battalion moved to Kingston, arrived on 12th.
	May 5.	Reserve battalion formed at Chichester.
	,, 12.	,, ,, embarked at Portsmouth for Kingston, Canada.
	July 6.	,, ,, arrived at Kingston.
	Mar. 19.	Depôt companies left Carlisle for Manchester.
	April.	,, ,, arrived at Chichester.
	May 18.	,, ,, ,, ,, Parkhurst, Isle of Wight.
1843.	Sept. 20.	First battalion left Kingston.
	,, 28.	,, ,, embarked at Quebec for Barbados.
	Oct. 23.	,, ,, arrived in Carlisle Bay.
	,, 26.	,, ,, three companies proceeded to Demarara.
	June 24.	Reserve battalion arrived at London, Canada.

CHRONOLOGICAL SUMMARY

1843.		Depôt companies at Parkhurst.
1844.		A goat was presented to each battalion by Queen Victoria.
	April 9.	First battalion companies rejoined from Demarara.
	Nov. 28.	,, ,, sailed for Trinidad, Grenada, Tobago.
		Reserve battalion at London, Canada West.
	May 19.	Depôt companies proceeded to Guernsey.
	June 15.	,, ,, returned to Parkhurst.
1845.		First battalion at Trinidad, etc.
	May 12.	Reserve battalion left London for Chambley.
		Depôt companies at Parkhurst.
1846.	Dec.	First battalion at Barbados.
		Reserve battalion at Chambley.
		Depôt companies at Parkhurst.
1847.	Mar. 16.	First battalion embarked at Barbados.
	April 3.	,, ,, disembarked at Halifax, N.S.
	July 21.	Reserve battalion moved to Montreal.
		Depôt companies at Parkhurst.
1848.	Sept. 16.	First battalion embarked at Halifax for England.
	Oct. 7.	,, ,, landed at Portsmouth and moved to Winchester.
		Reserve battalion at Montreal.
	,, 16.	Depôt companies joined first battalion at Winchester.
1849.	July 12.	First battalion new colours presented by H.R.H. the Prince Consort at Winchester; the old ones being placed in St. Peter's Church, Carmarthen.
		Reserve battalion at Montreal.
1850.	April 23.	First battalion embarked at Portsmouth, landed at Plymouth on 24th.
	May.	Reserve battalion moved to London, Canada West.
	,, 6.	,, ,, detachment drowned in Lake Erie.
1851.	Jan. 31.	Major-General George Charles D'Aguilar, C.B., was appointed Colonel in succession to General Sir James Willoughby Gordon, G.C.B., deceased.
	July.	First battalion moved to Chester, Liverpool, etc.
	Oct. 9.	,, ,, Queen Victoria visited Liverpool.
		Reserve battalion at London, Canada West.
1852.		First battalion at Chester, Liverpool, etc.
	May.	Reserve battalion moved to Toronto.
1853.	June.	First battalion moved to Isle of Wight.
	July 6.	Reserve battalion moved to Quebec.
	,, 11.	,, ,, sailed for England.
	,, 28.	,, ,, arrived at Parkhurst, and was amalgamated with the first battalion.
1854.	Feb. 23.	Battalion formed of eight service companies and two depôt companies.
	,, 24.	Battalion proceeded to Portsmouth.

CHRONOLOGICAL SUMMARY

1854.	April	4.	Embarked at Portsmouth for Turkey.
	,,	25.	Disembarked at Scutari.
	May	29.	Embarked for Varna, landed there on 31st.
	July	24.	Marched to Monastir.
	Aug.	30.	Embarked for the Crimea.
	Sept.	14.	Disembarked near Lake Kamichla.
	,,	20.	Battle of the Alma.
	Nov.	5.	,, ,, Inkermann.
1855.	Mar.	1.	St. David's Day Dinner held in hut before Sevastopol.
	,,	7.	Attack on the Redan.
	Feb.	8.	Reserve companies, two, formed at Winchester.
	.,,	20.	,, ,, landed at Malta.
	May	22.	Lieutenant-General Henry Rainey, C.B., appointed Colonel in succession to Lieutenant-General Sir George C. D'Aguilar, K.C.B., deceased.
	July.		Reserve companies, two additional formed. Depôt companies at Winchester.
1856.	Mar.	30.	Peace declared.
	June	14.	Embarked for England.
	July	21.	Disembarked at Gosport, proceeded to Aldershot.
	,,	24.	Four reserve companies joined from Malta.
	Nov.	4.	Depôt companies joined from Newport.
1857.	Feb.	9.	Proceeded to Portsmouth.
	May	16–23.	Embarked for China in three divisions; first division proceeded as far as Singapore.
	Aug.	7.	Second and third divisions diverted at the Cape to Calcutta on account of Indian Mutiny.
	Sept.	19.	Second division landed at Calcutta.
	,,	21.	First division landed at Calcutta from Singapore.
	Oct.	27.	Six companies reached Allahabad.
	Nov.	15.	,, ,, joined Sir Colin Campbell's force.
	,,	17.	Advance to relief of the Residency at Lucknow.
	,,	18.	Third division landed at Calcutta.
	,,	22.	Residency relieved, and evacuated.
	Dec.	6.	Capture of three guns from the Gwalior contingent.
	,,	12.	Third division joined headquarters before Cawnpore.
1858.	Jan.	29.	Grenadier and Light Infantry companies to be abolished.
	Feb.	19.	Left Cawnpore.
	Mar.	16.	Residency at Lucknow again taken.
	Nov.	9.	Capture of fort of Simree.
	Mar.	3.	A second battalion formed at Newport, Mon.
	Dec.	7.	Second battalion moved to Aldershot.
1859.	Jan.	15.	First battalion returned to Lucknow.
	Feb.	5.	Second battalion, ten service companies embarked at Portsmouth.
	,,	22.	,, ,, landed at Malta.

CHRONOLOGICAL SUMMARY

1859.	Dec.	21.	Second battalion, new colours presented.
1860.			First battalion remained at Lucknow.
	Dec.	26.	Lieutenant-General Sir W. J. Codrington, K.C.B., was appointed Colonel in succession to Lieutenant-General Henry Rainey, C.B., deceased.
			Second battalion remained in Malta.
1861.	Dec.	1.	First battalion left Lucknow.
	,,	9.	,, ,, arrived at Fyzabad.
			Second battalion remained in Malta.
1862.	Dec.	20.	First battalion moved to Agra.
			Second battalion remained in Malta.
1863.			First battalion remained in Agra.
	Oct.	28.	Second battalion arrived at Gibraltar.
1864.			First battalion remained in Agra.
			Second battalion remained in Gibraltar.
1865.	Dec.	6.	First battalion arrived in Jubbulpore.
			Second battalion remained in Gibraltar.
1866.			First battalion remained in Jubbulpore.
	June	23.	Second battalion embarked for Canada.
	July	13.	,, ,, arrived at Montreal.
1867.	Nov.	30.	First battalion left Jubbulpore.
	Oct.	16.	Second battalion embarked for England.
	,,	29.	,, ,, landed at Portsmouth, proceeded to Newport, Mon.
1868.	Jan.	2.	First battalion arrived at Poona.
	Mar.	10.	,, ,, ,, ,, Colaba, Bombay.
			Second battalion remained at Newport.
1869.	Oct.	8.	First battalion embarked at Bombay.
	Nov.	9.	,, ,, arrived at Portsmouth, proceeded to Devonport.
	May	14.	Second battalion moved to Aldershot.
1870.	Oct.	28.	First battalion proceeded to Newport, etc.
	Mar.	24.	Second battalion proceeded to Chatham.
1871.	Sept.	28.	First battalion proceeded to Pembroke Dock.
	Aug.	2.	Second battalion proceeded to Woolwich.
	,,	31.	,, ,, a wing sent to Windsor Castle.
1872.			First battalion remained at Pembroke Dock.
	Aug.	12.	Second battalion proceeded to Blandford for manœuvres.
	Sept.	13.	,, ,, ,, ,, Portsmouth for embarkation.
	,,	16.	,, ,, disembarked at Kingstown, proceeded to Mullingar.
1873.	July	26.	First battalion embarked, landed at Plymouth and proceeded to Dartmoor for manœuvres.
	Aug.	21.	First battalion proceeded to Aldershot.
	June	11.	Second battalion moved to the Curragh.
	Nov.	20.	,, ,, left the Curragh for Cork.
	,,	21.	,, ,, embarked at Cork for the Ashanti Expedition.
	Dec.	29.	,, ,, arrived off Cape Coast Castle.

CHRONOLOGICAL SUMMARY

1874. Mar. 12. First battalion took part in lining streets of London on the entry of the Duke and Duchess of Edinburgh.
Jan. 6. Second battalion right half landed at Cape Coast Castle.
,, 12. ,, ,, ,, ,, re-embarked.
,, 15. ,, ,, headquarters and 100 disembarked, and proceeded to the front.
,, 29. Second battalion capture of Borborassie.
,, 31. ,, ,, ,, Egginassie.
Feb. 4. ,, ,, entered Coomassie.
,, 6. ,, ,, left Coomassie for the coast, arrived on 20th; embarked on 22nd.
Mar. 20. Second battalion disembarked at Portsmouth, proceeded to Shorncliffe.
May 19. Second battalion proceeded to Aldershot for the day for Review.
Oct. 10. ,, ,, embarked at Portsmouth for Gibraltar, arrived on 17th.

1875. Mar. 16. Lieutenant-General C. Crutchley was appointed Colonel in succession to General Sir W. J. Codrington, transferred to Coldstream Guards.
Oct. 4. First battalion proceeded to Portsmouth, embarked for Ireland.
,, 7. ,, ,, arrived at Queenstown, proceeded to Cork, etc.
Second battalion remained at Gibraltar.

1876. May 10. First battalion proceeded to Dublin.
Second battalion remained at Gibraltar.

1877. May 14. First battalion, two companies proceeded to Enniskillen and two to Londonderry.
July 6. First battalion, two companies proceeded to Enniskillen and two to Londonderry.
,, ,, First battalion, two companies proceeded to Wrexham to help to form the 23rd Brigade Depôt.
Second battalion remained at Gibraltar.

1878. First battalion remained at Enniskillen, etc.
Second battalion remained at Gibraltar.

1879. May 6. First battalion left Enniskillen for Kingstown, arrived Woolwich on 9th.
June 30. First battalion, four companies stationed in Tower of London rejoined headquarters on July 26th.
Second battalion remained at Gibraltar.

1880. Aug. 16. First battalion, presentation of new colours by H.R.H. the Prince of Wales.
,, ,, First battalion embarked at Portsmouth for India.
Sept. 12. ,, ,, landed at Bombay, arrived Jubbulpore on 30th.
Dec. 31. ,, ,, left for Chakrata.
Feb. 14. Second battalion left Gibraltar for Plymouth, disembarked 21st
Mar. 1. Dinner of first and second battalions and depôt at Woolwich.

1881. Mar. 13. First battalion arrived at Chakrata.

CHRONOLOGICAL SUMMARY

1881.	July 1.	The number of the Regiment abolished, the Army reorganised under the Territorial system.
	Nov. 16.	Second battalion proceeded to Pembroke Dock.
1882.	Oct. 31.	First battalion proceeded by route march to Dum Dum.
	Dec. 29.	,, ,, arrived at Benares.
		Second battalion remained at Pembroke Dock.
1883.	Jan. 14.	First battalion marched to Dinapore and entrained for Calcutta.
	,, 18.	,, ,, arrived at Dum Dum.
	Nov. 20.	Second battalion moved to Queenstown, stationed at Templemore.
1884.		First battalion remained at Dum Dum.
		Second battalion remained at Templemore.
1885.	Nov. 2.	First battalion embarked at Calcutta for Rangoon, Burma.
	,, 8.	,, ,, left Rangoon, arrived Thayetmyo on 14th.
	,, 16.	,, ,, capture of Singboungweh.
	,, 25.	,, ,, ,, ,, Myngyan.
	,, 27.	,, ,, Ava Forts occupied.
	,, 28.	,, ,, entered Mandalay.
	Dec. 15.	,, ,, proceeded to Shwebo.
	,, 20.	,, ,, ,, ,, Bhamo.
	July 28.	Second battalion proceeded from Templemore to Fermoy.
1886.		First battalion split up into many detachments.
		Second battalion remained at Fermoy.
1887.	Mar. 2.	First battalion embarked at Bhamo for Mandalay and Rangoon.
	,, 24.	,, ,, ,, ,, Rangoon for Calcutta, disembarked 28th.
	April 2.	,, ,, arrived at Lucknow.
	Aug. 24.	Second battalion moved to Galway, Castlebar, etc.
1888.	Feb. 9.	First battalion medals for the Burmah Campaign presented by Sir F. (afterwards Earl) Roberts, V.C., at Lucknow.
		Second battalion remained at Galway, etc.
1889.		*Bicentenary of the Regiment.*
		First battalion remained at Lucknow.
		Second battalion remained at Galway, etc.
1890.	Nov. 8.	First battalion left for Peshawar, arrived on December 9th.
	July 15.	Second battalion left for the Curragh.
1891.	Mar. 9.	First battalion arrived at Darband for the Black Mountain Expedition.
	,, 14.	First battalion arrived at Tilli.
	,, 23.	,, ,, capture of Seri.
	,, 25.	,, ,, ,, ,, Darbanai.
	June 11.	,, ,, remained on Black Mountain on submission of the Hasanzai, etc.
	Nov. 9.	First battalion returned to Peshawar.
		Second battalion remained at the Curragh.
1892.	April 25.	First battalion moved to Cherat.
	Nov. 20.	,, ,, ,, ,, Peshawar, and to Nowshera on the 22nd.

CHRONOLOGICAL SUMMARY

1892.	Sept.	2.	Second battalion left the Curragh for a march through North Wales, and arrived at Bangor.
	,,	3.	Second battalion at Carnarvon; thence to Portmadoc, 8th; Festiniog, 9th; Bettws-y-coed, 13th; Denbigh, 15th; Ruthin, 17th; Corwen, 19th; Llangollen, 20th; Wrexham, 21st.
	,,	26.	Second battalion entrained for Aldershot.
1893.	Nov.	2.	First battalion left Nowshera by route march for Jhansi. Second battalion remained at Aldershot.
1894.	Feb.	7.	First battalion arrived at Jhansi, etc.
	Sept.	27.	Second battalion moved to Manchester.
1895.			First battalion remained at Jhansi, etc.
	Sept.	20.	Second battalion, unveiling of the west window in Wrexham Church.
1896.	Oct.	16.	First battalion left Jhansi for Aden, arrived on 28th.
	July	8.	Second battalion left Manchester for Malta, disembarking on 16th.
1897.	Nov.	21.	First battalion left Aden, arrived at Devonport on December 9th.
	April	6.	Second battalion embarked for Crete.
1898.	Mar.	31.	General Sir E. G. Bulwer, K.C.B., was appointed Colonel in succession to General Charles Crutchley, deceased.
	Aug.	3.	Second battalion embarked for Egypt.
	Sept.	11.	,, ,, ,, ,, Crete.
	Dec.	12.	,, ,, ,, ,, Hong-Kong.
1899.	Sept.	5.	First battalion moved to Pembroke Dock.
	Oct.	23.	,, ,, embarked for South Africa.
	Nov.	17.	,, ,, disembarked at Durban.
	Dec.	15.	,, ,, Battle of Colenso.
	Jan.	13.	Second battalion disembarked at Hong-Kong.
1900.	Feb.	14.	First battalion, capture of Hussar Hill.
	,,	19.	,, ,, ,, ,, Hlangwane Hill.
	,,	28.	,, ,, Relief of Ladysmith.
	April	15.	,, ,, embarked at Durban for Capetown.
	May	5.	,, ,, action at Rooidam.
	Aug.	7.	,, ,, ,, ,, Tygerfontein.
	Oct.	9.	,, ,, ,, ,, Dwarsvlei.
	,,	25.	,, ,, ,, ,, Frederikstad.
	June	2.	Authority approving of all ranks wearing on full dress " the Flash."
	,,	16.	Second battalion, A, C, and E companies embark for Tientsin.
	,,	22.	,, ,, Relief of Tientsin.
	July	21.	,, ,, headquarters and H company reached Tientsin.
	Aug.	6.	,, ,, capture of Yangtsun.
	,,	14.	,, ,, Relief of Pekin.
	Oct.	18.	,, ,, left for Tientsin.
	Nov.	3.	,, ,, arrived at Hong-Kong.
1901.	April	22.	First battalion action at Brakspruit.
	May	20.	,, ,, moved to Potchefstroom.
	Sept.		,, ,, ,, ,, Scandinavia Drift to occupy blockhouses.

CHRONOLOGICAL SUMMARY

1901.	Dec.		First battalion moved to Bothaville.
	,,	21.	H.R.H. the Prince of Wales was appointed Colonel-in-Chief of the Regiment.
	Mar.	14.	Second battalion, B and D companies embarked for Tientsin.
	,,	,,	,, ,, F and G companies embarked for Pekin.
1902.	May	31.	First battalion, peace concluded at Vereeniging.
	June	3.	,, ,, party left to represent the Regiment at the Coronation of King Edward VII.
	Sept.	17.	First battalion moved to Potchefstroom.
	Nov.	10.	Second battalion embarked for India, arrived at Meerut on 29th.
1903.	Jan.	12.	First battalion arrived at Cape Town.
	Feb.	4.	,, ,, disembarked at Southampton, proceeded to Lichfield.
	May	8.	,, ,, proceeded to Wrexham for the unveiling of the South African and China campaigns Memorial Window.
			Second battalion remained at Meerut.
1904.	July	19.	First battalion proceeded to Liverpool for the visit of King Edward VII.
	Sept.	19.	First battalion proceeded to Aldershot.
	Nov.	26.	Second battalion arrived at Agra.
1905.			First battalion remained at Aldershot.
			Second battalion remained at Agra.
1906.			First battalion remained at Aldershot.
			Second battalion remained at Agra.
1907.	Oct.	2.	First battalion arrived at Cork.
	Dec.	15.	Second battalion embarked at Calcutta for Rangoon.
1908.			First battalion remained at Cork.
	Jan.	8.	Second battalion arrived at Shwebo.
1909.			First battalion remained at Cork.
			Second battalion remained at Shwebo.
1910.	May	6.	H.R.H. the Prince of Wales, Colonel-in-Chief, succeeded as King George V, on the death of King Edward VII.
	Oct.	3.	First battalion arrived in Dublin from the Curragh.
	Dec.	9.	Major-General the Hon. Sir Savage Mostyn, K.C.B., was appointed Colonel in succession to General Sir Edward Bulwer, G.C.B., deceased.
	,,	31.	Second battalion left Rangoon for India.
1911.	May	16.	Centenary of the Battle of Albuhera.
	June	22.	First battalion detachment present at the coronation of King George V.
	July	13.	First battalion present at the Investiture of H.R.H. the Prince of Wales at Carnarvon, returned to Dublin.
	Aug.	18.	First battalion left Dublin for Warrington.
	,,	25.	,, ,, returned to Dublin.
	Jan.	9.	Second battalion arrived at Karachi.
	April	1.	,, ,, ,, ,, Quetta.

CHRONOLOGICAL SUMMARY

1911.	Dec.	7.	Second battalion took part in the ceremonies of the Durbar.
1912.	Nov.	21.	First battalion moved to Portland.
			Second battalion remained at Quetta.
1913.	Aug.	30.	First battalion moved to Windsor.
	Sept.	26.	,, ,, returned to Portland.
			Second battalion remained at Quetta.
1914.	Jan.	10.	First battalion embarked at Southampton for Malta.
	June	2.	Major-General Sir Luke O'Connor appointed Colonel in succession to Major-General the Hon. Sir Savage Mostyn, K.C.B., deceased.
	Sept.	3.	First battalion embarked for England.
	Feb.	16.	Second battalion embarked at Karachi for England.
	Mar.	10.	Second battalion disembarked at Southampton for Portland.

LIST OF ILLUSTRATIONS.

COLOURED PLATES

	FACING PAGE
THE COLOURS	52
OFFICER, 1820	52
BAND, 1848	52
PRIVATE AND BANDSMAN, 1852	52
OFFICER, 1857	52
PRIVATE, 1900	52
OFFICERS, SERGEANT, ETC., 1914	52

BLACK AND WHITE PLATES

THE KING'S COLOUR, 1826	16
"BILLY"	46
PORTRAIT GROUP, 1849	58
MEMORIAL SLAB AND INSCRIPTION AT PORT MAITLAND, CANADA	64
GUN CAPTURED BY CAPTAIN E. W. D. BELL, V.C., AT THE ALMA	74
BURMESE BELL, CAPTURED AT MANDALAY	74
LIEUTENANT-COLONEL E. W. D. BELL, V.C.	78
MAJOR-GENERAL SIR ARTHUR WELLESLEY TORRENS, K.C.B.	96
GENERAL SIR DANIEL LYSONS, G.C.B.	96
GENERAL CHARLES CRUTCHLEY	152

LIST OF ILLUSTRATIONS

	FACING PAGE
EATING THE LEEK, ST. DAVID'S DAY DINNER	159
GENERAL SIR EDWARD E. G. BULWER, G.C.B.	226
MAP OF THE RELIEF OF LADYSMITH	239
SOUTH AFRICAN AND CHINA WARS MEMORIAL	302
MAJOR-GENERAL THE HON SIR SAVAGE L. MOSTYN, K.C.B.	313
MAJOR-GENERAL SIR LUKE O'CONNOR, V.C., K.C.B.	332

REGIMENTAL RECORDS OF THE ROYAL WELCH FUSILIERS
VOL. II.

1816.

In January this year the regiment was quartered at Montmartre. The following month it moved to Hamelincourt and the neighbourhood, where it was cantoned, except for a few weeks, until April 1817. During the month 30 men joined from the depôt.

The strength of the regiment in February was 53 officers, 53 sergeants, 22 drummers, 48 corporals, and 760 privates. In April it was cantoned as follows :

At Hamelincourt (H.Q.)	6 officers,	53 men.
,, Boyelle	2 ,,	40 ,,
,, Moyenneville	3 ,,	64 ,,
,, Boiry St. Rictrude	4 ,,	34 ,,
,, Boiry St. Martin	—	26 ,,
,, Boisleux au Mont	2 officers,	39 ,,
,, Boisleux St. Marc	1 officer,	24 ,,
,, Hénin	2 officers,	40 ,,
,, Boiry Becquerelle	2 ,,	31 ,,
,, St. Léger	1 officer,	51 ,,
,, Croisilles	6 officers,	141 ,,
,, Bullecourt	3 ,,	45 ,,
,, Escont St. Mein	4 ,,	77 ,,
,, Mory	3 ,,	57 ,,

The regiment was inspected on the 20th of May at Hamelincourt by Colonel Sir Edward Blakeney, K.C.B., commanding the 7th Fusiliers.

A Division Order dated Cambrai, 2nd May, in reference to smoking is as follows : " It having been represented by the Civil Authorities that smoking out of doors of houses in the villages is contrary to the Public

Laws, from the danger to which the houses would be exposed from being generally low and thatched, Commanding Officers are requested to take measures to prevent it. Smoking can only be allowed inside the houses."

During the month of May 1 drummer and 20 privates joined from the depôt, and 23 privates were discharged as unfit for further service.

Captain (Brevet Lieut.-Colonel) W. M. Campbell was appointed Brigade Major to the 1st Cavalry Division and Captain H. S. Blanckley D.A.A.G. at headquarters.

On the first anniversary of the Battle of Waterloo the detachment at Mory celebrated the event as described in the following extract from a letter from a British officer in France to his friends in Dumfries:

"Dated MORY, 20 *June* 1816.

"The British Officers in this place celebrated, on Tuesday last, the Anniversary of the battle of Waterloo. It was at first proposed that a regimental dinner should take place at Arras, but, upon reflection, the idea was given up, as it might appear as if we meant to crow over and insult the feelings of the French. It was consequently resolved to spend the day in a jovial, but not in a tumultuous manner. We had horse-racing, gambols, and a dinner upon the ground. The *tout ensemble* of this *fête-champêtre* was delightful. Every thing went off in excellent style. About 60 persons sat down to dinner, when many appropriate toasts, and songs to correspond, were given: 'The Land of Cakes' was not forgotten, nor 'Honest Men and Bonny Lasses.' When the memory of Colonel Ellis was proposed, the following song, composed for the occasion, was sung in good style. The band attended on the occasion. After dinner dancing commenced, which was kept up with great spirit. As soon as the English Ladies retired, the village girls threw off their sabots, and tripped it until a late hour.

"Air—'Jessie the flower of Dumblane.'

"At evening the husbandman gaily was jesting,
  How full and how fair were his hopes of the year!
At night, on their bosom the valiant were resting,
  And crush'd were his hopes ere the morn did appear.
But who shall the harvest, he hoped for, gather?
  No sickle nor scythe its rich honours shall reap:
But musket and sabre, and cannon shall rather
  Strew fields of the mighty in many a heap.

"Oh! Waterloo's face, ere the toil of that battle,
  Blush'd, lovely and fresh, in the sun's beaming glow:
But, ah! ere that sun on the mountains did settle
  What torrents of blood o'er its beauties did flow!

>   Oh! dread was the shower of the death-bringing metal,
>   And loud was the thunder and piercing hurra:
>   And, ah! the rude charge of the bayonet was fatal,
>   And great was the harvest of death on that day.
>
> " Oh! bright are her smiles, while Britain is boasting
>   What honours she earn'd by the blood of the brave:
>   A tear too is mingled—for those she joy'd most in
>   Are silent for ever—are cold in the grave.
>   There Picton the dauntless, and Ponsonby's glory,
>   Macara, and Cameron, in brilliancy fell,
>   There thousands, whose deeds shall be written in story,
>   There Ellis who led us, and fought us so well.
>
> " Oh! fill the red goblet—'tis friendship invites us,
>   In memory of those who for honour have died:
>   Another—'tis gratitude's warmth that incites us—
>   To Ellis, our Colonel, our friend and our pride.
>   Still, still on this day shall thy worth be remembered,
>   And still the full cup to thy memory shall flow:
>   Still, still in our hearts shall thy virtues be numbered,
>   Still loved—still respected—the tribute we owe.
>   MILES."

On the 15th of July, out of a strength of 727, the regiment had only 1 man on the sick list.

On the 25th of August the bands of the 7th, 23rd, 43rd, and three Danish regiments competed at Arras for a gold medal given by the prefect of the department and the local civil authorities on the anniversary of St. Louis. The Royal Fusiliers were adjudged the winners.

On the 27th of September the regiment marched from its cantonments in the neighbourhood of Hamelincourt to Cambrai, where it remained until the 19th of October, when it marched to Denain to take part in a review of the Army of Occupation by the Dukes of Kent and Cambridge, at that place on the 22nd of the month. After the review a sham fight took place under the personal direction of the Duke of Wellington.

After the sham fight the regiment returned to its former cantonments, which were reached on the 25th of October. During the month 1 corporal and 26 men joined from the depôt.

The state of the regiment on the 25th of October was as follows: Present fit, 41 officers, 35 sergeants, 14 drummers, 36 corporals, 490 privates. Sick present, 1 sergeant, 1 drummer, 2 corporals, 30 privates. On command, 2 officers, 3 sergeants, 2 privates. Undersized men of poor physique on the march to Calais for return to the depôt, 3 sergeants, 1 drummer, 2 corporals, 126 privates.

The detachment was in charge of Captain James Milne, Lieutenant

Walter F. Kerr, and 2nd Lieutenant Thomas Baillie. These officers rejoined the regiment on the 22nd of November.

On the 30th of October the regiment was permitted to bear the word " MARTINIQUE " on its colours and appointments, and in connection with this it may be observed that the 23rd were instrumental in the capture of four Eagles now at the Royal Hospital, Chelsea. They were surrendered at Martinique in 1809 to the expedition of which the 23rd formed part. They are the three Battalion Eagles of the French 82nd Regiment of the Line, and one Regimental Eagle of the 26th Regiment of the Line. All four Eagles have the silken tricolour attached, as also has one surrendered at the same time at Guadeloupe. At that time a French regiment consisted of three battalions, and each had an Eagle. These had been granted on the 5th of December 1804. In 1808 Battalion Eagles were abolished and one Regimental Eagle substituted. The 82nd Regiment evidently had not returned their Battalion Eagles, and thus lost them. The French attached little value to the tricolour flag, the Eagle itself was everything; and in order to render the latter less conspicuous in action, the tricolour was generally removed. These Eagles were surrendered, not captured in action, which accounts for the tricolour's presence.

The regiment was inspected at Hamelincourt on the 11th of November by Major-General Sir James Kempt, G.C.B. His remarks as regards the privates were as follows : " A good serviceable body of men, though there are still many low men in the regiment. They appear to be very healthy and cleanly, and particularly well behaved in their quarters : their arms are in excellent condition."

1816.

Depôt.

The Depôt Company embarked from the Isle of Wight on the 1st of April, and disembarked at Dover on the 7th, being quartered at the Citadel Barracks. On the 13th of May it marched under Captain E. M. Brown to Deal, being quartered at the South Barracks; moving from the South to the North Barracks on the 1st of August.

1817.

During the month of February Captain E. M. Brown and Lieutenant Walter Kerr were placed upon half-pay, and the following officers declared to be supernumerary to the establishment : Lieutenants A. Clayhills,

E. Methold, W. R. Lloyd, A. Gledstanes, T. Lillie, G. Dunn, G. Stainforth, G. FitzGibbon, J. Drury, and T. Towers. On the 5th of February Captain H. Wynne, 2nd Lieutenants W. Gourlay and T. Baillie proceeded to Valenciennes to be instructed in the sword exercise.

On the 24th March 234 volunteers joined from the 1st [Royals], 3rd, 5th, 52nd, and 91st regiments.

By General Orders of 30th March the 4th Brigade was renumbered the 6th: on the 4th of April the volunteers who had lately joined the 23rd were paraded for the inspection of Colonel Sir Edward Blakeney.

On the 14th of April the regiment proceeded to Valenciennes to form part of the garrison of that town. Its strength then amounted to 887 all ranks.

Special precautions were ordered to be taken by the Brigade on occupying the Royal Barracks on account of an outbreak of ophthalmia having occurred among the troops previously quartered there.

On the 15th of May the regiment was inspected at Valenciennes by Colonel Sir Edward Blakeney, K.C.B., who remarks that " the battalion having received a great increase to its numbers by recent drafts from other corps did not appear so steady under arms as before."

During the month of June 42 privates were transferred to the 85th regiment and in the following month 24 privates joined from the depôt.

The following extract from a Brigade Order dated 5th July is interesting as showing the difference of range of musketry fire then and now: " The men are to fire singly, commencing at the distance of 80 yards, and those who hit the target at this distance will fire next time at the distance of 100 yards, and the distance will be increased to 130, 150, and 200 yards to those who hit the target at a less distance, but no man is to be permitted to fire at more than 80 yards until he hits the target at that distance; a Field Officer will superintend the practice, and the utmost attention is to be paid to it."

On the 23rd of August Lieutenant-Colonel Thomas Dalmer was placed on the half-pay of the 43rd Regiment. He was succeeded by Lieutenant-Colonel Thomas Pearson from the half-pay of the 43rd Regiment.

On the 6th of September the British and Danish contingents were reviewed by the King of Prussia near Prouvy. On the 10th the regiment marched to Cambrai and encamped on the glacis, where the whole of the infantry of the 1st Division was assembled.

In October the regiment returned to Valenciennes, where it was quartered during the rest of the year, being inspected there on the 22nd by Major-General Sir James Kempt, who remarked that the " band plays in correct time, and is in every respect an excellent one." He also observed that " the messes are good, and abundantly supplied with vegetables."

1817.

Depôt.

In April the recruiting parties seem to have been withdrawn, probably on account of the large number of men from other regiments drafted into the 23rd, when it was decided to retain the regiment in France. The strength of the depôt, which was still at Deal, was 5 sergeants, 3 corporals, 4 drummers, 31 privates.

1818.

The regiment continued to do garrison duty at Valenciennes until August. In April 2 sergeants and 49 privates were sent home for discharge. On the 29th of April the regiment was inspected at Valenciennes by Major-General Sir James Kempt. An extract from his report is as follows:

" It is impossible for any officer to evince more ability, zeal, and attention than Lieut.-Colonel Pearson has employed in his command of the 23rd.

" The Drummers appear to be very attentive and to understand the different beats.

" The Regimental Band is an excellent one.

" *Privates*.—A very excellent body of men with a very healthy and clean appearance.

" *Messing*.—Great attention appears to be paid to the messing; the men are supplied with abundance of vegetables, and the provisions supplied by the French Government are of a good quality. The officers mess together.

" The great coats are quite new.

" The men have 20 rounds of ball cartridge in their own possession: the remainder is in charge of the Royal Artillery.

" *Regimental School*.—Great attention appears to be paid to the Regimental School, which is well attended. In addition to the Schoolmaster an officer of the Regiment takes the general superintendence of it; the scholars appear to make considerable progress in reading and writing.

"The officers and men of the Regiment constantly attend Divine Service, which is performed every Sunday by the Chaplain of the Brigade."

On the 17th of August the regiment left Valenciennes and proceeded to a camp near Cambrai.

A weekly state of the British forces under the command of the Duke of Wellington, dated Headquarters, Cambrai, 27th September 1818, contains the following information respecting the regiment: Camp near Cambrai, 23rd Regiment—Present, 3 field officers, 8 captains, 17 subalterns, 4 staff, 36 sergeants, 20 drummers, 688 rank and file. On command, 1 sergeant, and 7 rank and file. During October the regiment was reduced to the extent of 1 officer (1 assistant surgeon instead of 2), 10 sergeants, 10 corporals, and 140 men.

Major-General Sir James Kempt again inspected the regiment on the 12th of October and made the following most favourable report: "Non-Commissioned Officers are as good and respectable in point of character, and appearance, as those of any Battalion in the service. All such as cannot write continue to attend the Regimental school. The privates are a very stout and healthy body of men and particularly cleanly and soldier-like in their appearance. The regiment is in the most efficient state in every respect."

On the dissolution of the Allied army in France the British troops began to evacuate that country in October.

In 1816, as in 1760, when Prince Ferdinand of Brunswick gave orders to the Allied army that "it is forbid on pain of death to all and every one to go a sporting, or to kill game of any kind," the innate love of Englishmen for sport, even during the perils of war, was the cause of orders, regulating sport, being issued from time to time during the occupation of France.

For instance, on 4th April 1816, a Division Order dated from Cambrai reads as follows: "The Lieutenant-General having been informed that officers and gentlemen attached to the army have got out nets from England, for the purpose of drawing the rivers, it is by no means his desire to prevent the amusement of fishing, but he positively prohibits the use of nets. It is not reasonable or can it be expected that the inhabitants will patiently submit to have their fish completely destroyed, which the use of nets will in a very short time effect, and of course with it, the amusement of fishing."

In November 1817 two General Orders were issued to the effect that if more care was not taken to avoid damage to the crops by hunting and shooting both forms of sport would be strictly forbidden. It had to be remembered " that in France (a country where hounds are unknown and greyhounds prohibited) the laws are particularly rigid." In spite of " Orders," etc., the keenness of the Briton for sport of any kind is exemplified in a general memorandum dated Valenciennes, 31st March 1818, as follows : " A complaint has been made by the Mayor that on the evening of the 29th instant, some servants were seen hunting with dogs the swans in the ditch to the left of the Paris Gate; any repetition of such a practice will be most severely punished."

On the 26th of October the regiment left Cambrai, and marched to Calais via Cantin, Lens, Lilliers, Racquingham, and Valles Aord Auguse : Calais being reached on the 31st.

Sir James Kempt bade farewell to his brigade—to which he was evidently greatly attached—in the following eulogistic terms :

"CALAIS, 1st November 1818.

" It having been a source of great satisfaction to Major-General Sir James Kempt to be placed during the last three years in command of a brigade composed of such distinguished regiments as the Royal Fusiliers, the Royal Welch Fusiliers, and the 43rd Light Infantry, it is with feelings of great regret that he parts from them on the breaking up of this army. During that long period he has had everything to commend, but nothing to blame. In all his reports he has had occasion to speak in terms of the highest praise of the excellent discipline that prevails in these regiments : of the spirit with which both officers and men are animated : of the great ability displayed by Colonel Sir Edward Blakeney, Lieutenant-Colonel Pearson, and Lieutenant-Colonel Patrickson, in their respective commands : and, if the brigade had been called into active service, Sir James Kempt has a perfect conviction that the regiments composing it would have been as exemplary for heroism and gallantry in the field as they have been for regularity and good conduct in quarters, each nobly supporting the fame and reputation they had so justly acquired in the Peninsula. For many of the officers Sir James Kempt has a personal regard, and he can never cease to take a deep interest in their welfare.

"[*signed*]   C. YORKE, *Brigade Major.*"

On the 1st of November the regiment embarked, and landed at Dover the following morning, being quartered at Dover Heights Barracks. On the 19th it marched to Deal and embarked on board the transports *Defence* and *Alfred* for Cork.

The following officers sailed on board the *Alfred* : Captains (Brevet

Lieutenant-Colonel) F. Dalmer (Grenadier Company), J. C. Harrison, T. Strangeways, (Brevet Major) H. S. Blanckley, and W. Walley. On board the *Defence* there were Captains (Brevet Lieutenant-Colonel) W. Campbell, H. C. Johnson, F. O'Flaherty, J. Milne, H. Wynne (Light Infantry Company).

On embarking the regiment mustered 26 officers, 43 sergeants, 22 drummers, 612 privates present fit—39 privates sick and 65 privates invalids.

The transports sailed for Cork on the 20th. On the 24th the *Alfred* transport arrived at the Cove of Cork with the Left Wing. On the 27th the Left Wing sailed in a steamboat to Cork and was quartered in the Barracks. On the 28th the Left Wing marched to Mallow. On the 30th the Left Wing marched to Buttevant Barracks. The Right Wing arrived in the Cove of Cork on the 28th November 1818 and sailed in a steamboat to Cork, and was quartered in the Barracks. On the 2nd December the Right Wing arrived at Buttevant. On the 9th and 10th the battalion marched to Limerick.

The establishment for this year was 800 rank and file, 107 officers and non-commissioned officers, total 907 all ranks.

1818.

Depôt.

Recruiting recommenced in May this year, parties being stationed at Dudley, Hereford, Wrexham, etc. In November the Depôt Company seems to have been absorbed into the regiment on its departure from France for Ireland.

1819.

On the 1st of May the battalion was inspected by Major-General O'Loghlin at the New Barracks, at Limerick.

"Lower Shannon District Order.

"Assistant Adjutant-General's Office,
Limerick, 1st May 1819.

"Major-General O'Loghlin feels much gratification in expressing to Lieutenant-Colonel Pearson and the Officers of the Royal Welch Fusiliers his unqualified approbation of the very soldierlike and steady appearance of that corps at the half-yearly inspection this day.

"The general good arrangement and consequent regularity in the internal economy of the Regiment, and the intelligence and steadiness of the Officers in the Field, are all highly deserving of commendation, and are such as may naturally have been expected from so distinguished a corps under an officer of Lieutenant-Colonel Pearson's capability and experience.

"By order,
[*signed*]   T. T. WOOLDRIDGE,
Major, Asst. Adjutant General."

On the 8th of October the battalion was inspected by Major-General Gordon at the New Barracks, Limerick.

"DISTRICT ORDER.
"HEAD QUARTERS, MUNSTER DISTRICT,
CORK, *October 30th*, 1819.

"Major-General Gordon is very much pleased with the appearance of the 23rd Regiment on parade. It is a very steady corps and performs the manœuvres according to His Majesty's Regulations with much precision and celerity.

"The economy of the Regiment is also most respectable, and the Major-General has not any deviation or deficiency to notice.

"[*signed*]   BENJ: GORDON, *Major-General*."

During the whole of this year the regiment was stationed at Limerick, its effective strength only varying between 640 and 650 men.

The establishment for this year was 650 rank and file, 96 officers and non-commissioned officers, total 746 all ranks.

1820.

The regiment remained at the New Barracks, Limerick (with detachments at Shanagolden, Tarbert Island, Carrick Island, Scabbery Island, Newport, and Kildimo), being inspected there on 12th May by Major-General Sir Thomas Brisbane, K.C.B. In June it moved to Ennis. From then until October it was split up into no less than 16 detachments varying from 5 to 25 privates, and non-commissioned officers in proportion. Towards the end of November the detachments were all withdrawn, and the return for the 25th of that month shows 8 companies at Ennis, and 2, viz. Nos. 5 and 6, under Captains Dalmer and Rentoul on the march to Dublin. The return for 25th December shows the regiment as being then stationed in Dublin (459 officers and men), Killaloe (25 officers and men), and O'Brien's Bridge (21 officers and men).

1821.

The regiment remained at Dublin until September, when it moved to Londonderry. During March and April a detachment of 1 officer and 49 non-commissioned officers and men was stationed at the Pigeon House Fort to relieve a similar detachment of the 78th Regiment. This was withdrawn in May, when a detachment under 2nd Lieutenant W. A. Gourlay of 1 sergeant and 17 men proceeded to Man-of-War (a hamlet in co. Dublin) to relieve another detachment of the 78th. In that month a detachment under Captain H. Wynne of 85 non-commissioned officers and men was stationed at Slane.

The following regimental order was issued on the 6th of September: "The Division consisting of 2, 4, 5, and 6 Companies under the command of Lieutenant-Colonel Hill will march to-morrow morning at 6 o'clock agreeable to their respective routes, and will be quartered as directed in conformity to the scale laid down by Colonel Pearson. All baggage to be loaded this evening: a proportion of non-commissioned officers and officers' servants will form the baggage guard, and to be dressed in the most uniform manner. The men to march in their white trousers, and the cloth trousers to be most carefully preserved. All young soldiers to be under the command and superintendence of commanding officers of companies. All parades to be the same as at headquarters.

"The 1st Division of the Corps under the command of Lieutenant-Colonel Hill will commence its march for Londonderry at 6 o'clock to-morrow morning, and the 2nd Division under the command of Lieutenant-Colonel Keightley on the following day."

The regiment while stationed at Londonderry was again broken up into small detachments, 18 in all—with 10 to 20 non-commissioned officers and men in each, there remaining at headquarters only 254 officers and men.

The battalion was inspected on 5th November by Major-General Egerton. The regiment received orders on 14th November to march to Strabane; the 1st division had already reached there when it was recalled and returned to Londonderry.

The establishment during this year was 650 rank and file, 96 officers and non-commissioned officers, total 746 all ranks.

1822.

The regiment remained at Londonderry until April, when it moved to Boyle, co. Roscommon, in four divisions: 1st division, which consisted of the Headquarters, Nos. 1 and 8 Companies, left Londonderry on 8th April; 2nd division, Nos. 2 and 5 Companies under Captain Harrison, left on the 9th; 3rd division, Nos. 4 and 7 Companies under Captain Sir William Crosbie, left on the 10th; 4th division, Nos. 3 and 6 Companies under Captain (Brevet Major) Smith, left on the 11th. There were then present at headquarters 205 officers and men; at Sligo 81 officers and men; and small detachments of about 20 men each at fourteen other stations.

On the 10th of May the regiment was inspected by Major-General Sir John Elley, who summed up his report by observing: "This corps is in a high state of discipline, perfectly equipped, and in every respect fit for any service."

The establishment for this year was 74 officers and non-commissioned officers, 576 rank and file, total 650 all ranks.

1823.

Major-General Sir James Willoughby Gordon, Bart., K.C.B., Quarter-Master General to the Forces, was removed from the Colonelcy of the 85th Light Infantry to that of the 23rd Royal Welch Fusiliers on the 23rd of April: in succession to General Sir Richard Grenville, who had died in London on the 22nd of April. The following letter was addressed to Colonel Pearson, commanding the 23rd Royal Welch Fusiliers, by Major-General Sir Willoughby Gordon, Bart., on his appointment to the Colonelcy of the regiment:

"HORSE GUARDS, 28*th April* 1823.

"DEAR SIR,

"The Commander-in-Chief having acquainted me that the King has been graciously pleased to appoint me to the Colonelcy of the Twenty-third Royal Welch Fusiliers, I take the earliest opportunity in my power to notify the same to you. I beg you will be assured that it has been to me a source of the highest gratification in having been thus selected for this honourable command: and that while I receive it as an additional proof of His Majesty's favour to me, I feel a pride in the national distinction of the corps, and in being thus associated with its long and hardly-earned honours and renown, which it will be ever one of my most anxious duties to endeavour to maintain and extend.

"It is also no small satisfaction to me to be immediately placed in communication with an officer under whose command this fine regiment has established so much of its fame and glory.

"I have, etc.,

[*signed*]   J. W. GORDON, *Colonel Royal Welch Fusiliers.*

"Colonel Pearson, C.B., commanding Twenty-third Royal Welch Fusiliers."

In May the regiment moved to the Richmond Barracks, Dublin, where it was inspected on the 3rd of June by Major-General Sir Colquhoun Grant, K.C.B., whose most satisfactory report reads as follows :

"Colonel Pearson is a most valuable Regimental Officer. A most exact and strictly enforced discipline is maintained in this excellent Corps, which in parade appearance, and field manœuvre, is not perhaps to be surpassed by any Battalion in the British service.

"The general appearance of the Corps evinces that an admirable system of drill is established.

"The non-commissioned officers appear to have been selected with great care and are a very respectable class.

"The Drummers are well chosen and the Drum-Major is in possession of a printed copy of the 'Regulations for the calls and beats of the drum.' The Band is composed of good musicians.

"*Privates.*—The Regiment is composed of a remarkably fine body of men, they are thoroughly drilled and their conduct good.

"The 23rd Regiment move in battalion with the utmost precision, and have a particularly imposing and soldierlike appearance under arms.

"The clothing of the regiment is particularly well made, and the utmost pains appear to have been taken in fitting it neatly to the men.

"The officers' mess is conducted on a footing of respectability, but with proper economy. The sergeants of the Regiment do not at present mess together. The meat and bread is furnished by contract, meat $3\frac{1}{2}d.$ per lb., bread $1\frac{3}{4}d.$ per lb.

"All ranks have attended Divine Service regularly, and a sermon has always closed the service.

"The School is conducted on the system of Dr. Bell; some of the boys are instructed in trades, but the girls are too young to learn knitting.

"*General remarks.*—The foregoing very favourable report of the 23rd precludes the necessity of much remark under this head. It will suffice to say that numerous as my inspections have been for the last three years, I have seen no corps surpass and scarcely any equal the Fusiliers, in appearance, movement, and discipline.

"Vaccine inoculation is always practised."

Orders for the embarkation of the regiment for Gibraltar were received in Dublin on the 7th of November.

Previous to the embarkation the following general order was issued by Lieutenant-General Lord Combermere, G.C.B., commanding the Forces in Ireland :

General Order.

"Adjutant-General's Office, Dublin,
24th November 1823.

"The Twenty-third Royal Welch Fusiliers being on the point of embarkation for a foreign station, Lieut.-General Lord Combermere feels he cannot, in too strong terms, express his approval of the general good conduct and discipline of this superb regiment during the time it has been under his orders.

"The Twenty-third, so eminently distinguished for its services in the field, has been uniformly conspicuous in this command for its soldierlike appearance and behaviour : and from the ample opportunity the Lieut.-General has had of personal observation, he is enabled to bear testimony to the merits of the system—evincing throughout the corps the greatest zeal, energy, and talent on the part of Colonel Pearson, as well as unremitting attention on the part of all under his command.

"By command of the Lieut.-General,

[*signed*]   J. Gardiner, *D.-A.-General.*

"Colonel Thomas Pearson, C.B., commanding Twenty-third Fusiliers."

Field-Marshal Viscount Combermere obtained his first commission, a 2nd Lieutenancy without purchase, in the 23rd, on 26th February 1790 ; he joined the regiment in Dublin the year after, became lieutenant 16th March 1791, and did duty with the regiment until 28th February 1793, when he was promoted to a troop in the 6th Dragoon Guards. He married as his third wife, in 1838, the grandniece of Major Gibbings, who was in command of the 23rd when the Field-Marshal served with the regiment forty-eight years before.

In December the regiment in four divisions embarked for Gibraltar.

The first division, Nos. 1 and 8 Companies, with the Band, under Lieutenant-Colonel Pearson, consisting of 7 officers and 158 non-commissioned officers and men, embarked on board the *William Harris* transport, and arrived at Gibraltar on 21st December. The second division, Nos. 3 and 7 Companies under Captain Harrison, consisting of 5 officers and 131 non-commissioned officers and men, embarked on board the *Fanny* transport, and arrived at Gibraltar on the 23rd of December. The third division, Nos. 4 and 5 Companies under Lieut.-Colonel Dalmer, consisting of 7 officers and 136 non-commissioned officers and men, embarked on board the *Indian Trader* transport, and arrived at Gibraltar on 4th January 1824. The fourth division, Nos. 2 and 6 Companies under Major England, consisting of 6 officers and 140 non-commissioned officers and men, embarked on board the *Prince of Orange* transport, and arrived at Gibraltar on the 23rd of January 1824.

On the departure of the regiment the depôt at Fermoy consisted of Captain Sir W. Crosbie, Bart., Lieutenant E. T. Ellis, 1 sergeant, 2 corporals, 1 drummer, and 3 privates.

1824.

On the 14th of May the regiment was inspected by General Sir George Don. The following is an illustration of the severity of the sentences of Courts Martial then passed on soldiers: "Private T. Roberts being sentenced to 7 years' transportation for (1st) Desertion, (2nd) Having sold or lost, or having made away with, 1 greatcoat, 1 red jacket, 1 pair of blue trousers, 1 pair of boots, 1 shirt, 1 forage cap."

The regiment was again inspected on the 8th of December by General Sir George Don, who commented on its fine appearance.

1824.

Depôt.

On 25th February the depôt was on board the transport *Joseph Swan* in Cove Harbour, Cork, en route for Albany Barracks, Isle of Wight, where it remained until April in the following year, the "privates fit" never exceeding 10 in number.

1825.

The regiment remained at Gibraltar during the whole of this year, being inspected by General Sir George Don on the 16th of May. In this report the Band is mentioned separately for the first time, as " Music, 1 corporal, 13 privates." From a return of " Nationality " compiled in April it appears that no fewer than 231 Irish privates were then serving in the regiment out of a total of 516.

By General Order 425 of the 25th of March each battalion of infantry, excepting those serving in the East Indies, was to consist of :

6 service Companies of 86 rank and file	. .	516
4 depôt ,, ,, 56 ,, ,,	. .	224
	Total	740

This augmentation was not made operative so far as the 23rd was concerned till 25th June.

1825.

Depôt Companies.

In April the depôt companies left Albany Barracks, disembarking at Plymouth on the 26th. On the 13th of July they re-embarked and landed at Swansea on the 16th, arriving at Brecon on the 20th.

1826.

On the 3rd of May and 6th December the regiment was inspected by General Sir George Don, who on both occasions reported " the regiment is in very high order in every respect." By General Order of 24th July 1826, attention was drawn to the neglect to establish Sergeants' Messes in several corps. This, however, did not refer to the 23rd Regiment, as in nearly all the reports the existence of a sergeants' mess is mentioned.

During the autumn of this year the affairs of Portugal were in a critical condition, owing to the machinations of the " Absolutist " or reactionary party, which was straining every nerve to undermine the Constitution, which had been granted to that country, some months previously, by its Sovereign John VI, who, however, did not live long enough to see his policy carried out.

Owing to these reactionaries being aided and abetted by Spain, the Princess Regent was compelled early in December to send an earnest appeal to King George IV for military assistance, as this country was by treaty obligation bound to come to the assistance of Portugal, when attacked from without.

THE KING'S COLOUR, 1826.

On the 11th of the month with the approval of Parliament it was decided to send to the Tagus an expeditionary force of 5,000 men under Lieutenant-General Sir Henry Clinton, consisting of the following regiments :

    10th Light Dragoons, 2 squadrons.
    12th   ,,   ,,   2   ,,
    1st battalion,   1st Foot Guards.
    2nd   ,,   3rd   ,,   ,,
    1st   ,,   60th, and 4th, 10th, 11th, 23rd, 43rd, and 63rd Regiments.

The equipping of this force was fitted out with a rapidity which could scarcely have been credited beforehand, so much so that by the end of the year all the regiments from home had arrived in the Tagus.

A new set of Colours presented by Lieutenant-General Sir James Willoughby Gordon, Bart., K.C.B., Colonel of the Royal Welch Fusiliers, was received, and consecrated on Friday, 1st December. They were presented on the Almeida at Gibraltar by Mrs. Pearson and received by Lieutenants Elliott and Stretton.

1826.

Depôt Companies.

On the 25th of March Major Harrison, commanding the depôt, in explanation of the desertion of 15 recruits states that " it is to be attributed first to the facility of escape, and the security from detection afforded in this country by the ready employment deserters have found in the neighbouring iron and copper works, and secondly from the little intercourse the people of this country have with the military ; the lower classes have very contracted notions of the service, and they have a disposition to aid and abet soldiers in this crime."

The depôt companies left Brecon on the 27th of April and disembarked at Guernsey on the 12th of May. In July a draft of 2 sergeants, 1 drummer, and 50 men was sent to the regiment.

At the beginning of September the depôt left Guernsey, and disembarked on the 19th of September at Pillgwenlly, arriving at Brecon on the 22nd.

1827.

The regiment, under the command of Colonel Pearson, C.B., embarked at Gibraltar for Lisbon on the 8th of January on board H.M.S. *Windsor*

Castle, but did not actually sail until the 13th, owing to strong westerly winds, and disembarked on the 20th, on which date a draft of 1 sergeant and 20 men under Captains W. Sloane, T. Bigge, and W. Tupper joined the regiment from the depôt.

The women and children who were not on the married establishment secreted themselves on the departure of the regiment, but managed to embark on a Portuguese vessel, which after running aground, and a most stormy passage of no less than 52 days instead of 6, eventually reached Belem.

The monthly return shows, present fit, 22 officers, 24 sergeants, 9 drummers, 26 corporals, and 467 privates.

The 4th, 10th, 23rd, and 1st battalion 60th regiments were formed into a brigade under the command of Major-General Sir Edward Blakeney.

On the 5th of February the regiment marched from Lisbon, and arrived at Coimbra on the 18th, where it remained until the beginning of June.

The regiment under Colonel Pearson, C.B., was inspected at Coimbra, on the 3rd of May, by Major-General Sir Edward Blakeney. In his "General Remarks" he states: "I can say nothing that can add to the well-earned renown of the Royal Welch Fusiliers. Their interior arrangements, appearance under arms, and steady discipline in the field are all of the most perfect description."

On the 19th of June it marched from Coimbra, and arrived at Leiria on the 21st, leaving there on the 25th July under the command of Major Harrison, and reached Mafra on the 27th of August. On the 25th of that month Sergeant-Major Samuel Brelsford was promoted 2nd Lieutenant, and appointed Adjutant in the 60th Rifles.

On Sunday the 29th of July, Nos. 1, 2, and 9 Companies returned to Caldas, as a guard of honour to Her Royal Highness the Princess Regent of Portugal, and rejoined headquarters at the end of August.

On the 8th of November Quartermaster-Sergeant Garrett More was appointed Quartermaster of the regiment, vice George Sidley, who retired on full pay of the 7th Fusiliers.

1827.

Depôt Companies.

At the end of March a detachment of 44 non-commissioned officers and men, and Lieutenants W. Gourlay, E. T. Ellis, and S. Powell, left

Plymouth on H.M.S. *Romney*, and joined the headquarters on 9th of April. In April a detachment under Captain R. Holmes and 2nd Lieutenant C. S. Bunyon, with 38 non-commissioned officers and men, was stationed at Usk. A further draft of 29 non-commissioned officers and men embarked on the 5th of October in the *Hope* transport, under Lieutenants M. Ross and the Hon. H. T. Stanley.

1828.

On the 11th of March the regiment left Mafra, and embarked at Lisbon on H.M.S. *Ocean* on the 12th. The following is an extract from the Captain's log: "Came on board the 23rd Regiment, consisting of 22 officers, 516 soldiers, 5 servants, 33 women and 53 children: weighed on the 14th, arrived at Gibraltar and landed troops on the 22nd." The loss sustained by the regiment during its stay in Portugal amounted to 27 men. The regiment was inspected on the 7th of May and 20th December by General Sir George Don. During the autumn an epidemic of yellow fever raged at Gibraltar, which prevented field exercises, etc., from being carried out. Even the schools had to be closed. In October the deaths amounted to 13, in November to 28, and in December to 7, the sick, however, in that month being still numerous, viz. 36.

1828.

Depôt Companies.

On the 24th July Major J. C. Harrison took over command of the depôt from Major W. Ross. On the 18th of November a draft of 96 non-commissioned officers and men was sent to the regiment under Major Ross: it embarked at Gosport on H.M.S. *Melville*: left there on the 1st of December, the vessel putting into Plymouth, where it remained until the 28th of December, arrived at Gibraltar on the 8th of January, and disembarked the troops on the 19th.

1829.

The six companies stationed at Gibraltar were Nos. 1, 2, 3, 6, 9, and 10. On the 19th of January Major Ross, Captains Bigge and Matheson, 2nd Lieutenants Bunyon and Lindsay, and Paymaster J. Macdonald joined with a detachment from the depôt.

On the 29th of April the regiment was inspected by Major-General Sir George Don, who reported that the privates were "a very fine body of men."

1829.

Depôt Companies.

The four companies stationed at Brecon were Nos. 4, 5, 7, and 8. In the first four months of this year the depôt sent to the service companies 2 sergeants and 92 privates, and in the beginning of November a further draft of 1 sergeant, 1 drummer, and 17 privates.

1830.

The regiment was inspected on the 9th of February, and again on the 3rd of May, by General Sir George Don, who in his earlier report remarks that the " orders contained in the circular of 24th June 1829, relative to the hair and beards of officers and men, has been strictly complied with." This referred to the practice of officers and men of certain infantry regiments allowing the " mustachio or the beard to grow on the chin." This malpractice is described in the circular as " officers and men being at liberty to vie with each other in disfiguring their faces as may best suit their individual taste and fancy."

His Majesty King William IV was pleased to promote Colonel Pearson, C.B., to the rank of Major-General, Commission dated 22nd July 1830.

On this event the Major-General addressed the following communication to Major Ross, commanding the Service Companies :

" United Service Club,
August 3rd, 1830.

" My dear Major,
" The most painful moment of my life has at length arrived when I am obliged to take a final leave of the Royal Welch Fusiliers, in which distinguished corps I have served Twenty-seven years. To separate myself from a Regiment with which my best interests have been identified, and in which I have passed the best and happiest days of my life, is an event of so trying a nature, that I find myself utterly at a loss for expression to describe my feelings on the occasion. The only sad duty left me to perform is to pronounce a sorrowing farewell to all. To Major Harrison, to you my dear Major, and to you my dear and valued brother officers I beg to offer my warmest acknowledgments for the zealous manner you have on all occasions afforded me your ready assistance in the maintenance of the General Discipline and best interests of the corps.

"Human nature is ever liable to err and in no situation more so than in the exercise of command; be assured that in those instances when in the execution of public duty I may unintentionally have given pain, the fault has proceeded from the head, and not from the heart, and it is now only permitted me to hope that the sentiments of affectionate regard which I have ever entertained for every member of the Royal Welch, will enable me to cherish the idea that when remembered it will not be with other feelings than those with which I now in the full sincerity of an overflowing heart subscribe myself your ever attached and truly affectionate friend.

"[signed]   T. PEARSON,
Major-General; Late Lt.-Col. R.W.F.

"To Major Ross and the Officers of the R.W.F., etc. etc."

Major Ross' reply.

"GIBRALTAR, 10th *October* 1830.

"MY DEAR GENERAL,

"I beg to acknowledge the receipt of your very kind letter of the 3rd August last addressed to myself and the Officers of the Corps conveying to us your feeling and sentiments on relinquishing the command of the R.W.F., in which you had served for so many years. Believe me, dear General, our feelings are in unison with your own on this occasion, and I have only to offer in my own name and that of the officers our sincere and warm congratulation on your promotion, to express to you our best wishes for your future happiness and prosperity, and I can with truth declare to you that nothing would afford us greater pleasure than to see you again in the full exercise of your profession with the Old Welch under your command. In the name of all your late Brother Officers allow me to subscribe myself your very faithful and obliged friend.

"[signed]   WM. ROSS,
Major Commdg. 23rd Fusiliers.

"To Major-General Pearson, C.B., etc. etc."

Major Harrison was appointed to the Lieutenant-Colonelcy of the Regiment vacant by the promotion of Colonel Pearson, C.B., and joined it on the 21st of October from England.

1830.

Depôt Companies.

A detachment of 2 sergeants, 1 drummer, and 40 privates under Captain G. Beauclerk and Lieutenant Lort Phillips was stationed at Newport, Mon., in April, being withdrawn in June, when it rejoined the depôt, which moved at the end of that month to Plymouth. On the 6th of October the depôt companies were inspected at Stonehouse, Plymouth, by Major-General Sir John Cameron, K.C.B.—no inspection having been made since May 1826. The depôt was then under the command of Major George Fielding, who died at Bath on the 29th November and was succeeded by Major R. P. Holmes. Sir John Cameron in his report states that the following officers were Welsh: Lieutenant W. A. Griffiths, 2nd Lieutenants J. Tucker and J. Lort Phillips. The present fit rank and file was 154—wanting 58. Establishment 212. "The officers and men were imperfectly drilled, but have every reason to be satisfied with the progress they made since." In November the depôt companies were moved to Drogheda: one company being stationed at Kingscourt under Captain Beauclerk.

1831.

On the 18th of May the regiment was inspected by General Sir George Don, who again reported it as "in a high state of discipline, and in every respect in excellent order."

It was again inspected on 26th October by Lieut-General Sir William Houstoun, G.C.B., who reported it as "a fine body of men."

The following is a copy of a letter addressed to this General Officer on the question of status of ensigns and second lieutenants:

"Horse Guards,
6 December 1831.

"Sir,

"Having submitted to the General Commanding in Chief your letter of the 9th ultimo with its enclosures from Lieutenant-Colonel Harrison, commanding the 23rd, preferring the claim of the Second Lieutenants of his Regiment to take rank of Ensigns, I am directed to acquaint you that the practice of the Service has always been that Second Lieutenants should rank before Ensigns and after all Lieutenants, without reference to the dates of their respective commissions, and this was considered to be the rule by the General Officers who were charged with the duty of affixing a price to commissions, and who went upon the principle of awarding so much for rank and so much for pay. Thus it is that the price of a 2nd Lieutenantcy exceeds by £50 that of an Ensigncy.

" I have the honour to be, Sir,
Your obedient Servant,
[*signed*]   FITZROY SOMERSET.

" Lieut.-General Sir William Houstoun, G.C.B., etc. etc. etc."

1831.

DEPÔT COMPANIES.

The depôt companies were inspected at Drogheda on the 31st of May by Major-General Sir E. Blakeney. There were present under arms 9 officers, 9 sergeants, 7 corporals, 3 drummers, and 153 privates, with a detachment of 41 non-commissioned officers and men at Kingscourt under Captain Lockett. He remarks that the depôt companies are in an excellent state of discipline, he gave Major Holmes great credit for the attention he had paid them, and stated that the *esprit de corps* was well upheld. Owing to some complaint having reached the General respecting abuse in the system of franking soldiers' letters, he makes the following special remark : " The mode of franking the soldiers' letters is by the officer of the company first signing his name, and afterwards signed by the officer commanding. I have made enquiry in this head in several of the regiments, and I have no reason to conclude that any improper use is made of this indulgence."

On the 6th of October a detachment of 3 officers and 104 non-commissioned officers and men, under Major Holmes, was dispatched to Cork, on the way to join the Service Companies.

On the 8th the depôt companies left Drogheda, and on the 10th arrived in Dublin.

On the 27th of October the detachment at Kingscourt rejoined the companies at Dublin. On the 31st the detachment at Cork under Major Holmes was reduced to 1 sergeant, 1 drummer, 1 corporal, and 72 privates, the remaining men joining the companies at Dublin. On the 2nd of November the companies under Major Ross were inspected in Dublin, by Major-General Sir Edward Blakeney, who reported that they were in every respect in most excellent order. On the 5th of December the detachment at Cork, with Major Holmes, Captain Cockell, Lieutenant

Deakins, and 2nd Lieutenant Granville, embarked on board the transport *Sylvia* for Gibraltar, where they arrived on the 13th of January 1832.

1832.

This year the regiment continued to be stationed at the Town Range Barracks until the 9th of November. In April the regiment through its commanding officer put forward a claim for " Ciudad Rodrigo " to be added to its Colours.

The following correspondence thereupon ensued :

"Horse Guards,
April 24th, 1832.

" My dear Sir,

" Upon the receipt of your letter relative to the claim of the regiment to inscribe the words ' Ciudad Rodrigo ' upon the Colours, I did not lose a moment in applying to the proper Authorities upon the subject, and I now enclose to you a copy of a letter which I have received from the Duke of Wellington, who commanded the army upon the occasion, explanatory of the Rules adopted upon that and similar cases.

" Yours faithfully,
[*signed*]   J. W. Gordon.

" Lieut.-Colonel Harrison, commanding 23rd Regiment, Gibraltar."

"Strathfield Saye,
April 19th, 1832.

" My dear General,

" In answer to your letter respecting the desire of the Commanding Officer of the Royal Welch Fusiliers to have the words ' Ciudad Rodrigo ' inscribed on the Colours of that Corps, I have to inform you that the Rule according to which I have been guided in respect to my recommendation of this mark of Distinction, has been to recommend that it should be granted only on an occasion which the King's Government has thought so important, as that the Commander of the Forces had been authorised to recommend Officers on whom the distinction should be conferred of wearing a medal for their conduct to be struck to commemorate the action, and that this distinction of having the name of the Action inscribed on the Colours of the Battalion or Regiment should be granted only to those whose officers should have been recommended for the distinction of the medal.

"The King's Government did direct that a medal should be struck to commemorate the Storm of 'Ciudad Rodrigo' for which the officers were recommended according to the usual Regulations who were employed in that operation.

"The Royal Welch Fusiliers was a Regiment in the 4th Division of the Infantry of the Army. This Division and the Regiments belonging to it were employed in the Siege of the Fortress, but they were not employed in the part of the operations commemorated by the grant of the medal. Their officers were not recommended for that medal. According to the rule, therefore, I cannot recommend that the words 'Ciudad Rodrigo' should be inscribed upon their Colours.

"These Rules were well considered at the time. I believe them to be well calculated to render the Honours desirable, the grant of which they were intended to restrain and regulate, and I am convinced that they cannot be departed from without great public inconvenience.

"Ever, my dear General,
Yours most faithfully,
[*signed*]   WELLINGTON.

"Lieut.-General Sir Willoughby Gordon, G.C.B., etc. etc. etc."

On the 23rd of April and the 25th of October the regiment was inspected by Lieutenant-General Sir William Houstoun. His general remarks on the latter date are as follows :

"The perfectly efficient and serviceable state of the Royal Welch Fusiliers in every branch merits high praise and reflects credit on the judicious system and soldierlike ability of Lieut.-Colonel Harrison, whose constant attention to the interests of his men and to their comfort is evinced both in their discipline in the field and interior arrangements.

"The officers are a fine set of young men, intelligent and well instructed, and second the C.O. with an *esprit de corps* tending to materially support the high state of discipline which this distinguished corps so fully maintains."

1832.

DEPÔT COMPANIES.

On the 27th of March the Companies left Dublin 229 strong and arrived at Newry on the 30th. On the 17th of April they left Newry, and arrived in Belfast on the 19th, sending a detachment the same day under Captain J. Brown to Portglenone. On the 15th the companies were inspected at Belfast by Major-General MacDonell, C.B., whose "General Remarks" include the following: "The treatment of soldiers in this Reserve is most kind and encouraging: marriage of soldiers is discouraged." On the 17th of May a further detachment under Lieutenant Alcock proceeded to Magherafelt. On the 14th of July the companies from Belfast marched to Naas, which was reached on the 24th: the detachments from Portglenone and Magherafelt joining en route. On the 31st July the companies left Naas, reached Carlow on the 1st of August, and returned to Naas on the 19th. The depôt was inspected on the 5th of November by Major-General Sir Edward Blakeney.

1833.

On the 8th of May and again on the 7th of October the regiment was inspected at Gibraltar by Lieutenant-General Sir William Houstoun, who again reported most favourably upon the condition of the regiment.

1833.

Depôt Companies.

The depôt companies in two divisions left Naas on the 15th and 16th February, 240 strong, for Fermoy, which was reached on the 23rd and 25th. On the 12th of March the companies left Fermoy for Clonmel, arriving there on the 13th. On the 9th of October a detachment under Captain J. Brown of 51 non-commissioned officers and men proceeded to Cork, and later embarked on the transport *Stentor* to join the service companies, and arrived at Gibraltar on the 14th of December.

1834.

On the 13th of May the regiment was inspected by Lieutenant-General Sir William Houstoun, who describes the privates as "a fine, serviceable, well-seasoned, soldierlike body of men, averaging nearly 30 years of age; there are four undersized men who are no acquisition to this fine corps."

On the 28th of October the right wing, 3 companies, 259 strong, under Lieutenant-Colonel Harrison, embarked on board the *Stentor*, and the left wing, 3 companies, 217 strong, under Major Holmes, on board the *Mary*. Previous to the embarkation the following Garrison Order was issued by

His Excellency the Lieutenant-Governor, Lieutenant-General Sir W. Houstoun :

"HEADQUARTERS, GIBRALTAR, 25th Oct. 1834.

"His Excellency the Lieutenant-General Commanding desires to express to the 23rd Royal Welch Fusiliers before they embark for England, his entire approbation of the orderly and soldierlike conduct they have evinced during the time they have been under his command, particularly in the exemplary manner in which they have performed their garrison duties.

"He begs to offer the officers, non-commissioned officers, and privates of this highly distinguished corps his cordial thanks, and sincere good wishes for their future welfare, as well as particularly to acknowledge the sense he entertains of the unremitting and able exertions of Lieutenant-Colonel Harrison, commanding the Regiment which he has so eminently led, both in the field and in quarters, to maintain the high state of discipline of this Corps, and which reflects so much credit upon that officer."

The right wing arrived in Portsmouth Harbour on the 8th of November, and on the 10th the companies disembarked from the *Stentor* and occupied Fort Monckton, Gosport, until the 14th, when they marched to Titchfield and Botley en route for Winchester. On the same morning the left wing landed from the *Mary* and marched to Fareham : the depôt companies under Major Ross moved from Portsmouth, where they had been stationed for a few weeks, to Waltham and Wickham. On the following day the 3 divisions assembled on the Downs near Winchester, and after exchanging hearty congratulations on the happy occasion, the 10 companies marched into the city and occupied the barracks. On the 28th of November the regiment was inspected at Winchester by Major-General Sir Thomas McMahon, K.C.B., who stated " it may be pronounced an excellent corps, in high order."

1834.

DEPÔT COMPANIES.

On the 4th of February the depôt marched from Clonmel, 236 strong, arriving at Templemore on the 5th, and sending a detachment to Thurles on the same day.

On the 16th of May the depôt was inspected by Major-General Sir J. Douglas. On the 27th the detachment at Thurles was withdrawn, and two companies were dispatched to Cashel.

On the 23rd of June the depôt, 157 strong, proceeded from Templemore to Fermoy, which was reached on the 26th: the two companies from Cashel joining on the 27th. On the 18th of August the depôt left Fermoy, 230 strong, arriving at the Cove of Cork on the 19th, and embarking the same day on board the *Stentor* transport, sailed on the 20th, and arrived at Portsmouth on the 22nd, disembarking on the following day and being stationed at Fort Cumberland, whence 1 sergeant and 12 privates were sent as an advance party to Winchester Barracks; on 15th November the depôt joined the service companies at Winchester.

They were inspected at Portsmouth on the 6th October by Major-General Sir Thomas McMahon, K.C.B., who commented upon the wearing of "the Flash" by the officers; the outcome of which is described in the Appendix on "the Flash."

1835.

The following letter dated Horse Guards, 20th March 1835, was addressed to Lieutenant-General Sir J. W. Gordon, Bart., G.C.B., the Colonel of the 23rd Regiment, viz.:

"Sir,

"I have the honour to acquaint you by direction of the General Commanding in Chief that His Majesty has been graciously pleased to permit the 23rd Regiment or Royal Welch Fusiliers to continue to bear on its second Colour the following device as authorized by the Royal Warrants dated 1st July 1751 and 19th December 1768, viz.:

"In the centre of the Colour, the Device of the Prince of Wales, viz. Three Feathers issuing out of the Prince's Coronet and the motto 'Ich Dien.'

"In the second and third corners of the Colour the ancient badges of the Regiment, viz. the 'Rising Sun' and the 'Red Dragon,' and

"In the fourth corner the 'White Horse' with the motto 'Nec Aspera terrent.'

"I am also directed to acquaint you that His Majesty has been pleased to permit the Regiment to bear the word 'Corunna' in commemoration of the services of its late second Battalion at the Battle of Corunna on the 16th January 1809, in addition to the other Badges and distinctions heretofore granted to the Regiment.

"I have the honor to be, Sir,
Your most obedient Servant,
[*signed*]   John Macdonald, A.G."

The battalion marched in 4 divisions from Winchester on the 18th, 20th, 25th, and 26th of May, to Weedon Barracks, Northamptonshire, which were reached on 26th, 28th of May, and 1st June, detaching two companies to Newcastle-under-Lyme.

The battalion marched from Weedon in 3 divisions on the 24th August, 31st August, and 14th September, and took up detached quarters in the Northern district. Headquarters and 2 companies at Blackburn, 3 companies at Bolton, 2 companies at Rochdale, 3 companies at Burnley, and 1 company at Nottingham.

The Headquarter Companies were inspected on the 9th of October by Major-General Sir H. Bouverie, K.C.B. The privates fit present were 176, absent 386. In his "General Remarks" he states that "the practice of this regiment is that every subaltern shall qualify himself for the duties of adjutant. This regiment is in exceedingly good order, Lieutenant-Colonel Harrison is most zealous and attentive, and thoroughly understands the duties of his profession, and there is no part of the corps which does not bear the strictest examination."

The headquarters and 6 companies marched into Manchester on the 19th November, leaving 2 companies at Bolton, 1 company at Blackburn, and 1 company at Rochdale.

1836.

Two companies marched from headquarters on the 23rd March to Chester, and two companies proceeded per railway to Liverpool 25th March, and were replaced by the companies from Bolton, Blackburn, and Rochdale.

The regiment was inspected at Manchester on 9th May by Major-General Sir H. Bouverie. Fifty-five recruits had joined since the date of the last inspection.

The headquarters and 5 companies, 359 strong, under Lieutenant-Colonel Harrison, proceeded per railway to Liverpool on the 13th September, and embarked that day on board the *Earl Roden* steamer for Ireland, and landed in Dublin the following day.

The remaining 5 companies, 290 strong, under the command of Major Holmes, embarked at Liverpool on board the *Erin* steamer on the 15th September, and landed in Dublin on the following day.

The battalion proceeded by different routes and took up detached quarters in the Eastern district: Headquarters and 4½ companies at Kilkenny on 21st September, 2 companies at Carlow on 21st September,

1 company at Maryboro' on 21st September, 1 company at Castle Comer on 21st September, 1 company at Carrick-on-Suir on 26th September, and half a company at Callan on 22nd September.

At the inspection on 13th December at Kilkenny Major-General Sir James Douglas commented on the lack of discipline and steadiness of the men present. This he ascribed to the fact that the companies had been much dispersed in England, and there were still 360 men on detachment, only 2 companies being present at headquarters.

1837.

In March Lieutenant-Colonel Harrison relinquished command of the regiment; the following regimental order was issued in connection therewith:

REGIMENTAL ORDER.

"His Majesty having been graciously pleased to allow Lieutenant-Colonel Harrison to resign the command of the Royal Welch Fusiliers and retire from active service, Lieutenant-Colonel Harrison cannot take leave of a Regiment in which he has served for so many years without conveying to the officers, non-commissioned officers, and soldiers his feelings of deep regret on the occasion, and of expressing to them his most cordial thanks for the support they have at all times afforded him in the discharge of his responsible duties since he had the honour of being placed at their head, and he begs to assure this gallant corps that wherever the Service of their King and Country may call them, they will have his most fervent wishes for their welfare and success.

"After thirty-two years and upwards of uninterrupted service in various countries and climates with the Royal Welch Fusiliers, Lieutenant-Colonel Harrison cannot but feel a deep interest in their future well-being, and in taking leave of them he does so with the feelings he would at parting with a tried and valued friend, or at the loss of a near and dear relative. He however consoles himself in the confident trust that the high character which his distinguished corps has so deservedly gained as well by its bravery in the field as the exemplary and soldierlike demeanour of both officers and men in quarters, will ever remain unsullied, and that the glorious deeds recorded in their annals and inscribed upon their colours will serve as incitements to additional acts of renown in those now composing the Regiment whenever an opportunity offers in their Country's cause.

"Lieutenant-Colonel Harrison again wishes to his comrades in arms, the Royal Welch Fusiliers, every éclat as a Corps, and every happiness as individuals and friends, for whom he shall ever entertain the sincerest esteem and regard.

"Kilkenny, 26 March 1837."

Lieutenant-Colonel Harrison was succeeded in the command by Lieutenant-Colonel Ross, who joined headquarters on the 30th March 1837 from Carlow, where he had been some time on detachment as Major.

The regiment was inspected at Kilkenny on 12th May by Major-General L'Estrange. The privates fit present numbered 340, on detachment 240. The total privates effective 610, wanting to complete 93: the recruits numbering 65. The Inspecting General observed that "the greatcoats are rolled and placed on the pack, not 'folded square and carried outside flat against the back of the pack.' The tin covers are painted black instead of 'unpainted canvas,' as directed by the circular letter dated Horse Guards, 19th June 1829, para. 7. The arms have been longer in use than is usual in the service, and are inferior to everything else in the corps."

The battalion marched from Kilkenny and the different outposts in five divisions, Headquarters and four companies commencing on the 25th May, and proceeded to occupy the Royal Barracks, Dublin, where they remained until the 26th October, when headquarters and four companies were moved to Beggars Bush Barracks in the same city, detaching 2 companies to Porto Bello Barracks, 3 companies to George's Street Barracks, leaving 1 company at the Royal Barracks.

On the 17th of October the regiment was inspected by Lieutenant-General Sir E. Blakeney. He reported as follows: "The Royal Welch Fusiliers made an excellent inspection and are in very high discipline, the equipment most complete. Lieutenant-Colonel Ross pays great attention to all points, and I have every satisfaction in making this favourable report of him. The appearance of the regiment remarkably fine."

1838.

On receiving an order to hold the battalion in readiness to proceed on Foreign Service the six service companies (which were ordered to be augmented to 600 rank and file) were separated from the depôt, and were inspected by Lieutenant-General Sir Edward Blakeney on the 14th March, who highly approved of the selection.

The service companies continued in Dublin until the 17th, and embarked for Cork in three divisions, viz. :

1st division—2 companies under the command of Major Matheson on board the *Emerald Isle* steamer on the 17th, and landed upon the 18th March.

2nd division—2 companies under the command of Captain Cockell on board the *Hercules* steamer on the 22nd, and landed upon the 23rd March.

3rd division—Headquarters and two companies under the command of Captain Crutchley on board the *Hercules* steamer on the 30th, and landed 31st March.

There they remained until the 22nd May, when they embarked in two river steamers, proceeded down to Cove, and were put on board Her Majesty's troopship *Jupiter* for Halifax, Nova Scotia, under the command of Lieutenant-Colonel Ross.

The *Jupiter* sailed from Cove on the 25th May, and after a pleasant and most excellent passage of 18 days arrived at Halifax on the 12th June; the service companies disembarked the following day, and proceeded to occupy the South Barracks, detaching 1 officer and 60 men to George Island. One man died on the passage and his body was committed to the deep on the 31st May.

On the 7th of July the service companies were inspected at Halifax, Nova Scotia, by Major-General Sir Colin Campbell, who reported that owing to an issue of two flannel shirts and two pairs of drawers to each man on leaving Ireland, the allowance of £10 per company had been exceeded in every case.

1838.

Depôt Companies.

The depôt was formed on the 1st of April at Dublin under Major R. P. Holmes and marched from there on the 8th May, arriving at Armagh on the 14th, where it was inspected on the 23rd by Major-General T. Pearson. Present, 9 officers and 69 non-commissioned officers and men, the establishment being laid down at 14 officers and 155 non-commissioned officers and men. He again inspected it on the 1st of November and reported most favourably on its discipline and appearance.

In June, 28 recruits joined; in July, 15; in August, 29 : the recruiting parties which were stationed at Newcastle-under-Lyme, Oxford, Ludlow, Wrexham, etc., being withdrawn in September. On the 19th October a draft consisting of 1 sergeant and 15 privates was transferred to the service companies.

1839.

Service Companies.

On the 12th of March the left flank company was detached to Annapolis, consisting of Captain Cockell, Lieutenants Rice and Capron, 4 sergeants, 1 drummer, and 70 rank and file. Much good feeling was manifested on this occasion by the inhabitants of the Province, who furnished sleighs for the party free of expense, the whole way—a distance of 130 miles.

The service companies were inspected at Halifax, Nova Scotia, on the 13th May by Lieutenant-General Sir Colin Campbell. He reported that " the 23rd Royal Welch Fusiliers are composed of a fine body of serviceable men, and are in high order."

On its being represented to the officers of the Royal Welch Fusiliers during the summer of this year that the grave of their late Colonel, Sir Henry W. Ellis, who fell at Waterloo, and who is buried in the churchyard there, was in a very dilapidated state, Lieutenant-Colonel Ross and the officers lost no time in causing the grave not only to be put in proper and substantial repair, but caused a handsome marble slab to be placed in the church at Waterloo, with the following inscription :

" Sacred to the memory of Colonel Sir Henry Walton Ellis, K.C.B., late of the 23rd Royal Welch Fusiliers, who, after serving with distinction in Egypt, America, the West Indies, and throughout the Peninsular War, fell gallantly at the head of his regiment on the plains of Waterloo, in the 32nd year of his age. This tablet is erected by Lieut.-Colonel Ross and the officers of the 23rd Fusiliers."

1839.

Depôt Companies.

Two companies, 87 strong, marched from Armagh on the 16th of April, arriving at Castlebar on the 26th; headquarters and the other two companies, 92 strong, left Armagh on the 25th and arrived at Castlebar on the 4th of May. On the 10th of May and again on the 10th of October the depôt was inspected by Major-General Sir W. P. Carroll, who on both occasions reported " the 23rd depôt is in the best possible order : Major Holmes is an excellent officer."

In September the strength of the companies was increased from 155 non-commissioned officers and men to 220, by the addition of 4 sergeants, 4 corporals, and 57 men ; and in consequence recruiting parties were again at work.

In November recruiting parties were stationed at Cheltenham, Leominster, Oxford, Shrewsbury, Wrexham, Dublin, and Limerick : 23 recruits being obtained in October, 21 in November, and 22 in December.

On Friday the 15th of November Major Holmes and the officers stationed at Castlebar presented Paymaster and Lieutenant George Dunn with a handsome gold snuff-box as a mark of their regard on his approaching retirement from the regiment, and in the evening there was a farewell dinner.

Lieutenant Dunn was present with the regiment at Waterloo. The other " Waterloo " officers then serving in the regiment were Lieutenant-Colonel William Ross, Major R. P. Holmes, Captain John Enoch, and Quartermaster Garrett Moore. As Lieutenant Dunn's name appears in the Army List as Paymaster of the 23rd as late as 1850, it is evident that he did not carry out his original intention.

1840.

Service Companies.

On the 4th of June the service companies were inspected at Halifax, Nova Scotia, by Lieutenant-General Sir Colin Campbell. The returns show 2 officers as " Welsh," namely Lieutenant G. W. Rice and Second Lieutenant A. W. W. Wynn. The General stated as follows : " I cannot speak in too high terms of the appearance, discipline, and high order which the 23rd Regiment has attained. Lieutenant-Colonel Ross, who commands, is a zealous and attentive officer, and is well seconded by the officers— all movements were performed in the most correct and soldierlike manner. Their arms, appointments, and clothing are of the best description. I have only to complain that desertion has been too frequent ; the encouragement and facility in getting away from hence to the United States is very great, but every possible means are adopted to prevent it."

The 1st division, consisting of headquarters, Nos. 2, 3, and 4 companies, 301 strong, commanded by Lieutenant-Colonel Ross, embarked at Halifax on Saturday morning, the 3rd October, on board the *Unicorn* steamer for Quebec, sailed the same evening, and arrived there on the 7th, were transhipped to the *St. George* river steamer, which proceeded the same night and arrived at Montreal, Lower Canada, the following evening. It disembarked the next morning and occupied Point au Callière Barracks.

The 2nd division, consisting of Nos. 1, 5, and 6 companies, 271 strong, under the command of Captain Crutchley, marched from Halifax to Picton, arriving there on the 15th, embarked on the 16th on board the *Unicorn*, and arrived at Quebec on the 19th. There it transhipped to the *Canadian Eagle*, arrived at Montreal on the night of the 21st, and joined headquarters. On the 15th of October a transfer of 5 sergeants, 4 corporals, and 42 privates was received from the 66th Regiment.

The following is an extract from the *Halifax Morning Herald* on the departure of the regiment: "The splendid steamer *Unicorn* passed down the harbour at a rapid rate and in splendid style at about six o'clock on the Saturday evening for Quebec with the right wing of the 23rd Regiment, who left this Province, bearing with them the high esteem of the community and its deep regret at their departure from a Garrison in which they have won the regard of its inhabitants.

"The sight was indeed an exciting and exhilarating one, and amidst the roar of cannon, the shouts of enthusiastic thousands, the sound of soul-stirring music, and the waving of hats and handkerchiefs we felt carried away by the tumult of our feelings with an admiration of and a pride in belonging to the greatest nation in the universe."

The following address was presented to the Corps upon leaving Halifax:

"To Lieutenant-Colonel Ross, commanding Her Majesty's Royal Welch Fusiliers:

"SIR,
    "We the Magistrates of Halifax and others, having learned that the distinguished Corps under your command is about to be removed from this Province, beg leave on behalf of ourselves and our townsmen, to express our admiration of that uniform propriety for which it has ever been celebrated.

"It is highly honourable to the Regiment, that while their bravery in the field has universally merited the applause of their fellow subjects and obtained so many proofs of Royal approbation, they also in times of tranquility exemplify that respect for the social arrangements of life, which so happily blends the character of the civilian with that of the soldier. While we regret their departure it still is to us a pleasing duty to accompany that event with this public declaration of our unqualified esteem, and to add our testimony that though time and the ravages of war may have swept away the greatest part of those who composed the Regiment, when many years ago it formed part of our garrison, their successors continue to maintain the exalted character for which the 23rd have ever been admired.

"We embrace the present opportunity to render to the officers, non-commissioned officers, and privates our thanks for the valuable services, which upon every emergency they have promptly afforded the inhabitants of this town.

"To you, Sir, and all under your command we wish every success in that career to which you and they do so much honour.

"We feel assured that, wherever our beloved sovereign requires the services of the Royal Welch Fusiliers, their deportment will prove alike honourable to themselves and gratifying to all with whom they may be associated."

Signed by the Magistrates, Clergy, and all the respectable inhabitants of the town.

To this address Lieutenant-Colonel Ross made the following reply:

"HALIFAX, 3rd October, 1840.

"GENTLEMEN,
"In offering to you on behalf of the Royal Welch Fusiliers my most sincere thanks for the distinguished honour conferred upon the Corps by the highly flattering address of the Magistrates of Halifax, it affords me the highest pleasure to find that the conduct of the officers, non-commissioned officers, and soldiers has been such as to obtain for them the approbation of a community distinguished alike for intelligence, loyalty, hospitality, and good feeling. Altho' time and the chances of war have swept away with one exception our predecessors, of whom you have been pleased to retain such favourable impressions, yet I trust that the kindness we ourselves have experienced and the generous sentiments now expressed towards us, will more strongly cement the bonds of friendship and long keep alive the grateful recollection of Halifax which have been handed down to us and render them in a manner hereditary with the Royal Welch Fusiliers.

"Permit me to add that we leave you with no ordinary feelings of regret, and wherever our destiny may place us it will always be the highest ambition of myself and my companions in arms to discharge faithfully our duty to our Sovereign and to merit the esteem of Fellow Citizens.

"I have the honour to be, Gentlemen,
With feelings of respect and regard,
Your obedient Servant,
[signed]   WILLIAM ROSS, *Lieut.-Colonel,*
commanding Royal Welch Fusiliers."

1840.

DEPÔT COMPANIES.

On the 22nd of April the headquarters and 2 companies, 95 strong, marched from Castlebar and arrived at Newbridge on 1st May; the other 2 companies, 68 strong, marched on 23rd of April, arriving at Newbridge on the 2nd of May. On the 26th of April 1 sergeant, 2 corporals, and 58 men were transferred to the service companies, arriving at Halifax, Nova Scotia, on the 6th of June in the transport *Stokesby*. The depôt was inspected on the 28th of May by Lieutenant-General Sir E. Blakeney. There were present 9 officers and 222 non-commissioned officers and men. It marched, 209 strong, from Newbridge on 10th June, and arriving at Kingstown on the following day embarked upon H.M. war steamer *Vesuvius* on the 12th. Liverpool was reached on the 13th, where the troops were put on board a river steamer, and disembarking at Eastham marched to Chester, being billeted there on the 14th, and taking over the barracks in the Castle on the 15th. Towards the end of July a destructive fire broke out at a draper's establishment at Chester. The men of the depôt, under the direction of Major Holmes, "contributed in an eminent degree in staying the devastating march of the consuming flames." The companies, who were then under the command of Major Matheson, were inspected on the 26th October by Major-General Sir C. Napier, who reported as follows: "It has, I am informed, been the practice of this depôt in 'marking time,' to stamp with one foot, without throwing it out, so as to beat time. I understand also that this is the practice with the service companies. I have forbidden this with the depôt companies as contrary to the clear directions in the book of field exercises." He also remarked that "the charge for mess is 2s. 6d. without beer, this appears to me to be dear."

1841.

The headquarters of the regiment, which consisted on the 1st of January of 23 officers and 608 non-commissioned officers and men, remained at Montreal during the whole of this year.

The regiment was inspected at Montreal on the 9th of July by Major-General Clitheroe. Out of a total of 613 non-commissioned officers and men 369 were English, 3 Scotch, and 241 Irish. The following are extracts from the General's report: "The drums and fifes of this regiment are unusually perfect"; "the men very steady under arms; it is a fine regiment, and in excellent order."

On the 15th of October Lieutenant-Colonel Arthur Wellesley Torrens, from the 1st Battalion the Grenadier Guards, was appointed to the Lieutenant-Colonelcy of the regiment, vice Lieutenant-Colonel Ross retired on half-pay.

1841.

Depôt Companies.

On 9th April a detachment under the command of Major Holmes, consisting of 2 sergeants and 50 men, marched to Deptford for embarkation on board the transport *Albion*, in order to join the service companies: they arrived at Montreal on the 29th of May.

The companies were inspected on 1st May at Chester by Major-General Sir C. Napier, and on the 5th the depôt, 216 strong, proceeded to Birkenhead, was billeted there, and embarked on the 8th on H.M. steamer *Albion*. It disembarked at Port Carlisle and marched into Carlisle Barracks on the 9th.

1842.

1st Battalion.

Charles Dickens paid a visit to Montreal in 1842 and took part in some theatricals in which several of the officers of the Royal Welch Fusiliers, with their wives, performed.

The following is an extract from the Life of Dickens:

"Dickens went to Montreal in May, 1842. He says, I think I told you I had been invited to play with the officers of the Coldstream Guards here. . . . The play came off last night: the audience, between 500 and 600 strong, were invited as to a party: a regular table with refreshments being spread in the lobby and saloon.

"We had the band of the Twenty-third, one of the finest in the service, in the orchestra; Sir Charles Bagot, Sir Richard Jackson, and their staff were present. I prompted myself when I was not on. I really do believe that I was very funny: at least, I know that I laughed heartily at myself.

"I send you a bill, to which I have appended a key.

"PRIVATE THEATRICALS.

Committee.

Mrs. Torrens.   Mrs. Perry.
W. C. Ermatinger, Esq.   Captain Torrens.
The Earl of Mulgrave.

Stage Manager: MR. CHARLES DICKENS.

Queen's Theatre, Montreal.

"On Wednesday evening, May 25th, 1842, will be performed—

'A ROWLAND FOR AN OLIVER'

Mrs. Selbourne	MRS. TORRENS.
Maria Darlington	MRS. GRIFFIN.
Mrs. Fixture	MISS ERMATINGER.
Mr. Selbourne	LORD MULGRAVE.
Alfred Highflyer	MR. CHARLES DICKENS.
Sir Mark Chase	HONOURABLE MR. METHUEN.
Fixture	CAPTAIN WILLOUGHBY.
Gamekeeper	CAPTAIN GRANVILLE, 23RD.

After which an interlude in one scene (from the French) called—

'PAST TWO O'CLOCK IN THE MORNING'

The Stranger	CAPTAIN GRANVILLE, 23RD.
Mr. Sadlington	MR. CHARLES DICKENS.

"To conclude with the Farce in one act entitled—

'DEAF AS A POST'

Mrs. Plumpley	MRS. TORRENS.
Captain Templeton	CAPTAIN TORRENS, 23RD.
Amy Templeton	MRS. CHARLES DICKENS.
Mr. Walton	CAPTAIN WILLOUGHBY.
Sophy Walton	MRS. PERRY.
Tristram Sappy	DR. GRIFFIN.
Sally Maggs	MRS. GRIFFIN.
Crupper	LORD MULGRAVE.
Gollop	MR. CHARLES DICKENS.

"Gazette Office.

"MONTREAL, *May* 24*th*, 1842."

On 17th June the battalion was inspected at Montreal previous to its departure by Major-General Sir J. A. Hope, who remarked as follows: " I have the highest opinion of the state and discipline of the 23rd Regiment."

Drafts as follows were received on the 1st of July:

	Sergeant.	Corporals.	Privates.
From the 56th Regiment	—	2	48
,, ,, 67th ,,	1	2	47
,, ,, 70th ,,	—	2	46

while 72 men were transferred to the Reserve Battalion.

While in Montreal Major Holmes's house was burnt to the ground, and the famous "Spurs of Toby Purcell," then in his possession as Senior Major of the Regiment, were lost to the Royal Welch Fusiliers for ever.

These spurs were worn at the battle of the Boyne by Major Toby Purcell, who was appointed Major in the regiment shortly after its formation: and from that time up to the date when they were unfortunately lost in the fire that destroyed Major Holmes's house, it was the proud privilege of each Senior Major in succession to keep and wear these spurs. "Toby Purcell's Spurs and St. David" is one of the toasts that is drunk to this day by the officers of the Royal Welch Fusiliers every 1st of March.

The battalion left Montreal in two divisions: the 1st consisting of 286 men on 5th July, the 2nd division consisting of 250 men on the 7th, arriving at Kingston on the 12th and 14th of the month, where it was joined by the Reserve Battalion.

In October No. 1 and No. 2 companies, under Captain Crutchley, were sent to Belleville to act in aid of the Civil power in suppressing disturbances at an election at that place.

1842.

Depôt Companies.

On the 19th of March the companies, 248 strong, marched from Carlisle, arriving at Manchester on the 26th: where they remained about three weeks, receiving 70 volunteers from the 68th Regiment and 93 from the 66th Regiment. They then proceeded to Chichester under command of Lieutenant-Colonel Torrens.

On the 5th of May orders were received to augment the regiment to 1,200 rank and file. In consequence of this the depôt companies were formed into a Reserve Battalion as from the 14th of April, and 8 sergeants,

2 drummers, 7 corporals, and 75 privates who were to form the depôt left Chichester on the 18th under Captain Seymour and proceeded to Parkhurst Barracks.

1842.

Reserve Battalion.

On the 5th May the Reserve Battalion, composed of the four depôt companies and two new companies, was formed, and proceeded on the 12th to Portsmouth, where it embarked on H.M.S. *Resistance*, 520 strong, under Lieutenant-Colonel Torrens, on the 13th, in excellent order, so as to call for the particular commendation of Major-General Sir Hercules Pakenham, although so hurriedly that the equipment of clothing, belts, arms, and caps was only put on board on the day of embarkation, and was not unpacked until the arrival of the battalion at Kingston, Canada West.

After a stormy passage of six weeks the battalion arrived at Quebec on the 25th of June, and transhipping into a river steamer reached Montreal on 30th June; from there it proceeded the same day by barges to Kingston, arriving there the 6th of July, 493 strong. Major Holmes commanded the Reserve Battalion, but was under the superintendence of Lieutenant-Colonel Torrens, commanding the 1st battalion. On 26th September it was inspected at Kingston by Major-General Sir R. Armstrong. Being a Reserve Battalion it carried no colours, and there was no band beyond fifes and drums.

1843.

1st Battalion.

On the 24th of March the battalion was inspected at Kingston by Major-General Sir R. Armstrong. He reported as follows: "This fine battalion is in excellent order. The men are cheerful, healthy, and without a complaint: and a strong *esprit de corps* appears to reign among them." On 20th April a detachment under Lieutenant John Wynne marched by almost impassable roads to Cornwall, to relieve the Provincial Militia. On 21st April a similar detachment under Lieutenant Baker proceeded to Prescott and Brockville on a similar errand.

Orders having been received for the 1st battalion to proceed to the West Indies, it left Kingston in two divisions under Lieutenant-Colonel Torrens and Major Matheson respectively, on the 20th and 22nd

September. Both divisions embarked in excellent order and with perfect regularity. They proceeded in barges towed by small " propeller " steamers down the whole course of the St. Lawrence, passing through all the rapids. Part of the 1st division made the passage with extraordinary rapidity, for, including a transhipment of the division with its baggage at Montreal, it reached Quebec in forty-six hours after having left Kingston, a distance of about 400 miles.

One of the " propellers," having on board two officers and several sergeants, was nearly lost in the Lachine Rapids, being dismasted by a squall and the wreck of the mast fouling the rudder during the instant of passing through the very intricate channel of this most difficult and dangerous rapid. The presence of mind and the intrepidity of the pilot (Mr. Roebuck) were on this occasion the means of saving the steamer and all on board.

On arriving at Quebec the regiment embarked on board H.M.S. *Resistance*; the ship's log contains the following details of the embarkation:

Date.	Officers.	Men.	Women.	Children.	Total.
22nd	6	206	9	11	232
23rd	3	85	9	17	114
26th	7	223	18	27	275

The ship sailed on the 28th of September, and after a favourable passage, without any casualty, anchored in Carlisle Bay, Barbados, on the 23rd of October. The headquarters and Nos. 1, 4, and 5 companies disembarked on the following day under the command of the Lieutenant-Colonel, and took up their quarters in the Stone Barracks in the garrison of St. Ann's. The remaining companies, under the command of Major Matheson, proceeded on the 26th to Demerara, whence No. 2 company, under Captain Alcock, was dispatched to Mahaica.

Fever soon showed itself at Demerara and some deaths unfortunately ensued, when after a temporary cessation of the sickness it suddenly appeared again in a most virulent form, and four men died on the same day. Immediate steps were most wisely taken for a change in the distribution of the troops. No. 3 company, under the command of Lieutenant Ferguson, proceeded at a few hours' notice to Berbice, and No. 6 company, under Captain Willoughby, which remained at Demerara, was moved to another barrack, detaching a part of the company to Mahaica (a healthy post). This for a time had the desired effect of checking the epidemic.

1843.

Reserve Battalion.

On the 30th of January the battalion was specially inspected by Major-General Sir R. Armstrong owing to the rather numerous desertions taking place. In a report to the D.A.G. Montreal, dated 14th February, he stated that he had inspected the battalion not only by companies, but had individually asked every man on parade whether he was satisfied with his messing accounts and general treatment. As he had expected, they were all perfectly contented, and he could not elicit a single cause of complaint, but only shuffling excuses. He comments on the fact that the highest proportion of desertions — 1 in 10 — occurs amongst the volunteers from regiments in England, while the proportion of desertions amongst volunteers from regiments in Canada was only 1 in 24, thus showing that enlistment was merely used as means of obtaining a free passage to Canada with every intention of deserting to the United States.

On the 31st of March it was again inspected by Sir R. Armstrong. He stated " there are no desertions since my special inspection." The battalion moved in two divisions from Kingston on the 16th and 17th of June, 513 strong, and arrived at London, Canada West, on the 24th and 25th June, where it was stationed.

1843.

Depôt Companies.

A draft of 2 subalterns and 51 men left the depôt on the 12th of May to join the 1st battalion, arriving at Kingston, Canada West, on the 17th of July. On the 23rd of August a further draft of 1 subaltern and 40 privates embarked on the *Java* transport for Barbados. During the period September to December 159 recruits joined the depôt.

1844.

1st Battalion.

In consequence of the continued illness among the detachment stationed at Demerara under Major Matheson it was recalled, leaving there 202 strong on 27th March in the transport *General Palmer*, and disembarking at Barbados on 9th April. From the time of their arrival in that Colony up to the date of rejoining headquarters these companies had lost by death, from yellow fever, 3 sergeants and 17 privates.

On the 8th of May Captain W. L. Willoughby was appointed to command the troops at St. Kitts. On the 24th Captain D. Lysons was appointed to command the troops at Tobago, rejoining headquarters in September. This officer was subsequently General Sir Daniel Lysons, G.C.B., Constable of the Tower, etc. On the 26th of June Lieutenant-Colonel Torrens embarked for St. Lucia, to command the troops there—a command which involved the administration of the Government of the island for 2½ years, and by the sanitary measures he pursued the health of the troops serving in the island was preserved with unprecedented success.

The correspondence on this subject was subsequently published, by command of His Grace the Duke of Wellington, Commander-in-Chief, for the information and guidance of General and other officers commanding at foreign stations, in a circular letter dated from the Horse Guards on the 18th of November 1847, in which it was directed that similar precaution should be taken at all military commands, where draining and cleaning were requisite: particularly pointing out the salutary effects of removing from the immediate vicinity of military stations all superabundant vegetation, brushwood, strong weeds, rank grass, etc. etc., by means of fatigue parties, as had been effected at St. Lucia.

The following table shows the several stations at which mortality had occurred among the men of the 1st battalion, 23rd Royal Welch Fusiliers, in the West Indies from October 1843 to the 15th March 1847, distinguishing the chief classes of disease:

Diseases.	Barbados.	Demerara.	Trinidad.	Grenada.	Tobago.	Antigua.	Dominica.	St. Kitts.	
	No. 6 Comp.	No. 3 Comp.	No. 3 Comp.	No. 2 Comp.	No. 1 Comp.	No. 3 Comp.	No. 1 Comp.	No. 2 Comp.	
Died from Fevers	1	20	13	6	3	1	—	3	47
,, Pulmonary Diseases	7	2	6	2	2	4	—	—	23
,, Puteric Diseases	8	—	4	—	—	9	—	—	21
,, Hepatic Diseases	1	—	—	—	—	—	—	—	1
,, Diseases of Brain and Nerve	—	—	6	1	—	—	—	1	8
,, Dropsies	1	—	—	—	—	—	—	—	1
,, Other causes	1	—	1	—	—	—	—	—	2
	19	22	30	9	5	14	—	4	103

No returns are recorded for Nos. 4 and 5 companies.

In the month of February 1847 Lieutenant-Colonel Torrens received the offer of the permanent Lieutenant-Governorship of the island from Earl Grey, Secretary of State for the Colonies, on an augmented salary of £1,200 a year, in consequence, as His Lordship was pleased to express himself, of the energy and ability of his administration. Lieutenant-Colonel Torrens, however, preferring to continue his service in the Royal Welch Fusiliers, declined the appointment. He rejoined the regiment on the 8th of February 1847.

On 6th July Sergeant-Major C. Grant from the Grenadier Guards was appointed Quartermaster.

During the autumn the race-course would appear to have been much frequented, as Captain Lysons in his *Early Reminiscences* records he rode many successful races on a horse named " Highlander," the property of Captain W. H. Wellesley, 81st Foot, A.D.C.

At the inspection on 27th November by Lieutenant-General G. Middlemore at St. Ann's, Barbados, he states that " the general appearance of the regiment is excellent, and imposing, extremely steady under arms, and perfectly equal to undertake any manœuvres."

On 28th November the headquarters and Nos. 3, 5, and 6 companies, 269 strong, under the command of Captain Granville (leaving one company under Captain Campbell at Barbados), embarked on board the ship *Imogen* and brigantine *Bermudiana*, and sailed for Trinidad the same day, disembarking on the 2nd and 3rd of December, and were stationed at St. James. Two companies, Nos. 1 and 3, proceeded in December to Grenada under Captain Lysons; and No. 4 company under Lieutenant Routh embarked at Barbados on the 24th of that month, arriving at Tobago on the 26th.

During this year the regimental goat died, and Her Majesty was pleased to direct that the two finest goats belonging to a herd in Windsor Park —the gift of the Shah of Persia—should be given to the regiment. One of these was sent to the 1st battalion, and the other to the reserve battalion in Canada. These goats were then, as their successors are now, " the observed of all observers."

In connection with the above event the following amusing extract is taken from the *St. Lucia Palladium* of 3rd January 1846 :

" It has been the custom of this regiment, from time immemorial, to be preceded in all its marches and accompanied in all its parades by a mighty goat, the emblem of old Cambria, whose venerable beard and grave aspect might inspire the fanciful idea, under the old superstition of the transmutation of souls, of being a fitting dwelling-place for the departed spirit of one of those ancient bards so famed in Cambrian song, and of whom the poet writes:

> His hoary beard and tangled hair
> Stream'd like a meteor in the troubled air.

The last representative of this horned and bearded dynasty lately accompanied the regiment from Canada to Barbados, where his knowledge of his place at the head of the drums, his correct and soldierlike demeanour, his grave and patriarchal aspect, so struck the dusky race of Afric's blood that, on watching his stately progress at the head of the corps, the exclamation has been heard ' He got tense [sense] same as Christian.' Poor Billy! whether the climate disagreed with him, or he missed his native mountains, or he found his coat too hot for our broiling region, did never appear, but, alas! he died; and great was the lamentation throughout the regiment. The circumstance happened to be mentioned at the table of our Gracious Monarch, and the Queen directed that two milk-white goats, of a magnificent Cashmere breed, be forthwith presented to the gallant 23rd to replace poor Billy's loss. To feel their service and value thought of in the Royal Palace, when far away guarding the distant possession of their mistress, will add, if possible, to the *esprit de corps* and devotion of this famous old regiment."

1844.

Reserve Battalion.

It was to have been inspected at London, Canada, on 11th March by Major-General Sir R. Armstrong, but the following extract from his report explains why he was unable to do so: " In the rigorous climate of Canada, and the next to impossible state of the roads to the westward at this season of the year, it is impracticable for me personally to visit London."

On 20th May it received a transfer of 1 sergeant, 1 corporal, and 40 privates from the 68th regiment, and on the 30th a draft of 60 non-commissioned officers and men from the depôt.

1844.

Depôt Companies.

The companies embarked at Cowes on the 19th of May, 148 strong, on board H.M.S. *Blazer*, and disembarked the next day at Guernsey. They re-embarked upon the *Transit* steamer on the 14th of June, and,

"BILLY."

landing the next day in the Isle of Wight, proceeded to Parkhurst Barracks. On the 15th of June Major Crutchley took over command of the depôt from Captain Granville.

1845.

1st Battalion.

During the whole of this year it was stationed at Trinidad, the strength on the 1st of January being 19 officers and 505 non-commissioned officers and men. The company at Barbados under Captain Campbell was moved in January to Tobago, and on the 19th of that month a draft of 71 men joined from the depôt. Major Crutchley joined the headquarters of the battalion at Trinidad, and assumed command on the 26th of July, Lieutenant-Colonel Torrens being still in command at St. Lucia.

Captain Lysons records as follows : " Lieutenant Peregrine Phillips of the Royal Welch Fusiliers, having been ordered home to England, came up to Barbados to wait for his ship, and stayed with me. He had collected a number of curious animals to take home, among them a large baboon, a handsome macaw, a very fine sloth, an electric eel, an armadillo, a small deer, some parrots, etc.

" One day we had been bottling off a quarter-cask of ' Fusilier ' punch, and had emptied out the thick bottom of the punch into a tub and left it on the verandah. The unfortunate baboon got at the delicious beverage, and not having taken ' the pledge ' exceeded considerably. When we came home we found him lying hopelessly drunk. Next morning he was very bad, and we had to tie a wet handkerchief round his head and nurse him like a baby.

" I could not get Phillips to make any preparations for embarking his menagerie : consequently when the ship arrived I had to take him and his animals out to her loose in an open boat. I took the big baboon on my lap, Phillips had the macaw on his hand, his servant had charge of a few parrots, the eel was in a bucket at our feet, and all the other creatures were knocking about in the bottom of the boat. Just as we were approaching the ship, the macaw took fright and flew away : in getting on to the companion ladder the baboon managed to tumble into the water, but was fortunately saved. The boat rowed off vigorously after the macaw, but the poor thing got tired before it reached the shore and was drowned.

" We carried all the menagerie down into Perry Phillips' cabin, and I left him sitting with the half-drowned baboon wrapped up in a blanket on his lap, the motionless sloth in his berth, the electric eel very lively in his wash-stand basin, half a dozen parrots flying about, screaming violently, and the armadillo crawling about the floor inspecting the dead corpse of the macaw."

1845.

Reserve Battalion.

It was inspected on the 1st of March at London by Major-General Sir Richard Armstrong, who remarked as follows: "On the opening of navigation this battalion is under orders to remove to Canada East. I should not do justice to that valuable good old soldier, Major Holmes, the commanding officer, or to the officers and men if I refrained from saying how much I regret at losing him, and the fine battalion he has formed, from under my command. He has been most assiduous in so doing, and being well seconded by his officers and non-commissioned officers has fully succeeded. The privates are a body of very fine young men, and I look upon the condition of this Reserve Battalion as highly creditable to all concerned. They carry with them discipline, regularity, and orderly conduct, those sure elements of that success I so heartily wish them, and which I have no doubt they will reap, whenever occasion may offer, and nobly sustain the renown of the old Corps."

On the 12th of May the headquarters and 3 companies, 255 strong, left London and arrived at Chambley, Canada East, on the Richelieu, on the 22nd of May, detaching No. 7 company under Captain H. G. Anderdon to Fort William Henry, or Sorel, which was the summer residence of the Commander of the Forces. The left division set out on the 20th, and arrived there on the 31st of May. During the late autumn there were several cases of frost-bite.

1845.

Depôt Companies.

They remained at Parkhurst during the year. Captain F. Torrens took over command on the 1st of July from Captain Baker, who proceeded with a draft of 2 subalterns and 55 men on the *Atholl* troopship to join the 1st battalion at Trinidad.

1846.

1st Battalion.

On the 1st of January the battalion was distributed as follows: 3 companies at Trinidad, 2 at Grenada, and 1 at Tobago. On the 16th of March No. 3 company under Captain Roebuck embarked at Trinidad for Dominica, and on the 3rd of April the headquarters and Nos. 5 and 6 companies for Antigua, arriving there on the 13th, and being stationed at the Ridge. On the 11th of May Nos. 1 and 2 companies proceeded from Grenada to St. Kitts, No. 4 company from Tobago rejoining headquarters at Antigua. On the 31st of December the entire battalion was reunited at St. Ann's, Barbados, preparatory to quitting the Windward and Leeward command.

Early this year a beautiful monument was erected in the parochial church of St. Peter's Port, Guernsey, to the memory of General Sir Thomas Saumarez, who had served in the regiment with distinction during the American War of Independence. In October 1781 he was taken prisoner with the garrison of Yorktown: Lord Cornwallis ordered that 1 captain and 3 subalterns from each regiment should remain with the prisoners, and Captain Saumarez proved the unlucky one; he marched with the regiment from Yorktown to Winchester and from there to Lancaster. On the 2nd of June 1782 he with the other 12 captains taken prisoners were ordered by the American Congress and General Washington to assemble at Lancaster to draw lots that one might be selected to suffer the death penalty by way of retaliation; the lot fell on Sir Charles Asgill, but the penalty was not carried out. Captain Saumarez, being the senior officer with the British troops whilst they were prisoners, had charge of them during their nineteen months' captivity.

1846.

Reserve Battalion.

The battalion was augmented this year by one lieutenant-colonel, a surgeon, and a quartermaster. Major Holmes, who had long commanded the battalion, was promoted to the Lieutenant-Colonelcy on the 14th of April, Surgeon Robert Smith was appointed from the Staff on the 7th of August, and Quartermaster-Sergeant Robert Fortune was appointed Quartermaster on 25th of August.

1846.

Depôt Companies.

On the 27th of May a draft was dispatched to the reserve battalion by Captain Torrens, in command of the depôt, by the *Florentia* freightship.

It consisted of 1 corporal and 50 privates, and reached the battalion on the 20th of July.

1847.

1st Battalion.

On the 16th of March the battalion embarked at Barbados on board the freightship *Herefordshire* and sailed on the following day for Halifax, Nova Scotia, where it arrived on the 2nd of April (to find the ground covered with snow), and disembarked on the 3rd, having left but one man behind, sick at Barbados.

On the 13th of June No. 5 company under Captain Rickford embarked at Halifax for Cape Breton; and No. 6 company under Captain Evans for Prince Edward's Island.

The battalion was inspected on the 26th of June by Lieutenant-General Sir John Harvey, and soon afterwards received a transfer of 2 sergeants, 3 corporals, and 57 privates from the 89th Regiment.

The efficient state of the 23rd Royal Welch Fusiliers after its service in the West Indies of three years and a half, including a separation into detachments for the greater portion of that time, received the marked commendation of His Excellency Lieutenant-General Sir John Harvey, K.C.B., K.C.H., commanding the troops in Nova Scotia.

The following is an extract from a letter from Lieutenant-General Sir John Harvey to General Sir W. Gordon, Colonel of the Royal Welch Fusiliers, dated—

"HALIFAX, *July 1st*, 1847.

"The state in which the Twenty-third Fusiliers were produced for my inspection within a few weeks of their arrival from the West Indies, where they had been dispersed throughout many islands, it has been my endeavour to bring to the favourable notice of the Commander-in-Chief in my confidential report which I am now engaged in making.

"This, however, cannot be forwarded just yet, and in the meantime it occurred to me that it could not be otherwise than gratifying to you to be assured that your regiment is all you could wish it, whether as respects health, description of men, discipline in the field of exercise, conduct in quarters, and complete efficiency in every other respect."

Surgeon E. Bradford of the battalion was the hero of the following adventure as narrated by Captain Lysons:

"One night I took old Bradford down the harbour in my skiff to spear lobsters by torchlight. It was curious sport. The bottom near Mac-Nabb's Island was beautiful, smooth, white sand, and we could see the big lobsters crawling about by the light of a red-cedar torch, which we fastened over the bow of the boat. When we lowered our spears towards them, they put up their claws and showed fight. We then had dexterously to thrust our spears down just behind their forearms, and bring them up with their legs and claws sprawling about and throw them into the bottom of the boat. That night we caught a lot of very large ones. The spears did not go through them: they were made of two springy pieces of wood that caught them on each side of their backs.

"Rowing back again up to Halifax, Bradford offered to take the oars. At first he did very well, but after a while, getting too confident, he caught a crab, and over he went backwards all amongst the lobsters! His cries were dreadful. I rushed to his rescue and pulled him up with a number of the great black-looking things hanging all over him—to his ears, head, and tail. It was some time before I could get them all off."

The following is another extract, but of a different nature:

"One day Captain Evans came to me boiling over with wrath and indignation. He said he had been grossly insulted by Captain Harvey, the Governor's son, and begged me to act as his friend. I agreed, provided he promised to do exactly as I told him. He consented.

"I called on Captain Harvey's friend, Captain Bourke, and we agreed to abide by the Duke of Wellington's order about duelling, which had just then been promulgated at Halifax. We carried out our intention as follows: We made each of our principals write out his own version of what had occurred. We then chose an umpire. We selected Colonel Horn, of the 20th Regiment, a clear-headed and much-respected officer. With his approval we sent him the two statements, and he directed us to come to his house the following morning with our principals.

"At the appointed time we arrived, and were shown into the dining-room. We bowed formally to each other across the table, and awaited the appearance of our referee.

"Colonel Horn soon entered, and addressing our principals, said: 'Gentlemen, in the first place I must thank you for having made my duty so light. Nothing could be more open, generous, or gentlemanlike than your statements. The best advice I can give you is that you shake hands and forget the occurrence has ever happened.' They at once walked up to each other, and shook hands cordially. They were the best of friends ever after.

"This was, I believe, the first case that occurred of a settlement.

on the Duke of Wellington's system, of an affair of honour. Poor Evans was afterwards killed at the battle of the Alma."

1847.

Reserve Battalion.

In June it received a transfer of 3 sergeants, 1 corporal, and 27 privates from the 52nd Regiment. It was inspected at Chambley on the 18th of June by Major-General the Hon. Charles Gore; on the 21st July the headquarters and 5 companies marched from Chambley, arriving at Montreal the same day, to relieve the 52nd Light Infantry ordered home; No. 10 company from Sorel rejoining on the 24th.

The battalion was inspected on the 2nd of August by Major-General Sir J. Hope, who stated that "the 23rd Royal Welch Fusiliers are in their usual good state of discipline, drill, and appearance."

1847.

Depôt Companies.

Recruits joined the depôt as follows: February, 30; March, 53; April 78, and in consequence on the 1st of May there were 160 "supernumeraries," the establishment of the depôt being only 92. On the 11th of that month a draft of 1 corporal and 50 privates under Lieutenant Hopton left in the *Apollo* troopship to join the reserve battalion.

1848.

1st Battalion.

On the 26th of May the battalion under Major Crutchley was inspected at Halifax by Lieutenant-General Sir John Harvey. In his general observations he remarks as follows: "In the field as in quarters the regiment's appearance is equally commendable, and reflects great credit on all ranks; it is in a highly efficient state."

On the 16th of September the battalion under the command of Major Crutchley embarked at Halifax on board H.M. transport *Java* for England, the strength being 17 officers, 25 sergeants, 6 drummers, 22 corporals, and 338 men: having transferred to the 1st battalion of the 97th, 3 sergeants, 1 corporal, and 45 privates. It landed at Portsmouth on the 7th of October and proceeded immediately to Winchester, where it was joined on the 16th by the depôt companies under Captain Phillott.

THE COLOURS.

[*Frontispiece*

OFFICER, 1820.

BAND, 1848.

PRIVATE AND BANDSMAN, 1852.

OFFICER, 1857.

PRIVATE, 1900.

OFFICERS, SERGEANT, ETC., 1914.

On the 28th of October it was inspected there by Major-General Lord F. FitzClarence, G.C.H., who reported as follows:

"*Officers.*—I never have seen officers so well instructed, and I never saw better Captains in every respect, both in the field and every situation.

"*Non-commissioned officers.*—Nothing can be better.

"*Field exercises.*—Nothing can be better.

"*Outpost duties.*—The only regiment that has come under my orders that has in the slightest degree attended to H.M. Regulations in this particular.

"*General Remarks.*—I cannot express myself too strongly in praise of Lieutenant-Colonel Torrens, the Major, Captains, and officers, and non-commissioned officers in general. The zeal, attention, and assiduity of the Lieutenant-Colonel coupled with his talents, assisted as he is by all, makes the Royal Welch, I truly think, the most perfect regiment I have seen since I have had the honour to be on the Staff. Lieutenant-Colonel Torrens' knowledge of his profession and his power of imparting it to those under him render him a most excellent and valuable officer; his good example seems to have given a military feeling and tone to all in this highly old established and distinguished regiment. I beg strongly to recommend this regiment to the Commander-in-Chief's most favourable commendation."

1848.

Reserve Battalion.

The battalion continued in Montreal with the 19th and 77th Regiments until the spring of 1849. It was inspected on the 20th of May, and the 11th of October, by Major-General the Hon. C. Gore. On the 29th of September a draft of 44 privates joined from England: and on the 30th of December a detachment of 1 sergeant and 36 privates proceeded to relieve a similar detachment of the 19th Regiment, stationed at Monklands, the residence of the Governor-General.

1848.

Depôt Companies.

On the 16th of October the depôt under Captain Phillott, with a strength of 1 captain, 3 subalterns, 7 sergeants, 2 drummers, and 234 privates, joined the 1st battalion at Winchester.

1849.

1st Battalion.

On the 1st of June the battalion was inspected by Major-General Lord F. FitzClarence. In the same month a draft of 2 officers, 1 sergeant, and 50 privates embarked on the troopship *Euphrates* to join the reserve battalion. Recruiting parties were stationed at Oxford and Southampton. The results of their efforts per month were as follows: 16, 18, 13, 6, 4, 4, 5, 22, 27, 34, 29, and 27. A comparison of these figures shows the usual falling off in recruiting during the summer months.

On the 12th of July, new colours were presented to the 23rd Royal Welch Fusiliers by Field-Marshal His Royal Highness the Prince Consort, at Winchester Barracks.

The regiment, being drawn up in line with the old colours in the centre, received His Royal Highness with the usual honours; the flank companies were then brought forward so as to form three sides of a square, to the centre of which the new colours were brought under escort and piled on an altar of drums. The Rev. George Gleig, M.A., Chaplain-General to the Forces, then consecrated them, after which His Royal Highness delivered them to Lieutenants Bruce and Sutton, making the following address to the battalion:

"Soldiers of the Royal Welch Fusiliers,—The ceremony which we are performing this day is a most important and to every soldier a most sacred one: it is the transmission to your care and keeping of the colours which are henceforth to be borne before you, which will be the symbol of your honour and your rallying points in all moments of danger. I feel most proud to be the person who is to transmit these colours to a regiment so renowned for its valour, fortitude, steadiness, and discipline.

"In looking over the records of your services, I could not refrain from extracting a few, which show your deeds to have been intimately connected with all the great periods in our history.

"The regiment was raised in 1689. Its existence, therefore, began with the settlement of the liberties of the country. It fought at the Boyne, under Schomberg: captured Namur, in Flanders, in 1695: formed part of the Great Marlborough's legions at Blenheim, Ramillies, Oudenarde, and Malplaquet: fought in 1743 at Dettingen, and at Fontenoy in 1745: decided the battle of Minden in 1759, for which the name of Minden is inscribed on the colours: showed examples of valour and perseverance in

America in 1775: at Bunker's Hill in 1777: at Brandywine in 1780: at the capture of Charlestown: and in 1781 at Guildford. The regiment accompanied the Duke of York to Holland, was amongst the first to land in Egypt in 1801, under the brave Abercromby, and was the last to embark at Corunna in 1809. Between those two important services it fought at Copenhagen, and was at the taking of Martinique; Egypt, Martinique, and Corunna are waving on these colours In the Peninsula the regiment won for its colours, under the Duke of Wellington, the names of Albuhera, Badajos, Salamanca, Vittoria, Pyrenees, Nivelle, Orthes, and Toulouse. The deeds performed at Albuhera are familiar to everybody who has read Napier's unsurpassable description of that action. The regiment was again victorious over a powerful enemy at the Duke's last great victory at Waterloo. Although you are all, of course, well acquainted with these glorious records, I have thought it right to refer to them, as a proof that they have not been forgotten by others, and as the best mode of appealing to you to show yourselves at all times worthy of the name you bear.

"Receive these colours—one emphatically called 'The Queen's,' let it be a pledge of your loyalty to your Sovereign, and of obedience to the laws of your country: the other—more especially the Regimental one—let that be a pledge of your determination to maintain the honour of your regiment. In looking at the one you will think of your Sovereign; in looking at the other you will think of those who have fought, bled, and conquered before you."

To which gracious address Lieutenant-Colonel Arthur Wellesley Torrens replied in these words:

"May it please Your Royal Highness, in the name of the Royal Welch Fusiliers I return to you the heartfelt thanks of the regiment for the honour you have conferred upon us this day.

"The eminent services of the Royal Welch Fusiliers during a lapse of 160 years are deeply impressed upon our memories, and while we welcome the responsibility, we feel the privilege of succeeding to so vast an inheritance of renown.

"Our hearts have beat with pride and exultation to hear those achievements so accurately remembered, and so gracefully recorded by your Royal Highness, the honoured Consort of the Sovereign to whose service we have devoted our lives.

"With the exception of a brave and skilful officer (Lieutenant-Colonel

Holmes), now absent in command of a battalion of the regiment in America, and of two highly-respected veteran officers present upon this parade (the Paymaster and the Quartermaster of the battalion), not one of the present generation of Welch Fusiliers here had a share in the acquisition of the glorious badges which are inscribed on their colours.

"But though it has not been our good fortune to have taken part in any of the campaigns since the termination of the great Continental War, the regiment has served faithfully, patiently, and honourably, though with less brilliant glory, indeed, during a prolonged foreign and colonial service in every climate—from the burning sun of the Mediterranean and of Portugal, to the snows of the Canadas, and the heat and pestilence of the West Indian Archipelago.

"Throughout I have seen the discipline of the regiment preserved, and its high spirit maintained: and, Sir, I know and feel that when the hour of trial shall arrive, it will be found that a discipline so patient and so enduring is animated yet by the selfsame determination which hurled back the French masses from Albuhera's heights, and stemmed their squadrons on the crowning field of Waterloo."

The new colours were then trooped, and took the place of the old ones, which were marched off the parade.

The battalion then marched past in slow and quick time.

His Royal Highness afterwards honoured the officers with his presence at luncheon. The old colours were lodged in the Church of St. Peter's, Carmarthen, on the 19th of November, with military honours.

Strange to relate, the War Office refused to grant a " route " or free pass for the escort.

The following account of the ceremony is taken from the private diary of the late C. Diggle Williams of Carmarthen (now in possession of the Carmarthen Antiquarian Society):

" Monday, 19th November 1849. The Mayor, Corporation, and a large number of the inhabitants of Carmarthen assembled in the Town Hall about 11 o'clock.

" Colonel Love, the Commandant of the district, accompanied by his aide-de-camp, Captain Mann, both in full dress uniform, rode up to Saint Peter's Church about the same hour—half an hour after which the soldiers of the garrison, consisting of a Troop of the 5th Dragoon Guards, commanded by Capt. Prime, with the left wing, about 200 rank and file of the 14th Regiment, commanded by Major Watson, arrived near the

Hall, and were joined by the Mayor, Corporation, and inhabitants. The procession was then formed in the following order :

Police Officers.
Town Crier, with insignia of office.
Mace-bearers with maces.
Sword-bearer with sword.
The Mayor in scarlet robes.
Aldermen, two abreast.
Troop of 5th Dragoon Guards on foot.
Fifes and Drums.

The Colours, borne by Lieut. Slater and Ensign Armstrong of the 14th Regiment, supported by two Colour-Sergeants.

About 200 rank and file of the 14th Regiment in marching order, with fixed bayonets.

Old Pensioners wearing their medals.

"The procession reached the Church in the above order. When it arrived there Archdeacon Bevan, the Vicar, in full canonicals, accompanied by both churchwardens, came out to meet the Mayor and Corporation, and conducted them into the Church, where they were met by Colonel Love and his aide-de-camp. The Infantry filed right and left in the Churchyard, the colours being placed in the centre. Some evolutions were performed, the Colours were saluted for the last time, and then carried through the western door into the Church, in the north aisle of which they were received by Colonel Love, who, taking one in each hand, and standing in the centre, addressed the assembly in an appropriate speech, and delivered the Colours over to Valentine Davies, Esq., Mayor, who replied in appropriate terms, upon receiving them. The Mayor then carried the Colours to the entrance to the chancel, and they were fixed by some workmen on each side of the arch which separates the chancel from the north aisle. The organ then struck up 'God Save the Queen,' which ended the ceremony in the Church. The company retired, and the Military were marched to their quarters.

"These Colours were presented to the Regiment in 1816, and bear on them the names following : Minden, Egypt, Corunna, Martinique, Albuhera, Badajoz, Salamanca, Vittoria, Pyrenees, Nivelle, Orthes, Toulouse, Peninsula, Waterloo.

"The conduct of the Mayor, Corporation, Clergy, and inhabitants of Carmarthen in receiving and depositing the Colours was so gratifying to the 23rd Regiment that the Commanding Officer wrote the letter (of which the following is a copy) to the Mayor:

"WINCHESTER,
30 *Nov.* 1849.

"SIR,

"I beg you will accept for yourself, and further do me the favour of communicating, as far as possible, to the other gentlemen of the Corporation and city of Carmarthen, the expression of the warm thanks of the officers, non-commissioned officers, drummers, and private soldiers of the Welch Fusiliers, for the respect which has been shown to the worn-out Colours of the Regiment on the occasion of their deposit in the Church of St. Peter in your city.

"The Royal Welch Fusiliers cherish proudly their connection with the Principality of Wales, and if anything could add to the devotion with which they serve Her Majesty and their native land it is their knowledge that their brethen in civil life sympathise with them as you do—that they remember their perils and appreciate their privations, and that they venerate, even with a soldier's reverence, those symbols of loyalty and patriotism which the Church (having in the first instance consecrated them) now welcomes back to their final resting place to one of her sacred and time-honoured edifices.

"I have the honour to be, Sir,
Your Worship's most obedient humble servant,
[*signed*]   ARTHUR W. TORRENS,
Lieutenant-Colonel Royal Welch Fusiliers, commanding 1st Battalion.

"To his Worship, the Mayor of Carmarthen."

The battalion remained at Winchester during this year.

1849.

RESERVE BATTALION.

On the 25th of April Lord Elgin, the Governor-General, proceeded to Parliament House, Montreal, to give Royal Assent to various Bills, including the Indemnity Bill, which was to allow compensation to the inhabitants of Lower Canada for losses they had sustained during the Rebellion of 1837-38. He was received with disapprobation and uproar: and in the evening the populace burst open the door of the Parliament House and proceeded to set fire to the building, which was completely

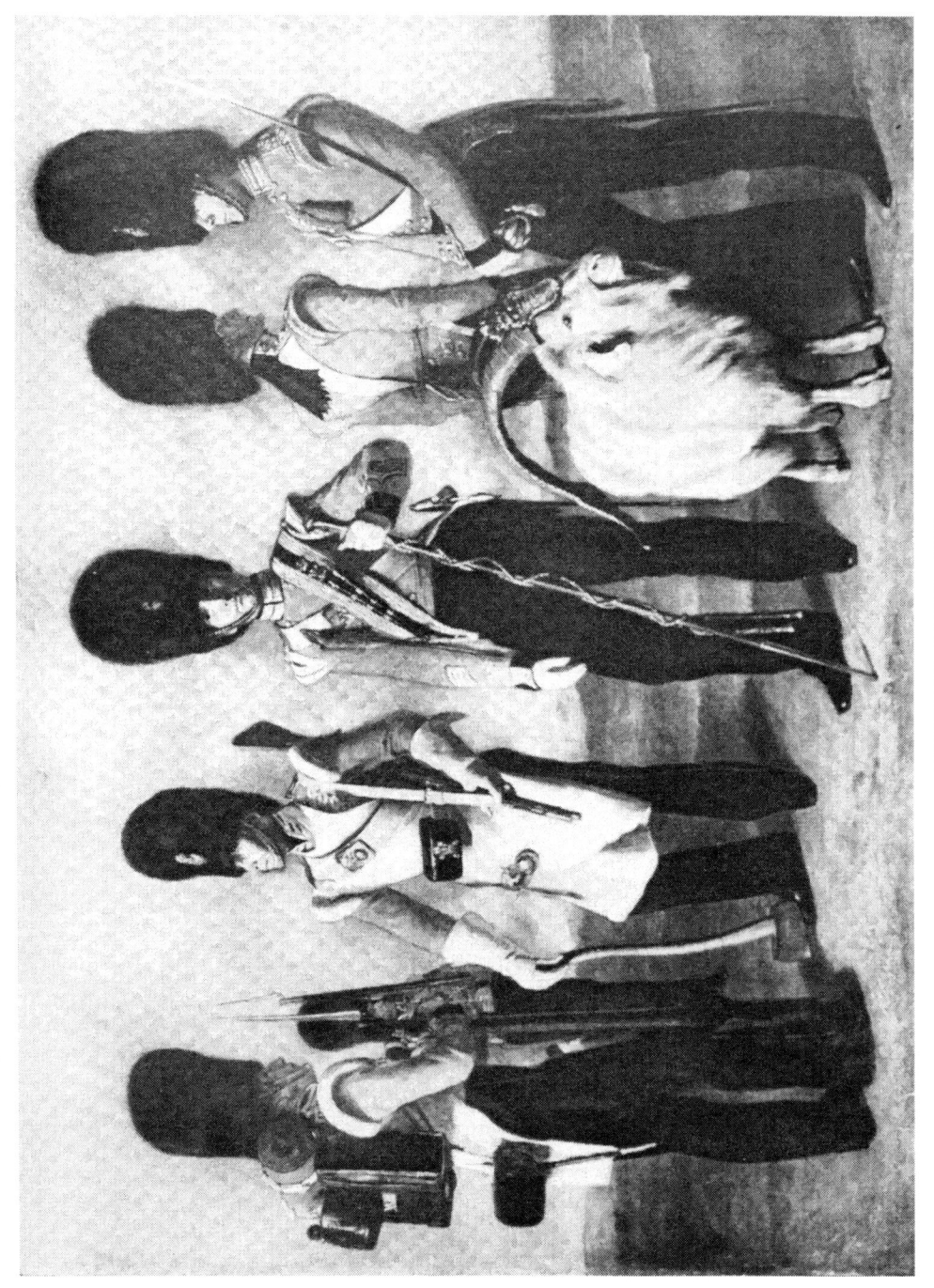

PORTRAIT GROUP, 1849.

Pte. Kennedy.　　Pte. Marsh.　　Pioneer Thompson.　　Drum-Major T. Noble.　　"Billy."　　Lt. F. B. Tritton.　　Lt. R. Bruce.

From the original painting at Wrexham Barracks.

gutted; the troops were called out and were reinforced by the 71st Light Infantry from St. John's, a fort on the River Richelieu.

Fortunately the riots were put down without bloodshed. The troops on that occasion received the thanks of His Excellency Sir Benjamin D'Urban, K.C.B., Commander of the Forces, for their forbearance, good temper, and discipline in the face of thousands of exasperated rioters.

On the 30th of June a detachment of 1 sergeant and 40 privates proceeded to Monklands, to furnish a guard at the residence of the Governor General, returning on the 16th of July.

The health of the regiment in July is described as "indifferent" owing to the outbreak of cholera in Montreal and many other cities of Canada: there was a daily average of 30 sick, and four privates died from cholera. One of the first victims was Lieutenant-Colonel R. P. Holmes, who died on the 23rd of July of cholera. He had served 38 years in the Royal Welch Fusiliers, and no officer was ever more lamented than this "Father of the battalion" as he was called by all ranks; he joined the regiment as 2nd Lieutenant on 14th February 1811, and served with it at Waterloo.

Captain H. G. Chester (afterwards killed at the head of the regiment at the battle of the Alma) took temporary command of the battalion until the arrival of Lieutenant-Colonel Crutchley, who had been promoted to the Lieutenant-Colonelcy.

The battalion was inspected at Montreal on the 16th of October by Lieutenant-General W. Rowan, who stated as follows: "This is a very pretty battalion. The officers and men are well drilled, and the latter are considerably above the average standard."

1850.

1st Battalion.

On the 1st of January the strength of the battalion was as follows: 25 officers, 37 sergeants, 31 corporals, 13 drummers, and 685 privates.

On the 23rd of April the headquarters and Nos. 1, 2, 4, and 5 companies left Winchester by rail, and embarking at Portsmouth on board H.M.S. steam frigate *Birkenhead*, landed at Plymouth next morning, when they occupied the Citadel. Nos. 3 and 6 companies left Winchester on the 29th, and embarked the same day on board the *Birkenhead*, landing at Plymouth next day. In May a draft of 2 sergeants and 82 men proceeded in the troopship *Java* to join the reserve battalion in Canada. It was inspected at Plymouth on the 3rd of June by Major-General the Hon. H. Murray, who remarked as follows: " I consider the state of the Royal Welch Fusiliers to be more perfect than that of almost any regiment that I have seen." He again inspected it on the 10th of October. In his general observations he remarks as follows: " The 23rd is in very high order. The officers are much liked in Society, and off duty are fond of hunting, which gives them active habits and knowledge of the country. I am persuaded that in any circumstances in which the regiment may be called upon for exertion, it will fully answer expectation."

1850.

Reserve Battalion.

The battalion, which had been stationed in Montreal since July 1847, was ordered to move to London, Canada West, on the 1st, 11th, and 21st of May, for the purpose of relieving the reserve battalion of the 20th. It proceeded by the River St. Lawrence and Lakes Ontario and Erie. Unfortunately the steamer *Commerce*, having on board Captain Phillott, 2nd Lieutenants Sir Henry Chamberlain and Radcliffe, and Assistant Surgeon Grantham, with No. 8 Company and several women and children, in all about 112 persons, was run down by the steamer *Despatch* on Lake Erie at 11 o'clock on the night of the 6th May, and Assistant Surgeon Grantham, 3 sergeants, 1 drummer, 2 corporals, 19 privates, and 8 women were drowned.

The circumstances are detailed in the official account of the accident addressed by Captain Phillott to the Assistant Adjutant-General at Kingston.

"*On board*, H.M.S. '*Minos*,'
Port Maitland,
8th May 1850.

" Sir,

" In connection with the telegraphic despatch I forwarded to Major-General Gore yesterday, it now becomes my painful duty to report to you for the information of the Major-General Commanding the Western District, the particulars of the melancholy disaster that has befallen the Detachment of the 23rd Fusiliers under my command.

" The *Commerce* and the *Cathcart* arrived at Port Maitland on the Monday morning; the latter having damaged her paddles was detained until half-past 10 o'clock that night, as my orders were to remain in company with her, and as we were much the fastest sailer the Captain of the *Commerce* allowed the *Cathcart* to precede us and the *Commerce* therefore did not sail from hence until about 11 o'clock p.m. of Monday night the 6th instant.

" The men were all asleep on the covered deck, except a guard of 1 sergeant and 12 men with 4 sentries stationed at the gangway and an Orderly Sergeant at a ladder, leading to the Hurricane Deck above, and a Sergeant and Corporal on that deck. These precautions I had adopted with the view of preventing any desertion through the Welland Canal, as well as other places we had touched at on our voyage from Montreal. At the distance of about three miles from Port Maitland and standing our straight course for Port Stanley, I was awoke in my berth on the upper deck by a violent concussion and loud cries from the sailors outside. I immediately called up all the officers, and finding that the steamer *Despatch* had stove in our bows got the men and women on the upper deck instantly.

" At first for a moment or two there was some confusion, the women screaming loudly, but the men fell in at my desire immediately, and remained in very good order and quiet as far as circumstances would permit. The sailors then endeavoured to lower a boat: but did not succeed in getting her wholly into the water; four or five soldiers jumped into it and fell from her into the water. I extricated one and three more clambered back again, but one or perhaps two sank.

" By this time our vessel began to sink at the bows, the water coming up to the deck and the lower deck being full to the top of the ladder. She then heeled to starboard, righted, and gradually began to settle down. The *Despatch* had after the collision kept away. I understand when I first observed her she was about four hundred yards from our starboard bow. We hailed her to draw nearer, but for some minutes she did not appear to move. I entreated the men to remain quiet and stay with me, and explained that the *Commerce* would not sink altogether for some time; the greater part obeyed me and encouraged each other to ' hold on,' but I have since learnt that three or four married men jumped with their wives into the water to swim to the *Despatch*, but were drowned. The steamer plunged once and then gradually heeled over to starboard, leaving her larboard side from the keel upwards. The men followed me and clung on as well as they could, the water being about half a foot up our legs. The sea was running rather high and the rolling of the wreck caused all who could not find anything to grasp to fall into the water, and here the great loss of life took place. It was utterly out of my power to help them. The Captain, Dr. Grantham, two men, and young Rogers had climbed to the top of the mast; the men descended, but sad to relate, Dr. Grantham, who could not swim, and young Rogers then perished.

"By this time half an hour had elapsed when to our great relief the *Despatch* closed us, and 3 officers, 92 men, 12 women, and 9 children, some by swimming, and others hauled up by ropes, gained her deck. I think it right to add that I remained on the wreck until the last person had left it.

"I shouted loudly for Grantham, but could neither see nor hear him, and then I swam to the *Despatch* and was pulled up. On landing I applied to Mr. Hatch the Master-Gunner in charge of the *Minos*, and with the greatest promptitude he received us on board and with the greatest kindness administered to the wants of the men and women, some of whom were in their shirts only and all only half clad, so impossible was it to save anything but our lives. The arms, accoutrements, packs, and baggage of officers' mess were all below in the hold, and all are lost. I have contracted with a butcher and baker in the village to supply the men with bread and meat, but I fear the price will be more than the Commissariat contract.

"The magistrates have taken up the loss of life with a great determination to enquire most strictly into the particulars, and have notified to me that they require the presence of an officer and witnesses to identify the bodies.

"As some things have already been washed ashore and pillaged, and others may be so, I propose with the approbation of the Major-General to leave Sir Henry Chamberlain, 1 sergeant, and 2 privates for that purpose should the *Cathcart* return from Port Stanley to embark us. I beg to add that the expense of communicating by telegraph is exceedingly expensive, the nearest post being St. Catherine's, a distance of 35 miles, and the cost of a man and a horse 3 dollars each trip, besides the expense at the office.

"In conclusion I would take leave to add that the conduct and bearing of my subalterns, Lieutenant Sir Henry Chamberlain and 2nd Lieutenant Radcliffe, during the trying time of our disaster was most soldierlike and excellent. Both exerted themselves to their utmost to assist me; Sir Henry Chamberlain narrowly escaped with his life, having been washed off the wreck and pulled on board in an exhausted state. The kindness of the inhabitants and magistrates towards us has been most gratifying.

"I have, etc.,

[*signed*] FRED PHILLOTT, *Captain*,
Commanding Detachment, 23rd Fusiliers.

"Lieut.-Colonel Young, K.H., Asst. Adjutant-General, Kingston."

The Commander-in-Chief was pleased on this occasion to express his approbation of the conduct of the troops in the following terms :

"HORSE GUARDS, *8th June* 1850.

" Memo. for the Qr.-Mr. General.

" The Military Secretary begs to return the papers transmitted by the Quarter-Master General in his memorandum of the 5th instant and to acquaint him that they have been submitted to the Commander-in-Chief, who has received similar reports from the Lieut.-General Commanding the troops in Canada and has been pleased to express his approbation of the conduct of both the officers and men on board the *Commerce* under most trying circumstances.

" [*signed*]   FITZROY SOMERSET."

There can be little doubt that the loss of life would have been much greater but for the self-possession, courage, and activity of Captain Phillott, who, with the other officers, was the last to quit the wreck.

The following additional details are gleaned from the *Hamilton (Canada) Spectator* of Saturday, 2nd May 1914. From this it appears that the *Commerce*, pursuing her usual course S.S.W., directly on leaving the port descried a steamer bearing towards her which proved to be the *Despatch* from Port Stanley to Buffalo. The *Commerce* bore away in order to give her a wide berth, but, strange to say, the *Despatch* continued to approach.

The *Commerce* then deviated still further from her course, always keeping her own side, until finally, when the *Despatch* appeared determined to cross her bows, her helm was put hard to port.

Immediately afterwards the collision took place. The *Despatch* struck the *Commerce* a few feet from the bow : the hold filled with water and the vessel lay with her bows downwards at an angle of 45 degrees. The engineer opened the safety valve of the engine and thus doubtless prevented an explosion.

On the sixty-fourth anniversary of the loss of the *Commerce*, viz. 6th May 1914, the rector (the Rev. Canon P. L. Spencer) and churchwardens of Christ Church, Port Maitland, decided to put the grave of the victims in perfect order, and otherwise show respect to their memory.

On the last-mentioned date a memorial service was held by the rector and clergy of the rural deanery of Haldimand County ; the Hamilton Army and Navy Veterans' Association also took part, placing a wreath bearing the colours of the Royal Welch Fusiliers on the grave.

The inscription on the memorial slab is as follows :

"The officers, non-commissioned officers, and privates of the Reserve Battalion, 23rd Royal Welsh Fusiliers, have erected this stone to mark the spot where lie the remains of Assistant Surgeon Grantham and twenty-four men, women, and children of that regiment, who perished near this shore by the sinking of the steamer *Commerce* on the night of the 6th of May 1850, whilst on their route from Montreal to London, Canada West."

1851.

1st Battalion.

On the 31st of January, Major-General George Charles D'Aguilar, C.B., was appointed Colonel of the 23rd, in succession to General Sir James Willoughby Gordon, G.C.B., deceased.

The battalion remained at Plymouth until July, when the headquarters, recruits, and one company under command of Lieutenant-Colonel Torrens proceeded to Chester, 1 company under Captain Tritton to the Isle of Man, and 4 companies under Major Lysons to Liverpool.

The regiment furnished 3 guards of honour on the occasion of Queen Victoria's visit to Liverpool in October. On Thursday the 9th of October Her Majesty passed through the principal streets of the town, and at the Landing Stage, St. George's Pier, "a guard of honour, composed of the 23rd Royal Welch Fusiliers, arrived at the pier at 10 o'clock from Chester, in great-coats and heavy marching order. They were accompanied by their celebrated regimental goat, a present from Her Majesty. The animal is of the white Cashmere species, and bears on its forehead a massive silver plate recording its presentation to the regiment by Her Majesty. The Earl Cathcart, General commanding the district, with Colonel Torrens and a brilliant staff of officers, came about the same time to await Her Majesty's arrival."

The explanation of the "three guards of honour" as stated above is given by Captain Lysons in his *Early Reminiscences*, as follows :

"Her Majesty the Queen visited Liverpool, and I had three guards of honour under my command at different places, but only one band and one goat, the gift of Her Majesty to the regiment. As soon as I had given my royal salute at one place I had to take a short cut and hurry away to the next, with the band and goat. Fortunately Billy behaved remarkably well. The vast mob were very good-humoured and much interested to get us along. I believe, if it had been necessary, they would have

THE OFFICERS.
Noncommissioned Officers
and Privates of the Reserve
BATTALION.
23rd Royal Welch Fusiliers, have
Erected this Stone to mark the Spot
where lie the Remains of
ASSISTANT SURGEON GRANTHAM.
and Twenty Four Men Women
and Children of that
REGIMENT.
Who Perished near this Shore, by the
Sinking of the Steamer
COMMERCE.
On the Night of the
6th of May 1850, whilst on
their Route from
Montreal to London, C.W.

MEMORIAL SLAB AND INSCRIPTION AT PORT MAITLAND, CANADA.
From photographs kindly supplied by the Rev. Canon P. L. Spencer of Port Maitland.

carried Billy. However, we were always in time with the goat, colour, band, and all complete, much to the amusement of the young Princes, who looked out for him at each guard and were evidently much pleased to see Billy always at his post."

A short time after the arrival of the 1st battalion at Chester, Lieutenant-Colonel Torrens was employed on particular service and proceeded to Paris. The command then devolved upon Major Lysons, who retained it until relieved by Lieutenant-Colonel Crutchley at Parkhurst Barracks, Isle of Wight, early in 1853.

On the detachment from the Isle of Man rejoining headquarters, the following address, signed by the principal inhabitants of the place, was presented to Captain Tritton:

"We, the undersigned, on behalf of the inhabitants of Castletown, and its vicinity, render you our thanks for the able, peaceable, and satisfactory manner you have conducted yourselves during your residence amongst us.

"It must be satisfactory to you to feel, as it is a pleasure for us to state, that during that period the most perfect good feeling and unanimity have existed.

"We therefore assure you that you leave us with our sincere regret, and with our best and kindest wishes for your future prosperity."

1851.

Reserve Battalion.

On 12th June the battalion was inspected at London by Major-General the Hon. C. Gore, who noticed that "a small voluntary subscription has been entered into by some of the officers for brass drums, the wooden ones being found ill-suited to the climate." On this the Adjutant-General's remarks were as follows: "The subscriptions here alluded to must be peremptorily prohibited."

In July No. 12 company under Captain W. P. Campbell, consisting of 2 subalterns, 4 sergeants, 4 corporals, 2 drummers, and 76 men, was detached to Hamilton West in aid of the civil power. It remained there for some months.

1852.

1st Battalion.

During the whole of this year the battalion remained at Chester, Liverpool, and the Isle of Man. The Queen's goat died in Chester Castle towards the end of the year, and Her Majesty was graciously pleased to present another goat to the regiment in its place early in the following year.

1852.

Reserve Battalion.

In May the headquarters of the battalion and 2 companies marched to Hamilton, and embarked for Toronto, where they were joined by No. 12 company and also a draft from England; Nos. 7, 9, and 10 companies remained at New London under the command of Major Chester.

1853.

1st Battalion.

In consequence of the death of the regimental goat already referred to the following regimental order was issued:

"The commanding officer has much pleasure in announcing to the battalion that Her Majesty has been graciously pleased to confer a distinguished mark of attention on the Royal Welch Fusiliers in presenting them with a successor to their late goat."

The following letter from Colonel Phipps was received:

"Windsor Castle, *March* 31, 1853.

"My dear Torrens,

"I have had the honour to submit to Her Majesty the Queen the intelligence contained in your letter of the 29th instant of the death of the goat formerly presented by Her Majesty to the Royal Welch Fusiliers.

"Her Majesty has been pleased to command me to notify her gracious intention of presenting a successor to that distinguished corps.

"If you will request the Commanding Officer of the regiment to place himself in communication with Seymour, at Windsor Park, he will take the necessary steps for carrying out Her Majesty's intentions.

"Very sincerely yours,

[*signed*]   C. B. Phipps."

On the 2nd of May Lieutenant-Colonel Crutchley returned to England from Canada, and relieved Major Lysons, who was in command of the 1st battalion; Colonel Torrens having been appointed A.Q.M.G. of the

Horse Guards a short time before. On leaving the regiment Colonel Torrens published the following farewell address:

" Having had the honour to have been appointed to the headquarter staff, Colonel Arthur Wellesley Torrens now bids farewell to the Royal Welch Fusiliers.

" During a command of more than eleven years he has seen the regiment in various climates go through a succession of colonial services, less brilliant indeed, yet perhaps scarcely less trying than a campaign.

" Throughout these it has been his pride to have seen undisturbed the efficiency, high spirit, good feeling, and unsurpassed reputation of the regiment, and to this circumstance he cannot but in a great measure attribute the great distinction which has befallen him. He is bound, therefore, now more than ever, thankfully and proudly to acknowledge the assistance which all ranks have afforded him in conducting so arduous a trust, and it is with the warmest feelings of goodwill that he bids his esteemed comrades farewell.

" Stirring times may perhaps be at hand, and Colonel Torrens may yet see the colours of the Royal Welch Fusiliers wave again a proud and glorious defiance through the smoke of a hostile fire. Though he may then be pardoned a passing feeling of regret that the glory of leading such a regiment at such a moment had not been reserved for him, he will as proudly and confidently watch the calm and steady determination which he knows the Young Twenty-third will then show to imitate the hard-won glories of the Old Regiment."

Colonel Torrens's words were prophetic! The Crimean War broke out shortly afterwards, and the Young Twenty-third fulfilled all he had prophesied of them, and at the Alma and Inkerman well upheld the glorious name the Old Regiment had won.

On the 21st of May the battalion under the command of Major D. Lysons proceeded to Parkhurst Barracks, Isle of Wight, where it furnished detachments at Osborne House and Sandown: on the 13th of June one company under Captain F. E. Evans proceeded to Chobham Park.

1853.

Reserve Battalion.

The battalion in May received, very unexpectedly, orders to proceed home. Lieutenant-Colonel Crutchley was transferred to the 1st battalion, vice Lieutenant-Colonel Torrens, who had been appointed to the Head-Quarters Staff.

Nos. 8, 11, and 12 companies, having been relieved by the headquarters and 1 company of the Royal Canadian Rifles, embarked on Lake Ontario, and proceeded down the St. Lawrence via Kingston and Montreal to Quebec, where they embarked on H.M. troopship *Vulcan* on 6th July. They were joined next day by Nos. 7, 9, and 10 companies from New London.

The *Vulcan* sailed on the 11th, and, after a pleasant voyage of 16 days, anchored in Cowes Roads on the 27th. The battalion disembarked on the 28th, and marched to Parkhurst Barracks, Isle of Wight, where it joined the 1st battalion, from which it had been separated for ten years. On the 4th of August an order was received to amalgamate the two battalions into one regiment of ten companies, which was immediately carried out.

Nos. 2 and 8 companies were broken up, and several alterations were made in the numbers of the remaining companies. Lieutenant-Colonel Crutchley commanded the regiment on its amalgamation.

On the fusion of the battalions Lieutenant-Colonel Chester, Captains Raynes, Tritton, Lieutenants Dickens, Carnegie, Jervoise, Surgeon Burke, and Quartermaster Fortune were placed on half-pay. This closes the service of the " Reserve " battalion, which had existed, distinct from the " First," from 14th of April 1842 to 31st July 1853.

1854.

On the 1st of January the state of the regiment was as follows : 45 officers, 64 sergeants, 55 corporals, 21 drummers, and 997 privates.

In February the regiment received orders to hold itself in readiness for service in Turkey, and was removed in two divisions from Parkhurst Barracks, Isle of Wight, to the Clarence Barracks, Portsmouth, on the 24th and 25th of February. It was divided into 8 service companies and 2 depôt companies, by authority dated Horse Guards, 23rd February, in which the establishment was arranged as follows :

Service Companies, officers, 34 ; non-commissioned officers and men, 913.
Depôt   ,,   ,,   6   ,,   ,,   ,,   ,,   162.

During March the regiment remained at Portsmouth making preparation for active service, two companies being stationed at Fort Cumberland.

Lieutenant-Colonel Crutchley, who from ill-health was unable to accompany the regiment, was permitted to retire from the command,

and was succeeded by Lieutenant-Colonel Chester, who had previously commanded the reserve battalion.

On the 4th of April the service companies, under command of Lieutenant-Colonel Chester, proceeded by rail to Southampton, and embarked on the steamship *Trent*.

The following was the strength of the battalion: Field-officers, 3; captains, 7; subalterns, 16; staff, 5; sergeants, 45; corporals, 41; drummers, 15; privates, 808; of these N.C.O.s and men, 570 were English, 331 Irish, and 8 Scotch.

The following is a list of the officers who embarked: Lieutenant-Colonel H. G. Chester, Major D. Lysons, Major H. W. Bunbury; Captains A. W. W. Wynn, E. W. D. Bell, F. E. Evans, J. C. Conolly, W. P. Campbell, R. Bruce, C. E. Hopton; First-Lieutenants C. G. Sutton, E. G. Bulwer, Sir W. N. Young, Bart., G. H. Hughes, F. E. Drewe, F. Sayer, F. P. R. Delmé-Radcliffe, H. Bathurst, G. T. John, A. Applewhaite; Second Lieutenants J. Duff, D. Dyneley, B. Granville, H. Anstruther, F. F. Vane, J. H. Butler; Paymaster H. Hall Dare, Adjutant H. D'O. Torrens, Quartermaster J. Aston, Surgeon W. G. Watt, Assistant-Surgeon E. A. Jenkin.

On the 5th of April the *Trent* steamed through Southampton Water; on the 9th at midday passed the Rock of Lisbon; on the 11th anchored opposite the New Mole at Gibraltar at 7.30 a.m., and found the *Orinoco* there with the 7th Fusiliers on board. On the 12th the *Trent* having completed her coaling left Gibraltar; on the 18th she anchored at the Grand Harbour of Malta, leaving again at 5 p.m.; on the 23rd she arrived at Gallipoli, leaving on the 24th, and arrived at Scutari on the 25th. The regiment disembarked on the 25th and encamped on the ground between the Cemetery and the Military Hospital. On the 27th of April the British troops at Scutari were reviewed by Seraskier Pasha, the Turkish Commander-in-Chief.

A seemingly trivial dispute in 1853 for precedence between the Monks of the Greek and Latin Churches in the Holy Land was the primary cause of the Crimean War.

Nicholas, the Czar of all the Russias, naturally espoused the cause of the Greek Church, while the Latin Church found a strong supporter in Louis Napoleon, the Emperor of the French.

The two potentates approached the Sultan of Turkey for a decision in favour of their respective clients. The Sublime Porte, as might be expected, endeavoured to trim its sails, but only succeeded in partially satisfying the Emperor. The Czar, taking, or pretending to take, great umbrage at the result of the referendum, sent his Minister, Prince Menschikoff, as Envoy to Constantinople to demand special powers, and backed it up by dispatching two army corps to the borders of the Danubian Principalities.

The Sultan's Ministers promptly refused to entertain Menschikoff's proposals, the result being that on the 2nd of July 1853 Russian troops crossed the River Pruth, and entered the Principalities.

The Great Powers attempted to mediate between the disputants, but all to no purpose. On the 5th of October 1853 the Sultan declared war on Russia. In a series of contests at Kalafat the Turks proved themselves to be superior to the Russians, and equally so in their valiant defence of both Silistria and Shumla after the war became general.

The real object of the Czar, which was to grind Turkey to dust, becoming apparent to France and England, both these Powers addressed an ultimatum to him on the 27th of February 1854, requiring the evacuation of the Danubian Principalities by the 30th of April. To this demand he gave no heed, the result being that war with Russia was declared on that day.

Previous to this an offensive and defensive alliance had been concluded between France and England on the 10th of April. The feature of a plan of campaign decided upon by France and England in the autumn of 1853, in the event of a rupture with Russia taking place, provided for a joint attack upon Sevastopol and the fortifications by which it was defended.

On the 1st of May the Light Division was formed under the command of Lieutenant-General Sir George Brown, K.C.B. The First Brigade, commanded by Brigadier-General Airey, consisted of the 7th Fusiliers, 23rd Royal Welch Fusiliers, the 33rd (The Duke of Wellington's) Regiment, and the 2nd Battalion Rifle Brigade. The 2nd Brigade, commanded by Brigadier-General Buller, consisted of the 19th, 77th, and 88th Regiments.

During May the rank of " Second Lieutenant " was abolished and that of " Ensign " substituted for it.

The distribution of the regiment was then as follows :

	Officers.	Sergeants.	Drummers.	Corporals.	Privates.
Service Companies	33	57	21[1]	50	950
Depôt Companies	12	20	8	20	380

On the 25th of May a review of all the troops took place at Scutari in honour of the Queen's Birthday.

On the 29th the regiment embarked on board the screw steamer

[1] Including Drum Major.

Andes; steaming up the Bosphorus and disembarking on the 31st, it encamped outside the walls of Varna with the Light Division. On the 5th of June it marched with the rest of the Light Division to Aladin, where it was reviewed by General Canrobert. On the 30th the Light Division marched from Aladin to Devna, where its camp was visited on the 3rd of July by Omar Pasha. Assistant Surgeon D. Woods joined the battalion on the 18th of June. On the 10th of July No. 6 company, under Captain Hopton, Lieutenant J. Duff, and Ensign J. H. Butler, was sent to Varna as a depôt.

Major Broughton-Mainwaring states in his *Historical Record* of the regiment that " from the time the division left Aladin the food became very bad and insufficient, the meat was chiefly buffalo beef, which is scarcely ever eaten, and the bread was of very bad quality. There was no supply of vegetables issued, and scarcely any condiments, such as salt, pepper, etc., and the health of the men became much deteriorated.

" On the 22nd of July cholera made its appearance in the division, a man of the Twenty-third Royal Welch Fusiliers being the first attacked.

" The supply of medicines was unfortunately very limited, there being only what was contained in the regimental panniers, and this was soon exhausted. Scarcely any was obtained from Varna, although it was constantly asked for. At one time some of the medical officers were so badly in want of astringents that they took the bark of the oak-trees, and made a decoction of that to supply the need."

On the 24th of July the division marched to Monastir; on account of the soil on which the regiment was encamped having become insanitary it was moved to the opposite side of the village.

On the 2nd of August Assistant Surgeon E. A. Jenkin died of cholera: the Royal Welch Fusiliers having the lamentable distinction of being the heaviest sufferers therefrom.

On the 26th of August the Light Division marched to Yanksacola; on the 28th to Karagoli; on the 29th to the camp near Varna; and on the 30th embarked on board the screw steamship *Victoria* together with 3 companies of the 7th Fusiliers; the depôt company under Captain Hopton rejoined the regiment.

On the 1st of September Major-General Codrington was appointed to the command of the 1st Brigade Light Division vice Brigadier-General Airey appointed Quartermaster-General of the Army.

On the 7th of September the 23rd Regiment sailed for the Crimea, and at daybreak on the 14th the vessel anchored opposite the salt lake known as Lake Kamichla. In accordance with the instructions which were issued by Lord Raglan at Varna on the 3rd of September, the Light Division was the first to land.

In beautiful weather, and favoured by a sea whose surface was scarcely ruffled, the landing was effected on a long, low, narrow strip of beach which separated the lake from the sea. A boat of H.M.S. *Britannia* laden with men of No. 1 company under the command of Major D. Lysons landed the first British troops to set foot in the Crimea. No sooner were they landed than they were called upon to intercept about a dozen " Arabas " or small bullock-waggons, containing for the most part firewood, which were being driven along the coast road by Tartar peasants, who made no attempt to escape. One waggon was, however, laden with small pears of excellent flavour, which were speedily devoured by the men.

On the night of the 15th of September there was a false alarm of attack which caused the Light, 1st, 2nd, and 3rd divisions to turn out instantly under arms. It was occasioned by a loose horse galloping furiously through the camp. On the following day Captain C. G. Sutton, who had been left on the *Victoria* suffering from cholera, breathed his last.

The British force under the command of Lieutenant-General Lord Raglan consisted of 1,000 cavalry, 26,000 infantry, and 60 guns. The French under Marshal St. Arnaud numbered 28,000 infantry and 68 guns. A small force of 7,000 Turks acted under the Marshal's orders.

Owing to the scarcity of water the Allied armies moved forward towards Sevastopol, distant twenty-five miles, on the morning of the 19th of September.

As the French were without cavalry they advanced on the right next the sea. The Light Division headed by the 23rd Regiment led the British infantry, which was about to traverse a part of the Crimea, chiefly under grass with occasional patches of cultivation. Although the men marched without knapsacks their first march was a most trying one, owing to the intense heat of the sun, and the absence of water, which told heavily upon frames in many cases enfeebled by recent attacks of cholera in Bulgaria. Their spirits, which for the time being had been maintained, owing to their being permitted during the frequent halts to hunt the numerous hares that sprang up on all sides, began early in the afternoon to flag, but were revived by the sight of the River Bulganak, a small, slow-running stream but nevertheless very welcome to the weary soldiers, many of whom as they approached it broke their ranks, and rushed forward to assuage their thirst.

To the credit of Major-General Codrington's brigade it must be recorded that though so sorely tempted, it was one of those in which discipline was proof against such an irregularity. Not a man moved until permission was given for the brigade to drink in comfort.

The Allied armies bivouacked that night for the sake of the water on the southern bank of the Bulganak. In the distance groups of Russians were clearly to be seen scattered along the banks of the River Alma: the sight of them fired the men with enthusiasm.

At a late hour that night Marshal St. Arnaud called at Lord Raglan's headquarters and arranged with him the following plan of operations. The Marshal with a portion of his army was to assail the enemy's left by crossing the Alma at its junction with the sea, while the remainder of the French divisions were to move up the heights on their front. To the British army was assigned the task of attacking the right and centre of the enemy's position, which was held by 3,400 horsemen, about 20,000 infantry, and 86 guns, under the command of Prince Menschikoff.

Between 9 and 10 a.m. on the 20th of September the Allied armies advanced towards the River Alma on the same alignment, the British being formed as follows: The Light Division in double column of companies, together with the 2nd Division on the right, formed the first line; the second was composed of the 3rd Division on the right and the 1st Division on the left. The 4th Division and the Light Cavalry were held in reserve to protect the left flank and rear from possible attacks by the enemy's cavalry, large bodies of which were seen in those directions.

On approaching the river the Light and 2nd Divisions, which were leading, came under a formidable fire from a twelve-gun Russian field battery, which was planted in an earthwork on the eastern slope of the Kourgané Hill, necessitating their being halted and deployed without delay. "The deployment of the Light Division was effected by each regiment with beautiful precision."

After a short halt, during which the men stretched themselves on the ground, the two Divisions again advanced. Sir George Brown, noticing that the Light Division was being galled by the enemy's battery, halted it, and altered the formation from contiguous quarter-distance columns to open column, but this was not adhered to as he soon reverted to his line formation.

The Division, on arriving within three hundred yards of the Alma, was compelled to force its way through orchards, vineyards, and over stone walls and felled trees, all the time ejecting Russian skirmishers, which caused it to lose much of its line formation. When the river was reached it was seen that its steep banks were both rugged and broken, presenting serious obstacles to further progress. This difficulty, to which was added the unequal depth of the river, did not deter the Light Division from speedily effecting the crossing, and gaining the opposite bank with luckily little loss. Upon a narrow strip of ground it endeavoured to regain its two-deep formation, under cover of a rocky bank quite ten feet high, which for the moment gave protection from the enemy's artillery, but left it exposed to a severe fire from the skirmishers, who lined the top of the bank in force, causing several casualties. Before the 23rd could re-form, a strong enemy column bore down upon it, and was not perceived until it was within less than a stone's throw. Captain Conolly of the regiment sprang forward, and calling upon the men to follow him succeeded in clambering up the bank, only to fall dead on reaching the top, having been shot by the Russians.

For some years past the 23rd had been commanded by unusually proficient officers, who set a good example, with the result that the men were proud to follow leaders in whom they both believed and trusted.

For a moment all was confusion, the men of the 1st Brigade and the 19th and part of the 95th Regiments belonging to the 2nd Brigade being mixed up together. Fortunately the practised eye of General Codrington discovered a break in the scarped face of the bank. Calling out to the broken and disordered mass of men, " Never mind forming! come on anyhow!" he gallantly led it " in numberless waves " up the slope of the Kourgané Hill, making for a redoubt about 400 yards distant known as the " Great Redoubt." This redoubt consisted of an earthwork, about breast high, armed with fourteen guns of heavy calibre, and was regarded as the key of the position.

When the greater part of the slope had been traversed, Ensign Joseph H. Butler, who was carrying the regimental colour, was shot dead. It was instantly picked up by Lieutenant-Colonel Harry G. Chester, commanding the regiment, who was leading it on foot owing to his horse having been shot under him. Colour in hand he had proceeded but a few yards when he was struck in the breast by a ball, and, to the inexpressible grief of the regiment, by whom he was beloved, was instantaneously killed.

Sergeant William Stait, who was close beside his Colonel, remained alone with the body under very heavy fire for some time after the regiment fell back, until he was able to carry the Colonel's body to the rear, and hand it over to the surgeon. This act was performed in the immediate presence of the enemy, and evinced great courage as well as devotion to his commander. Throughout the siege Sergeant Stait also displayed on all occasions great zeal, coolness, and courage.

GUN CAPTURED BY CAPTAIN E. W. D. BELL, V.C., AT THE ALMA; AND BURMESE BELL TAKEN FROM THE INCOMPARABLE PAGODA, MANDALAY.

From a photograph by Algernon Smith, Wrexham.

Just as Codrington's men reached the earthwork they perceived, through the smoke of battle, to their amazement that artillery teams were rapidly drawing away the heavy guns with which it was armed. One gun, however, a sixteen-pounder to which only two black horses were attached, was captured by Captain E. W. D. Bell of the 23rd, as it was being drawn to the rear. Bell ran up to the driver, and holding a pistol to his head ordered him to dismount, a command which the man promptly obeyed, the gun being then taken to the rear. The horses were afterwards used in the "Black Battery." This was the first and only effective gun captured from the enemy.

For his daring feat—of which the following is the official account in the *London Gazette* of 24th February 1857 : " Recommended for his gallantry, more particularly at the Battle of the Alma, where he was the first to seize upon and capture one of the enemy's guns, which was limbered up, and being carried off. He moreover succeeded to the command of that gallant regiment, which he brought out of action : all his senior officers having been killed or wounded "—Captain Bell received the " Victoria Cross " when it was instituted by Queen Victoria.

A few moments before this incident occurred Ensign Henry Anstruther, who was carrying the Queen's Colour, was shot dead. It was instantly picked up by Private Wm. Evans, who handed it to Corporal E. Luby, who shortly afterwards handed it over to Sergeant Luke O'Connor, one of the centre sergeants. O'Connor, who but a moment before had been severely wounded in the shoulder, ran forward as quickly as his wound would permit, and despite a heavy fire from a Russian column, that was posted higher up the hill, succeeded in planting it on the redoubt. After carrying the Colour for some time he handed it to Ensign Bevill Granville. The gallant O'Connor was soon after commissioned in the regiment, and awarded the V.C. for his bravery.

Codrington's regiments on entering the earthwork proceeded to line the parapet, and extend themselves on both sides of it. A disabled brass 32-pound howitzer was discovered in the works. A corporal of the 23rd found himself alone in the enemy's battery, and actually bayoneted three men before assistance came to him. He was immediately promoted to be sergeant.

Flushed with success the Light Division again advanced up the hill, pouring in repeated volleys after the retreating Russians. At this moment a compact column noiselessly descended one of the hills. A mounted officer called out, " The column is French : for God's sake, men, don't fire." The supposed French column, which in reality consisted of four battalions of the Vladimir Regiment, 3,000 strong, when it arrived within musket range deployed in line, and before the error could be discovered poured a fearful volley into the British ranks. The 23rd suffered severely and six officers fell on the spot.

The order to " Retire " was sounded by a bugler. At first the remaining officers of the 23rd declined to go back, feeling confident there was some mistake ; but as it was repeated several times along the whole line, they had no alternative but to give the hated command. The redoubt fell into the hands of the Russians once more.

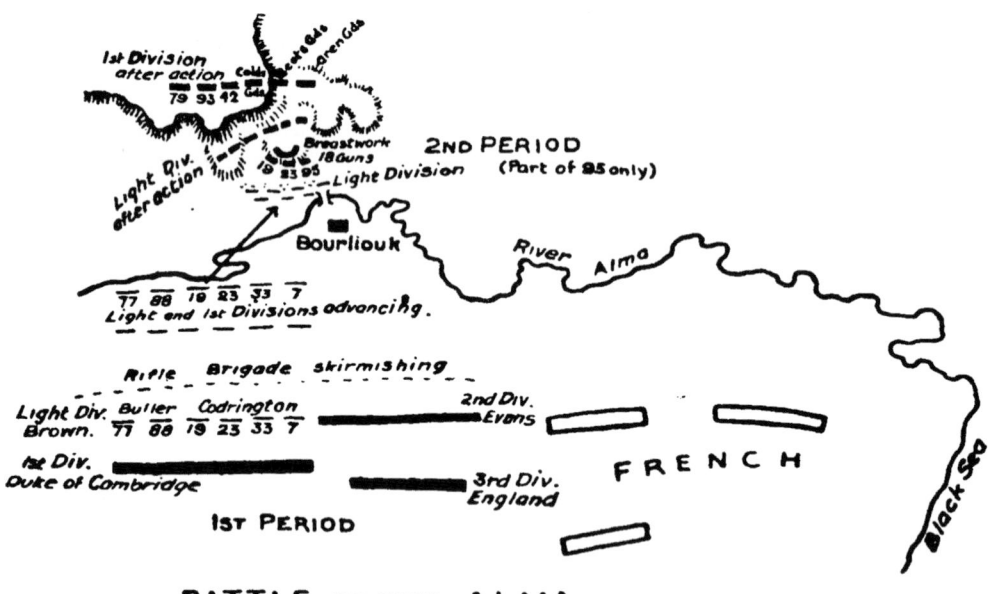

BATTLE OF THE ALMA.

The 1st Division, which was some distance in the rear, at once deployed, and supported by the Highland Brigade under Lieutenant-General Sir Colin Campbell, advanced with a rush and recaptured the redoubt at the point of the bayonet. The Light Division then rallied and advancing again formed the second line. The key of the position having now been secured, and the enemy's left being threatened by the French, the Russians had no alternative but to retreat on all sides.

Lord Raglan in his dispatch of the 23rd of September containing an account of the Alma observes as follows : " The mode in which Lieutenant-General Sir George Brown conducted his Division under the most trying circumstances demands the expression of my warmest approbation. The fire to which his division was subjected, and the difficulties he had to contend against, afford no small proof that his best energies were applied to the successful discharge of his duty." In a later dispatch dated the 28th of September His Lordship observes that Lieutenant-General Sir George Brown speaks in the highest terms of Lieutenant-Colonel Chester of the 23rd, who was unfortunately killed, and of Captain Bell, who succeeded to the command and brought the regiment out of action. He adds that Lieutenant-General Sir De Lacy Evans eulogises the conduct of Major Lysons of the regiment acting as Assistant Adjutant-General of the 2nd Division.

Where all behaved so well it would be difficult to mention the name of any one man as more gallant than another. The conduct of Sergeant Luke O'Connor, Corporal Luby, and Corporal Chadwick, however, was conspicuous.

The zeal and ability of the surgeon of the regiment, Mr. Watt, were most highly spoken of, whilst the kindness and attention shown to the wounded soldiers of the regiment by Purveyor's Clerk Harrington, who volunteered his valuable assistance in the field hospital, should never be forgotten by the Royal Welch Fusiliers.

The Regimental Colour, which was pierced by sixteen balls, was carried out of action by Sergeant Henry Smith. The Queen's Colour, after the action was over, was found to have been pierced by twenty-six balls, and in addition the staff was badly broken by another.

During the action the Regimental Colour of the 7th Fusiliers was found lying on the ground by Captain Pearson of that regiment, A.D.C. to Sir George Brown. He picked it up, and, no officer of the 7th being near, General Codrington desired him to give it to Captain Bell, observing, "It cannot be in safer keeping that that of the Royal Welch." The colour was accordingly placed between those of the 23rd, and was carried by a sergeant of the 7th during the remainder of the action.

The British losses in this battle fought on the 20th September amounted to 2,002 of all ranks; the Russian losses, according to their published statement, amounted to 5,709.

The following is a list of the officers of the Twenty-third Royal Welch Fusiliers killed and wounded at the battle of the Alma:

Killed: Lieut.-Colonel H. G. Chester; Captains A. W. W. Wynn, J. C. Conolly, F. E. Evans; Lieutenants F. P. R. Delmé-Radcliffe, Henry Anstruther, Sir W. N. Young, Bart., J. H. Butler. Wounded: Captains W. P. Campbell, wounded in the arm, C. E. Hopton; Lieutenants H. Bathurst, F. Sayer, wounded in the ankle.

Lieutenant and Adjutant A. Applewhaite was mortally wounded, and died on board ship on the 22nd of September.

There were 44 non-commissioned officers and men killed, including Sergeant-Major Jones, and 154 non-commissioned officers and men wounded.

The following is a statement of the losses of the 23rd Royal Welch Fusiliers at the battle of the Alma :

Killed : Field officers, 1 ; captains, 3 ; subalterns, 4 ; sergeants, 3 ; drummers, 1 ; privates, 40 : total, 52. Wounded : captains, 2 ; subalterns, 3 ; sergeants, 10 ; drummers, 4 ; corporals, 12 ; privates, 128 : total, 159. Total : field officers, 1 ; captains, 5 ; subalterns, 7 ; sergeants, 13 ; drummers, 5 ; corporals, 12 ; privates, 168 : total, 211.

Seven of the officers who fell were buried in a trench with the officers of the 7th Fusiliers, the other two were buried elsewhere.

A handsome monument was erected in the Crimea to their glorious memory. The following is the inscription :

"Sacred to the memory of Lieut.-Colonel Harry George Chester, Captain Arthur Watkin Williams Wynn, Captain Francis Edward Evans, Captain John Charles Conolly, First Lieutenant Sir William Norris Young, Bart., First Lieutenant Frederick P. R. Delmé-Radcliffe, Second Lieutenant Joseph Henry Butler, Augustus Applewhaite, Henry Anstruther, Officers of her Britannic Majesty's Twenty-third Royal Welch Fusiliers. They were killed at the battle of the Alma, 20th September 1854, and the first-named seven lie buried under this monument. If we be dead with Christ we shall also live with Him, St. Paul. Love one another, St. John."

A subscription of £1,892 5s. 8d. was raised by some noblemen and gentlemen connected with the principality of Wales, who were desirous of recording the high esteem they entertained of the services of the regiment in the Crimean War, and especially of its gallant conduct at the battle of the Alma.

This subscription was invested for the benefit of deserving widows and orphans of non-commissioned officers and privates belonging to the regiment, and is called "The Alma Fund."

The gun captured by Captain Bell as already narrated, and known in the regiment as "Bell's Gun," was in due course conveyed to England. In 1885 it was sent to the brigade depôt at Wrexham, where it still stands in front of the Officers' Mess.

For its distinguished conduct at the Battle of the Alma the 23rd was permitted, on the 3rd of October 1855, to add the word "Alma" to those already borne on its colours.

LIEUTENANT-COLONEL E. W. D. BELL, V.C.
From a photograph at Wrexham Barracks.   Photo. by Algernon Smith, Wrexham.

On the 21st of September Major Lysons took command of the 23rd, his promotion to Lieutenant-Colonel being subsequently antedated to the date of his taking over command. The Allied armies halted on the banks of the Alma, from the afternoon of the 20th until the morning of the 23rd, during which period the working parties were busily engaged in burying over 700 British and Russian dead, and helping to remove the sick and wounded of both nationalities on board the fleet.

On the 23rd of September the army marched for the Katcha River, on the southern bank of which it established itself for the night. Daylight disclosed a veritable land of milk and honey! Instead of a barren and hilly country which had been traversed the greater part of the previous day, an undulating plain unfolded itself clothed with vineyards and orchards. In less than no time the soldiers were partaking of the richest of grapes, and the choicest of pears and apples. Even the horses were revelling in feeds of corn. Several of the companies of the 23rd being left without officers, Lieutenants G. R. Beresford, G. R. Browne, and E. D. Radcliffe of the 88th Regiment were temporarily attached to it. It may here be incidentally stated that these officers were made honorary members of the mess for life.

At noon in sweltering heat the army resumed its march, and soon leaving the fertile district, traversed a hilly region covered with scrub and trees, where very little water was to be obtained; later on, however, the configuration of the country changed for the better.

In the afternoon the River Belbeck was reached, and the village and left bank of it occupied by the troops.

Lord Raglan and Marshal St. Arnaud having " after due deliberation " decided to endeavour by a flank march to get round Sevastopol, and seize Balaklava, a march began " which deserves to be classed among the boldest movements ever made by any military commander in the face of an enemy."

Towards midday on the 25th of September the army started on its march for Balaklava, and after traversing for some time the high road from Belbeck to Sevastopol, it was obliged to pass through a densely wooded country, where marching in the proper direction could only be effected by compass. On emerging from the wood into the open, it found itself in the immediate presence of a large body of Russian infantry, which was moving at right angles to it, proceeding from Sevastopol to Bakshe-Serai.

This proved to be the baggage guard of a column, which had traversed the same route while the British army was threading its way through the forest. As soon as possible it was attacked by the Horse Artillery and portions of the 8th and 11th Hussars, supported by the Light Division, the 23rd leading the column. After firing a few rounds the Russians broke and fled precipitately, leaving behind them many waggons, containing an immense quantity of wearing apparel, some jewellery, and a considerable supply of small-arm ammunition. As this was legitimate plunder the troops were permitted, under proper supervision, to take what they liked, and make the most of it. The plunder put the soldiers in great good humour and they marched on the whole day with elastic step.

A halt was made at the little hamlet of Traktir, on the Black River adjoining Mackenzie's Farm, so called from a Russian Admiral of Scottish descent who had made a plantation of trees there. After resting for a while the army resumed its march, and on reaching the Tchernaya River bivouacked for the night on its banks. On the morning of the 26th the march was resumed across the valley of the Tchernaya towards some low hills behind which Balaklava lay.

As the head of the column approached the village of Balaklava it was suddenly fired upon from an old Genoese Castle, thereupon Lord Raglan occupied two flanking heights with the Light Division, and part of a troop of Horse Artillery. After a show of resistance the Commandant, Colonel Monto, hung out a flag of truce, and surrendered with his garrison, which consisted of about 70 militia men, most of them Greeks, who belonged to Balaklava or the neighbourhood. The guns taken were small brass mortars.

On the 27th the Light Division was one of two divisions which were ordered by Lord Raglan to move up to the immediate neighbourhood of Sevastopol, and effect a reconnaissance of its defences from the southern side of it. On the following day it was sent to the front, where it deployed and bivouacked near Upton's House.

On the 1st of October the Light Division marched to the right of the line adjoining the Woronzoff road, and there the 2nd Brigade deployed. Next day the 1st Brigade deployed to the right of the 2nd. Both brigades occupied this position until the termination of the war.

On the 4th of October, in consequence of the heavy losses sustained by the regiment at the Battle of the Alma, it became necessary to rearrange it into 6 companies instead of 8 as hitherto.

During the night of the 7th October the Division was busily engaged in constructing a half-sunken battery, Green Hill Battery, on the heights to the extreme right of the British position, about 2,800 yards from the enemy's nearest works, for a long-range gun of the "Lancaster" pattern.

It was hoped that its fire might reach the Malakoff, then called the White Tower.

During the whole day on the 10th of October the Russian batteries played on the high ground in front of the Light Division, ploughing it up in all directions, luckily with no damage to life, as the men were screened by the heights from the direct range of the guns. During the following night a working party consisting of 400 men from both the Light and 2nd Divisions under Captain Gordon, R.E., was engaged in constructing trenches for conversion into batteries. The men worked with such good will that by the morning of the 12th nearly 400 yards of trench on Green Hill were ready. Early in the afternoon of that day a sortie was made by the Russians. The Light and 2nd Divisions turned out with the field guns attached to them, and opened fire with the latter upon the advancing enemy. After the conflict had lasted about half an hour the enemy broke and fled, on being charged by the 8th Regiment.

The morning of the 17th of October ushered in the " most tremendous conflict of artillery which up to that time the earth had ever witnessed." The Allied artillery opened throughout their extent upon the Russian works. The British batteries succeeded in demolishing the Round Tower of the Malakoff, but not the works around it ; also silencing about a third of the guns in the Redan, and blowing up a large magazine there. Unfortunately two French magazines were blown up by the enemy, after the contest had lasted for some hours, which almost reduced their batteries to silence.

Some ammunition in a waggon in the trenches was exploded by a shell, but happily little harm was done. Volunteer sharp-shooters were employed on this occasion, and Corporal Dawson was in charge of the party of the Royal Welch Fusiliers, which consisted of ten men, all of whom behaved extremely well.

At dusk the cannonade ceased everywhere.

The casualties in the 23rd during the period October 13th to 17th inclusive amounted to 1 corporal and 5 privates wounded.

Early in the morning of the 25th of October the Russians made a determined attack on the Allied front before Balaklava, and succeeded in carrying some redoubts, from which they were ejected later in the day by the 1st and 4th Divisions, aided by two remarkable charges made by the Heavy and Light Cavalry Brigades. The Light Division stood to arms, but did not leave its camp.

On the following day a strong sortie was made by the enemy, the brunt of the attack falling upon the left of the 2nd Division. Reinforce-

II—6

ments were rushed up, with the result that the Russians were speedily repulsed. Some guns of the Light Division rendered useful assistance on this occasion, and a company of the 23rd under Lieutenants W. H. Poole and G. T. John, on piquet in the " White Horse Ravine," kept up a brisk fire on the flank of the enemy with considerable effect. In this action, known as " Little Inkerman," one private wounded was the only casualty in the 23rd.

Dawn on the 5th of November, on the heights and valley of Inkerman, was ushered in by a fog so dense, that it was impossible to see more than a couple of yards. A sharp-eared sergeant, of an outlying piquet of the Light Division, hearing what he believed to be the sound of wheels in the valley below the hills, reported the matter as speedily as possible to an officer, who happened to be Major H. W. Bunbury of the 23rd Regiment.

That officer came to the conclusion that it was caused by ammunition carts proceeding to Sevastopol by the Inkerman Road. Soon afterwards Major-General Codrington, who, in accordance with his usual practice, was visiting the outlying piquets of his own brigade, was startled to hear the sharp rattle of musketry down the hill to the left of the Light Division. Putting spurs to his horse regardless of consequences in the thick fog, he proceeded in the direction of the firing, but presently galloped back with the object of warning his brigade.

Half the 23rd was at the moment on duty: one company under Lieutenant J. Duff being on piquet in the " White Horse Ravine," and two companies under Lieutenants F. F. Vane and S. C. Millett were in the " Five Gun Battery."

Dense columns of grey-coated Russians seemed to spring out of the ground. The advanced piquets of the 2nd Division, which covered the right of the position, were the first to feel their presence, and though behaving with admirable gallantry were forced to retreat step by step owing to close and very heavy volleys of musketry. The piquets of the Light Division were next assailed, and though stubbornly contesting every inch of ground were compelled by weight of numbers to fall back upon their main body.

While this outpost struggle was in progress the 2nd Division with its guns managed to get into position. The Light Division under Sir George Brown was brought to the front with the least possible delay : Codrington's Brigade being posted on the long slopes towards Sevastopol with the object of protecting the battery on its right, and guarding against attack on that side. Buller's brigade was formed up on the left of the 2nd Division. " Now commenced the bloodiest struggle ever witnessed since war cursed the earth." The Russians fought with incredible fury, time after time charging with the bayonet to be resisted with cold steel.

To attempt to describe the Battle of Inkerman would be futile. For the most part it resolved itself into a series of sanguinary hand-to-hand fights, and desperate assaults, either in the glens, or amidst the thick

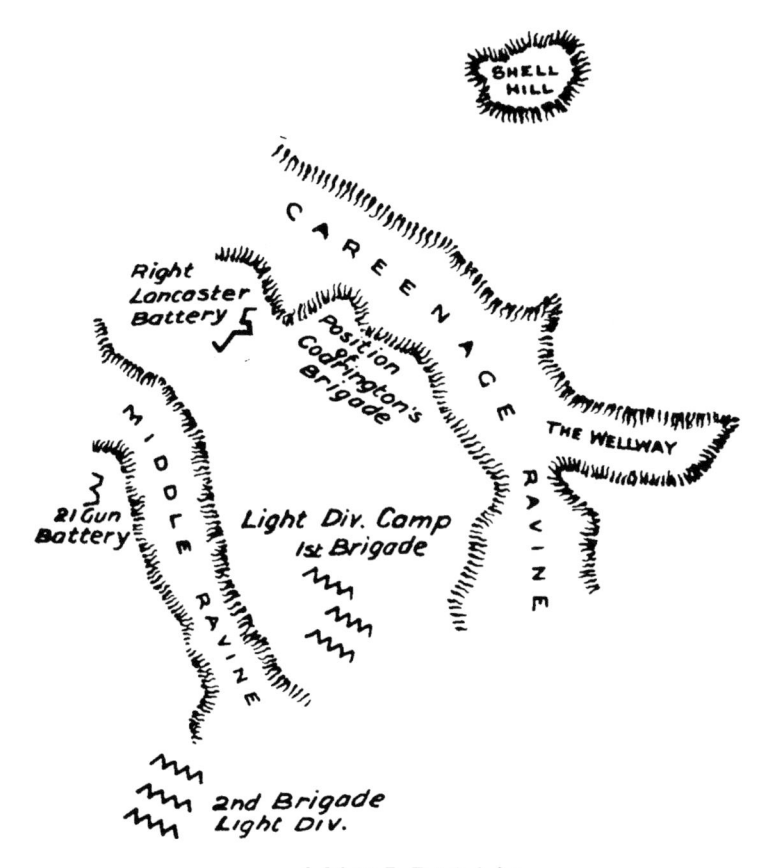

INKERMAN.

upland brushwood. This ding-dong struggle lasted until 1.40 p.m., when the Russians retreated, their left flank being assailed by a detachment of the Light Division which was posted on the Victoria Ridge.

During the engagement Major McKenzie rode back to the camp and ordered all the batmen, men on guard, and any of the sick who could carry arms, to turn out " at once," stating that he feared that the " Five Gun Battery " would be taken. No officer being in camp, Lieutenant-Colonel

Lysons, who was then recovering from an attack of fever, got up and took command of the parties of the three regiments of the 1st brigade. The Royal Welch Fusiliers turned out over sixty men—every man who could stand volunteering to go out. They went to the front in support of their comrades, but no serious attack was made in the direction of the Light Division, although the fire from the enemy's field pieces across the front, especially at the "Five Gun Battery," which was completely enfiladed, and near the "Old Redoubt," was very heavy.

Sergeant William Coleby noticing that Sergeant Richard Dunkley lay severely wounded on the front of the redoubt in rear of the "Five Gun Battery" collected some of the band who were acting as stretcher-bearers, which was a part of their duties at this period, and proceeded with them under heavy fire to remove him to the camp, which was successfully accomplished.

Late in the afternoon, after a severe struggle, the enemy was gradually forced back, and compelled to retire, and the celebrated Battle of Inkerman was won. In this engagement Sir George Brown was badly wounded, being shot through the arm, and General Codrington assumed the command of the division.

The casualties in the Twenty-third Royal Welch Fusiliers were 8 men killed ; Lieutenant Vane and 21 rank and file wounded ; whilst, owing to the heights on the right having been left unguarded during the night, Lieutenant Duff, Sergeant J. Newman, and 11 privates were surrounded, and taken prisoners in the "White Horse Ravine."

When Lieutenant Duff found that he was surrounded he hid his watch in a cave, which he explained in a letter to Lieutenant-Colonel Lysons, who went to look for it, and found it where he stated it to be. He was afterwards conveyed to Odessa, and after his return on the 22nd of September 1855, he reported that when there he was asked by a staff officer what regiment he belonged to, and he replied "The 23rd Fusiliers." "Oh," said the staff officer, "Colonel Lysons' regiment : we know him well, and want to get hold of him."

Major Bunbury was called upon during the action to take command of a battery owing to Major Sir Thomas Troubridge of the Royal Fusiliers being obliged to quit his post on being desperately wounded. Major Bunbury's gallant conduct on this occasion being brought by Major-General Codrington to the notice of Lord Raglan, the latter mentioned him in his dispatch of the 11th of November. Another officer of the 23rd, Lieutenant H. D'O. Torrens, then acting as a brigade major in the 4th Division, was mentioned in this dispatch.

"The admirable behaviour" of both Lieutenant-General Sir George Brown and Major-General Codrington on the 5th of November had already been brought to the notice of the Secretary of State by Lord Raglan in his dispatch of the 8th of November.

No praise is too great for the steadfast men who fought on that memorable 5th of November in the "Soldiers' Battle" of Inkerman.

Another battle honour—that of Inkerman—was added by Royal authority, dated 3rd of October 1855, to those already borne on the colours of the Royal Welch Fusiliers.

On the 9th of November Lord Raglan issued a General Order of which the following is an extract: "The Commander of the Forces returns his thanks to the Officers and troops for their conduct in the Battle of Inkerman, on the 5th instant, in which, aided by their gallant Allies, they succeeded in completely repulsing and defeating the enemy, by whom they were attacked in very superior numbers, with masses of artillery both of field and position, as well as of ship guns.

"The army have thus taken an advantage of distinguishing themselves, and of showing that, under all circumstances, and in presence of every difficulty, their determination to devote their best energies to the service of their country is still the same."

Early on the morning of the 14th of November a terrific gale from the south-west sprang up accompanied by torrents of rain which wrought havoc among the tents of the besiegers, making a clean sweep of them. Lieutenant-Colonel Lysons collected the three companies of the Royal Welch Fusiliers that were in camp with their arms, accoutrements, and the colours, and they sought what shelter could be obtained in the "Middle Ravine" and there remained, cold and hungry, until nightfall, when both wind and rain abated. Twenty-one vessels in or adjoining the harbour of Balaklava, all laden with stores which were urgently needed for the troops, were dashed to pieces. One in particular, the *Resolute*, contained ten million rounds of rifle and gun ammunition.

Towards the end of that month the regiment was augmented by 3 supernumerary Lieutenants and 3 supernumerary Ensigns.

From the memorable 14th of November onwards the weather was very broken: torrents of rain falling at frequent intervals greatly interfering with the efforts of the troops to provide hutting for themselves, and also with the conveyance of provisions over seven miles of quagmire from Balaklava. In consequence the Light Division was frequently about this time on half rations, sometimes on even less.

Despite these hardships Lord Raglan was able to inform the Secretary of State in his dispatch of the 28th of November that " The men . . . notwithstanding their privations, their exposure to the weather, and the constant labour required of them, exhibit the same cheerfulness, the same ardour in the discharge of their duty as they have manifested throughout the extensive operations in which they have been engaged."

On the 6th of December the regiment was augmented to 16 companies divided into 8 service companies of 1,120 all ranks, and 8 depôt companies, 1,098 all ranks : of the latter 4 companies were stationed at Malta and 4 at Newport.

On the 11th Captain G. H. Hughes died of typhus fever at Constantinople.

On the 12th of December Captains W. P. Campbell and E. W. D. Bell were promoted to the Brevet rank of Major in the army for distinguished service in the field.

By the 18th of that month a considerable portion of warm clothing had been received, and issued to the troops, which conduced materially to their comfort.

On the night of the 20th of December the enemy made a serious sortie on the advanced trenches in front of the " Twenty-one Gun Battery," and succeeded in occupying them for a short time. The trenches, however, were quickly retaken, and the Russians retired to their own works : a company of the Royal Welch Fusiliers, under Lieutenant Poole, was on duty there at the time, and Corporal Dawson, who had shown great coolness on a former occasion, again distinguished himself by remaining at his post with Privates Godden, O'Beirne, and Pearce, and firing on the enemy for some time after the rest of the company had been driven back. The casualties on that night were 1 private killed, 10 privates wounded, and 9 privates missing. Of these last, who had been taken prisoners, 6 died in Russia.

During this month the weather became most severe, and the duties more and more arduous. Both officers and men were frequently on duty two and three nights in succcession, without any shelter from the snow and rain, whilst provisions and forage, owing to the want of transport, became very scarce. This told on the troops, and more especially on the young soldiers, who were unable to withstand the hardships and fatigues, and numbers died in consequence. The almost entire lack of transport is well illustrated by the following anecdote extracted from General Sir Daniel Lysons' *The Crimean War* : " One day old Colonel Yea's beautiful grey charger got loose, and strayed into our lines : he was immediately sent off to Balaklava for a load. A few minutes after he had started, old

Yea came over to our camp storming and swearing dreadfully : of course, no one knew anything about it.

"He then came to me, and I inquired about his horse, which was not then quite out of sight. The quartermaster at last came out of his tent and said, ' Oh yes, a strange horse strayed into our lines : we did not know what to do with him, so he was sent down to Balaklava to be fed and taken care of.' So he was : but he returned with two large boxes of boots on his back for the men, and was then sent to his master with my compliments."

In November the "Queen's goat" died at Sevastopol from the effects of the inclemency of the weather. On the death of the goat becoming known at Windsor, Her Majesty the Queen was pleased to send the following most gracious letter to Lieutenant-Colonel Lysons, a mark of Her Majesty's favour which was highly esteemed by the Royal Welch Fusiliers :

"WINDSOR GREAT PARK, *January 18th*, 1855.

"Colonel Seymour presents his compliments to Lieut.-Colonel Lysons, and is commanded by the Queen to inform him that Her Majesty, having heard of the death of the goat belonging to the Twenty-third Royal Welch Fusiliers, has been graciously pleased to signify a wish to replace him by another of the same breed from Windsor Park. The Queen being aware, however, of the difficulties that may attend the conveyance of the goat to the Crimea, and of its maintenance during so arduous a campaign, has been pleased to instruct Colonel Seymour to ascertain from Lieut.-Colonel Lysons whether it is the wish of the regiment to have it sent to the Crimea immediately, or to have it forwarded to the depôt, or to be kept in Windsor Park until the termination of the contest in which the Twenty-third Royal Welch Fusiliers are bearing so distinguished a part.

"Lieut.-Colonel Lysons, Commanding Twenty-third Royal Welch Fusiliers."

To which Lieutenant-Colonel Lysons replied as follows :

"CAMP BEFORE SEVASTOPOL, *6th February* 1855.

"Lieut.-Colonel Lysons presents his compliments to Colonel Seymour, and begs that he will convey in the most suitable terms to the Queen the sincere feeling of gratitude entertained by the officers and soldiers of the Royal Welch Fusiliers, for the high mark of distinction conferred on them by Her Most Gracious Majesty. The fate of the late goat induces

Lieut.-Colonel Lysons to request that his successor may be allowed to remain in Windsor Park until the army may have the good fortune to carry back to their ever mindful Sovereign peace and glory.

" Colonel Seymour, Windsor Great Park."

1854.

Depôt Companies.

These 2 companies were formed on 23rd February, and were to consist of 6 officers and 162 non-commissioned officers and men. They were stationed at Fort Cumberland under Captains A. J. Herbert and F. T. Brock. The depôt removed from Fort Cumberland Barracks to Winchester on the 10th of April, having recruiting parties at Monmouth, Carmarthen, Carnarvon, and Oxford, which from May to December enlisted 520 recruits. On the 29th of June a draft under Ensign W. H. Poole of 2 sergeants and 100 rank and file left for the East, and joined the battalion on the 26th of July. In July 2 additional companies were formed at the depôt under Captains R. T. Raynes and E. Crofts. In September a detachment of 127 non-commissioned officers and men under Captain F. B. Tritton was stationed at the Tower of London, and remained there until March 1855.

On the 26th of October another draft of 2 sergeants and 130 rank and file with Major A. J. Herbert, Lieutenants W. C. Clerke, T. S. Bigge, and Ensign F. W. Jebb left for the Crimea in the steamer *Queen of the South*, landing at Balaklava and joining the regiment on the 22nd of November.

On the 29th of October another draft of 102 non-commissioned officers and men under Ensign R. H. Somerville left on the *Ottawa*, joining the regiment on the 28th of November. Again, on the 30th of December another draft of 3 corporals and 99 men under Captain E. Crofts and Lieutenant the Hon. S. Mostyn left on the *Imperatrix*, joining the battalion on the 26th of January 1855.

1855.

During the greater part of January the weather remained very severe, so much so that the hair on the men's faces was often covered with icicles. Numbers of them died in the trenches from cold and exhaustion, despite the fact that about the middle of the month every man in the army had—to quote the words of Lord Raglan—"received a second blanket, a jersey frock, flannel drawers and socks, and some kind of winter coat in addition to the ordinary great-coat." In this one month alone 96 men of the regiment succumbed to cold and innutrition.

The casualties in the regiment during this month were 1 private killed and 4 wounded.

On the 10th of February the first hut for the hospital of the regiment was completed; it was the second that was put together in the camp, Colonel Yea of the Royal Fusiliers having finished one a few hours earlier.

On the 22nd of February Lieutenant-General Sir George Brown resumed command of the Light Division " in perfect health."

During the second half of the month the weather considerably improved, so much so that the condition and appearance of the men made great progress. Instead of wretched half-starved spectres in tatterdemalion rig crawling down to the trenches, possibly never to return alive, one saw, as February came to an end, well-dressed and well-set-up men marching to them, revelling in the bright sunshine, heedless of the snow which still lay upon the ground.

The vitality of the regiment was marvellous: " it seemed to rise from its ashes with renewed strength and vigour," despite the shadow cast over it by the death in hospital this month of no less than 92 men of the regiment. The only war casualty recorded during the month was one private wounded.

This marked improvement in the health of the troops was most opportune, as it induced both officers and men of the 23rd, on the 1st of March, to keep up the time-honoured custom of observing St. David's Day in a manner befitting the occasion. The Royal Welch Fusiliers had the credit of erecting the first mess hut in the camp. In this hut " The Day " was celebrated. The following incident in connection with it is narrated by General Sir D. Lysons in his *The Crimean War*:

" The hut was papered with newspapers, with brown paper panels. In the centre of each was a picture cut out of the *Illustrated London News*: red sashes were festooned round the top: the colours at the end over my head. We sat down thirty-two: General Codrington on my right, poor Egerton, 77th, on my left. We had tablecloths, plates, tumblers, etc., borrowed from the *Trent* steamer. Each servant cooked what he could do best. The dinner went off capitally.

" By the way, Lord Raglan happened to be passing our camp as our table was being laid for the dinner: he came and looked into the hut, and was much interested and pleased with this early effort to get up something jolly. The drum-major came in with the leeks, and to our surprise a goat (our old goat had died) led by a chain. After he had presented the leeks to the young Welchmen, the goat sat up on his hind legs and drank a glass of champagne, much to the amusement of the company. He proved to be Styles, my groom, dressed up in a sheepskin coat, with the old goat's head stuck on his cap.

" I proposed the health of the Queen : and handed over the Welch toasts to Herbert, who made several good little speeches with much fun in them. I then proposed Codrington's health in a speech that was received with great applause : it ran about thus : ' There was a grey horse. This grey horse was seen at the Battle of Alma constantly passing backwards and forwards in the ranks of the Royal Welch Fusiliers. This grey horse carried an officer who, by his example and cheery voice, encouraged the men of the regiment in the moment of extreme danger. Since then we have to acknowledge many an act of kindness and courtesy extended to us by him (tremendous cheering). I need hardly say the toast I propose is the health of General Codrington (renewed cheering)—health, and three times three.'

" I then proposed the health of Colonel Vaughan of the Monmouth Militia, who was staying with us, and had furnished us with a large quantity of volunteers from his regiment of Militia. I compared him to a nurse who kept a capital nursery of very fine children for the regiment : this caused a good deal of fun and brought a good answer from him ; he speaks remarkably well. Several other healths were drunk, the band played, one or two songs were sung, and all went off well."

On the recommendation of Lieutenant-Colonel Lysons, Hospital Sergeant Simpson of the regiment was awarded on the 1st of March a silver medal, with an annuity of £30, for " Distinguished and meritorious service and gallant conduct in the field."

An alteration was made in the establishment of the regiment this month as follows : for 1 Lieutenant-Colonel and 3 Majors, 2 Lieutenant-Colonels and 2 Majors were substituted, and 24 Lieutenants and 16 Ensigns were replaced by 26 Lieutenants and 14 Ensigns.

On the night of the 22nd of March a sortie, mainly directed against the French works opposite the Malakoff tower, was made by the enemy. So high was the wind that the heavy firing which took place was not heard in the British camp, consequently the troops did not turn out. Captain Drewe, Lieutenants Poole and Radcliffe, 3 sergeants, and 110 rank and file were in the trenches at the time, and behaved with great gallantry in assisting to expel the enemy from a portion of them, which they had succeeded in capturing for a short time.

Major Campbell died of fever at Scutari on the 22nd of March.

On the 26th of March, silver medals, with gratuities as under, were awarded to the undermentioned non-commissioned officers and men of the 23rd Royal Welch Fusiliers, for distinguished conduct in the field: Sergeant-Major W. H. Smith, £15. Corporals—James Dawson, £10; Thomas O'Donohue, £10; Edward Luby, £10; Thomas Rees, £10. Privates—Thomas Callan, £5; James Chadwick, £5; Thomas Kellen, £5; Thomas McGwire, £5; Michael Manning, £5; William Willwood, £5; Joseph Molyneux, £5; John O'Beirne, £5; John Owens, £5; Joseph Thomas, £5.

Sergeant Frederic Nixon and one private were wounded during this month.

On the 5th of April Major Bell's name was mentioned in General Orders for being of great assistance to the Engineer officers when constructing a demi-parallel.

At daylight on the morning of the 9th of April, the second bombardment of Sevastopol was started by the British and French siege batteries opening fire upon it. The garrison was evidently taken by surprise, as, except on the extreme left, it did not respond to the attack for nearly half an hour.

On the 19th the bombardment practically ceased " for reasons now known to be connected with the proposed visit of the French Emperor to the Crimea." It is computed that during its progress the Allies threw 130,000 projectiles into Sevastopol.

On the same night the Russian rifle pits afterwards known as " Egerton's Rifle Pits " were attacked, and carried by assault in the most gallant manner by a detachment of the 77th Regiment under Colonel Egerton. At daylight on the following morning Captain Drewe with a party of the 23rd took charge of the captured pits; and although there was very little cover in them owing to the gabions being in many places only half filled, the party worked with such goodwill that by midday the parapet was made fairly secure.

The casualties in the regiment during the month of April amounted to 5 privates killed and 7 wounded.

On the 10th of May Corporal Richard Lowry of No. 7 Company while on duty in the advanced trenches noticed a soldier of the 9th Regiment lying wounded in front of Green Hill Battery. He obtained permission of Lieutenant O'Connor to cross the ravine with the object of removing him to a place of safety, but was himself severely wounded, and afterwards brought in with the man under a flag of truce.

Dr. John Hall, Inspector-General of Hospitals at the seat of war, in his report on the weekly state of the sick of the army from the 6th to the 12th of May, remarks with regard to the Light Division : " In this Division, as in all others, fever is the prevalent disease, but only two deaths have occurred from it during the week. Seven men have died from wounds and two of cholera—one in the 77th and the other in the 23rd Regiment."

On the 21st of May Lieutenant-General Sir George C. D'Aguilar, K.C.B., died, and was succeeded in the Colonelcy of the regiment by Lieutenant-General H. Rainey, C.B., K.H.

The casualties in the regiment this month amounted to 1 corporal and 16 privates wounded.

At 3 p.m. on the 6th of June the third joint bombardment commenced, the object being to capture the White Works (so called from the chalky soil on which they stood), the Mamelon, and the Quarries which were situated about 400 yards in front of the Redan.

At 6 p.m. on the 7th the tricolour was observed to be fluttering over the Mamelon. This was the preconcerted signal for the British to attack the Quarries. The storming party consisted of detachments from the Light and 2nd Divisions—in all 1,500 men, 700 being for the immediate assault and 600 in close support with the 62nd Regiment, and strong working parties in reserve, the whole under Colonel Shirley of the 88th Regiment, who was then acting as General Officer of the Trenches.

On the British guns ceasing to fire on the Quarries, the 700 men led by Lieutenant-Colonel Campbell of the 90th Regiment made a rush for the flanks of the work, from which they speedily drove the Russians with a loss of 100 men. Repeated attempts were made by the latter to recapture the Quarries. While the preparations for the first of them were in progress, Major Herbert with a party of the 23rd was holding the advanced trench near the Dockyard Ravine. An officer who had just returned from visiting the advanced posts informed him that, to the best of his belief, he had detected a column forming up facing the Quarries. Herbert at once withdrew all the men from the trench, and made them lie down in a slight dip of the ground. As the column passed within easy range he ordered his men to commence " independent firing " at its flank, which was unable to reply effectually.

Herbert's well-executed movement materially helped to frustrate the object of the enemy on this occasion, and brought about his mention by Lord Raglan in his dispatch of the 9th of June.

The Allied commanders decided late on the night of the 17th of June to simultaneously attack the Malakoff and the Redan the following morning. The supports to the storming party of the Light Division consisted of detachments of the 7th, 23rd, and 33rd Regiments under Lieutenant-Colonel Lysons. The detachment of the 23rd was not, however, engaged, as Sir George Brown, considering that the attack was doomed to failure, stopped it from advancing.

Lieutenant-Colonel Lysons was mentioned in dispatches for his services on this occasion and appointed C.B. on the 5th of July, and subsequently promoted Brevet Colonel, " for distinguished service in the field."

He had been severely wounded on the morning of the 18th of June, being the only casualty in the 23rd on that day.

On the evening of the 28th Lord Raglan, whose health had of late been none too good, mainly due to care and overpowering anxiety, passed peacefully away, to the great regret of the army. He was succeeded by Lieutenant-General James Simpson. The Royal Welch Fusiliers were represented at his funeral by Major Herbert, Captains Drewe, Vane, and Lieutenant Radcliffe, with 50 N.C.O.s and men.

On the 29th of June Lieutenant W. Owen, a very promising young officer of the regiment, was struck by a piece of shell whilst on duty in the advance trench in front of the Quarries and mortally wounded. He lingered for a few hours and died early on the morning of the following day.

The casualties during the month were: killed, 1 officer (Lieutenant W. Owen) and four privates; wounded, 1 officer (Lieutenant-Colonel Lysons), 1 sergeant (Michael Coyle), 3 corporals, and 30 privates.

The casualties in the regiment in July were 2 privates killed, 1 corporal and 10 privates wounded.

The casualties in the regiment during August were 1 corporal and 4 privates killed, Colour-Sergeant Daniel Chamberlain, Sergeant J. Edwards, 5 corporals, and 49 privates wounded.

Early in the morning of the 5th of September the final bombardment of Sevastopol began, and lasted until the 7th.

The following order was published on the latter day: " The Lieutenant-General has great pleasure in referring to the good conduct of two men of the 23rd Royal Welch Fusiliers named Wm. Brown and Thomas Symonds, who brought in from the front a corporal of the 97th Regiment, who had been severely wounded and left in a very exposed position, to which they went out most gallantly and humanely, at the risk of their own lives. The Commander of the Forces in wishing their names to be publicly noticed desires they may have a gratuity of £3 each."

Also on the same fateful 7th of this month the following after order was promulgated: " The Redan will be assaulted after the French have assaulted the Malakoff."

The regimental order that was issued for the storming of the Redan was as follows: " The regiment will parade at a quarter before nine o'clock to-morrow morning in coatees, black trousers, and forage caps, every man's water-bottle to be quite full." The task of carrying out the assault was assigned to the 2nd and Light Divisions owing to " the circumstances of their having defended the batteries and approaches against the Redan for so many months, and from the intimate knowledge they possessed of the ground."

On the morning of the 8th of September, the troops moved down to the trenches to prepare for the attack. The Royal Welch Fusiliers were placed in the left boyau, next to the 22nd Battery, instead of in the right boyau, as previously ordered.

Exactly at twelve, noon, the signal for the French to advance and attack the Malakoff was given, and their columns moved quickly out to the front.

It so happened that the Russians in the Malakoff were at their dinners at the time, and being totally unprepared for the attack offered no resistance to the French, who occupied the position without any loss.

The signal for the English to advance was then given, and the different parties proceeded to carry out the orders they had received. They crossed the long space between the fifth parallel and the Redan, a distance of 285 yards, under a heavy fire, and the losses were heavy; but holding steadily on, the ditch was reached, the ladders lowered and fixed, and the storming parties rushing in carried the salient angle, and even got as far as the third or fourth embrasure, but there they were stopped, no further advance could be made against the tremendous fire of the enemy. Seeing this the Royal Welch Fusiliers were moved up to the fifth parallel, and Sir W. Codrington ordered Colonel Lysons to take out a wing of the regiment and attack the proper right flank of the Redan. Five companies were at once formed up, and at the word of command the gallant Fusiliers jumped over the parapet, and advanced in line in splendid style, all the young officers waving their swords in front and cheering on their men. These companies continued to advance, leaving the other parties swarming on the salient angle on the right, until they approached the re-entering angle, when the enemy's fire became so terrific—the guns on the flank were throwing grape and canister into their very teeth, and the infantry on the face of the Redan were firing down on to their right shoulders, and in the front were standing up on the parapet ready to receive them—that it was impossible to advance.

Colonel Lysons was severely wounded in the thigh close to the ditch. Fourteen officers out of eighteen were hit, and over ninety-seven non-commissioned officers and men had fallen. The few men who remained, therefore, not being sufficient to attempt an attack fell back into the trenches. Some men, however, with British doggedness, did get across the ditch, and bravely met their death fighting on the parapet.

Lieutenant and Adjutant Dyneley, one of the wounded officers, was hit in the head, and in attempting to get back to the trenches got confused, and entered a kind of cave under the Russian works. Hearing of this, Assistant-Surgeon Sylvester volunteered to go out and dress his wounds, which he successfully accomplished under a galling fire; and when the regiment was ordered to return to camp, Captain Drewe, with Corporal Shields, Privates M. Aherne, James Taylor, John Green, and Thomas Kennedy, asked leave to remain behind to endeavour to bring in their adjutant: this being granted they waited till dusk, and then went out over the open, under a heavy fire, to the cave where Lieutenant Dyneley was lying, and carried him in safety back to the camp. Private Thomas Harris, who had faithfully remained with Lieutenant Dyneley the whole of the time, came in with him. For their gallantry on this occasion Assistant-Surgeon Sylvester and Corporal Shields were awarded the Victoria Cross.

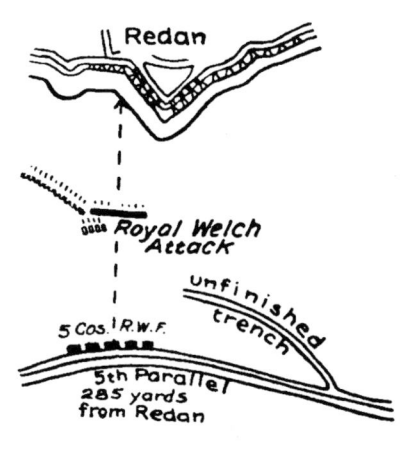

ATTACK ON THE REDAN

Many deeds of heroism were performed that day, and the "old corps" behaved splendidly. Unfortunately, however, the attack was unsuccessful, and the losses exceedingly heavy.

The following is a list of the killed and wounded in the 23rd Royal Welch Fusiliers at the attack on the Redan:

Killed: Lieutenant R. H. Somerville, 2 colour-sergeants, 2 sergeants, 2 corporals, and 35 privates.

Wounded: Colonel Lysons, C.B.; Captains F. E. Drewe, F. F. Vane, and W. H. Poole, who died on the 24th of September; Lieutenants—Lieutenant and Adjutant Dyneley, who died on the 9th, L. O'Connor, G. P. Prevost, S. C. Millett, C. Beck, who died on the 29th of September at sea on board the *Robert Clive*, F. M. Hall Dare, J. De Vic Tupper, E. S.

Holden, who died on the 9th, J. Williamson, and T. S. Bigge ; Sergeant-Major H. Smith, 2 colour-sergeants, 1 drum major, 9 sergeants, 2 drummers, 5 corporals, and 123 privates ; and there were twenty-three privates missing.

Total of killed—Subaltern, 1 ; sergeants, 4 ; corporals, 2 ; privates, 35 ; wounded—Colonel, 1 ; captains, 3 ; subalterns, 10 ; sergeants, 13 ; drummers, 2 ; corporals, 5 ; privates, 123 ; missing—23 privates : total —Colonel, 1 ; captains, 3 ; subalterns, 10 ; sergeants, 17 ; drummers, 2 ; corporals, 7 ; privates, 181. Of these one captain, three subalterns, and many men died of their wounds.

The following names were mentioned in Sir W. Codrington's dispatches : Colonel Daniel Lysons, C.B., afterwards familiarly known as "Redan Lysons," and Lieutenant-Colonel Bunbury, C.B.

During the following night loud explosions were heard, and huge fires were seen in the town, and it soon became known that the Russians were retreating from the south side, that the defences were abandoned, that the great "Siege of Sevastopol" was at an end, and that the fortress had fallen.

For the gallant part it played in this memorable siege the 23rd was permitted on the 3rd of October to add the word "SEVASTOPOL" to those already emblazoned on its colours.

The following appeared in regimental orders :

"The Commanding Officer begs to thank the officers, non-commissioned officers, and soldiers of the Royal Welch Fusiliers for the gallant manner in which they advanced from the fifth parallel on the 8th instant under an extremely heavy fire. He deeply feels the loss the corps has suffered, many old and tried soldiers having fallen. He views moreover with pride the determination of the younger men to preserve the character of the regiment that has hitherto been so celebrated : it would be invidious, where so many behaved gallantly, to mention individuals, as many equally deserving have escaped notice. The Commanding Officer has, however, preserved a list of those whose names have been brought to his notice."

The Commanding Officer has been pleased to make the following promotion : "For distinguished conduct in the field"—To be Corporal, No. 2945 Lance-Corporal Shields.

Corporal Shields was afterwards awarded the Cross of the Legion of Honour by the Emperor of the French.

When presenting it to him at Aldershot on the 18th of August 1856, Colonel Bunbury made the following speech to the regiment :

"Whilst decorating Corporal Robert Shields with the Cross of

GENERAL SIR DANIEL LYSONS, G.C.B.
From a photograph by Messrs. Elliott & Fry.

MAJOR-GENERAL SIR A. W. TORRENS, K.C.B.
From a mezzo by L. Dickenson kindly lent by Messrs. T. H. Parker, Berkeley Street, W.

Chevalier of the Legion of Honour awarded to him by His Imperial Majesty the Emperor of the French for distinguished gallantry on the 8th of September 1855, the Commanding Officer deems it incumbent on him to publish for general information the names of the four brave and devoted soldiers who volunteered on that day to follow and assist Corporal Shields in bringing in Lieutenant and Adjutant Dyneley, who lay mortally wounded near the Redan. This voluntary duty was nobly and successfully performed under a very heavy fire, and Colonel Bunbury will see that the names of Private James Taylor, Private Thomas Kennedy, Private John Green, and Private Michael Aherne are duly inscribed in the records of the regiment as bright examples for the future."

Their names *have* been entered in the regimental records, and as each 8th of September comes round their gallant and devoted conduct will be remembered with pride.

The duties now became very light, the principal employment being the making of roads from Balaklava to each division.

In October of this year Colonel Lysons was appointed to the command of the 2nd Brigade of the Light Division, which appointment he held until the Division was broken up on the return of the troops to England.

The command of the 23rd Royal Welch Fusiliers then devolved upon Lieutenant-Colonel Bunbury, C.B.

During the month Captain C. G. C. Norton, Lieutenants A. L. Tobin, A. M. Law, P. H. Knight, and J. Tilly joined the regiment.

On the 13th of November the magazine of the French right siege train exploded, and destroyed the greater part of the Light Division camp. Privates J. Durkin and M. Sheppard were both killed, and six other privates wounded.

The regiment remained stationed in huts before Sevastopol during the whole of the winter.

The numerous gifts that were sent from home to the regiment included three cases of warm clothing that were dispatched by Lord Dynevor towards the close of the year.

Colonel Lysons states that on New Year's Eve " I had a capital little party of Royal Welchmen. We had a round game at my round table and a supper—we sat down ten. The supper was declared perfection. Bell made the mull: we had some songs, and drank the health of 1856, all in proper style."

1855.

Reserve Companies.

On the 8th of February a draft of 7 sergeants, 2 drummers, 6 corporals, and 115 privates under Captain R. T. Raynes, with Lieutenant F. Horsford, Ensigns E. S. Holden, J. B. Hackett, and E. G. Blane, left the depôt at Winchester for Malta, where they formed the nucleus of the two reserve companies. They arrived about the 20th of February. Lieutenant Horsford died a few days after landing. In July 2 additional reserve companies were formed, the companies being numbered 13, 14, 15, and 16. From May to September the companies supplied 11 officers and 500 non-commissioned officers and men to the regiment in the Crimea.

1855.

Depôt Companies.

On the 26th of January a draft of 102 non-commissioned officers and men under Captain E. Crofts and Lieutenant the Hon. S. Mostyn was sent to the Crimea.

The depôt under command of Captain Raynes supplied 130 non-commissioned officers and men on the 8th of February to form the reserve companies in Malta.

On the 24th another draft under Lieutenant H. D. Radcliffe and Ensign W. Owen of 1 sergeant and 99 privates was sent to the Crimea.

On the 4th of May a draft of 6 sergeants, 2 drummers, 6 corporals, and 144 privates was sent to Malta, with Lieutenants Prevost, Hon. N. Fiennes, Lawrence, Williamson, and Lewis.

On the 30th of June Captain Bruce left the depôt in command of a draft of 4 sergeants, 2 drummers, and 94 privates for Malta; also Lieutenants Tupper, Griffiths, Hall Dare, and Ensigns Beck and Gregorie.

On the 10th of August Captain Granville left with a further draft of 61 non-commissioned officers and men for Malta, which was reached on the 22nd.

On the 29th of October yet another draft of 2 sergeants, 6 drummers, and 130 men under Captains G. Heigham and J. C. Jervoise proceeded to Malta, arriving on the 9th of November.

From January to December the depôt received 483 recruits and 275 from the Militia, principally from the Montgomeryshire and South Down Militia.

1856.

The New Year was ushered in by a fall of snow, and Colonel Lysons, then temporarily in command of the 2nd Brigade Light Division, took the opportunity of varying the usual marches, ball firing, etc. etc., by encouraging a sham fight, with snowballs, between the 1st and 2nd Brigades. Many prisoners were taken on both sides. The Royal Welch Fusiliers succeeded in capturing fourteen officers, and made them all pay 2s. 6d. each as ransom; the soldiers paid one penny.

In the spring drill was commenced, field days and reviews taking place in the plains near Balaklava.

In February theatricals were started in the regiment, the 7th Fusiliers uniting with it in erecting a temporary theatre; some of the scenery was painted by Colonel Lysons.

On the 30th of March peace with Russia was concluded.

The regiment remained at Sevastopol until the 14th of June, when it marched to Kamiesh and embarked on board H.M.S. *London*, 90 guns, together with the 33rd Regiment, and after a long and tedious voyage arrived at Spithead on the 19th of July, disembarking at Gosport on the 21st, and proceeding by rail to Aldershot, where it was encamped; the four reserve companies from Malta joined on the 23rd.

On the 31st of July the regiment was inspected by H.M. Queen Victoria, who was accompanied by H.R.H. the Prince Consort and H.R.H. the Duke of Cambridge.

Early in August the regiment moved into huts, and was brigaded with the 7th Fusiliers and 90th Light Infantry, under Major-General Lord William Paulet, C.B.

On the 4th of November the four depôt companies from Newport joined the regiment at Aldershot and were amalgamated with the service companies.

The establishment, privates only, was as follows:

September	8 companies	950
October	8 ,,	810
November	8 ,,	760
December	12 ,,	952

The total loss of the regiment during the Crimea was as follows:

	Officers.	Sergeants.	Drummers.	Rank and File.
Killed	14	11	2	196
Died of wounds or diseases	6	1	1	526
Missing	—	—	—	38
	20	12	3	760

404 N.C.O.s, drummers, and privates were invalided to England during the war in addition to the above.

The following is a list of the officers of the Royal Welch Fusiliers who were killed in action, or who died of their wounds, or of disease, from July 1854, up to the taking of Sevastopol on the 9th of September 1855:

Rank and Name.	Killed.	Died.
Lieut.-Col. Harry George Chester	Alma	
Capt. Arthur W. W. Wynn	Alma	
Capt. Francis E. Evans	Alma	
Major W. P. Campbell		December 1854, of fever and wounds received at Alma.
Capt. J. C. Conolly	Alma	
Capt. C. G. Sutton		Of cholera on board the *Victoria*, 16th September 1854.
Lieut. F. P. R. Delmé Radcliffe	Alma	
Capt. G. H. Hughes		Of fever at Pera, 12th December 1854.
Lieut. Sir W. N. Young, Bart.	Alma	
Lieut. and Adj. A. Applewhaite		28th September 1854, on board the *Andes*, of wounds received at Alma.
Lieut. and Adj. Douglas Dyneley	Attack on Redan, 8th September 1855	
Second-Lieut. Henry Anstruther	Alma	
Second Lieut. J. H. Butler	Alma	
Capt. W. H. Poole		Of wounds received at the Redan, September 1855.
Lieutenant F. Horsford		At Malta, of fever, 1854.
Asst.-Surgeon E. A. Jenkin		Of cholera at Monistir, August 1854.
Lieut. R. H. Somerville	Attack on Redan, 8th September 1855	
Lieut. E. S. Holden		9th September 1855, of wounds received at the Redan.
Lieut. W. Owen	In the trenches before Sevastopol	
Lieut. C. H. Beck		29th September 1855, of wounds received at the Redan.

The following is a list of the officers of the Royal Welch Fusiliers who were wounded from the time of the regiment landing in the Crimea, up to the capture of Sevastopol:

Rank and Name.	Severely or otherwise.	Description of wound.	On what occasion.
Lieut.-Col. Daniel Lysons	Severely	Leg	First attack on Redan.
Col. Daniel Lysons	Severely	Ball lodged in thigh	Second attack on Redan.
Capt. H. D'O. Torrens	Slightly	Head	Inkerman.
Capt. F. E. Drewe	Slightly	Arm	Second attack on Redan.
Lieut. H. Bathurst	Severely	Right arm broken	Alma.
Lieut. F. Sayer	Severely	Ankle	Alma.
Lieut. F. F. Vane	Slightly	Head	Inkerman.
Capt. F. F. Vane	Severely	Ankle	Second attack on Redan.
Lieut. S. C. Millett	Severely	Left arm broken	Second attack on Redan.
Lieut. T. S. Bigge	Slightly		In the trenches before Sevastopol.
Sergt. L. O'Connor	Severely	Shoulder	Alma.
Lieut. L. O'Connor	Dangerously	Both legs	Second attack on Redan
Lieut. H. D. Radcliffe	Slightly		Second attack on Redan.
Lieut. G. Prevost	Slightly		Second attack on Redan.
Lieut. J. De Vic Tupper	Severely	Ankle	Second attack on Redan.
Lieut. J. Williamson	Severely	Leg	Second attack on Redan.
Lieut. F. M. Hall Dare	Severely	Head	Second attack on Redan.
Capt. C. E. Hopton	Slightly	Left side	Alma.

A handsome monument to the honoured memory of the officers, non-commissioned officers, and men who fell during the Crimean War was erected in 1858 at Carmarthen by subscription from the officers serving, or who had served, with the Royal Welch Fusiliers. The inscription on the monument, which also bears the names of the campaigns in which the regiment has taken part, is as follows:

SACRED TO THE MEMORY OF

THE OFFICERS AND SOLDIERS OF THE "ROYAL WELCH FUSILIERS"

WHOSE NAMES ARE INSCRIBED ON THE ADJOINING TABLETS,

WHO FELL IN THE SERVICE OF THEIR COUNTRY

DURING THE WAR WITH RUSSIA IN 1854 AND 1855.

THIS MONUMENT WAS ERECTED A.D. 1858

AS AN ENDURING RECORD OF THE GALLANT DECEASED,

BY THE OFFICERS THEN SERVING OR WHO HAD SERVED IN

THE CORPS.

"Fear not them which kill the body, but are not able to kill the soul."—St. Matt. x. 28.

ALMA, SEPT. 20TH, 1854.

Lieut.-Colonel : Harry George Chester.
Captains : Arthur Watkin Williams Wynn, Francis Edward Evans, John Charles Conolly.
First-Lieutenants : Sir William Norris Young, Bart., Frederick P. R. Delmé Radcliffe, Augustus Applewhaite (Adjt.).
Second-Lieutenants : Henry Anstruther, Joseph Henry Butler.
Sergeant-Major : H. Jones.   Colour-Sergeant : R. Hitchcock.
Sergeants : J. Burke, F. Edmonds, J. Kerr.
Corporals : J. Jones, W. Winter.
Drummers : J. Collins, J. Royal.
Privates : W. Andrews, C. Badcock, C. Barnett, M. Clack, T. Conroy, W. Cruize, M. Clarke, G. Dobson, S. Draper, G. Evans, J. Evans, I. Fry, J. Fry, J. Groom, H. Goddard, J. Handrahan, H. Hine, J. Harrington, J. Hall, H. Huban, J. Harris, H. Hall, E. Jones, J. Knightley, T. Lynch, W. Lines, G. Lowman, J. Maloney, H. Marsh, W. Martin, W. Milden, J. Miles, W. Neal, G. Nichols, T. Owens, P. Paterson, D. Povey, J. Powell, C. Randall, T. Seymour, J. Stevens, T. Spiller, J. Sockett, C. Thrupp, T. Taylor, E. Williams, J. Williams, R. Walters, J. Warburton, J. Wells.

REDAN, SEPT. 8TH, 1855.

Captain : William Halsted Poole.
Lieutenants : Douglas Dyneley (Adjt.), Reginald Hugh Somerville, Edward S. Holden, Charles Henry Beck.
Colour-Sergeants : J. Gillogly, J. Ungless.
Sergeants : T. E. Roberts, J. Wilkinson.
Corporals : J. Kelly, E. Malone, T. Stoat.
Privates : J. Appleford, J. Abbotson, R. Biddle, W. Brown, T. Barnes, G. Brown, J. Bradbury, J. Bedford, J. Barrett, J. Brown, N. Bath, T. Box, R. Brown, T. Boyer, C. Bass, H. Churchill, M. Curran, G. Clarke, C. Constable, W. Crutcher, M. Clarke, F. Davies, G. Downer, J. Donovan, E. Dwyer, W. Davies, C. Fox, J. Frankhum, W. Fowles, B. Fielding, J. Gardiner, T. Giles, T. Harvey, P. Hayes, G. Hobbs, W. Hudson, T. Hall, P. Hillen, R. Horne, D. John, W. Jones, J. M. Jones, W. Jelly, J. Jones, E. Jones, W. Johnson, J. Kilroy, G. Kemish, R. Longman, J. Lawless, J. Lamb, T. Millington, T. McEvoy, R. McCrum, W. Mason, W. Martin, J. Nasmyth, W. Nunan, T. O'Brien, F. Owens, C. Perkins, H. Perkins, C. Payne, W. Price, G. Plant, J. Robinson, R.

Richards, S. Reed, J. Rush, J. Redding, H. Stone, J. Singlefield, W. Smith, W. Sparks, G. Saunders, D. Taylor, J. Walsh, L. Williams, J. Wright, J. Whitehead, H. Ware, H. Whilrican, T. Williams, J. Woodall.

INKERMANN, NOV. 5TH, 1854.

Sergeant: R. Dunkley.

Privates: H. Aitkin, W. Brown, J. Batten, W. Carr, J. Eustace, V. Gallagher, G. Harris, J. Hetherington, J. D. Murrin, D. Saunders, J. Williams, J. Webb.

IN TRENCHES BEFORE SEBASTOPOL, 1854 AND 1855.

Lieutenant: William Owen. Sergeant: T. Casey.
Corporals: W. Clayton, R. Gibbs, J. J. Shawe.

Privates: J. Aubrey, J. Arnott, J. Bennett, W. Brumwell, E. Buckingham, T. Bull, T. Bryan, H. Clarke, R. Chalkley, M. Dix, J. Durkin, H. Elms, G. Edwards, T. Evans, W. Foley, J. Goff, R. Hollister, J. Hanny, H. Hedges, L. Haynes, W. Holmes, T. H. Jones, J. McMahon, P. Maskell, J. McCorey, G. Morris, J. Murray, G. Meeton, T. Neville, J. Painting, J. Ryan, T. Reese, S. Russell, T. Reycroft, T. Roberts, O. Shine, M. Sheppard, E. Spent, S. Shafford, T. Stokes, W. Taylor, J. Willis.

OF DISEASE DURING THE WAR.

Major: William Pitcairn Campbell.
Captains: George Henry Hughes, Cornelius Graham Sutton.
Asst.-Surgeon: E. A. Jenkin.
and 526 Non-commissioned Officers, Drummers, and Private Soldiers.

The inhabitants of Chester placed a beautiful stained-glass window in St. Mary's Church, Chester, in loving memory of the officers and men of the Royal Welch Fusiliers who died in the war.

The window bears the following inscription:

"In memory of the officers and men of the Twenty-third Regiment Royal Welch Fusiliers who fell in the Crimea, from the victory of the Alma to the storming of Sevastopol, September 1854 to September 1855."

1856.

Reserve Companies.

On the 27th of February Captain Raynes with a draft of 103 non-commissioned officers and men left for the Crimea, and on the 9th of March the last draft of 50 non-commissioned officers and men under Lieutenant G. W. H. Russell left to join the regiment. The four companies proceeded early in July to England, where they joined the regiment on the 24th of July at Aldershot.

1856.

Depôt Companies.

Drafts were sent to Malta as follows: on 14th January 98 non-commissioned officers and men, and on 19th February 71 non-commissioned officers and men.

On the 7th of June the companies moved from Winchester to Newport (Mon.).

In August a detachment was stationed at Brecon under Ensign G. Pack, and another at Cardiff under Ensign Annesley Cary.

The four depôt companies marched under Captain Bathurst from Newport to Aldershot, on the 4th of November, where they were amalgamated with the regiment.

The recruits from January to April numbered 110, and 150 joined from the Militia.

1857.

In January Colonel Lysons published the following order on relinquishing the command of the regiment:

"Colonel Lysons regrets much that he cannot accompany the Royal Welch Fusiliers on foreign service. In taking leave of the distinguished regiment which he has had the honour of commanding on active service under circumstances of peculiar trial and danger, he has to return his sincere thanks to the officers, non-commissioned officers, and men, who have so gloriously won renown for the old corps, for the support he has always received from all hands.

"Colonel Lysons has to assure his late comrades that his warmest wishes for their happiness and welfare will ever accompany the good old ' Welch Fusiliers.' "

He was succeeded in the Lieutenant-Colonelcy by Lieutenant-Colonel Samuel Wells from the 25th Foot.

In the early part of this year Queen Victoria was pleased to send to the regiment the goat she had so graciously presented to it, to replace the one that had died at Sevastopol.

On the 1st of February the regiment received orders to move to Portsmouth, and again prepare for active service, China being its destination on this occasion; it marched from Aldershot to Portsmouth on the 9th of February.

No. 11 and No. 12 companies were selected as depôt companies and proceeded to Fort Monckton.

The regiment left England for service in China in three divisions.

The 1st division, consisting of Nos. 2, 3, and 4 companies under Lieutenant-Colonel R. Pratt, embarked on the 20th of May in H.M.S. *Adventure*; 11 officers and 294 N.C.O.s and men.

The 2nd division with the headquarters, and Nos. 1, 7, 8, and 9 companies under command of Lieutenant-Colonel S. Wells, embarked in the steamship *Cleopatra* on the 16th; 22 officers and 353 N.C.O.s and men.

The 3rd division, Nos. 5, 6, and 10 companies under Lieutenant-Colonel E. W. D. Bell, V.C., embarked in H.M.S. *Melville* on the 23rd; 15 officers and 291 N.C.O.s and men.

All the officers embarked with their companies except Captain Bulwer, who had not returned from diplomatic employment abroad, and Lieutenant Luke O'Connor, who was specially retained in England to be decorated with the Victoria Cross, by H.M. The Queen in person. Surgeon McFarlane died on the voyage, and was buried at sea on the 23rd of July.

The regiment, however, was not destined to reach China, for its services were urgently required elsewhere.

For some time past an extensive conspiracy had been in existence in Northern India, having for its object the abolition of British rule in that country, by sowing discontent in the minds of the native army. The Hindu soldier, by nature readily inclined to believe everything at first hand, was secretly, but none the less thoroughly, led to believe that it was the settled policy of the Indian Government to belittle his faith, and by that means induce him to embrace Christianity.

The following incident formed the pretext for changing his loyalty, which had stood the test of exactly one hundred years, into the rankest treason.

In the early part of this year the Enfield rifle, which superseded the one hitherto in use known as the Minié rifle, was introduced into Bengal. To render it thoroughly effective it was necessary that the cartridge should be greased. This fact was used by the conspirators as a powerful lever to further their ends. A report was sedulously set on foot that the grease was a mixture of the fat of cows and pigs—abhorrent to both Hindus and Mahommedans—and that Queen Victoria had been petitioned by the missionaries to make use of the greased cartridges, as a means of forcing the natives to discard their faith.

With a view to counteracting this false report the Governor-General of India, by means of a proclamation, made it known to the army of Bengal, that nothing had been done, or would be done, by the Government to interfere with the religion, or the caste, of any class of the community; but all to no purpose.

The flame which was destined to set Bengal ablaze was kindled at Meerut, where, on the 10th of May, two native regiments rose in mutiny and shot their officers. From there it spread to Delhi, thence to Allahabad, and so on until by the end of June native troops had broken out into open mutiny at no less than twenty-two stations.

The Bombay Government being anxious to obtain reinforcements, as quickly as possible, dispatched a special steamer to the Cape of Good Hope, bearing an urgent request to the Governor to intercept all vessels with troops on board, and send them to India without a moment's delay. H.M.S. *Adventure* with Lieutenant-Colonel Pratt's division had sailed ten days before the special steamer arrived, and had proceeded as far as Singapore before news of the Mutiny reached her. She arrived at Calcutta on the 19th of September, and the division, landing on the 21st, marched into Fort William.

The steamship *Cleopatra*, after having been detained two days at Madeira, and five days at Ascension, for coaling purposes, arrived at Table Bay on the 7th of August, simultaneously with the special steamer. The Governor, Sir George Grey, directed that the *Cleopatra* should coal at once, and proceed to Calcutta, which was reached on the 18th of September, where Lieutenant Luke O'Connor, V.C., who had come out by mail steamer, reported himself on board. The headquarters and the four companies under Lieutenant-Colonel Wells disembarked on the 19th and marched into Fort William. The seven companies remained in Fort William, occupying the Royal Barracks until the 11th of October.

H.M.S. *Melville*, however, with Lieutenant-Colonel Bell's division, was delayed by adverse winds, etc., and did not arrive at Calcutta until the 18th of November, when the division disembarked and proceeded up-country to join headquarters. It did not arrive in time to share in the relief of the Residency, but took part in the subsequent operations.

On the 11th of October the first Company left Calcutta by bullock train for Allahabad, which was the rendezvous; the other companies followed at the rate of one company per diem. No. 1 company was, however, left at Benares to protect the station, with orders to follow when relieved by the corps following after.

On the 27th of October six companies, Nos. 2, 3, 4, 7, 8, and 9, reached Allahabad, and encamped under the walls of the fort there. On the following day Major Bruce, with Captain Norton's company of the Royal Welch Fusiliers, a company of Royal Engineers, and the Naval Brigade under Captain William Peel, R.N., proceeded by railway to railhead at Lohunga, which was forty miles distant from Allahabad. At Lohunga a temporary depôt was established for cattle and transport, and for the transmission of troops and stores towards Cawnpore.

On the 31st of October Captain Peel's force marched to Fatehpur, which was reached at midnight. At daylight on the 1st of November, Peel, leaving the company of the Royal Welch Fusiliers there to hold the camp, marched to Kudjwa, and attacked the Sepoy mutineers of the Dinapore Regiment, utterly routing them.

On the 3rd of November the company of the regiment which was commanded by Brevet-Major Torrens proceeded by rail to Lohunga, in charge of part of a battering train which was being got together for the relief of the Lucknow Residency.

On the following day Lieutenant-Colonel S. Wells, with the headquarters and two companies of the regiment, accompanied by Captain Longdon's battery of artillery, joined Brevet-Major Torrens' company at Lohunga, Lieutenant-Colonel R. Pratt being directed to follow with the other three companies.

On the 6th of November Lieutenant-Colonel Wells left Lohunga with the object of joining the force under General Sir Colin Campbell, the Commander-in-Chief, which left Cawnpore on the 9th of November to relieve Lucknow.

On the morning of the 14th of November the companies of the Royal Welch Fusiliers joined the rear-guard of the relief force, after the march had commenced. The rear-guard did not close up to the column until late on the 15th, as the enemy hung on to it until daylight closed on the previous day.

Lieutenant-Colonel Pratt, with the three companies of the regiment already referred to, having now joined those under the command of

Lieutenant-Colonel Wells, the whole, together with two and a half companies of the 82nd Regiment, were constituted the 5th Infantry Brigade under the command of Brigadier D. Russell.

On the 16th of November Sir Colin Campbell was in a position to advance against the Secundra Bagh, which lay to the south-east of the Lucknow Residency. It was a high-walled enclosure about 120 yards square, strongly built and loopholed all round. It was held in strength by the mutineers. After an attack which lasted about an hour and a half it was brilliantly carried by storm. During the attack the 5th Brigade was inactive, being halted a short distance off waiting for orders.

During this period of enforced inactivity both the Royal Welch Fusiliers and the 82nd Regiment suffered several casualties.

On the 17th of November the 5th Brigade was moved up the road on the left of the line, in the direction of a barracks which was occupied by 300 men of the 93rd Highlanders. When it arrived within a short distance of this barracks, Lieutenant-Colonel Wells with three companies of the Royal Welch Fusiliers took post at two long, thatched, barrack-like buildings on the right side of the road, and at a mud-walled village opposite to them. As soon as this was done a company of the Royal Welch Fusiliers, together with a piquet of the 53rd Regiment, proceeded to occupy a trench and bank extending from the north angle of the barracks yard wall, with the object of watching the right front.

The enemy kept up an incessant fire on the buildings occupied by the Royal Welch Fusiliers, from the effect of which Lieutenant J. J. Henderson was slightly wounded. On the afternoon of the following day the enemy made a sharp attack on the piquets covering the centre of the line. A company of the Royal Welch Fusiliers and another of the 53rd Regiment were sent to their support, aided by Captain Remmington's troop of Horse Artillery, which " opened fire with extraordinary rapidity and precision " : the mutineers were speedily driven back.

About the same time Brigadier Russell commanding the 5th Brigade was severely wounded whilst in charge of his line of posts. His place was taken by Lieutenant-Colonel G. Biddulph, Head of the Intelligence Department, who was killed almost immediately afterwards when making his disposition for the attack on the hospital fronting the enclosure of the " D " Bungalows.

The command of the brigade then devolved upon Lieutenant-Colonel Hale of the 82nd Foot, who as quickly as possible led the attack upon the hospital, from which, and also from the building in the cramped suburbs, a most galling fire was kept up by the enemy. The hospital was captured, but the thatched roof catching fire necessitated the evacuation of the building, and the retirement of Lieutenant-Colonel Hale's force to the " D " Bungalows.

Lieutenant-Colonel Crawford, R.A., commanding the R.A. Field Force, witnessed an incident during this assault which so impressed him that he wrote an account of it to the Assistant-Adjutant-General, Brigadier Grant's Field Force. The following is a copy of the letter in question :

" SIR,   " CAMP ALUMBAGH, *November 25th,* 1857.

" I have the honour to report, for the information of His Excellency the Commander-in-Chief, that about 5 o'clock on the 18th instant, when visiting a detached party of Royal Artillery, with three five-inch mortars on the left of our position at Secundra Bagh, I there witnessed a most gallant and humane act performed by Lieutenant Hackett, H.M. Twenty-third Fusiliers : Lieutenant Harrington of Captain Boucher's Field Battery : Gunner 8955, John Ford : Gunner 7614, John Williams : and Band Boy 5202, George Monger, H.M. Twenty-third Fusiliers.

" A corporal of the 23rd was lying in the open ground outside the bungalow occupied by Brigadier Russell. The man was badly wounded. Lieutenant Hackett came forward and called for volunteers to assist him in getting in a wounded man. Lieutenant Harrington, Gunners Ford and Williams, immediately came forward. They left the house, crossed the road, exposed to a heavy musketry fire, brought in the corporal, and with them Band Boy Monger, who remained the whole time with, and attended to the wounded man, the boy bringing in the rifle of the corporal. It was a gallant act, and in my opinion, deserving of good reward.

" [*signed*]   LIEUT.-COLONEL CRAWFORD,
Royal Artillery.
Brigadier Commanding Royal Artillery Field Force.

" To the Assistant-Adjutant-General,
Brigadier Grant's Field Force."

For their gallantry on this occasion Lieutenant T. B. Hackett and Drummer George Monger were awarded the Victoria Cross.

The following notices appeared in the *London Gazette* of the 12th of April 1859 :

" HACKETT, LIEUTENANT THOMAS BERNARD.
23rd Regiment.

Date of Act of Bravery : 18th November 1857 (India).

For daring gallantry at Secundra Bagh, Lucknow, on the 18th of

November 1857, in having, with others, rescued a corporal of the 23rd Regiment, who was lying wounded, and exposed to a very heavy fire. Also, for conspicuous bravery, in having, under a heavy fire, ascended the roof and cut down the thatch of a bungalow, to prevent its being set on fire. This was a most important service at the time."

"MONGER, PRIVATE GEORGE.
23rd Regiment.

Date of Act of Bravery: 18th November 1857 (India).

For daring gallantry at Secundra Bagh, Lucknow, on the 18th of November 1857, in having volunteered to accompany Lieutenant Hackett, whom he assisted in bringing in a corporal of the 23rd Regiment, who was lying wounded in an exposed position."

From the 19th to the 22nd of November an incessant fire from the batteries was kept up on the Kaiser Bagh, which was occupied by the rebels. The whole of the relief force then formed one outlying piquet which was " constantly subject to annoyance from the enemy's fire."

As the mutineers were led to believe that an assault was imminent, orders were issued for the retreat of the garrison through the lines of piquets at midnight on the 22nd. As the hour for the evacuation of the Residency approached, the Commander-in-Chief requested that two officers of the 23rd Royal Welch Fusiliers might be sent to him to convey the necessary information as to when the garrison had passed to the rear. Lieutenants Monsell and Williamson were selected for this duty, and were sent to the Commander-in-Chief, who, with his staff, was waiting within the angle formed by the two roads meeting at the Secundra Bagh, the 93rd Highlanders being formed there as the last support.

It had been arranged that the posts on the left of the Secundra Bagh should be held until the Residency garrison and the posts on the right had safely retired, followed by the Commander-in-Chief with his staff, and the 93rd Highlanders in support. On receiving notice of this, Lieutenant-Colonel Ewart's detachment in the barracks was to retire by the rear of the " D " Bungalows, giving notice as it passed by, when Colonel Hale and his brigade would also retire on the La Martinière. In the meantime the headquarter companies, 23rd Royal Welch Fusiliers, were to watch the front, and, after allowing sufficient time for the evacuation of the barracks and " D " Bungalows, were also to retire on the La Martinière.

This programme was effectually carried out. No. 4 company of the 23rd Royal Welch Fusiliers had previously been moved out of the trench, that it had occupied for five days and nights, and extended in skirmishing order towards the right front. No. 7 company formed on the road as a support, while No. 2 company was moved to the rear by the sandy track through the village to hold the open space beyond, until No. 4 company should have been withdrawn, file by file, followed by No. 7. So quietly, and in such perfect order, were the movements carried out that the enemy was totally unaware of the withdrawal of the entire Residency garrison, and of the different piquets, and posts of the relieving force.

The night of the 22nd of November was dark and very still. The utter silence and quiet observed by officers and men were beyond all praise. One solitary shot was fired by the enemy, which passed close over No. 7 company and lodged in the mud wall in its rear. This occurring in the middle of the night, and in the great stillness, had a very startling effect, but nothing took place to delay the movement to the rear. The Commander-in-Chief's directions were successfully carried out, and the 5th Brigade assembled in the La Martinière enclosure soon after 1 a.m. on the 23rd of November.

On that day Brigadier J. Inglis, late commanding the Residency Garrison, took over the command of the 5th Brigade. On the following day it removed from the La Martinière enclosure, and joined the forces at the Alum Bagh.

The casualties in the Royal Welch Fusiliers during the relief operations were: killed, 3 rank and file; wounded, 1 officer (Lieutenant Henderson) and 18 rank and file. Lieutenant-Colonel Wells was mentioned in General Sir Colin Campbell's dispatch of the 18th of November.

Leaving Major-General Sir James Outram with his division (4,000 strong) to occupy a position before Lucknow, the Commander-in-Chief accompanied Brigadier-General Hope Grant's division, to which was assigned the task of conveying the women, children, sick, and wounded of the Lucknow garrison, and the wounded of the relief force, across the Ganges—an operation which was successfully performed by the 30th of November.

Grant's division with its encumbrances then marched for Cawnpore, which was found to be in possession of the rebels. By order of the Commander-in-Chief it occupied a position which enabled communication between Fatehpur and Allahabad to be restored.

By the 5th of December all the non-combatants and wounded had been dispatched to places of safety. On the following day the right of the enemy's position, which lay partly in and partly outside Cawnpore, occupied by the Gwalior Contingent, was successfully attacked. Its camp was captured at 1 p.m. and the flying enemy pursued for fourteen miles. Both Brigadier Inglis, commanding the 5th Infantry Brigade, and Lieutenant-Colonel Wells were mentioned in Sir Colin Campbell's dispatch of the 10th of December.

The Royal Welch Fusiliers did not join in the pursuit, as both it and a wing of the 38th Regiment were ordered to remain in the captured camp with a view to safeguarding it.

Whilst it was in the act of piling arms, a party of the enemy, with three guns, suddenly appeared and opened fire. Colonel Wells at once ordered two companies, under Major Torrens, to advance in skirmishing order, with one company in support.

The enemy's guns kept up a pretty sharp fire of grape during the advance, and George Rogers, the smartest man in No. 3 company, was killed, and another man was wounded.

When the skirmishers arrived at about 200 yards from the enemy, Major Torrens gave the word to " double," and the men simply raced for the guns, the enemy flying in all directions. Colour-Sergeant Knightley, afterwards Sergeant-Major, and later on Quartermaster, was the first to reach the guns. He at once scratched on them with his bayonet, " No. 3 Company, Royal Welch Fusiliers." Two of the guns were taken back to camp at once : the third, which had a wheel broken, was brought in the next day.

These guns were known for a long time afterwards as " No. 3 Company Guns." This was a very brisk and exciting affair, and reflected no little credit on the regiment.

On the 12th of December Nos. 5, 6, and 10 companies under Lieutenant-Colonel Bell, which had landed at Calcutta on the 18th of November, joined the headquarters before Cawnpore. On the 22nd No. 1 company joined from Benares. On the 24th of December the Royal Welch Fusiliers marched with the force under Sir Colin Campbell which left the camp before Cawnpore with the object of striking a blow at the rebels then holding Fatehgarh. The same day a halt was made at Chowbepore, where Sir Colin remained until the 26th, when he marched to Poorah and thence to Arrown, which was reached on the following day. On the 28th Major-General Windham, C.B., was dispatched with the 5th Brigade, the 4th Punjaub Infantry, a squadron of irregular cavalry, and a battery of artillery, to Futtiah, with the object of capturing and blowing up a rebel fort there. As the fort was found to have been evacuated, the Engineers quickly demolished it. Windham's brigade then marched to Tirooah and back again to Futtiah.

During this year the undermentioned past and present officers and men of the regiment were the recipients of the Sardinian War Medal conferred in 1857 by the King of Sardinia, viz. :

>Colonel D. Lysons, C.B.
>Major F. E. Drewe.
>Captain S. C. Millett.
>Lieutenant Luke O'Connor.
>Corporal E. Luby.
>Corporal T. Symonds.

The Sultan of Turkey awarded in March the Imperial Order of the Medjidie to the undermentioned past and present officers of the Royal Welch Fusiliers in approbation of their distinguished services before the enemy during the late war :

>Colonel Daniel Lysons, C.B.
>Lieutenant-Colonel H. W. Bunbury.
>Lieutenant-Colonel A. J. Herbert.
>Brevet-Lieutenant-Colonel E. W. Bell, V.C.
>Brevet-Major H. D'O. Torrens.
>Captain F. Sayer.
>„ J. Duff.
>„ F. F. Vane.
>„ S. C. Millett.
>„ T. S. Bigge.
>Lieutenant Luke O'Connor, V.C.
>Surgeon W. G. Watt.

1857.

Depôt.

On the 1st of May the depôt which had been formed by Nos. 11 and 12 companies at Fort Monckton, Portsmouth, was under the command of Captain F. F. Vane.

In July it moved to Chatham ; recruiting parties being stationed at Wrexham, Oxford, Newport, and Reading, with the result that they obtained 120 recruits from October to December.

1858.

On the 1st of January the regiment rejoined Sir Colin Campbell's headquarters camp at Goorsai Gunge.

On the 2nd of January the regiment crossed the suspension bridge over the Kali Nadi, from which the enemy had been driven, with a loss of eight guns and upwards of 200 men, by the brigade of Highlanders and the 53rd Regiment earlier in the day.

The regiment bivouacked about three miles from the river, and marched the next morning to Fatehgarh, which was found evacuated by the enemy, who had fled, leaving guns and stores of all descriptions undestroyed in the hands of the British.

On the 7th of January Nos. 6 and 7 companies were sent on detachment to Firozabad to relieve two companies of the 82nd Regiment. On the 9th two companies of the regiment under Brevet Lieutenant-Colonel Bell marched to Berrar for the purpose of receiving a convoy expected from Delhi; he had been promoted to Lieutenant-Colonel in the 14th Foot on the 8th of January.

On the 11th of January a redistribution of regiments took place. The Royal Welch Fusiliers together with the 2nd and 3rd battalions of the Rifle Brigade now constituted the 5th Brigade of the 1st Division, under the command of Brigadier-General Walpole.

On the 13th of January Walpole's brigade, together with a battery of artillery, two guns under Captain Peel, C.B., R.N., and one squadron of the 6th Dragoon Guards, marched from Fatehgarh to the Ramganga, where it camped and remained there from the 14th to the 31st of January, engaged in sending out piquets to watch the enemy on the opposite side of the river.

On the 1st of February Walpole's Brigade vacated its camp on the Ramganga, and set out for Cawnpore, marching via Fatehgarh, Jellahabad, and Poorah, reaching there on the 11th of February.

Another redistribution of regiments now took place. The Royal Welch Fusiliers, the 79th Regiment, and the 1st European Bengal Fusiliers, now the Royal Munster Fusiliers, formed the 5th Brigade under Brigadier-General Douglas, which, together with Colonel Horsford's 6th Brigade, composed the 3rd Division under the command of Brigadier-General Walpole; 7 subalterns from the Hon. East India Company's service were attached from now onwards to the regiment.

On the 19th of February the 5th Brigade left Cawnpore and arrived at Bunterah on the 26th and 27th of February, the Royal Welch Fusiliers reaching there on the latter date.

The present state of the Royal Welch Fusiliers on the 2nd of March was as follows: officers, 54; rank and file, 825: total, 879.

On the same day Sir Colin Campbell, who had now 20,000 men and 180 guns under his orders, commenced his final advance for the capture of Lucknow. Leaving Bunterah early in the morning of that day, he arrived before the Dilkusha Palace, Lucknow, in the afternoon. A skirmish took place, the result being that it was captured, and occupied as an advance piquet.

The Royal Welch Fusiliers and the 79th Regiment, forming an escort for the heavy siege guns, did not leave Bunterah until 11 a.m. on the 2nd of March, and after a weary tramp in the dark joined Sir Colin Campbell in the park of the Dilkusha Palace at 11 a.m. on the following day.

On the evening of the 5th of March the 3rd Division, forming part of a force under Sir James Outram, crossed to the left bank of the Gúmti River, by two pontoon bridges that had been thrown across that river during the afternoon.

The order received by Sir James Outram was to push up the left bank of the Gúmti, and render untenable the enemy's strong position on the canal which abutted on the right bank of the Gúmti, thus preparing the way for Sir Colin's direct attack from the Dilkusha.

On the morning of the 6th of March Outram disposed his force in three lines, and after advancing up the river for some distance wheeled to the left, and marching direct for Lucknow pitched his camp in front of the Chaka Kothi, which was the key of the enemy's position.

On the morning of the 7th the enemy attacked Outram's advanced outposts, but was speedily driven back.

On the following day Outram erected a battery with the object of shelling the enemy on his line of works along the canal.

At daybreak on the 9th the battery opened fire " with excellent effect." Seeing this, Outram, who had divided his force into a right and left column, directed General Walpole, who commanded the right column, to attack the enemy's left, while he advanced with the left column, in which the Royal Welch Fusiliers were included, towards the Badshah Bagh, near which he hoped to join hands with the right column. While the latter was successfully assaulting the Chaka Kothi the left column forded a small tributary of the Gúmti called the Kakrail, and advanced to a position where it could be joined by Walpole as soon as he had succeeded in driving back the enemy's left. This operation having been successfully performed, both columns pressed forward to the Badshah Bagh. The fortified gates of this strong walled enclosure were blown open, the garden occupied, and two guns captured by the troops.

The 10th of March was spent by Outram in strengthening his position. The Royal Welch Fusiliers spent that day at the Badshah Bagh, and at night sent working and covering parties to a battery, which was being erected there with the object of shelling the Mess House and the Kaiser Bagh.

All the preparations for a simultaneous attack on both sides of the River Gúmti having by now been completed Sir Colin Campbell directed Outram to advance on the morning of the 11th of March against the position held by the rebels in the suburbs and push them back on to the iron and stone bridges, then to occupy the left bank of the river and erect additional batteries to play upon the centre of the city. The Commander-in-Chief on his part was to storm and capture a large block of palaces called the Begum Kothi.

The right column of Outram's force, under the immediate command of Brigadier-General Walpole, was led by the former in person. It worked its way through the suburbs until it reached a mosque which commanded the iron bridge distant about half a mile. Leaving the 1st European Bengal Fusiliers to occupy the mosque, Outram pushed on with the remainder of his force, and succeeded in penetrating to the head of the stone bridge without encountering serious opposition. As, however, he found that his men were exposed to both artillery and musketry fire, he retired to the mosque already occupied by the Bengal Fusiliers.

The left column, which consisted of the Royal Welch Fusiliers, the 2nd Punjaub Infantry, and 5 guns under the command of Lieutenant-Colonel Pratt of the former regiment, moved forward through the suburbs adjoining the Gúmti, and met with considerable opposition.

It succeeded, however, in occupying all the houses down to the river bank and the head of the iron bridge, but withdrew from them in the afternoon by Outram's orders, and retired to the camp at Badshah Bagh, but without the Royal Welch Fusiliers, who were left to guard a new battery which had been constructed adjacent to the iron bridge.

In the action at the iron bridge the Royal Welch Fusiliers sustained the following casualties: Captain G. P. Prevost wounded slightly, Lieutenant G. W. H. Bussell wounded severely, Sergeant James Holland wounded slightly, also four privates.

Sir Colin Campbell, operating on the south side of the Gúmti, succeeded in capturing the entire block of buildings already referred to, and inflicted great loss on the enemy.

On the night of the 13th of March a party of the Royal Welch Fusiliers guarded a breastwork of gabions, which had been constructed by a working party of the 79th Regiment, across the centre of the iron bridge.

On the following night the headquarters and 4 companies of the regiment returned to the camp at the Chaka Kothi, followed by the remainder of the regiment on the night of the 14th of March. On the 15th a bridge of casks was constructed over the Gúmti opposite the Secundra Bagh.

On the morning of the 16th Outram with Douglas's Brigade (the 23rd, 79th, and 1st European Bengal Fusiliers) crossed the river by this bridge of casks, and proceeded to join Sir Colin Campbell at the Kaiser Bagh. On the approach of the brigade Sir Colin Campbell rode out to meet Outram, and personally instructed him to take the Residency, also the iron bridge in reverse (which was Sir Colin's principal object); then to advance for over a mile and storm the Machi Bawan and the Great Imambara. He also informed Outram that he had strengthened the brigade by the addition of the 20th Regiment, and the Ferozepore Regiment of Sikhs, and that no time was to be lost in pressing the movement. What followed is briefly described by Sir James Outram in his memorandum on the operations carried on, under his command, at the siege. "I immediately ordered the advance and took possession of the Residency, with little opposition, the 23rd Fusiliers charging through the gateway, and driving the enemy before them at the point of the bayonet, the remainder of the Brigade following them in reserve. The enemy having been dislodged from the Residency, two companies of the 23rd under Lieutenant-Colonel Bell, accompanied by Captain Gould Weston, who pointed out the road, pressed rapidly forward, and captured the brass gun, which was in position to sweep the Iron Bridge, after some opposition."

The Royal Welch Fusiliers bivouacked for the night in the Residency. Lieutenant A. L. Tobin of the regiment was severely wounded in the early part of the day's operations, and Private White belonging to No. 1 company was killed.

On the 17th of March Outram, with a force which included the headquarters and the right wing of the Royal Welch Fusiliers, advanced against a block of buildings known as Shurfooddowlah's house, which was occupied without opposition, the enemy precipitately retreating therefrom. The regiment then proceeded to occupy the Great Imambara.

On the morning of the 19th of March Sir James Outram proceeded with a column, in which the Royal Welch Fusiliers were included, to attack the Músa Bagh—the last stronghold of the enemy—which was held by a force estimated at about 5,000 men with 12 guns.

As the enemy appeared to be in great strength on the road a field battery, together with skirmishers from the Royal Welch Fusiliers and the 79th Regiment, was ordered forward. Their fire soon silenced that of the enemy. Two squadrons of the 9th Lancers had in the meantime made a flank movement to the enemy's left. Outram's force then advanced, whereupon the enemy fled precipitately, abandoning all his guns. Leaving the 2nd Punjaub Infantry to occupy the Músa Bagh, Outram withdrew the rest of the troops to their quarters in the city—the Dowlat Khana being that of the Royal Welch Fusiliers.

On the 21st of March the last body of the rebels was expelled from Lucknow.

On the same day Lieutenant-Colonel Wells was compelled by illness to relinquish the command of the regiment, and return to England. He was succeeded by Lieutenant-Colonel Pratt.

On the 22nd of March the Commander-in-Chief published a congratulatory order in which he stated that every regiment employed had won much distinction, and that every man employed could rest assured that he had deserved well of his country.

Sir James Outram in his report of the operations carried out by the force under his command states that " Lieutenant-Colonel Wells records the services of Major Bruce, Captains Prevost, Duff, and Norton of the 23rd Fusiliers," and he also records that Brigadier Douglas mentioned with approbation " Lieutenant Utterson, 23rd Fusiliers, his Aide-de-Camp and Orderly Officer."

In a Roll of Officers who served under Brigadier-General R. Walpole, commanding the 3rd Infantry Division during the operations at Lucknow in March 1858, and who were considered deserving of honourable mention, the following appears : " Lieutenant-Colonel Wells, 23rd Regiment, commanded his regiment and distinguished himself during the operations, including the actions of 9th and 11th."

" Lieutenant-Colonel Pratt, 23rd Regiment, commanded a column, consisting of the 23rd Regiment and 2nd Punjaub Infantry, on the 11th, when the iron bridge was secured, and distinguished himself on this occasion."

" Captains Duff and Prevost, 23rd Regiment, recommended by Lieutenant-Colonel Wells, commanding 23rd Regiment, for having distinguished themselves in the advance on the iron bridge, on the 11th instant."

The casualties sustained by the regiment during the operations before Lucknow from the 2nd to the 21st of March inclusive were as follows :

killed, 3 privates; wounded, Captain G. P. Prevost, Lieutenant G. W. H. Bussell, Colour-Sergeant Christopher Lester, Sergeants Elijah Adams, James Holland, and Jabez Carr, and 12 privates.

Queen Victoria, in commemoration of the services of the Regiment in restoring order in Her Majesty's Indian Dominions, was graciously pleased on the 8th of August to command that the word "LUCKNOW" should be borne on their colours and appointments.

From the 1st to the 30th of April the companies of the regiment were either scattered in encampments in the environs of Lucknow, or formed part of a movable column that had been formed for the dispersal of bodies of rebels stated to be collecting near Bunnee Bridge.

On the 1st of May this column returned to Lucknow, and from that day until the 10th of September the whole regiment remained at Lucknow. On the 28th of May Ensign H. J. Richards died of fever there. In July the regimental goat breathed his last at headquarters in the Kaiser Bagh, to the great grief of all ranks.

At 10.30 on the night of the 22nd of September a force, in which two companies (180 men) of the Royal Welch Fusiliers were included, left Lucknow under the command of Major E. G. Bulwer of that regiment with the object of operating against a body of rebels, estimated at about 3,000 strong with 4 guns, occupying an entrenched position at Selimpore, situated on the right bank of the Gúmti, and which was in direct communication with a large force of double that number on the opposite side of the river. As speedily as possible the enemy's position was surrounded. Major Bulwer then gave instructions for the fire from two field guns and two mortars, covered by a company of the Royal Welch Fusiliers under Captain C. Monsell and a company of the 88th Regiment, to be brought to bear upon the south and west of the enemy's position. Bulwer, observing the commotion soon caused by the accuracy of his artillery fire, directed the infantry and skirmishers to storm the position, which they did with such gallantry that the entrenchment was speedily carried, numbers of the mutineers being mown down as they frantically endeavoured to escape by the only gateway.

The casualties sustained by the detachment of the regiment in this most creditable affair were: killed, 1 rank and file, wounded, Sergeant Wm. Brady and 3 rank and file, one of whom, Private John Lloyd, subsequently died of his wounds.

Major Bulwer in his report of the 25th of September dispatched from his camp at Goorsaingunge speaks highly of the conduct of Captain Heigham, who commanded the two companies of the regiment, and also of Ensign Wildes, who was Major Bulwer's Orderly Officer. The Commander-in-Chief expressed his high opinion of the brilliant manner in which Major Bulwer conducted the operations entrusted to him.

While Bulwer was hotly engaged a force under his commanding officer, Lieutenant-Colonel R. Pratt, which contained 200 men of the regiment under Captain Norton, was engaging a larger body of rebels encamped on the opposite bank of the Gúmti, near the scene of Bulwer's operations.

The 6 guns that accompanied the expeditionary force, supported by the infantry, opened fire at 500 yards with such telling effect that in a short time the enemy dispersed in all directions.

On the 1st of October an outlying piquet of the column at Goorsaingunge was attacked at about one o'clock at night, but the enemy was driven back.

On the 11th of October the column left Goorsaingunge and marched to Kurjowlee, proceeding to Jubrowlee on the following day. Whilst on the march from Kurjowlee to Jubrowlee, Lieutenant Tobin, who had never thoroughly recovered from the severe wound he had received at the attack on the Residency, died of dysentery, and was buried in the maidan in front of the camp.

On the 23rd of October the enemy attacked the column in force, but were repulsed with great slaughter. Their loss on this occasion amounted to upwards of 200 killed and wounded, and four guns were captured; whilst on the British side a considerable number of the Native cavalry attached to the column were killed, and some were wounded. Lieutenant Metford, commanding Hodson's Horse, was wounded.

On the 26th of October the column marched for Poorah, where it encamped next day.

Whilst the column was in the act of changing its position on the 29th of October, the rebels suddenly came up and attacked it in great numbers, when some severe fighting took place. The enemy were eventually defeated and driven back, with a loss of upwards of 600 killed and wounded, and 2 guns. The Native cavalry and infantry attached to the column suffered greatly in this action.

On the 31st of October Colonel Eveleigh, of the 20th Regiment, who had with him detachments of the 20th and 80th Regiments, joined the column and assumed the command.

At six o'clock on the morning of the 8th of November Colonel Eveleigh, commanding a movable force in which 250 men of the Royal Welch Fusiliers were included, left Poorah with the intention of attacking a body of rebels, 4,000 strong with 3 guns, which occupied the village of

Morar Mow. Major Bulwer with No. 6 company of the regiment was left in charge of the camp.

As the approach to the village was very difficult Colonel Eveleigh dispatched a troop of cavalry to the right of it, and another to the left, with the object of turning the enemy's flank. This manœuvre was immediately successful, the enemy commencing a retreat which was speedily transformed into an utter rout. Two of his guns were captured, and about 100 men, principally sepoys of the Bengal army, were killed.

At six o'clock on the following morning the column left its camp at Morar Mow for the purpose of attacking the strong fort of Simree, which was situated in a dense jungle.

On the position of the fort being located, two companies each of the Royal Welch Fusiliers and the 80th Regiment, with the necessary supports, were ordered to extend and advance with the object of clearing the enemy's numerous skirmishers out of the jungle. The skirmishers advanced, driving the enemy before them, and, to their surprise, came most unexpectedly close upon the fort, and observing the wall in one part to be rather low, and a few bushes only in front of a wicket gate, they gave a cheer and rushed boldly on, when the enemy ran bodily from the walls and bastions into the jungle behind.

Colonel Eveleigh in his report remarks as follows : " The advance of the 80th under Captain Young and also of the Royal Welch Fusiliers under Captain Heigham excited my warmest approbation." No loss was sustained by the detachment of the regiment on this occasion.

On the 17th of November Colonel Eveleigh's column, which was making westward in accordance with instructions, overtook about 5,000 men forming part of a hostile force under the command of Rana Banee Madho and dispersed it, taking three guns.

Major Bulwer, in command of the company which had been left at Poorah, joined the column the same day with a large convoy of " hackeries," containing a month's supplies for the force.

On the 23rd of November the column reached Nuggur, where it was joined by the Commander-in-Chief, Lord Clyde, better known as Sir Colin Campbell.

On the following day two companies of the regiment under the command of Captain Monsell were sent to Buxar Ghaut on patrol duty.

On the 24th of November Lord Clyde attacked the Rana at Doundeakeara, completely breaking and dispersing his forces. A detachment of Royal Welch Fusiliers on this occasion formed part of the left brigade under Colonel Jones of the 6th Dragoon Guards. One rank and file wounded was the only casualty this day.

On the 3rd of December the column arrived at Lucknow. On the 6th of December a movable column was formed under the command of Lieutenant-Colonel Gordon with the object of pursuing the Rana Banee Madho, and driving him to the banks of the Gogra. A detachment of the Royal Welch Fusiliers formed part of his force. The remainder of the regiment was employed under Brigadier Purnell in reconnoitring the country adjoining the Gogra in a north-westerly direction, until the beginning of the following year.

A draft of 248 men under Lieutenant Winstanley joined the battalion on the 19th of December whilst on the march.

By Circular Memorandum from the Adjutant-General, dated 29th January 1858, it was laid down that the Grenadier and Light Infantry Companies of regiments were to be abolished; but it was not until a few years later that they finally disappeared. In future the companies were distinguished by a letter instead of a number.

In June of this year Lieutenant-Colonel Samuel Wells was one of nineteen officers in the service of Her Majesty Queen Victoria, and of the East India Company, who, by a special statute of the Order of the Bath, were made extra members of the Military Division.

1858.

Depôt.

The depôt in January sent a draft of 32 men to the service companies; in March 147 men; on the 12th of April a draft of 230 men to form the nucleus of the 2nd battalion; and in June another draft of 248 men to the 1st battalion.

During the year 497 recruits joined the depôt.

1858.

2nd Battalion.

The mutiny of the Native troops, comprising the Bengal Army in India, having necessitated an increase in Her Majesty's Army, the Colonel of the 23rd Royal Welch Fusiliers, Lieutenant-General Henry Rainey, C.B., K.H., received an intimation from the Secretary of State for War, dated 16th March, that Her Majesty the Queen had been pleased to issue an order for the formation of a 2nd battalion for the regiment under his command, from the 3rd of March. It was to consist of 12 companies of 42 officers, 3 surgeons, 1 sergeant-major, 56 sergeants (including staff sergeants), 50 corporals, 24 drummers, and 950 privates: total, 1,126.

On the 12th of March the General Commanding-in-Chief (His Royal Highness the Duke of Cambridge) directed the transfer of 4 sergeants, 1 drummer, 43 rank and file, and 157 of the last-joined recruits from the depôt of the 1st battalion.

This draft left Chatham on the 12th of April under Captain Vane and proceeded by rail to Newport, Mon., the station fixed upon at which to raise the new battalion. The draft reached its destination on the 13th of April.

On the 17th Major Gubbins joined the battalion upon appointment and took command, of which he was relieved on the 20th of June by Lieutenant-Colonel Bell, V.C., from the 14th Regiment.

On the 19th of April a notification was received from the Secretary of State for War that the establishment had been reduced from the 1st of April by 2 sergeants, 2 corporals, and 48 privates.

On the 9th of June recruiting parties were sent to Aberdare, Merthyr Tydvil, Carnarvon, Swansea, and Oxford. For the first four months the average recruiting was from twenty-five to thirty men a week, but during the succeeding two months the ranks became so rapidly filled with volunteers from the militia, that the Commanding Officer was enabled to report, on the 23rd of September, that the establishment of the battalion was filled up, when an order was issued that recruiting for the regiment should be stopped. Those recruits and volunteers who had enlisted for the 2nd battalion previous to the receipt of instructions to discontinue the recruiting, and who had been sent to other districts on its discontinuance, were permitted to join the battalion, special authority for their being borne on the strength of the regiment being granted.

The total number of men who had joined the 2nd Battalion Royal Welch Fusiliers by the 12th of October, that is to say within seven months of the receipt of the orders for its formation, was 1,218.

The following list will show whence the men were received:

Transfers from the depôt of the 1st Battalion Royal Welch Fusiliers	230
Recruits raised at headquarters, etc.	425
Volunteers received from the militia	549
Transfers from Line regiments	14
Total	1,218

On the 26th of July three companies of the battalion, under Major Lumley, proceeded on detachment duty to Brecon.

This detachment was augmented on the 6th of September by No. 9 company from the battalion, and fifty more men were sent to it on the 15th of September, and forty more on the 11th of October.

On the 22nd of October No. 7 company, under the command of Brevet-Major Vane, proceeded to Cardiff, where it was stationed until the 8th of December. On the 7th, 8th, and 10th of December the battalion moved in three divisions to Aldershot, where it was posted to the 3rd Brigade, under command of Major-General Lawrence, C.B., and occupied huts in the South Camp.

On the departure of the battalion from Newport, the following complimentary address was presented by the Mayor and Town Council of the borough to the officer commanding the battalion:

" Sir,

" The Mayor and Town Council of this borough cannot allow the 2nd Battalion of the Twenty-third Regiment to leave Newport without expressing the high sense they entertain of the general good conduct of the regiment, and considering the force has been newly raised within the last few months it must be highly satisfactory to you that your watchfulness for the maintenance of military discipline has been so ably supported by the officers and non-commissioned officers under your command, and they trust that men who have commenced their career so creditably will add fresh laurels to those already borne by the Royal Welch Fusiliers, a regiment in which the county of Monmouth must always feel a deep interest.

" I have the honour to be,
  [signed] T. Woolett.

" Lieut.-Colonel Bell, commanding 2nd Battalion
  Twenty-third Royal Welch Fusiliers, Newport.
Dated at Newport, Monmouthshire, 8th December 1858."

1859.

1st Battalion.

On the 6th of January the regiment marched out of Lucknow to Nanpara, returning, however, on the 15th to the old cantonments at Merriow.

The battalion remained at Merriow, furnishing detachments periodically in the city, until the 12th of October, when it marched to the new cantonments at Dilkusha, remaining in camp there until the 4th of November, when regular quarters were given over to the regiment.

The depôt under Captain Lees remained at Chatham the whole year.

1859.

2ND BATTALION.

On the 31st of January the battalion was separated into 10 service and 2 depôt companies, the former to consist of 39 officers, 861 non-commissioned officers and men, the latter of 6 officers, 162 non-commissioned officers and men.

Orders having been received for the battalion to embark for Malta, the 1st division left Aldershot on the 5th of February, proceeding to Portsmouth and embarking the same day on board H.M.S. *Perseverance*: the division was under the command of Major Gubbins, and consisted of 10 officers, 431 non-commissioned officers and men. It sailed on the 6th, and arrived at Malta on the 22nd of February.

The 2nd division and headquarters left Aldershot on the 8th by the same route, and embarked on board H.M.S. *Urgent*. The division was under the command of Lieutenant-Colonel Bell, V.C., and consisted of 19 officers and 535 men. It sailed on the 9th, put into Plymouth on the 10th from stress of weather, sailed again on the 14th, and arrived at Malta on the 24th of February. The battalion marched into the barracks at Fort Ricasoli.

On the 26th of September the battalion moved from Fort Ricasoli to Lower St. Elmo Barracks, Valetta.

On the 21st of December colours were presented to the 2nd Battalion Royal Welch Fusiliers by His Excellency Sir John Gaspard Le Marchant.

The ceremony took place at 2 p.m. on the " Florian " parade ground, for which purpose the regiment was drawn up in position in line, forming three sides of a square. The two centre subdivisions composed the escorts and were commanded by Captain Prevost and Captain Tupper.

The colours, having next been blessed by the Venerable the Archdeacon Le Mesurier, were then handed to His Excellency by Major Gubbins and Major Granville, who placed them in the hands of Lieutenant Law and Lieutenant Henderson.

Owing to a heavy wind blowing at the time, His Excellency deemed it advisable to postpone his address, and accordingly forwarded a written one to Lieutenant-Colonel Bell, V.C., which was read to the battalion afterwards. This address and Colonel Bell's reply are as follows :

"Address to the 2nd Battalion Royal Welch Fusiliers on the presentation of their Colours by His Excellency Sir Gaspard Le Marchant, 21st December 1859 :

"OFFICERS, NON-COMMISSIONED OFFICERS, AND SOLDIERS OF THE TWENTY-THIRD ROYAL WELCH FUSILIERS,—I have been requested by your Commanding Officer to present to you your new colours. I accept with pleasure so distinguished an honour, for it must ever be to a soldier a source of much congratulation to be associated in the history of a regiment so distinguished as that I now see on parade. If there is no ceremony more imposing in our service than the presentation of colours to a young regiment, there is no ceremony more solemn, and which imposes deeper obligations on every individual connected with a corps, than the one which I am about to perform. If on a soldier entering the service he swears allegiance to his Queen and country, so in like manner does he bind himself by an oath no less solemn to defend the colours of his regiment, and he must feel, either in peace or war, that they represent the honour of his corps, and that every one individually must, if necessary, sacrifice his life in support of them.

"To trace back the career of the Twenty-third Fusiliers it would be almost necessary to read the history of the last 200 years, for since the year 1689, in which it was first raised, it has ever borne a most distinguished and conspicuous part in every great battle that has recorded the glory of our country.

"In 1690 the Royal Welch first saw fire at the battle of the ' Boyne.' There, in support of the constitutional liberties of England, you established your fame and your reputation to the character of good soldiers.

"At the battle of ' Blenheim ' you served under that great commander the Duke of Marlborough, and after seeing great and distinguished service in the French wars against the great Monarch, Louis XIV, I again trace you as a highly distinguished regiment under George I.

"At the great battles of ' Dettingen ' and ' Minden,' the Royal Welch ever stood signally conspicuous for their gallantry. At ' Bunker's Hill ' and ' Guildford,' in the war of American Independence, you supported the fame of the old corps.

"In Egypt, under Abercromby, the Welch were repeatedly noticed for their intrepidity, and at ' Corunna ' you fought under Moore.

"In the ' Peninsular War ' with our great Duke of Wellington, this corps took part in all the engagements of the day, and whether it be at 'Albuhera,' 'Badajoz,' 'Salamanca,' 'Vittoria,' 'Pyrenees,' 'Nivelle,' 'Orthes,' or 'Toulouse,' it is difficult to say in which fight your gallantry was best displayed. In the closing scene of that great war at the battle of Waterloo no corps probably on the ground was more proudly distinguished than your own, and certainly no military body could have more brilliantly resisted the repeated charges of the cuirassiers of the Imperial Guard than your gallant regiment. That deed was then the theme of admiration, and it must ever be, so long as your corps lasts, a subject of pride to all, and a point of emulation to every young soldier who finds himself enrolled under your colours. After this day your regiment passed a period of some thirty years in peace, but the breaking out of war with Russia again brought the 'Old Welch' in front of the enemy. Regard your colours, and they will best speak of the glories won in that campaign. 'Alma,' 'Inkerman,' and 'Sevastopol,' each will tell you of the struggles and the hand-to-hand fight in which your regiment was engaged, and no corps in Her Majesty's service came out of that brilliant campaign with a prouder step than the Old Welch Fusiliers.

"While you may thus look with a natural feeling of pride upon the gallant deeds and distinguished honours which were won, you may drop a tear to the memory of those whom Providence ordained should not survive the glories of those days.

"In that short campaign, so severe was your fighting, so unflinching your gallantry, when opposed to the enemy, that but very few of those gallant soldiers who marched for the shores of the Crimea are now left to tell amongst you their triumph and their victories.

"It was now only wanting to complete the chain of gallant deeds recorded in honour of your corps for the colours again to be found in India at the 'Relief of Lucknow,' restoring to the protection of their country the last remnants of the wives, widows, and children of your slaughtered countrymen and comrades in arms who had fallen a sacrifice in the fury of that terrible rebellion.

"In presenting these colours, I wish I could sufficiently impress upon the minds of all whom I address the sacredness of the trust reposed in them. All soldiers, from the day of enlistment, become members of that great military family which England looks to to support the honour of the Crown and the institutions of our country. Reflect, therefore, men, how much is expected of you, and on the duties you are called upon to perform.

"No man can disconnect himself from his regiment. If he acts the part unbecoming a soldier, he brings discredit on his corps, for a soldier is known less by his name than by that of the regiment into which he has entered, and in like manner intrepidity in the field and bravery in action shed additional lustre on his comrades and the colours of his regiment.

"The minister of God, our Very Reverend Archdeacon Le Mesurier, has blessed the colours about to be confided to your care. May his sacred call bring down on us protection of a Higher Power, Who watches over and preserves us equally, whether it be in the quiet walks of private life, or in the strife of a hard-fought battlefield.

"Though there may not be many in this young 2nd battalion who can boast of sharing in the glories of their elder comrades, yet their appearance on parade, their admirable soldier-like bearing, leads me to predict with confidence that opportunity alone is wanting for their adding to the records names of equally distinguished actions. Soldiers! preserve with care and fidelity the colours I have now the honour to present to you. The one represents your Queen and your allegiance as soldiers: the other is the emblem and represents the honour of your regiment: and when you regard it, think of the proud deeds it represents, and of the brave soldiers and gallant hearts who have fallen in the strife which speaks so home to your pride and to your hearts' blood.

"This corps has ever been distinguished not only for its remarkable gallantry, but especially for its esprit de corps, the pride and attachment of the soldiers to their officers, and the deep solicitude with which the officers have always watched over the interests of their men.

"As a soldier myself, and an old regimental officer, I can give you no better advice than to maintain those feelings. The bond of union between the officer and his men is an element alone sufficient to make a corps happy and distinguished. I congratulate the regiment on being commanded by an officer so distinguished as Colonel Bell, and one who has ever been with you from his first entrance into the service to the present day.

"I am sure it must be a source of pride to every officer to see his Commander wear on his breast the 'Victoria Cross'—an honour alone conferred for distinguished bravery before the enemy. Let every man who now regards that cross of chivalry bear in mind that the like honour is equally open to the soldiers as well as to the General, and that our Gracious Queen places this decoration on the breast of the private soldier with the same feeling of acknowledgment for his services to his Crown and country as she would on the most distinguished officer of her army.

"Recollect that, and let it be the beacon that should direct the soldier and cheer him onwards in the path of his duties to his Queen and country.

"Soldiers! three cheers for your Queen."

The following was the reply made by Lieutenant-Colonel Bell, V.C., commanding the 2nd Battalion Royal Welch Fusiliers:

"Sir Gaspard Le Marchant,—On the part of the Royal Welch Fusiliers I beg to return you most sincere thanks for the honour you have this day conferred upon us. It is most gratifying to the regiment to hear the careful manner in which you have recapitulated its history from the first raising of the corps down to the present time. We are fully aware of the vast inheritance of renown that is entrusted to our safe keeping, and accept with pleasure its responsibilities. I feel confident that the conduct of the young soldiers of this battalion, whether in quarters or in the field, will fully justify the encomiums you have this day passed on them: and that should these standards be unfurled in the day of battle —mindful of the proud position the Royal Welch has always held—we shall be found staunch to our colours, and ready, if need be, to lay down our lives for our Queen and country."

The following is an extract from a local newspaper of the period:

"The Officers of the Royal Welch Fusiliers gave a Grand Ball on Wednesday night, December 21st, at the Auberge de Provence, at which upwards of 500 persons were present. We have not space for a list, but amongst them we may mention H.R.H. Prince Alfred, His Excellency Sir G. Le Marchant, accompanied by a brilliant Staff, the foreign Consuls, the officers of all the regiments stationed in Malta, officers from every man-of-war in harbour, and the leading English and Maltese families in the Island. The whole of the extensive rooms belonging to the Union Club, kindly lent by the members for the occasion, were tastefully decorated and thrown open to the visitors: while the nationality of the gallant regiment was brought forcibly to the minds of all present, by the groups of Welch women attired in the ancient and picturesque costume of their country, and by the celebrated harper of the regiment, who dressed in his Bardic Robes played several spirited airs whilst the company was arriving.

"Dancing was commenced immediately on arrival of His Excellency Sir G. Le Marchant, and kept up with great spirit till twelve o'clock, when the Supper Room, which was beautifully adorned with flags, stars of swords, and bayonets, and other appropriate devices, was thrown open, and the dancers hastened to partake of a most magnificent supper. The festivities were shortly resumed, and the day was dawning ere the last guest left the Ball Room.

"The goat presented to the Regiment according to ancient custom by Her Most Gracious Majesty, was also present, and received the most marked attention from the Fair Sex."

The Colours presented on this occasion are still (1922) carried by the battalion.

The depôt was augmented by 2 sergeants and 2 corporals, but reduced by 2 privates.

On the 1st of March it proceeded from Aldershot to Walmer by train: 4 officers and 108 non-commissioned officers and men under command of Captain D. Reid.

1860.

1st Battalion.

During the whole of this year the battalion remained at Lucknow: transferring in March 23 men to the Bengal Artillery, and receiving a draft of 3 corporals and 60 men on the 29th of October. Assistant Surgeon Charles F. Morris died at Lucknow on the 30th of June.

Lieutenant-General Henry Rainey, C.B., K.H., Colonel of the Regiment, died at Brighton on the 26th of December, and was succeeded in the Colonelcy by Lieutenant-General Sir W. J. Codrington, K.C.B.

1860.

2nd Battalion.

The battalion remained in Lower St. Elmo Barracks, Malta, during the whole of this year. No. 6 company moved to Marsa Muscetto on the 26th of May. The depôt remained at Walmer and sent a draft of 30 privates on the 4th of May to the battalion.

1861.

1st Battalion.

The battalion remained at Lucknow cantonments, and furnished a weekly detachment of 2 companies to guard and garrison the arsenal at Muchee Bawn.

In February it received a draft of 20 privates from the 1st battalion 24th Regiment.

In March it received the following transfers:

From the 24th and 37th Regiments	. . .	33 men
,, ,, 64th ,, 73rd ,,	. . .	22 ,,
,, ,, 1st battalion, 5th Regiment	. . .	54 ,,
		109 ,,

On the 15th of March Lieutenant Charles Wrench died, and on the 6th of May Captain and Brevet-Major Heigham died at Lucknow of smallpox.

The establishment of regiments serving in India was reduced on the 3rd of May to 10 service companies of 40 officers and 918 rank and file. The two depôt companies were also reduced to 6 officers and 114 rank and file.

The battalion marched from Lucknow en route for Fyzabad on the 1st of December and arrived at that station on the 9th of the same month.

The depôt moved on the 29th of August from Chatham by rail to Dover, and marched from there to Deal.

1861.

2ND BATTALION.

On the 26th of March the battalion moved from Lower St. Elmo Barracks and was quartered as follows:
Headquarters and three companies at Bola Gate.
Three companies at St. Francesca de Paola.
One company at Elema Gate.
Three companies at Polo Cristo.
The depôt sent a draft of 30 men to the battalion in January, and one of 20 men to the battalion in July.

1862.

1ST BATTALION.

On the 3rd of December the battalion proceeded under Lieutenant-Colonel Wells, C.B., from Fyzabad to Agra, which was reached on the 20th of that month. This move, which was out of the usual course of the reliefs, was made in exchange with the 35th Regiment, which it was considered desirable to remove from Agra on account of excessive sickness amongst the men.

1862.

2ND BATTALION.

On the 5th of April the establishment was reduced, in accordance with Horse Guards circular No. 196, by 30 privates.

On the 30th of May the battalion proceeded to Pembroke Camp Barracks, St. George's Bay.

On leaving the Cottonera district the following appeared in brigade orders :

"2ND BRIGADE OFFICE, 29th May 1862.

"BRIGADE ORDERS.

"No. 8.—The Brigadier-General wishes to express to Lieutenant-Colonel Bell and the officers and men of the Royal Welch Fusiliers before they leave his brigade his entire satisfaction with the conduct of the regiment since it has been under his command. The regiment is in high order, creditable alike to officers and men, and the Brigadier-General regrets that the requirements of the service should necessitate the removal of the regiment from his brigade."

On the 6th June His Royal Highness the Prince of Wales, who was returning to England after a tour made in Egypt, Syria, Constantinople, etc., and had landed in Malta on the 4th June, visited the Barracks at Pembroke Camp.

Having first laid the foundation stone of a Soldiers' Library and Reading Room, which was in course of erection, he then proceeded to review the " Royal Welch," who were drawn up in line ready to receive him. After riding down the ranks, the battalion was broken into open column and marched past in quick time.

His Royal Highness complimented Lieutenant-Colonel Bell in the most gracious manner on the soldierlike appearance of the battalion under his command, expressing his satisfaction at the steadiness of the men under arms, and desiring that the same might be communicated to them.

On the 11th of June two companies proceeded to Lower St. Elmo Barracks, Valetta, and were followed by the headquarters on the 4th of July.

The battalion was inspected by Major-General R. B. Wood, C.B., commanding 1st Brigade, at Lower St. Elmo Barracks, on the 3rd of November.

The depôt sent a draft of 2 sergeants and 30 privates to the battalion on the 7th of September.

1863.

1ST BATTALION.

During the whole of this year the battalion remained at Agra.

In March 1 corporal and 81 privates were transferred to the 107th Regiment.

Whilst at Agra the regiment took a prominent part in all the amusements at the station, and at the annual race meeting this year greatly amused the garrison by a race that took place amongst the officers, which was called the " St. David's Race," and wherein all the competitors were dressed in fancy dress.

The following is an extract from an Indian newspaper which contained an account of the Agra carnival in 1863:

" The second day's races came off to-day: the scene was enlivened considerably by a novel entertainment on the turf— ' a fancy dress race '—when fifteen riders, mounted on animals varying in size from a very small bazaar-tat to a large horse, and dressed in costumes which I should be bold were I to attempt to describe, tried the mettle of their steeds. This was the ' St. David's Stakes,' especially in honour of the Royal Welch and their patron saint, towards whom the time-honoured traditions of the corps enjoin the utmost reverence, culminating on the famous 1st of March almost to hero worship.

" On this occasion the memory of the patron saint was duly honoured by one of the jockeys in the long flowing beard and the exact counterpart of the costume St. David is well known always to have worn.

" Nobody can say that St. David, with all his minor accomplishments, couldn't ride a race, though the irreverence of a free-thinking age might have been manifested in the worshippers of the saint not allowing the object of their adoration to win the stakes."

This custom was kept up for some time, and at the annual regimental games one of the principal features was the " St. David's Race," when the officers in every conceivable fancy dress afforded the utmost amusement to the onlookers, and rode a desperate race for a cup and " St. David."

The depôt supplied a draft under Captain Bussell to the battalion: it reached India on the 7th of November.

1863.

2ND BATTALION.

On the 1st of April the battalion returned to Pembroke Barracks, St. George's Bay.

The establishment was reduced by 90 men on that date.

On the 15th of August an order was received to hold the battalion in readiness to embark for Gibraltar. On the 24th of October it was inspected previous to its departure by His Excellency Sir John G. Le Marchant, G.C.M.G., and embarked immediately afterwards on board H.M.S. *Orontes* under command of Colonel Bell, V.C., the embarkation strength being 23 officers, 47 sergeants, 20 drummers, 38 corporals, 719 privates. It arrived at Gibraltar on the 28th of October; headquarters and five companies occupied barracks at Europa, the other five companies being at Buena Vista.

The depôt, which was still stationed at Walmer, was reduced on the 1st of April by 10 men; its establishment now consisting of 6 officers, 10 sergeants, 4 drummers, 10 corporals, and 110 men.

1864.

1st Battalion.

The battalion remained at Agra.

The establishment was reduced by one assistant surgeon on the 20th of September.

On the 4th of November a draft consisting of 1 sergeant, 3 corporals, and 37 privates landed, and joined the service companies at Agra on the 30th of November. With this draft there also arrived a goat which Her Majesty Queen Victoria had presented to the battalion to replace the one which died at Lucknow in July 1858.

On the 27th of January of this year there died, and was buried at Llanfor, Merioneth, a pensioner of the regiment named John Williams. His record of service, which is almost unique, is recorded on his tombstone and reads thus:

"IN MEMORY
OF
JOHN WILLIAMS
PENSIONER 23RD (ROYAL WELCH
FUSILIERS) REGIMENT OF FOOT
DIED 27TH DAY OF JANUARY 1864
AGED 87 YEARS.
HE FOUGHT FOR HIS COUNTRY AT
27 BATTLES, AMONG WHICH WERE
MARTINIQUE, ALBUHERA, CIUDAD RODRIGO, BADAJOZ, SALAMANCA, VITTORIA,
PYRENEES, ST. SEBASTIAN, NIVELLE, ORTHES, TOULOUSE,
WATERLOO."

1864.

2ND BATTALION.

The battalion remained at Europa Barracks, Gibraltar, during the whole of the year. Two companies proceeded to the North Front for rifle practice in September, rejoining headquarters in December.

The depôt remained at Walmer.

1865.

1ST BATTALION.

On the 29th of October No. 8 company proceeded by rail from Agra to Allahabad, being followed on the 1st of November by headquarters and Nos. 4, 6, 7, and 9 companies; and on the 5th by Nos. 1, 2, 3, 5, and 10 companies. It marched on the 11th of November from Allahabad for Jubbulpore; and on the 22nd, Nos. 1, 9, and 10 companies were detached to Nagode under the command of Captain C. Monsell. On the 6th of December the battalion arrived at Jubbulpore, relieving the 91st Highlanders, and moved into barracks on the 11th of that month.

The depôt furnished a draft consisting of 2 sergeants, 1 drummer, and 21 privates under Captain F. Gerard, which joined the battalion on the 1st of November.

The following Horse Guards Circular Memorandum, dated 10th June of this year, abolished the system under which the companies of a regiment of infantry were known by numbers and substituted lettering for them in lieu:

"His Royal Highness the Field-Marshal Commanding-in-Chief is pleased to direct that, in place of being designated by numbers, the companies of Infantry shall be distinguished in each regiment by letters from 'A' to 'M' (excluding 'J') for all purposes of interior economy.

"On parade they will be numbered from right to left, the Company actually on the right being number one."

1865.

2ND BATTALION.

The battalion remained at Gibraltar the whole of this year. As already stated, the word "LUCKNOW" had been granted to the regiment for its services in the Indian Mutiny, and on the 5th of September the embroidered scrolls which had arrived at headquarters, Gibraltar, were affixed to the colours.

1866.

1st Battalion.

The battalion remained at Jubbulpore.

On the 1st of April the establishment was reduced by 60 privates.

The regiment suffered from a severe type of fever during the rainy and cold weather months—the disease affected both officers and men.

1866.

2nd Battalion.

Orders having been received on the 19th of April for the battalion to proceed to Canada, it embarked, under the command of Colonel Bell, V.C., on board H.M.S. *Orontes* and sailed on the 23rd of June. The strength on embarkation was as follows: 29 officers, 44 sergeants, 21 drummers, 40 corporals, 668 privates. On the voyage the ship touched at Fayal, where the band was landed and played in the public gardens. The battalion arrived at Quebec on the 11th of July, when, finding orders waiting for it to proceed to Montreal, it disembarked, and, re-embarking the same day on the Canadian steamer *Quebec*, sailed for Montreal, arriving there on the 13th of July.

A curious incident occurred when the ammunition for the newly issued Snider rifle arrived. Instructions were sent to the storekeepers to place it in the ordinary magazines, it being stated that there was no danger in so doing, as the new cartridges could not possibly explode except in the rifle. Whilst the first supply was being placed in the Great Magazine, on the island of St. Helen's opposite Montreal, one of the cartridges was accidentally dropped, when it immediately exploded.

1867.

1st Battalion.

On the 26th of November the Nagode detachment rejoined headquarters at Jubbulpore preparatory to the march of the battalion to Nagpore in the Bombay Presidency. Strength was as follows: 2 field officers, 5 captains, 14 subalterns, 2 staff, 41 sergeants, 20 drummers, 32 corporals, and 548 privates. The march commenced on the 30th November under command of Colonel Pratt, C.B., and the battalion went into camp on the 20th December at Nagpore, and remained there until the 31st, on which day headquarters and the right wing proceeded by rail to Poona.

1867.

2ND BATTALION.

On the 1st of April the establishment was reduced from 800 rank and file to 620. It now consisted of 38 officers, 70 non-commissioned officers, and 540 privates, with a depôt of 6 officers, 14 sergeants, and 80 privates.

On the 10th of June the battalion proceeded from Montreal to Point Levis, where it remained under canvas until the 15th of October, being employed under the Royal Engineer Department on the Government works there.

On the 22nd of August orders were received to prepare for embarkation to England: the battalion embarked on the 16th of October, under the command of Major the Hon. S. Mostyn, on board H.M.S. *Himalaya*, with a strength of 25 officers, 49 sergeants, 21 drummers, 38 corporals, and 569 privates, and arrived at Portsmouth on the 29th of October.

On arrival in England orders were received for the distribution of the battalion as follows: headquarters and 4 companies, Newport; 4 companies, Brecon; 2 companies, Cardiff; they arrived at their destination on the evening of the 30th of October.

On the same day the establishment was again reduced, the whole battalion to consist of 38 officers, 70 sergeants, and 600 privates.

1868.

1ST BATTALION.

On the 1st of January the left wing of the battalion, under the command of Brevet-Lieutenant-Colonel Elgee, proceeded by rail from Nagpore to Poona. At Bhowsawal Junction the left wing sent a detachment of two companies under Captain John Tilly to the fortress of Asirgurh.

The headquarters arrived at Poona on the 2nd, and was joined by the left wing on the 3rd. It remained at Poona until the 9th of March, when it proceeded to Colaba Barracks, Bombay, relieving the 108th Regiment. The march to Poona quite restored the health of the battalion.

The depôt supplied a draft of 80 non-commissioned officers and men under Captain T. S. Holroyd, which joined the battalion on the 21st of April.

1868.

2nd Battalion.

During the whole of this year the regiment was quartered at Newport, Brecon, and Cardiff.

1869.

1st Battalion.

On the 1st of April the battalion was reduced by 10 corporals and 300 privates.

In June the battalion, its tour of Indian service having been completed, was called upon for volunteers who were desirous of prolonging their service in India for regiments remaining there, whereupon 1 sergeant, 3 corporals, 5 drummers, and 102 privates decided to remain in that country, and were struck off the strength.

On the 8th of October the battalion, after a service of twelve years and twenty-one days in India, embarked at Bombay on board the *Malabar* under the command of Brevet-Colonel R. Pratt, C.B. At Suez the battalion landed, and was railed to Alexandria, where it embarked on board H.M.S. *Crocodile*. It landed at Portsmouth on the 9th of November, and occupied temporary quarters pending the arrival of H.M.S. *Orontes*.

On the 16th of November it embarked on board the *Orontes* for conveyance to Plymouth, and on arrival there proceeded to occupy quarters in the Raglan Barracks, Devonport.

On the 19th of November the depôt, consisting of 7 officers and 107 non-commissioned officers and men, was amalgamated with the service companies.

1869.

2nd Battalion.

On the 27th of April the battalion was reduced by 40 privates, leaving the establishment 520 privates, the other ranks remaining the same.

The battalion was moved from Newport and Brecon by special trains on the 14th of May to Aldershot. On arrival it was encamped on Rushmore Bottom until the 18th of June, when it moved in to C and D Lines

Barracks, South Camp : they were attached to the 1st Brigade under Major-General Daniel Lysons, C.B., an old commanding officer of the Royal Welch Fusiliers.

Before the battalion left Newport, the officers were entertained at a banquet given by the county of Monmouth and the town of Newport, the High Sheriff of the county, John Lawrence, Esquire, of Crick, presiding, the Mayor of Newport, James Murphy, Esquire, occupying the vice-chair. After dinner the High Sheriff presented the officers with a handsome silver kettle, which bore the following inscription :

" Presented to Colonel Bell, V.C., and the officers 2nd Battalion Twenty-third Regiment Royal Welch Fusiliers, at a farewell banquet given to them by their Monmouthshire friends, the High Sheriff, John Lawrence, Esquire, in the chair, the Mayor, James Murphy, Esquire, in the vice-chair."

Soon after the arrival of the battalion at Aldershot a handsome silver inkstand was sent by the inhabitants of Brecon, where one wing of the battalion had been stationed. The inkstand bore the following inscription :

" Presented to the Officers of the 2nd Battalion Twenty-third Royal Welch Fusiliers by the many and sincere friends made by a detachment of the regiment quartered in Brecon."

On the 1st of September Lieutenant-Colonel the Honourable S. Mostyn was promoted to the command of the 2nd battalion, vice Colonel Bell, V.C., C.B., placed on half-pay.

On Colonel Bell's relinquishing the command of the 2nd battalion, the following appeared in regimental orders :

" I cannot leave the Royal Welch Fusiliers without expressing how grateful I feel to the officers, non-commissioned officers, and men for the ready obedience they have accorded to me. It is nearly twenty-eight years since I joined the regiment, and I have served uninterruptedly in it ever since. I cannot sever my connexion with the Royal Welch Fusiliers without expressing how proud I feel in having participated in some of its glories, and how glad I shall always be to hear of its continued prosperity."

1870.

1st Battalion.

By Army Circular dated 24th August the establishment of the rank and file was increased to 40 corporals and 660 privates as from the 15th of that month. On the 3rd of September Major G. P. Prevost of the 2nd battalion was promoted to the Lieutenant-Colonelcy of the battalion rendered vacant by the placing of Brevet-Colonel Pratt, C.B., on half-pay.

On 28th of October the battalion marched from Devonport, the headquarters and 5 companies to Newport under Lieutenant-Colonel Prevost, and 5 companies to Brecon under Brevet-Lieutenant-Colonel Elgee.

1870.

2ND BATTALION.

On the 11th of February a wing of the battalion, under Major Millett, proceeded to Gravesend, where it was employed in erecting and repairing rifle butts. The work was so remarkably well done, and in such a short space of time, that the battalion was complimented by Major-General Freeman Murray on a full parade at Chatham on the 29th of March.

On the 24th of March the headquarters of the battalion, under the command of Lieutenant-Colonel the Honourable S. Mostyn, left Aldershot for Chatham, and was quartered in St. Mary's Casemate Barracks, the wing from Gravesend rejoining it on the 26th.

By a General Order the depôt battalion at Walmer was broken up, and the depôt of the battalion arrived at Chatham on the 26th of March, accompanied by the depôt of the 2nd battalion of the 21st Royal North British Fusiliers, which was attached to the battalion.

On the 19th of May the strength of the battalion was reduced from 520 privates to 460, the other ranks remaining the same.

War having been declared between France and Prussia, and England having guaranteed the neutrality of Belgium, and undertaken to use force in the event of the neutrality being broken by either of the belligerents, the British Army was increased by 20,000 men, when the battalion was increased from 460 to 760 privates.

1871.

1ST BATTALION.

From the 1st of February the establishment of rank and file of the battalion was reduced to 40 corporals and 560 privates.

On the 14th of March two companies (A and F) of the battalion from Newport, and one company (H) from Brecon, proceeded on detachment to Fort Hubberstone, Milford Haven, under command of Brevet-

Lieutenant-Colonel Elgee: Brevet-Lieutenant-Colonel Torrens, C.B., assuming command of the Brecon detachment.

On the 16th of April the Queen's goat died at Newport of a severe cold, having served seven years in the battalion.

On the 28th of September the battalion moved from Newport and Brecon to Pembroke Dock, two companies (F and H) remaining on detachment at Fort Hubberstone, and one company (G) being sent to Penally.

The rank of "second-lieutenant" was substituted for that of "ensign" by the Royal Warrant dated the 30th of October.

On the 15th of December the detachment at Fort Hubberstone rejoined headquarters.

1871.

2ND BATTALION.

On the 1st of February the establishment was increased by 50 privates, making a total of 810 privates.

On the 1st of April two companies of the battalion, under Captain Willes, proceeded to the Isle of Grain, where they were employed by the Royal Engineers at work on the fort of Grain. On the return of these two companies on the 31st of May, a letter was received from Lieutenant-Colonel Kerr, commanding Royal Engineers at Sheerness, who in expressing his entire satisfaction at the manner in which the detachment performed its duties, stated: "The superintending officer of the Royal Engineers has reported to me frequently, verbally and by letter, that during the whole period the non-commissioned officers and men have worked remarkably well and with excessive goodwill, having executed all work given them to his entire satisfaction. The quantity of work they have done, together with the expert handling of their tools, has proved this regiment to be, in my estimation, a very superior one for labour in the field."

On the 2nd of August the battalion, with the depôt of the 21st Royal North British Fusiliers attached, was moved from Chatham to Woolwich.

On the 31st of August a wing of the battalion, under command of Major Hackett, V.C., proceeded to Windsor to perform the duties at that place whilst the Grenadier Guards were taking part in the autumn manœuvres. The smart appearance, soldierlike bearing, and general good conduct of this wing earned for it the esteem and approbation of all. The detachment rejoined headquarters on the 26th of September.

On the 16th of October the battalion was inspected by His Royal

Highness the Field-Marshal Commanding-in-Chief, when he expressed in the highest possible terms his extreme satisfaction, not only with the general appearance of the regiment under arms, but also with the smartness and steadiness with which the various manœuvres were executed, more especially the " bayonet exercises," which were remarked by His Royal Highness to be " perfection."

1872.

1st Battalion.

On the 7th of March Queen Victoria presented a goat to replace the one which had died at Newport on the 16th of April last.

From the 1st of April the establishment of the battalion was fixed as follows : 33 officers, 48 sergeants, 18 drummers, 40 corporals, and 480 privates : total, 619 all ranks.

1872.

2nd Battalion.

On the 1st of May the establishment of the battalion stood at 32 officers, 66 sergeants and drummers, 40 corporals, and 480 privates : total, 618 all ranks.

On the 3rd of August the depôt of the 21st Royal North British Fusiliers left the battalion, proceeding by steamer from Woolwich to join its own regiment in Scotland.

On the 12th of August the battalion proceeded by rail from Woolwich to Blandford, to take part in the autumn manœuvres on Salisbury Plain. The manœuvres were completed on the 12th of September, and on the following day the battalion marched from the camp at Amesbury to Salisbury, and proceeded from there by rail to Portsmouth, where it embarked on H.M.S. *Tamar* and sailed for Ireland. The battalion arrived at Kingstown on the 16th of September, and disembarked the next day, when headquarters and three companies were sent to Mullingar, and detachments were dispatched to the following places : one company to Oldcastle, one company to Kells, one company to Navan, one company to Trim, one company to Sligo, two companies to Boyle, three companies remaining at headquarters.

On the 14th of October a farewell dinner was given to Surgeon-Major Tydd on his leaving the battalion, when a silver centre-piece and an address were presented to him, as a testimony of the love and esteem entertained for him by the regiment.

1873.

1st Battalion.

On the 26th of July the battalion embarked at Pembroke Dock on board H.M.S. *Euphrates* and proceeded to Plymouth, arriving at that place on the following day, when headquarters and eight companies, under the command of Lieutenant-Colonel G. P. Prevost, disembarked and marched to the camp on Dartmoor, to take part in the autumn manœuvres. Two companies, C and H, under Brevet-Major J. Tilly, with the women and children and heavy baggage, proceeded in H.M.S. *Euphrates* to Portsmouth, en route for Aldershot.

At the conclusion of the Dartmoor manœuvres on the 21st of August the battalion proceeded to Aldershot, and was attached to the 3rd Brigade in the North Camp, under Brigadier-General Herbert, C.B., who had himself served many years in the Royal Welch Fusiliers. On the 29th the battalion was moved into the South Camp, and was attached to the 1st Brigade, under Major-General Parke, C.B.

As mentioned in the record of the 2nd battalion for this year, two transfers of men were made to the 2nd battalion in November for service in Ashanti.

1873.

2nd Battalion.

On the 1st of April Brevet-Colonel W. D. Bell, V.C., C.B., was appointed Lieutenant-Colonel commanding the newly constituted 23rd Infantry Brigade depôt.

On the 11th of June headquarters and D and F companies moved from Mullingar to the Curragh, the other companies having preceded the headquarters there.

Early in September the battalion was placed under orders to proceed on active service to the West Coast of Africa to take part in the Ashanti Expedition, which was brought about under the following circumstances.

By a treaty dated the 17th of February 1872, the Dutch ceded to Great Britain, among other forts and possessions on the Gold Coast, one in particular at Elmina over which Koffee Kalkalli, the King of Ashanti, claimed suzerainty, for which he stated he received a yearly head rent. The British Government repudiated this claim when it was put forward by this African potentate. Prolonged negotiations then ensued, resulting eventually in the Ashantis invading British territory, and attacking the Fantis, a tribe then living under the protection of Great Britain.

The available forces in the colony proving powerless to do more than protect the forts and the ground surrounding them, the Government decided to dispatch a punitive force from home of three regiments, viz. the 2nd battalion of the Royal Welch Fusiliers, the 42nd Highlanders, and the 2nd battalion of the Rifle Brigade, which, together with local levies, were under the command of Colonel (local Major-General) Sir Garnet Wolseley, G.C.M.G., C.B.

On the 7th of November fifty men were transferred from the 1st battalion, and on the 20th of November a further draft of thirty men, under Lieutenants H. R. Boyle and R. B. Mainwaring, having been received from the 1st battalion, the battalion left its lines at 11.30 o'clock at night, marched to the Curragh Camp Station, and proceeded by rail to Cork.

The popularity of the regiment was so great that the whole of the troops in camp—the 12th, 27th, and 57th Regiments, the Royal Engineers, and Royal Artillery—turned out, and every man bearing a lighted torch in his hand, formed a continuous avenue from the camp to the station, through which the battalion (which was clothed in the new grey service uniform), headed by the massed bands of all the regiments, marched to the troop train awaiting it at the camp siding.

At Cork the officers were hospitably entertained by the officers of the 8th and 35th Regiments, previous to embarking in steam tugs for conveyance to H.M.S. *Tamar* at Queenstown.

On the 21st of November the battalion, under Lieutenant-Colonel the Honourable S. Mostyn, embarked at Queenstown on board H.M.S. *Tamar* and sailed for Cape Coast Castle, West Coast of Africa.

The strength of the battalion was 8 companies, consisting of 31 officers and 650 non-commissioned officers and men. The following is the list of officers who embarked with the battalion: Lieutenant-Colonel the Honourable S. Mostyn, in command; Major Millett, Major Hackett, V.C.; Captains Hutchison; (Brevet-Major) O'Connor, V.C.; R. F. Williamson, E. Morgan, F. Hutton, G. B. Luxford, H. Roe; (Brevet-Major) J. De Vic Tupper; Lieutenants Graves, Hutton, Shepherd, Gilbert, Cowan, Honourable D. de Moleyns, Johnston, Palk, Boyle, Bernard, Mainwaring, Griffiths, Clough; Lieutenant and Adjutant W. Phibbs, Quartermaster P. McCormick; Paymaster Major Leet; Surgeon-Major Alder; Surgeon Bolton. The following officers were attached for duty: Lieutenant

Barton, 1st battalion 7th Fusiliers; Lieutenant Auchinleck, 2nd battalion 21st Fusiliers; and Lieutenant Liptrott, 104th Fusiliers.

H.M.S. *Tamar* arrived at Cape Coast Castle on the 29th of December, but, finding that the arrangements for landing were not completed, sailed out again on a short cruise, returning on the 5th of January 1874, when orders were received for the battalion to disembark on the following day.

1874.

1st Battalion.

Notification from the Horse Guards was received on the 7th of January that recruits were to be raised in the 33rd, 34th, 41st, 42nd, 43rd, 45th, 47th, 48th, and 50th Sub-Districts, and the London District, for the 23rd Brigade Depôt, and sent to the battalion.

On the 12th of March the battalion took part in the ceremony of lining the streets on the occasion of the public entry into London of their Royal Highnesses the Duke and Duchess of Edinburgh, returning to Aldershot the same day.

On the 1st of May the establishment was fixed as follows: 26 officers, 42 sergeants, 16 drummers, 40 corporals, and 480 men: total all ranks, 604.

1874.

2nd Battalion.

Ever since the first arrival of troops at Cape Coast Castle the transport department had experienced great difficulty in collecting carriers for the baggage, and it was only by dint of threats and bribes that it had at length succeeded in obtaining a sufficient number from the friendly tribe of Fantis for the use of the regiment. The annoyance, therefore, was very great when, on the morning of the 6th of January, as the battalion was preparing to disembark, it was discovered that more than half of the carriers had run away during the night. Sufficient, however, remained for the right half-battalion, which disembarked and marched to Accrofol; here, however, it was checked, as the coolies in front, having run away all along the line, those carrying the baggage of the regiment had to be sent on to replace them, and the half-battalion was obliged to return to Cape Coast Castle, where it re-embarked on the 12th of January in good health.

When it was found that the regiment could not proceed up-country on account of the Fanti carriers having run away, the disappointment was immense, and the whole of the regiment—officers and men—volunteered their services to act as carriers for the force. It was found, however, impracticable to accept the offer, which nevertheless reflected great credit on the regiment.

On the 15th of January headquarters and 100 men, under the command of Lieutenant-Colonel the Honourable S. Mostyn, with Captain H. F. Hutton, Lieutenants Graves, G. H. Hutton, Shepherd, and Gilbert, and Lieutenant and Adjutant W. Phibbs, disembarked and proceeded to the front, together with a wing of the 42nd Regiment.

On the 17th the goat presented by Her Majesty Queen Victoria to the battalion died at Inquabim.

The River Prah was crossed by the 42nd on the 22nd of January, and on the following day by the Royal Welch Fusiliers. Moinsey, the first town in Ashanti proper, was reached on the 25th of January, and on the following day Quisa. That evening the 42nd and the detachment of the battalion were inspected by Major-General Sir Garnet Wolseley. Captain Henry Brackenbury, Assistant Military Secretary to the former, records that "the appearance of the 42nd was most admirable; and the 23rd, though not looking so strong, were reported to be in good health."

On the 28th of January the headquarters and detachment of the battalion marched to Kiang Boassu, and were attached to the advanced guard under Colonel M'Leod, commanding the 42nd Highlanders.

On the following day the headquarters and the detachment of the battalion, numbering 1 field officer and 79 non-commissioned officers and men, formed part of a force that advanced against the village of Borborassie, which scouts reported to be occupied by Ashantis estimated at from 300 to 1,000 men. At 11 a.m. the force arrived before the village, taking it quite by surprise. The Ashantis were quickly driven out of it and bolted on every side for the bush.

On the return of the force to camp " the 23rd Regiment formed the advanced guard, and a brisk fire was kept up between them and the Ashantis, who were blowing their horns and shouting in all directions."

On the 31st of January the headquarters and the detachment of the battalion formed part of the front column under Brigadier-General Sir Archibald Alison, who was directed to advance against the enemy, believed to be concentrated near the village of Egginassie. At 9 a.m. the column was heavily engaged with the enemy, who offered a most determined resistance. At 9.45 a.m. Sir Archibald Alison with the headquarters of the battalion entered the village of Egginassie. The detachment of the battalion—83 of all ranks—was then ordered by Major-General Wolseley to support Alison, who discovered the enemy in great force beyond a swampy stream to the north of Egginassie.

The Ashantis held their ground steadily for some time; but on the detachment of Royal Artillery with two 7-prs., under the command of Major Rait, finding a firm spot—the ground being rather swampy—from which the guns could play upon the enemy, and then firing about fourteen rounds into the dense masses of the enemy, caused such a slaughter of them as shook their firmness and enabled the position to be carried.

Sir Garnet Wolseley in his dispatch of the 1st of February, written at Amoaful, states that "the headquarters and detachment of the 2nd Battalion 23rd Royal Welch Fusiliers under Lieutenant-Colonel Mostyn behaved steadily and coolly under the trying conditions of a fight in dense bush."

The detachment suffered on this occasion the following casualties: wounded, Lieutenant G. H. Hutton (severely), Lieutenant and Adjutant Phibbs (slightly), Private A. Goodwin (severely), Private J. Tourish (dangerously), Private J. North (severely).

On the 1st of February Sir A. Alison was directed to make an attack upon Becquah, about a mile to the west of Amoaful. His force was divided into an advanced guard and main body. The latter, which consisted of the detachment of the battalion and five companies of the 42nd Regiment, was held in reserve. The town was set on fire.

On the following day the whole force, divided into an advanced guard and a main body, advanced from Amoaful. The detachment of the battalion formed part of the main body under Sir A. Alison. Both the advanced guard and the main body reached Aggemamu soon after midday, where a halt was called, the force being then about fifteen miles from Coomassie. Sir Garnet Wolseley there and then determined to make his further advance upon Coomassie as a flying column.

On the 3rd of February the march was resumed, and, although strong opposition was encountered near the River Ordah (where Private J. Maynard of the detachment was slightly wounded) and at the village of Ordahsu, Coomassie was entered next day.

On the 5th of February Sir G. Wolseley issued a special General Order addressed to the Soldiers, Seamen, and Marines of the expeditionary force, from which the following has been extracted: "You have penetrated far through a dense forest, defended at many points with the greatest obstinacy. You have repeatedly defeated a very numerous and most courageous enemy fighting on his own ground in well-selected positions."

At 6 a.m. on the 6th of February the troops commenced to march off on their return to the coast, which was the signal for the King's palace to be blown up and the town to be set on fire: it became a heap of smoking ruins.

The Naval Brigade, the small-arm ammunition column, and the headquarters and detachment of the battalion, marched to Amoaful with orders to continue their march to Cape Coast Castle, picking up and taking on the four companies of the battalion which had disembarked on the 22nd of January under Major Millett, and had proceeded up-country as far as Ahkam Coomassie in charge of stores.

Cape Coast Castle was reached on the 20th of February. The Royal Welch Fusiliers embarked on board the *Tamar*, which sailed for England on the 22nd of February, and arrived at Portsmouth on the 19th of March.

Six officers, Captains Morgan, Williamson, Hutchison, Lieutenants Mainwaring, Johnston, and Surgeon-Major Alder, and a large number of men were invalided from the effects of the climate: one of the former, Lieutenant Johnston, a most promising officer, died on board H.M.S. *Victor Emmanuel*, and was buried at sea on the 28th of February 1874. The following privates died of wounds or disease; Privates Tourish, McCue, Phillips, Brooks, and Baker.

The names of Lieutenant-Colonel the Honourable S. Mostyn, Captain H. F. Hutton, Lieutenant G. H. Hutton, and Lieutenant and Adjutant W. Phibbs were mentioned in dispatches.

Lieutenant-Colonel Mostyn was created a C.B., Captain Hutton received a Brevet-Majority, and Lieutenant Phibbs was promoted Captain in the 54th Regiment, whilst medals for "distinguished conduct in the field" were awarded to the undermentioned non-commissioned officers and man: Colour-Sergeant R. Elphick, Sergeant G. Attiwell, Private T. Commin.

For the services rendered by the battalion during this expedition the regiment was permitted on 16th October 1876 to bear on its colours the word "ASHANTEE," which in June 1914 was altered to "ASHANTEE, 1873-4."

On the 20th of March the battalion disembarked, and met with a most enthusiastic reception from the inhabitants of Portsmouth.

A magnificent banquet was provided for both officers and men, when the Mayor, on behalf of the inhabitants of the town, in most flattering terms presented the battalion with a goat which had been specially obtained from Wales.

Colonel Mostyn, in a short speech, accepted the gift as a mark of the good feeling of the people of Portsmouth, but intimated that it could not be called the "regimental goat," as that was always the gift of Her Most Gracious Majesty the Queen. This goat lived with the battalion for many years, and was always on most amicable terms with his royal brother.

After the banquet the battalion proceeded by train to Shorncliffe, there to be stationed. On entering the train at Portsmouth it was found that the hospitable inhabitants had placed in each carriage a quarter of a pound of tobacco, a pipe, and a box of matches for every man. On the 21st of March His Royal Highness the Field-Marshal Commanding-in-Chief inspected the regiment at Shorncliffe, when he made the following speech :

"Colonel Mostyn, Officers, and Men of the Royal Welch Fusiliers,—As Commander-in-Chief of the Army I hasten to thank you on behalf of the Queen and country for your gallant services, for the perseverance you have displayed in a victorious march through pathless jungles and deadly swamps, and for the courage exhibited at every step by those of your regiment. I am sorry, Colonel Mostyn, that the whole of your regiment was not able to participate in the final operations, but you and your men and your officers will know as soldiers that the exigencies of the service sometimes render it impossible to gratify all that brave hearts and arms desire : it is enough to know that those of the regiment who did go up country kept up the glorious old reputation of the Royal Welch. I am proud to say that I remember the gallantry and devotion to the Queen of the officers and men of the regiment at the battle of Alma. Since then I have often, as Commander-in-Chief, had reason to admire you, and to believe that your old valour and readiness to maintain the honour of the country remain with you. The best proof of my confidence in you is shown by my selection of the regiment for the war now happily ended. I knew the traditions of the past would be kept. I know you too well, and too well do I know the gentleman-like spirit which prevails in all ranks of your regiment, to suppose that any want of cordiality can exist between the Royal Welch and the troops more generally fortunate at the front. I again congratulate you on your return to England, and while doing so cannot but express my astonishment at the good appearance of the regiment. I have been given to understand that the battalion landed as invalided, but I may safely say, that though I have watched over the Army for many years, I never saw a regiment look more soldier-like."

On the 30th of March the whole of the troops engaged in the Ashanti war were reviewed by Queen Victoria in the Great Park, Windsor.

A memorial tablet with the following inscription was placed in Wrexham Church:

IN MEMORY OF
LIEUTENANT W. A. JOHNSTON
AND
PRIVATES J. BROOKS, J. McCUE, G. McPHERSON,
W. PHILLIPS, J. TOURISH, AND G. BAKER
ALSO OF
SURGEON E. T. McCARTHY
FORMERLY OF THE REGIMENT
WHO DIED SERVING THEIR COUNTRY DURING THE ASHANTEE CAMPAIGN
1873–1874.
ERECTED BY THEIR COMRADES OF ALL RANKS.

On the 19th of May the battalion proceeded to Aldershot to take part in a review in honour of the Emperor Alexander II, Czar of all the Russias, and returned to Shorncliffe the same day. This was the first occasion on which the two battalions of the regiment had met on duty, and, after the review, the officers, non-commissioned officers, and men of the 2nd battalion were cordially entertained by their comrades of the 1st battalion. At the review, in which 30,000 men took part, the Czar was exceedingly struck with the appearance of the troops. He especially noticed the Royal Artillery and the Highlanders, and greatly admired the bearskins worn by the Fusilier regiments. A curious incident occurred on that day. The Czar, accompanied by His Royal Highness the Duke of Cambridge, Field-Marshal Commanding-in-Chief, and a brilliant staff, inspected the whole of the troops, which were drawn up in the "Long Valley." When the royal party arrived opposite the Royal Welch Fusiliers during the ride down the line previous to the march past, the Czar noticed the tattered colours of the 1st battalion, which were proudly carried by Lieutenants Clough-Taylor and Evans. Turning to His Royal Highness the Duke of Cambridge, His Imperial Majesty asked the reason of the colours being in such a ragged condition. His Royal Highness informed him that they were the colours that had been carried by the Royal Welch Fusiliers during the Crimean War, where they had been much torn. What the feelings of the Czar were on hearing this may be better imagined than described, but with grave solemnity His Imperial Majesty saluted the colours and passed on.

On the 1st of October the troops at Shorncliffe were inspected by

His Royal Highness the Field-Marshal Commanding-in-Chief, and, at the conclusion of the inspection, His Royal Highness ordered the 2nd Battalion Royal Welch Fusiliers, which was under orders to proceed to Gibraltar, to be closed on the two centre companies, and addressed it as follows :

"Colonel Mostyn, Officers, and Men of the Royal Welch Fusiliers,—As this is most probably the last occasion I shall see you before your departure from England on foreign service, I cannot let you leave without expressing my entire approbation of your conduct and discipline whilst serving in England. Whether it is the commanding officer, the adjutant, the non-commissioned officers, or men, I cannot say, but wherever the praise may be due, you are a pattern to regiments, and I am very sorry to lose you, and hope soon to see you home again."

On the 10th of October the battalion proceeded to Portsmouth, and, embarking on H.M.S. *Tamar*, sailed for Gibraltar the next day.

The following was the strength of embarkation: Field officers, 3; captains, 6; subalterns, 12; staff, 3; colour-sergeants, 7; sergeants, 33; drummers, 17; rank and file, 549.

The battalion arrived at Gibraltar on the 17th of October, and disembarked the same day. The right half-battalion was quartered in Europa Flats, the left half-battalion at Windmill Hill.

1875.

1st Battalion.

On the 16th of March General Sir W. J. Codrington, G.C.B., was transferred to the Colonelcy of the Coldstream Guards, and Lieutenant-General C. Crutchley was appointed to the Colonelcy of the Royal Welch Fusiliers, from the 80th Foot. The following letters were received by the commanding officers of each battalion of the regiment:

"110 Eaton Square, S.W.
April 4th, 1875.

"Dear Colonel Prevost,

"You will have seen in the *Gazette* that I am transferred to my old regiment, the Coldstreams. Although there were rumours and suppositions, it was not till late on the 27th of March that I had semi-official knowledge of the intention. I cannot forget my very first and my continued acquaintance with the regiment, and I should have been well contented to have remained in the position in which war service with the light division had placed me, but choice is not given in such matters when authorities settle affairs, and you may believe there was no asking on my part. I will ask you to read the enclosed, and, if you see no objection, to let it appear in your battalion orders, as a communication to you put in by you as commanding officer, because I do not think a titular honorary colonel should put in a regimental order.

" If you see nothing to object to, I will send a similar one to Colonel Mostyn at Gibraltar with a note to the same effect.
" Yours sincerely,
[signed]   W. J. CODRINGTON, *General.*

" I hope I may attend your dinner in May, as a former officer of the Twenty-third."

Letter from General Sir W. Codrington, G.C.B. :

" Her Majesty having been pleased to transfer my name from the Colonelcy of the Twenty-third Royal Welch Fusiliers to that of the Coldstream Guards, in which I formerly served for many years, my immediate connexion thus ceases with the Twenty-third Royal Welch Fusiliers ; but though it ceases in form and fact, it ceases not in recollection of the 1st brigade of the light division of the Crimea, of which the Twenty-third Regiment formed a part under my command. Those were times of earnest preparation, of hard fighting, of success, of sickness, of difficulties ; but on all occasions, whether in the earlier battles or the hard work of the trenches and assaults, the Twenty-third Royal Welch Fusiliers, with a strong regimental feeling, maintained the high character it had always borne. It was gratifying to me when Her Majesty gave me an honourable peace connexion as Colonel of a regiment with which I had seen more serious service. It is with a feeling of regret on my part that the connexion must cease, but my interest can never cease in the wellbeing and credit of the Twenty-third Royal Welch Fusiliers, with which I was so long and intimately connected by service in the field.
" [signed]   W. CODRINGTON, *General.*
" EATON SQUARE, *April* 13*th,* 1875."

The following letter from General Crutchley was received by Colonel Prevost :

" I have this morning received a letter from the Duke of Cambridge, informing me that Her Majesty has been graciously pleased to approve of my appointment to the Colonelcy of the Royal Welch Fusiliers in

GENERAL CHARLES CRUTCHLEY.
From a photograph in Wrexham Barracks.   Photo. by Algernon Smith, Wrexham.

succession to General Sir W. Codrington, G.C.B., transferred to the Coldstream Guards. I can assure you that I am most grateful to His Royal Highness for this mark of consideration, and that it is a great satisfaction to me to be once more associated with the distinguished corps in which I passed the best part of my life, and in the welfare and renown of which I have never ceased to feel the warmest interest.

" [*signed*]   C. CRUTCHLEY, *Lieutenant-General.*

" 2nd April, 1875."

On the 4th of October the battalion left Aldershot with the following strength : 28 officers, 555 non-commissioned officers and men, together with the depôt of the 2nd battalion, 2 officers, 35 non-commissioned officers and men, and embarked at Portsmouth on H.M.S. *Himalaya* for conveyance to Ireland, arriving at Queenstown on the 7th of October.

The headquarters, five companies, and the depôt of the 2nd battalion proceeded to Cork, there to be stationed. Three companies, under Major Shadwell, were stationed at Carlisle Fort, and two companies at Haulbowline Island.

On the 1st of November the three companies from Carlisle Fort, and one company from Haulbowline, were moved to Camden Fort, and one company was sent to Youghal.

On the 30th of November one company was sent to Bantry.

1875.

2ND BATTALION.

General Codrington, G.C.B., the Colonel of the regiment, on being transferred to the Colonelcy of the Coldstream Guards addressed a letter to Colonel the Hon. S. Mostyn at Gibraltar in similar terms to the one dated 13th April addressed to Colonel Prevost, already set forth in the record of the 1st battalion for this year.

1876.

1ST BATTALION.

Notification was received from the Horse Guards on the 22nd of March that all recruits raised in the 19th and 20th Brigade depôts at Lichfield were to be sent to join the battalion.

On the 10th of May, all the detachments having joined headquarters, the battalion proceeded to Dublin, and was quartered in Ship Street, and Linen Hall Barracks.

In commemoration of the services rendered by the 2nd battalion during the Ashanti Expedition of 1873-74, the regiment was permitted on the 16th of October to bear on its colours the word "ASHANTEE." which in June 1914 was altered to "ASHANTEE, 1873-4."

1876.

2ND BATTALION.

On the 15th of April the battalion furnished a guard of honour under command of Captain F. Stringer and Lieutenants Lord E. Somerset and G. Parry at the Convent on the occasion of His Royal Highness the Prince of Wales landing at Gibraltar, on returning from his tour in India.

On the 27th the battalion moved from Wellington Front, and Town Range Barracks, to the Casemate Barracks.

At a brigade parade, held at the North Front, Gibraltar, on the 30th of December, the following Garrison General Order was read to the troops, Sergeant G. Morris, and Privates Cox, Houghton, Doznin, and Kirby, 2nd battalion Royal Welch Fusiliers, being called to the front:

"On the night of the 30th of November the boat of a Spanish gunboat was upset in a squall near Catalan Bay. It was very dark and stormy, and the position of the wreck was indicated only by the cries of the boatmen. A guard of the 2nd battalion Royal Welch Fusiliers on duty at the eastern beach, assisted by three Spanish boatmen, with difficulty launched a boat, and being joined by one of the wrecked crew, rescued four exhausted men who were clinging to the wreck. On reaching the shore it was ascertained that one of the crew was missing: the boat was again put off. Privates Cox, Doznin, and Kirby swam about the wreck in search of the missing man, whose body was subsequently recovered.

"General Lord Napier of Magdala feels much pride in communicating these details to the garrison.

"The soldier-like conduct of Sergeant G. Morris, and the men of his guard, and especially of Privates Cox, Houghton, Doznin, and Kirby, have merited His Excellency's warm approval, which Major-General Somerset is requested to be so good as to convey to the sergeant and his guard at the head of the infantry brigade.

"By command,

M. DILLON, *Colonel A.-A.-General.*"

1877.

1st Battalion.

On the 14th of May A and H companies proceeded to Enniskillen, F and G to Londonderry respectively.

On the 6th of July the remainder of the battalion proceeded from Dublin as follows: B and D companies and band to Enniskillen, C and E to Londonderry, J and K companies were left behind for the purpose of proceeding to Wrexham to form, with two companies of the 2nd battalion, the 23rd Brigade depôt, under the command of Colonel C. Elgee. The strength of the two 1st battalion depôt companies was 4 officers, 30 non-commissioned officers and men.

1877.

2nd Battalion.

On the 19th of October the battalion moved from the Casemate Barracks to Buena Vista Barracks.

On the 22nd of October a draft, under the command of Captain Graves, joined the battalion from England.

At a brigade parade, hold on the Almeda on the 30th of November, Privates Cox, Houghton, Kirby, and Doznin, of the battalion, were presented with medals granted to them by the Royal Humane Society for saving life on the 30th November 1876. Privates Cox, Kirby, and Doznin were presented with the silver medal, and Private Houghton with the bronze medal.

1877.

Depôt.

The "Brigade Depôt" system having been introduced on the 1st of April 1873, very fine barracks were built at Wrexham at a cost of £30,000, and here the depôt of the Royal Welch Fusiliers was formed.

Two companies each of the 1st and 2nd battalions forming the depôt arrived at Wrexham on the 17th of August, when the following address of welcome was presented by the Town Clerk, accompanied by the Mayor, on behalf of the town. The address, which is surmounted by the Wrexham borough arms, and is a beautiful example of illuminative art, was enclosed in a splendid frame, and read as follows:

"To Lieutenant-Colonel Elgee commanding, the Officers, Non-Commissioned Officers, and Men of the Royal Welch Fusiliers,—On behalf of the Mayor and Corporation of the Borough of Wrexham, I beg to offer you a hearty welcome to this old Welch town, which has been selected by the War Office authorities as the future depôt of the regiment.

"We are not unmindful of the glorious services rendered to our country, and the daring deeds of fame performed by our gallant Welch Fusiliers, nor how, under the most trying and difficult circumstances, it has always upheld the prestige and renown of the British Army.

"The names of 'Minden,' 'Egypt,' 'Martinique,' 'Corunna,' 'Albuhera,' 'Badajoz,' 'Salamanca,' 'Vittoria,' 'Pyrenees,' 'Nivelle,' 'Orthes,' 'Toulouse,' 'Peninsula,' 'Waterloo,' 'Alma,' 'Inkerman,' 'Sevastopol,' 'Lucknow,' and 'Ashantee,' recorded on your banners, alone suffice to show the terrible struggles you have been engaged in, and the noble victories you have achieved on behalf of the British Crown and people. We trust that while you are stationed here there may exist between yourselves and the inhabitants of the borough the most kind and cordial good feeling, resulting to both the military and civil authorities and the people in peace, happiness, and concord.

"Signed, on behalf of the Mayor and Corporation,
J. BEIRNE, *Mayor*."

1878.

1st Battalion.

On the conclusion of hostilities between Russia and Turkey, Lord Beaconsfield deemed it advisable on the 19th of April to call out the Army and Militia reserve with a view to safeguarding British interests. In April and May, 252 Army reserve and 274 Militia reserve joined the battalion, its strength on the 1st of June being 24 officers and 1,069 non-commissioned officers and men.

On the report that the Army and Militia reserves were about to return to their homes on demobilisation the inhabitants of Enniskillen, in order to show their thorough appreciation of the orderly behaviour of the reserve men, presented the following address to Colonel Prevost, commanding 1st battalion Royal Welch Fusiliers:

"TOWN COMMISSIONERS' OFFICE, TOWN HALL, ENNISKILLEN,
24th July 1878.

"At a meeting of the Commissioners of the Borough of Enniskillen, held on the 24th of July 1878, it was proposed by Mr. Wm. Teele, seconded by Mr. James Maguire, and unanimously resolved, That, having heard that the Army and Militia reserve force quartered in this town are immediately to be dismissed to their homes, the Government no longer requiring their services, the Town Commissioners of Enniskillen cannot allow the occasion to pass without marking their high appreciation of the orderly, steady, good conduct and soldier-like bearing of the men of the reserve during their stay amongst us: and we feel that much credit is due to Colonel Prevost, the officers, non-commissioned officers, and men of the Twenty-third Royal Welch Fusiliers, who have contributed so largely, both by discipline and example, to such a result: and they would add that these men carry with them the best wishes, not only of the Commissioners themselves, but also of the inhabitants of the town and neighbourhood. It was also resolved that Colonel Prevost be requested to convey the above to the men previous to their departure.

" Signed, on behalf of the Town Commissioners,
JEREMIAH JORDON, *Chairman*.
JOHN CLELAND, *Town Clerk*."

On the 31st of July the reserves were demobilised consequent upon the satisfactory condition of affairs brought about by the Treaty of Berlin.

On the following day the strength of the battalion was as follows: 24 officers and 540 non-commissioned officers and men.

1878.

2ND BATTALION.

On the 28th of November the battalion moved from Buena Vista Barracks to the South Front.

1879.

1ST BATTALION.

On the 1st of April the establishment was fixed at 24 officers and 538 non-commissioned officers and men.

The battalion left Enniskillen on the 6th of May, and proceeded to Kingstown, embarking on board H.M.S. *Assistance*, and arriving at Woolwich on the 9th, being quartered at Cambridge Barracks: the detachment at Londonderry joined the headquarters at Kingstown.

On the 30th of June four companies of the battalion under Major

Shadwell proceeded to the Tower of London for duty to relieve the Guards, and rejoined headquarters on the 26th of July.

On the 6th of October the garrison of Woolwich was inspected by His Royal Highness the Field-Marshal Commanding-in-Chief (the Duke of Cambridge), on which occasion the following memo. was received from the Adjutant-General:

"The steadiness under arms of the 1st Battalion Twenty-third Royal Welch Fusiliers, and their faultless equipment, especially attracted the attention of His Royal Highness."

On the 10th of November Major-General E. W. D. Bell, V.C., died whilst in command of the Belfast District, when Major-General Torrens, C.B., late of the Royal Welch Fusiliers, was appointed to command the Belfast District, vice Major-General Bell, V.C.

1879.

2ND BATTALION.

During the year the battalion remained at Gibraltar, receiving on the 11th of June a draft from the depôt of 1 sergeant and 82 privates under Lieutenant W. F. J. Cowan.

The sad death after a few days' illness at Gibraltar of Brevet-Colonel S. C. Millett, which occurred on 3rd August, was notified to the Garrison by General D. Anderson, Commanding the Infantry Brigade, in the following order:

"GENERAL ORDERS.

"GIBRALTAR, 4th August 1879.

"The Major-General Commanding desires to record his regret at the loss the Service has sustained, and more especially the 2nd Battalion Twenty-third Royal Welch Fusiliers, by the death after a few days' illness of Colonel Sydney Crohan Millett whilst in temporary command of the 2nd Battalion Twenty-third Royal Welch Fusiliers.

"Colonel Millett joined the Twenty-third Regiment while it was on active service in Turkey at the commencement of the War which ended in the Crimea, and was wounded at the second attack on the Redan.

"He subsequently returned with his Regiment and was present with it in the Ashantee Campaign.

"In life the welfare of his Regiment was ever present to Colonel Millett's mind, and among his last thoughts was his express desire that he should be carried to the grave by soldiers of the Regiment under his command."

EATING THE LEEK, ST. DAVID'S DAY DINNER.

From a drawing by Caton Woodville, by kind permission of the " Illustrated London News." Photographed from a colour print by Burwoods, Walham Green.

1880.

1st Battalion.

On the 1st of March, "St. David's Day," on the return of the 2nd battalion from Gibraltar, the officers of the two battalions and the depôt dined together at Woolwich. This was the first time the two battalions had dined together on St. David's Day since the formation of the 2nd battalion, and the muster of "Royal Welchmen" past and present was a very large one, and included many distinguished names, among others General Sir William Codrington, Sir Daniel Lysons, and Colonel Bigge. The latter, a fine specimen of the old school, had been Lysons's Captain, and was in 1880 over 90 years of age, which had not prevented his thorough enjoyment of the reunion with his brother officers. These three very senior officers had driven down from London to Woolwich together. When taking their departure to return to Town, Colonel Bigge, who was smoking a big cigar, looking round at the other two before stepping into the carriage, exclaimed: "What, neither of you two fellows smoking! You boys of the present day aren't worth a d—, you neither drink nor smoke." Both the "boys" were approaching, if they had not reached, their allotted span of 70 years.

It is at the "St. David's Day Dinner" that the ceremony of "eating the leek" takes place. It consists of every subaltern attending his first St. David's Day Dinner, and every guest who has not previously done so eating a leek. This is done between the giving of the toasts, usually after "the Prince of Wales" has been drunk. The subaltern or guest stands on a chair, with the goat, sergeant-drummer, and a drummer behind him. The sergeant-drummer hands up a leek which the subaltern or guest eats, while the drummer beats a roll on his drum. After eating it he is handed a cup of champagne, and then resumes his seat; no officer is considered a full blown "Royal Welchman" until he has eaten his leek.

On the 1st of April the establishment was increased by 320 privates.

On the 21st of June Brevet-Colonel G. P. Prevost was placed upon half-pay, when Brevet-Colonel C. Elgee succeeded to the command of the 1st battalion.

On Brevet-Colonel Prevost's leaving the battalion, the following appeared in regimental orders:

"Colonel Prevost regrets to have to notify to the battalion the approaching severance of his connexion with the regiment after a service in it of over twenty-five years.

"He is, however, thankful to think that owing to the hearty co-operation of all who have served under him during the last ten years he is enabled to hand over the battalion to his successor in a very satisfactory condition. He has now nothing further to do than to wish every happiness and success to those who have made his ten years' period of command a time that, notwithstanding his own shortcomings, he will always look back upon as the happiest part of his life."

On the 29th and 30th of June four companies of the battalion, under command of Major J. Williamson, proceeded to London for duty at the Tower, rejoining headquarters on the 23rd of July.

Major Broughton Mainwaring, in his *Historical Records of the Royal Welch Fusiliers*, states that when these companies were leaving the Tower of London the Lieutenant of the Tower (Lieutenant-General Maitland, C.B.) presented the officers with a handsomely bound copy of the *History of the Tower of London*, and in a letter to Major Williamson remarked, "I have been very much struck with the intelligent and smart way in which your men perform their duty, the sentry duty especially."

On the 29th of July the 1st battalion was suddenly ordered to proceed to India on active service, on account of the Maiwand disaster in Afghanistan, and having received 138 men from the 2nd battalion (which had just returned from Gibraltar), and 38 men from the brigade depôt, Wrexham, it proceeded in two trains to Portsmouth on the 16th of August, and embarked at once on H.M. troopship *Malabar*. The women and children were left behind to follow the battalion at a later date.

Before leaving Woolwich the battalion was inspected by Major-General J. Turner, C.B., who expressed himself as "extremely pleased with the rapidity with which the battalion has been got ready for service." He also said he felt "great sorrow in saying farewell to the battalion, as I have never had under my command so well-behaved, smart, and well-drilled a regiment." This praise was, indeed, well deserved, for Brevet-Colonel Prevost had spared neither time nor pains to make the battalion efficient, and Colonel Elgee succeeded to the command of a battalion complete in every respect.

Previous to the embarkation of the 1st battalion, new colours were presented to it by His Royal Highness the Prince of Wales, who, with Her Royal Highness the Princess of Wales and His Royal Highness the Duke of Edinburgh, went to Portsmouth in the Royal yacht for that purpose. The battalion was formed up in line of the Garrison Recreation Ground in "open order," and their Royal Highnesses closely inspected each rank. The drums were then piled in the centre, and new colours brought forward,

Major Tilly carrying the Queen's Colour and Major J. Williamson the Regimental Colour.

The Chaplain of the garrison, the Rev. C. A. A. Craven, having consecrated them, His Royal Highness the Prince of Wales received the new colours in succession, and handed them to Lieutenants Evans and Carey, who received them kneeling. His Royal Highness then addressed the battalion as follows:

"Colonel, Officers, Non-Commissioned Officers, and Men of the Royal Welch Fusiliers,—I consider it a very great privilege to have been asked to present your regiment with new colours on the eve of its departure for India. It occurs to me in performing this gratifying ceremony that the colours I hand to you are to replace those which were given you about thirty-one years ago by my lamented father, colours which during three campaigns your regiment has carried with honour and success. You will in a few years celebrate the two-hundredth anniversary of your formation.

"During that long period your regiment has served in nearly every quarter of the globe, seeing as much or more real service, perhaps, as any regiment in the Army within the limits of the present century. You have served at Corunna, Salamanca, the Peninsula, Waterloo, Alma, Inkerman, Sevastopol, Lucknow, while coming down to more modern times, Ashantee.

"I know the distinguished character of the regiment, and I feel sure that those now in its ranks will seek to emulate what has been done in the past, and therefore I feel certain that its good name will continue to be maintained as pre-eminent as it is now. On the eve of your departure for India, nobody can wish you more heartily than I do 'God-speed,' and I feel sure that whatever service you may be called upon to perform, it will be carried out in a way to bring fresh credit for the courage and steadfastness for which the name of the Twenty-third Royal Welch Fusiliers has ever been so justly celebrated."

Colonel Elgee in reply said:

"Your Royal Highness,—We sincerely thank you for the distinguished honour you have conferred on the Royal Welch Fusiliers in presenting our colours to-day, the more so that our title and nationality connects us with the Principality of Wales.

"The memory of this occasion will be handed down to future generations of the Royal Welch, and we, who have had the good fortune to take part in the ceremony, will preserve the impression of it for the rest of our lives: and I am sure, wherever these colours are carried, whether before the enemies of our country in the field, or to perform our duties in time of peace, we shall always maintain the high reputation the regiment now bears.

"Before leaving on foreign service we beg to offer our heartiest wishes for the welfare and happiness of Her Most Gracious Majesty, of Her Royal Highness the Princess of Wales, and the other members of your Royal Highness's family."

The battalion then marched past, and re-forming, the line advanced in "review order" to within a few paces of the Royal party.

At His Royal Highness's request each officer was then presented to him in turn.

His Royal Highness the Prince of Wales having expressed a wish that the "old colours" might be retained by him at Marlborough House, they were taken on board the Royal yacht: the Queen's Colour in charge of Lieutenant Sir R. A. W. Colleton, Bart., and the Regimental Colour in charge of Lieutenant R. H. Dunn, escorted as usual by a company with the band and drums. On arrival at the quay along which the *Osborne* was lying, these officers with their immediate escort of colour-sergeants proceeded on board the Royal yacht to the quarter-deck, where the Prince and Princess of Wales, etc., were standing. By direction of His Royal Highness the colours were crossed on the wheel of the yacht and a Guard of Royal Marines was placed over them. The escort then landed and marched to the *Malabar*.

This great honour caused some disappointment to the inhabitants of Wrexham, who had made preparations to receive the old colours and to deposit them in their church. Every effort has been made to trace the whereabouts of these colours, both at Windsor Castle, Buckingham Palace, Sandringham, and Osborne House, but unfortunately without success, despite the efforts of General Sir Dighton Probyn, V.C.

The ceremony of the presentation concluded at 2 o'clock. After luncheon the whole party from the Royal yacht proceeded on board the *Malabar*, on which the battalion had already embarked, where they stayed three-quarters of an hour and made a thorough inspection of the ship. For the previous two hours during which the ship lay alongside the jetty, waiting for the tide, the fore and main shrouds, as well as the bulwarks of the ship, had been crowded with Fusiliers, who cheered every distinguished person as he appeared, and addressed facetious remarks to the crowd. The band of the Royal Marines ashore played "The March of the Men of Harlech" and "Cheer, Boys, Cheer," while the troops responded by singing "Auld Lang Syne."

At 3 p.m. the *Malabar* sailed.

Their Royal Highnesses the Prince and Princess of Wales and their family in the royal yacht *Osborne* on the starboard side, and His Royal Highness the Duke of Edinburgh in his yacht on the port side, accompanied the *Malabar* on her journey for about an hour, and before leaving the following signal was received from the Royal yacht *Osborne*: " His Royal Highness the Prince of Wales and Her Royal Highness the Princess of Wales wish you all God-speed "; whilst from the other side of the *Malabar* His Royal Highness the Duke of Edinburgh, from his yacht, signalled, " Farewell to you all."

The strength of the battalion on embarkation was as follows: Lieutenant-Colonel, 1 ; majors, 2 ; captains, 6 ; subalterns, 12 ; staff, 2 ; paymaster, 1 ; staff-sergeants, 10 ; sergeants, 41 ; corporals, 40 ; drummers, 16 ; privates, 782.

The following are the names of the officers who embarked with the battalion : Colonel C. Elgee ; Majors J. Tilly, J. Williamson ; Captain and Brevet-Major J. H. Tulloch ; Captains L. J. W. Hadden, A. R. Hutchinson, A. Taylor, R. T. Webber, C. G. A. Mayhew ; Lieutenants O. de B. Carey, E. R. Evans, H. E. Baker, A. S. Chapman, F. Morris, Sir R. A. W. Colleton, Bart., J. H. K. Griffith, R. H. Dunn, H. T. Lyle, W. R. H. Beresford, C. Lysons ; Lieutenant and Adjutant R. B. Mainwaring ; Quartermaster P. McCormick ; Paymaster Captain G. Bampfield.

Having lost three men from heat apoplexy in the Red Sea, the battalion landed at Bombay on the 12th of September, and proceeded to Deolali, arriving there on the following day.

On the 27th of September the battalion left Deolali, and proceeded to Jubbulpore, arriving at that station on the 30th of September, where it relieved the 1st Battalion The Royal Scots.

A detachment of three companies, under command of Major J. Williamson, was sent to Saugor.

On the 9th of November Her Majesty's goat, which had been presented to the battalion by Her Majesty Queen Victoria in 1872, died at Jubbulpore, having served in the battalion over eight years.

On the 31st of December the battalion, under command of Colonel Elgee, moved by route march from Jubbulpore to Chakrata, N.W.P., being joined on the march by the detachment from Saugor.

1880.

2ND BATTALION.

On the 14th of February the battalion, under command of Colonel the Hon. Savage Mostyn, C.B., embarked on board the hired transport *Ontario* at Gibraltar for conveyance to England.

Strength as under, viz.: 8 companies, 3 field officers, 6 captains, 13 subalterns, 3 staff, 8 staff-sergeants, 28 sergeants, 16 drummers, 34 corporals, 463 privates.

Leaving Gibraltar on the afternoon of the 14th February, the battalion arrived in Plymouth Harbour on the morning of the 20th, after an unusually rough voyage, and disembarking on the following morning marched into the Citadel Barracks, Plymouth, there to be quartered. Strength as above. A detachment of 5 companies, 1 captain, 4 subalterns, 16 sergeants, 12 corporals, 221 privates, was then sent to Millbay Barracks, the remainder of the battalion being quartered at headquarters.

On the 1st of March, as already recorded in the narrative of the 1st battalion, the officers of the two battalions dined together at Woolwich.

On the 10th of April Colonel the Honourable S. Mostyn's name appeared in the *London Gazette* as retired on half-pay, and appointed to the command of the 23rd Brigade Depôt, Wrexham.

On the 12th of April Colonel Mostyn took leave of the battalion in the following speech, which appeared in regimental orders on that day:

" Colonel Mostyn having relinquished the command of the 2nd battalion, Royal Welch Fusiliers, cannot take leave of the battalion without conveying to the officers, non-commissioned, and men, his feelings of very deep regret on the occasion. He begs to assure them that he will always look back upon the 27 years that he has served in the Royal Welch Fusiliers as the happiest years of his life, and that though he will be henceforth to a certain degree separated from them, their interests will still remain what they have always been to him. He also begs to express to all ranks his cordial thanks for the hearty co-operation, support, and assistance, that has always been afforded him, more especially during the last ten years that he has had the honour of commanding them, and he also assures them that this support, which has always been so cheerfully and readily given both in times of peace and in times of war, has materially lightened the responsibility of the important duties he has had to discharge. In conclusion he trusts that all ranks will do their utmost to uphold that esprit de corps which has gained for the Royal Welch Fusiliers the very great name they have always borne : so that when their services are again required in the field they may be found what they are now, one of, if not the smartest and most efficient regiments in Her Majesty's service. He begs to wish all non-commissioned officers and men of the battalion every good fortune, happiness, and success."

On Monday, 12th inst., Colonel Mostyn dined with the Officers of the regiment : during dinner the following telegram was received from the officers of the 1st battalion Royal Welch Fusiliers quartered at Woolwich : " We hear Colonel Mostyn is dining with you to-night ; we drink his health and wish him God-speed and every happiness and success."

In returning thanks after dinner, Colonel Mostyn alluded to the " happy family that the Royal Welch had always been during the whole of his service in them, trusting that they would always remain so." He sat down amidst much cheering, the band playing " Auld Lang Syne."

On Tuesday, 13th inst., Colonel Mostyn visited the Sergeants' Mess, where his health was drunk. In returning thanks, he stated that he always looked upon the sergeants of the regiment as a class above and superior to those to be found in any other regiment.

At 2 p.m. he walked out of the Citadel Barracks, the men being at the gate to cheer him away, the Band meanwhile playing the regimental marches. At the Millbay Barracks, where he called in to say " Good-bye," the men were drawn up to receive him ; he was drawn to the station in a carriage by the sergeants, being heartily cheered by the men as he passed out of the gates. All the officers present with the regiment were at the station to see him off.

On the 21st of June Brevet-Colonel Luke O'Connor, V.C., assumed command of the battalion.

On the 6th of August a draft consisting of 3 officers, 4 sergeants, and 114 privates proceeded by rail to Woolwich under command of Captain Blyth, to join the 1st battalion, on transfer, to proceed with it on service to India. The following officers were transferred to the 1st battalion : Lieutenant Carey, 2nd Lieutenants Knight and Lyle.

On the 10th August Quartermaster P. McCormick left the battalion to join the 1st battalion at Woolwich on transfer to proceed with it to India.

The following recognition of his services was published in Regimental Orders of the 9th inst., viz. : " Colonel O'Connor in losing the valuable services of Quartermaster McCormick cannot allow this officer to leave the battalion in which he has served so long without expressing to him his sincere regret at the loss which he personally, and the battalion at large, sustains by his departure; he assures him that wherever he may go the good wishes and interest of his brother officers and the non-commissioned officers and men of all ranks will always accompany him."

1881.

1st Battalion.

On the 13th of March the battalion arrived at Chakrata, having completed the distance from Jubbulpore, 706 miles, in 72 days, including halts; two men died on the line of march.

On the 1st of July the organisation of the Army was altered. The following extracts from General Order 41 show the principal changes which took effect from that date:

"*Paragraph II. Organization.*—The Infantry of the Line and Militia will in future be organized in Territorial Regiments, each of four battalions for England, Scotland, and Wales, and of five battalions for Ireland: the 1st and 2nd of these being Line battalions and the remainder Militia. These regiments will bear a territorial designation corresponding to the localities with which they are connected: and the words 'Regimental District' will in future be used in place of 'Sub-District' hitherto employed."

"*Paragraph IX. Uniform.*—The uniform of all the battalions of a Territorial Regiment will be the same. The title of the regiment will be shown on the shoulder strap."

Under the foregoing general order the regiment lost its numerical designation, and ceased to be the "Twenty-third" or Royal Welch Fusiliers, and the following became its precedence, title, composition, and uniform, as a territorial regiment:

Territorial Regiments.		Composition.	Headquarters or Regimental District.	Uniform.		
Precedence.	Title.			Colour.	Facings.	Lace.
23	The Royal Welch Fusiliers	1st Bn. 23rd Foot 2nd Bn. 23rd Foot 3rd Bn. Royal Denbigh and Merioneth Militia 4th Bn. Royal Carnarvon Militia	Wrexham	Scarlet	Blue	Rose pattern

The regiment will henceforward be known as the Royal Welch Fusiliers.

It was through the exertion of Lord Powis that this title, the pride of the regiment since its formation, was preserved to it.

It had been decided that the title of the regiment should be " The North Wales Regiment "; but Lord Powis, a staunch Welshman, being jealous of the old name, brought the matter before the House of Lords, asking the question, " What has this splendid regiment done to forfeit its glorious old name?" and earned for himself the sincere thanks of all past and present " Royal Welchmen," whilst in the future all will without doubt feel that they owe Lord Powis a deep debt of gratitude that the regiment can still be styled the Royal Welch Fusiliers.

In October the following non-commissioned officers were made warrant officers, viz.: Regimental Sergeant-Major, Bandmaster, and Schoolmaster, after twelve years' service, and the old title of " Drum-Major " was abolished, that of " Sergeant-Drummer " being substituted in its place.

On the 22nd of November a draft, under the command of Major R. F. Williamson, joined the battalion from England.

A goat, which Her Imperial Majesty Queen Victoria had been pleased to present to the 1st battalion in place of the one that had died at Jubbulpore in 1880, accompanied the draft.

1881.

2ND BATTALION.

In July the territorial system was adopted for the Army as outlined in the narrative of the 1st battalion for this year.

On the 16th of November the battalion, under the command of Brevet-Colonel Luke O'Connor, V.C., proceeded by rail from Plymouth to Pembroke Dock, strength as follows: 13 officers, 41 sergeants, 418 privates.

On the 23rd of December the regiment suffered a severe loss in the death of Colonel James De Vic Tupper. A tablet bearing the following inscription was erected to his memory in Wrexham Church:

" In affectionate remembrance of Colonel James De Vic Tupper, 2nd Battalion Royal Welch Fusiliers, who died at Pembroke Dock on the 23rd of December 1881, after a service of twenty-seven years in the regiment, including the Crimea, Indian Mutiny, and Ashantee Campaigns.

" Erected by Officers who served in the regiment with him."

1882.

1ST BATTALION.

On the 31st of March His Excellency Sir Donald Stewart, G.C.B., the Commander-in-Chief in India, arrived at Chakrata accompanied by all his Staff. On the 1st of April he made a minute inspection of the battalion, barracks, hospital, etc. The regiment paraded 8 companies of 43 files, 44 sergeants, band, drums, and pioneers : total, 790. On this occasion His Excellency was pleased to remark to the Commanding Officer, Colonel Elgee, as follows : " Yours is a magnificent battalion, one of the finest bodies of men I have ever seen. The barracks, hospital, etc., are perfect. I shall have much pleasure in writing a most favourable report to His Royal Highness the Field-Marshal Commanding-in-Chief."

On the 26th May Lieutenant-General Sir R. O. Bright, K.C.B., commanding the Meerut Division, made his annual inspection of the battalion. The strength of the regiment on parade that day was as follows : 4 field officers, 3 captains, 14 lieutenants, 3 staff, 2 warrant officers, 44 staff sergeants and sergeants, 14 drummers, 63 corporals, 665 privates.

After the inspection the General addressed the battalion in the following terms : "Colonel Elgee and Officers of the Royal Welch Fusiliers, I have much pleasure in congratulating you on the satisfactory condition of the regiment. I find it in appearance, in health, and in drill quite what I expected it to be. I am very sorry that I am shortly to lose you out of my Division, but I feel sure that wherever you go you will find it hard to get a regiment to beat you."

On the 31st of October the battalion commenced its march from Chakrata to Dum Dum in three parties as follows : on 31st October, B and C companies, under Lieutenant-Colonel Tilly ; 1st November, headquarters, A, D, and E companies, band and goat, under Colonel Elgee ; on 2nd November, F, G, and H companies and drums, under Major L. J. W. Hadden.

The battalion halted at Kalsi, 27 miles from Chakrata, at the foot of the Himalayas, to allow of it being got together on the 3rd November, and on the 4th November fairly started on its long march.

On the 8th November the battalion halted at Saharunpur, 80 miles from Chakrata : here intimation was received that the regiment would be entrained at Dinapore, thereby saving 344 miles of marching through Lower Bengal.

From Saharunpur the battalion proceeded on its way, marching and halting at the principal places as follows :

Meerut	14th and 15th November.
Cawnpore	10th and 11th December.
Allahabad	21st and 22nd ,,
Benares	29th and 30th ,,

1882.

2ND BATTALION.

The battalion was quartered at Pembroke Dock during the whole of this year.

1883.

1ST BATTALION.

On the 14th of January the battalion marched into Dinapore, having completed the distance from Chakrata, 781 miles, in 76 days, including 9 halts; the men were in perfect condition and healthy. The battalion halted on the 15th, and on the 16th at 5.30 p.m. headquarters with E, F, G, H companies, band, and goat left by special train, arriving at Howrah Station, Calcutta, at 2 p.m. on the 17th of January under command of Colonel Elgee.

On the 17th A, B, C, D companies and drums, under Lieutenant-Colonel Tilly, left by a second special train at the same hour, reaching Howrah at 2 p.m. on the 18th of January.

From Howrah the two wings proceeded to Dum Dum by route march (8 miles), and on the evening of the 18th of January the whole regiment was once more safely lodged in barracks after a period of over $2\frac{1}{2}$ months under canvas. The whole march was most successful. There was no sickness whatever, the road was on the whole very good, the weather charming, and the transport excellent throughout; everything went off most satisfactorily and not a single hitch occurred. This concluded the second march of over 700 miles done by the regiment since its arrival in India in September 1880.

On the 29th of May the battalion goat died: this goat had arrived in India with a draft on the 22nd November 1881. On the 19th of November a draft of 140 non-commissioned officers and men under Lieutenant C. H. Milford arrived. This draft brought out a new goat graciously presented by H.M. Queen Victoria to replace the one that had died on the 29th of May.

1883.

2ND BATTALION.

On 1st of April the establishment of the battalion was increased by 6 sergeants and 40 privates, making a total of 608.

On the 13th of September two goats were received by the battalion from Windsor. One was forwarded to the 1st battalion in India, the other remained with the 2nd battalion. They were the gift of Her Majesty Queen Victoria.

On the 20th of November the battalion moved from Pembroke Dock on board H.M.S. *Assistance* to Queenstown, and was quartered at Templemore, whence a detachment of 2 officers and 40 rank and file was stationed at Killarney.

The strength of the battalion on embarkation was 15 officers and 406 non-commissioned officers and men.

1884.

1st Battalion.

On the 11th of December the battalion, 551 all ranks, proceeded from Dum Dum to Calcutta, a distance of 8 miles, and encamped on the Maidan in readiness to take part in the ceremonies attendant on the entry of the new Viceroy, the Earl of Dufferin, into Calcutta.

On the 12th December the battalion took part in a field day and parade of the whole of the troops in garrison (6th and 23rd British Infantry; 2nd, 12th, and 17th Native Infantry) under Brigadier-General H. C. Wilkinson, C.B., commanding the Presidency District: His Excellency the Commander-in-Chief in India being present on parade. The regiment on this occasion acquitted itself with the greatest credit, earning unlimited praise for its marching past.

On the 13th December the battalion assisted in the lining of the streets on the occasion of the entry of the Viceroy, the Earl of Dufferin, into Calcutta.

On the 15th the battalion was similarly employed on the departure of the late Viceroy, Lord Ripon, for England.

On the 17th December the battalion returned to quarters at Dum Dum.

On April 11th Mrs. Jennie Jones died at Tal-y-Llyn, Corris, Merioneth, where a monument is erected to her. She was born in Scotland in 1789 and was, with her husband, who belonged to the 23rd Royal Welch Fusiliers, at the Battle of Waterloo, and was on the field for three days.

1884.

2ND BATTALION.

The battalion was stationed at Templemore during the whole of this year.

It was inspected on the 11th of August by Major-General G. S. Young, commanding the Cork District. In his report he gave "unqualified praise of the manner in which the battalion performed the Manual and Bayonet Exercises."

1885.

1ST BATTALION.

On the 4th of April a draft of 144 non-commissioned officers and men, from the 2nd battalion at Templemore, arrived in charge of Captain R. B. Mainwaring and Lieutenant J. D. Vyvyan.

On the 1st of April telegraphic instructions were received for the battalion to "prepare at once for active service." This order was the result of fresh complications arising out of the Russo-Afghan Boundary question. The battalion was ordered to form part of the "First Army Corps" destined to proceed to the Pishin Valley, Baluchistan.

On the 2nd of April the battalion was medically inspected and found to be in a wonderful state of physical fitness. On the 9th April the battalion was inspected in "service uniform" by Brigadier-General H. C. Wilkinson, C.B., commanding the Presidency District. At the close of the inspection the General expressed his satisfaction to the officers in the following terms : " I congratulate you, Colonel Elgee, in handing over this magnificent regiment in such an efficient condition : I congratulate you, Colonel Tilly, on receiving over the responsibility of the command of such a regiment, and I congratulate you all, gentlemen, on being about to proceed on service with such comrades."

The strength of the battalion on parade was 744 all ranks ; this is after deducting 136 men on command at Barrackpore and at Darjeeling, and the daily "duties."

On the 9th of April, after a service of twenty-three years in the regiment, Colonel C. Elgee was retired on half-pay at the expiration of five years' command of the battalion.

The command of the battalion devolved on Lieutenant-Colonel J. Tilly, who joined the regiment on the 6th April.

The following appeared in Regimental Orders on the occasion of Colonel Elgee handing over the command:

"The Colonel commanding, in taking leave of the battalion on the expiration of his period of command, takes the opportunity of thanking the officers, non-commissioned officers, and men for the cordial and uniform support they have always rendered him. The zeal with which all ranks have performed their duties has made his term of command a very happy and pleasant one. He also wishes to thank Sergeant-Major Hector, and Lieutenant and Adjutant Griffith, for the very able and cheerful assistance they have uniformly given him.

"In saying farewell to the battalion Colonel Elgee wishes every one in it a prosperous and happy future, and he will always follow their career with the greatest interest.

"DUM DUM, 9th April, 1885."

On the 19th of October the battalion was directed to proceed by route march from Dum Dum to Lucknow. This order was cancelled shortly afterwards.

On the 23rd of October, in consequence of the strained relations between the King of Burmah and the Indian Government, several regiments (the Royal Welch Fusiliers being one) received orders "to be prepared for embarkation at a moment's notice."

On the 31st of October intimation was received that the 1st Battalion Royal Welch Fusiliers would be in the Bengal Brigade, under the command of Brigadier-General F. B. Norman, C.B., which was to form part of the Burmah Expeditionary Force, under Major-General H. Prendergast, V.C., C.B., and on the 1st of November it was notified that the battalion would embark at Calcutta on the following day.

In accordance with the above order the battalion left Dum Dum on the 2nd to proceed on active service to Burmah. Starting in the morning, headquarters and 7 companies proceeded by route march to Calcutta, and there embarked on board the hired transport *Nerbudda* for passage to Rangoon, being joined on board ship by the detachment from Barrackpore, consisting of D Company under command of Captain Norris.

Strength of battalion on embarkation was 17 officers and 730 non-commissioned officers and men.

The following officers embarked with the battalion:

    Colonel John Tilly.
    Major R. F. Williamson.
    Captain R. B. Mainwaring.
        „ F. Morris.
    Lieutenant and Adjutant R. H. W. Dunn.
    Lieutenant H. T. Lyle.
        „ W. R. H. Beresford.
        „ C. Lysons.
        „ A. W. G. L. Cole.
        „ A. C. King.
        „ J. D. Vyvyan.
        „ A. P. G. Gough.
        „ J. A. H. Walford.
        „ P. R. Mantell.
        „ L. de R. Jervis.
        „ J. H. Gwynne.
    Quartermaster W. Gray.
    Surgeon-Major G. D. N. Leck was attached to the Battalion for duty.

A battalion depôt under command of Major Hadden was left at Dum Dum; strength, major, 1; subaltern, 1; staff-sergeants, 3; sergeants, 7; corporals, 9; privates, 111.

The *Nerbudda* sailed from Calcutta about 9.30 a.m. November 2nd for Rangoon, where she arrived on November 6th. The battalion at once disembarked from the *Nerbudda* and re-embarked in the river steamer *Aloung Pyah*, which had a large flat on each side, being the first European regiment of the Expedition to arrive at Rangoon.

On the 8th of November the battalion left Rangoon in the steamship *Aloung Pyah*, and after a somewhat tedious journey up the River Irrawaddy, arrived on the 14th of November at Thayetmyo, which was the frontier station of British territory in Burmah, and was where the rendezvous had been ordered.

An amusing incident occurred this day, as, about 2 p.m., the "alarm" was suddenly sounded from the headquarter ship, and orders were issued for the troops to turn out instantly and line the bank of the river in expectation of an attack from the enemy, who was reported to be coming down the river. This was promptly done, and the excitement became very great when a Burmese war-vessel was discerned slowly steaming down the river. On its near approach, however, it was seen that the white flag of St. George was waving above the green dragon of King Theebaw, and it turned out that this was one of the King of Burmah's war-steamers which had been sent down to reconnoitre the British advance, and which a party of blue-jackets, under Lieutenant Trench, R.N., in the steam-launch *Kathleen*, had cut out and brought away from under the very guns of the fort at Singboungweh. The gallant sailors were heartily cheered as the prize steamed alongside the headquarter ship.

That the misapprehension was not confined to the British force was apparent from the fact that the moment the alarm, "One of the King's ships coming down the river," was heard, the whole of the natives left their houses and shops and fled into the jungle, and when the regiments returned to their ships it was through an entirely deserted town that they marched. A guard of the Royal Welch Fusiliers, under Lieutenant C. Lysons, was placed on board the captured vessel, which was afterwards known as Prize No. 1.

On the 15th of November the flotilla, consisting of twenty-eight vessels, most of which had a large flat on each side, containing the Expeditionary Force, left Thayetmyo early in the morning, and having crossed the frontier line at 4 p.m., anchored for the night in Burmese waters, when as one of the officers of the regiment remarked, "the green line was rubbed out of the map, leaving the red line to be moved considerably higher up!"

On the 16th of November the battalion with the 9th Battery 1st Brigade Cinque Ports Division Royal Artillery (Mountain Battery), under the immediate command of Brigadier-General F. B. Norman, landed on the left bank of the river, with orders to attack and destroy the fort of Singboungweh, which was situated on some rising ground some little distance inland. The remainder of the force proceeded up the river towards Fort Minhla, and was engaged during the day in attacking and destroying some earthworks and stockades on the right bank.

The battalion formed up on the river bank, and A company under Captain Mainwaring, and B company under Lieutenant King, having been extended as skirmishers, the advance commenced through dense jungle. The advance continued very slowly for about four miles, when a report was received that the enemy had fired on some Bhisties, who were following the skirmishing line. The force pushed on till a small hill overlooking the stockade and village of Singboungweh was reached. Brigadier-General Norman here ordered up two guns, and a couple of shells were fired into the stockade, which was apparently empty. C and G companies, under command of Major Williamson and Lieutenant Beresford, then advanced, and lined the dry bed of a river below the hill. The enemy could now be distinguished running away on the right ; on continuing the advance the village was found to be empty. The stockade was burnt, and after a halt the force marched back to the ship, which was reached about 8 p.m. The battalion, having been delayed by the previous day's expedition, proceeded to follow up the remainder of the flotilla, arriving opposite Minhla Fort after it, and the Kole Kone Redoubt on the opposite bank of the river, had fallen.

On the 18th of November the Expeditionary Force was formed into brigades. The 3rd Brigade, under command of Brigadier-General F. B. Norman, C.B., consisted of 1st Battalion Royal Welch Fusiliers, 2nd Bengal Native Infantry, and 11th Bengal Native Infantry.

On the 19th of November the whole of the force proceeded up the river, and on the 22nd of November anchored off Pagan, after a fort at that place had been shelled and destroyed by H.M.I.M.S. *Irrawaddy*, the pioneer vessel of the flotilla.

On the 23rd of November the Expedition arrived at Myngyan, where a large force of the enemy, said to number over 5,000, with several guns, had entrenched themselves. At about three miles off a large body of the enemy could be seen, which was supposed to be the Commander-in-Chief's body-guard, as there were many elephants and gold umbrellas visible, and the men were clothed in red. At 5 p.m. the flotilla was halted about half a mile from the town, and those vessels which had the Naval Brigade and the artillery on board steamed on, and commenced to shell the entrenchments, the enemy returning the fire with vigour. The bombardment was kept up till 1 a.m., but no attack was made by the infantry.

On the 25th of November the 1st and 3rd Brigades were landed below Myngyan, with orders to attack the town on the north-east side, whilst the 2nd Brigade attacked the front. On landing, however, it was found that the town was deserted, the enemy having retired during the night, leaving their guns and ammunition behind. The force accordingly re-embarked, and proceeded up the river, leaving a strong party to garrison the place.

On the morning of the 26th of November the following orders were issued relative to the contemplated attack the next day on the celebrated fortress of Ava :

" The 3rd Brigade, composed of the Mounted Infantry, the Hazara Mountain Battery, the 1st Battalion Royal Welch Fusiliers, the 1st Madras Pioneers, and half a company of Sappers, under the command of **Brigadier-General F. B. Norman, C.B.**, will land on the left bank of the

Irrawaddy just above the creek, about one mile from the Ava Redoubt, sometimes called 'Tsn Kyun,' and will direct its attack on the south-west angle of the town wall, and will endeavour to bring a fire to bear upon the great bridge leading from the town to the south, if Burman soldiers should be crossing it. The object is to drive the King's army eastward over the Myit Ngay River, and to prevent its retreat to the south. The 3rd Brigade will preserve connexion with the 2nd Brigade on its left, and will protect its own right flank during the operations.

"General Norman will, if possible, advance to the east face of Ava town: if assistance be required, he will send a written request for reinforcements to Brigadier-General Foord, commanding the 1st Brigade in reserve, stating the number of troops wanted, the place at which they are required, and the object to be attained.

"If possible, an officer of the 3rd Brigade should see the operations performed and report accordingly to the officer commanding the 3rd Brigade.

"It is recommended that close formation should, as a rule, be preferred to extended order, but the working of scouts should be specially enforced."

About five o'clock in the afternoon a gilded State barge, with two large white flags flying, manned by fifty-four rowers, in the bows of which two personages of importance were seated, was seen coming down the river from the direction of Ava, from which it was surmised that King Theebaw wished to treat with General Prendergast. Such, indeed, proved to be the case, as the barge contained envoys from Mandalay with a flag of truce, consisting of the "Minister of the Interior" and the "Under-Secretary of State," who were received on board the headquarter ship. The Minister of the Interior presented General Prendergast with a letter from King Theebaw, in which an armistice was asked for in order that "a friendly treaty, by which intercourse between the two nations may be resumed," might be entered into.

General Prendergast's answer, which was most peremptory, was couched in the following terms:

"No armistice can at present be granted, but if King Theebaw agrees to surrender himself, his army, and his capital to the British arms, and if the European residents in Mandalay are all found uninjured in person and property, General Prendergast promises to spare the King's life and respect his family."

It was demanded that the reply to this communication should reach General Prendergast by four o'clock next morning. The envoys, looking very depressed, and promising to send the King's answer in the required time, entered the State barge and returned to Ava.

During the interview General Prendergast, in order to impress the envoys with the strength of the British force, had anchored the headquarter steamer in mid-stream and caused the whole flotilla to pass by and proceed up the river, thus bringing it clearly before the Ministers that the means to enforce his demands were in the hands of the officer commanding the British arms. The flotilla anchored for the night about eighteen miles below Ava.

The following morning, as no answer to the General's ultimatum had been received, the flotilla steamed towards Ava at six o'clock. Shortly after ten Ava and the Segiun forts were reached, and the steamers drew up within range of the forts, and preparations for landing were made. No answer had as yet been received to his peremptory demands, but General Prendergast, humanely allowing the enemy two hours' grace, gave orders that if at the end of that time the reply had not arrived a signal gun was to be fired from the headquarter ship, when the artillery was to open fire, and the infantry to land and carry out the attack.

The excitement was intense, and it was a curious sight to see those armies facing each other waiting for the two hours to pass. On the one side a long line of ships, whose big guns were loaded and run out ready for the command to fire, their sides manned with armed men silent in their excitement and impatience to land and meet their enemy at last; on the other, the bank of the river, scarce a pistol-shot distant, lined with thousands of Burmese soldiers carrying every description of arm, from the native spear and dah to the Italian Martini rifle, lying carelessly about laughing and smoking cigarettes, apparently perfectly indifferent as to what might happen at the end of the two hours.

As the hour of twelve noon approached there was much speculation as to whether it had been remembered to counter-order the firing of the midday gun, for one gun was the signal for the attack.

But the twelve-o'clock gun was not fired, neither was the signal gun for the attack, for almost as the hour of grace elapsed the gilded barge appeared, coming down the river, and once more the Ministers of King Theebaw were received on board the headquarter ship. They were no longer serious or depressed, but wore smiling faces. They presented a telegram to General Prendergast from the Council of State accepting the terms of unconditional surrender, and by their behaviour seemed exceedingly glad that a peaceful solution had been arrived at. And so the British were doomed to disappointment! There was to be no fighting, for the great redoubt of Ava had surrendered without a shot being fired, and several thousands of the enemy were prepared to lay down their arms without striking a single blow for their King and country! The 1st Battalion Royal Welch Fusiliers was at once landed, and proceeded to the redoubt to superintend the disarmament of the Burmese troops.

Five Burmese regiments, one of which was the King's body-guard, clothed in red, and armed with Italian Martini rifles, and which was one of the regiments noticed at Myngyan, filed past and marched out, after laying down their arms and ammunition, whilst it was conjectured that upwards of 2,000 men, who were destined afterwards to give much trouble as " Dacoits," had fled into the country, carrying their arms with them. The guns, arms, and ammunition having been placed on board, the battalion re-embarked, the flotilla remaining anchored off Ava for the night. On the 28th of November the Expedition proceeded up the river. A short distance above Ava the Burmese had sunk a line of ships across the river at a place where it narrows considerably, and which is completely commanded by the guns of a very strong fort, which is called the Thambyadine Redoubt, built in mid-stream; they had, however, left a narrow opening for their own use, through which the flotilla passed in safety, and, advancing close by the left bank, where mud forts with guns in them had been placed every one hundred yards or so, arrived opposite Mandalay at twelve noon.

Immediately on arrival, intimation was received that King Theebaw surrendered unconditionally, and the force was ordered to disembark forthwith, and proceed by different routes to the palace, which was about two miles from the river.

The 3rd Brigade marched by the " D " road, and secured the north and west gates of the palace enclosure. A strong party having been left to guard the palace, the force returned to the ship.

On the 29th of November, it having been decided to deport King Theebaw at once, a brigade composed of the Mounted Corps, 9th Battery 1st Brigade Cinque Ports Division R.A., 1st Battalion Royal Welch Fusiliers, and 23rd Madras Infantry, under the command of Brigadier-General F. B. Norman, C.B., disembarked at 9 a.m., and proceeded to the palace to escort the King to the steamship *Thooreah*, which had been selected for his conveyance down the river to Rangoon. On arrival at the east gate of the palace, B Company Royal Welch Fusiliers, under Lieutenant A. C. King, proceeded into the enclosure to form King Theebaw's personal escort, the remainder of the brigade lining the streets.

The brigade was formed in column of route in the following order:

23rd Madras Infantry, 9th Battery 1st Brigade Cinque Ports Royal Artillery, the carriage containing King Theebaw escorted by B Company Royal Welch Fusiliers, and proceeded through the city by the least frequented roads to the river, where the King was placed on board the steamer *Thooreah*, under the charge of Colonel Le Mesurier, with the headquarter companies of the King's Liverpool Regiment, who had been selected to form the escort down the river.

The march from the palace to the river was a most trying one, as the feelings of the people seemed to have been thoroughly awakened at the sight of their King and Queen being carried away as prisoners. The women shrieked and wept and tore their clothes as the escort with the royal prisoners in its midst passed by, whilst the men looked on sullen and scowling. It had grown quite dark before the river bank was reached, and several shots were fired into the rear-guard, happily without effect. Sir H. Prendergast's relief must have been great indeed when this very difficult business was completed without any rising of the people having taken place, nor could there be many in the brigade that formed the escort that day who would wish ever again to take a part in the dethronement of a king.

On the 10th of December orders were received for the battalion to hold itself in readiness to proceed up the river, taking five days' provisions, and disembark at a spot which would be subsequently pointed out. Accordingly, on the following morning the steamship *Aloung Pyah*, having on board the battalion, a party of blue-jackets with explosives, and two guns of the Hazara Mountain Battery, the whole under the command of Brigadier-General F. B. Norman, C.B., steamed up the river and anchored that same evening opposite Shemnagar, a village on the right bank of the river.

On the 12th of December the force disembarked, and leaving two companies of the Royal Welch Fusiliers, under Captain Morris, in charge of the ship, marched to Shwebo, where it arrived without any serious opposition on the 15th of December. Finding that the surrounding country was tranquil, and as there were no provisions for the European troops obtainable, the force marched, on the 16th of December, for Kyouk Myoung, a village some little way up the river above Shemnagar, and on the 17th of December embarked on board the *Aloung Pyah*, which had been directed to await the arrival of the troops at that place.

On the 19th of December, when about to start on the return journey, three steamers arrived from Mandalay. Major-General Sir H. Prendergast was on board one of these ships, and he had with him a force, consisting of Naval Brigade, Royal Artillery, and Native Infantry, which was destined for Bhamo. The headquarters of the battalion and A, B, F, and H companies, under the command of Colonel J. Tilly, were ordered to join this brigade, and were transhipped to the steamship *Palow*. C and G companies, under Major R. F. Williamson, were directed to return to Shwebo, and remain there till further orders ; D and E companies, under Captain Morris, were to return to Mandalay in the *Aloung Pyah*.

From this date the battalion was split up into numerous detachments in various parts of the country (at one time there were as many as twelve detachments, some of which were commanded by sergeants), nor was it reunited again until, its tour of Burmese service having expired, it returned to India in March 1887.

1885.

2ND BATTALION.

On the 21st of June Brevet-Colonel Luke O'Connor, V.C., was placed on half-pay on completion of five years in command of the battalion, and was succeeded by Lieutenant-Colonel James Williamson.

On Brevet-Colonel O'Connor, V.C., leaving the battalion, the following farewell order was published :

"Colonel L. O'Connor, having completed his five years in command of the 2nd Battalion Royal Welch Fusiliers, feels most keenly leaving the distinguished Regiment which he had the good fortune when quite a young man to join.

"It will, however, always be with pride that he can look back, and know that he had the good luck to have shared in so many of its brilliant Campaigns and Battles, in different parts of the world, for which he was recommended and received many honours and decorations, and also for having attained the proud position of commanding a Battalion of the Royal Welch Fusiliers during the last five years of his service in it.

"Colonel O'Connor need hardly say that he will ever take the greatest interest in the welfare of the Regiment and wishes all in it every good fortune and happiness: he feels sure that the high discipline and esprit de corps which has distinguished the Royal Welch Fusiliers, since the formation of the Regiment, will always be maintained.

"He now begs to thank the Officers, Non-Commissioned Officers, and Men of the Battalion for the ready support he has received from them on all occasions, during his period of command.

" In bidding farewell to all, he would wish to give a few parting words of advice to the Non-Commissioned Officers and Men of the Battalion, which at the moment is chiefly composed of such very young soldiers.

" That they must take interest in the service and particularly in the distinguished Regiment to which they belong, learning their drill and duties as quickly as possible.

" That they must always obey their superiors in everything, thus preventing much crime in the Battalion.

" Lastly, that they must remember that everything is done for their comfort and happiness, being fairly well paid, well clothed, fed, and educated, and that by leading a steady life while in the service, they will not only be a credit to their Regiment, but also well fitted when discharged for civil employment."

On the 28th of July the battalion proceeded from Templemore to Fermoy, with a strength of 17 officers and 351 non-commissioned officers and men.

On the 10th of November the establishment of the battalion was fixed at 25 officers, 2 warrant officers, 39 sergeants, 16 drummers, 40 corporals, and 560 privates: total, 682 all ranks.

On the 15th of December a draft—strength, 2 sergeants, 234 rank and file—proceeded by special train and embarked on H.M.S. *Malabar* at Queenstown to join the 1st battalion. The draft was under the command of Captain H. Archdale, Lieutenants G. F. Barttelot, C. A. Edwards, and R. S. Webber.

It would appear from the annual courts martial return for this year furnishing particulars as to discipline of the Army amongst the infantry battalions at home, that " the best disciplined regiment, judging by the number of courts martial, minor punishments, and desertion, is the 2nd Battalion Royal Welch Fusiliers."

1886.

1st Battalion.

On the 31st of December 1885 the Bhamo Brigade arrived at Bhamo, and occupied the town without resistance. A strong force, of which A and H companies Royal Welch Fusiliers, under the command of Captain R. B. Mainwaring, formed a part, was left to garrison the place; and on the 4th of January 1886 the headquarters, with B and F companies, were dispatched down the river to Modah, where F company, under Lieutenant

C. Lysons, was disembarked. On the following day, however, this company was re-embarked, and the headquarters proceeded down the river to Htigyaing, where it remained until the 6th of February; when, leaving F company, under Lieutenant C. Lysons, to garrison the village and stockade, it returned to Mandalay, arriving there on the 9th of February, and was quartered in the Kyoungs under Mandalay Hill, near the " Incomparable Pagoda."

On the 12th of February the battalion furnished a guard of honour of 100 men at the palace on the arrival of His Excellency the Earl of Dufferin, the Viceroy of India, at Mandalay. His Excellency the Commander-in-Chief, Sir F. S. Roberts, V.C., G.C.B., who accompanied the Viceroy, was pleased to express his great satisfaction at the appearance and smartness of the guard.

On the 5th of February the battalion furnished a guard of honour at the palace on the occasion of the Levée held by the Viceroy; and on the 18th of February it furnished the guard of honour on His Excellency's departure from Mandalay.

On the 3rd of March the headquarters left Mandalay in the steamship *Colonel Fytche*, and proceeded up the river to Bhamo, where it arrived on the 11th of March, taking up its quarters in huts that had been built for its accommodation.

With so many companies detached from the headquarters, each more or less actively employed, the records of the regiment could never be said to be complete unless the fortunes of the detachments that took prominent parts in the subjection of the country were followed up.

As their services constitute the records of the regiment this has accordingly been done, and the records of the more important detachments are shown in detail, from the time of their quitting headquarters till the date of their rejoining.

Mandalay Detachment.

On the arrival of D and E companies at Mandalay from Shemnagar on the 19th of December 1885, Lieutenant A. L. Cole, with fifty men of E company, was detailed as part of a small force, under Major Fenwick, Madras Pioneers, and ordered to proceed down the long-disused telegraph line from Mandalay to Myngyan to clear the country of the enemy, repair the line, and reopen telegraph communication between the two towns.

This force returned to Mandalay on the 21st of January 1886, having, after a month's hard marching through a district which had not hitherto been traversed by British troops, harassed the whole time by a disaffected population, successfully accomplished its task.

After halting a couple of days, Lieutenant Cole's party accompanied a force, under Major Warner, of the Madras Lancers, on an expedition to Kyouksai, at that time held by the Myngyan Prince. After some pretty severe fighting the place was taken, and the force returned to Mandalay. Lieutenant Cole and his party were shortly afterwards dispatched to form part of the garrison of the newly-formed post at Kyouksai.

As this was the only post between Mandalay and Myngyan, the garrison was continually employed in scouring the country and clearing it of the enemy, who were able to collect in large numbers in this unoccupied district.

Casualties, hardships, and continuous marching in the heat of the day had so diminished the numbers of Lieutenant Cole's party, that when it was ordered, at the beginning of May, to join headquarters at Bhamo, barely twenty men of the original detachment marched into Mandalay.

E company, under Lieutenant Cole, rejoined headquarters at Bhamo on the 15th of May. On the detachment leaving Kyouksai, Major Warner complimented Lieutenant Cole and his party on the courage and endurance with which they had performed the arduous duties allotted to them.

The Major-General commanding the Burmah Expeditionary Force was pleased to speak in the highest terms of the work done by this detachment, and Lieutenant A. L. Cole's name was mentioned in dispatches in General Orders.

Bhamo Detachment.

During the months of January and February 1886 the force at Bhamo was actively employed in repairing the stockade, digging entrenchments, and throwing up earthworks, whilst frequent flying columns scoured the surrounding country.

Two large redans were constructed in the north-east and south-east corners of the stockade, which were the cause of some good-humoured rivalry between the Royal Welch Fusiliers, who were employed on the north-east redan, and the Bengal Sappers and Miners, who were making the redan at the south-east corner, as to whose work should be done in the best manner and in the quickest time. Both redans were so remarkably well and quickly built, that the engineers were unable to decide to which corps to award the palm; but as, some months later, a band of marauding Chinese effected an entrance into the stockade over the south-east redan, the Royal Welch Fusiliers claimed to have built the better work.

On the 13th of February a force, consisting of Mounted Infantry, 3 guns of the Hazara Mountain Battery, 2 companies of the Royal Welch Fusiliers, with Lieutenants H. T. Lyle and J. A. H. Walford, one company of the 25th Madras Infantry, and a party of Bengal Sappers and Miners, the whole under the command of Major R. B. Mainwaring, Royal Welch Fusiliers, was dispatched from Bhamo to Mogoung, an important town on the borders of Yunan, to open up communications and to establish law and order in the country.

The expedition proceeded in two divisions, one under Captain Wace, R.A., moving up the river, passing through the "first defile," which, up to this time, had been deemed almost unnavigable; the other, under Major Mainwaring, having crossed the river at Phaten, proceeded overland across the mountains, both parties uniting at Mogoung. The work done by these divisions was of the hardest and most trying kind. The indefatigable energy of all, however, overcame every obstacle, and the force occupied Mogoung without resistance on the 4th of March.

On the 9th of March Major R. B. Mainwaring, with Lieutenant Walford and forty men of the Royal Welch Fusiliers, and a few of the Mounted Infantry, proceeded on a reconnaissance through the entirely unexplored country between Mogoung and the River Irrawaddy.

On the 12th of March, having forced its way through the bush, this party struck the Irrawaddy, crossed it, and occupied the town of Myena, on the left bank of the river. This is the most northern Burmese settlement on the river, and it is a little above this town that "the red line" spoken of when crossing the frontier on the 15th of November 1885 should be found on the map.

On the 13th of March Major Mainwaring's party proceeded to explore the country on the left bank of the river: and, after losing its way several times in the thick jungle, arrived at Talogye on the 15th of March.

At Talogye orders were received directing the recall to Bhamo of the Mogoung force. Dispatching by boat to Bhamo the whole of his party except an escort of five Mounted Infantry and ten of the Royal Welch Fusiliers, Major Mainwaring crossed the river at Hokat, and proceeded across country to Mogoung, reaching that place on March the 19th.

On the following day the whole of the force left at Mogoung quitted that place en route for Bhamo, part proceeding, as before, by river in boats.

The difficulties to contend with on the return were small in comparison with those met with on the upward journey: and the whole force arrived in Bhamo on the 25th of March, having traversed and explored and surveyed several hundreds of miles of hitherto unknown country.

On arrival at Bhamo the detachment rejoined the headquarters, which had arrived there on the 12th of March.

Major Mainwaring was highly complimented by the Brigadier-General on the manner in which he had carried out his political, as well as his military duties, and his name was mentioned in General Norman's dispatches.

The following extract from a letter to the A.A.G. from Brigadier-General Norman regarding the work done by the Mogoung Expedition was published in orders:

"All the troops had to rough it more or less and behaved admirably, but the hardest work fell upon the men of the Royal Welch Fusiliers, and whether they were employed in cutting a road through the thick jungle, pulling boats round rocks, or stripping and jumping into the water to haul a boat up or lower it down a rapid, the manner in which they worked gained commendation from all the officers with the force, and fairly astonished the villagers and boatmen."

On the 5th of April a force under the command of Captain Wace, R.A., consisting of 3 guns Hazara Mountain Battery, 50 rank and file of the Royal Welch Fusiliers, under the command of Captain Lyle with Lieutenant Jervis, and 120 of the Bengal Sappers and Miners, was dispatched from Bhamo to Choung Dauk, a village at the foot of the Kachin Hills, with the object of opening up the roadway for caravans from China.

On the 12th of April the force advanced into the hills, but finding the enemy very strongly posted in the passes, was compelled, after some sharp skirmishing, in which several men were wounded, to retire. Captain Wace, R.A., was wounded early in the day, when the command of the force devolved upon Captain H. T. Lyle, Royal Welch Fusiliers. On the following day this force, with Captain Lyle in command, again advanced into the hills. The enemy, however, were even more strongly posted than on the previous day, and after several hours' severe fighting, in which the casualties—amongst whom was Captain Lyle, who was severely wounded —were very numerous, the force was again compelled to retire, and fell back on Mansi, where a strong fort had been constructed.

Captain Lyle's name was mentioned in dispatches, and he was created a Companion of the newly established "Distinguished Service Order." Lieutenant Jervis's name was mentioned in Brigadier-General Norman's dispatches.

On the departure of Brigadier-General Norman, the command of the brigade devolved upon Colonel J. Tilly, Royal Welch Fusiliers, Major R. B. Mainwaring assuming the command of the regiment.

On the 26th of April, on the arrival of Brigadier-General R. Griffiths, Colonel J. Tilly resumed the command of the Royal Welch Fusiliers.

On the 19th of April Lieutenant C. Lysons died of enteric fever whilst in command of the detachment at Katha.

On the 15th of May E Company, under the command of Lieutenant A. L. Cole, rejoined headquarters.

On the 18th of May a large force, under the command of Lieutenant-Colonel Fitzgerald, 26th Punjab Infantry, of which 3 officers and 130 non-commissioned officers and men of the Royal Welch Fusiliers, under the command of Major L. J. Hadden, formed a part, was dispatched to Mansi to operate against the Tswaba of Pupkhan, in the Kachin Hills. For political reasons, however, this force did not advance beyond Mansi, but returned to Bhamo, leaving a garrison at Mansi.

During the cold weather, and whilst actively employed in marching about the country, throwing up earthworks, strengthening the defences, etc. etc., the health of the men had been excellent; but now that there was nothing much to occupy the troops, a reaction set in, and the mortality became very great. Sickness was rife in all the detachments, both amongst the officers and men, and frequent changes were made, so as to give all the benefit of a voyage up or down the river. At Rangoon H.M.I.M.S. *Tenasserim* was turned into a hospital ship, and made frequent trips to sea, which improved the health of the troops considerably.

The health of the regiment, however, was so completely shattered, that it was not till many months after its arrival at Lucknow that it could be again pronounced fit for service.

On the 3rd of August the headquarters moved into permanent wooden barracks, which had been built outside the stockade.

A welcome addition to the garrison at Bhamo was made on the 6th of November, when a draft of 230 non-commissioned officers and men of the Royal Welch Fusiliers, under the command of Captain H. Archdale, with Lieutenant Barttelot, arrived from the depôt at Lucknow.

On the 9th of November the detachment from Shwebo (strength, 149 non-commissioned officers and men), under the command of Captain F. Morris, with Lieutenants A. C. King, A. P. Gough, and P. R. Mantell, rejoined headquarters after a separation of eleven months, during which time it had greatly distinguished itself, and worthily upheld the name of the regiment.

THE SHWEBO DETACHMENT.

On the 20th of December 1885 C and G companies Royal Welch Fusiliers (strength, 160 non-commissioned officers and men), under the command of Major R. F. Williamson, with Lieutenants Beresford, Gough, and Mantell, embarked on the steamship *Pulu* and proceeded up the River Irrawaddy.

On the 22nd of December the detachment arrived at Kyouk Myoung, where it disembarked and marched to Shwebo. On nearing the town it was found to be occupied by the enemy, who had thrown up some breastworks and barricaded the gates. An attack was at once made, and after a smart skirmish, the Burmese evacuated the place, which was immediately occupied. Five of the enemy were found dead inside the gates.

No casualties occurred in the Royal Welch Fusiliers.

On the 25th of December a force of 2 officers and 102 rank and file, under the command of Major Williamson, marched on the village of Shadaw, which was held by a strong body of the enemy, who, however, fled as soon as fire was opened upon them. The force returned to Shwebo the same day.

On the 27th of December a party of 51 non-commissioned officers and men, under the command of Lieutenant J. H. Gwynne, arrived from Mandalay. On this day a force of two officers and 100 non-commissioned officers and men, under the command of Major Williamson, marched on the village of Zeedaw, which was occupied by the enemy in great numbers. The village was enclosed by strong walls, and the enemy made a most determined stand. After some heavy firing on both sides, the village was rushed and carried at the point of the bayonet, when the enemy fled, leaving fifty dead and many wounded inside the stockade.

The casualties of the Royal Welch Fusiliers were heavy. One lance-corporal, J. G. Coleman, C company, was killed and eleven men wounded, two of whom died of their wounds a short time afterwards.

On the 28th of December a force of 2 officers and 100 non-commissioned officers and men, under the command of Major Williamson, marched to the village of Sibok Taya, where the enemy was assembled in force under Prince Moung Hmat, a Pretender to the Burmese throne. After a few volleys were fired the enemy retired and the village was burnt. Seven of the enemy who were wounded were taken prisoners. The force returned to Shwebo on the 1st of January 1886.

On the 11th of January a force, consisting of 3 officers and 163 non-commissioned officers and men of the Royal Welch Fusiliers, under the command of Major Williamson, and 2 officers and 83 men of the 12th Madras Infantry, the whole under the command of Colonel Simpson, 12th Madras Infantry, marched from Shwebo for the purpose of dispersing a body of the enemy who had assembled at the village of Kadu, under Prince Moung Hmat. On approaching the village the enemy opened a heavy fire, when Lieutenant-Colonel Simpson, 12th Madras Infantry, and Lieutenant Gwynne, Royal Welch Fusiliers, were wounded almost simultaneously. On Lieutenant-Colonel Simpson being wounded, Major Williamson assumed the command of the force, which advanced with a rush and carried the village, the enemy retiring precipitately, leaving upwards of sixty dead and many wounded behind them. The casualties of the force were: Lieutenant-Colonel Simpson, 12th Madras Infantry, dangerously wounded; Lieutenant Gywnne, Royal Welch Fusiliers, severely wounded; Lieutenant Carnegy, 12th Madras Infantry, slightly wounded; and one non-commissioned officer, Corporal Flaherty, and two men of the Royal Welch Fusiliers, wounded: one of the latter died of his wounds a few days later.

On the 18th of January D company (strength, 52 non-commissioned officers and men), under the command of Captain F. Morris, arrived from Mandalay.

On the 26th of January a force, consisting of 1 officer and 2 guns Royal Artillery, 3 officers and 176 non-commissioned officers and men of the Royal Welch Fusiliers, 2 officers and 50 men of the 12th Madras Infantry, 15 sowars of the 2nd Madras Cavalry, the whole under the command of Major Williamson, marched to attack and disperse a body of the enemy, under Prince Moung Hmat and Boh Hla-oo, who had taken up a very strong position at Mee Taw Goung, a small village on the left bank of the River Moo.

The bank of the river was strongly defended, breastworks made of large logs of timber, cartwheels, brushwood, and mud having been constructed, whilst trenches had been dug about thirty yards from the river. The enemy opened a very heavy fire, and, in spite of the shells from the two guns and the volleys from the infantry, made a determined resistance. At last a shell from one of the guns having set fire to a part of the village, Major Williamson and Lieutenant Beresford, with half a company of the Royal Welch Fusiliers and the Madras Cavalry, forded the river under cover of infantry fire, and rushed the village, when the enemy fled, leaving fifty-three dead bodies on the ground. In spite of the very heavy fire of the enemy there were no casualties in the force, which then marched to the village of Si Eni and encamped. The arms had scarcely been piled, and the men taken off their accoutrements, when a sudden attack was made by a body of the enemy who had approached unseen. The attack was, however, repulsed without any loss, several of the enemy were killed, and a brass gun, some standards, and a large number of muskets, spears, and dahs were taken.

On the 28th of January the force returned to Shwebo.

On the 31st of January a force, consisting of 1 officer and 2 guns Royal Artillery, 3 officers and 173 non-commissioned officers and men of the Royal Welch Fusiliers, 2 officers and 60 men of the 12th Madras Infantry, and 15 sowars of the 2nd Madras Cavalry, the whole under the command of Major Williamson, marched to the village of Taloung, and on the next day proceeded to Betagachin, one of the outposts of the enemy: both villages, however, were found deserted.

On the 2nd of February the force advanced to Tabien Myo, where Prince Moung Hmat and Boh Hla-oo, with a following of 2,000 men, had entrenched themselves. The position was a very strong one, the town being surrounded by walls which were covered with thick bushes, whilst a wide moat had been dug the whole way round it.

On arrival, the guns opened fire, and the infantry advanced with a rush. There was little resistance, the enemy retiring the moment they saw the bayonets fixed, leaving behind them all their stores and baggage and many arms.

The town was burnt, and the force returned to Shwebo on the 4th of February.

On the 10th of February a force, under Major Williamson, consisting of 1 officer and 2 guns Royal Artillery, 3 officers and 150 non-commissioned officers and men of the Royal Welch Fusiliers, 2 officers and 80 men of the 12th Madras Infantry, and 15 sowars of the 2nd Madras Cavalry, marched to disperse a mixed body of Burmese and Shans that had assembled at Zezin under Prince The-Tang-Thit, another Pretender to the Burmese throne.

The force arrived at Kinnoo on the 11th of February, but found the enemy had retired on Pinden.

On the following day the force marched to Pinden, which was found deserted, the enemy having evacuated it during the night and retired in the direction of the River Irrawaddy. As no reliable information could be obtained of the enemy's movement, the force returned to Shwebo on the 13th of February.

On the 19th of February a force, consisting of 1 officer and 2 guns

Cinque Ports R.A., 2 officers and 105 non-commissioned officers and men of the Royal Welch Fusiliers, 2 officers and 40 men of the 12th Madras Infantry, and 13 sowars of the 2nd Madras Cavalry, under the command of Captain F. Morris, Royal Welch Fusiliers, was dispatched to scour the country south of Shwebo. This force destroyed several fortified villages and stockades, and, with the exception of a few slight skirmishes, meeting with no resistance, returned to Shwebo on the 26th of February.

On the 29th of March Major Williamson left Shwebo for England on promotion to the second Lieutenant-Colonelcy of the 2nd battalion, when Captain F. Morris assumed the command of the detachment.

On the 1st of May G company (strength, 1 officer and 63 non-commissioned officers and men), under Lieutenant Gough, proceeded to Ye-u, there to form an outpost.

On the 9th of May B company (strength, 1 officer and 61 non-commissioned officers and men), under the command of Lieutenant A. C. King, arrived from Mandalay.

On the 29th of May C company, under Lieutenant Mantell, proceeded on detachment duty to Kyouk Myoung.

On the 12th of June a force, consisting of 20 men Royal Welch Fusiliers, as mounted infantry, 1 officer and 50 men of the 5th Bengal Light Infantry, and 15 sowars of the Madras Cavalry, the whole under Lieutenant A. C. King, Royal Welch Fusiliers, marched to co-operate with a column from Sagaing for the purpose of clearing the country between the two places. A few prisoners were taken, but no fighting took place, and the force returned to Shwebo on the 15th of June.

On the 15th of July the same force marched to attack Yuatha, a walled town which was strongly held by the enemy. As soon as the column appeared the enemy opened a heavy fire, but the distance was too great for the Burmese small arms, and the musket-shots fell short, whilst the gingal-balls passed harmlessly overhead. The town was then rushed at the point of the bayonet, when the enemy fled, leaving 38 killed and 87 prisoners, besides arms and ammunition.

The casualties in Lieutenant King's force were 2 men, 5th Bengal Light Infantry, severely wounded. On the following day the defences of Yuatha were destroyed, and the force marched to and occupied Htantabin, from which the enemy fled on the approach of the column.

On the 28th of July the force returned to Shwebo.

On the 18th of August the same force, with Lieutenant Williams, 5th Bengal Light Infantry, in command, Lieutenant King in charge of the mounted infantry, marched to attack a small town on the banks of the

River Moo, where Boh Hla-oo had entrenched himself with a strong body of the enemy.

As soon as Lieutenant Williams's covering party opened fire the enemy, after firing wildly for a few minutes, fled precipitately. The column returned to Shwebo on the following day.

On the 7th of September a force, consisting of 30 sowars of the Madras Cavalry, 2 guns Cinque Ports R.A., 50 men of the Royal Welch Fusiliers (30 of whom were mounted infantry), under Lieutenant King, 50 men of the 21st Madras Light Infantry, with some Punjab police, the whole under Major W. Aitken, R.A., marched to Htantabin to form a post at that place.

On the 10th of September a portion of this force moved to Tabine, which was held by the enemy. As on former occasions, however, the place was evacuated as soon as the column appeared. The cavalry and mounted infantry pursued the enemy for some distance, killing a large number. One sowar killed was the only casualty in Major Aitken's force.

On the 14th of September, leaving a garrison at Htantabin of 50 men of the Royal Welch Fusiliers, under Lieutenant Mantell, and 50 men of the 21st Madras Infantry, the whole under the command of Captain Waugh, 21st Madras Infantry, the column returned to Shwebo.

On the 30th of October Lieutenant Mantell's detachment rejoined at Shwebo, having been relieved by the King's Own Light Infantry.

On the 31st of October the outpost from Ye-u, under Lieutenant Gough, rejoined at Shwebo.

On the 2nd of November the Shwebo detachment, under command of Captain Morris, left Shwebo for Bhamo, arriving there and rejoining headquarters on the 9th of November.

The services of this detachment were highly commended by the general officer commanding the Burmah Expeditionary Force, and Major Williamson, Lieutenants Beresford, King, Gough, and Gwynne were mentioned in dispatches in general orders.

Lieutenant-Colonel R. F. Williamson afterwards received a Brevet-Colonelcy for his services, both as military commander and political officer, the duties of which latter position he had exercised for some time with much ability.

Katha Detachment.

On the 14th of November B, F, and H companies, under command of Lieutenant-Colonel Creek, were dispatched from Bhamo to Katha (where A company was already quartered) to form part of a force, under the command of Brigadier-General Cox, ordered to operate against the Tswaba of Woontho, who had declined to acknowledge the British rule and who was creating disturbances in the Woontho district.

These companies landed at Katha on the 16th of November.

On the 17th of November B company, under Captain Archdale, was sent on detachment duty to Kyundoung, whence it returned to Bhamo, and rejoined headquarters on the 9th of December.

On the 29th of November F company, under Major Evans, with Lieutenant Edwards, formed part of a column, under Lieutenant-Colonel Home, 5th Bengal Light Infantry, which attacked and captured Mawlu, a town where the enemy had entrenched themselves behind a strong stockade.

Lieutenant Edwards and one sergeant were slightly wounded in the attack, and a private was knocked over by a bullet which struck him in the chest. Beyond a severe bruise, however, he sustained no injury, the bullet having hit a bag of rupees which the man had in his breast coat-pocket.

Lieutenant-Colonel Home highly commended Lieutenant Edwards, and Privates Bibbings and Carless, for their conduct on this occasion.

The following extract from a private letter of an officer of the regiment who was present gives a spirited account of the attack on Mawlu:

" . . . About a mile from Mawlu we emerged into an open, paddy plain, and saw immediately in front of us Mawlu and Nga Kiyis's strong stockade. We then deployed into line, and after the guns had fired a few rounds, advanced steadily across the plain. Mawlu and the stockade were situated on the further bank of a river which we knew was there, but could not see on account of the steepness of the banks. When we got about 150 yards from the river, we were met by a tremendously hot fire, so we doubled to the river, crossed it (it was about fifty yards wide), and got up on the other bank at the foot of the stockade, where the bullets simply rained all around us, but as no one was hit, I suppose they all went over our heads. We found it impossible to get into the stockade, and were ordered to get down into the river, under shelter of the bank, whilst the guns bombarded the place.

" The Burmese bullets whizzing over us one way, and our own shells the other, made a pretty good row, I can tell you : but the shells were too much for the Burmese, for when we again attacked the stockade, and managed to cut our way through one of the gates, we found the enemy flying as fast as they could.

" Edwards, who did very well on the right with a handful of men, had a narrow escape, a bullet striking the butt of his revolver, and glancing down his hand. Private Mathers was knocked over by a bullet, but as it struck a collection of rupees in his left-hand breast-pocket, he suffered no further injury than a severe bruise. Sergeant Evans had a finger grazed by a bullet. All the men behaved splendidly, and did not seem to care for anything.

" The marvel is, with the tremendous fire poured on us from the fort, that no one on our side was killed.

" We found ten of the Burmese dead in the stockade, and a number of wounded."

On the 30th of November two companies of the Royal Welch Fusiliers, under Lieutenant-Colonel Creek, were moved from Katha to Nahakoung, about twenty miles on the road to Woontho.

At Nahakoung Lieutenant-Colonel Creek received orders to march to Thila, about five miles from Manteik, for the purpose of relieving the inhabitants, as it was reported that the town had been besieged by the Tswaba of Woontho for several months.

On the 3rd of December a force consisting of 2 guns Hazara Mountain Battery, 2 companies of the battalion, 1 company 5th Bengal Light Infantry, and a detachment of Bengal Sappers and Miners, the whole under Lieutenant-Colonel Creek, Royal Welch Fusiliers, marched to Manleh, on the road to Woontho. On the next day, having been joined by another company of the 5th Bengal Light Infantry and a company of the 26th Punjab Infantry, the column marched to Manteik, and encamped near a ford across the River Merza, on the opposite bank of which Thila was situated.

The enemy, reported to be upwards of 1,000 strong, had surrounded Thila with a series of stockades, within which they had entrenched themselves.

On the morning of the 5th of December the column crossed the river at daybreak, and, rushing the stockades, completely surprised the enemy, who fled precipitately, leaving their arms and ammunition behind them.

The stockades were destroyed, and, leaving a garrison of 1 Native officer and 25 Sepoys in Thila, and half a company of the Royal Welch Fusiliers, under Lieutenant Barttelot, in support at Manteik, the column returned to Manleh.

The above detachments were withdrawn a few days later.

On the 12th of January 1887 the column advanced from Manleh to Talwyn Pass, where the enemy had erected a series of extremely strong stockades: they were, however, found deserted, and were accordingly destroyed. It having been ascertained that the Tswaba had evacuated

Woontho and was retiring northwards, Brigadier-General Cox directed Lieutenant-Colonel Creek to push on and secure the town. Marching at 1 a.m. on the 15th of January, Lieutenant-Colonel Creek arrived at and occupied Woontho, which was found almost deserted, at 4 p.m. that day.

At eleven o'clock on the following morning the remainder of the force, under Brigadier-General Cox, arrived, when the detachment of Royal Welch Fusiliers was quartered in a fort north of the town.

On the 24th of February the detachment of Royal Welch Fusiliers was selected to escort the Burmese Minister, Kin-Wun Min Gye, to Htigyaing, which place was reached on the 27th of February. The detachment remained at Htigyaing until the 6th of March, when it rejoined the headquarters, which was proceeding down the river in the steamship *Pulu* en route for India. Lieutenant-Colonel E. S. Creek's name was mentioned in Brigadier-General Cox's dispatches.

1886.

1st Battalion.

Depôt in India.

On the 26th of February the depôt (strength, 130 rank and file), under the command of Major Hadden, with Lieutenant Helbert, left Dum Dum for Lucknow, arriving at that station on the 2nd of March, where it was joined by a draft of 236 non-commissioned officers and men, under the command of Captain H. Archdale, with Captain R. Gwynne and Lieutenants Barttelot, Webber, and Edwards, which had arrived at Lucknow from England on the 23rd of January.

All the men of the regiment who were invalided from Burmah to India were borne on the strength of the depôt.

On the 11th of June Major Mainwaring arrived from headquarters in Burmah to take over the command of the depôt from Major Hadden, who was ordered to join the service companies.

On the 31st of September a draft, consisting of 230 non-commissioned officers and men, under the command of Captain Archdale, with Lieutenants Barttelot and Webber, left Lucknow en route for Burmah.

1886.

2nd Battalion.

During the year the battalion remained quartered at Fermoy.
At his inspection of the 2nd battalion, Major-General His Serene

Highness Prince Edward of Saxe-Weimar questioned the right of the regiment to the distinction of its Pioneers wearing white buckskin aprons and gauntlets.

The original authority not being forthcoming, application was made to the War Office, when the following letter was received :

"Horse Guards, War Office,
27th January 1887.

"His Royal Highness the Field-Marshal Commanding-in-Chief has been pleased to approve of white buckskin aprons and gauntlets being continued to be worn by the Pioneers of the Royal Welch Fusiliers, provided no extra expense is incurred against the public.

" [signed]   T. Elliot, A.G."

During the year the regimental goat died at Fermoy.

1887.

1st Battalion.

On the 16th of February the following welcome telegram was received by the headquarters at Bhamo: "Fusiliers will embark at Bhamo about 1st of March, and Katha 3rd of March, for return to India."

On the 2nd of March the headquarters embarked at Bhamo on board the steamship *Pulu*, and being joined by the detachments at the following places—Shwegoogyee, 17 men, under Lieutenant Delmé Radcliffe; Katha, 77 men, under Major Evans; Htigyaing, 72 men, under Lieutenant-Colonel Creek, with Lieutenants King and Edwards—arrived at Mandalay on the 10th of the month.

On the 14th of March the battalion embarked at Mandalay on the steamship *Shoay Myo* and proceeded down the river to Prome, where it arrived on the 23rd of March, and at once continued its journey by rail to Rangoon.

On arrival at Rangoon the trains containing the regiment were met by the Bishop of Rangoon, Dr. Strahan, and Colonel Jackson and officers of the Royal Scots Fusiliers; the latter regiment entertained the Royal Welch Fusiliers with great kindness, in remembrance of the depôt of the Royal Scots Fusiliers having been attached for so long a time to the Royal Welch.

On the 24th of March the battalion embarked on board H.M.S. *Dalhousie* and sailed for India.

On the 28th of March the battalion disembarked at Calcutta, and proceeded on the following day by rail to Lucknow, where it arrived on the 2nd of April, and was quartered in the left infantry lines.

On the arrival of the battalion, 12 officers and 484 rank and file, at Lucknow, having been one year and four months on active service, the depôt was amalgamated with it. Previous to the departure of the battalion from Burmah the following farewell order was published by Brigadier-General Cox:

"The Royal Welch Fusiliers being about to return to India, the Brigadier-General cannot allow them to leave his command without placing on record his appreciation of the way in which officers and all ranks have always cheerfully performed all duties, and the most exemplary behaviour of the non-commissioned officers and men. In bidding them farewell the Brigadier-General wishes them a speedy and pleasant voyage to India."

The following officers were mentioned in dispatches for good service during the campaign :

>Colonel J. Tilly (twice mentioned and C.B.).
>Colonel R. F. Williamson (Brevet of Colonel).
>Lieutenant-Colonel E. S. Creek.
>Captain H. T. Lyle, D.S.O.
>Captain W. R. H. Beresford.
>Lieutenant A. W. G. L. Cole.
>Lieutenant A. C. King.
>Lieutenant A. P. G. Gough (twice mentioned).
>Lieutenant J. H. Gwynne.

The following casualties occurred in the battalion during the campaign :

Officers wounded.

Captain H. T. Lyle, gunshot wound in groin.
Lieutenant J. H. Gwynne, gunshot wound in knee.

Died of disease.

Lieutenant C. Lysons.

Invalided to England from disease.

Major L. J. W. Hadden.
Captain and Adjutant R. H. W. Dunn.
Captain W. R. H. Beresford.
Captain R. B. Firman.
Lieutenant F. de C. Helbert Helbert.

Invalided to England from accidental injuries.
Lieutenant J. D. Vyvyan.
Lieutenant J. A. H. Walford.

Invalided to India from disease.
Lieutenant L. de R. Jervis.
Lieutenant R. S. Webber.
Lieutenant G. F. Barttelot.

NON-COMMISSIONED OFFICERS AND MEN.

Killed.
Lance-Corporal J. G. Coleman.

Died of wounds received.
Private F. Davey.
Private H. Crawley.
Private S. Gould.

Wounded.
Corporal J. Flaherty.
Private D. Roberts.
Private E. Rees.
Private G. Smith.
Private W. Blake.
Private M. D. Terranean.
Private W. Lewis.
Private G. Davies.
Private W. Davies.
Private G. Ranfield.
Private J. Plenderleath.

Non-commissioned officers and men invalided to England, 14.
Non-commissioned officers and men invalided to India, 327.
Non-commissioned officers and men died of disease, 87.

Of the 17 officers and 730 men who left Calcutta on the 2nd of November 1885, only 6 officers and barely 300 rank and file marched into Lucknow on the 7th of April 1887, and yet only 4 men had been killed by the enemy.

When in Mandalay the battalion obtained two magnificent large bells from the Incomparable Pagoda, near which it was quartered: one of these was sent to the brigade depôt at Wrexham, where it now hangs in the barrack-square, next to "Bell's Gun." (See page 75.) The other one stands in front of the 1st battalion quarter-guard, and its wonderfully pure tones can be heard at a great distance as the hours are struck on it by a stalwart sentry.

A third bell, smaller but beautifully engraved, was sent from Katha to the 2nd battalion in Ireland.

On the 21st of November 1890 H.M. Queen Victoria authorised the regiment to add "BURMA 1885-87" to those honours already borne on its colours.

On the 1st of July Colonel J. Tilly was placed on half-pay on completion of six years as a Lieutenant-Colonel, and was succeeded in the command of the battalion by Lieutenant-Colonel E. S. Creek. On Colonel Tilly's leaving the regiment, the following farewell order was published:

"After more than thirty-two years' service in the 1st Battalion Royal Welch Fusiliers, Colonel Tilly takes an affectionate farewell of the regiment. The support that he has universally received from officers and non-commissioned officers will cause his regimental service to be a time that he will always look back upon with pride and happiness.

"From them and from the private soldiers he now takes leave with feelings of the profoundest regret. Colonel Tilly is desirous of recording his obligations to the members of his regimental staff for their zeal and ability under the exceptional, trying circumstances of the recent campaign in Burmah, where the battalion was broken up into so many detachments.

"The adjutant, Captain Dunn; the Acting Adjutant, Lieutenant Cole; Quartermaster Gray, and Sergeant-Major Hammond, never failed in rendering him the most willing assistance.

"While to the Paymaster, Major Brett, who, all ranks will regret to learn, is about to sever his connexion with the battalion, his best thanks are also due."

A concentration of troops was made at Lucknow for manœuvre purposes: it commenced on the 16th of November and concluded on the 10th of February 1888. The battalion took part in all of the manœuvres.

In the autumn the attention of the battalion was called to a correspondence which had taken place between Major W. T. Walker, 3rd Middlesex Rifle Volunteers, and the 2nd battalion, respecting the original Crimean tombstone: this is fully set out in the record of the 2nd battalion for this year.

1887.

2ND BATTALION.

A letter dated the 15th of March was received by the Officer Commanding the 23rd Regimental District from Major W. T. Walker, 3rd Middlesex Rifle Volunteers, formerly attached for instruction to the 1st Battalion, in which he stated that when travelling recently in the Crimea he had come across the original tombstone erected there to the memory of the officers of the regiment who fell at the Battle of the Alma, which had been replaced by a monumental tomb also erected by the regiment: that as the tombstone was broken and had been cast aside, he had obtained permission to bring it to England, where it was in a still further dilapidated condition, having suffered in transit.

Major Walker requested to be supplied with any information respecting the stone that could be obtained from the regimental records.

Thereupon Colonel Browne, commanding the depôt, wrote to Colonel J. Williamson, commanding the 2nd battalion of the regiment, suggesting that Major Walker should be asked to present the stone to the regiment, and that if he consented to do so it should be erected at the depôt, Wrexham. This course was adopted, Major Walker writing to say he would gladly present the relic to the regiment: the stone was forwarded to Wrexham.

On the 14th of April a mess meeting of the officers of the 2nd battalion was held at Fermoy, at which it was resolved that a letter of thanks inscribed on parchment should be forwarded to Major Walker, and that he be made a permanent honorary member of the mess. It was also decided to acquaint the 1st battalion, then in India, with these resolutions.

The stone was dispatched to Wrexham in the beginning of September and reached its destination safely. It was then erected in the Barrack Square, but was subsequently removed and re-erected in the Regimental Memorial Chapel of the Parish Church.

On the 2nd of April Brevet-Colonel J. Williamson retired with the rank of Major-General, when Brevet-Colonel R. F. Williamson succeeded to the command of the battalion.

Her Majesty Queen Victoria was pleased to present a goat from the herd in Windsor Park to replace the one that had died last year: it reached the battalion with a draft from the depôt on the 27th of May.

On the 24th of August the battalion moved from Fermoy to Galway, headquarters, 3 companies, and band proceeding there, 3 companies and drums to Castlebar, 1 company to Oughterard, and 1 company to Gort.

On the battalion leaving Fermoy, the following complimentary " resolution " was received from the magistrates of Fermoy :

" Resolved : That we, the Magistrates assembled at Fermoy Petty Sessions, beg to record our unanimous approval of the conduct of the 2nd Battalion Royal Welch Fusiliers while stationed here for the past two years, there not being, to the best of our recollection, a civil case against them during that period, and that our Clerk be directed to send a copy of this resolution to Colonel Williamson, in command of the regiment.

"[*signed*]   GEO. MONTGOMERY,
Chairman.

" Fermoy Petty Sessions, 12th September 1887."

1888.

1ST BATTALION.

During his visit to Lucknow, in February, His Excellency the Commander-in-Chief in India, Sir F. S. Roberts, V.C., G.C.B., at a special parade on the 9th of February, presented to the battalion the medals granted for the Burmah campaign, when His Excellency was pleased to pin the medals on the breasts of the officers and men with his own hands, an honour that was greatly appreciated by the regiment.

During the year the battalion remained quartered at Lucknow.

On the 15th of October a draft of 103 non-commissioned officers and men under Major E. R. Evans joined from the 2nd battalion.

A concentration of troops was again formed at Lucknow on the 1st of December for manœuvre purposes, in which the battalion took part.

1888.

2ND BATTALION.

By Army Order dated the 7th of May the establishment of the battalion was fixed at 23 officers, 2 warrant officers, 40 sergeants, and 736 rank and file : total all ranks, 801.

On the 7th of September a draft of 105 non-commissioned officers and men, and on the 25th of December another of 82 non-commissioned officers and men, proceeded to join the 1st battalion.

1889.

1st Battalion.

On the 6th May Her Majesty the Queen was pleased to approve, on the recommendation of His Royal Highness the Commander-in-Chief, of the grant of an annuity of £10 together with a silver medal to Quartermaster-Sergeant John Beer, late 1st Battalion Royal Welch Fusiliers, as a reward for his long and highly meritorious service, including the Crimean and Indian Mutiny Campaigns.

Colonel R. S. Liddell was appointed to command the 23rd Regimental District (The Royal Welch Fusiliers) vice Colonel C. H. Browne, C.B., deceased 3rd June.

The figure of merit of the battalion in the Musketry Season of 1888–89 was 155·39, showing an increase of 37·11 points on the previous year. The battalion was 10th in order of merit in the list of British Infantry Regiments in India for the current season.

A concentration of troops was again formed at Lucknow during the winter of 1889, commencing on the 1st December, and concluding on the 10th January 1890, in which the battalion took part.

His Excellency the Commander-in-Chief in India made the following remarks on the Annual Musketry training of the battalion for the season 1888–89:

"The very great improvement in the shooting of the 1st Battalion Royal Welch Fusiliers during the season 1888–89 is highly creditable to those concerned, and the Commander-in-Chief is much pleased to observe that all ranks of this battalion have striven with success to obtain a high standard of musketry efficiency."

In December the battalion sent up teams to compete at the Central Meeting of the Bengal Presidency Rifle Association held at Meerut, N.W. Provinces. They were successful in winning the non-commissioned officers' cup with a total of 335 points, the victorious team consisting of—

> Quartermaster-Sergeant R. S. Ransom.
> Colour-Sergeant W. W. Jones.
> ,, J. Evans.
> ,, H. Coleman.
> ,, W. Veale.
> Sergeant P. Cush.
> Coach—Captain Sir R. A. W. Colleton, Bart.

and the cup became the property of the Sergeants' Mess of the battalion.

The team entered for the Inter-Regimental Cup, consisting of—
>Captain Sir R. A. W. Colleton, Bart.
>Quartermaster-Sergeant R. S. Ransom.
>Colour-Sergeant W. W. Jones.
>,, H. Coleman.
>,, W. Veale.
>Sergeant P. Cush.
>Private M. Collins.
>,, J. Griffith.
>Coach—Captain Sir R. A. W. Colleton, Bart.

succeeding in beating all the other teams sent up by regiments of the Regular Army in India with a total of 682 points, although only securing the third prize, the winning and second teams belonging to Volunteer Corps. Sir R. Colleton's score of 97 was the highest made in this competition, which was shot under very difficult conditions of a strong crosswind and dust. In addition to the above the following were successful in winning 1st prizes in the individual matches as stated:

>Colour-Sergeant W. W. Jones: "The Durbungah."
>Private M. Collins: "The Benares."

And numerous other prizes were won by Captain Sir R. A. W. Colleton, Bart., and Colour-Sergeant H. Coleman.

Lieutenant-General Sir C. Gough, V.C., K.C.B., Commanding the Oudh District, was pleased to forward his hearty congratulations to the battalion on their splendid shooting when the above results were made known.

1889.

2ND BATTALION.

The battalion goat died on the 9th of March of acute inflammation and was replaced, as before, by Her Majesty Queen Victoria sending one from the herd in Windsor Park on the 30th of July.

The battalion continued to be stationed at Galway.

1890.

1ST BATTALION.

On the 21st of February the following order was published:

"Under instructions from the Horse Guards the undermentioned officers are appointed to exchange to the Battalions specified against their names provided the public be put to no expense by the arrangement.

Royal Welch Fusiliers.
Colonel R. F. Williamson, 1st Battalion.
Lieut.-Colonel E. S. Creek, 2nd Battalion."

On the 25th of February the following order was published: "The following extract from the Annual Report on the Musketry Instruction of the British Regiments serving in the Bengal Presidency, for the year 1888–89, is published for information.

" The Company with the highest figure of merit is letter ' A ' Company of the 1st Battalion, Royal Welch Fusiliers, with 192·73 points."

On the 1st of March, the following was published in Regimental Orders: " The Commanding Officer feels great pleasure in publishing for the information of the Battalion the following speech made by Lieut.-General Sir Charles Gough, V.C., K.C.B., Commanding Oudh District, on the completion of the annual inspections dated 17th January 1890.

" Colonel Creek, Officers and Men, Royal Welch Fusiliers,—It has given me much gratification to make this inspection, and I am glad to say I shall be able to submit a very favourable report of the drill, discipline, and general efficiency of the regiment.

" The men are clean and well turned out, and steady under arms, the clothing is remarkably well fitted. There has been a great improvement in musketry, and it is hardly necessary in these days to impress its great importance on you all; the perfect control of fire renders your shooting more effective, and this can only be obtained by practice and discipline. . . ."

On the 10th of March the following farewell letter from Lieutenant-Colonel E. S. Creek was published in Regimental Orders:

" Officers, Warrant Officers, Non-Commissioned Officers and Men, 1st Battalion Royal Welch Fusiliers,—I regret much that owing to ill-health I am not able to take leave of you personally, and that I am obliged to say the words of farewell in an order, after thanking you all for having rendered my command such a pleasant duty. I beg most particularly to recognise the support I have received from Major Norman as 2nd in command, and from the Field officers generally, also from Captain Dunn as Adjutant, and Captain Gray as Quartermaster; the battalion is fortunate in having officers like these, who have served from youth to manhood among you, and whom you can all respect and trust.

" I feel sure that maintaining the old regimental system of mutual reliance and community of interest between officers and men, you will continue to be an example to the Army of good behaviour in quarters, and a smart performance of duty in the field, and on the line of march. You will never forget the magnificent inheritance of glory that has come down to you from those who have gone before, and that for intrepidity in action and courage in bearing heavy loss the Royal Welch Fusiliers have always been unsurpassed.

"You are, I believe, to march next autumn to the Frontier, where chances of distinction may soon come. I wish success to you all."

The battalion won the Commander-in-Chief in India's Musketry Cup, which was a very handsome heavy Burmese bowl, and a purse of one hundred rupees open to all British regiments serving in the Bengal Presidency.

The terms were teams of ten from each regiment; seven rounds at 200 yards and seven rounds at 800 yards, Wimbledon targets.

The names of the team are given below:

> Sergeant-Major A. E. Hammond.
> Quartermaster-Sergeant R. S. Ransom.
> Colour-Sergeant W. W. Jones.
>   ,,   H. Coleman.
>   ,,   W. Veale.
> Sergeant P. Cush.
> Private M. Collins.
>   ,,   J. Griffith.
>   ,,   J. Llewellyn.
>   ,,   G. Boast.

The following telegram was sent from His Excellency the Commander-in-Chief to the General Officer Commanding Oudh District:

"Please convey to the Royal Welch Fusiliers my congratulations on winning my prize. I am delighted at this proof of the Battalion's proficiency in musketry, and am very pleased to see that the successful team includes the names of the Sergeant-Major, the Quartermaster-Sergeant, and three Colour-Sergeants."

On the 16th of July Major-General Æneas Perkins, C.B., R.E., Commanding Oudh District, presented the Commander-in-Chief in India's cup to the battalion, making a complimentary speech and congratulating the battalion on its success.

On the 11th of June Lieutenant J. D. Vyvyan died at Lucknow of meningitis.

On the 27th of October an advanced party of 2 officers and 76 non-commissioned officers and men left Lucknow for Peshawar by rail under command of Captain Morris.

On the 8th of November the headquarters of the battalion left Lucknow for Peshawar by rail as far as Rawal Pindi, reaching the latter station on the 12th of November. From Rawal Pindi the battalion marched to Khysabad on the Indus, where it took part in the camp of exercise held there, and was in the Southern or defending force commanded by Major-General Elles, C.B., in the 2nd Infantry Brigade commanded by Colonel Waller, 19th Punjab Infantry. Colonel Williamson was during the camp of exercise in command of the 3rd Infantry Brigade; the battalion being commanded by Major Norman. On the breaking up of the camp the battalion resumed its march to Peshawar, where it arrived on the 9th of December.

1890.

2ND BATTALION.

On the 28th of January Brevet-Colonel R. F. Williamson left the 2nd battalion, and exchanged with Lieutenant-Colonel E. S. Creek to command the 1st battalion.

On the 15th of July the headquarters and outlying detachments proceeded to the Curragh Camp, and were quartered in B lines.

On the 14th of September Lieutenant-Colonel E. S. Creek joined and took command.

On the 20th of February a draft of 103 non-commissioned officers and men, and on the 19th of September another draft of 165 non-commissioned officers and men, embarked at Queenstown for Bombay to join the 1st battalion at Lucknow.

1891.

1ST BATTALION.

It so happened that this year St. David's Day fell on a Sunday, consequently on the depôt parading for Divine Service, the battalion being en route for the Black Mountain, every officer and man wore a leek in his helmet. The strong scent of opium in the church attracted the notice of the congregation, who were unaware of this regimental custom.

The reason for wearing the leek is as follows: St. David is credited with having advised the Britons on the eve of a battle with the Saxons to wear leeks in their caps so as to easily distinguish friend from foe, and thus to have helped to secure a great victory.

In the Iola MSS. it is stated that at Crécy " the Welsh acquired great fame for their brave achievements in support of Edward the Black Prince." (This in all probability accounts for the adoption of the badges of the Black

Prince by the regiment on their colours.) " It was at this time that Captain Ladwgan Voel called to the Welsh desiring them to put leeks in their helmets, the battle there being in a field of leeks : and when they looked about they were all Welsh in that locality except 130, and it was from this circumstance that the Welsh took to wearing leeks."

To this event, and to the custom of wearing the leek on St. David's Day, Shakespeare alludes when in *King Henry V* he caused Fluellen to say : " The Welshmen did good service in a garden where leeks did grow, wearing leeks in their Monmouth caps : which, your Majesty knows, to this hour is an honourable badge of the service, and I do believe your Majesty takes no scorn to wear the leek upon Saint Tavy's Day."

King Henry V : " I wear it for a memorable honour : for I am Welsh, you know, good countryman."

In January it was decided to send an expedition under command of Major-General W. K. Elles, C.B., against the Hazanzai and Akazai, two Black Mountain tribes. The object of this expedition was to enforce recognition and compliance with the Government demands, which had been agreed to by these tribes after the Black Mountain Expedition of 1888.

The main advance was to be made up the Indus Valley, as it would lead straight to the centre of population, and the ground was more open than if the advance was made from the eastern side of the Black Mountain.

The concentration of the Expeditionary Force was made at Darband, about 16 miles north of Attock, on the Indus, and at Oghi, about 20 miles to the north-east of Darband, the force consisting of 3 brigades.

The 1st, under Brigadier-General R. F. Williamson, consisted of No. 1 Mountain Battery R.A., 3 guns ; No. 2 Derajat Mountain Battery R.A. ; 2nd Battalion Seaforth Highlanders ; 4th Sikhs ; 32nd Bengal Infantry ; Pioneers, 4 companies ; 37th Dogras ; and Guides Infantry.

The 2nd, under Brigadier-General A. G. Hammond, V.C., D.S.O., of the Guides, consisted of No. 9 Mountain Battery R.A. ; 1st Battalion Royal Welch Fusiliers ; 11th Bengal Infantry ; 32nd Bengal Infantry ; Pioneers, 4 companies ; 2nd Battalion 5th Gurkhas and Khyber Rifles.

The 3rd, under Brigadier-General Sir W. S. A. Lockhart, K.C.B., C.S.I., consisted of No. 1 Mountain Battery R.A., 3 guns ; 11th Bengal Lancers, 1 squadron ; 1st Battalion King's Royal Rifles ; 19th Bengal Infantry ; and 27th Bengal Infantry.

Divisional Troops : 11th Bengal Lancers, 1 squadron ; No. 4 company Bengal Sappers and Miners.

On account of the bad weather some delay occurred in the start, but on the 12th of March the 1st Brigade was ordered to move up the left bank of the Indus on Kanar, while the 2nd Brigade moved along the western slopes of the Black Mountain on Tilli. From a diary kept by Captain Sir Robert Colleton, Bart., who acted as Brigade Major to the 2nd Brigade under Brigadier-General Hammond, most of the following information as regards the expedition has been drawn.

On the 9th of March the battalion (20 officers and 612 N.C.O.s and men), Guides Infantry, and the Khyber Rifles arrived at the Camp at Darband, making the Hazara Field Force complete (Brigadier-General R. F. Williamson arrived with the battalion and assumed command of his Brigade, the 1st); 72 shelter huts were issued to the Battalion, the invention of Colonel J. Cook, for trial and report at the end of the campaign. On the 11th orders were received for the advance, which commenced at 8 a.m. on the 12th; the roads were found to have disappeared, and the 2nd brigade did not arrive at Tilli till Saturday, the 14th. A bridge of boats brought up from Attock was put in hand at Kotkai.

Heavy rain fell and thunderstorms occurred during the next few days, interfering with the road-mending parties, which were also frequently sniped at. General Elles visited Tilli on the 15th from Kotkai, and on finding the difficulties of supply so great with the column, decided to alter his plans by leaving detachments at Tilli, Ril, and Makranai, and then bringing the 2nd brigade down into the Indus Valley to concentrate with the 1st Brigade, the river column, at Palosi: the 1st Brigade would then operate on the right, and the 2nd Brigade on the left bank of the Indus.

On the 17th of March there was a continuous storm of wind, rain, hail, and sleet all day, stopping the working parties, and necessitating an extra free issue of rum and meat to all. On the night of the 18th a determined attack was made about 3 a.m. on an advance post at Ghazikot held by a company of the 4th Sikhs, but they beat the enemy off successfully; 4 Sikhs were killed, 16 wounded and 1 officer.

On the 20th the weather cleared, and orders were issued for an advance on Ril and Seri, the troops being divided as follows: for Seri, 200 men of the Royal Welch Fusiliers, 100 from the 32nd Pioneers, 200 2/5th Gurkhas, and 200 Khyber Rifles; for Ril, 2 guns No. 9 Mountain Battery R.A., 100 Royal Welch Fusiliers, and 100 2/5th Gurkhas. There was only slight opposition, and both places were occupied.

On the 23rd of March Seri was burnt, and on the 24th the Brigade left Tilli at 9 a.m. and reached Palosi about 3 p.m., crossing the Indus by the bridge of boats at Kotkai; it was a very trying, hot march of about 11 miles. On arrival at Palosi the Khyber Rifles were ordered to Bakrai.

On the 25th the column paraded at 6.30 a.m. in preparation for an advance on Darbaurai; it crossed the Indus by boats and a flying bridge at Bakrai, and opposition by the enemy commenced soon after leaving Led. Darbaurai was rushed by the Gurkhas, and a running fight ensued as far as Surmul, the Royal Welch Fusiliers carrying the neck in front of Surmul and the Khyber Rifles clearing the heights on the right. Lieutenant C. H. M. Doughty, Royal Welch Fusiliers, was severely wounded in the knee and one sepoy of the Khyber Rifles was also wounded, the enemy's loss being 30 or 40.

On the 26th General Hammond tried to open negotiations with the enemy, with the object of inducing them to turn on the water supply, but without effect.

The battery took up a position to the north-east of the village, whilst the Khyber Rifles moved up the hill to reach the water supply. The Royal Welch Fusiliers, 11th Bengal Infantry, and 2/5th Gurkhas moved down the hill on Surmul. The enemy were in great force and began firing directly the advance commenced. Private A. Godfrey of the Royal Welch Fusiliers was hit in the right shoulder; he died on the 15th of April. The Royal Welch Fusiliers, supported by the 11th Bengal Infantry, attacked in front, the Khyber Rifles on the right, whilst the 2/5th Gurkhas took the village on the left, when the enemy who were collected behind, about 600 in number, fled: this was about 10 a.m. The Rifles burned two or three small villages and turned on the water supply. The enemy's casualties were estimated at about 80. Brigadier-General Hammond in his dispatch observed " that no troops could have behaved more steadily or shown more eagerness to get to close quarters than the Royal Welch Fusiliers and 2/5th Gurkhas."

On the 28th a force of 400 men, made up of 100 each from the Royal Welch Fusiliers, Gurkhas, 11th Bengal Infantry, and Khyber Rifles, was sent on reconnaissance to find a good alignment for the road, but was not successful: no opposition was met with, but a few rocks were rolled down-hill. On the 30th another reconnaissance, under Major Mainwaring, with 150 Royal Welch Fusiliers, 100 Gurkhas, and 50 Khyber Rifles, was carried out in the hills.

On the 2nd of April Major C. Norman was appointed to command the battalion vice Colonel Williamson, who had completed four years' command. Colonel Williamson was retained as supernumerary to the Establishment until the 16th June, when he was placed on half-pay.

On April 3rd the detachment of 100 Royal Welch Fusiliers at Led rejoined the headquarters at Darbaurai.

On April 5th Major E. R. Evans of the battalion died at Palosi, in hospital, from pneumonia, contracted during the advance from Darband.

On April 6th a force, consisting of 1½ companies Royal Welch Fusiliers, 75 Khyber Rifles, 50 2/5th Gurkhas, and 2 companies of the 11th Bengal Infantry, under Colonel Stead, left Darbaurai before daybreak, and reaching Sabé burnt it and other small villages and returned without opposition.

On the 10th it was proposed to hold a Gymkhana to vary the monotony of road-making, village-burning, repairing the water supply, etc., and a very successful meeting was carried out on Monday the 13th: on the 11th orders had been received to transfer the base from Darband to Oghi, the mail route being changed to the Seri and Oghi road.

On the 24th another effort to relieve the monotony was made by the Royal Welch Fusiliers, who gave a very successful smoking concert at the headquarters at Darbaurai; this was followed by another Gymkhana held at Seri on the 27th, and Sports on 4th of May, and another smoking concert by the Royal Welch Fusiliers on the 6th.

On the 7th, headquarters of the Royal Welch Fusiliers and No. 9 Battery R.A. marched for Seri and Panji Gali, followed by the right half of the battalion on Saturday, 9th of May. On the 29th of May orders were received for the concentration of the 2nd Brigade by the 1st of June, as the submission of the Hazanzai and Akazai was complete, and on June 11th the main body of the Hazara Field Force started on its return to India, leaving No. 9 Mountain Battery R.A., 1st Battalion Royal Welch Fusiliers, 4th Sikhs, 28th Bengal Infantry, 1st Battalion 1st Gurkhas, 4 companies 32nd Pioneers (till 10th July), and No. 4 Company Bengal Sappers and Miners, to occupy the Black Mountain and Oghi until the British terms were fully complied with. The Black Mountain was held till the late autumn, when a settlement being finally made, the British force withdrew, leaving 200 Border Police to preserve order. The battalion returned to Peshawar, arriving there on the 9th of November.

1891.

2ND BATTALION.

The following letter was published in Regimental Orders:

"WINDSOR CASTLE,
16th March 1891.

"DEAR COLONEL CREEK,

"I am commanded by the Queen to convey to you Her Majesty's best thanks for the three Kashmir goats which you have procured for the Royal herd.

" They arrived here in safety and good condition, and no doubt will soon get accustomed to their new home.

" Yours very truly,
   [*signed*] ARTHUR BIGGE, *Major*.

" Colonel E. S. Creek,
  Royal Welch Fusiliers."

The foregoing letter had reference to the following circumstances. Colonel Creek when in command of the 2nd battalion at Lucknow in 1889 saw, on the road to Thibet, several goats exactly like those in the Royal herd at Windsor: on a previous occasion hearing that that herd was in want of fresh blood he communicated with Sir Fleetwood Edwards, and received a reply that Her Majesty would be pleased to have some of these goats. Colonel Creek, having by that time returned to the plains, sent a photograph of one of the best specimens of Regimental Goats to Colonel Parry Nisbett, the resident in Cashmere, and with the assistance of this gentleman and the good offices of Colonel John Ardagh, C.B., R.E., private secretary to the Viceroy, Lord Lansdowne, the above-mentioned goats were obtained and conveyed to their destination.

On the 1st of July Lieutenant-Colonel S. B. Blyth took over command of the 2nd battalion from Brevet-Colonel E. S. Creek, who was placed on half-pay, and who reverted to full pay upon being appointed Assistant Adjutant-General, Chester.

1892.

1ST BATTALION.

On the 25th of April the headquarters of the battalion left Peshawar for Cherat, arriving at the latter place on the 27th of April, and remaining there during the hot weather.

On the 28th of October Her Majesty's goat, which had served with the battalion since 1883, died at Cherat.

On the 20th of November the headquarters of the battalion moved from Cherat to Peshawar, and on the 22nd by rail to Nowshera in relief of the 2nd battalion Northumberland Fusiliers.

During the hot season, while stationed at Peshawar, the battalion suffered greatly from sickness, losing 63 non-commissioned officers and men, 2 women and 1 child.

1892.

2ND BATTALION.

On the 5th of April the battalion goat died at the Curragh Camp from inflammation, and on notification of the fact to Her Majesty, she was pleased to direct that another should be forwarded from the Royal herd at Windsor, and it duly arrived at the Curragh on the 12th June, in charge of Colour-Sergeant Wade, 2nd Battalion Royal Welch Fusiliers.

A march of the battalion through North Wales having been decided upon, the following letter was received by Colonel R. S. Liddell, commanding the 23rd Regimental District :

"70 BROOK STREET,
GROSVENOR SQUARE, W.
26th July 1892.

" DEAR COLONEL LIDDELL,

" May I ask you kindly to convey through the proper channel to the officers and men of the Battalion of the Royal Welch Fusiliers, which is to visit Anglesey, the sense of pleasure with which we in Anglesey look forward to their visit, and at the same time express my hope that they will accept such hospitality as it will be in my power to offer them during the few hours they will be in the County.

" I understand that after visiting Llanfair you are inclined to select some fields near the station as the most convenient place for the Regiment to be lunched.

" If this is so I should be glad, as it appears to me that it will be also very convenient for the numbers of people who will come by train to see them.

" Next to the soldiers I think the convenience of the Public should be studied.

" If it should be practicable, as I have no doubt it would be desirable, to arrange for an inspection or parade of the troops, I would invite Deputy Lieutenants of the County and any others whose presence may be desirable, to attend in uniform and to meet the Officers at luncheon in a marquee in the field.

" Yours faithfully,
[*signed*] R. DAVIES,
H.M. Lieutenant for Anglesey."

Copy of resolution passed unanimously at a public meeting held at the County Hall, Carnarvon, on 6th August:

"That the County of Carnarvon is much gratified to hear of the intended visit of the Royal Welch Fusiliers, and begs to offer them a hearty welcome."

The March through Wales.

The regiment, with the exception of D and F companies, left the Curragh at four in the morning of the 2nd of September, the officers being: Lieutenant-Colonel S. B. Blyth in command; Majors R. B. Mainwaring and H. J. Archdale; Captains C. H. Milford, G. F. Walker, B. H. Philips, S. B. Bright-Smith, and E. L. Engleheart; Lieutenants C. E. Bancroft, R. S., Webber, H. W. McMahon, R. C. B. Throckmorton, H. M. Richards, W. G. Braithwaite, R. E. P. Gabbett, H. Rotherham, G. E. Pigott, A. Hay, and J. D. Crosbie (Adjutant).

On arrival at Holyhead after a rough passage the men disembarked, and marched to the Market Hall, where breakfast was given by the Local Board. Hence by train to Llanfair. Here the regiment was met by the Anglesey Volunteers, and formed up in the grounds of the High Sheriff, Mr. Harry Glegg, and were inspected by Major-General Julian Hall in the presence of the Lord-Lieutenant of Anglesey and a considerable concourse of visitors. An address of welcome was read by Mr. Lloyd Griffith of Holyhead, Clerk of the Peace for Anglesey, which was replied to by Colonel Blyth in suitable terms. Both officers and men were afterwards entertained at luncheon. At 2 o'clock the regiment marched to Bangor over Menai Bridge, at the Carnarvon side of which they were met by the Mayor of Bangor, Major H. Savage, in command of the Cheshire and Carnarvon Artillery Volunteers, by whom they were escorted into Bangor, where they encamped on ground placed at their disposal by Councillor Williams.

In the evening a banquet was given to the officers and supper to the men.

The band of the regiment gave a concert in the evening.

Here Captain J. H. K. Griffith, 4th R. W. Fusiliers, met them charged with conducting the regiment through the first half of the march.

Leaving Bangor on Saturday morning the 3rd of September at 10 o'clock the battalion marched to Carnarvon, lunching on the way at Llanfair Hall, where Captain Wynne Griffiths provided luncheon.

On arriving at 3 o'clock at Carnarvon, which was profusely decorated, the battalion entered by the east gate, proceeded to the Cross, and then to Castle Square; there Mr. Greaves, the Lord-Lieutenant, presented an address on behalf of the county, while Mr. Davies, the Mayor, gave the regiment a cordial welcome to the town ; the men then marched to their camping ground at Cal Tolpes. At night the town and castle were brilliantly illuminated by Messrs. Brock, and at 6 o'clock dinner and a special entertainment were given by the town to the men in the Eisteddfod Pavilion.

On Sunday the 4th of September, after church parade, the Castle was thrown open to the soldiers.

At Carnarvon the battalion remained till September 8th, during which time they enjoyed all sorts of festivities—a concert in the Pavilion, athletic sports, special train to Llanberis on Monday to see the Quarries, where they were entertained to lunch by Mr. Assheton-Smith, county ball, etc.

On Thursday the 8th the battalion left by special train for Pwllheli, where they detrained and marched to Bron Eifion, Criccieth, the seat of the Lord-Lieutenant of Carnarvonshire, Mr. T. G. Greaves, who entertained the officers and men and a large party to lunch.

After lunch the battalion went through physical drill and an officers' race took place, the prize being given by the ladies of the county.

The battalion then marched up to Bron Eifion, where the Lord-Lieutenant wished them good-bye ; they then resumed their march to Portmadoc via Criccieth. At Portmadoc they encamped the night just inside the town, which was beautifully decorated ; a display of fireworks and a military tattoo were the excitement of the evening. Next morning, the 9th, the battalion left for Penrhyndeudraeth, marching over the embankment and through Minffordd to Penrhyndeudraeth station, where they entrained, and were taken to Harlech Castle, the expense of the special train being defrayed by W. Osmond Williams, Chairman of Merionethshire County Council. On arrival at the station the battalion detrained and marched into the Castle, where they were addressed by Mr. W. Wynne, Constable of the Castle and Lord-Lieutenant of the County, in Welsh and English. Afterwards the men had luncheon in the Castle and the officers in the Town Hall. After a short musical drill the regiment left amidst deafening " cannonading " from the Castle Hill and defiled down the slopes to the station, where they were entrained and taken to Minffordd Junction and thence per narrow-gauge railway to Blaenau Festiniog, where they were greeted with rock cannon salutes. The next day, without their baggage and in Field Day " Order," the regiment proceeded to Dolgelly by special train, where they were reviewed by Colonel Creek, late Colonel of the Regiment. They here performed several exercises, the most popular being " the trooping of the Colours." After dinner to the men, and luncheon to the officers, given by the County and Mrs. Richards of

Caerynwch, a return was made to Blaenau Festiniog, where the Lord Mayor of London, himself a Welshman, met the regiment—an address being presented. An exhibition of fireworks, more thunder of rock cannon salutes, and a concert in the evening closed the day.

The next day was so wet that the men had to evacuate camp for quarters in the Town Hall.

The 13th of September saw the regiment again on their march, in drizzling rain and driving fog, saluted by volley after volley of rock cannon, moving towards Bettws-y-Coed.

On reaching Dolwyddelan a halt was made for luncheon for both officers and men, provided by Colonel C. Mainwaring, 1st Volunteer Battalion Royal Welch Fusiliers. Here Colonel Creek again met the regiment. Bettws-y-Coed was reached in the late afternoon, and on passing over the well-known Waterloo Bridge, which was beautifully decorated with an evergreen arch, the regiment found themselves at their camping-ground by the river. Here Captain Griffith's duty ended of conducting the regiment through Anglesey, Carnarvon, and Merioneth—an onerous task, which had been performed in a highly successful manner.

The next day, the 14th, the regiment proceeded to Llangerniew, where they encamped the night in Haifordunas Park, their march being marked by much enthusiasm and gay bunting displayed in every available space. Half-way in the market square at Llanrwst an address of welcome was presented by Mr. R. James. After the Colonel had responded in suitable terms the men were supplied with refreshments, the officers being entertained at luncheon at the Victoria Hotel. The next day, Thursday the 15th, the regiment proceeded to Abergele. A fatal accident occurred there to the goat, which, being too young to march, was conveyed on a waggon, from which it fell, a wheel passing over its body. The Lord Mayor on hearing of this offered and finally sent the battalion a Welsh goat with beautiful horns. The goat which accompanied the battalion during the remainder of the march was kindly lent by the 3rd Battalion Royal Welch Fusiliers. The regiment then proceeded to St. Asaph.

The little city was gaily decorated. On arrival officers and men attended a special service in the cathedral. A brief service was gone through, the Bishop of St. Asaph officiating and at the close delivering a short address, taking as his text, "A devout soldier." The men were afterwards supplied with an excellent dinner, the officers being entertained by the Bishop of St. Asaph at the Palace, at which the Duke of Westminster proposed the toast, "The Welch Fusiliers," which was briefly responded to by Colonel Blyth.

Afterwards W. A. V. Kyrke, Esq., High Sheriff of Flintshire, on behalf of the magistrates of the county presented the regiment with a beautifully illuminated address. The regiment then proceeded the same day, Thursday the 15th, to Denbigh; here they were received by Colonel Cornwallis West, Lord-Lieutenant of the County, and the men supplied with refreshments.

They encamped here, remaining two days—a smoking concert, sports, illuminations, and a ball to the officers taking place.

On Friday an address was presented to the regiment in the old castle grounds by Major Edwards, the Mayor. The town was beautifully decorated.

On Saturday the 17th the march was resumed to Ruthin. The regiment was received by the Ruthin Volunteers and a troop of the Denbighshire Hussars. Flags, bunting, and all sorts of decorations met the eye everywhere. The regiment halted in the market square, where an address of welcome was read by the Mayor (Mr. Roberts) and responded to by Colonel Blyth. They then marched to their camping-ground on the Corwen Road. Later on luncheon was supplied to every man, the band and sergeants being entertained at dinner, the officers being entertained by Colonel Cornwallis West and Major R. G. G. Ellis and Lieutenant Blizzard. In the evening the town was illuminated, and a concert by the band held in Ruthin Castle grounds.

On Sunday the troops attended Divine Service at St. Peter's, and in the afternoon the band played selections in the ground of Ruthin Castle.

The next morning, Monday the 19th, the march to Corwen commenced. A halt was made at Nantclwyd Hall, where the regiment was magnificently entertained by Mrs. Naylor Leyland, the officers lunching at her house; the village was decorated, and a triumphal arch erected at the entrance to the Park.

Corwen was reached on Monday afternoon. The morning was wet and miserable but cleared partially. The camping-ground was at the bottom of the town. After pitching tents, tobacco and drinks were served out and the men invited to a variety entertainment in the Assembly Rooms.—fireworks taking place later, and the streets being gaily decorated. The officers attended a ball at Dolgelly given in their honour by the ladies of Merioneth.

The following morning, Tuesday the 20th, the regiment left for Llangollen. Llangollen was reached in pouring rain and tents pitched under most unpleasant conditions. The band gave a concert in the afternoon at the Assembly Rooms, and a smoking concert was held in the evening. A banquet was given to the officers at the Grand Hotel, at which Sir

Theodore Martin, K.C.B., proposed the health of the regiment in an excellent speech. On Wednesday the regiment left camp at 10 a.m. and marched through the town, which was nicely decorated, on its way to Wrexham. Cefnmawr was reached at midday; the heights were lined with people, who gave the Fusiliers a hearty welcome. The men were supplied with refreshments, the band afterwards giving a selection of music. The march was then continued in heavy rain to Ruabon, which was well decorated; no halt was made here, and Wrexham was reached about 3.30 p.m. on Wednesday the 21st. They were accorded a most hearty welcome in this their depôt town, which was gaily decorated for the occasion with bunting of every description, and evergreen arches bearing various inscriptions.

On arrival, the Parish Church bells rang out a merry peal, and the regiment marched up the town hill and into High Street and halted in quarter-column of half-companies opposite the Wynnstay Arms. Here they received an address from the Mayor (Mr. Soames), which was replied to by Colonel Blyth, on conclusion of which the troops marched to their camping-ground on the race-course. The streets and square were kept by troops from the Regimental Depôt, Police, and the Wrexham Volunteer Companies. After pitching tents each man was supplied with refreshments. On Thursday a cricket match took place at Marckwiel Hall, with the band in attendance, and the regiment visited the depôt the same day, marching through the town in drill order. In the evening a Military Tattoo and torchlight procession took place. Friday saw sports on the race-course, and a ball in the evening given by the Mayor and Mayoress (Mr. and Mrs. Soames), a smoking-concert at the Conservative Club for the men, and a sergeants' dance at the depôt Barracks. On Saturday morning Major-General Sir Julian Hall, commanding North-Western District, inspected the regiment. The usual manœuvres were gone through, including the march past, physical drill, and trooping the colours. In the afternoon the officers of the depôt gave a garden party, which was very largely attended. On Sunday the troops attended the Parish Church, and in the afternoon the sergeants and their wives drove over to Eaton, and were entertained by the Duke of Westminster. An address by the boys of Oswestry Grammar School was also presented this day. On Monday morning, 26th September, the regiment entrained for Aldershot, where they arrived the same afternoon and proceeded to Talavera Barracks.

The following is a copy of Sir Julian Hall's speech to the Royal Welch Fusiliers at their inspection at Wrexham:

" Colonel Blyth, Officers, Non-Commissioned Officers, and Men,—

I am very glad to have this opportunity of telling you how very gratifying it was to me, as I knew it was to you, to see the great enthusiasm that was shown by the people of all ranks and classes throughout North Wales in offering you so hearty and unprecedented a reception. Your march is nearly over and it is with feelings of the greatest gratification that I have noticed your good conduct and soldierlike bearing under the varied temptations you have had to meet.

" Nothing is of greater service to an army as a whole, or a regiment in particular, than the evidence you have given of how a well-conducted regiment lives.

" I had no misgivings as to your conduct, but it gives me the greatest pleasure to be able to tell you how pleased I am, and I hope you will during your stay at Aldershot bear the same unsullied reputation in the face of all the many temptations thrown in your way there."

The following is a copy of a letter from the Deputy Adjutant-General, War Office, to the General Officer commanding the troops, Aldershot :

"Horse Guards, War Office,
3rd November 1892.

" Sir,

" I have the honour by the desire of the Commander-in-Chief to acquaint you that His Royal Highness has been much pleased with the conduct of the 2nd Battalion Royal Welch Fusiliers during the march through North Wales, which it so successfully carried out in September last ; and to request that you will be so good as to convey His Royal Highness's appreciation thereof to all concerned.

" I have, &c.,
[*signed*] Chas. M. Clarke, D.A.G.

" G.O.C., The Troops, Aldershot."

The regimental goat having been killed accidentally during the march through Wales, Her Majesty was graciously pleased to allow the battalion another from the herd in Windsor Park.

This goat reached the 2nd battalion the third week in October.

1893.

1st Battalion.

On the 21st of March the medals for the Hazara Campaign of 1891 were issued to the battalion.

On the 27th of March A and E companies, under the command of Major Sir R. Colleton, Bart., left Nowshera by rail for Jhansi to take over the barracks, etc., from the 2nd Battalion Wiltshire Regiment.

On the 2nd of November headquarters, consisting of "B," "C," "D," "F," "G," and "H" companies, left Nowshera by route march for Jhansi, Nowgong, and Sipri.

1893.

2ND BATTALION.

On the 29th of August a force numbering about 17,000 men took part in manœuvres on the borders of Berkshire and Wiltshire.

The battalion was brigaded with the 1st West Yorkshire Regiment, the 1st Wilts, and 1st Durham Light Infantry, under Major-General Utterson, and formed part of the 1st Division under Lieutenant-General Davies.

The battalion was formed into four companies under Major H. J. Archdale, Captains G. F. Walker, R. B. Firman, and B. H. Philips, as near as possible at war strength, totalling 596. They arrived at Liddington on the 2nd of September, from which date, until the 15th, they were engaged in manœuvres over an area of about sixty square miles. The return journey was commenced after a field day and a defile past on the 15th, arriving at Aldershot on the 19th; the health of the regiment was good, and the weather all that could be desired.

On the 8th of December a draft of 145 non-commissioned officers and men under Captain A. F. Cooper embarked at Portsmouth, for service with the 1st battalion, taking out with them a goat from Her Majesty's herd at Windsor.

1894.

1ST BATTALION.

On the 17th of January a young goat, the gift of Her Majesty the Queen, arrived from England with a draft of 145 non-commissioned officers and men, under the command of Captain A. F. Cooper; 2nd Lieutenant W. Keen also arrived with this draft.

On the 27th of January the battalion resumed its march to Jhansi; "C" company under the command of Captain Mantell branched off at Old Gwalior on the 1st February for Sipri to form the garrison there.

On the 7th of February headquarters arrived at Jhansi.

On the 10th of February "D," "F," and "G" companies under command of Major Morris left Jhansi for Nowgong, reaching the latter place on the 15th of February.

On the 15th of November a letter was received from the Horse Guards intimating that Her Majesty the Queen had been graciously pleased to approve of the "Rising Sun" to be borne on the Regimental Colour in the first and fourth corners, the "Red Dragon" in the second, and the "White Horse" in the third, with the number of the battalion in the first corner also.

1894.

2ND BATTALION.

On the 27th of June the following letter was received from the War Office :

"HORSE GUARDS, WAR OFFICE, S.W.
26th June 1894.

"In reference to previous correspondence I have the honour by desire of H.R.H. the Commander-in-Chief to acquaint you, for the information of the Officer Commanding the 2nd Battalion of the Regiment, that Her Majesty has been graciously pleased to approve of the badges carried in the corners of the Regimental Colour of the Royal Welch Fusiliers being rearranged as follows :

"In the first and fourth corners the 'Rising Sun,' in the second the 'Red Dragon,' and in the third the 'White Horse.'

"The number of the Battalion will be placed beneath the badge borne in the first corner."

On the 27th of September the battalion moved from Aldershot to Manchester : one company ("E") proceeding to Fleetwood.

On the 8th of March a draft of 88 non-commissioned officers and men, and on 23rd of November a further draft of 165 non-commissioned officers and men, left for service with the 1st Battalion at Jhansi.

1895.

1ST BATTALION.

On the 1st of January "D," "E," "F," and "G" companies from Nowgong, and "C" company from Sipri, concentrated at Jhansi for manœuvres with headquarters

On the 1st of February "D," "E," "F," and "H" companies, under command of Major A. J. E. Wrench, left Jhansi for Nowgong by route march, arriving at the latter station on the 6th of February.

On the 2nd of April Major H. W. Griffith succeeded Lieutenant-Colonel C. Norman in the command of the battalion.

On the 6th of November " D," " E," " F," and " H " companies marched from Nowgong, and arrived at Jhansi on the 12th of November, concentrating for Winter Drill.

1895.

2ND BATTALION.

On the 5th of May the goat presented by Her Majesty died of pneumonia.

On the 1st of July Lieutenant-Colonel R. B. Mainwaring assumed command of the battalion vice Lieutenant-Colonel S. B. Blyth, who went on half-pay.

On the same date four companies moved to Chipping Camp for musketry and field training; on the 10th the remaining four companies joined them, returning to Manchester on the 30th of August and 3rd September.

The Royal Welch Fusiliers, having their Regimental District Headquarters at Wrexham, resolved upon erecting in the Parish Church a window to the memory of departed comrades; to this end both battalions and depôt contributed a day's pay per man. The removal of the old organ, with the gallery which previously held it, came most opportunely, and the suggestion made by the Officers of the regiment, that the space at the west end of the nave of the church, adjoining the tower, should become a regimental chapel was cordially accepted by the vicar and churchwardens, and was approved by the parishioners in vestry, and the organ and gallery were removed.

The order for the window, which was given to Messrs. Clayton & Bell, was beautifully carried out by them, in the style peculiar to the fifteenth century. It is divided into five long lights up to the springing of its arch, above which the smaller tracery lights are in three tiers and number ten in their subdivisions. In the upper part of the lower lights are full-sized figures of St. Deiniol of Bangor, St. Michael, St. David of Wales, Edward the Black Prince, and St. Giles. Below are subsidiary subjects illustrating episodes in their lives. In the tracery openings are introduced twenty-four smaller figures of saints especially connected with Wales. At the apex of the window is represented the Badge of the regiment, and at the base the inscription runs as follows :

"To the Glory of God, and in memory of those who have faithfully served their Queen and country in the Royal Welch Fusiliers, this window is erected by their comrades and friends."

The monuments which were already in the church and dedicated to the memory of departed members of the regiment were collected and re-erected in the regimental chapel. These consisted of: A mural brass monumental tablet with the following inscription: "In memory of Major Charles Arthur Baldwin Knyvett Leighton, 1st Battalion Royal Welch Fusiliers, who died at Naini Tal, N.W.P., India, on the 11th of May 1889. Erected by his brother officers." A mural brass monumental tablet with the following inscription: "In memory of Lieutenant Charles Lysons, 'F' Company, 1st Battalion Royal Welch Fusiliers, who died on active service while commanding a detachment of his regiment at Katha, Upper Burmah, on the 19th of April 1886, aged twenty-five years. Erected by the non-commissioned officers and men of his company." A mural stone monument, containing in the centre, upon a black shield-shaped tablet, the following inscription: "In memory of Lieutenant W. A. Johnston, Privates J. Brooks, W. Phillips, J. McCue, J. Tourish, C. McPherson, C. Baker, 23rd Royal Welch Fusiliers, also of Surgeon E. T. McCarthy, formerly of the regiment, who died serving their country during the Ashantee Campaign, 1873-74. Erected by their comrades of all ranks"; and a mural monument consisting of a brass tablet fixed upon a stone slab, which tablet bears the following inscription: "In affectionate remembrance of Colonel James De Vic Tupper, 2nd Battalion Royal Welch Fusiliers, who died at Pembroke Dock the 23rd December 1881, after a service of twenty-seven years in the regiment, including the Crimean, Indian Mutiny, and Ashantee Campaigns. Erected by officers who served in the regiment with him."

A brass monumental tablet has also been erected to the memory of the late Major Ernest Riddle Evans.

The original tombstone erected in the Crimea to the memory of the Royal Welch Fusiliers who fell at the Battle of the Alma was removed from the Barrack Square, where it was being affected by the weather, and placed in the regimental chapel.

The memorial fund which is kept up by a donation from each officer on first appointment erects brasses to each Colonel of the regiment and every V.C. on their death; the other brasses are put up by the battalions to all officers who die during their service.

The unveiling of the west window took place on Friday, 20th September, the anniversary of the Battle of the Alma. The 2nd Battalion Royal Welch Fusiliers under Colonel R. B. Mainwaring came from Manchester with the Colours, and a Guard of Honour of 100 men under command of Major Griffith, and the band under Mr. F. Gregory.

The ceremony, which was a very impressive one, was attended by the Mayor of Wrexham and Corporation, many old officers of the regiment and those serving in both battalions, together with the Militia, Volunteers, and gentry of the surrounding neighbourhood. The service was conducted by the Bishop of St. Asaph, assisted by the Rev. Canon Fletcher, vicar, and many others. The new window was unveiled by the Dowager Lady Williams Wynn. Sir Edward Bulwer, on the unveiling of the window taking place, addressed the vicar and churchwardens, handing over the window to their care and keeping. After an address by the Bishop the ceremony was concluded, and the visitors were entertained by the officers of both battalions at luncheon at the depôt and a garden party later on by the officers of the depôt. The committee which had charge of collecting the funds for the new window were General Crutchley (Colonel of the regiment), President ; General Sir D. Lysons, G.C.B. ; General Sir E. G. Bulwer, K.C.B. ; Major-General the Hon. Savage Mostyn, C.B. ; Lieutenant-Colonel Howard Vincent, C.B., M.P. ; and the Officers commanding the 1st and 2nd battalions Royal Welch Fusiliers and 23rd Regimental District, *ex officio* members.

Major E. H. Clough-Taylor was secretary, and Captain Dunn had charge of the local arrangements.

In September a draft of 100 non-commissioned officers and men left Manchester for Southampton for service in India with the 1st battalion at Jhansi.

1896.

1st Battalion.

On the 1st of March " E " and " G " companies, under command of Captain J. L. Locke, proceeded to Nowgong by route march to form the detachment there.

On the 4th of March Major C. C. H. Thorold was appointed to command the battalion vice Lieutenant-Colonel H. W. Griffith.

On the 16th of October Lieutenant-Colonel Thorold, 17 officers, 731 non-commissioned officers and men left Jhansi by rail en route for Aden, embarking on the 3rd of October in the S.S. *Victoria* and landing at Aden on the 28th of October. Major H. T. Lyle, D.S.O., and 250 non-commissioned officers and men continued the voyage to join the 2nd battalion at Malta.

1896.

2ND BATTALION

The regimental goat having died last year of pneumonia, Her Majesty Queen Victoria was pleased to send another in its place from Windsor Park; it arrived at Manchester in the second week in June.

On the 8th of July the battalion left Manchester for Malta, disembarking there on the 16th.

On the same day the establishment was increased by 4 subalterns, 7 sergeants, and 200 privates.

On the 6th of November a draft of 250 men under the command of Major H. T. Lyle, D.S.O., arrived, being transferred from the 1st battalion on its moving from Jhansi to Aden. Lieutenant C. M. Dobell was also transferred, and did duty with this draft. On the 18th of that month a draft of 153 men under Major the Hon. R. H. Bertie joined from the Provisional Battalion at Shorncliffe.

1897.

1ST BATTALION.

On the 21st of November Lieutenant-Colonel Thorold, 16 officers, and 618 rank and file embarked at Aden in the S.S. *Dilwara* en route to Devonport.

On arrival in Devonport on the 9th of December, headquarters and four companies proceeded to Fort Tregantle, three companies (" D," " E," and " F ") going to Millbay, and " C " company to Bull Point; and on the same day 2 officers and 116 non-commissioned officers and men joined from the Provisional Battalion.

1897.

2ND BATTALION.

Turkish misrule in Crete had at the commencement of this year reached such a pitch that pillage, murder, and incendiarism were rampant, the Turkish Government being impotent to stop them.

On the 8th of February the Cretan insurgents proclaimed union with

Greece, which thereupon sent a flotilla of torpedo boats, followed by a force of over 1,500 men and two batteries, to Crete.

As a counterblast to this expedition, Canea, the capital of the island, was occupied by detachments of sailors from the fleets of the Great Powers. Despite the presence of an international force, fighting took place between the Greeks and Turks. The situation became so critical that on the 2nd of March the Powers addressed a joint Note to the Greek Government, in which they stated in plain terms that, under existing circumstances, they would not permit of the annexation of Crete to Greece.

With a view to coercing the latter the Powers proclaimed a blockade of the Cretan ports, and followed it up by dispatching a mixed force to occupy the island.

Consequently on the 30th of March the headquarters and four companies of the battalion were ordered to hold themselves in readiness to proceed there at an early date.

They embarked on the 6th of April in the hired transport *Malacca*, and landed at Candia on the 9th and 10th of April.

The following was the embarkation strength: Lieutenant-Colonel R. B. Mainwaring; Majors H. J. Archdale, J. H. K. Griffith; Captains S. G. Everitt, B. K. Hanbury; Lieutenants H. Rotherham, O. S. Flower, G. F. H. Dickson, J. A. Higgon; 2nd Lieutenants F. C. France-Hayhurst, H. Hill, W. Lloyd, R. B. Johnson, G. J. P. Geiger; Lieutenant and Adjutant C. M. Dobell, Hon. Lieutenant and Quartermaster J. E. F. Barr, Sergeant-Major Hickman, 22 sergeants, 18 corporals, 8 drummers, 324 privates: total all ranks, 389. Captain B. H. Philips had previously been selected to act as Staff Officer to Colonel Chermside, C.B., C.M.G., commanding the British troops in Crete.

On the 6th of July a draft of 67 privates reached headquarters from the wing at Malta, under command of Lieutenant G. E. Rickman, who returned to Malta the same day. This brought the strength at headquarters up to 400 rifles.

On the 30th of July at 9.30 p.m. orders were received for the wing at Malta to proceed to join headquarters in Crete at once. At 2 p.m. on the 31st of July "A," "B," "D," and "F" companies embarked on board H.M.S. *Tyne*, arriving in Candia, Crete, on the 3rd of August.

The following was the strength of the wing: Captains J. H. Gwynne, C. H. M. Doughty; Lieutenants R. A. Berners (acting Quartermaster), A. Hay (acting Adjutant); 2nd Lieutenants F. J. Walwyn, F. A. Stebbing, C. A. Ball-Acton; 17 sergeants, 18 corporals, 9 drummers, 370 privates.

After the departure of the wing, a depôt company was formed under command of Lieutenant G. E. Rickman with Lieutenant E. T. Le Marchant. This company remained in Verdala Barracks, Malta.

The celebration of the Diamond Jubilee of Her Majesty Queen Victoria was held on 22nd June 1897. The Admirals of the International Fleets with their flagships assembled at Candia, Crete, to participate in the celebration.

A review of the British troops at Candia was held in honour of the occasion.

The troops were inspected by the Admirals and afterwards marched past as follows :

    4th Mountain Battery.
    2nd Battalion Royal Welch Fusiliers.
    1st Battalion Seaforth Highlanders.

On the withdrawal of the 1st Seaforth Highlanders from the island, consequent on the reduction of the British force in Crete, the 2nd Battalion Royal Welch Fusiliers was called upon to furnish a detachment of 2 companies, 220 of all ranks, at Canea. " C " and " D " companies were detailed for this duty, and on the 21st November proceeded there under command of Major H. J. Archdale.

On the 1st of December the 1st Battalion Royal Welch Fusiliers touched at Malta en route from Aden to Devonport. A draft of 100 privates was disembarked for service with the 2nd Battalion.

Lieutenant O. de L. Williams, who had been transferred from the 1st battalion to the 2nd battalion, accompanied this draft.

The draft joined headquarters in Crete on the 8th of January 1898.

1898.

1st Battalion.

On the 10th of January 2 officers and 32 non-commissioned officers and men proceeded to Aldershot for a course of instruction in " Mounted Infantry Duties," returning on the 16th of March.

General Sir Edward Gascoyne Bulwer, K.C.B., was appointed Colonel of the regiment, vice General C. Crutchley, deceased, 31st March.

On the 1st of April Sergeant J. Rogers was awarded the medal for Long Service and Good Conduct.

Six officers and 150 rank and file proceeded to Newport in aid of the Civil Power on the 14th June, returning on the 22nd June.

On the 27th of July 8 officers, 200 rank and file proceeded to South Wales, distributed as follows:

	Rank and file.	Officers.
Newport	100	4
Mountain Ash	50	2
Aberdare	50	2

and on the 30th July the force was augmented by 2 officers and 50 rank and file proceeding to Merthyr Tydvil.

On the 3rd of September 4 officers and 100 non-commissioned officers and men rejoined the battalion on completion of special duty in South Wales.

On the 9th of September the battalion moved into the Raglan Barracks, Devonport.

On the 13th of September 4 officers and 100 non-commissioned officers and men rejoined the battalion on completion of special duty in South Wales.

In accordance with a War Office letter dated 8th December approval was given for the letter " R " to be prefixed to the " W.F." already worn on the shoulder straps of the regiment.

The annual report of Musketry Instruction in India for the year 1897–98 shows the battalion to be the best shooting battalion in India for that year.

1898.

2ND BATTALION.

On the 30th of March General Charles Crutchley died, and was succeeded in the Colonelcy of the regiment by General Sir Edward Bulwer, K.C.B.

Colonel Sir Herbert Chermside, K.C.M.G., C.B., Colonel on the Staff commanding the British troops in Crete, inspected the battalion at Candia on 11th, 12th, 13th, and 14th April.

Owing to the troops in Egypt being engaged in the Nile Expedition, the 2nd battalion was ordered from Crete to do garrison duty in Cairo.

The battalion embarked at Candia on the 3rd August 1898, on H.M. hired transport *Jelunga*, and arrived at Cairo on the 6th and 7th of August.

The following was the strength on reaching Cairo: 26 officers, 2 warrant officers, 41 sergeants, 16 drummers, 878 rank and file.

Headquarters and five companies were quartered at the Citadel, and three companies at Kasr-el-Nil Barracks.

GENERAL SIR EDWARD E. G. BULWER, G.C.B.
From an engraving by Walton.

On the 6th of September the Moslem population of Candia, Crete, rose, attacked the Highland Light Infantry who formed the British garrison, and massacred the Christians. It was therefore considered necessary to send more British troops to Crete, and on 10th September the battalion was ordered to be held in readiness to return to Crete at an early date.

On the same evening the battalion left Cairo in two trains for Alexandria, and on the 11th embarked on S.S. *Matiana*, and disembarked at Candia on the 13th of September.

The battalion was encamped on the ramparts.

On the 12th of December the embarkation of the battalion from Candia for Hong-Kong, on hired transport S.S. *Avoca*, was commenced.

Owing to the strong wind and heavy sea it was not until the evening of the 14th that all were aboard.

At Suez on the 17th the depôt company from Cairo joined headquarters.

The strength, including a draft of 114 non-commissioned officers and men from 1st battalion which had arrived on S.S. *Avoca*, was: 20 officers, 2 warrant officers, 38 sergeants, 16 drummers, 33 corporals, 888 privates.

1899.

1st Battalion.

The battalion went through the ceremony of Trooping the Colours on the 1st of March, at which were present a majority of the old officers of the regiment, including General Sir E. Bulwer, K.C.B., Colonels Holroyd, Creek, Williamson, and Norman.

On the 11th of May the battalion formed a Guard of Honour to the Commander-in-Chief (Lord Wolseley) on the occasion of an official visit to Devonport.

At the Royal Military Tournament on the 25th of May the Regimental Team secured the third place in the Bayonet Exercise Competition open to the Army.

At the Annual Inspection of Signalling in 1899 the Battalion Figure of Merit was 132·66 out of a possible 135: the D.A.A.G. for Signalling having occasion to note the admirable performance of the battalion.

On the 8th of August the battalion proceeded to Salisbury Plain for the Autumn manœuvres, returning therefrom on the 5th of September, proceeding direct to Pembroke Dock in relief of the South Wales Borderers.

The following is an extract from the report of the G.O.C. Western District on his inspection:

"The G.O.C. having completed his annual inspection of the unit

(28th July) has much pleasure in placing on record his satisfaction with the general appearance of the Battalion on parade and their conduct in garrison.

"The strong esprit de corps which animates all ranks has a very good influence in the Battalion.

"The result of the signalling examination was highly creditable."

In a Convention between Great Britain and the Transvaal signed in 1884, the former as the paramount power in South Africa defined the conditions under which, and the extent to which, the latter as a dependent State would be permitted to manage its own affairs. Hardly, however, was it signed before Paul Kruger, President of the South African Republic, set about making it a dead letter, with the object of establishing a sovereign international state in South Africa, which would strike a deadly blow at British interests there.

Eventually the question of the enfranchisement of British subjects in the Transvaal (styled "Uitlanders" by the Boers) brought matters to a crisis. "The spectacle of thousands of British subjects kept permanently in the position of helots" was steadily undermining the influence and reputation of Great Britain.

As the counter proposals of President Kruger for the settlement of this burning question could not be entertained by the British Government, it became evident that war was inevitable. On the 7th of October 1899 an order was issued from the War Office directing the immediate mobilisation of a field force for service in South Africa.

On the 8th of October the battalion received orders to mobilise for active service in South Africa, the Reservists being mobilised on the 9th, and on the 23rd of that month it proceeded from Pembroke Dock to Southampton and embarked on the S.S. *Oriental* under orders for East London to join the 6th Fusilier Brigade under Major-General Geoffrey Barton, which, together with the 5th Irish Brigade under Major-General Fitzroy Hart, composed the 3rd Division commanded by Lieutenant-General Sir W. Gatacre, D.S.O.

The following embarked with the battalion : Lieutenant-Colonel C. C. H. Thorold, Major H. J. Archdale ; Captains A. Gough, P. R. Mantell, R. M. O. Glynn, G. F. Barttelot, H. Delmé-Radcliffe, R. C. B. Throckmorton, and R. G. B. Lovett ; Lieutenants G. F. H. Dickson, O. de L. Williams, G. E. S. Salt, F. A. Stebbing, and W. M. Kingston ; 2nd Lieutenants D. Powell, H. Maddick, F. C. A. Hurt, C. C. Norman, F. H. Nangle, A. H. Reynolds, E. A. T. Bayly, W. J. H. Hughes, and H. V. V. Kyrke ; Captain and Adjutant W. G. Braithwaite, Lieutenant and Quartermaster R. S.

Ransome, Major B. Langley Mills, R.A.M.C., and 1,074 warrant officers, non-commissioned officers, and men.

From the above the battalion furnished a section composed of 30 non-commissioned officers and men under Lieutenant the Hon. C. R. Clegg-Hill to the 2nd Battalion Mounted Infantry.

The early events of the war having necessitated a change in the distribution of the units of the South African Field Force from that originally contemplated, the battalion on arrival at Cape Town on the 13th of November received fresh orders to proceed to Durban in order to form part of a special force, under the command of Major-General Sir Francis Clery, for the protection of Natal, and the relief of Sir George White's force, which was besieged in Ladysmith.

The battalion arrived at Durban on the 17th of November and at once entrained for Mooi River, which was reached on the following morning, dropping en route at Pietermaritzburg Lieutenant Stebbing with 25 sick and 18 other details to form a divisional base. Both officers and men had a trying time at the Mooi River owing to hard work and outpost duties.

On the 22nd of November and the two following days the camp was shelled by the Boers from a hill estimated to be 8,000 yards distant, at which range the field guns were unable to reply; however, very little damage was done.

On the 26th of November the battalion left Mooi River for Estcourt, a march of 23 miles, which was accomplished in seven hours. While there Captains R. S. Webber and G. E. Rickman joined the battalion.

On the 9th of December the battalion marched to join Major-General Sir F. Clery's Division at Frere. The regimental goat left there on the 10th for the General Depôt, Pietermaritzburg. At 1 a.m. on the 11th the Royal Welch Fusiliers, the 2nd Battalion Royal Fusiliers, and half of the 2nd Battalion of the Royal Scots Fusiliers made a night march and seized a ridge beyond Chieveley, which was occupied at 8 a.m. by the naval guns. A bombardment of the Colenso position was commenced immediately afterwards at a range of 10,900 yards.

On the afternoon of the 14th of December Sir Redvers Buller determined to attempt the passage of the Tugela at Colenso on the following day.

The main attack was to be made in the direction of Colenso by General Hildyard's 2nd Brigade, which was to cross the river by the Iron Bridge at Colenso, and gain possession of the kopjes north of that point. The 5th [Irish] Brigade (Major-General Hart's) was to cover the left flank of the main attack.

The Mounted Brigade was to move at 4 a.m. with 1,000 men and 1 battery Royal Field Artillery to cover the right flank of the general movement. The 6th Fusiliers Brigade (Major-General Barton's), less half a battalion escort to the baggage, was ordered to move at 4 a.m. east of the railway in the direction of Hlangwane to a position whence it could protect the right flank of the 2nd Brigade, and, if necessary, support the mounted troops moving against Hlangwane. The 4th Brigade (Major-General Lyttelton's) was to be in reserve.

In accordance with Sir Redvers Buller's orders the Fusilier Brigade moved at 4 a.m. on the 15th of December, the Royal Artillery forming the advance guard, with the two batteries of No. 1 Brigade Division (and naval 12-pounders attached) on the left of the Brigade; Dundonald's Mounted Troops and the 7th Battery Royal Field Artillery on the right, the former scouting well to the right front and flank in the direction of Hlangwane.

There is a conflict of evidence as to the exact formation of the Royal Welch Fusiliers, and the distribution of the companies, but by comparison of the various sources (official and private) of information available, it appears that at the commencement of the advance the battalion had six companies in line, each having a sub-section in its front, and the remaining two companies in regimental reserve.

The 2nd Battalion Royal Scots Fusiliers, less half the battalion at Frere, was in echelon of companies on the left flank. The 2nd Battalion Royal Fusiliers was in echelon of companies on the right flank, and the 2nd Battalion Royal Irish Fusiliers, less half the battalion on baggage guard, was some 1,500 yards in rear of the leading battalion.

After a time the respective directions assigned to the guns and Fusilier Brigade diverged, and Major-General Barton detailed two companies of the Royal Scots Fusiliers to accompany the guns as immediate escort.

At 5.30 a.m. Barton halted his Brigade when the leading battalion was still about two miles from the river, but Colonel Long's guns were pushed on in advance of the infantry to reach a position from which they could cover the attack of the 2nd Brigade on the Colenso kopjes. When these guns, having been brought into action within effective rifle fire, were beginning to suffer heavily, four companies of the Royal Irish Fusiliers were pushed forward to assist the escort of two companies of the Royal Scots Fusiliers.

In order to meet any advance of the enemy from the bush near the river on the right front of the guns, the Brigadier had moved the Royal Welch Fusiliers some 1,000 yards nearer the point where they had first halted.

The final position of the battalion was about 1,500 yards from the river facing north by east. Counting from left to right " H," " G," " D," and " C " companies formed the firing line and supports, with " F," " E," " B," and " A " companies in reserve.

The battalion remained in this position under shell fire, which did but little damage, until the order to retire was given about 3.30 p.m. When the disaster occurred to Colonel Long's guns " H " company under Captain Rickman, supported by " G " company under Captain Glynn, was pushed forward in order to assist the companies of the Royal Scots Fusiliers and Royal Irish Fusiliers in repelling any attempt by the Boers to cross the river and carry off the guns.

The order for the retirement did not reach " H " company of the battalion, which was then close to the river, consequently Captain Rickman only retired just in time to avoid capture by the Boers, who took possession of the ten abandoned guns of the 16th and 44th batteries.

As it did not fall to the lot of the Royal Welch Fusiliers to take a conspicuous part in the engagement the casualties suffered were correspondingly few—three men only, Privates W. Meek, J. Horner, and David Jones, being wounded. This slight loss was also probably due to the fact that the Boer fire, long reserved, was chiefly directed in this part of the field on Long's guns.

The crashing sound caused by the outburst of hostile fire when it did come is described by several officers as terrific. Lieutenant Harris in his diary states: " When within easy rifle-range—my scouts (' D ' company Royal Welch Fusiliers) were beginning to climb the hill (Hlangwane)—there was a terrific rattle of musketry: sounding like a very heavy hailstorm on a tin roof, and I looked round wondering why no bullets had arrived, then I saw what the Boers were firing at. Colonel Long's two batteries were then galloping back from a line of thick bush close to the river and soon unlimbered and opened fire." The same officer remarks : " It was the general opinion of all that the guns could have been saved by leaving a force entrenched within rifle fire, and then removing them under cover of darkness."

On the 17th of December the Brigade settled down in a new camp near Chieveley station.

1899.

2nd Battalion.

On the 13th of January the battalion disembarked at Hong-Kong, and was quartered as follows: headquarters and 3½ companies at Murray and Queen's Road Barracks, 3 companies at Mount Austin Barracks, 1½ companies at Gun Club Hill, Kowloon.

The following are extracts from the *London Gazette*:

"10th March 1899.

Royal Welch Fusiliers."

Lieut.-Colonel R. B. Mainwaring to be Brevet-Colonel.

Captain Sir H. W. McMahon, Bart., D.S.O., to be Brevet-Major.

Lieutenant C. M. Dobell is noted for consideration for the Brevet rank of Major on promotion to the rank of Captain.

"26th May 1899.

Captain C. M. Dobell, The Royal Welch Fusiliers, to be Major in recognition of his services during occupation of Crete, dated 8th March 1899.

"20th June 1899.

The Queen has been graciously pleased to give directions for the following promotions in, and appointments to, the Most Distinguished Order of Saint Michael and Saint George.

"To be ordinary members of the Third Class or Companion of the said Most Distinguished Order.

"Lieut.-Colonel and Brevet-Colonel R. B. Mainwaring for services rendered in Crete, dated 3rd June."

Lieutenant-Colonel and Brevet-Colonel R. B. Mainwaring left on the 21st June on giving up command to take up the appointment of A.A. General at Portsmouth.

The battalion assisted in the taking over of the additional territory recently leased from the Chinese at Kowloon, over which the British flag was hoisted on the 16th of April.

Lieutenant-Colonel the Hon. R. H. Bertie arrived on the 15th of December and took over command of the battalion.

1900.

1st Battalion.

With the exception of a demonstration towards Colenso in January intended to divert the attention of part of the Boer forces then engaged in the grand attack on the Cæsar's Camp and Wagon Hill defences of Ladysmith, the Fusilier Brigade remained quietly in their camp at Chieveley, employed in strengthening its defences until the commencement of Sir Redvers Buller's movement on the 10th of January towards Springfield, which resulted in the operations about Spion Kop and Vaal Krantz.

During these latter operations Major-General Barton's force, by constant demonstrations against Colenso, shelling their works, and vigorous patrolling, succeeded in keeping considerably more than 3,000 of the enemy immobile round Colenso, in spite of urgent and reiterated appeals from Louis Botha to Lucas Meyer for help on the Upper Tugela.

After the failure to relieve Ladysmith by way of Spion Kop and Vaal Krantz Sir Redvers Buller decided on the 7th of February to make another attempt by getting possession of Hlangwane. The Boers, however, always nervous since the 15th of December for the safety of their left flank, isolated as Hlangwane was on the south bank of the river, had by this time constructed strong entrenchments all along the front overlooking the northern slopes of the Gomba Valley from Hlangwane to Green Hill, with their left flank thrown back via Monte Cristo to the river.

The discovery of this fact by a reconnaissance carried out by a mixed force consisting of the 2nd Cavalry Brigade, Royal Welch Fusiliers, a battery of Royal Field Artillery, and some Royal Engineers on the 11th of February caused some delay, and it was not until the 13th that orders were issued for the advance on Hussar Hill by the 2nd and 5th Divisions on the 14th of February.

At 7 a.m. that day Sir Redvers Buller moved out of Chieveley Camp with Dundonald's Cavalry Brigade, the 2nd Division under Lyttelton, and the 5th Division under Sir Charles Warren, to which was attached Barton's 6th Fusilier Brigade which led the advance, with the Royal Fusiliers and Royal Welch Fusiliers as advance guard, making for the highest point of Hussar Hill, supported by the 5th Division on the left rear, while the 2nd Division, working out of sight, moved along the valley of the Blauw Krantz in the direction of Mooi Kraal.

The Boer skirmishers under pressure of the Fusiliers' advance evacuated

Hussar Hill and took position in the dongas north-west and north-east of it, leading to the Gomba stream, whence they sniped for the rest of the day. As the two leading companies, "D" and "H," under command of Captains Barttelot and Rickman respectively, crossed the crest line, they were subjected to a very hot fire at close range. Half of "D" company, under Lieutenant Harris, occupied a kraal to the front and spent the rest of the day there under fire at 600 yards. The remainder of the battalion spent the day in entrenching the position under an annoying shell fire of Creusot guns and Pom-poms, in spite of which the battalion had only 9 men wounded. Private Vipond, however, died of his wounds.

On the 15th of February the 2nd Division occupied Mooi Kraal Hill: Sir Charles Warren connected the right of the 5th Division with Lyttelton by dispatching the Fusilier Brigade to seize a wooded spur about one mile east of Hussar Hill. On the 16th and 17th the 61st Howitzer Battery, Royal Field Artillery, escorted by "D" company Royal Welch Fusiliers, shelled the enemy's position on Green Hill, making fine practice.

Lyttelton having captured Cingolo on the 17th, Monte Cristo was attacked on the 18th by the 2nd Division assisted from the east by Dundonald's mounted troops. As soon as the crest of the hill was won, the 6th and 4th Brigades, which had previously, in anticipation of the order, been extended facing Green Hill and the ridge connecting it with Monte Cristo, were directed to carry those positions, which were taken with the loss of 1 private, W. Williams, killed, and 6 privates wounded, only to find the Boers in full retreat towards Hlangwane. Major-General Barton was anxious to push on in pursuit towards the Boer bridge below the waterfall, only four miles distant, and had immediately after the successful attack reorganised the Fusilier Brigade for the purpose, but was ordered to stop. Thus a splendid opportunity was lost for inflicting heavy loss on the Boers, encumbered as they were with waggons and baggage in their retreat across the only bridge which connected them with their main force on the left bank of the Tugela.

During these operations the troops suffered greatly from want of drinking water, as the Gomba stream was found to be dry. A certain amount of water was obtainable by digging about six inches down in the sandy bed of the river, but unfortunately it proved to be contaminated, thereby laying the seeds of the severe outbreak of enteric fever which took place at Modder Spruit after the relief of Ladysmith, costing the Royal Welch Fusiliers the life amongst others of Lieutenant Salt.

On the 19th of February the Fusilier Brigade, supported by the 10th Brigade under Colonel (local Major-General) Coke, occupied Hlangwane unopposed, the Royal Fusiliers being on the right and the Royal Welch Fusiliers on the left of the first line.

Owing to a misunderstanding the kopjes north of Hlangwane were not occupied by the Brigade until the 20th: the Boer snipers on these kopjes, as well as the riflemen in the hills on the left bank, and the hostile guns in the Colenso kopjes, subjected the troops to an annoying cross fire.

From the top of Hlangwane thousands of Boers and miles of waggons could be seen in full and disorderly retreat towards the north, and it looked as if Ladysmith would be relieved without further fighting.

The enemy, observing the comparative inaction of the British on the 19th and 20th of January, and the entire absence of any pursuit, took heart again, and were persuaded by Botha to reoccupy their formidable positions on the left bank of the Tugela, from which they were only dislodged after heavy loss.

By seven o'clock on the morning of the 20th of February reconnoitring patrols found Colenso deserted and that no Boers were left south of the Tugela. Shortly afterwards the crest of the hills on the right bank of the river was occupied by the 2nd Division, while on the left Sir Charles Warren moved part of the 6th Brigade along the spur which, jutting out from the northern end of Hlangwane, overlooks the Tugela near the Boer bridge below the waterfalls.

The Royal Scots Fusiliers held this spur; the Royal Welch Fusiliers held Hlangwane with the rest of the Brigade about three-quarters of a mile to the rear in support.

By the evening of this day, with the exception of Hart's Brigade at Chieveley, a battalion of the 2nd Brigade (Hildyard's) at Monte Cristo, Thorneycroft's Mounted Infantry watching the left flank of the army, Dundonald's vedettes on Monte Cristo and along the Tugela to the junction of the Blauwbank, nearly the whole of Buller's force was concentrated in the space bounded by the river west of Hlangwane, Naval Hill, Bloy's Farm, and Hussar Hill.

At 5.30 a.m. on the 21st the Royal Welch Fusiliers and Royal Irish Fusiliers had been moved down to the river bank to cover the construction by the Royal Engineers of the heavy pontoon bridge west of Hlangwane.

The troops streamed across this bridge all night, so that by the morning of the 22nd the greater part of the infantry was concentrated on the left bank of the Tugela. Major-General Barton's Fusiliers extended along the heights overhanging the right bank of the river as far as the Boer bridge and guarded the pontoon bridge, which, owing to the Colenso bridge being broken, constituted the only sure means of passage over the otherwise impassable Tugela.

At 2 p.m. on the 22nd of February the 11th Brigade (Wynne's) advanced to the attack of the hill that now bears his name, otherwise known as Hedge Hill. Thanks to the support of the artillery and the long-range covering fire of the Fusilier Brigade from the western slopes of Naval Hill, the 11th Brigade effected a lodgment with little loss on that part of Wynne's Hill which overlooked the railway; but on pushing on towards the stone breastworks occupied by the Boers on the further crest they found themselves subjected to a severe cross fire from Terrace Hill, the broken ground about the Langewacht Spruit, Grobelaar Mountain, and above all from Horse Shoe Hill, which had not been occupied by troops of another brigade, as Colonel (local Major-General) Wynne had understood would be the case when he planned his attack on Hedge Hill. The attack was thereby brought to a standstill until part of the Rifle Reserve Battalion succeeded in making a lodgment on the south-eastern crest of Horse Shoe Hill, by which time, however, night had fallen, thus obliging the British artillery to cease fire, and enabling the Boers to make a vigorous counter-attack on Wynne Hill, which caused severe pressure on the 11th Brigade until the East Surrey and Devon Regiments were brought up to reinforce them.

Orders were given for the attack of Terrace Hill—afterwards known as Hart's Hill—on the 23rd of February by the 5th [Irish] Brigade (Hart's).

At 6 p.m. on this day Major-General Barton was ordered to send two battalions across to the left bank of the Tugela to Horse Shoe Hill to replace two battalions lent by Lyttelton to Hart. The battalions selected for this duty were the Royal Fusiliers and the Royal Welch Fusiliers, who arrived at Horse Shoe Hill after dark. The battalions were posted, as well as the darkness would permit, on the southern crest of the flat-topped kopje, the Royal Fusiliers being on the right in touch with the Queen's on Wynne's Hill.

At dawn on the 24th these battalions found themselves engaged in front at 300 to 400 yards range by the Boer trenches lining the northern crest of the Horse Shoe Hill, enfiladed on both flanks—some of the enemy's trenches on the left being only 200 yards distant—while the position was completely commanded by the Boer guns on Grobelaar Mountain.

Arriving on the position after dark when it was impossible to see the nature of the ground, the sangars which had been built during the night only afforded cover from frontal fire, and gave no shelter from that coming from the flanks.

All that day the battalion lay exposed to a fire so severe, and delivered at such close range, that the diaries kept by some of the officers of the regiment record that it was impossible to raise a finger above the skyline without instantly drawing fire. The whole of the Royal Welch companies were engaged—half a company being in the firing line, half in support in rear of the crest.

The Boers had the range to a nicety, and Lieutenant Harris relates in his diary that by 10 a.m. about 11 men in his half-company (" D ") had been hit, some in three or four places. Those who were unable to crawl down the hill had to remain where they were, as it was impossible to move them, or to bring up rations or water until darkness set in.

The casualties this day were Lieutenant-Colonel C. C. H. Thorold, Lieutenant Stebbing, Corporal J. Evans, Privates G. Cox, S. Pike, R. Birkett, E. Evans, and R. Joyce killed, and Lieutenant C. C. Norman and 29 rank and file wounded, one of whom, Private J. Smith, died on the 27th. In Lieutenant-Colonel Thorold the battalion lost a most popular and able commanding officer, whose death was universally deplored.

The Boers attacked the position during the night, and a terrific fusillade lasted for about two hours, the Royal Welch Fusiliers alone expending 5,800 rounds of ammunition; one man, Private W. Jephcote, was killed, and two wounded. That the attackers got pretty close was proved by the fact that one of their loaded rifles was picked up next morning by Lieutenant Dickson within twenty yards of the sangar he occupied.

On the 26th Lieutenant Salt and his maxim-gun detachment greatly distinguished themselves by keeping the gun in action under a heavy close-range fire, by which the non-commissioned officer and No. 1 of the detachment—Corporal Roberts and Private Clarke—were dangerously wounded. Lieutenant Salt then worked the gun by himself until the foresight was shot away and the gun jammed owing to the piercing of the water-jacket by a bullet. Salt had a bullet through his helmet and there were 51 bullet holes in the gun and carriage. He was recommended for the D.S.O. by Sir Redvers Buller, but never lived to wear it, owing to his untimely death by enteric fever at Modder Spruit shortly after the relief of Ladysmith.

On the 27th of February Hart's, Railway, and Pieter's Hill were captured after hard fighting which put an end to the long and strenuous resistance of the Boers on the Tugela; on the 26th 1 private was wounded, and on the 27th Private W. Williams was killed and 8 privates wounded.

On the 3rd of March the battalion took part in the formal entry of Buller's army into Ladysmith. The casualties of the Brigade from the

22nd to the 26th of February were 18 officers and 350 rank and file killed and wounded.

After the relief of Ladysmith the 5th Brigade (Hart's) and the 6th [Fusilier] Brigade (Barton's) were formed into the 10th Division under Major-General Sir Archibald Hunter, K.C.B., D.S.O. On March the 12th the Fusilier Brigade marched to Modder Spruit, about 5½ miles north-east of Ladysmith, which proved to be an excellent camping-ground. While in this camp the battalion was reinforced on the 15th by the arrival from England of 2nd Lieutenants Williams and Ellis, 100 Reservists of Section D, and on the same afternoon the Volunteer Company (114 all ranks) under the command of Captain Keene, and Lieutenants Jones, Parry, and Bamford, which brought the strength of the battalion up to 31 officers and 1,200 non-commissioned officers and men.

The following is a copy of a commendatory letter received about this time from Major-General H. Hildyard, commanding the 2nd Infantry Brigade:

"SURPRISE HILL CAMP, 6th March, 1900.

"The 2nd battalion Royal Fusiliers under Lieutenant-Colonel Donald and the 1st battalion Royal Welch Fusiliers under Lieutenant-Colonel Thorold were attached to my Brigade from 24th to 27th February 1900. Exceptional coolness and gallantry were exhibited by all ranks during a very trying period. They were exposed daily to a close frontal fire from the enemy's trenches at a range in some cases of 200 yards, and were also subjected to a harassing enfilading fire, both rifle and artillery, and at night to a series of alarums very trying to their morale. Their conduct throughout was most gratifying and was worthy of the high reputation of both regiments. I deeply regret the loss of Colonel Thorold, who was killed while going round his defences. The command was then assumed by Captain Gough. Lieutenant-Colonel Thorold had been placed by me in charge of the left section of the defence, which after he was wounded was taken over by Colonel Donald, who conducted it in an efficient manner until the withdrawal."

The regimental goat rejoined the battalion for duty on the 25th of March.

On the 3rd of April Lieutenant Salt, whose gallant conduct has been already narrated, died, greatly regretted by all ranks.

On the 7th of April orders were received for the 10th Division to proceed to Cape Colony. On Good Friday, April 13th, the strength of the battalion was 29 officers and 1,271 N.C.O.s and men. The battalion

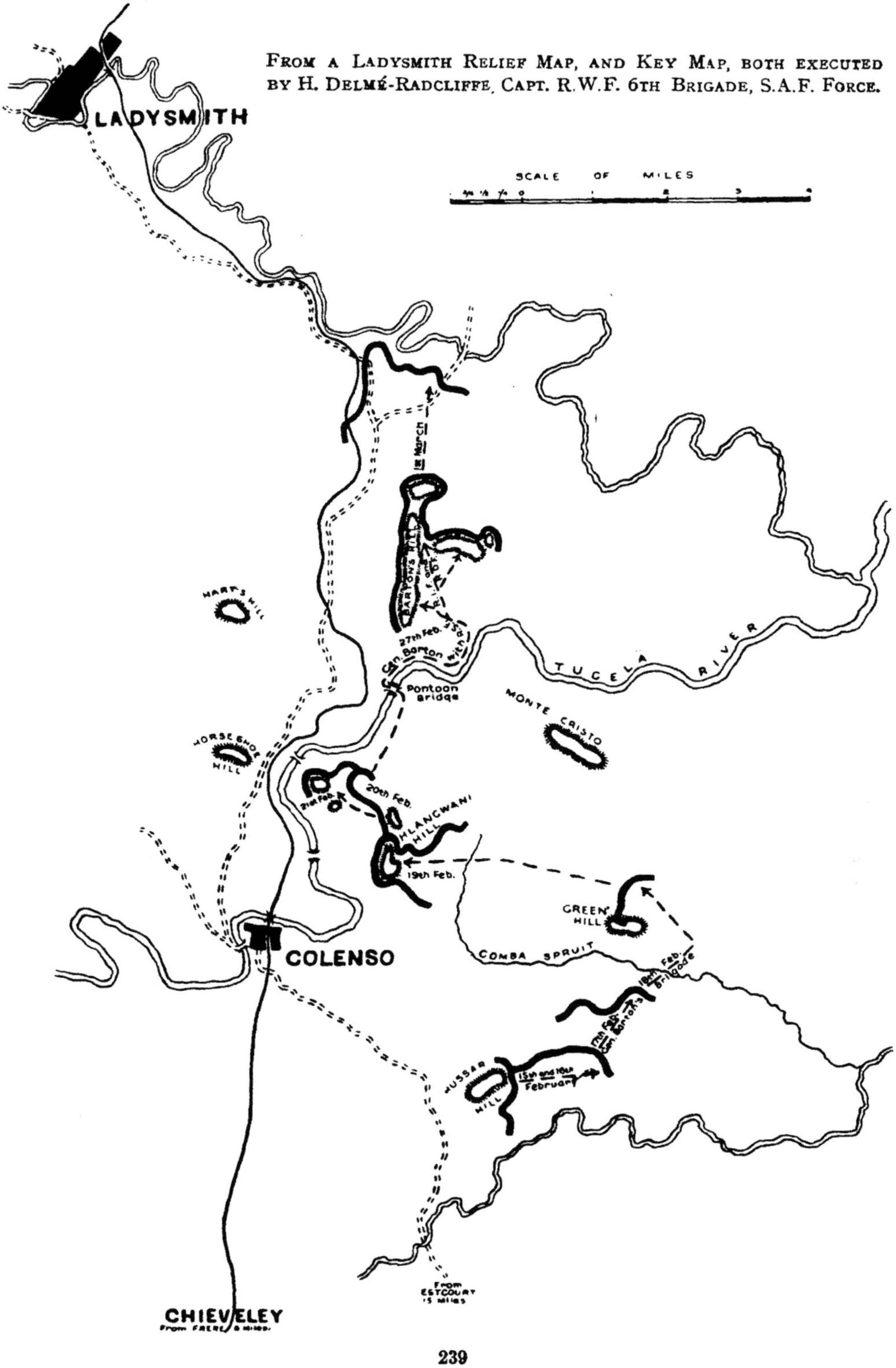

FROM A LADYSMITH RELIEF MAP, AND KEY MAP, BOTH EXECUTED BY H. DELMÉ-RADCLIFFE, CAPT. R.W.F. 6TH BRIGADE, S.A.F. FORCE.

left Ladysmith on the 14th at 4 p.m. in four special trains and embarked at Durban on Easter Sunday, the 15th of April, in the *Hawarden Castle* in under 2½ hours and sailed at 4.45 p.m.; arriving at Cape Town on the 19th. Owing to a paucity of rolling stock the battalion did not disembark until the 25th of April, when it entrained, and arrived at Dronfield Camp about six miles north of Kimberley on the 28th.

A draft from England of 100 men joined the battalion at this camp, bringing its effective strength up to 27 officers and 1,099 non-commissioned officers and men, exclusive of 225 sick left behind in Natal and at Cape Town, mostly suffering from enteric and dysentery.

On the 21st of April General Sir A. Hunter arrived at Kimberley, and was entrusted by Lord Roberts with the task of relieving Mafeking. It was decided to form a flying column in which was included a body of 100 picked infantry of which each battalion of the Fusilier Brigade furnished 25 men representing the United Kingdom. The honour of commanding those drawn from the Royal Welch Fusiliers fell to 2nd Lieutenant V. V. Kyrke.

On the 1st of May Captain Gough commanding the battalion went sick with fever, and Captain P. R. Mantell assumed command.

The flying column, under Colonel Mahon, started from Barkly West on the 4th of May. In order to protect Mahon's march Sir A. Hunter moved on the 5th towards Rooidam, where Generals Liebenberg and S. P. du Toit had taken up a position, the Royal Welch Fusiliers in advance guard. Sir A. Hunter resolved to turn the Boer right, and deployed his troops for this purpose.

The 2nd battalion Royal Scots Fusiliers and the 2nd battalion Royal Irish Fusiliers were sent to the east to guard the right flank by threatening the Boer left, and to prevent them from coming down on Windserton. Hunter pressed on with the 2nd battalion Royal Fusiliers, the 1st battalion of the Royal Welch Fusiliers, and the 28th and 78th batteries Royal Field Artillery. Major-General Barton on the left flank was directed to work through the scrub with the Royal Fusiliers and the Royal Welch Fusiliers, but not to cross the open ground until the artillery had had time to shell the position.

The advance began about noon, when a Boer gun firing black powder opened from a kopje on the enemy's left. The Royal Welch Fusiliers were extended to ten paces, having "A," "B," "C," and "H" companies in the firing line, in the order named from left to right; "G" company was echeloned to the right rear of the firing line; "D," "L" (the Volunteer Company), "E," and "F" being in reserve in rear of "A," "B,"

"C," and "H" companies respectively. The Royal Fusiliers followed on the left rear of the Royal Welch Fusiliers in echelon of companies, right in front. The right of the Royal Welch Fusiliers was directed on a point believed to be about the centre of the Boer position.

After advancing about 1,500 yards it was found that the main position, instead of being parallel to our line, had its right too much retired, while on the left of the Royal Welch Fusiliers their line was thrown forward, forming a salient along a row of most formidable rocky kopjes covered with scrub which gave admirable cover to the enemy. These kopjes enfiladed the advance of the battalion, but "A" and "B" companies, being a little to their right, supported by the cross fire of the others, stormed the foremost kopje. Captain Lovett, who had led "A" company in the most gallant manner, was mortally wounded in the head. He had endeared himself to all ranks, by whom his death was greatly regretted.

It was now apparent that if the Royal Welch Fusiliers, swinging round their left flank, were to continue to advance over the wide open space on front, the attack would become a direct frontal one and the loss heavy. The advance was therefore checked until the Royal Fusiliers, who were engaged in a wider enveloping movement, could come up and prolong the left flank. "A" company, under Lieutenant Dickson, ably assisted by Colour-Sergeant King, being in a very exposed position, were at this time subjected to a heavy fire which caused several casualties, but they were considerably assisted by the hot fire poured in by a handful of men of "B" and "D" companies, who had seized a stone enclosure near a Kaffir kraal, close up to a Boer position. By 2 p.m. the left of the line had worked round far enough to allow the left centre to push forward.

The final advance took place about 3 p.m. The Boers, threatened on their left by the Royal Irish Fusiliers, and turned on their right by the Imperial Yeomanry and Royal Horse Artillery, gave way before the advance of the Royal Fusiliers and Royal Welch Fusiliers, who carried the position after a stout resistance about 3.15 p.m. The Boers fled in the direction of Fourteen Streams, pursued for some miles by the Imperial Yeomanry.

The casualties suffered by the battalion in this action were: killed, Captain R. G. B. Lovett, Sergeant J. W. Graham, Privates F. Ballard, M. Maurice, F. Ledbrook, J. Leadbetter, J. Davies, and W. Dodd; wounded, Captain P. R. Mantell, commanding the battalion, Captain and Adjutant W. G. Braithwaite, and 14 rank and file.

Captain Braithwaite's behaviour on this occasion was admired by all. He was hit by two bullets while stooping down to carry a wounded man.

Colour-Sergeant W. G. King also distinguished himself by his leading of " A " company after Captain Lovett was mortally wounded. Captain McMahon of the Royal Fusiliers having been wounded, Captain Braithwaite took over the duties of Brigade-Major, 6th Brigade, and Lieutenant Dickson those of Adjutant of the 1st battalion of the Royal Welch Fusiliers.

On the 7th of May the force marched unopposed to Fourteen Streams and remained in the neighbourhood of that place until the 15th of the month.

On the 11th of May Captain Alan Gough on arrival from Kimberley took over command of the battalion from Captain Mantell. Orders having been received for the advance on Christiania, the force crossed the Transvaal border on May the 15th, being the first troops to cross the border.

The column was joined some eight miles from Fourteen Streams by the Scottish Yeomanry. On the 16th the march was resumed, the battalion being in the advanced guard. The force was halted about 1½ miles short of Christiania when Lieutenant-General Sir A. Hunter, escorted by 1 officer and 25 men from each of the battalions of the Fusilier Brigade (the Royal Welch Fusilier detachment being under 2nd Lieutenant Bayly), went forward and received the surrender of the town. The Union Jack was hoisted and three cheers given for the Queen. Boer arms and ammunition were collected and the former smashed.

On the 17th of May a flying column of which the Fusilier Brigade formed part moved in a northerly direction and occupied Schaapfontein on the following day. Tents were pitched here for the first time in three weeks.

On the 22nd of May the column marching along the railway arrived at Taungs.

On the 25th the battalion entrained at Taungs Station, and went to Vryburg. It left there on the 27th, and marching via Maribogo, De Klipdrift, and Kalkspruit, arrived at Lichtenburg on the 4th of June, where three days later the whole of the 10th Division was concentrated.

On the 7th 2nd Lieutenant Kyrke rejoined the battalion with his detachment after having taken part in the relief of Makeking under General Mahon. The detachment had earned high praise for its excellent marching: Lieutenant Kyrke himself marched 34 miles the first day, was on piquet the same night, and then marched 24 miles the following day without getting in the carts which had been provided for the tired men of the detachment of the Fusilier Brigade, who, it must be remembered, were the only unmounted men with Mahon's column, which moved to the relief of Mafeking by forced marches.

On the 10th of June the Royal Welch Fusiliers left Lichtenburg and marched to Potchefstroom, which was reached on the 14th. It remained there until the 22nd of June, when it entrained, and arrived at Krugersdorp the same day.

The 10th Division was now broken up after having done good work during its short existence. Much excellent marching was done by the Fusilier Brigade when forming part of the 10th Division. In one march of two days the Fusiliers covered 45 miles, and during the whole time hardly a dozen men fell out from exhaustion.

The force under Major-General Sir G. Barton which remained in garrison at Krugersdorp consisted of—The Lothian and Berwick Company Scottish Imperial Yeomanry, the 78th Battery R.F.A., the 2nd battalion Royal Scots Fusiliers, and the 1st battalion Royal Welch Fusiliers.

On the 24th of June Lieutenant-Colonel Sir Robert Colleton, Bart., who had been appointed to succeed Lieutenant-Colonel Thorold, arrived from England and took over command from Captain Gough. Captain C. H. M. Doughty, who had also joined from England, left on the 25th to join the Mounted Infantry.

On the 6th of July "D" and "F" companies of the battalion, under Captains Barttelot and Madocks with 2nd Lieutenants Nangle, Reynolds, and Kyrke, were detached to form part of a force, under the command of Major Heyworth Savage, R.F., consisting of 200 men of the Royal Scots Fusiliers, 200 of the Royal Welch Fusiliers, 2 guns 78th Battery R.F.A., and a few Imperial Yeomanry, which was railed to Potchefstroom, reported to be threatened by a Boer commando.

On the 11th of July Major Alan Gough left to take up the appointment of Commandant of Potchefstroom, but the danger having passed he returned with the whole force to Krugersdorp on the following day.

On the 13th Major Dobell, D.S.O., Captain Doughty, Lieutenants O. de L. Williams, Dickson, Hugh Hill, and 106 rank and file proceeded to Cape Town en route to reinforce the 2nd battalion of the regiment at Hong-Kong embarking on the 20th. Captain P. R. Mantell was appointed Acting-Adjutant vice Lieutenant Dickson.

A few days later news was received that the Boers had captured a hospital train in which Lieutenant Harris and 20 other sick of the battalion were proceeding to hospital at Johannesburg from Potchefstroom. They were well treated and returned on the 29th of July.

On the 18th of July Potchefstroom was occupied by a force under

Major Alan Gough, consisting of 40 Imperial Yeomanry, 2 guns 78th Battery R.F.A., 2 companies of the Royal Scots Fusiliers, and "D" and "F" companies of the battalion under Captains Barttelot and Madocks, Lieutenants Kyrke and Bayly.

Lord Methuen in pursuit of De Wet was moving from Scandinavia Drift to Venterskroon, and having with his mounted troops outmarched his infantry he ordered Gough's detachment on the 6th of August to move out and occupy the defile at Rooikraal some four miles south-east of Potchefstroom. During the night of the 6th–7th a further message was received directing the detachment to join his force at Tygersfontein at daybreak on the 7th. De Wet, who had crossed the Vaal at Schoeman's Drift the previous day, had moved on the right bank up-stream towards Van Vuren's Drift under cover of three parallel lines of hills.

Methuen's mounted troops having driven the enemy off some low kopjes on the north side of the Tygersfontein valley soon after daybreak, the junction of the two forces was effected.

The Boer rear-guard had fallen back on to a high ridge called the Tygersberg, which Gough was ordered to take. The position was a strong one, commanding an open valley about 2,000 yards in breadth traversed by a small stream. Isolated kopjes on the right and left of the main ridge increased the front to about 3,000 yards and gave facilities for bringing a cross fire on Gough's four weak companies, which could only muster about 250 rifles. The advance across the open was made with the four companies in line without supports: the Royal Scots Fusiliers being on the right and the Royal Welch Fusiliers on the left.

The Tygersberg was taken without a check, but as our troops reached the summit they masked the fire of our own guns, and the enemy opened fire from a ridge about 300 yards distant on the left front. This hill was taken with the bayonet. About 200 Boers with a gun took temporary shelter behind an isolated kopje. These when forced to retire came under a very heavy fire at 1,300 to 1,600 yards.

Major Gough ordered a further advance to a plateau one mile further to the south, which was occupied without loss. As, however, the plateau was exposed to a heavy fire from two hills lying south-east across a deep gorge the infantry was withdrawn under cover of the northern edge of the plateau, where they re-formed. Major Gough, having been wounded, here handed over command to Captain Madocks, who ordered an advance half left to a more favourable position. A party of the battalion under Lieutenant Bayly occupied a rocky kopje on the right of the line. "D" company under 2nd Lieutenant Kyrke occupied a high hill on the left overlooking the valley of the Vaal River. The Scots Fusiliers were in the centre. Second Lieutenant Kyrke with 13 men was able to push on to a position completely commanding the Venterskroon Road at a distance of 600 yards, from which his fire inflicted considerable loss in men and horses on the enemy retiring towards Venterskroon.

In his wire to Lord Roberts Lord Methuen made special mention of the gallantry displayed by the Royal Scots Fusiliers and the Royal Welch Fusiliers in this brisk little action, in which the casualties of the latter were Privates G. Wilkinson and P. Miller killed and 7 wounded (including Major Gough and Captain Barttelot slightly and 2nd Lieutenant Bayly severely).

On the 15th of August Private A. Stadden of "A" company reported his arrival, having escaped from De Wet, who had derailed a train at Horning Spruit, Orange River Colony, on 21st of July and captured some 200 unarmed men returning from hospital. Of these, 14 rank and file belonged to the Royal Welch Fusiliers, which gave rise to an alarming head-line in the English newspapers : " Capture of the Welch Fusiliers." The battalion was reinforced on the 23rd of August by a draft from England of 114 rank and file, and on the 24th and 25th by Major H. Lyle, D.S.O., 2nd Lieutenants Hughes and Price, with 92 rank and file who had been taking part in General Sir A. Hunter's operations about Wittenberg, which resulted in the surrender of Prinsloo with 4,140 men and 3 guns.

About this time much pleasure was caused in the regiment by the announcement that by War Office letter dated 2nd June 1900, Her Majesty was pleased to approve of all ranks of the line battalions of the Royal Welch Fusiliers wearing on their full dress a "Flash" somewhat similar to that worn by the officers of the regiment.

While at Krugersdorp General Barton decided that the battalion should form a section of Mounted Infantry (1 officer and 25 rank and file), who were mounted chiefly on captured ponies. The section was not at first officially recognised, but was so later. It was eventually increased to 50 or 60 strong and performed most useful service for the remainder of the war. Under command of Lieutenant Kington it played a distinguished part in the action of Wildfontein on the 24th of March 1901.

A gymkhana race meeting was held on the 21st of September, when two events were won for the battalion by Lieutenants Kington and Price.

On the 28th of September a draft of 101 N.C.O.s and men joined from England under Lieutenant H. I. Webb-Bowen, 3rd battalion.

At 5 a.m. on October the 5th General Barton left Krugersdorp with a force which included the Royal Welch Fusiliers (900 strong) and the Mounted Infantry section of the battalion. The advanced guard, which included four companies of the battalion, was commanded by Sir Robert Colleton, who was directed to secure the passage of the Crocodile River at Mulders Drift on the Pretoria Road.

The force bivouacked for the night about three miles east of Zwartz Kop and marched on the 7th to Roodeval. On the next day it marched in a westerly direction and halted at Tweefontein, driving the Boers before it. On the 9th the march was resumed, the Royal Welch Fusiliers being on rear-guard. About 7.30 a.m. on approaching Dwarsvlei heavy firing was audible on the right front. Sir R. Colleton hurried to the head of the baggage with the intention of parking it if necessary. He found there General Barton, who had already issued orders to that effect, and who directed him to take two companies of the battalion to reinforce Major Duncan Carter, R.F.A., who had left camp at 3 a.m. with mounted troops, " A," " F," and " H " companies of the battalion, 2 guns R.F.A., and a pom-pom, to surprise a commando and a lot of cattle reported to be laagered between Tweefontein and Dwarsvlei. Leaving orders for the two companies to follow, Lieutenant-Colonel Colleton galloped about 1½ miles towards the sound of the guns, and found them in action on a ridge facing a much higher range of flat-topped rocky heights which was held by the Boers, who were keeping the mounted troops in check in the intervening valley, as although under fair cover they could neither advance nor retire without exposure to serious loss from the enemy's fire at 1,000 to 1,200 yards' range.

The enemy's main position was a very strong one, and extended for several miles, precluding a flank attack, except at one place where there was a gap about 800 yards wide; their main position seemed to be east of the gap, and the hill on the west of it seemed to be unoccupied or at any rate but weakly held. However, to safeguard the main attack as far as possible from a cross fire from the western hill it was shelled by the 4·7 Naval gun and a section of field guns. " A " company of the battalion under Captain R. P. Gabbett was ordered to occupy the hill, while " F " company under Captain Madocks was directed to advance to a lower rocky ridge about 1,600 yards from the Boer position, and engage the enemy from there, pending the arrival and deployment of the other companies which made the flank march from right to left under cover of a fold in the ground.

" B " and " L " (Volunteer) companies being in rear with the baggage, only seven companies were available for the attack. They were disposed as follows: The left of " D " (Barttelot) to direct and to march on the shoulder of the hill east of the gap; " E " (Delmé-Radcliffe) to prolong the line on the right of " D "; " H " (Rickman) on the left of " D " had orders to push into the gap, and then wheel to his right and assist " D's " attack by taking the eastern hill in flank; " G " (Best) to follow " H," and if " A " was strongly opposed to assist by taking the hill west of the gap in flank, after which, leaving " A " in occupation, it was to follow as reserve to " H "; " C " (Webb-Bowen) was to follow as reserve to " E," and " F " as reserve to " D," when the latter should have passed through it. The maxim gun (Reynolds) to advance on the left of " D " and take position on the kopje occupied by " F." Firing line and supports, " H," " D," and " E " extended to 10, and Reserve to 5, paces.

The artillery, one 4·7 Naval gun and 4 guns 78th battery R.F.A., covered the advance, which began about 10.30 a.m. and was continued until the front companies reached Madocks' kopje, when a heavy machine-gun and rifle fire was opened on the ridge, during which the reserve companies reached the kopje and took up the fire. On their arrival the firing line and supports again pushed on. Their advance across the valley was covered by the artillery, machine-gun, and reserve companies firing over their heads.

In the meantime " A " company's advance on the western hills had been strongly opposed. 2nd Lieutenant Williams-Ellis was killed as the company crossed the Hekpoort road, and Captain R. P. Gabbett dangerously wounded before the company reached the two rocky knolls, about 800 yards from the hill, which were its preliminary objective, and then command of the company devolved on Colour-Sergeant W. G. King.

The result was so to delay " A " company's advance that it reached its objective in line with, instead of before, the main attack. However, it fully carried out its mission of protecting the left flank of the main attack from enfilade, Commandant Steenkamp and the 130 Boers who held the western side of the gap being kept fully occupied in defending their own position.

The Boers retired as soon as the attacking companies reached the dead ground at the foot of the slope, and by the time the infantry had crossed the ridge they had disappeared into the Hekpoort Valley. It was ascertained that General de la Rey was in command of the enemy's force, which was composed of the commandos of Piet de la Rey, Sarel Alberts, Van der Heuver, Steenkamp, and Van Zyl, with a total of about 650 men in all.

The casualties suffered by the battalion were: 2nd Lieutenant Williams-Ellis and Private J. Nolan killed; Captain Gabbett, 2nd Lieutenant Kyrke,

Sergeants F. R. Mellor, E. Riley, J. Tomlinson, and 5 men wounded. Lieutenant Kyrke was shot in the head above the left ear, but the bullet fortunately grazed, without penetrating, the skull. Having had first aid applied, he ran on and overtook his company (" D ") before it had carried the position. Colour-Sergeant W. G. King distinguished himself by his able leading of " A " company after Captain Gabbett and Lieutenant Williams-Ellis were disabled. 2nd Lieutenant Price and Privates G. Duglord and J. Butterworth were also brought to notice for gallantry in bringing under cover Private Nolan, who was lying wounded and exposed to a heavy fire.

In his report to Lord Roberts of this engagement General Barton remarked : " The Royal Welch Fusiliers, admirably led by Sir Robert Colleton, behaved very well."

General Barton had hoped by this attack, not only to give the enemy a lesson, but to drive them into the arms of the column under Major-General R. A. P. Clements, which was then operating in the Hekpoort Valley, and he intended to continue his operations to that end with his mounted troops the next day. But the opportunity of catching De la Rey between two fires was lost, and the situation suddenly changed by a telegram from Lord Roberts directing General Barton to proceed with all speed south to the Buffelsdoorn pass in the Gatsrand, and at all hazards to prevent De Wet from going north to join Steyn and Botha.

Accordingly on the 10th of October the force reached Brandvlei after a long and tiring march, and Bank the next day. On the 13th the march was resumed at 3.30 a.m. to Welverdiend, 13 miles from Bank. The force had no sooner pitched camp than two 9-pounder Creusot guns opened fire from a ridge, 5,300 yards to the south, through which ran the road to the Buffelsdoorn pass 5,000 yards further on. The 4·7 Naval gun and the 78th Battery R.F.A. replied to this fire, making excellent shooting, and the mounted troops and the Royal Scots Fusiliers moved out : whereupon the enemy retired, and the hills commanding the road defile were occupied as an outpost by " A," " B," " C," and " D " companies, Royal Welch Fusiliers.

On the 15th the column marched at 4 a.m. to the attack of the Buffelsdoorn pass, a very strong position, but which fortunately proved to be but weakly held. A long line of rocky hills of an average height of 200 feet—affording no opportunity for flank attack—completely commanded the valley, about 5,000 yards in width, across which the assailants had to advance.

Colonel Carr, Royal Scots Fusiliers, commanded the right column, consisting of some Imperial Bushmen, 2 guns 78th Battery R.F.A., 2 companies each of the Royal Scots Fusiliers and Royal Welch Fusiliers, which had the task of containing the enemy, who occupied a tract of rocky hills, connecting the Gatsrand and the hill occupied by the Royal Welch Fusiliers outpost, and thus threatened the right flank of the left column in its advance on the Buffelsdoorn. The 4·7 Naval gun shelled the pass from Outpost Hill.

The left column, under the command of Lieutenant-Colonel Sir R. Colleton, Royal Welch Fusiliers, was disposed for the attack of the pass as follows: echeloned in front of the left flank, 19th company Imperial Yeomanry, to the left rear of whom was Marshall's Horse, " H," " G," " F," and " E " companies Royal Welch Fusiliers formed the firing line and supports, the right of " E " marching on the pass. Behind these were " C," " L," and " D " companies in reserve, followed by 4 guns of the 78th battery R.F.A. Two thousand yards to the right rear, marching by the Welverdiend road direct on the pass, were the Royal Scots Fusiliers (less 2 companies) as General Reserve. As soon as the advance commenced the hostile guns opened fire from the hill on the left of the pass, but were speedily silenced by the Naval gun.

About half-way across the valley on the east of the Welverdiend road a low kopje forms the western end of a low grassy ridge, which is covered with thin thorn scrub and dwindles away to nothing about 1,500 yards from the kopje. On arrival of the firing line at this ridge the whole line wheeled half-right and attacked the pass direct, supported by the fire of the Naval gun and 78th battery R.F.A., which latter had come into action under cover of the grassy ridge.

The enemy riflemen now opened a hot fire on Marshall's Horse and on the front, flank and rear of " H " company. " E " and " F " companies were also fired on from the pass at about 700 yards, but the pass was occupied, and the heights on either side were carried without loss. The absence of casualties was probably due to the Boers being misled by the original direction of the advance into thinking that the hills east of the pass were the objective, and having hurried to their right to defend that flank, and the ground on top of the ridge being very rocky and bad for horses, they were unable to return in time when the real point of attack was disclosed.

The force bivouacked at Deelkraal three miles south-west of the Buffelsdoorn, and remained there on the 16th and 17th of October.

On the 18th the force marched to Frederikstad in two columns, north and south of the main ridge of the Gatsrand, and parallel to it, the northern column under Colonel Carr—19th Company Imperial Yeomanry,

2 guns 78th battery R.F.A., and 4 companies of the Royal Scots Fusiliers—being intended to turn any flanking position the enemy might take up on the main range. A running fight ensued all the way; the enemy always evacuated their position in time to avoid encirclement. The final stand made by the rear-guard, on the long ridge south of the railway station at Frederikstad, forced the main column to deploy for attack, thus delaying its march for over two hours, during which time the waggons, cattle, etc., escaped to the north of the Mooi River—a very pretty example of rear-guard tactics.

On arrival at Frederikstad station the force bivouacked. The exigencies of the situation obliged General Barton to take up a more extended position than was altogether desirable. South Hill, from which the Boer rear-guard had just been driven, commanded the railway station, 1¼ miles to the north of it, and all the slope beyond to the Mooi River.

The Hill was held by Marshall's Horse, 6 companies of the Royal Scots Fusiliers, and 2 guns R.F.A. The water in the dam by the railway bridge east of the station being scanty and bad, the Royal Welch Fusiliers were quartered on the south bank of the Mooi, and 1½ miles from the station where General Barton had his headquarters. The remaining guns and transport were on the slope between the river and the station.

The force rested on the 19th of October. Early on the 20th Major Lyle, D.S.O., Royal Welch Fusiliers, was ordered to proceed with the 19th Company Imperial Yeomanry, 2 guns R.F.A., and " E " and " G " companies Royal Welch Fusiliers half-way to Welverdiend to meet a convoy and escort it back to camp, where it arrived safely.

In the Official and *Times* Histories of the War in South Africa this detachment has been confused with the detachment (3 companies, " A," " C," and " D " Royal Welch Fusiliers, 2 guns R.F.A., and Imperial Light Horse) under Lieutenant-Colonel Sir Robert Colleton, Royal Welch Fusiliers, ordered to reconnoitre towards Potchefstroom. In order to make the movements of this last detachment clear, General Barton's order is given verbatim:

" The following force will march at 8.30 a.m. to-day under command of Lieutenant-Colonel Sir Robert Colleton, Bart., 1st battalion Royal Welch Fusiliers, on the following duty—

" (1) To reconnoitre the river bed towards Potchefstroom as far as the second bridge, about five miles distant from camp.

" (2) To examine the bridges and drifts.

" (3) To put the mill at first bridge out of gear and remove the grain.

" (4) To visit any farms in the area, and remove any forage or grain, waggons, cattle and horses.

" (5) To report on the crops.

" (6) To examine residents living on their farms.

" (7) Houses from which, or near which, any firing of the enemy takes place to be at once destroyed.

" 2 waggons and 2 spare spans of oxen will be at the camp at 8.30 a.m.

" The bridge near camp will be passable for guns and waggons by noon to-day.

"By order,
W. G. BRAITHWAITE, *Captain,*
" Frederikstad, 20/10/00."   *Brigade Major, 6th Brigade.*

During the outward march small parties of Boers were seen on both flanks and front. While the mill and the houses near the first bridge, three miles from camp, were being cleared an order was received from General Barton that the detachment was to return to camp with all speed, no reason being given. The retirement commenced, being covered on the right rear by the Imperial Light Horse under Colonel Wools Sampson. "D" company Royal Welch Fusiliers moved along the north bank of the river as left flank-guard.

On the arrival of the infantry and guns at the railway bridge over the Spruit at Buffelsvlei, about two miles from camp, the Imperial Light Horse, who were by this time hotly engaged on the hills south of the railway, were ordered to retire under cover of the fire of the guns. Lieutenant-Colonel Colleton then ordered Colonel Wools Sampson and the guns to retire covered by the infantry, and to take up a position which would cover the infantry's retirement in their turn. But by some misunderstanding the Imperial Light Horse and 2 guns trotted straight back to camp. Whereupon a party of about 300 Boers emerged from a neck in the hills and galloped down on the unsupported infantry. "A" and "C" companies at once lined the railway embankment in extended order, and a hot musketry fight at 900 to 1,000 yards ensued with the Boers, who had dismounted under cover of a quarry and low rocky ridge south of the railway.

The battalion had several casualties : Privates J. Godfrey, J. Jones, and J. Lockett killed, and Sergeant-Major E. Parker and 3 privates wounded. Private Isidore Simpson, Imperial Light Horse, orderly to Sir Robert Colleton, was mortally wounded and the latter's horse killed. Lance-Corporal James, Royal Welch Fusiliers, earned the D.C.M. by assisting his commanding officer to carry Private Simpson under cover. Lieutenant-

Colonel Colleton, finding that the Imperial Light Horse and guns did not respond to his message asking for support, and as ammunition was running short, decided to continue the retirement, which was carried out by alternate companies, the Boers following up on foot. On arrival in camp the whole force was found to be engaged with the enemy on all sides.

After the departure of Lyle's and Colleton's detachments, the Brigade Signalling Officer, Lieutenant Kington, Royal Welch Fusiliers, had gone up to the South Hill to look out for the Colonial Division, which in consequence of information to that effect received from headquarters, Pretoria, General Barton believed to be in pursuit of De Wet.

Seeing a large body of horsemen advancing from the south in regular formation, Kington turned his helio upon them, when they broke up hurriedly into several parties, and it became evident that they were Boers. On receipt of this information General Barton issued orders for the return of Lieutenant-Colonel Colleton, who was attacked by the enemy's left wing during his retirement as above related, but his stand of two hours held off the enemy's left wing until the camp had been struck and the transport loaded and inspanned.

The new-comers proved to be De Wet, who was bringing his Free State commandos to the assistance of Liebenberg, who had also called in his scattered commandos, thus bringing the enemy's concentration up to a total of about 2,500 mounted men and 6 guns.

It was obvious that if such a mobile enemy were attacked by a force mainly consisting of infantry, he could easily evade the shock and pass it on either flank.

But as General Barton's orders were to prevent De Wet at all costs from going north, and having received a telegram from Army Headquarters at Pretoria informing him that the Colonial Division had crossed the Vaal at Schoeman's Drift (35 miles from Frederikstad) at daybreak on the 19th, he decided to keep De Wet in play by a passive defence until the arrival of the pursuing columns and then smash the enemy between the hammer and the anvil.

The British Commander maintained his position until nightfall on the 20th, when he withdrew the troops between South Hill and the river to a new, more concentrated position on the south of Gun Hill, about two miles east of the station, while still retaining his hold on South Hill by means of Colonel Carr's detachment.

Encouraged by the passive attitude of the British force, the Boers on the 21st and three following days pressed the attack by the fire of 6 guns posted on the Gatsrand and a pom-pom north of the Mooi, and musketry from all sides. On the 23rd the Royal Scots Fusiliers on South Hill bore the brunt of the attack, the Boers pushing forward along the ridge, amid the rocks and bushes west of their position to within 400 yards of the defences.

On the 24th of October the Royal Welch Fusiliers were the most heavily attacked. The troops about Gun Hill depended for their water on a large spring, which gave rise to a small tributary of the Mooi about a quarter of a mile in length. Towards sunset on the 24th the enemy rushed a piquet of the Imperial Light Horse, and drove them from a low strong kopje which commanded this water supply. It was reoccupied after dark by " E " company Royal Welch Fusiliers, who strengthened the position, and held it in close proximity to the enemy all next day, Captain Delmé-Radcliffe being slightly wounded in the head; Lieutenant F. H. Nangle was also wounded, besides other casualties.

It must be mentioned here that Barton's force left Krugersdorp with only 200 rounds per rifle and 200 per gun, not expecting to be away for more than a week. No further supply having been received, ammunition was now running very short, so that by the 25th it was reduced to 80 rounds per rifle and 40 per gun.

In consequence of this scarcity orders had been given to economise ammunition as much as possible, and not to fire more than was absolutely necessary to prevent the enemy from advancing. Telegraphic communication with Welverdiend, although intermittent, had not been entirely interrupted by the Boers, who by tapping the wires were kept informed of all messages passing between General Barton and headquarters. They were thus aware of the shortage of ammunition, and the early arrival of a reinforcing column with convoy.

De Wet therefore realised that if he was to be successful there was no time to be lost, and resolved on a bold stroke. Seven hundred Free Staters and Transvaalers of Froneman's and Liebenberg's commandos, under Sarel Celliers and Wessels, were ordered to leave their horses, and take up a position after dark in the donga near the railway station bridge, where they would be favourably placed for rushing Gun Hill during the night.

On the other hand, in the event of failure, an enforced retirement during daylight from this position would necessitate crossing on foot a mile and half of open ground swept by the British artillery—a contingency that weighed heavily with men accustomed to trust in retreat to the speed of their horses. The order, therefore, was not at all to the liking of the majority of those affected by it, and when the commandants, who were to lead the stormers, arrived at the rendezvous they found the numbers at their disposal far too few to give any hope of the success of the enterprise. They therefore remained concealed in the donga.

General Barton was made aware of their presence before daybreak on the 25th by the capture of the water-cart sent by the Royal Scots Fusiliers to water at the dam by the railway bridge. This, however, afforded no clue to the strength of the enemy holding the position.

On the supposition that only a few snipers had to be dealt with, a company of the Royal Scots Fusiliers under Captain Bailey about 8 a.m. was ordered to advance from Gun Hill south of the railway and drive them away. The opposition encountered showed that the donga was held in force, and the company had to retire with the loss of their captain and several other casualties.

It being now evident that the donga was strongly held, General Barton organised an attack on a larger scale. " A," " C," and " E " companies Royal Welch Fusiliers, under Major H. Lyle, D.S.O., were ordered to make a frontal attack parallel to, and north of the railway, supported by a squadron of the Imperial Light Horse, who were to follow mounted and echeloned on the right rear of the Royal Welch Fusiliers, in readiness to pursue the enemy when he should be driven from the shelter of the donga. Two companies of the Royal Scots Fusiliers were to make a simultaneous flank attack on the railway bridge from South Hill.

The attack started about 3 p.m. and was met by a very hot fire, the Royal Welch Fusiliers suffering from a cross fire from the river bed as well as from the front, and the squadron of Imperial Light Horse was obliged to retire. The Royal Welch Fusiliers, however, continued the advance and closed with the enemy with the bayonet. The enemy after making a stout resistance broke and fled in great disorder across the flat open ground, in a westerly and north-westerly direction towards the river, and suffered severely during their retirement from the fire of the artillery, who made splendid practice. The Imperial Light Horse had again advanced after their repulse, but on foot, whereby a good tactical opportunity for mounted pursuit was lost.

Disheartened by this reverse, and the arrival during the action of the relieving convoy containing the much-needed ammunition, and its escort under Colonel Hicks, the Boers fled in all directions. De Wet, giving up the attempt to strike north, fell back towards the Vaal, with a much weakened and demoralised following, and made but a feeble resistance to the attack of the column under Sir C. Knox at Rensburg Drift on 27th October.

The casualties suffered by the Royal Welch Fusiliers in the six days' fight were 12 rank and file killed (Privates W. Thomas, A. Morris, J. Foley, H. Williams, G. Jones, W. Evans, E. Underwood, R. Jones, T. Thomas, F. Barnett, R. Roberts, J. Edwards), Captain Delmé-Radcliffe, Lieutenant Nangle, Lieutenant Best, and 33 rank and file wounded.

On the evening of the 25th the following order by General Barton was received: "The G.O.C. desires to thank the Royal Artillery, Royal Scots Fusiliers, and Royal Welch Fusiliers for the excellent services rendered by them to-day. The gallantry with which the men of the above battalions drove the enemy from their strong positions to-day and followed them up is deserving of the highest praise, and accords with the highest traditions of the distinguished regiments."

The following telegram was received from Field-Marshal Commanding-in-Chief to General Barton:

"FREDERIKSTAD, *October 25th.*

"I heartily congratulate you and the troops under your command on your success this morning.—ROBERTS."

The official summary of news, dated Pretoria, October 25th, contains an account of the ceremony of proclaiming the Annexation of the Transvaal to Her Majesty's Dominions. Representatives of the troops furnished by England, Scotland, Ireland, and the Colonies were present, and the summary adds: "Wales would have been represented by the Royal Welch Fusiliers, but that distinguished corps is engaged to-day adding fresh laurels to its splendid reputation."

On the 28th of October Captain Keene, Lieutenants Bamford and Atherley Jones, and the 1st Volunteer Company Royal Welch Fusiliers, 31 strong, left Frederikstad for England, after having performed a year's excellent service.

On the 29th, leaving a strong garrison at Frederikstad under Sir R. Colleton, General Barton marched with a column of all arms, including "E," "F," "G," and "H" companies Royal Welch Fusiliers under Major Lyle, D.S.O., to Potchefstroom, and, having installed half a battalion Somerset Light Infantry and 2 guns as garrison, returned to Frederikstad on the 31st of October. Potchefstroom was not again abandoned during the war.

On the 13th of November the battalion moved to Potchefstroom, half by rail, and the remainder with the transport by road. On the 14th General Barton in command of a column of all arms, including the Royal Welch Fusiliers, marched for Klerksdorp, which was occupied on November the 16th simultaneously with Major-General Douglas's Column. Klerksdorp was garrisoned permanently for the rest of the war. General Barton returned with his column to Potchefstroom on the 18th.

On November the 20th General Barton made over command of the column to Major-General Babington, and left to assume control of the line of communications between Pretoria and Walverhoek. On his departure General Barton made the following farewell speech:

"I do not know if there are any men of other regiments here, but I wish to say a few words especially to the men of the Royal Welch Fusiliers. I went to your camp this morning to say good-bye to the regiment, but found the camp empty. I supposed your Commanding Officer had taken you for some kind of drill or parade, but I was touched and gratified to learn that you had gone to the Railway Station to say good-bye to me. I think it very kind of you. Without wishing in any way to disparage any of the other regiments of the Fusilier Brigade, I may say for the past twelve months I have always looked on you as my special regiment. I came out with you on the same ship, and except for a few days on Horse Shoe Hill you have never been separated from me for more than twenty-four hours, and it is for this reason I look upon you as my special regiment.

"During those twelve months you have always done what I have asked of you willingly and cheerfully, whether it was toiling along over rough ground on flank guard, or attacking a difficult position. The work has always been well done in a satisfactory manner. I think one of the chief reasons for your success is the good feeling existing in the regiment between the officers and the rank and file, and as you have come here of your own free will I am glad to think that feeling is extended even to me.

"During these twelve months you have suffered heavy losses, but they are the inevitable losses that must occur in war, and you may congratulate yourselves that you have never suffered avoidable and unnecessary losses through the carelessness and inefficiency of your officers.

"You belong to one of the most distinguished regiments in the British Army, and you may pride yourselves that you have not only maintained the reputation of your regiment but have greatly increased it. I say increased it because although many glorious deeds were done by your predecessors in the Peninsula, Crimea, and Indian Mutiny, nothing was done equal to what you have done in this campaign: for no army but our own has had to contend against smokeless powder, and whatever people may say who sit in their arm-chairs, knowing nothing about it, and who say this and that ought to have been done, it is a very different and much more difficult task to attack a position, occupied by an invisible enemy, when losses begin at ranges over 3,000 yards, and bullets come from all sides, one cannot tell from where, than it used to be when you could see your enemy, and the damage did not begin until you had arrived at comparatively close ranges.

" I hope that you may soon get home to enjoy the reputation you have earned so well, and I now wish you ' good-bye.' I should like to shake hands with every man of you, for I look on every one of you as my friend, but as it is impossible to shake hands with you all, I will do so with your Sergeant-Major as your representative—' good-bye.' "

The General then entered his carriage, and departed with the affectionate regret of all ranks.

On the 26th of November Private Tubbs and Lance-Corporal Newnes pluckily attempted to save the life of Trooper Davidson, Brabant's Horse, who was drowned while bathing in the Mooi River. Tubbs dived several times to try to extricate Davidson from the weeds by which he was entangled. He was awarded the medal of the Royal Humane Society.

On the 26th of December General Babington with a column consisting of about 500 mounted men, including 45 Royal Welch Fusiliers Mounted Infantry, 3 guns R.F.A. and 3 pom-poms, and the 1st Battalion Royal Welch Fusiliers (less " F " and " B " companies at Tygersfontein), and 100 of the Derbyshire Regiment attached to the Royal Welch Fusiliers, marched to Buffelsdoorn, 19 miles west of Potchefstroom.

On the 27th another 19 miles march was made to Witpoortje, and after a further march of 18 miles the column reached Ventersdorp on the 28th, where a junction was effected with the columns under Broadwood and Kekewich, the latter of which was placed at the disposal of General Babington, who divided his force into two movable columns, known as Kekewich and Colleton's columns.

1900.

2ND BATTALION.

A formidable organisation known as " the Boxers," having for its object the expulsion of all foreigners from China, became this year a serious menace as the Imperial Chinese Government was either too weak to attempt to suppress it, or, what is more probable, secretly encouraged " the Boxers " while pretending to resist them.

The outrages committed by these fanatics became more frequent and serious as time went on, especially at Pekin, where on the 20th of

June the whole foreign community crowded into the British Legation for safety, and a state of siege immediately commenced.

For nearly eight weeks the besiegers gallantly defended themselves until relieved by an international force of which the 2nd battalion of the Royal Welch Fusiliers was the only representative of the British infantry. The share taken by the battalion in this enterprise will now be narrated.

Instructions were received on the 9th of June to hold 300 men in readiness to proceed to North China at an early date. " A," " C," and " E " companies, under command of Major F. Morris, with Captains Gwynne and Richards, Lieutenants Rotherham, Flower, Walwyn, and Owen, with 329 non-commissioned officers and men, embarked on H.M.S. *Terrible* on 16th June for passage to Tientsin.

The *Terrible* arrived at Taku at daybreak on the 21st (the forts had already been taken by the Allies), and the force disembarked at once, the Royal Welch Fusiliers entering the river in H.M.S. *Fame*, Commander Keys.

On landing at Tong Ku the Royal Welch Fusiliers, and 150 seamen and marines under Captain Craddock, proceeded by train until about seven miles from Tientsin, where the train was partially derailed: then the party bivouacked and the next day, 22nd of June, came up with American marines and Russians, who had suffered a check.

At first the Chinese showed but little disposition to oppose the advance, the activity being spasmodic only; but presently their opposition increased, causing the whole of the attacking troops to open out in extended order.

The progress of the Allies was necessarily slow owing to the number of villages on the left flank which had to be reconnoitred and cleared in succession. About noon the Russians met with a check, and their casualties became so numerous that in view of the repulse which they had sustained two days previously, some doubt arose as to the feasibility of their reaching their destination. It was, nevertheless, decided to push forward vigorously, Tientsin being only about four miles distant. The advance was continued with the Americans on the right of the leading line. The Naval brigade marched next between the railway and the river in attack formation, while the Fusiliers prolonged the line to the extreme left. Each corps furnished its own supports.

After clearing several villages, the Fusiliers on the Allied left arrived within about five hundred yards of the position, and, as the enemy's shots began to tell, the intervening distance was traversed at a run. The Chinese made off as soon as they saw the gleam of bayonets, though their marksmen kept up a brisk fire from among the streets and houses, from which they were speedily dislodged. Meanwhile the Russians had deflected in a north-easterly direction towards the railway station, which their countrymen within the Settlement, together with some British marines, had been holding for some days past in the face of an overwhelming number of assailants.

The main body of the relief force making for the Concessions, with a persistent determination to overcome all difficulties, held straight on, and dispersing the enemy entered the European quarter by the raft and native boats shortly after noon. They had thus relieved Tientsin.

The total casualties amongst the Allies was about 600. The Royal Welch Fusiliers only lost 1 killed (Private Power) and 2 wounded, probably owing to the colour of their dress. Major Morris was also slightly wounded.

The International Forces advanced on the 24th to relieve Admira Seymour, who was in difficulties near the Siku arsenal, having got so far on his return from his attempt to relieve Pekin. Two hundred of the Royal Welch Fusiliers accompanied this force, which started at night, and arrived at the opposite side of the river to that on which Admiral Seymour was at daybreak. Admiral Seymour had been in great straits, having almost exhausted his supplies. He had attacked and taken the arsenal and found in it great stores of arms and munition of war, and all manner of scientific instruments. They had with them 220 wounded. Admiral Seymour's force having been got across the river, the whole force retired on the Settlement, which they reached at 11 a.m. on the 25th.

The Russians endeavoured to capture the Pei-Yang arsenal, and being unable to do so asked for reinforcements, which were sent out by the British and other nations, the Royal Welch Fusiliers being with the British Force : the arsenal was now captured.

Desultory fighting went on from day to day until 3rd July, when three big guns arrived from H.M.S. *Terrible* and the bombardment of the native city was begun in earnest.

The Chinese artillery practice was very good, and their information appeared good, for on the 6th of July they directed their fire upon the houses occupied by senior officers.

Major Morris was invalided home and left for Hong-Kong, and Captain Gwynne assumed command.

In an official dispatch from Major Morris to the G.O.C. China, the following officers were noted for favourable consideration as under:

" Captain J H. Gwynne—this officer has done most excellent work, and was conspicuous in leading some of the principal attacks on the various villages.

"Lieutenant F. J. Walwyn—this officer managed under great difficulties to make local arrangements to bring up the reserve ammunition into the firing line, and assisted in saving the killed and wounded from falling into the hands of the enemy.

"Lieutenant O. S. Flower afforded me valuable assistance as Staff Officer."

On the 8th of July a shell burst in the Royal Welch Fusiliers barracks, whereby No. 4014 Private Porter was killed and Privates Street and Cartwright wounded.

As the enemy appeared to be trying to outflank the Settlement a force was formed on the 9th to eject them, and of this the Royal Welch Fusiliers composed the firing line. The enemy were driven out and lost heavily: in this action No. 3644 Private Porter was killed and Privates King, 4533 Innes, and 4786 Wilson were wounded.

On the 10th the enemy made a determined attack upon the railway station, which was held by the British, and " E " company was ordered to reinforce, and the attack was repulsed.

The station after the siege presented an extraordinary appearance, the iron sheds having the appearance of nutmeg graters, and the walls of the engine house being literally riddled with shell holes.

On the 13th at 3 a.m. the troops, consisting of 3 columns, " A," " B," and " C," were assembled to attack the walled city of Tientsin ; " A," the French 500 strong, were to take the right along the mud wall ; " B," the Japanese 3,200 strong, the centre ; and " C," the British 500 strong and the Americans 1,000 strong, the left.

" B " and " C " columns advanced to within 200 yards of the walls under a terrific fire, and as arranged remained there until the Japanese should have blown in the gate. They were unable to do this, however, owing to the failure of the Russians to carry out their part of the contract, which was to hold the enemy to the west of the city, and thus remove pressure from the south where " B " and " C " columns were operating. After remaining all day in this position the columns were withdrawn, the losses of the Royal Welch Fusiliers being : 4478 Private Tomlinson, 4728 Private Mansfield, 4342 Private Scott, 4517 Private Crew, 4480 Private Thomas killed, and 2737 Corporal Wilson, 5157 Private Evans, 4906 Lance-Corporal Burke, 4621 Private Taylor, 4040 Lance-Sergeant Pearce, 4079 Private Bonner, 5435 Private Richardson, 3469 Private Owens, 3217 Sergeant Deane, 4346 Corporal Kellock, 4056 Private Pitt, and 5272 Private

Voyce wounded. Private Doodson was noted for his gallantry in carrying out of action Lance-Sergeant Pearce when wounded, and afterwards a Japanese soldier. Private Crew was killed when carrying Private Bonner out of action. The total casualties amounted to over 800 killed and wounded.

The 7th American Infantry lost very heavily owing to their advancing in close formation, apparently owing to a mistake.

While this action was in progress the enemy commenced a heavy shell fire on the railway station, in which was a piquet of the Royal Welch Fusiliers : one shell killing 5 men of various corps and wounding 11 ; 6 of the latter being Royal Welch Fusiliers, viz. 4562 Corporal Hanmer, 3472 Private Radford, 5122 Private Tindall, 4428 Private Greaves, and 4190 Private Kenny.

Captain Johnson, 3rd Punjaub Cavalry, attached to the 2nd battalion Royal Welch Fusiliers, who was in command of the piquet, displayed remarkable coolness.

The total casualties in the Royal Welch Fusiliers were 5 killed and 19 wounded out of 200 engaged, or 12 per cent.

On account of the retirement of the main body, the Japanese were enabled to blow in the South gate, and enter at daybreak, closely followed by the Royal Welch Fusiliers, who had orders to seize and hold the North gate. Passing beyond the North gate as far as the canal, a yard containing about 200 Imperial junks was captured, also a river steamer.

On the 16th, consequent upon a rumour that the enemy had abandoned some guns in a fort to the west of the city, Captain Gwynne and Lieutenant Flower, with 18 men Royal Welch Fusiliers, all mounted on ponies seized in the Settlement, and Major Waller, American Marines, with 5 of his men, went to reconnoitre and brought away two 4-inch Krupp guns and three field guns.

A detachment was sent to the junk yard already mentioned on the 17th, at first 12 men but later on increased to 60.

Favourable mention was made in dispatches of Captain Gwynne and Lieutenants Flower and Walwyn.

Telegraphic instructions from the War Office were received by the G.O.C. China on 11th July to send headquarters and another company to Taku at once, and in consequence headquarters and 1 company (" H ") under the command of Lieutenant-Colonel Hon. R. H. Bertie embarked on board the S.S. *Taisang* at Hong-Kong for passage to Taku, to join the detachment 2nd Royal Welch Fusiliers at Tientsin. The following was the embarkation strength : 5 officers (Lieutenant-Colonel Bertie,

Lieutenants Hay, Johnson, and Vyvyan, Lieutenant and Quartermaster Cleeve), Sergeant-Major Hickman, and 130 non-commissioned officers and men.

After calling at Wei-hai-Wei on the 19th July, the *Taisang* arrived at Taku on the 20th at daylight. Disembarking baggage into lighters was commenced at once, and on completion in the afternoon the troops also disembarked into the lighters, and were towed up the Peiho River as far as Sinho, where the lighters were anchored for the night.

A start was made about 6 a.m. on the 21st of July and Tientsin was reached at 5 p.m. the same day. Accommodation was provided for the men in "go-downs" belonging to Messrs. Osborne. On arrival the total strength of the Royal Welch Fusiliers was as under: 10 Officers (Lieutenant-Colonel Hon. R. H. Bertie, Captains J. H. Gwynne, H. M. Richards, Lieutenants H. Rotherham, O. S. Flower, R. B. Johnson, C. S. Owen, W. G. Vyvyan, Lieutenant A. Hay (acting-Adjutant), Lieutenant and Quartermaster J. F. Cleeve, one warrant officer, Sergeant-Major Hickman, and 451 non-commissioned officers and men.

On the 23rd a party of 40 non-commissiond officers and men, under Lieutenant Johnson, was sent out to a village on the canal, about four and a half miles to the north of Tientsin, to capture a number of junks lying there, and to bring them down to Tientsin.

On the 24th a party of 27 non-commissioned officers and men, under 2nd Lieutenant Vyvyan, was sent out to the village of Siku to relieve a similar party under 2nd Lieutenant Owen, who returned to headquarters. This party had been guarding some junks captured the previous week. Lieutenant Johnson returned to headquarters in the evening, having brought down the junks.

Lieutenant F. J. Walwyn rejoined headquarters on the 26th from Wei-hai-Wei, having been sent there sick. General Sir A. Gaselee arrived with his staff and took over command of the British North China Field Force from Brigadier-General Dorward on the following day.

Instructions were received on the 28th to hold 300 men in readiness for active operations; 150 men of the battalion, under Captain Richards, with Lieutenants Vyvyan and Walwyn and 2 machine guns, were to remain as part of the garrison. The other troops comprising the force for the advance were as under:

1st Bengal Lancers	400 sabres.
7th Bengal Infantry	500 rifles.
1st Sikhs	500 rifles.

24th Punjaub Infantry	. . . . .	250 rifles.
12th Battery R.F.A.	. . . . .	6 guns.
Hong-Kong Artillery	. . . . .	1 12-pounder.
		4 maxims.
Navy	. . . 3 12-pounders and about	450 men.
Royal Welch Fusiliers	. . . . .	300 rifles.
Hong-Kong Regiment	. . . . .	100 rifles.
1st Chinese Regiment	. . . . .	100 rifles.

No. 7 Ammunition column
Detachment Royal Engineers.

Captain Johnson, I.S.C., ceased to be attached to the Royal Welch Fusiliers on the 30th of July, and Mr. H. Grant Smith (Shanghai Volunteer Corps) was attached for duty from this date.

On 31st of July the heavy baggage was stored and kits placed in a "go-down" for custody during the absence of the force; men's light kits were packed in the junks, which were towed up the river in the afternoon to Siku.

The Royal Welch Fusiliers were attached to the 1st Brigade China Expeditionary Force under Brigadier-General Sir Norman Stewart, Bart.

The following order was received on the 4th of August, at 7 a.m.:

"The enemy is in position in the direction of Pei-Tsang on both sides of the Peiho. The position is believed to be entrenched with outposts thrown forward. The Russian, French, and German Forces will operate on the left bank of the River Peiho. The British, American, and Japanese on the right bank. The British Forces will march to Siku to-day, where they will bivouac for the night. The British Force will march in the order given below:

"Royal Welch Fusiliers (3 companies) with advance guard of 1 company, detachment Royal Engineers, 1 Field Troop 1st Bengal Lancers, H.Q. Staff of Division (½ company Sikhs G.O.C.'s escort), 12th battery Royal Field Artillery, No. 7 Ammunition Column, Hong-Kong Artillery, Brigade Staff, 7th Rajputs less 1 company, 1st Sikhs, Chinese Regiment, 1st Bengal Lancers, Divisional and Brigade Headquarter Transport, Commissariat and Transport, Field Hospitals, Rear Guard 1 company 7th Rajputs."

With reference to above "A" company with Lieutenant O. S. Flower furnished the advance guard.

Siku was reached about 4.30 p.m. and the force bivouacked for the night in the fields at the side of the road.

The enemy was discovered in position astride of the River Peiho before Pei-Tsang. Dispositions were made to attack at dawn the following day: Russians, French, and Germans were on the left bank of the river; the remainder of the Allies were on the right bank.

The advance commenced at about 3 a.m. on the 5th of August. The men had nothing but their great-coats, which were carried on mules throughout the march, as their waterproof sheets and blankets had been put on board the junks, together with the reserve supplies and spare ammunition. Thus they had to bivouac as best they could. Each man carried 150 rounds of ammunition and rations for two days, so his load, including the whole of his kit and his rifle, amounted to about 45 lb., a heavy burden in the intense and trying heat of a Chinese summer. The enemy's position was found at about 4.30 a.m., being about two miles in extent on the right bank. The artillery opened the action at 4.50 a.m., and the enemy were practically driven out of their advanced trenches by 6.45 a.m., but continued to fight until 9.30 a.m. Colour-Sergeant Jones ("A" company) was wounded in the knee about 7 a.m. Firing was continued until 3.30 p.m. The position had been well selected, the trenches, breastworks, etc., having been dug in the crops, which were from 12 to 18 feet high. The Japanese bore the brunt of the action, and, as they fought in shoulder-to-shoulder formation, lost considerably. The Royal Welch acted as a reserve to the British force. The force bivouacked for the night at Pei-Tsang.

The advance commenced at 5.30 a.m. on the 6th of August. At Yangtsun, along the east bank of the River Peiho, the enemy were found in an entrenched position covering Yangtsun, and a halt was made while dispositions were made for the attack.

The main attack fell to the lot of the British and Americans, who advanced simultaneously on each side of the railway: the combined cavalry, American, British, and Japanese, covered the right flank and the Russians advanced on the left. At 10.30 a.m. our artillery opened fire at a range of 2,800 yards and the enemy was driven out of his first position about noon, the advance having been very rapidly pushed through in the most intense heat.

Private Jackson of the battalion performed a plucky action: a village having been occupied by our troops, unknown to the artillery of some of the Allies, became subject to shell fire: thereupon Private Jackson got up on an embankment in full view, and under the fire of both the Allies and the enemy, and signalled the fact that the village had been already occupied by the Allies.

The Fusiliers lost 2 men killed and 8 wounded at Pei-Tsang; the Japanese hardly took any part in the action, having arrived late. The Allies bivouacked north and south of Yangtsun that night.

Lieutenant-Colonel the Hon. R. H. Bertie in his diary of the Expedition to North China states as follows : " The Royal Welch Fusiliers were awfully done up after yesterday's battle. The heat, and a run in of quite half a mile, pumped the men and we could only muster 100 out of 200 at the finish : 29 cases of sun and 22 missing came in later. The rest stopped for water as soon as we reached the village, as the ' cease fire ' had sounded. I collected about 50 there soon after, and the rest were accounted for all right. Captain Gwynne was so beat that he looked fit to drop. I was fairly done up too. I don't think that any of the troops were fit to go on till rested and watered : fortunately there was no need to do so. All our officers played up well, and were quite cool under fire. Private Cook ('A' company) and Dr. O'Neill were near me yesterday throughout the action and were quite cheery. Poor Baker, Royal Welch Fusiliers, a private, had a fearful wound in the groin. I saw him and all the wounded to-day, and a large bit of iron from a shell, which was extracted from his wound, the gash being a frightful one. We rest to-day and go on again to-morrow, probably fighting."

The 7th was a day of rest for all the troops, except the Japanese, who pushed forward, and was spent in drawing upon the junks, which arrived in the course of the afternoon, for such requirements as were needed.

The Indians and the white troops disported themselves in the Peiho, muddy as it was, and the British camp had quite an air of comfort, the men having by this time become very handy at rigging up shelters made with bits of bamboo or matting, interwoven with the long stalks of the maize. These small shanties afforded some protection from the scorching sun, though not impervious to wet.

This day's halt was of great benefit to all, as after the trying marches and fighting of the two previous days a short repose was sorely needed.

The march was resumed at 7 a.m. on the 8th of August, the Royal Welch Fusiliers in rear of the force passing some very strong and well-constructed entrenchments in the village of Yangtsun, which had never been utilised by the enemy : the force bivouacked for the night at Tsai-tsn.

At starting on the 9th there was some confusion in time, with the result that the troops had little or no breakfast : the march, however, commenced at 7 a.m., the Royal Welch Fusiliers leading the British contingent. The heat became terrific, and on reaching the river the column halted for two hours to place exhausted men in junks. The force reached Ho-Shi-Wo at 4 p.m. thoroughly exhausted.

The enemy had evacuated a very strong defensive position, having loopholed the walls of the mud houses, and cleared a belt of ground in front, and made a most effective entanglement by leaving a foot or so of the stalks of the crops and twisting them: they had also evidently intended to flood the country over which the Allies had to advance, as an almost completed canal was found dug from the Peiho to the country which was lower than the river. It was extremely fortunate that they were unable to carry out their intention, as, in addition to making the advance of the Allies most arduous, they would have made the river too dry for the junks to ascend.

The march was continued at 4 p.m. on the 10th of August, the Russians impeding the march by their baggage train: the heat being so intense that a halt was called until the sun had gown down, when the march was continued, arriving in a camp short of Matao, at 1 a.m., after a short halt at Anping. The battalion marched into Matao at 5 a.m. on the 11th.

Having halted during the heat of the day, the march was resumed at 6 a.m. to Chang-chi-wan, a walled town which had been the scene of a big fight in the 1860 campaign.

On the 12th Tung-chow, the objective of the following day, was found to be strongly held by the enemy, who were quickly driven out by the Japanese before the arrival of the Allies, the garrison retiring on Pekin.

The Royal Welch Fusiliers arrived here at 12.30 p.m., but halted by the river about a mile and a half from the town: the force remained here until the morning of the 14th instant, a reconnaissance having proceeded in the direction of Pekin, consisting of the 7th Rajputs, cavalry, and 2 guns.

Some consternation was caused in the British camp, that was situated on the river's edge at Tung-chow, on discovering the fact that a party of forty of the Welch Fusiliers, who were expected to rejoin their corps at Chang-chi-wan from Matao, had failed to arrive. They were known to have left the junks, and the camp at Matao, and to be following the tracks of their own contingent; but from the time of their starting on the morning of the 12th, in charge of two Colour-Sergeants, Kelly and Murphy, no tidings had been heard of them, nor was any news of them forthcoming till three days later. They were, nevertheless, in good company and under most able guidance, as their non-commissioned officers had tracked their countrymen to the outskirts of Tung-chow, but, unable to ascertain the exact situation of the British camp, and finding themselves at some cross roads, they concluded that the English contingent must have set out for the capital.

Accordingly they made up their minds to reach Pekin, if possible, forthwith, and had, by help of a map, set their faces in that direction, when they fell in with the advance guard of the Russians bent on the same errand. The commander of the latter allowed them to accompany it, and the small party of Fusiliers eventually found themselves under the city walls, some twenty hours before any other units of the British force arrived within sight of Pekin.

The British force commenced what turned out to be their final march at 3.30 a.m. on the 14th, coming up with the reconnoitring force at 5.30 a.m. in the act of moving off; the South-east gate of the Chinese city was reached and found to be shut but undefended, the guard having doubtless been drawn off by the Americans who were bombarding the East gate, and by the Russians who were attacking the East gate of the Tartar city, and by the Japanese to the north of the Russians: the wall was scaled and the gate opened, and the British force, the 1st Sikhs and the Royal Welch Fusiliers leading, was the first to enter the city at 4.45 p.m., and relieve the Legation by entering the Tartar city by the Water Gate.

Inside the British Legation, after the arrival of the relief column, there was not so much excitement among those rescued as might have been expected after so long an incarceration. The enthusiasm which had been roused to a high pitch on first realising that help was really at hand, the wild, delirious joy of liberty, had evaporated as twelve hours or more had elapsed since the fact originally became known that deliverance was nigh. There could be no doubt that the rescuers were welcome, but the reaction was too great, and the occasion too solemn for those who had been liberated to give free vent to their feelings by noisy demonstrations.

The ladies looked very pale and the rest of the inmates haggard and worn, but all seemed wonderfully cheerful after the anxiety and suspense which they had undergone. They had first realised the presence of their liberators by seeing a Sikh soldier enter followed by a few others, among whom were the headquarter staff as well as Major Vaughan, commanding the Rajputs, and his Adjutant, Lieutenant Lock, whose men relieved the defenders at their posts and with the Sikhs cleared the enemy out of the Mongol Market.

While at one of the loopholes, which had been closed with a brick against stray bullets, an Indian, prompted by a natural curiosity to see what was going on at the other side, withdrew this obstacle to his view from the aperture, with the result that, while peeping through it, a ball hit him in the mouth and travelling downwards passed out of his arm. Mr. Knobel, the Dutch Minister, and a Belgian, both of whom had been unscathed during the siege, were wounded this afternoon.

The scene presented on the Legation lawn was that of a garden party at which ladies and children neatly attired in cool white dresses, and men in comfortable flannel suits, busied themselves in dispensing tea, bread, and such refreshments as their limited stock could supply to the troops. The latter in their khaki, stained with perspiration and covered with dust, unkempt and unshaved, showed unmistakable signs of their ten days' march, and formed a strange contrast to the dainty toilettes of the women who attended to their wants.

The British main force had covered quite seventeen miles that day, and had been on the move from 2.15 a.m., on very little food, till 5 p.m., and the sun had taken most of the backbone out of all.

The following is an extract from Lieutenant-Colonel Bertie's diary:
" I brought in only 50 Royal Welch Fusiliers out of 160 starters : we covered about 16, nominally 13, miles during the day, and had nothing but tea or cocoa and a biscuit to go upon all those hours in a burning sun."

The British lost between the 8th and 14th 2 killed, 5 wounded, and 1 missing.

The troops were most fortunate in having had no rain to impede the march, or make the roads heavy till the 13th, as in China rain generally means a deluge. Under all circumstances, looking to the imperative necessity of the speedy relief, the heat, intolerable as it was, was preferable to the wet.

In the evening the officers were entertained by Sir Claude Macdonald in the Minister's dining-room, where a table d'hôte open to all comers furnished a welcome meal, the chief component of which was pony, disguised under various forms. Meat had become scarce, and the defenders had consequently fallen upon their riding and draught animals; but one thing had not failed, and that, champagne, had been invaluable to the patients in the hospital.

The Royal Welch Fusiliers bivouacked for the night in the Imperial Carriage Park, an enclosure next the Legation wall, from the coach-houses of which a heavy fire had been continually kept up by the Chinese.

Two companies of the battalion, under Captain Gwynne, were sent to hold the Llama Temple in the Imperial City, distant about half a mile from the Legation as the crow flies, but a hole had to be made in the South wall to admit of communications. From this date on, the city of Pekin was given up to pillage by all nations, but the looting was carried out in a systematic manner by the British : all things from unoccupied houses being placed in store and sold by public auction, the money being divided into shares.

The work of pacification and of cleaning the streets was now commenced.

The following details are extracted from Colonel Bertie's diary:

"August 19th.—The men are recovering now from fatigue; Sergeant-Major Hickman, Mr. Cleeve, Captain Richards, and Quartermaster-Sergeant Patterson have come up to time again."

"August 20th.—A convoy with Cleeve left yesterday to get our small kits from Tung-chow."

"August 24th.—We sent 60 Fusiliers under Captain Richards, and 240 Baloochis, to the gates which the Chinese had agreed to open at 7 a.m.; as usual the Chinese evaded their promises, so the force came back, instead of blowing the gates in, which would have been a better mode of dealing with the Celestials."

"August 28th.—The so-called triumphal march of the Allies through the Forbidden City came off. We paraded at 7 a.m. in the outer court. After an inspection by the Russian General the Russians led off headed by their band, then came the Japanese with their bugles in front, the British, Americans, French, Germans, Austrians, and Italians following in order. The Royal Welch Fusiliers were represented by myself, Captain Hay, Mr. Flower, and 30 men."

"August 29th.—We sent 100 men under Captain Richards and Mr. Flower to Coal Hill to relieve the Marines, who go back with the Naval Brigade."

"September 14th.—Some 80 tons of cordite were to be destroyed at Tung-chow, where 30 Royal Welch Fusiliers and some Indians are stationed. Part of it had been successfully destroyed when the remainder accidentally ignited. The Royal Welch Fusiliers have lost 6 out of 10 men."

"September 17th.—A force of about 3,000 Germans, Americans, and British proceeded to destroy some temples 12 miles N.E. of the Chinese city used by 'the Boxers' as a stronghold. The Royal Welch Fusiliers were under Major Dobell, with Captain Hay and Mr. Johnson—100 men in all. The force returned on the 22nd, having accomplished its object without any loss."

"October 14th.—We leave this on the 18th, probably for Tientsin."

The Royal Welch Fusiliers were relieved on their departure by part of the Australian contingent which had landed on the 15th of September.

On leaving Pekin the following Field Force Order respecting the Royal Welch Fusiliers was issued:

"The Lieutenant-General Commanding cannot allow Lieutenant-Col. the Hon. R. H. Bertie and the 2nd Battalion Royal Welch Fusiliers to leave his command without expressing his appreciation of their soldierly conduct during this campaign. Nothing could have exceeded their dogged endurance during the march on Pekin, and in Pekin their discipline, conduct, and appearance have, with few exceptions, been most satisfactory.

"The Lieutenant-General feels sure from what he has seen of the Royal Welch Fusiliers that the British Infantry is as good now as it ever has been."

In addition the following Brigade Order was promulgated by Brigadier-General Sir Norman Stewart, Bart.:

"In saying good-bye to the 2nd Battalion Royal Welch Fusiliers, General Stewart thanks Lieut.-Col. the Hon. R. H. Bertie and all ranks for the manner in which the Battalion has conducted itself in the Field and in quarters, and congratulates them on having earned one more distinction for the Colors of the Regiment they, and the whole Army, are so proud of. The distinction in their case is unique, for whilst the 1st Battalion in South Africa have been adding to the long list of honours already gained, the 2nd have been doing the same several thousand miles away in a different direction, an opportunity which has seldom or never fallen to the luck of any Regiment of Her Majesty's Army. It will always be a proud boast of General Stewart's to be able to say he had the honour of having the 2nd Battalion Royal Welch Fusiliers under his command on service, and he wishes them all success in the future."

The battalion embarked on board the transport *Salamis*, and on the 29th of October the following Regimental Order was issued on board:

"The Commanding Officer desires to thank all ranks for their hearty co-operation during the march to Pekin and subsequently, which so greatly facilitated the performance of his duties and has earned for the Battalion at large the commendations of the Lieut.-General in command, and of their Brigadier. He regrets that a few exceptions should latterly have discounted the otherwise admirable conduct of the Non-Commissioned Officers and men during their advance and on first arrival in the Chinese Capital, and trusts that their comrades will, on reaching Hong Kong, maintain the good reputation which characterised them while on active service. He takes this opportunity to place on record his appreciation of the excellent services rendered at Tientsin by the Detachment between 21st June and 21st July, which reflects great credit on all concerned. Realising the temptations to which all will necessarily be exposed on return to the normal conditions of garrison life, he hopes that crime will be reduced to a minimum, and that no act on the part of the Soldier, individually or collectively, will occur to bring into discredit the good name which their discipline, and general behaviour, has procured for the Regiment in North China."

The following is a summary of the casualties:

Officers

Invalided: Major Morris, Captain Rotherham.

N.C.O.s and Men

Killed	9
Died of wounds	3
Drowned	1
Killed by explosion	7
Died of disease	8
Transferred to base hospital (11 returned to duty to 31st October)	52
Wounded	37
Sick at Pekin	7
Additional death on 1st November	1
,, ,, 5th December	5

On arrival at Hong-Kong on 3rd November the men were landed in launches at Murray Pier, and marched along the Praya, headed by the Royal Welch band, and drums and fifes, to a position close to the Queen's statue. The men were in command of Colonel Bertie, and the other officers on parade were Captains Gwynne, Cadogan, Hay, and Richards, Major and Adjutant Dobell, Quartermaster Cleeve, Lieutenants Flower, Walwyn, Vyvyan, Johnson, Owen, and Grant Smith. The last-named officer was a son of Mr. John Grant Smith of Hong-Kong, and as a Tientsin volunteer was attached to the regiment for service. Three companies of the regiment came direct from Pekin previous to embarkation, leaving five men behind on the sick list. The remainder were awaiting their arrival on board the steamer. About half-past four o'clock Major-General Gascoigne, C.M.G., accompanied by Colonel The O'Gorman, D.A.A.G., Major Morris, and Captain the Hon. H. W. Trefusis, A.D.C., arrived, and was received with a general salute. The General walked down the lines and then addressed a few words of welcome to the men.

The General said: "Colonel Bertie, officers and men of the 2nd Battalion Royal Welch Fusiliers and the detachment of the Royal Engineers,—I am very glad indeed to welcome you back into my command. We who have had to stay behind—your other half battalion, myself, and the staff—should like to have gone forward, but some must stay behind, but we have nevertheless looked with the most genuine interest on the way you have acquitted yourselves.

"It certainly is a magnificent thing for a regiment—that one battalion should have been serving for twelve months, doing hard work in South Africa, and another battalion of the regiment should be doing equally good work in the north of China. It is a very proud thing indeed for a regiment to have such a record as that. I am not going to detain you any longer, only I wished to welcome you here. I know there are other welcomes that will be given, but it was my pride and my privilege to be able to be the first one to welcome you back into the command. One last word. I am certainly not against the men enjoying themselves thoroughly, but I cannot help remembering that there are a good few of your comrades left behind, who have found graves in the north of China. All honour to them. They died, some on the field of battle, some from wounds received in battle, and many from sickness the result of the hard work and privations they endured. For the mercy that Almighty God has shown every one of you who are listening to me, I ask you to show your gratitude for the blessings vouchsafed to you by taking your pleasures discreetly. Now, men, we have been standing in the shadow of the statue of the Empress-Queen, whose servants we are proud to think we are. Take your helmets and join with me in giving three cheers for Her Most Gracious Majesty Queen Victoria."

The request was acceded to with great enthusiasm.

On the call of the General, the band played the National Anthem.

General Gascoigne having intimated his desire to march at the head of the regiment to the barracks, the men formed up and marched off to the strains of the drums and fifes, the band of the regiment taking the lead later with "Men of Harlech" and the regimental march. A number of their comrades gave the men a hearty reception on entering the barracks.

In the barrack square General Gascoigne exchanged greetings with the officers.

The men were dismissed immediately, and were served with a cold collation.

The following, taken from a local paper on November 5th, is a description of a reception give by the Sergeants' Mess to their comrades on their return from Pekin:

"The Sergeants' Mess, Murray Barracks, was on Saturday night the scene of one of those gatherings which go to prove the meaning of the term ' esprit de corps ' and to show how the friendly relations amongst the Non-Commissioned Officers of a Battalion are so well augmented in the Regiment generally.

"The occasion was the reception given by the Sergeants' Mess, Royal Welch Fusiliers, on the return of their comrades from the North, and was the outcome of a mess meeting held as soon as it was known that the latter were rejoining the Garrison. The arrangements were placed in the hands of an able and energetic committee, composed of Colour-Sergeant H. Yates, Sergeants Y. Payne, Glazebrook, C. Notmen, and H. Malone, and the catering was deputed to Thomas' Grill Rooms. The dinner was to the guests a most enjoyable and sumptuous repast, and had full justice done to it, over eighty seats being occupied.

"Then followed the inevitable smoker, at which Quartermaster-Sergeant Holloway presided, the following officers being present : Lieutenant-Colonel the Hon. R. H. Bertie, Majors Everitt and Dobell, Captains Gwynne, Hay, Doughty, Cadogan, Richards, Lieutenants Flower, Geiger, Gwyther, Owen, Walwyn, and Cleeve, and Lieutenant Cargill, R.E. There were in addition representatives from the different messes in garrison, from the S.S. *Salamis*, the trooper which brought the troops from the North, and a fair sprinkling of civilian friends.

"The time-honoured toasts, ' The Queen,' ' The Prince of Wales,' and ' The Army and Navy,' were drained with customary spirit.

" ' The Officers ' was proposed by the Chairman, who said that it was, he felt sure, a matter of pride to them all present to know how well their officers had acquitted themselves in the field, and he would mention in particular Lieutenant-Colonel the Hon. R. H. Bertie, upon whom he would call to reply.

"Colonel Bertie, who was suffering from a cold, and who was received with cheers, said it was with great pleasure that he rose to thank the members of the Non-Commissioned Officers' mess for the way in which they had entertained the officers that night. What gave him greater pleasure still was to have returned to Hong-Kong and have met so many old faces from the other battalion. Commenting upon the Chairman's remarks with reference to the officers he said he thought it would be very hard if British Officers ever failed to do their duty. The General, in his speech yesterday, had read the most flattering order from the G.O.C., North China. There had been very little crime in the half battalion, and that fact was very pleasing to him. Regarding their fighting North he could, he thought, say with certainty that sanction would be obtained for ' Pekin ' being inscribed on the Regimental Colours, and he understood that the Sergeant-Major had already secured a good portion of the White Ensign. He had heard many remarks about the officers doing well, but he would remind all that it was the Non-Commissioned Officers who helped them in their work. The gallant officer referred in brief to Major Dobell shortly vacating the post of adjutant, and said that all ranks would miss him.

"Major Dobell feelingly replied, and said he could only congratulate his successor, Captain Cadogan. Other speeches were given during the evening, Sergeant-Major Hickman's possessing particular importance in its reference to the social feeling existing in the regiment, which had been so enhanced by that night's entertainment.

"Throughout the evening a most enjoyable evening was spent in music, and was brought to a close promptly at midnight."

By submission to King Edward VII the regiment was permitted on the 29th of October 1902 to bear the distinction "PEKIN, 1900" upon its colours.

1901.

1st Battalion.

On the 2nd of January, leaving 70 Royal Welch Fusiliers under Major Glynn as part of the garrison of Ventersdorp, Colleton's column, consisting of 2 squadrons 14th Hussars, Royal Welch Fusiliers, and Gloucester Mounted Infantry, the Imperial Light Horse, and 3 guns, marched to Modderfontein, distance 10 miles, next day 13 miles to the source of the Mooi River, thence on the 4th 13 miles to Rietfontein.

On the 5th of January Colleton's column was ordered to march towards Blauwbank, to drive the Boers up the Hekpoort Valley, co-operating with the column under General Gordon, the whole operation being under the direction of General Babington.

After marching about 2½ miles Gordon was heard in action on the left front, and the Boers were seen on the left flank, and rear, descending from the Naauwpoort Hill and the Mafeking–Krugersdorp road. Babington had ordered the Royal Welch Fusiliers to occupy the hill, but subsequently ordered the Imperial Light Horse to do so instead, hoping to forestall the enemy in its possession.

The Boers, having reached the summit first, lay concealed in the long grass, and gave the Imperial Light Horse, whose line during the gallop had become somewhat crowded, a very warm reception, obliging them to retire with a loss of 2 officers and 10 rank and file killed and 33 wounded. Late in the afternoon the Royal Welch Fusiliers were ordered to occupy the hill, which they did without opposition : Colleton's column halted that night at Naauwpoort.

On the 6th of January the column started on its return to Ventersdorp, which was reached without incident on the 9th. Major Lyle, with a detachment of all arms, making a detour to clear the valley of the Mooi River, reached Ventersdorp on the 11th, bringing with him " H " company, which had been on detachment at Du Preez drift.

Colonel Kekewich having been incapacitated by an injury caused by his horse falling on him, his column was amalgamated with Colleton's under the direct command of General Babington.

On January the 24th information having been received that General Cunningham was engaged with De la Rey, south of Oliphant's Nek (one of the passes of the Magaliesberg, south of Rustenburg), the column marched at 2.30 p.m. from Ventersdorp to his assistance. Klipkrans, 17 miles distant, was reached that afternoon, the baggage not reaching camp till 10 p.m. On the 25th the column marched 20 miles to Vlakfontein, which was reached about 2 p.m., from which " D " and " G " companies were at once pushed on to gain touch with Cunningham, who had had 68 casualties, including 9 killed. In consequence of Babington's arrival the Boers retired. " D " and " G " companies Royal Welch Fusiliers had thus marched 40 miles between 2 p.m. on the 24th and 7 p.m. on the 25th, the remainder of the battalion having covered 37 miles in 24 hours over a bad veldt road.

Sir R. Colleton received the following complimentary note from General Babington : " Could you kindly let all ranks of your battalion know how very pleased I am with their fine marching on the 24th and 25th inst., and also that I have told General French of it."

Cunningham's force joined Babington's on the 26th at Vlakfontein.

On the 27th Major Mantell having been placed on the sick list with pneumonia, Major Beresford-Ash took over the duties of Acting-Adjutant from him.

On January the 28th the two columns marched with slight opposition towards Naauwpoort, where Babington's encamped, Cunningham's going on next day to Krugersdorp to refit. The column remained at Naauwpoort nearly six weeks, the Royal Welch Fusiliers being principally employed strengthening the position, and finding detachments for convoy duty to and from Krugersdorp from time to time. Lieutenant Hunt left to join the Royal Welch Fusiliers Section, 2nd Mounted Infantry, in General Cunningham's column, vice Lieutenant the Hon. C. R. Clegg-Hill.

About 9 a.m. on March the 7th General Babington sent for Sir R. Colleton and informed him that the small garrison of Lichtenburg was attacked by much superior numbers under De la Rey, and that he had been ordered to proceed with all speed to the relief of the garrison. Also that time being of such importance he proposed to take mounted men and a few guns only, and proceed by forced marches of such length that he feared the infantry would be unable to keep up, and he therefore intended to leave Colleton to bring the infantry and rest of the column back to Ventersdorp by ordinary marches.

Colleton asked if it was the intention of the General Officer Commanding to take any baggage and supply waggons with his flying column, and was told that it would be necessary to take a small quantity of transport only. The commanding officer Royal Welch Fusiliers then represented that the regiment would be greatly disappointed if they were left behind, and not allowed to share in the relief of their comrades, and that he would undertake that the infantry could march as fast and as far as the transport. The General Officer Commanding said in that case he would take them, and the whole column was ordered to start at 11 a.m. for Ventersdorp en route to Lichtenburg.

On parade before starting Colleton addressed the infantry, and informed them of the G.O.C.'s first intention to leave them (viz. the Royal Welch Fusiliers and half-battalion Somerset Light Infantry) behind, and of the undertaking he had given, and asked them to make a special effort for the relief of their gallant and hard-pressed comrades of the Northumberland Fusiliers at Lichtenburg. The faces of the men showed their appreciation of the trust reposed in them. It began to rain soon after starting, which greatly increased the difficulties of an already bad road: the infantry had to assist the mules and oxen, by man-handling the waggons at many of the drifts, over the swollen and unbridged streams. Nevertheless 22 miles were covered by 12 o'clock that night. The last of the transport waggons, however, did not arrive in bivouac until 3.30 a.m.

The march was resumed at 8 a.m. next day, the 8th March, in heavy rain, the country being more or less under water. Ventersdorp was reached at 5 o'clock that evening, the total distance of 44 miles being covered in 30 hours, with no stragglers. The men were quite prepared to resume the march next day, but further effort was not required of them, news having been received that De la Rey's attack had been beaten off, and that he had retired from Lichtenburg.

On the 10th the following letter, dated 9th March 1901, was received from General Babington, commanding the force:

" I hope you will make known to your Regiment my very high appreciation of their performance on the 7th and 8th instant, and that I shall certainly bring the same to the notice of the Commander-in-Chief. The Regiment was called upon to make an exceptional effort, and responded in a manner it would be impossible to beat . . . I am indeed proud to have such men under my command."

The thanks of Lord Kitchener were conveyed to the regiment by General Babington a few days later.

On the 14th of March " E," " B," and " F " companies rejoined headquarters from detachment, also Captains J. B. Cockburn and Throckmorton. Lieutenant the Hon. C. R. Clegg-Hill, having been appointed Adjutant, took over the duties from Major Beresford-Ash.

On March the 15th the force marched 10 miles to Koppiesfontein on the Lichtenburg Road: the next day 12 miles to Putfontein, 17 prisoners being brought in. On the 17th after a march of 10 miles Doornhoek was reached, where the bulk of the column halted, while General Babington and some mounted troops rode on about 10 miles further to Lichtenburg and returned the same night, 8 more prisoners being brought in.

The next day the force covered 20 miles to Nicholas Water in heavy rain, which made the roads very bad for men and transport. On the 19th the force left at 6 a.m. and marched 10½ miles to Kaffirs Kraal, whence, after a midday halt to cook and eat, the march was resumed for another 14 miles to Geduld (Patience)—a fitting name for the end of a very trying and severe march, the difficulty of which was aggravated by heavy rain, and a bad drift about a mile from camp. The last of the waggons did not come in until 9.30 a.m. and only one company reached camp before dark, about 6 p.m. The Boers retired before the force and split up into several small columns.

On the 20th a march of 8 miles through a pass in some low but steep hills brought the force to Hartebeestfontein, but, the camp being commanded from the hills, it was moved in the afternoon 1 mile further south nearer Klerksdorp. The next day " B " and " F " companies proceeded with a convoy to Klerksdorp, and returned on the 22nd.

On the 23rd of March a start was made towards the north at 5.30 a.m. The infantry and transport, under Lieutenant-Colonel Sir R. Colleton, halted at Geduld 1½ hours, and then continued its march to Palmietfontein, where they halted for the night. General Babington allowed false reports to be spread saying he was going to march at 3 a.m. on the 24th on

Ventersdorp, etc. etc., with the result that the Boers fell into the trap, were pressed back, and eventually routed with a loss of 22 killed and 140 prisoners, 2 guns, 4 maxims, and much transport.

In the meantime Colleton moved out from Palmietfontein at 5.30 a.m. with orders from General Babington to pick up Shekleton's transport at Syferkuil, and proceed from there with the combined convoy to join him at Putfontein. The guide not knowing the way led the convoy direct across the Vlei towards the drift over the Kaal Spruit. When the leading waggon arrived within a mile of the Spruit, the ground became so swampy that it was impossible to proceed. It being now broad daylight, a search revealed a fairly good road to the north of the track first taken. The low kopje under which the column had bivouacked the previous night was held by the 8th Mounted Infantry (detached from Shekleton's force) supported by " C " and " E " companies.

The leading waggon reached the drift at 9 a.m. The head of the column halted for breakfast at Shekleton's camp. Animals were outspanned, watered, and turned out to graze as each waggon got over the drift, which, owing to its being the rainy season, was in a bad condition, so that the last waggon did not get over till 10.45 a.m.

At Syferkuil the column was reinforced by 2 guns " P " battery R.H.A., 1 pom-pom, and 100 men Kitchener's Horse detached by Shekleton for that purpose. The combined convoy of Babington and Shekleton, consisting of 200 mule and ox waggons, besides Cape carts and 1st line transport, moved on at 11 a.m. The difficulty of defending this convoy, which was some 8 miles in length, is evident.

When the head of the main body had passed Rietfontein the sound of the guns of the rear-guard in action was heard, and the Black boys, some 200 in number, riding the spare horses of the mounted troops, came charging up the road in a dense mass in panic, causing a dangerous stampede of the mule waggons, several of which were upset in the Rietfontein Spruit before it could be checked.

These undisciplined Black boys on spare horses had been a source of danger on several occasions; instead of being allowed to ride at will and independently alongside the waggons, as was the current practice in this war, they should have been made to ride in separate bodies by regiments, each under charge of an officer, with a proportion of reliable non-commissioned officers.

Colleton immediately sent orders to Major Madocks, commanding " F " company Royal Welch Fusiliers, to seize a wooded hill which commanded the nek over which the road passed (to the east of it) at short range, and dispatched " D " company under Lieutenant Kyrke to assist the rear-guard, no mounted troops being available for the purpose. Colonel Colleton, having ridden forward to select a suitable place to park the convoy, gave orders for all waggons to park in the hollow near the farmhouse of Vaalbank, which stands by the roadside on the right bank of another branch of the Taaibosch Spruit. The two R.H.A. guns and the howitzer escorted by " B " and " H " companies were at first directed to take post on the hill east of the road, from which it was hoped a view of the rearguard fight would be obtained. As, however, nothing could be seen from there, the guns with their escort were ordered to move over to the hill west of the road. The hill on the east of the road was held by " G " and half of " D " company, which latter connected with Kitchener's Horse, who held the farm buildings of Vaalbank, which commands the drift by which the road crosses the Spruit. Beyond Vaalbank the left flank was held by " A " company on the north-eastern side of the hill west of the road.

By this time the last of the mule convoy was seen to have crossed the nek seized by Major Madocks, but Sir R. Colleton was informed that the ox waggons were cut off by the enemy. They had, however, been forestalled by Major Madocks, commanding " F " company, who seeing the vital importance of this position had anticipated the order to hold it.

Leaving Brevet-Lieutenant-Colonel Lyle, D.S.O., in command at Vaalbank, Lieutenant-Colonel Colleton was about to take " H " company Royal Welch Fusiliers back to the assistance of the rear-guard, when the first ox waggons were seen coming over the nek ; and all crossed without further hindrance, and parked in safety with the rest of the convoy. The attacking force consisted of 400 to 500 men of Vermaas' and other commandos under General Liebenberg.

The enemy made several attempts to seize positions on the high ground on the left flank and rear, which would enable them to fire on the convoy at effective rifle range ; but all their attacks were beaten off by the skilful handling of the rear-guard under Major Beresford-Ash, ably seconded by Lieutenant Howell in charge of the 2 guns of the 78th battery R.F.A., and Major Madocks, Captain Delmé-Radcliffe, and Lieutenant Webb-Bowen commanding " F," " E," and " C " companies Royal Welch Fusiliers.

General Liebenberg's son, who was his adjutant on this occasion, informed Sir R. Colleton, after the declaration of peace, that 600 men had been detailed for the attack on the convoy, but about 200 fell out on the march, their horses being done up, so that only about 400 were available for the attack. That the Boers were confident of the result is proved by the remarks of several of the prisoners captured by the mounted troops to the effect : " Ah well, you have got our convoy, but Liebenberg has got yours."

When the long convoy had been parked under cover in the hollow, Liebenberg, seeing no chance of success against the concentrated escort, broke off the action ; but some apprehension was caused by the appearance of about 200 mounted men coming from the north, who were at first thought to be Boers, who had cut in between the mounted troops and the convoy. They turned out, however, to be " Roberts's Horse," under Major Carrington-Smith, sent back by General Babington, when he heard the sound of the guns, to the assistance of the convoy. The new-comers brought the good news of Babington's success.

It was now about 5 p.m., with only one hour of daylight left. The transport animals being very tired, and there being a possibility of a night attack on the convoy, Lieutenant-Colonel Colleton directed Major Hare, D.A.A.G., to select a defensible camping-ground on a ridge on the left bank of the branch of the Taaibosch Spruit, on which Vaalbank farm-house is situated ; but just then a helio message was received from General Babington saying " Use every endeavour to reach here to-night."

Consequently the march was resumed, and after much difficulty, owing to the bad state of the drifts over the several flooded spruits, the drizzling rain and intense darkness, the head of the convoy reached General Babington's camp at Wildfontein at 9 p.m. after a trying march of 22 miles. Owing to a bad drift just outside camp the last of the waggons and the rear-guard did not arrive in camp till 6 a.m. on the 25th of March. The march was resumed about 12 noon on the 25th, and Ventersdorp, 18 miles distant, was reached the same evening.

No march on the 28th. A football match, Royal Welch Fusiliers *v.* Loyal North Lancashire Regiment, was won by the Royal Welch Fusiliers by 1 goal to *nil*.

On the 1st of April Babington's column left Ventersdorp and marched 9 miles to Wolvepan, and thence on the 2nd to Rietfontein, 13 miles, where it was joined by Rawlinson's (late Shekleton's) column. The march was continued at 5.30 a.m. on the 3rd in a north-easterly direction to Rietpan, a very trying march of 18 miles for the infantry on a bad road and in heavy rain. The rear-guard did not reach camp till 8 p.m. Tafel Kop (8 miles) was reached at 11.30 a.m. on the 4th, the hill being secured by the erection of a blockhouse garrisoned by Lieutenant Norman and 25 men of the Royal Welch Fusiliers.

On the 5th the empty convoy, escorted by Roberts's and Kitchener's

Horse, with the Royal Welch Fusiliers riding in waggons under command of Sir R. Colleton, left Tafel Kop and reached Ventersdorp, 23 miles, at 9.30 a.m. on the 7th: the rear-guard reaching camp at 11 a.m.

On the 8th Major R. Beresford-Ash left with an empty convoy to take up his appointment as second in command of the 2nd battalion Royal Welch Fusiliers in India.

On the 10th of April the column started on trek again, and camped at Buls Kop, 13 miles south of Ventersdorp; it reached Doornfontein, 14 miles farther, on the 11th, and Witpoort, 6 miles farther, on the 12th, whence "A" and "G" companies Royal Welch Fusiliers under Major Lyle proceeded with a convoy to Klerksdorp, and returned without incident the next day, bringing Major Mantell, who had returned from sick-leave. Meanwhile camp was moved, at 4 a.m. on the 14th, 4 miles to Brakspruit with the idea of using a standing camp as a base for the mounted troops of Babington's and Rawlinson's columns while clearing the neighbouring country.

On the 16th Captain Throckmorton left in charge of a convoy, escorted by "B" and "H" companies, for Klerksdorp, which rejoined next day at Rietkuil, whither the combined column had moved on the 17th.

The mounted troops found the enemy in force on the 18th holding the pass at Hartebeestfontein, and after a skirmish withdrew. The force marched 12 miles in a northerly direction on the 20th of April to Lapfontein, where it was joined by Major Mantell's convoy, which had gone to Klerksdorp the preceding day. On the 21st the force marched 13 miles to Syferkuil, where an entrenched camp for the two combined columns was formed as a base for the mounted troops.

On the 22nd of April an empty convoy under command of Major H. Lyle, D.S.O., left Syferkuil for Klerksdorp via the Drift over the Schoon Spruit at Brakspruit. The escort to the convoy consisted of 150 mounted infantry, 2 guns 78th battery R.F.A., and 200 men of "A," "D," and "E" companies Royal Welch Fusiliers, the infantry being carried in the empty waggons. The right flank was further protected as far as Brakspruit by mounted troops under Colonel Cookson, who after seeing the convoy safely over the Drift returned to camp.

The convoy after halting at Brakspruit to water and feed left there about 1 p.m. After it had marched about 8 miles the Boers were seen streaming out of the Hartebeestfontein Hills. They crossed the Schoon Spruit by the Brakspruit Drift in rear of the convoy at Witpoort on the right flank. The convoy was pushed on as fast as possible, "E" company Royal Welch Fusiliers being extended in rear, and "D" company on the right flank supporting part of the mounted infantry, who were holding some kopjes west of the road. The Boers closed in rapidly and drove in the mounted infantry rear-guard, and tried to rush the guns. They got to within 300 yards of the artillery, and brought a cross fire to bear on the guns from the rear and right flank. The guns limbered up and galloped towards the convoy, and the Boers were checked at close range by " E " company, whose appearance was probably a surprise to the enemy, as the infantry who had been riding in the waggons had dismounted and extended under cover of a fold in the ground. The fire of the Boers delivered from horseback did little damage. In the meanwhile " D " company, and the mounted infantry on the right flank, had checked the enemy, and the convoy had got some distance on.

After this a running fight ensued, the Boers following up within 2 miles of Klerksdorp. A few of the enemy who had got round on the left front captured 1 officer and 4 men of the mounted infantry. But after the first rush the enemy never got to closer range than 1,000 yards of the escort. The casualties were 2 killed, 6 wounded, and 8 prisoners, all mounted infantry, while it was reported afterwards that the Boers acknowledged to 75. They were 700 strong and commanded by Smuts.

On the 5th of May Babington's mounted infantry went out and met Lord Methuen's column about 15 miles from camp. One hundred and twenty Royal Welch Fusiliers of " A " and " E " companies escorted an Elswick high-velocity 12-pounder gun, which was posted in support of the mounted troops on a hill about three miles from camp.

On the 6th of May the whole force moved from Syferkuil to Geduld. The cavalry found a 9-pounder Krupp gun concealed in a donga. On the 7th the force marched in a north-westerly direction 7 miles to Brakspan and next day 8 miles to Palmietfontein, 20 prisoners and 25 waggons and Cape carts being captured.

After this the stages were: 10th May, 18 miles, south-west to Rhenosterspruit; 11th May, 16 miles south-west by south to Doornkuil. This was a very trying march, as it was hot and dusty with no water obtainable on the road.

On the 12th of May a march of 13 miles in a south-easterly direction brought the force to Doornfontein. On the 13th of May after a march of 16 miles due east Jackalsfontein was reached. On the 14th of May Welverand, 13 miles, through thick bush the first part of the march. Enemy sniped rear-guard and cavalry—no casualties.

On the 15th of May the force after a march of 7 miles reached Klerksdorp, and camped 1 mile west of the town. General Babington, on his departure to take over command of the Cavalry Brigade in the Eastern Transvaal, made the following farewell speech to the Battalion:

"Colonel Colleton, Officers and men of the Royal Welch Fusiliers,—I am not good at expressing what I mean, as I am no speaker, but I wish to say a few words to thank you for all that you have done for me. You have had a hard time, and have under all circumstances performed your duties in an exemplary and soldierlike manner. You have had a poor time as far as fighting goes, as your fighting has been confined of late to being attacked when on convoy duty. This is, I know, not to your liking, and you would far prefer to have had it the other way round and attacking the enemy. You have been constantly marching and had no chance of going for the enemy in the way I know you wished to. I am sorry I could not show you more fighting, but I required you for the important duties of guarding the camp and convoy, and felt that I could thoroughly rely on you, and you have never failed me. What has struck me most, and everybody who has seen you has made the same remark to me, is the exemplary manner in which you perform all your duties. However long the march, I know that you have always performed your duties in the most satisfactory manner. After marching great distances, I know that you have always carried out your outpost duties just as if you had been resting for a week or more. I have seen a good many regiments, but I know none to equal this regiment in its discipline and the way all duties are performed. I cannot fully express my gratitude to you, and the affection I feel for all, and I sincerely trust that you will get to your homes safely, and I wish one and all of you the very best of luck for the future. Good-bye."

With reference to the above speech it is interesting to record that the reputation of the battalion for hard marching earned it the honourable sobriquet in the column of "Babington's Foot Cavalry," while so great was the reliance on the regiment that it used to be said in the column headquarters mess: "Who is on outpost to-night? The Royal Welch Fusiliers. Ah then, we may go to bed in pyjamas."

On the 20th of May the battalion left by train for Potchefstroom, where the headquarters was stationed. "A," "C," and "G" companies, 175 strong, and 1 maxim were detached under Major Mantell to garrison Frederikstad, while the railway line between Potchefstroom and Frederikstad was protected by detachments of 25 men each under Lieutenant Bayly and 2nd Lieutenants Price and Kyrke at Buffelsvlei, Naauwpoort, and Mooi River bridge respectively.

On the 22nd of May Captain Throckmorton and 2nd Lieutenant Hughes left with "B" company to form part of the escort of the weekly convoy to Ventersdorp. It had been the custom for some time for the full convoy from Potchefstroom to meet the empty convoy from Ventersdorp at Witpoortje, and pass the night there together : the escorts exchanging convoys and returning to Potchefstroom and Ventersdorp on the following morning.

At 5.30 on the morning of 23rd May the convoys parted and started from Witpoortje on the return journey. The detachment of the Ventersdorp garrison in charge of the full convoy was under the command of Captain Purchas, South Wales Borderers, and consisted of 2 officers and 40 men of the Dorsetshire Yeomanry, 1 gun 78th Battery R.F.A., Captain A. Hay and 50 men of the 1st battalion Royal Welch Fusiliers, and 1 officer and 50 men of the Loyal North Lancashire Regiment.

On the left of the road to Ventersdorp there is a farm-house, and a few scattered houses known as Kaalfontein. On the head of the convoy nearing the farm, it was found that the Boers were holding it, and a ridge on the right of the road, and curving round to a wood on the right flank. They also held a ridge running parallel to and about 3,000 yards from the left of the road. The ambuscade was discovered by one of the Yeomanry right flankers riding over a Boer, who was lying concealed in the long grass. The Boer fired and gave the alarm, and the fight became general.

While the convoy was held up by the Boer position in front and right flank, about 200 Boers appeared over the crest of the ridge on the left flank, and after hesitating a few moments rode down on the rear of the convoy, which was thus almost surrounded. A hot fight ensued all along the road between Witpoortje and Kaalfontein. Three of the R.F.A. gun detachment were hit at the very start, and, the detachment being thus short-handed when unlimbering, the horses with the ammunition waggon broke loose and galloped down the road towards Witpoortje, through the rear-guard, which was composed of the 1st Battalion Royal Welch Fusiliers. The waggon would certainly have fallen into the hands of the enemy but for the presence of mind of Sergeant Fisher, 1st Battalion Royal Welch Fusiliers, who by shooting one of the horses enabled the drivers to regain control of the other horses.

The rear-guard was under a heavy cross fire from the road on the right flank, and two small kopjes on the left rear. Just then shells were seen bursting on Witpoortje, fired from the gun of the Potchefstroom convoy. The Boers who were holding Witpoortje, and so intercepting the communication between the two convoys, were obliged to clear off the road, and the Ventersdorp convoy was reinforced by 40 Imperial Light Horse, and 50 "B" company Royal Welch Fusiliers under 2nd Lieutenant

Hughes from the other convoy. The wood on the right, and the two kopjes on the left rear, were cleared by the Imperial Light Horse and 20 Royal Welch Fusiliers. The firing in front having now ceased, Captain Purchas decided to continue his march protected by the reinforced escort.

The road from Kaalfontein is quite level, and the ground on either side of it open until it crosses the Rietfontein Spruit, beyond which the ground rises to a ridge commanding the drift at a range of about half a mile. On this ridge a short distance from the right of the road is a group of deserted kraals to which the enemy had retired after the first attack. A party of the Imperial Light Horse had been left in occupation of Kaalfontein.

When the rear of the convoy was about a mile from Kaalfontein this party of the Imperial Light Horse, which had hitherto checked the Boers from riding down from their ridge on the left of the road, had to withdraw to avoid isolation. When the Imperial Light Horse began to slowly withdraw, the Boers in their turn began to follow up. As the waggons could only pass the drift in single file, the convoy was obliged to halt, and the Imperial Light Horse galloped through the Royal Welch Fusiliers rear-guard to pass through, and hold the left flank. Consequently there was nothing to prevent the Boers pressing the rear-guard, which was extended across the road about a mile from the spruit, where the ground begins to drop towards the stream.

The Royal Welch Fusiliers rear-guard was now exposed to a heavy and accurate fire from both flanks and rear: especially from a small party of Boers who had crept unperceived through the long grass into a small donga less than 100 yards from the rear-guard. While thus exposed to fire from both sides two stretcher-bearers, Privates Thomas and Morris, behaved with the greatest gallantry and coolness while attending the wounded. After dressing the wounds of three men completely in the open, and while attending to a fourth, Private Thomas was killed, and Private Morris severely wounded.

In the meanwhile the detachment of the Loyal North Lancashire Regiment reinforced by 20 Royal Welch Fusiliers was ordered to clear the kraals in front. They were starting to do this when the shells of a gun sent out from Ventersdorp caused the Boers to scatter hastily to the flanks. By about 4 p.m. the greater number of the waggons had crossed the spruit, the enemy, having apparently abandoned the hope of capturing the convoy, gradually drew off, the convoy was able to resume its march, and Ventersdorp was finally reached at 9 p.m. the same evening. Only two waggons were lost, which, owing to the greater part of their teams being shot, had to be left behind.

The total casualties were 6 killed and 40 wounded, of which the battalion lost 1 killed (Private P. Thomas) and 12 wounded, the latter including Captain A. Hay, slightly wounded in the head. The attack was carried out by about 500 men of Liebenberg's commando.

Captain Purchas, South Wales Borderers, commanding the convoy, reported that had it not been for the splendid behaviour of the Royal Welch Fusiliers he would have lost more than half the convoy.

On the evening of the 29th of June 2nd Lieutenant Sir F. Rose Price, Bart., received information from a native that 12 Boers slept regularly in a farm-house between 6 and 7 miles from his post at Naauwpoort. 2nd Lieutenant Price left at midnight with 7 men and surrounded the farm, but found only 4 Boers, who were captured with arms and ammunition and 8 horses.

On the night of the 18th of July 2nd Lieutenant de Burgh Edwards, who was then in command of the detachment of Royal Welch Fusiliers at Naauwpoort, received information from a native that Commandant Jan Smuts with a party of 11 Boers was spending the night at a kraal about 3 miles from his post. At 10 p.m. 2nd Lieutenant Edwards with 10 rank and file proceeded to the kraal, halting for an hour within 300 yards of it to allow the enemy to settle down for the night. Lieutenant Edwards then directed Sergeant Cottrell with 5 men to advance direct on the enemy's laager while he with 4 men made a detour with the object of attacking from the opposite side of the kraal. The night was pitch dark. When within a few yards the Boer sentry challenged, and fired, whereupon Lieutenant Edward and Sergeant Cottrell gave their men the order to charge. In the encounter which ensued, chiefly bayonet work, 4 Boers and 2 natives were killed and 4 taken prisoners, 2 of whom were wounded. Commandant Smuts escaped in the darkness. Lieutenant Edwards had only 1 native wounded. The capture included 1 Cape cart and 25 horses, 1 mule, 4 rifles and bandoliers.

The following telegram was received by 2nd Lieutenant Edwards: " Lord Kitchener to 2nd Lieutenant Edwards.—I am very pleased to hear of your successful encounter with Boers, which does you and your men great credit. Can you tell me anything of Smuts' movements?"

For their gallant conduct in this affair 2nd Lieutenant Edwards received the D.S.O., Sergeant Cottrell the D.C.M., and Privates Duglord and No. 2990 Davies were made King's Corporals.

In Lord Roberts's dispatch of the 4th of September published in the

London Gazette of the 10th, the following officers, warrant officers, non-commissioned officers, and men are mentioned, viz. :

Major H. T. Lyle, D.S.O.
Major A. P. G. Gough.
Major P. R. Mantell.
Captain G. F. Barttelot.
Captain H. Delmé-Radcliffe.
Captain G. E. Rickman.
Captain W. G. Braithwaite.
Lieutenant W. M. Kington.
Lieutenant F. H. Nangle.
Second-Lieutenant H. V. V. Kyrke.
Quartermaster and Honorary Lieutenant R. S. Ransome.
Sergeant-Major E. A. Parker.
Colour-Sergeant W. Gregory.
Colour-Sergeant W. Jones.
Colour-Sergeant W. G. King.
Colour-Sergeant G. J. Vale.
Colour-Sergeant C. Whinyates.
Sergeant S. Hotchkiss.
Sergeant W. Huffy.
Sergeant F. R. Mellor.
Sergeant J. J. Tomlinson.
Pioneer-Sergeant H. A. Legge.
Corporal T. Jenkins
Private T. Cahill.
Private M. Clark.
Private J. Marshall.
Private G. Mills.
Private J. Price.
Private J. Smith.
Private G. Wilkinson.

Mounted Infantry.

Captain and Brevet-Major C. M. Dobell.
Lieutenant the Hon. C. R. Clegg-Hill.
Lance-Sergeant W. Hill.
Private T. Evans.

On September the 15th Lieutenant Kington, 2nd Lieutenant Sir F. Price, Bart., and all the battalion mounted infantry left for Bank, to form part of a column under Colonel Hickman which was to operate in the Gatsrand Lieutenant-Colonel H. T. Lyle, with Lieutenant Reynolds as galloper, left on the 17th to take command of the mounted troops of the column. Captain Rickman, Lieutenants Harris and Edwards were detached with 101 rank and file to garrison blockhouses on the railway from Naauwpoort to Rocky kopjes (north of Frederikstad).

On the 23rd of September, with the exception of the mounted infantry, Captain Courtney Throckmorton's detachment of 30 men at Rooikraal, and Captain Delmé-Radcliffe's detachment of 60 men at Machavie (on the railway half-way between Potchefstroom and Klerksdorp), all detachments were called in, and the battalion concentrated at Potchefstroom.

On the 25th " A," " G," and " H " companies left Potchefstroom for Scandinavia Drift on the Vaal River 16 miles south of Potchefstroom, where they relieved the Scots Guards in the occupation of the blockhouse line from Scandinavia Drift on the Vaal River—about 16 miles south of Potchefstroom—to a point a few miles south of Reitzburg, Orange River State, whence the line was continued by the Oxfordshire and Buckinghamshire Light Infantry to kopjes south of Wolverhoek, on the Vereeniging-Bloemfontein railway; the rest of the battalion left on the 26th.

On arrival at Scandinavia Drift the battalion (18 officers and 509 rank and file) was employed in completing the barbed-wire fence between the blockhouses, and strengthening the defences of the headquarter camp, situated on the Orange River side of the Drift. The line was inspected on the 1st and 2nd of October by Major-General Mildmay Wilson, commanding Western Transvaal.

On the night of 1–2 October, and following night, small parties of Boers tried to cross the line, but were driven back.

As the battalion was employed for the remainder of the South African War in the erection and guarding of a succession of blockhouse lines, it may be well to give here a brief description of the purposes these lines were intended to fulfil and the mode of construction.

The immense extent of country which was comprised in the Cape, Natal, Orange River, and Transvaal Provinces made the guerrilla tactics adopted by the Boers after the taking of Pretoria very difficult to deal with. A mobile enemy composed of mounted men, each of whom had one or more spare horses, knowing the country perfectly, could laugh at the pursuit of a large column of all arms necessarily encumbered with a long train of mule and ox transport. On the approach of such a force the

Boers dispersed and split up into small commandos, or returned to their homes and became peaceful farmers until the danger was past.

This necessitated the formation on our side also of a large number of small columns of 400 or more mounted men with a few light guns and the minimum of mule transport. The co-operation of a number of such columns against an active enemy in a vast tract of undeveloped and sparsely watered country was most difficult, owing to the imperfect means then existent of intercommunication between columns, which depended chiefly on the heliograph. Under such circumstances a small column ran great danger of being isolated and overwhelmed by a concentration of largely superior forces.

To overcome these difficulties and hamper the movement of the Boer commandos, the blockhouse system was invented in 1901, and gradually developed until the end of the war in May 1902.

Blockhouses were originally adapted as a quick and economical means of guarding railway bridges and other important points, and the fortification of central points, such as Pretoria and Bloemfontein. The plan of guarding the railway lines by large detachments several miles apart was found to afford very imperfect protection to the line, and to absorb extravagant numbers of troops. A continuous line of blockhouses connected by a barbed wire fence was found more efficient and economical in every respect, and had the great additional advantage of converting the railway lines, thus protected, into serious barriers to the movements of the Boer commandos.

From this it was a natural step further to connect the railways by other blockhouse lines until the country gradually became cut up into large enclosures with sides of anything from 10 or 20 to 70 miles in length. The first blockhouses were built of stone, and were of various sizes according to the strength of the garrison they were intended to hold.

But when it became a question of erecting lines of blockhouses far from the railway, it was necessary to employ a more portable and economical material. After many experiments the circular blockhouse invented by Major Rice, R.E., was adopted as the standard pattern. It consisted of a double circular skin of corrugated iron, loopholed, and the space between the inner and outer skins filled with shingle to make it bulletproof. It was further protected up to the level of the loopholes by earth banked up against the outside, or a rough wall of uncemented stone. An umbrella-shaped roof and a water tank, both of corrugated iron, completed the accommodation for the garrison of 1 non-commissioned officer and 6 men. The blockhouse was surrounded by a ditch where the nature of the ground permitted, and a barbed-wire fence and entanglement.

Such a stronghold was of course not proof against field artillery, but at this stage of the war only the largest commandos encumbered themselves on special occasions with guns; while against musketry fire only, the garrisons were able to put up a stout defence—so much so indeed that, although the Boers were aware that it was possible by a determined attack to take one or more blockhouses before help could arrive, the capture of the very few men comprising the garrison, with one or two boxes of ammunition and a few tins of bully beef and biscuits, was not worth the probable loss and effort required.

On railway and veldt lines the blockhouses were as a rule placed 1,000 yards apart with supporting patrols where necessary and connected by a barbed-wire fence and a wire apron on both sides, to which as the system developed was added a V-shaped ditch to hinder the passage of wheeled transport. On river lines it was obviously a waste of effort and material to guard those stretches of river which were unfordable by a man on foot or on horseback, therefore only well-known drifts and possible fords were blockhoused. The search for possible drifts involved careful reconnoitring, which was not without danger of ambuscade, difficult to guard against owing to the fringe of scrub and thorn trees, 100 to 200 yards broad, which bordered the banks of the river in many places.

The usual routine of construction consisted in the establishment of a central entrenched camp for the headquarters of the column, from which working parties of infantry worked under the skilled superintendence of the R.E. protected by an escort of a company, and the mounted infantry. These parties worked as much as 5 miles on either side of the main camp; when the distance became too great for safety or convenience the headquarters camp moved on.

The mounted infantry was employed in patrolling the approaches, and cleared the country in the vicinity of live stock, and the farm-houses of their inhabitants, who were brought into concentration camps. It is beyond the scope of a Regimental History to discuss the pros and cons of Lord Kitchener's policy of clearing the country, and the consequent establishment of concentration camps: but it may be mentioned in passing that so long as the inhabitants and stock were allowed to remain unmolested, each of these farms became a potential magazine, and supply depôt for the commandos, which greatly facilitated the maintenance of the guerrilla warfare.

As each blockhouse was completed it was immediately garrisoned. A company section of the line consisted of seven or eight blockhouses, according to strength, and a company headquarters post or strong point in an entrenched farm-house or group of blockhouses. It will thus be seen that as the length of the completed line grew, and the distance from its base of supplies increased, so the strength of the headquarters column was diminished by the garrison it had provided, until at last it became a difficult task to find adequate escorts for the ox waggon supply convoys, while retaining a sufficient force in hand for the protection of the headquarters of the column, and support in case of attack for any threatened part of the line.

On October the 13th Lieutenant-Colonel Sir R. Colleton with the mounted infantry, " F " company Royal Welch Fusiliers, and " C " pontoon troop R.E. (Major G. Travers), left Scandinavia Drift for Machavie Station to erect a new line of blockhouses between the Potchefstroom-Klerksdorp railway and Kromdraai Drift on the Vaal. This line was garrisoned by " F " company. On the 19th Sir R. Colleton, the mounted infantry, and part of the R.E. returned to Scandinavia Drift. The line between the Mooi and Vaal Rivers was dismantled on the 20th, having become unnecessary by the construction of the Machavie-Kromdraai line to the west of it.

As the country in the vicinity of a blockhouse became clear of the enemy a new line was constructed, to protect the recently cleared area, either in substitution or addition to the line behind it.

In accordance with this policy the battalion headquarters with " B," " C," and " D " companies, mounted infantry, and R.E. moved on the 21st of October from Scandinavia to Witrand, with orders to construct a line on the left bank of the Rhenoster River from its junction with the Vaal east of Parady's Kop to Klip Drift inclusive, whence the line was carried on by the Oxfordshire and Buckinghamshire Light Infantry via the Lace Diamond mines to Kroonstadt.

On the 22nd of October the column was strengthened by the arrival of a draft of Royal Welch Fusiliers 83 strong with 2nd Lieutenants Morgan Jones, V. Barker, and Lieutenant Ball and a pom-pom section R.F.A., and on the 27th by the arrival of the 2nd Volunteer Company Royal Welch Fusiliers (56 rank and file) under Captain Meredith-Jones and Lieutenant Griffiths.

Most of the rivers of South Africa run between steep, high banks and are noted for their sudden floods without previous warning, usually due to heavy rain in the mountainous country where they have their source. The Rhenoster had a particularly bad reputation in this respect. The headquarters camp at Witrand was situated, owing to considerations of safety and supply, on the right bank, and was thus separated by the river from the blockhouses on the left bank. Advantage was therefore taken of the presence with the column of Major Travers's pontoon troop to secure communication between the two banks by means of a suspension bridge, the roadway of which was 25 feet above the river, which at this spot was only a few inches deep. As will be seen later, the construction of this bridge proved a fortunate precaution.

On the 19th of November Lieutenant-Colonel Sir R. Colleton with the pom-pom section, No. 7 company R.E. (Lieutenant Johnson), returned to headquarters at Witrand, after constructing blockhouses along the Vaal from Kromdraai Drift (where the Machavie line joined that river) to the junction of the Vaal and Schoonspruit, south of Klerksdorp. This line was held by "F" company, 2nd Lieutenant H. J. Phillips being at Wolmarans Drift with 20 men, Lieutenant Reynolds and 25 men at Vermaas Drift, with Captain A. Hay and 23 men at Coal Mine Drift.

On the 20th of November the Rhenoster Line being practically finished was organised as follows: Vaal to Kaffir Drift inclusive, Major P. R. Mantell and "C" company; Kaffir Drift to Klip Drift inclusive, Captain Barttelot and "D" company. The new line was inspected by Major-General M. Wilson, 23rd to 25th November. On the latter date 2nd Lieutenant Frere and 23 rank and file occupied the blockhouses erected on Parady's Kop and established a signal station, whence a wide view was obtained from Hartebeestfontein north-west of Klerksdorp, to Rhenoster Kop north of Kroonstadt.

Orders having been received to blockhouse the Vaal from Coal Mine Drift to Bothaville, the camp at Witrand was dismantled on the 3rd of December and the ox convoy sent across the Rhenoster the same evening, and laagered under the protection of the blockhouses guarding the drift.

The next day the battalion (less the detachments garrisoning the blockhouses in the Rhenoster and the Vaal between Kromdraai Drift and the junction of the Schoonspruit) marched at 5 a.m. just before daybreak. As the head of the main body cleared the camp a message from the O.C. advance guard reached the C.O. to say that the river had risen in the night, and was washing the road bearers of the suspension bridge, and it was doubtful if the mule waggons would be able to cross. After a delay of about half an hour on the river bank it became apparent that the water had reached its highest level, had even fallen a foot or so, and the battalion crossed, followed with some difficulty by the transport. The river remained unfordable for about six weeks.

The crossing accomplished without accident, the march was resumed via Jackalsfontein to Taaiplaats (11 miles), where camp was made, the oxen being completely done up by the hot sun and sandy soil. Coal Mine Drift was reached early next day. About 20 Boers were seen by the mounted infantry soon after leaving Taaiplaats, who sniped the left flank-guard.

The new Vaal line from Coal Mine Drift to Bothaville was commenced on the 6th, the first two blockhouses at Sand Drift near the junction of the Schoonspruit being garrisoned by Lieutenant Reynolds and 23 men of " B " company.

The column moved headquarters to Jonkers Kraal on the 11th, and to Yzer Drift on the 13th. This camp was situated on rising ground opposite the junction of the Yzer Spruit. The Vaal was divided here into two channels by a wooded island, which with the scrub thorn on the banks of the river facilitated a surprise attack. The camp was therefore carefully entrenched and the island secured by a blockhouse.

On the 15th of December a convoy left to bring supplies from Coal Mine Drift, escorted by 1 squadron South African Constabulary, the mounted infantry and " H " company (100 strong) Royal Welch Fusiliers, the whole under Lieutenant-Colonel Lyle, D.S.O. A Boer native spy was captured who reported that a large force of Boers was at Bothaville under General Liebenberg, who was expected to attack the camp that night. The whole force stood to arms at 2 a.m. till daybreak, but nothing happened. The interval between the departure and return of a convoy was always an anxious time for the column commander, whose small headquarter force was thus split into two parts, either of which would have had difficulty in successfully defending itself against a determined attack.

On the 18th Lieutenant Kington and the mounted infantry went out about 9 p.m. to try to capture some Boers reported at a farm-house at Zandfontein. The night was pitch dark and the mounted infantry lost their way, and about 12.30 a.m. attacked Lieutenant Webb-Bowen's post in a fortified house at Dood's Drift. Heavy firing went on for twenty minutes, when the mounted infantry returned to camp. The whole force in camp, alarmed by the firing, turned out, and manned trenches in expectation of an attack. Lieutenant Webb-Bowen reported next morning having beaten off an attack by a large force, and his garrison was very proud of itself. The mounted infantry were equally pleased with themselves. Both sides were much chagrined when they learnt that they had been fighting their own comrades, and were considerably chaffed by the rest of the column. Anyone who has had experience of the velvet blackness of South African darkness will understand how easy it was to make the mistake. As nobody was hit on either side, except one man grazed by a splinter or stone, the incident was amusing, but might have been tragic.

On the 19th the column commander with the mounted infantry about 23 strong went out to reconnoitre the drifts on either side of the Koodoesdrai, and select a site for the headquarters camp. About 50 Boers were seen a few miles off on the left bank of the Vaal, and the C.O. and staff while searching for drifts were sniped from the right bank.

On the 21st of December information was received that His Royal Highness the Prince of Wales had been appointed Colonel-in-Chief of the Royal Welch Fusiliers.

The same day information was received that a commando of 300 Boers under John Botha was in the neighbourhood supported by other commandos, and that they intended to attack the camp. The defences of the camp were still further strengthened on this and two following days.

On the 22nd two Boers came in and surrendered and stated they belonged to Ferreira's commando. As it was suspected that they were spies, special precautions were taken to prevent their escape, and all the men slept in their boots in readiness for instant action.

It may be of interest here to state how the large area of the camp was defended by the small force available when the convoy was absent. The garrison allotted to each post pitched their tents on the spot. First, a semicircular trench was dug about five yards in front of each tent. The next step was to connect the trenches of each pair of tents, and then repeat the process on the rear side of the tents. Each pair of tents was therefore enclosed by a dumbbell-shaped trench, which was surrounded by a barbed-wire fence and stocked with ammunition, water, and provisions, and thus formed a self-contained post which could continue its resistance even if some other part of the camp was rushed. In case of attack the tents would be immediately struck and the garrison in their places in the minimum of time. The maxim machine gun was posted well sand-bagged and wired on a small rocky hillock inside the perimeter, where it could fire in any direction.

1901.

2ND BATTALION.

On the 20th of February a draft of 118 non-commissioned officers and men under 2nd Lieutenant W. B. Garnett arrived from England.

On the 14th of March " B," " D," " F," and " G " companies under the command of Major S. G. Everitt embarked on the S.S. *Chingtu* for China to relieve the Australian contingent.

" B " and " D " companies under Captains Doughty and Bancroft proceeded to Tientsin.

" F " and " G " companies under Brevet-Major Sir H. W. McMahon, Bart., D.S.O., and Brevet-Major C. M. Dobell proceeded to Pekin to act as Legation Guard. The strength of each company was 110 men.

The following is an extract from Lieutenant-General Sir A. Gaselee's dispatch of the 17th of January : " Royal Welch Fusiliers. As the only British Infantry Corps with the force this regiment was invaluable to me. I understood they did good service at Tientsin before my arrival, and I certainly am much indebted to them for their services on the march to Pekin. I trust Lieutenant-Colonel the Hon. R. H. Bertie's services will be recognised."

In the *London Gazette* of the 25th of July the following rewards and promotions in the battalion are shown :

    Lieutenant-Colonel the Hon. R. H. Bertie awarded the C.B.
    Lieutenant F. J. Walwyn awarded the D.S.O.
    Captain J. H. Gwynne promoted to be Brevet-Major.

The following non-commissioned officers and men received the medal for distinguished conduct in the field :

    Sergeant C. W. Taylor.
    Private W. Crew.
        ,,   J. Doodson.
        ,,   T. Jackson.

On the 21st of December H.R.H. the Prince of Wales was appointed Colonel-in-Chief of the Royal Welch Fusiliers, an event which led to the issue of the following Regimental Order :

" In publishing the following letters of respectful salutation to H.R.H. the Prince of Wales on his being appointed Colonel-in-Chief of the Royal Welch Fusiliers, the officer commanding the 2nd Battalion feels sure that all ranks fully appreciate the honour conferred upon the Regiment, and cordially re-echo the sentiments of loyalty so ably expressed and conveyed therein, both to His Majesty the King and H.R.H. the Prince of Wales.

" The distance from home and consequent delay in receiving an official notification of His Royal Highness' appointment unfortunately prevented this Battalion from telegraphing their loyal respects on that auspicious occasion."

1902.

1st Battalion.

On January the 22nd, " E " company under Captain Delmé-Radcliffe took over the section of the line from Dood's Drift to Diepfontein. The column was reinforced on the 23rd by the arrival of 3 officers, 144 other ranks, and 93 horses, South African Constabulary.

On the 24th the column moved to Middelburg near Koodoesdraai Drift. Considerations of defence necessitated the placing of the camp on rising ground about 1¼ miles from the river, the only available water. As Boers were seen on the opposite bank of the river, in order to protect the transport animals when watering, two blinded armoured ox waggons moved down the hill, about a mile apart towards the river. These at a distance looked like ordinary tilted waggons and the Boers began to snipe at them as they approached the water. They were much astonished when the blinds were rolled up and disclosed that the innocent-looking ox waggons were in reality moving blockhouses capable of vigorous retaliation.

Lieutenant Norman with Lieutenant Ball took over command of the section on Captain Delmé-Radcliffe's left with headquarters at Middelburg Drift on February the 3rd.

On the 5th camp was moved to Doornhoek.

On the 21st No. 6473 Private E. Morris was accidentally killed by another sentry.

Two more troops S.A.C. under Captain Hoel Llewellyn joined the column on February 4th, followed by four other troops under Major Madoc on the 7th. Bothaville was occupied without opposition on the 13th and became the headquarters of the column. A line of blockhouses was erected on the left bank of the Vaalsch from its junction with the Vaal to Bothaville—6 miles up-stream ; the line was continued from Bothaville to Kroonstadt by the Oxford and Bucks Light Infantry.

While at Bothaville the mounted troops of the column, which included the Royal Welch Fusiliers Mounted Infantry, were employed in clearing the country west of the Vaalsch, inflicting the following losses on the Boers: 3 killed, 2 wounded, 19 prisoners (including G. Rademeyer, late Landrost of Bothaville and Abraham Pulter his clerk), 80 horses, 32 mules, 180 cattle, 3,600 sheep, 6 rifles, and 6 waggons and Cape carts.

On March 1st the South African Constabulary officers, Lieutenant Johnson, R.E., and Lieutenant Fuller, Oxford and Bucks Light Infantry, were guests at St. David's dinner.

During the night of the 13th about 100 Boers attacked the blockhouse on the heights west of the Vaalsch. About 50 succeeded in crossing, Steyn and De Wet supposed to be among them.

On the 14th Major Mantell rejoined with " B," " C," and " D " companies, which had been holding the Rhenoster line.

Orders having been received to extend the blockhouse line on the left bank of the Vaal as far as Commando Drift, Colonel Colleton went out to select a new advance supply depôt. A suitable place was found on the right bank of the Vaalsch near its junction with the Vaal. This post was garrisoned by 2nd Lieutenant H. J. Phillips and 22 men of " B " company.

On the 20th Bothaville and the portion of the Vaalsch line between it and the Vaal having been handed over to the Oxford and Bucks Light Infantry, the column marched to Palmietfontein, about 9 miles. The column marched on the 22nd and camped at Modderfontein, about 7 miles.

On the 1st of April the force moved camp to Strydfontein, about 7 miles.

On the 11th of April, the line having been completed and garrisoned as far as Commando Drift, the headquarters Royal Welch Fusiliers and R.E. marched for the Junction post. The South African Constabulary left the column for Hoopstadt. The column reached Junction post next day. A suitable site having been found about a mile from the Junction, it was strengthened and became the headquarters camp of the Vaal line between Coal Mine and Commando Drifts, the supply depôt being moved to the new camp, and one blockhouse left at the Junction to guard the flying bridge over the Vaalsch. The section of the line between the Junction and Commando Drift was placed under Major Mantell.

Parties of Boers varying in strength from about 200 downwards, with ox and other transport, attempted to cross the Vaal from the Transvaal side, and escape the drives of the mounted columns on the 6th, 12th, 18th, 20th, 21st, and 31st May. Most of these attempts were in the Krantz Drift sector of the line, which was commanded by Lieutenant W. Harris (now Harris St. John). Only on two occasions did a few succeed in crossing the line, but without transport, the remainder being driven back.

On the 1st of June a telegram was received from the Chief Staff Officer, Klerksdorp, saying that Peace had been concluded at Vereeniging the previous night.

On the 2nd orders were received from Lord Kitchener, Commander-in-Chief, South Africa, to send 1 officer, 3 non-commissioned officers, and 7 privates to Cape Town en route for England to represent the Royal Welch

Fusiliers at the Coronation of King Edward VII. This party, in charge of 2nd Lieutenant H. V. V. Kyrke, left next day.

On the 7th 21 Boers and 1 native with 18 rifles, 377 rounds S.A.A., 17 bandoliers, 1 revolver, 31 horses, 4 mules, and 1 Cape cart, surrendered to " A " company at Brand Drift. They were given one day's rations and sent on to join and surrender with Kritzinger's commando.

On the 13th the 3rd Volunteer Company Royal Welch Fusiliers, strength 2 officers and 36 other ranks, which had been garrisoning the Schoonspruit line between Klerksdorp and the Vaal, left en route for England.

On the 30th of June Colleton's column, having been broken up, the 1st battalion Royal Welch Fusiliers left for Klerksdorp, arriving at Diepfontein on 1st July and Vaal Camp on the 2nd. On the 5th a competition for the Liebig Extract Company's Cup took place, " G " company winning the inter-company knock-out, and in the final stage Sergeant Cawley took first place; he represented the battalion in the final competition at Pretoria on the 11th.

On the 7th the first batch of Reservists, 100 strong, under Lieutenant T. L. Pritchard, 4th battalion Royal Welch Fusiliers, left for Cape Town en route for England.

On the 16th Regimental Sports were held. Frequent football matches were played against the 2nd battalion Cheshire Regiment and the 2nd battalion Border Regiment.

On the 2nd of August a further batch of Reservists, 150 strong, under Captain A. Hay and Lieutenant Ball-Acton, left for England; a third batch of 100 under Lieutenant D. Powell left on the 11th; the remainder of the Reservists, 19, leaving on the 16th.

On the 27th Captain Gabbett and 65 non-commissioned officers and men left for Kimberley to join the 7th Mounted Infantry.

On the 11th of September " B," " C," " D," and " E " companies, 102 non-commissioned officers and men, left by train for Potchefstroom under Major P. Mantell, D.S.O., being followed on the 15th by the remainder of the battalion, 7 officers, and 193 other ranks, by route march, arriving there on the 17th.

On the 22nd of October a draft of 80 non-commissioned officers and men under 2nd Lieutenant R. N. Phillips left for Durban en route to India to join the 2nd battalion.

1902.

2ND BATTALION.

On the 10th of November the battalion embarked at Hong-Kong on the transport *Wakool* for India; it arrived at Calcutta on the 24th, and proceeded by rail to Meerut, arriving there on the 29th. Strength, 19 officers, 2 warrant officers, and 453 non-commissioned officers and men. There were left at Hong-Kong 356 non-commissioned officers and men for passage home for transfer to the Reserve.

On the 21st of November a draft from the 1st battalion of 80 non-commissioned officers and men arrived at Meerut to join the battalion on its arrival, and on the 29th a draft from England of 148 non-commissioned officers and men arrived.

On the 2nd of December a detachment of 4 officers and 100 non-commissioned officers and men proceeded to Delhi for duty at the Durbar.

On the 7th of December medals for South Africa and China were presented to non-commissioned officers and men.

1903.

1ST BATTALION.

On the 3rd of January orders were received for the battalion to return home. On the 6th it entrained at Potchefstroom en route for Cape Town at 8 p.m. The band of the 2nd battalion Somersetshire Light Infantry, and the drums of the 2nd battalion Norfolk Regiment, played the battalion down to the station: many officers and men of the garrison came to the railway station to say farewell to the battalion.

On the 8th the battalion arrived at Bloemfontein and picked up Lieutenant Nangle, 2nd Lieutenant H. J. Phillips, and 101 non-commissioned officers and men from the 7th battalion Mounted Infantry, who had marched in from Modder River Station.

On the 12th the battalion arrived at Cape Town at 6 a.m., and, after some delay owing to traffic on the line, embarked on the transport *Ortona*: Captain Gabbett with the remainder of the mounted infantry company and their heavy baggage also arrived on board.

The transport sailed on the 14th at 9 a.m., and on the 4th of February the battalion disembarked from South Africa at Southampton (strength 11 officers and 338 other ranks, 10 officers and 1 warrant officer being already in England on leave), and proceeded to Lichfield, where it was stationed in the hutments adjoining the Barracks.

The following telegram was received on disembarkation from His Royal Highness the Prince of Wales :

"I heartily wish all ranks welcome home after their long and trying campaign."

The following was sent in reply on the 5th of February :

"All ranks of the 1st battalion Royal Welch Fusiliers thank Your Royal Highness, and are much gratified by the gracious message of welcome from their Colonel-in-Chief."

From the 1st of February 1903, 478 non-commissioned officers and men were taken on the strength of the 1st battalion from the Details, Royal Welch Fusiliers, which had formed part of the 4th Provisional Battalion.

The Colours which had been kept at the Rifle Depôt, while the regiment was on active service in South Africa, arrived from the depôt on the 21st of February.

On the 26th of February H.M. the King signified his gracious acceptance of the goat brought home from South Africa by the 1st battalion (this goat had been purchased on the 20th of August 1900 for the sum of £2 near Krugersdorp), and also his intention to present to the battalion a goat from the herd in Windsor Park to replace it.

On the 7th of March 2nd Lieutenant H. V. V. Kyrke proceeded to Windsor with the goat brought from South Africa, and brought back the goat presented by the King.

On the 10th of March Lieutenant-Colonel Sir Robert Colleton, Bart., C.B., wrote to the Deputy Ranger, Windsor Park, and asked him to convey to H.M. the King the grateful thanks of all ranks of the battalion for His Majesty's gift, and their high appreciation of the latest mark of the gracious favour His Majesty had shown to the regiment.

On the 12th of March a draft of 51 non-commissioned officers and men under command of Captain G. W. D. B. Lloyd embarked for India at Birkenhead per S.S. *Olympia* to join the 2nd battalion in India.

On the 12th of March the Regimental goat died of syncope. H.M. the King graciously presented another goat to replace the one that died, which arrived on the 17th of April.

On the 7th of April the Commander-in-Chief, Field-Marshal Lord Roberts, K.G., V.C., visited Lichfield, and expressed his satisfaction at the appearance of the troops and state of the barracks during his inspection.

On the 8th of May the battalion proceeded to Wrexham by special train (strength, 24 officers, 607 other ranks), on the occasion of H.R.H. the Prince of Wales unveiling a Memorial in Wrexham Church to the officers, non-commissioned officers, and men of the regiment who fell in China during the War of 1900, and in South Africa during the War of 1899–1902.

The battalion formed a Guard of Honour to H.R.H. the Prince of Wales on this occasion. The Memorial, designed and sculptured by Mr. Thomas Rudd of Clapham Common, S.W., measures 10 feet by 7 feet, and is of pure English alabaster: the side niches contain white marble statues, representing an officer and private of the regiment, in a mourning attitude. The centre marble panel contains the names of 204 officers, non-commissioned officers, and privates who laid down their lives in South Africa during the years 1899 to 1902, and in the Expedition to Pekin in 1900.

After the ceremony of unveiling the Memorial in Wrexham Parish Church had concluded the battalion marched to the Barracks, Wrexham, where H.R.H the Prince of Wales presented the Queen's and King's South African and China Medals, to officers, warrant officers, non-commissioned officers, and men entitled thereto. A number of Distinguished Conduct Medals were also presented, also a Medal for Long Service and Good Conduct (to Colour-Sergeant W. G. King).

The Prince addressed the regiment in the following terms:

" Lieutenant-Colonel Sir Robert Colleton, Officers, and Non-Commissioned Officers, and men of the 1st Battalion Royal Welch Fusiliers,— It is a great satisfaction to me that my first duty as Colonel-in-Chief of your Regiment should have been to assist in doing honour to the memory of your comrades who laid down their lives for their Sovereign and Country, and I am very proud to have been able to present you with the medals to-day which you have so well earned during your long and arduous campaign in South Africa. I don't propose to recapitulate the deeds which have added fresh fame to the glorious records of the Royal Welch Fusiliers. Lord Roberts, Lord Kitchener, General Barton, and General Babington have testified in no uncertain language to the splendid work achieved by the battalion from the time it landed in Natal in November 1899 until the close of the War, and we must not forget that upwards of 350 of your Militia Battalion and three Volunteer Companies also took part in the War. I congratulate you all on your safe return home. I am very glad to meet you here to-day at the headquarters of our Regimental District, and I trust that such gatherings as these may stimulate the military instinct and draw to the ranks the best of her sons, keen to emulate the example of those whose brave deeds have added to its laurels, and help to maintain the proud traditions of the Regiment."

Colonel Sir Robert Colleton in reply said:

"Your Royal Highness,—On behalf of all ranks of all battalions of the Royal Welch Fusiliers, I beg you to accept our most sincere and hearty thanks for the great honour you have done the Regiment in coming here to-day to unveil the memorial of those comrades who have fallen in campaigns in South Africa and China, and to present the medals to the survivors. We desire also to place on record our high appreciation of the gracious kindness of Her Royal Highness the Princess of Wales in coming so far at so much trouble to herself to be present on this memorable occasion. The past services of the Regiment to which Your Royal Highness has alluded in such gracious and laudatory terms, together with the records of the other Welsh regiments, may, I hope, be taken as sufficient proof that Welshmen of modern times are no less stubborn fighters than their ancestors, whose conquest by Edward I was only assured when he gave his eldest son to be Prince of Wales. King Edward VII having long since achieved the conquest of the hearts of all his subjects, it only remained for His Majesty to complete the conquest of the Welsh by the appointment of your Royal Highness as Colonel-in-Chief of the senior regiment of the Principality. I venture to hope that as long as the regiment continues to merit the great honour by the maintenance of its reputation for valour and conduct in the field, the name of the heir to the throne may always be found at the head of its roll of officers."

Their Royal Highnesses the Prince and Princess of Wales, and other distinguished visitors, were entertained at luncheon by Colonel Mainwaring, C.M.G., commanding the Wrexham Depôt, and the officers of the Royal Welch Fusiliers. Their Royal Highnesses returned to Eaton Hall about 4 p.m.

The battalion returned to Lichfield the same day.

The appearance of the battalion and the smart work at Wrexham were much appreciated by past officers of the regiment who were present on that occasion.

Colonel Sir Arthur Bigge, Private Secretary to H.R.H. the Prince of Wales, forwarded the following letter to Colonel R. B. Mainwaring, Commanding 23rd R.D.:

"The Prince of Wales, who has just got back, desires me to write and tell you how much pleased he was with everything connected with

THE SOUTH AFRICAN AND CHINA WARS MEMORIAL IN THE REGIMENTAL CHAPEL IN WREXHAM PARISH CHURCH.

the visit to Wrexham. It was a great pleasure to H.R.H. to see for the first time the First Battalion, and he was greatly struck with their fine appearance on parade."

On the 4th of August the battalion proceeded to Milntown Camp, Isle of Man.

On the 11th of August the battalion returned to Lichfield.

1903.

2ND BATTALION.

On the 12th of March the battalion proceeded by march route to Chakrata, arriving on the 24th.

On the 8th of May the Memorial in Wrexham Church erected by the regiment to the officers and men who fell in the China War of 1900 and the South African War of 1899-1902 was unveiled by H.R.H. the Prince of Wales. A description of the ceremony will be found under the record of the 1st battalion.

On the 21st of August Lieutenant-Colonel the Hon. R. H. Bertie, C.B., gave up command of the battalion, and was placed on half-pay.

His farewell order was as follows:

" In bidding farewell to the battalion, in which he has passed the greater part of his service, Lieutenant-Colonel Bertie regrets that he is not handing it over to his successor in as satisfactory a condition as he could have wished.

" He feels sure, however, that, now the difficulties which militated against it, while split up in China and on first arrival in India, no longer exist, the battalion will speedily regain its efficiency.

" Already, at Chakrata, a marked improvement in shooting and drill has been noticeable. He deplores the recrudescence of crime in the last two months, particularly that of an insubordinate character, the more so as, during the previous half-year, the general behaviour of the men had been distinctly creditable.

" He exhorts them to shun the bad companionship and evil example of the malcontents, and to realise how disadvantageously the interests of a whole battalion may be prejudiced, and how easily a bad reputation can be gained for it, by the conduct of a few disaffected men.

" While thanking those of all ranks who by individual co-operation have assisted him in his duties, the Commanding Officer records his appreciation of the fact that, during his period of command, an additional honour

'PEKIN' has been added to the Colours, and assures those who have joined from South Africa that he values the privilege of having become associated with men, now serving under him, who nobly sustained the traditions of their Corps in that quarter of the Empire.

"Though the time has come to sever his personal connection with the 2nd Battalion Royal Welch Fusiliers, Lieutenant-Colonel Bertie will, nevertheless, continue to follow its fortunes with interest and, in taking leave of his comrades, he wishes them, one and all, good luck and success throughout their career."

He was succeeded by Lieutenant-Colonel H. T. Lyle, D.S.O.

On the 29th of October the battalion proceeded by march route to Meerut, arriving on the 12th of November, and taking part in the hill manœuvres between Chakrata and Dehra Dun.

A draft of 131 non-commissioned officers and men arrived at Meerut on the 23rd of December from the 1st battalion.

1904.

1st Battalion.

On the 1st of March the battalion was presented with a Silver Shield and Chain by the Mayor and Citizens of Lichfield to mark the gift of a goat to the battalion by His Majesty the King, while stationed at Whittington. The presentation was made in the Market Square, Lichfield, the battalion parading in Review Order under Lieutenant-Colonel Sir R. A. W. Colleton, C.B.

On the 20th of March a party of 50 rank and file under Major R. E. P. Gabbett and 2nd Lieutenant G. F. Hatton, proceeded to London to attend the funeral of H.R.H. the Duke of Cambridge, K.G., returning on the 21st inst.

On the 11th of May Lieutenant-Colonel (Brevet-Colonel) Sir R. A. W. Colleton, C.B., relinquished the command of the battalion on completion of the term of appointment.

On the 12th of May Lieutenant-Colonel B. H. Beresford-Ash took over the command of the battalion in succession to Lieutenant-Colonel Sir R. A. W. Colleton, Bart., C.B.

On the 19th of July 22 officers, 500 rank and file, with band and drums, proceeded to Liverpool to line the streets on the occasion of a visit made to that city by His Majesty the King. On the same date this party left Liverpool for Delamere Forest, for the Annual Training Camp, which had already been prepared near Oakmere by the advanced party of 2 officers and 130 men.

On the 28th of August the battalion returned to Lichfield.

On the 19th of September the battalion (strength, 24 officers, 2 warrant officers, and 818 rank and file) proceeded from Lichfield to Aldershot on change of station. The battalion was quartered in Maida Barracks, Stanhope Lines, and formed part of the 3rd Brigade, 2nd Division.

1904.

2ND BATTALION.

On the 12th of March the battalion proceeded by march route to Chakrata, arriving on the 24th.

A draft from England arrived on the 6th of April, consisting of 184 non-commissioned officers and men from the 1st battalion.

On the 21st of October the battalion proceeded by route march to Agra, where it arrived on the 26th of November, having halted at Meerut from the 3rd to the 12th of November for examinations in tactical fitness for command.

On the 6th of November the goat presented by Her Majesty the late Queen Victoria died at Meerut.

On the 22nd of December a draft of 106 non-commissioned officers and men arrived at Agra from the 1st battalion.

1905.

1ST BATTALION.

On the 12th of May Prince Eitel Fritz of Prussia, accompanied by the General Officer Commanding-in-Chief, Sir John French, inspected the Barrack Rooms of the battalion.

On the 20th of May, the annual competition for the Connaught Shield was won by the stretcher-bearers section of the battalion.

The battalion, numbering 17 officers and 595 rank and file, took part in a Review before Their Majesties King Edward VII and King Alfonso of Spain on June the 8th. His Royal Highness the Prince of Wales rode at the head of the battalion as Colonel-in-Chief of the regiment in the march past.

On the 18th and 19th of July 1 officer and 86 men took part in a grand military Fête and Torchlight Tattoo in the grounds of Government House,

Aldershot. Lieutenant E. A. T. Bayly and 50 non-commissioned officers and men formed the 3rd Brigade Guard of Honour. One non-commissioned officer and 8 men took part in the pageant dressed in the uniform of 1854.

On the 22nd of September the battalion took part in the Army Corps Manœuvres from the 22nd to the 29th of September.

1905.

2ND BATTALION.

On the 8th of January the battalion was inspected in drill and instruction (war training of infantry) by the Commander-in-Chief's Committee, and gained the highest number of marks in the Eastern Command.

On the 26th of October a draft of 1 corporal and 40 men arrived at Agra from the 1st battalion, bringing with them a goat to replace the one that died in the previous November.

During the visit of the Prince and Princess of Wales to Agra, from the 16th to the 20th of December, the battalion participated in the ceremonials connected with the stay of Their Royal Highnesses there.

1906.

1ST BATTALION.

In January the names of the Companies of the 1st battalion were changed from Nos. I, II, III, and IV to W, X, Y, and Z.

On July 10th and 11th 1 officer and 58 men took part in the Grand Military Fête and Torchlight Tattoo in the grounds of Government House, Aldershot. Lieutenant W. G. Jones and 50 non-commissioned officers and men formed the Welch Guard of Honour. One non-commissioned officer and 4 men dressed in the uniform of 1854 took part in the pageant.

On September the 1st the battalion Judging Distance Team, composed of members of " W " company, won the 3rd Brigade Judging Distance Cup, presented by Brigadier-General T. O. Pilcher, C.B., A.D.C.

On September the 13th to the 21st the battalion took part in the Aldershot Army Corps Manœuvres near Chichester. On the conclusion Major-General Sir Bruce Hamilton, K.C.B., commanding the 2nd Division, expressed his approval of the battalion, and the manner in which it had performed its duties in the field.

1906.

2ND BATTALION.

The battalion remained at Agra during the year. Two drafts arrived from the 1st battalion, one of 90 non-commissioned officers and men on the 11th of February, and another of 42 non-commissioned officers and men on the 15th of March.

1907.

1ST BATTALION.

On May the 16th His Royal Highness the Prince of Wales, Colonel-in-Chief of the regiment, accompanied by the Princess of Wales, inspected the battalion on Maida Barracks Parade Ground, Aldershot. The battalion (strength, 22 officers and 447 rank and file) was drawn up in line in Review Order at 4.30 p.m.

After the inspection Their Royal Highnesses visited the Barrack Rooms, Dining Halls, and Institutes of the battalion. They took tea with the officers at their mess, leaving barracks at about 6.15 p.m.

In a letter received by General Sir Edward Bulwer, G.C.B., from H.R.H. the Prince of Wales, His Royal Highness expressed his satisfaction at the appearance of the battalion on parade, and his appreciation of the arrangements which were made for his inspection.

On June the 12th the battalion took part in a review at Aldershot at which H.M. the King was present. H.R.H. the Prince of Wales marched past at the head of the battalion.

From the 13th to the 22nd of September, the battalion took part in the Aldershot Command Manœuvres in Buckinghamshire.

On the 26th of September a party of 1 officer and 27 rank and file proceeded to Cork to take over barracks on change of station.

On the 1st of October the battalion, consisting of 18 officers and 549 rank and file, left Aldershot for Cork, on change of station, arriving at Cork on the morning of October the 2nd. Two officers and 47 rank and file proceeded to Longmoor for duty with the mounted infantry.

1907.

2ND BATTALION.

In connection with the ceremonies of the visit of the Amir of Afghanistan in which the battalion took part, the following is an extract from the Special Command Concentration Orders, dated 9th January : "The Amir has requested the General Commanding the Eastern Command to express to the troops who paraded this morning in honour of his arrival his regret that they got wet. Desiring to show his appreciation of the soldierlike manner in which the troops turned out, and at the same time to share their discomfort, he refrained from cloaking himself during the procession, as they were not cloaked."

The battalion took part in a review of 30,000 men at Agra on the 12th of January held in honour of the Amir.

On the 21st of August Major P. R. Mantell took over command of the battalion from Brevet-Colonel H. T. Lyle, D.S.O., on the expiration of his period of command. The following farewell message from Colonel Lyle was published in Regimental Orders for Wednesday the 21st of August : " In saying good-bye to you all I should like to let you know that during my command I have been backed up in every way by officers, non-commissioned officers, and men. Whatever I wanted done has been most willingly carried out. I shall always be proud, like any other time-expired Welchman, of having belonged to the Regiment, and I wish you every chance of adding to that long list of honours by which you have already made your name."

The battalion moved from Agra, " A " and " D " companies forming an advance guard on the 12th of December, and proceeding to Calcutta by rail to load the baggage : the remainder of the battalion, with the exception of the time-expired details, proceeded to Calcutta by rail on the 13th, and arrived there on the 15th of December. They sailed on the R.I.M.S. *Northbrook* for Rangoon, and arrived there on the 19th, where they remained under canvas until the 24th. They then embarked on the flats drawn by the R.I.M.S. *Irrawaddy* and proceeded up the Irrawaddy River.

1908.

1st Battalion.

On the 12th of May Colonel R. H. Beresford-Ash went on retired pay on completing his period of command. Lieutenant-Colonel H. A. Iggulden, from the Sherwood Foresters, was promoted to command the battalion.

On the 30th of May the battalion (strength, 20 officers, 450 other ranks) left Cork and marched to Kilworth Camp, a distance of 28 miles, for training and musketry.

On the 29th of June the battalion returned from Moore Park, where it had moved from Kilworth Camp on the 27th, to Cork on completion of Musketry and Company Training. Brevet-Colonel E. S. Bulfin, promoted substantive Colonel, was removed from the regiment on appointment to the Staff.

On the 3rd of September the battalion left Kilworth Camp at 6 a.m., where it had arrived on the 25th of August, for Brigade Manœuvres; it marched to Faegarrid, where it halted for the night, and on the 4th moved on to Belleville Park, near Cappoquin, reaching Aglish Camp for Divisional Training, where it remained until September the 18th, when it marched to Youghal, and entrained for Cork, the original intention of marching to Cork being abandoned owing to the wet weather.

On the 18th of September the battalion returned to Cork on the conclusion of Summer Training, having marched during the training season over 500 miles, exclusive of manœuvres, etc., and having been nearly 3½ months under canvas.

1908.

2ND BATTALION.

The battalion arrived at Shwebo on the 8th of January: " E " and " G " companies proceeding to North Lines, and the remainder to South Lines. " D," " F," and " H " companies were under canvas, the remainder in bungalows.

The battalion was inspected by Brigadier-General E. S. Hastings, C.B., D.S.O., on the 3rd, 4th, 5th, and 6th of February. On the 3rd of February the battalion marched from Shwebo Barracks to Umbuk, formed a perimeter camp, and marched back. On the 4th the books were inspected and the battalion seen in movable column, knot tying, tent pitching, swimming, one mile double with 100 rounds of ammunition, kit inspection, etc. On the 5th the battalion was seen in the " Kitchener's " Field Test (marched 15 miles with 100 rounds of ammunition), and the attack, bivouacked for the night, and formed a rear-guard action back to barracks on the 6th. General Sir A. Hunter, K.C.B., D.S.O., was present.

The battalion took part in the " Burma Divisional Manœuvres," forming part of the Shwebo Force marching out of Shwebo on the evening of the 16th of February, and reached Saigang Shore on the 22nd, entrained at Saigang Shore for Shwebo on the 23rd.

A draft from the 1st battalion arrived at Shwebo on the 25th of February, consisting of 175 non-commissioned officers and men.

On the 8th of March " E," " G ," and " H " companies made up to 230 strong proceeded to Bhamo on detachment under command of Major G. W. D. B. Lloyd.

The following were the remarks of the Brigadier-General Commanding Mandalay Brigade on the Efficiency Test of the battalion for the year 1907-1908 : " The training has been very thorough and on sound lines : officers and non-commissioned officers smart and well kept up in their duties and men quick to grasp and carry out orders. Drill movements very smart and accurate. In preparation for war the regiment is expert. Musketry has improved since last year, and is good. Signalling very good. Discipline in this Brigade good, an increase over last year's crime statistics owing to Kailana Depôt. Marching powers very satisfactory. Physical appearance and training very satisfactory. Last draft satisfactory. Welfare of soldier satisfactory. Documents and records satisfactory. Personnel very satisfactory. Training satisfactory. Officers show resource and self-reliance ; there is no undue centralization. Interior economy sound.

"*General conclusions.*—A Corps in good training, both physical and professional for war, with a good tone and great esprit de corps. Above the average in efficiency. Fit for service. Maximum marks, 2,200. Amount obtained by the battalion, 1,694. Deductions for 2nd class shots, etc., 302."

1909.

1st Battalion.

On the 5th of August the battalion (strength, 8 officers and 223 rank and file) left Cork at 5 p.m., and marched to Kilworth Camp for Annual Training, being joined on arrival by 6 officers and 143 non-commissioned officers and men already at Kilworth, and on the 8th by 3 officers and 69 non-commissioned officers and men from the Curragh.

On the 12th of September the battalion (17 officers and 365 non-commissioned officers and men) returned to Cork on conclusion of Divisional Training.

1909.

2nd Battalion.

On the 10th of February " B," " D," and " F " companies moved to Bhamo in relief of " E," " G," and " H " companies, which rejoined headquarters. On the same day a draft consisting of 151 non-commissioned officers and men arrived at Shwebo from the 1st battalion.

The following is an extract from the report on the inspection which took place in February: " It has given the G.O.C. great pleasure to report very favourably on your battalion, which he considers above the average in efficiency and fit for service. I am to add that the condition of the Bhamo detachment, under the command of Major Lloyd, reflected great credit on that officer."

On the 27th of November a draft of 205 non-commissioned officers and men arrived from England.

" A " and " H " companies moved to Bhamo on the 1st of December, in relief of " B," " D," and " F " companies; " C " company moved there on the 8th.

1910.

1st Battalion.

On the 7th of May the following telegram was sent to the Colonel-in-Chief (King George V) on the occasion of the death of His Majesty King Edward VII:

" The officers and all ranks of the Royal Welch Fusiliers beg respectfully to tender their great sorrow, and sincerest sympathy, to their Colonel-in-Chief on his irreparable loss "; and the following was the reply received:

" The King sincerely thanks the officers and all ranks of the Royal Welch Fusiliers for their kind sympathy."

On the 11th of May the battalion furnished a Guard of Honour to attend the Proclamation of H.M. King George V. in the City of Cork. This consisted of 100 rank and file together with the band and drums, and was under the command of Captain C. I. Stockwell, with Lieutenant W. B. Garnett and Lieutenant E. O. Skaife carrying the King's Colour. The Proclamation was read by the Lord Mayor at the City Hall, the Law Courts, and at the Father Matthew Statue in Patrick Street. At the last place Brigadier-General R. C. A. Berwick-Copley, C.B., called for three cheers for the King, after which the battalion returned to Victoria Barracks.

On the 20th of May the battalion (C. of E.) attended the Memorial Service held at St. Luke's Church, Cork, at the same hour as the funeral of His late Majesty King Edward VII.

Other denominations also attended memorial services on this date.

On the 2nd of June the following letter was received from His Majesty King George V. by General Sir E. G. Bulwer, G.C.B., Colonel of the Royal Welch Fusiliers, and was published in Regimental Orders:

"MARLBOROUGH HOUSE, PALL MALL,
31st May 1910.

"DEAR SIR,
"I am commanded by the King to inform you that His Majesty has much pleasure in continuing to be Colonel-in-Chief of the Royal Welch Fusiliers.

"Yours very truly,
[signed] ARTHUR BIGGE.

"General Sir E. G. Bulwer, G.C.B.
45 Hans Place."

Reply :

"45 HANS PLACE,
1st June 1910.

"DEAR SIR,
"I have the honour to acknowledge your letter of the 31st ult., announcing His Majesty's intention of continuing to be Colonel-in-Chief of the Royal Welch Fusiliers, and in reply on behalf of the Regiment to convey their deep sense of the honour conferred on them, and of their assurance that they will always endeavour to be worthy of such honour.

"I remain, yours very truly,
[signed] E. G. BULWER, *General*.

"Colonel Sir A. Bigge, G.C.V.O., K.C.B.
Marlborough House, Pall Mall."

On the 11th of June the battalion furnished a party of 1 non-commissioned officer and 20 privates to represent the regiment at the Army Pageant at Earl's Court, London.

On the 21st of July the battalion left Cork for Ballyvonare for annual Summer Training.

On the 27th of July the battalion moved from Ballyvonare to Kilworth, owing to very inclement weather, and swampy state of camping ground.

On the 9th of September the battalion left Kilworth for Irish Command Manœuvres, and formed part of Blue Force arriving at the Curragh, Kildare, on Sunday the 18th of September.

On the 3rd of October the battalion entrained at Curragh Siding for Dublin on change of station, and was quartered in Royal Barracks.

The following appeared in the *London Gazette* on the 12th of October :

"Major and Brevet-Colonel Charles MacPherson Dobell, D.S.O., to be an Aide-de-Camp to His Majesty, 4. 11. 10."

On the 9th of December the news was received of the death of

MAJOR-GENERAL THE HON. SIR SAVAGE L. MOSTYN, K.C.B.
From a photograph at Wrexham Barracks. Photograph by Algernon Smith, Wrexham.

General Sir Edward Bulwer, G.C.B., Colonel of the Royal Welch Fusiliers, at 11. a.m. on the 8th of December. Orders issued for officers to wear mourning for one month.

A letter of condolence was sent from the battalion to the relatives of the late General Sir Edward Bulwer, G.C.B., and a reply was received thanking all ranks for their kind sympathy.

The following is an extract from the *London Gazette* of the 23rd of December :

"Royal Welch Fusiliers, Major-General the Hon. Sir S. Mostyn, K.C.B., from the Devonshire Regiment, to be Colonel."

1910.

2ND BATTALION.

On the demise of King Edward VII. on the 6th of May, the Colonel-in-Chief of the Royal Welch Fusiliers, H.R.H. the Prince of Wales, succeeded to the throne as King George V ; and General Sir Edward Bulwer, Colonel of the regiment, sent the following telegram to Marlborough House : "Royal Welch Fusiliers offer their sincere sympathy and whole-hearted allegiance to His Majesty, their Colonel-in-Chief," receiving in reply the following : "The King deeply appreciates the loyal and sympathetic message of the Royal Welch Fusiliers."

On the 12th of November the goat which had been presented by His Majesty the late King Edward VII. died at Shwebo, Burmah.

The General Officer Commanding the Division, before leaving the station after his Test inspection in November, expressed to the Commanding Officer his great satisfaction with all he had seen at his recent inspection. He was especially pleased with the fine physical condition of the regiment, and with the keenness, willingness, and energy which they had shown on all occasions.

He also wished to thank the officers, warrant officers, non-commissioned officers, and men of the battalion for the support which they had given in upholding all kinds of sport, and for the great assistance given him at Divisional Assault-at-Arms and Boxing Tournaments.

On the 14th of December after the inspection by General Sir E. Barrow, G.C.B., the Medal for Long Service and Good Conduct was presented by him to Sergeant-Major M. Murphy.

On the 15th the Bhamo detachment rejoined headquarters.

On the 18th of December the headquarters left Shwebo and embarked on the *Sladen* and *Custodian*, arriving at Rangoon on the 29th.

The headquarters and 5 companies left Rangoon on the R.I.M.S. *Hardinge* on the 31st of December for India. The Bhamo detachment and drums were left behind at Rangoon owing to there being insufficient accommodation in the *Hardinge* : they proceeded to camp near the Arsenal.

The following farewell order was published by the G.O.C. Mandalay Brigade :

" Before the 2nd Battalion Royal Welch Fusiliers leave Burma, en route to Quetta, the Major-General commanding the Brigade desires to place on record his appreciation of the good work, soldierly bearing, and fine sporting spirit shown by this Battalion throughout their stay in the Mandalay Brigade.

" The Battalion has the whole time been split up, furnishing a detachment at Bhamo, which notwithstanding the depressing influences of the heavy rains and malarial fever at that station has vied with the headquarters in the conscientious performance of its duties.

" The leading part taken in all sports by the Royal Welch Fusiliers during their stay in Burma will long be remembered by all the garrison, as well as the hospitality with which all comers to their stations were entertained by the officers and other ranks of the battalion.

" In bidding farewell with great regret to the 2nd Battalion Royal Welch Fusiliers Major-General Hastings thanks all ranks for their good service and soldierly conduct whilst under his command, and wishes them every success and good fortune in the coming years."

On the 8th of December General Sir Edward Bulwer, G.C.B., Colonel of the Royal Welch Fusiliers, died, and was succeeded in the Colonelcy by Major-General the Hon. Sir Savage Mostyn.

The following is an extract from the annual inspection of Signallers held at Shwebo :

" An excellent result and an improvement on last year. All the Signallers have qualified as first class. A keen, well-trained body of Signallers, who have well maintained their high standard of efficiency. Equipment in excellent order, and well cared for. One or two of the latest trained Signallers require accuracy, and rapidity in helio-setting."

1911.

1st Battalion.

On the 16th of May the occasion of the Centenary of the Battle of Albuhera was marked by combined Trooping of the Colours of the 1st battalion the Buffs, 1st battalion the Royal Fusiliers, and the 1st battalion the Royal Welch Fusiliers, which battalions had all taken part in that glorious fight. The Royal Welch Fusiliers attach great importance to this battle, as there is no other regiment which has the distinction of having fought at Fontenoy, Minden, and Albuhera. The ceremony, which took place on " the Fifteen Acres," Phœnix Park, Dublin, was honoured by the presence of His Excellency the Lord Lieutenant of Ireland, the Earl of Aberdeen, K.T., attended by General the Right Honourable Sir Neville Lyttelton, G.C.B., and Major-General W. Pitcairn Campbell, C.B., commanding the 5th Division.

His Excellency, on arrival, was received with a Royal Salute by the troops, who were drawn up in line.

The Trooping then commenced, the Colours being carried by Lieutenant E. O. Skaife and 2nd Lieutenant J. G. Bruxner-Randall. Major and Brevet-Colonel C. M. Dobell, D.S.O., A.D.C., was in command of the combined escorts. After the troops had executed a march past they advanced in Review Order, gave three hearty cheers for the King, and, having formed three sides of a square, were addressed by His Excellency, who expressed himself as very pleased with the smartness with which the evolutions had been carried out and announced that he intended to send a telegram to His Majesty the King describing the ceremony, and giving an assurance on behalf of the three regiments of their loyalty and devotion to his person. The three regiments then marched back to their respective barracks.

The following telegram was received the same night:

" Colonel Iggulden, Commanding Welch Fusiliers, I have much pleasure in transmitting the following telegram handed in at Buckingham Palace, 8.5 p.m. :

" Lord Lieutenant, Dublin,

" I thank you for your telegram describing interesting commemoration of the Centenary of the Battle of Albuhera. Please express to the Officers Commanding the three Regiments which took part in the ceremony my high appreciation of their loyal assurances.

" G.R.I."

On the 27th of May the battalion took part in a parade held in honour of the birthday of His Majesty the King, the Colours being carried by 2nd Lieutenants J. G. Bruxner-Randall and M. D. G. Parry. The troops were inspected by His Excellency the Lord Lieutenant of Ireland, the Earl of Aberdeen, who was accompanied by the G.O.C.-in-C. the Forces in Ireland.

A feu-de-joie was fired, and the parade concluded with a march past, an advance in Review Order, and the giving of three cheers for the King.

On the 20th of June a representative detachment from the battalion consisting of Major H. O. S. Cadogan, Captain A. Haig, Lieutenant E. O. Skaife, and 50 non-commissioned officers and men, with the goat, left for London to attend the Coronation of King George V.

They formed part of " B " composite battalion, which was encamped in Regent's Park East, under the command of Colonel H. A. Iggulden, with the following members of the regiment as Battalion Staff :

Brevet-Major R. E. P. Gabbett	Adjutant.
Lieutenant E. A. P. Parker	Quartermaster.
Sergeant-Major S. Williams	Sergeant-Major.
Q.M.-Sergeant F. Cottrill	Quartermaster-Sergeant.

On the 22nd of June, the day of the Coronation, the detachment was posted at the southern end of Whitehall, and on this occasion the goat excited much curiosity among the foreign Royalties in the procession.

On the 23rd of June, the day of the Royal Progress through South London, the detachment was at the east end of Pall Mall. It left London the same day and returned to Dublin.

On the 8th of July the battalion lined part of Clyde Road on the occasion of the State Entry of H.M. the King into Dublin. Lieutenant E. O. Skaife and Lieutenant J. G. Bruxner-Randall carried the Colours. Afterwards a Guard of Honour was furnished for the opening of the Royal College of Science by His Majesty the King. This consisted of 100 rank and file under the command of Captain the Hon. C. R. Clegg-Hill, D.S.O., with Lieutenant L. D. A. Fox and Lieutenant E. O. Skaife carrying the King's Colour.

On the 9th of July a Guard of Honour was furnished at the Castle with the King's Colour, carried by Lieutenant W. H. C. Pery-Knox-Gore.

On the 11th of July the battalion took part in a Royal Review at " the Fifteen Acres," Phœnix Park. Their Majesties arrived at 11 a.m., accompanied by the Prince of Wales and the Princess Mary, and were received by a Royal Salute, after which they inspected the line, and returned to the Saluting Base for the march past. On the conclusion of this, His Majesty presented new Colours to several battalions. The Review was concluded by an advance in Review Order and another Royal Salute. The battalion marched back to barracks, and an hour afterwards left for North

Wall and embarked for Wales. Carnarvon was reached about 11 p.m. and the battalion went into camp at Coed Helen.

On the 11th of July No. 9818 Private E. Musson showed prompt and intelligent action when, on the occasion of a woman catching fire on an electric tram, by his readiness of resource in quickly obtaining a blanket and enveloping her in it, he did his best to save her life.

On the 13th of July, on the Investiture of H.R.H. the Prince of Wales the battalion lined a great part of the square in Carnarvon, and also furnished a Guard of Honour at the Water Gate of Carnarvon Castle. His Majesty the King inspected the Guard, and was pleased to express his satisfaction at its smartness. The Guard was under the command of Captain W. B. Garnett with Lieutenant C. H. R. Crawshay and Lieutenant J. G. Bruxner-Randall, who carried the King's Colour. Major-General the Honourable Sir Savage Mostyn, K.C.B., Colonel of the Royal Welch Fusiliers, and Colonel H. A. Iggulden, Commanding the 1st battalion, had the honour of being in the procession in attendance on the Prince of Wales in the Castle.

On the 14th of July the battalion left Carnarvon for Bangor by train. During their stay in Carnarvon they had been encamped alongside the 3rd Battalion (S.R.) of the regiment, with whom the most cordial relations were maintained. At Bangor the battalion furnished a Guard of Honour at the railway station for the arrival of Their Majesties, under the command of Captain A. Hay, with Lieutenant W. C. H. Pery-Knox-Gore and 2nd Lieutenant M. D. G. Parry, who carried the King's Colour. The remainder lined the route to the New University, which was opened by His Majesty the King, and also the return route. His Majesty the King was again graciously pleased to compliment the commander of the Guard of Honour on its smartness. Both officers and men were provided with tea by the generosity of Colonel Platt, late of the Royal Welch Fusiliers.

The return journey to Dublin was made the same night, barracks being reached at 2 a.m.

Captain and Brevet-Major R. E. P. Gabbett was promoted to the rank of Major, and appointed to the command of the Regimental Depôt.

On the 18th of August at 12.30 a.m. the battalion was warned to embark at 6 a.m. on account of the threatened railway strike, and at 2.45 a.m. they were told to be in readiness to embark as soon after 4 a.m. as possible. The battalion arrived at North Wall at 4.27 a.m. and crossed to Holyhead with the 2nd Wiltshire Regiment. Chester was reached at 1 p.m. and both battalions encamped on the Roodee. After a stay of 24 hours the 1st battalion Royal Welch Fusiliers moved to Warrington, and were accommodated in the depôt of the 8th and 40th Regimental District at Orford Barracks. During the night it was necessary to send a detachment to protect a signal-box which was being attacked by strikers, and also Warrington Station. "B" company, under the command of Captain H. I. Webb-Bowen and Lieutenant M. I. H. Anwyl, was detailed for this work and successfully accomplished it, without coming into contact with the strikers. They were withdrawn about 10 a.m. on the 21st of August.

On the night of the 19th of August 150 men were requisitioned for the protection of the goods station at Salford, and at Victoria Station, Manchester. "A," "C," and "E" companies, under the command of Colonel C. M. Dobell, D.S.O., A.D.C., were sent at once and arrived at about 3.30 a.m. This detachment returned to Warrington on the 23rd of August.

On the 24th of August orders were received at 1 p.m. that the battalion was to entrain at 6 p.m. and return to Dublin. The battalion reached Royal Barracks at 6.30 a.m. on the 25th.

On the 20th of September, the anniversary of the Battle of the Alma, in honour of this occasion, and also of Major-General Luke O'Connor, V.C., C.B., being present in Dublin, a parade at 12 noon in Review Order was held in Royal Barracks. General O'Connor was received with a salute and inspected the battalion; quarter-column was then formed, and he gave an address in which he recalled with pride the part taken by the battalion in that battle, and how it assisted in winning further honour for the regiment. The parade was then dismissed, and the remainder of the day observed as a holiday.

1911.

2ND BATTALION.

The headquarters, etc., arrived at Karachi on the 9th of January; the Bhamo detachment and drums left Rangoon on the 7th on R.I.M.S. *Dufferin*, and arrived at Karachi on the 19th. A draft of 37 non-commissioned officers and men arrived from England on the 25th of February, and brought out a goat, the gift of H.M. King George V, to replace the one that had died at Shwebo. The battalion proceeded to the rest camp at Karachi, and remained there under canvas until the 31st of March. They left there on that day and arrived at Quetta on the 1st of April, being played in by the bands and drums of the Royal Irish Fusiliers and the Essex Regiment.

On the 2nd of June the goat presented by H.M. King George V. died at Quetta.

On the 20th of August Lieutenant-Colonel P. R. Mantell, having been placed on the half-pay list, relinquished command of the battalion. The command was taken over by Lieutenant-Colonel H. Delmé-Radcliffe.

A draft of 81 men from the 1st battalion at Dublin arrived on the 3rd of December and brought out with them another goat, the gift of King George V, to replace the one which had died at Quetta.

The following is the report on the annual inspection of the Signallers of the battalion held at Quetta on the 27th November : " A very satisfactory inspection. A thoroughly efficient body of Signallers, the standard of efficiency attained being a very high one."

The battalion furnished a special detachment consisting of Lieutenant-Colonel H. Delmé-Radcliffe, Captain R. B. Johnson, Sergeant-Major Murphy, Sergeant Jones, Corporal J. K. Jones, Lance-Corporal John Hughes, Drummers Taylor and Osborne, and 16 selected privates, i.e. 2 per company, to represent the Royal Welch Fusiliers at the various ceremonies of the Durbar.

The following duties were performed by the Special Detachment, viz. :

Thursday 7th December; State Entry of Their Majesties into Delhi.

The detachment was drawn up on the Selimgarh Bridge on both sides of the roadway at the end nearest to the Selimgarh railway station, distant about 100 yards from the bridge. A Guard of Honour was drawn up by the station, and also the Indian Mutiny and other veterans. Their Majesties were received with a Royal Salute by the Guard of Honour, and the King then inspected the Guard and the Veterans. Then commenced the historic " State Entry." As the Royal procession approached the Selimgarh Bridge, the detachment Royal Welch Fusiliers presented arms, the band striking up the National Anthem on hearing the word of command for the " Royal Salute " being given by the Officer Commanding Royal Welch Fusiliers. The detachment were thus the first troops to give the " Royal Salute " to Their Majesties at the commencement of their great " State Entry," and thus inaugurated the first act in the series of great and imposing ceremonies of the Coronation Durbar.

The detachment had an excellent view of the reception of the principal officials by Their Majesties on the station platform.

The Royal Procession passed between the ranks of the detachment across the bridge to the Reception Shamiana in the Fort. The roadway was narrow, and Their Majesties passed within four feet of the ranks of the detachment on either side.

Monday 11th December, Morning; Presentation of Colours.

On this morning His Majesty the King presented new Colours to nine battalions. It was a fine spectacle and the weather was cloudless; Her Majesty the Queen watched the ceremony from the Royal Pavilion at the side of the grounds. The King rode on to the ground opposite the Pavilion, and dismounted and walked forward to the place where he presented the Colours after the Consecration Service.

The detachment Royal Welch Fusiliers lined the edge of the ground in front of the Royal Pavilion and were the nearest troops to the place where the King rode on to the ground. The Sergeant-Major was on duty in the Pavilion handing leaflets of the "Form of Prayer" to the members of the Royal Family and other exalted personages and high officials.

Monday 11th December, Afternoon; Final of Polo Tournament.

On this afternoon Their Majesties watched the final match in the Coronation Durbar Polo Tournament, won by the Inniskilling Dragoons, the runners up being the King's Dragoon Guards: the detachment of the Royal Welch Fusiliers and Royal Irish Fusiliers being on the right of the Pavilion within a few yards of Their Majesties.

His Majesty noticed, after he had been there about five minutes, that the detachments were standing at "Attention" and sent an equerry to the commanding officers to tell them to let the detachments "Stand Easy."

Tuesday 12th December; The Durbar.

During the Coronation Durbar, which took place in the morning in the great amphitheatre, the detachment was drawn up in single rank, lining the east side of the circular road in the western half of the amphitheatre. Their Majesties drove by this road to the Royal Pavilion, distant about 100 yards from where the detachment was drawn up. Adjoining the detachment lining the edge of the cross-roads running to the Imperial Thrones were companies of the Royal Fusiliers, of which regiment the King is also "Colonel-in-Chief."

From the flank of the detachment up to the Royal Pavilion was an open space, so that the detachment had a fine view of the ceremony: 12,000 spectators, mostly Europeans, filled the smaller grand stand at the south side of the amphitheatre. An immense crowd of natives filled the many great stands all round the northern side of the amphitheatre, their number being estimated at something near 200,000. Inside the amphitheatre 20,000 troops were in array. At the foot of the dais, on which were the Imperial thrones, were drawn up four Guards of Honour, viz.: on the east side the 36th Sikhs of Saraghai fame, on the west side the Black Watch, at the northern side on either side of the main central road, the Naval Guard and the Royal Marine Artillery Guard. From the centre of this main central road, and facing Their Majesties seated on their thrones, the Delhi Herald, General Peyton, read out the Imperial Proclamation, and after he had concluded it was again read out in Hindustani by the Native Herald.

An Imperial Salute of 101 salvos of artillery (i.e. 606 guns) was then fired by batteries stationed outside the amphitheatre. After the 34th salvo had been fired, a feu-de-joie was fired by troops lining both sides of the road from the King's camp to the amphitheatre, a distance of about 3 miles. It commenced at the amphitheatre, ran up to the King's camp and back again, a distance of about 6 miles in all. After 33 more salvos had been fired the feu-de-joie was repeated, and again after 34 more salvos. The massed bands of 1,500 musicians then played the National Anthem, all spectators rising to their feet, and the whole of the troops giving the "Royal Salute."

Their Majesties then went back in procession from the thrones to the Royal Pavilion, where they entered the state coach and drove away amidst loud and prolonged acclamations of the assembled multitudes. The scene was one of unparalleled splendour. Their Majesties wearing their crowns and State robes, and the many varieties of uniforms, made a very brilliant scene in the amphitheatre. The homage of the Native Chiefs, clad in their finest uniforms and State robes, for the occasion, was also a wonderful spectacle. This took place before Their Majesties moved in procession from the Royal Pavilion for the Proclamation to the Imperial thrones on the dais, distant about 60 yards from the Royal Pavilion.

Captain Hill, M.V.O., of the 2nd battalion, as extra A.D.C. was in close attendance on Their Majesties during the ceremonies. Sergeant-Major Murphy was on duty in the grand-stand distributing leaflets of the King's Proclamation to the spectators.

Thursday 14th December, Morning; Royal Review.

About 50,000 troops were reviewed by His Majesty the King on the specially prepared Review Ground.

The detachment was on duty lining the enclosure, the left flank being only a few yards from where His Majesty sat on his horse at the Saluting Point during the Review. Her Majesty the Queen sat in the Royal Pavilion close behind the King. A feature of the Review was the large number of Imperial Service Troops, who marched past led by their own Rajahs, such as Bikaner, Gwalior, Jodhpur, etc.

Thursday 14th December, Night; Royal Investiture.

His Majesty the King invested many high personages and officials with orders and insignia, the first to be decorated being Her Majesty the Queen with the Grand Cross of the Star of India.

Lieutenant-Colonel and Mrs. Delmé-Radcliffe were present and had a good view of this interesting ceremony. The Sergeant-Major was on duty in the Reception Shamiana conducting people to their seats.

Friday 15th December; Presentation of Portraits.

His Majesty the King received the commanding officers of the regiments of which he was Colonel-in-Chief, and personally presented to them portraits of himself and Her Majesty the Queen with their autograph signatures at foot of the pictures. His Majesty the King addressed the officers commanding, and told them he wished these portraits put up in the messes of the regiments as a memento of the Coronation Durbar. Lieutenant-Colonel H. Delmé-Radcliffe received the portraits for the 2nd battalion Royal Welch Fusiliers.

Saturday 16th December; State Departure.

The detachment was on duty in the Royal Camp quite close to Their Majesties' tents, lining both sides of the road.

The following is the Review Report of the G.O.C. Southern Army on the Inspection Report of the battalion for 1911:

"A very fine regiment with great esprît de corps."

1912.

1st Battalion.

On the 9th of February the Commanding Officer had the following act of gallantry brought to his notice by the Secretary of the Royal Humane Society, Liverpool:

"On the 29.12.11 Bandsman Herbert Llewellyn gallantly stopped a runaway horse attached to a cab in Liverpool." The Society forwarded a framed Certificate of their thanks to Bandsman Llewellyn.

On the 16th of February "B" company's team won the Inter-Regimental Shooting Competition in the Brigade Competition.

Total scores made by the 1st R.W.F. ("B" company), 684 points.
,, ,, ,, R. West Kent Regt. (2nd best), 551 ,,

On the 20th of February "B" company won the Monro Challenge Cup of the Inter-Company Physical and Musketry Competition, and were awarded marks as follows: the next best were the 1st Buffs, whose marks are also given below:

	Gyms.	Cross-coun'try Running.	Rifle Shooting.	Total.	Order.
1st Royal Welch Fusiliers	338	191	685	1214	1
1st Buffs	437	168	542	1147	2

On the 24th of February "B" company's team took 2nd prize of £2 5s. in the Inter-Company Bayonet Fighting Competition, 13th Infantry Brigade.

On the 12th of April the regimental goat presented to the battalion by His Majesty King Edward VII, in April 1903, died at Dublin.

On the 18th of April H.M. the King graciously signified his intention of presenting a goat to the battalion, which arrived at Dublin on the 26th of April, to replace the one deceased.

On the 26th of April the Regimental (1st) Football Team won the Irish Army Football Association Cup, defeating The Royal Scots by 4—2 goals.

On the 29th of April the battalion took part in a "Farewell" Parade of all units in Dublin Garrison to General the Right Hon. Sir N. G. Lyttelton, G.C.B., Commanding-in-Chief the Forces in Ireland, which was held on the "Fifteen Acres," Phœnix Park, Dublin.

On the 3rd of May the battalion marched to Kilbride Camp for Annual Course of Musketry.

On the 4th of May Lieutenant-Colonel and Brevet-Colonel C. M. Dobell, D.S.O., A.D.C., was promoted to the command of the 2nd battalion Bedfordshire Regiment.

On the 6th of May the battalion furnished a Guard of Honour under Captain W. M. Kington, D.S.O., consisting of band, drums, and 50 rank and file, at Westland Row Station, Dublin, on the departure of General the Right Hon. Sir N. G. Lyttelton, G.C.B., the Commander-in-Chief of the Forces in Ireland, on the termination of his period of command. The General Officer Commanding inspected the guard, band, drums, and expressed his pleasure at the smart and soldier-like appearance of all.

On the 11th of May Lieutenant-Colonel and Brevet-Colonel H. A. Iggulden having completed his term of command (four years) was placed on half-pay.

Major H. O. S. Cadogan, 1st battalion, was promoted Lieutenant-Colonel, and took over the command of the battalion.

On the 15th of May Brigadier-General T. Capper, C.B., D.S.O., commanding 13th Infantry Brigade, presented the Dublin Garrison Football League Cup and Medals, also the Irish Junior League Cup and Medals, which were won by the 1st and 2nd Regimental Teams during the season 1911–1912.

On the 18th of May the battalion proceeded to Doolystown Camp, near Trim, for Battalion Training, returning on the 3rd of July.

On the 30th of May Sergeant M. Wood won the Silver Medal for the highest score in the Roupell Cup at the All Army Championship Meeting at Pirbright.

On the 13th of June the battalion took part in a parade held in Phœnix Park in celebration of the birthday of His Majesty the King. The Colours were carried by 2nd Lieutenant G. O. de P. Chance and 2nd Lieutenant D. M. Barchard.

On the 10th of July the Annual Inspection of the battalion by the Brigadier-General Commanding 13th Infantry Brigade took place, commencing with a parade in review order on the Esplanade, on the conclusion of which the Brigadier-General Commanding commented on the smart and soldierly appearance of the battalion, and expressed his regret that the battalion would shortly be leaving the Irish Command.

On the 20th of July the battalion marched to Kilbride for field practices, returning to Dublin on the 3rd of August.

On the 13th, 14th, and 15th of August Regimental Sports were held on the Esplanade. Three events open to the Irish Command were won by Private Kelly, " B " company, 1st battalion Royal Welch Fusiliers.

On the 2nd of September the battalion marched to Kill, en route for Curragh Camp to commence brigade training, thence to Coolmorey Camp on the 7th of September, at which camp, owing to the prevalence of foot and mouth disease, the proposed brigade and divisional training was cancelled, and the units returned to Dublin on the 12th of September.

According to the *Western Daily Mail* of the 5th of October, an exciting scene was witnessed in Queen Street, Cardiff, on Friday afternoon, 4th of October, in which the central figure was Private George Brown, of " G " company 1st battalion Royal Welch Fusiliers.

It was just after 3 o'clock when a runaway pony attached to a light trap, owned by Mr. Saunders, butcher, St. Mellons, dashed under the Taff Vale Railway Bridge into the crowded and busy thoroughfare. In the trap were Mrs. Saunders and her young child. It appears that when near the Power Station at Newport Road the reins somehow got caught by the shaft and the pony bolted. Mrs. Saunders with a child naturally lost control, and the pony galloped along the Newport Road at a furious pace, greatly to the consternation of the pedestrians.

Several ineffectual attempts to stay its progress were made, but the most plucky and determined one was made by Brown. The Fusilier was riding a bicycle, and, pedalling quickly after the runaway, first got alongside the trap in Queen Street, when he surprised the spectators by throwing himself off the machine right into the trap. Unfortunately, like Mrs. Saunders, he too was useless on account of the now broken rein, but after Police Constable Allen had failed to stay its progress, the runaway ran into a heavy " carter " drawing one of the corporation carts. Mrs. Saunders, who had her child in her arms, was thrown out, but escaped with a severe shaking and a slight bruise on her arm. The child was unhurt, and so was Brown, while the pony also escaped. The Council's horse, however, sustained extensive injuries, and had to be taken to the stables : after a short rest Mrs. Saunders was able to proceed home.

On the 21st of November the battalion moved to Portland, on change of station (less " C " and " E " companies to Dorchester), where it joined the 9th Brigade. Brigadier-General T. Capper, C.B., D.S.O., commanding the 13th Infantry Brigade, after a farewell speech on the Royal Barracks Square, Dublin, in which he praised the battalion on their smartness on parade, and zealousness in performing duties allotted to them during their stay in Dublin, and regretting that the battalion was leaving his command, proceeded with it from the Royal Barracks to the North Wall, where the battalion earned praise for the expeditious manner in which the embarkation was carried out, the whole embarkation of troops taking 17 minutes.

1912.

2ND BATTALION.

The goat presented by His Majesty King George V. in 1911 died at Quetta on the 21st of September.

The following is an extract from a letter from Lord Stamfordham, Private Secretary to His Majesty the King, to General Sir Savage Mostyn, K.C.B., Colonel Royal Welch Fusiliers :

" The King would be pleased to give a goat to the 2nd Battalion Royal Welch Fusiliers, but His Majesty is inclined to think it is a pity to send out goats from Windsor to India, where they seldom live long.

"His Majesty would be glad to buy a goat in India, and give it to the Regiment, and at the same time give a goat from the herd at Windsor to the Regimental Depôt."

With reference to the above the commanding officer requested General Sir Savage Mostyn to convey the thanks of all ranks of the 2nd battalion Royal Welch Fusiliers to His Majesty the King, for his kindness in promising to present a new goat to the battalion on its return to England.

The following are extracts from the General Officer's observations made in the Inspection Report of the battalion for the year ending 31st December:

"The Battalion is doing well and is very efficient. Regimental Standing Orders have arrived from England and will be a great boon to the Officers and Non-commissioned officers. Men are clean, healthy, and cheerful. There is tremendous esprît de corps, the Officers pull well together and unanimity prevails.

"I consider the Battalion has improved much during its stay in Quetta.

"Decentralization is more pronounced, and initiative is well developed all through the Battalion.

"The men work well and keenly, quite fit for active service."

1913.

1st Battalion.

On the 2nd of January His Majesty King George V. was graciously pleased to accept a Regimental Calendar for 1913.

On the 3rd of January the battalion team obtained 7th place (with same score as 6th) in the A.R.A. "young soldiers" competition, scoring 355, the winners 380.

On the 15th of March the Regimental Football Team won the Dorset Senior Cup, without having a goal scored against them throughout the competition.

On the 20th of March the battalion furnished a representative detachment, consisting of Lieutenant and Adjutant E. O. Skaife and 5 non-commissioned officers and 8 men, to attend the funeral of the late Viscount Wolseley in London.

The following successes were gained by non-commissioned officers and men of the battalion at the undermentioned Boxing Competitions:

Southern Command Championship, 26th February.

Middleweight: No. 10210 Corporal L. H. Spalding.
Featherweight: Private Willis was beaten in the Final.
Lightweight: Private Walker was beaten in the Final.
Welterweight: Corporal Callis reached the Semi-Final.
Lightweight: Private Lee reached the Semi-Final.

Army Boxing Championship Meeting.

Featherweight Champion, 1913: Private Willis.

The battalion was second in the Regimental Championships with 16 points to the 1st battalion Loyal North Lancashire Regiment's 19 points.

On the 17th of April the battalion marched to Bovington Camp, Wool, for musketry, battalion, and company training.

On the occasion of his birthday His Majesty was pleased to make the following promotions and appointments to the most honourable Order of the Bath:

To be Knight Commander (K.C.B.), Colonel and Hon. Major-General Luke O'Connor, C.B.

To be Companion (C.B.), Colonel Edward S. Bulfin, both late Royal Welch Fusiliers.

On the 13th of June the battalion returned by march route to Portland and Dorchester. During their stay in Bovington Camp the Regimental goat presented to the battalion in 1912 by H.M. King George V. was kicked by a horse, and one of its horns was broken off.

On the 30th of June, No. 10884, Private Watson, "D" company, earned the following notice which appeared in Battalion Orders of the 11th of July:

"The Commanding Officer is pleased to record the following action of No. 10884 Private W. Watson, who stopped a horse and cart in Oswestry, whilst on furlough. Police-Sergeant Mamlet reports that on Monday 30th June a horse attached to a heavy spring cart ran away up Oswald Road, Oswestry. Private Watson, who was standing on top of the road, jumped at the horse's head, and turned it into the pavement, where it was overturned. In doing this the wheel passed over his leg and broke it. The Police Superintendent also reports that the plucky action of Private Watson undoubtedly averted what would have been a very serious accident."

On the 7th of July a new goat presented by H.M. King George V. to replace the one damaged in Bovington Camp arrived from Windsor. On the departure of the battalion for Malta in 1914, the damaged goat was sent to Mr. W. Carlyle, Newport Pagnell, Bucks, to be cared for.

On the 23rd and 24th of July a team consisting of 4 officers and 12 non-commissioned officers and men competed at the Army Athletic Meeting at Aldershot. 2nd Lieutenant Courage won the Officers' High Jump. Lieutenant Chance was third in the Officers' Quarter-mile. The Relay team were third in the Army Relay Championship and won a cup.

On the 17th of August the battalion proceeded by train to Bulford Camp for battalion training, returning on the 26th.

On the 28th of August an advanced party of 3 officers and 52 other ranks proceeded to Windsor under command of Captain and Adjutant E. O. Skaife to take over guard duty and barracks from the 3rd Battalion Coldstream Guards, who had been detailed to attend divisional training and manœuvres. On the 29th of August the Guard was taken over at Windsor Castle; Lieutenant A. G. C. T. Dooner was in command.

On the 30th of August the battalion entrained for Windsor, and was quartered in the Victoria Barracks.

On the 9th of September an intimation was received that "The King will be very glad to become Patron of the Royal Welch Fusiliers Old Comrades' Association."

By a Special Army Order dated 16th September the organisation of an infantry battalion was changed from 8 companies to 4. The Order to take effect from 1st October.

In honour of the anniversary of the Battle of the Alma, on September 20th, the battalion carried out a special Review Order Parade, at which Major-General Sir Luke O'Connor, V.C., K.C.B., was present. Major-General Sir Savage Mostyn, K.C.B., was prevented from coming by a railway strike.

The battalion was formed up in three sides of a square facing the Officers' Mess, and the Colours, carried by Lieutenant E. C. Hoskyns and 2nd Lieutenant J. M. J. Evans, were brought on to parade in slow time. Sir Luke O'Connor came on parade, and was received with a General Salute and inspected the battalion. The battalion marched past first in slow, and afterwards in quick time. Sir Luke O'Connor then addressed the battalion, and expressed his great pleasure in again inspecting it on "Alma Day." He also impressed on the young soldiers, in particular, that he considered that the honour conferred on him by His Majesty in the Birthday Honours was conferred on the regiment through whom he had won all his honours. Sir Luke was again accorded a General Salute, after which the battalion marched away to their quarters. The officers entertained a large number of past and present officers of the regiment, the

Mayor and Mayoress of Windsor, and friends of the regiment. Three pensioners from Chelsea Hospital were entertained by the sergeants in addition to several old members of the Mess.

On the 24th of September, No. 10675 Lance-Corporal Blacktin, No. 9257 Private Broomhall, and No. 9017 Private Llewellyn were mentioned in Battalion Orders for " prompt and valuable assistance " by which an old woman was saved from a fire in Sydney Place, Peascod Street. The Mayor of Windsor wrote expressing his appreciation of their conduct.

On the 26th of September the battalion returned to Portland on completion of duty, leaving a party under Captain and Adjutant E. O. Skaife, and a guard on duty under Lieutenant G. O. de P. Chance.

1913.

2ND BATTALION.

The following telegrams were sent, and received, on the occasion of His Majesty the King advancing Major-General Luke O'Connor, V.C., C.B. (late commanding 2nd battalion Royal Welch Fusiliers) to the rank of Knight Commander of the Bath.

" To Major-General Sir Luke O'Connor.

" Warmest congratulations from all ranks 2nd Battalion Royal Welch Fusiliers."

" To 2nd Battalion Royal Welch Fusiliers.

" Heartfelt thanks to you all for all your sincere congratulations.
LUKE O'CONNOR."

1914.

1ST BATTALION.

On the 10th of January the battalion left Portland at 10.45 a.m. for Southampton to embark on H.M. troopship *Rewa* for conveyance to Malta. Lieutenant E. C. Hoskyns was left behind for duty with details. The Colours of the battalion were carried by 2nd Lieutenant L. A. A. Alston and E. Woodehouse. The departure of the battalion about 2 p.m. was witnessed by numerous friends. Previous to sailing, telegrams were received from many connected with the battalion, and a loyal message was sent to His Majesty the King, Colonel-in-Chief, to which the following reply was received by Marconigram :

"Sandringham, 10. 1. 14. O.C. 1st R.W.F. Transport *Rewa* at sea. Please convey to all ranks my sincere thanks for their kind message contained in your telegram. I wish you all *bon voyage*, and the Battalion every success during its tour of foreign service.—GEORGE R.I., *Colonel-in-Chief*."

On the 17th of January the battalion arrived at Malta about 12 noon.

At the Royal Naval Athletic Sports held on 19th of February the following successes were gained :

Half-mile "Corradino Championship." Open to all ranks of the Navy and Army :
  First, Captain and Adjutant E. O. Skaife.
  Third, No. 10387 Private W. Brooks, "A" company (first of the rank and file).

Quarter-mile open to the Army :
  Second, Private Kelly.
  Third, Private Broomhall.

St. David's Day was celebrated on the 2nd of March, as the 1st fell on a Sunday ; leeks, however, were worn on the 1st. The 2nd battalion Royal Welch Fusiliers under the command of Major A. Hay arrived about 8 a.m. in the Grand Harbour in His Majesty's transport *Dongola*, and disembarked the turnover of 6 sergeants and 327 rank and file. By the kindness of His Excellency Sir Leslie Rundle, Governor and Commander-in-Chief, the ship was detained until midnight, and the officers of the two battalions dined together, and St. David's dinner was celebrated under one roof by both battalions once more. The sergeants of the two battalions held a smoking concert.

On the 17th of March the battalion won the cup presented by His Excellency the Governor for Association Football, beating the 2nd battalion Middlesex Regiment by 3 goals to 2. His Excellency presented the cup on the conclusion of the match.

The Navy and Army (Malta) Boxing Meeting concluded this day. There were 22 entrants from the battalion.

Sergeant H. Spalding won the Welterweight Championship.

Private Edwards reached the Final of the Middleweight Competition. Boy Soames reached the Finals of the Boys' Lightweights. Lance-Corporal Redman and Private Morgan were in the Semi-Finals of the Welterweights. Private Claney was in the Semi-Final of the Featherweights. Private Willis was in the Semi-Finals of the Lightweights. Five other entrants got into the third series.

On the 4th of June news was received of the death of Major-General Sir Savage Mostyn, K.C.B., Colonel of the Royal Welch Fusiliers, which occurred on the 2nd of June.

On the 3rd of September the battalion embarked at Malta on S.S. *Ultonia* for England, arriving at Southampton on the 12th; soon to re-embark for the Continent and take its part in the Great War.

1914.

2ND BATTALION.

The battalion, consisting of 16 officers, 2 warrant officers, 34 sergeants, and 909 rank and file, under the command of Major A. Hay, left Quetta, Baluchistan, on the morning of the 15th of February, arrived at Karachi on the 16th of February, embarked on the H.T. *Dongola*, and sailed the following morning, arriving at Malta on the 2nd of March, where a turnover consisting of 6 sergeants and 327 rank and file, was posted to the 1st battalion.

This occasion is worthy of note, as it was the first time since 1880 that the battalions had met.

The battalion arrived at Southampton Dock on the morning of the 10th of March and entrained for Portland.

A number of officers from the Wrexham Depôt, including Captains Walwyn, Samson, Geiger, and Brigadier-General Sir Robert Colleton, Bart., who commanded the 1st battalion in South Africa, were on the quay to welcome the battalion. As the trooper hove in sight the band of the battalion conducted by Bandmaster W. J. Clancy, which was on the officers' deck, struck up the regimental march, "Men of Harlech," followed by "Hen Wlad fy Nhadau" ("Land of my Fathers"), and finally Brindley Richards's famous refrain, "God Bless the Prince of Wales."

One of the most touching incidents during the disembarkation was the visit of Private John Mellor, of Romsey, a Crimean veteran of 84, and a former member of the 1st battalion Royal Welch Fusiliers. As the Colours were being brought ashore, Mellor, who was becoming somewhat infirm and short-sighted, as the result of an injury he met with in the Crimean trenches, boldly stood to attention as the bugle sounded. He was anxious to see the old Colours, and Major Hay gave the order to have them unfurled. Another veteran in attendance was Sergeant-Major John Russell, who went out with the battalion in 1896, and wore four medals.

It may be mentioned that only six men of those who formed the original composition of the battalion, when it left the shores of England eighteen years ago, remained with the battalion, viz. : Sergeant H. Yeates, of Port Dinorwic (afterwards Lieutenant and Quartermaster), Sergeant-Major Murphy, who went out as a sergeant, Colour-Sergeants J. Jackson and F. Jones, who were only privates in 1896, Lance-Corporal P. Wilton, and Private R. Williams.

The strength of the battalion on disembarkation was 16 officers, 2 warrant officers, 28 sergeants, and 582 rank and file.

The battalion dispatched a detachment to Dorchester consisting of 3 officers, 4 sergeants, and 90 rank and file under the command of Captain G. J. P. Geiger.

The following letter was received from His Majesty King George V :

"His Majesty desires you to convey from their Colonel-in-Chief to all ranks who have come back with the Battalion, a hearty welcome home after nearly 18 years of foreign service, during which time the Battalion has been stationed in Malta, Egypt, Crete, Hong-Kong, and India, all of which places His Majesty has visited."

The goat which His Majesty King George V. graciously presented to the battalion arrived from Windsor on the 21st of March.

On the 2nd of June Major-General the Hon. Sir Savage Mostyn, K.C.B., Colonel of the Royal Welch Fusiliers, died at Ashby-de-la-Zouch, and was succeeded in the Colonelcy by Major-General Sir Luke O'Connor, V.C., K.C.B.

The battalion moved to camp at Wool, Dorset, by march route on June 11th for musketry, company, and battalion training.

Orders were received at 8 p.m. on July 30th for all units training at Wool to return to Peace Stations immediately. The battalion struck camp and proceeded to Portland by march route, arriving there at 5.30 a.m. on the 31st of July.

On the 4th of August Great Britain presented an ultimatum to Germany respecting the neutrality of Belgian territory, which brought about her participation in the Great War of 1914–1918.

The part taken by the regiment will be recorded in due course in Volume III of the Regimental Records.

MAJOR-GENERAL SIR LUKE O'CONNOR, V.C., K.C.B.
Photograph of the oil painting in Wrexham Barracks by Algernon Smith, Wrexham.

APPENDIX I

SUCCESSION OF COLONELS OF THE ROYAL WELCH FUSILIERS

SIR JAMES WILLOUGHBY GORDON, BART., G.C.B., G.C.H.
Appointed 23rd April 1823.

HE was a son of Captain Francis Grant, R.N. (who took the name of Gordon in 1768), by his wife Mary, daughter of Sir Thomas and sister of Sir Willoughby Aston, Bart. Appointed on 17th October 1783 to an ensigncy in the 66th (Berkshire Regiment), joined the regiment in the West Indies in 1786; Lieutenant 5th March 1789; in the spring of 1792 again joined the regiment in the West Indies and accompanied it to Gibraltar in 1793. Was present as a volunteer on board Lord Hood's fleet at Toulon in 1793, rejoined the regiment at Gibraltar in October, and was sent to England in 1794; Captain 2nd September 1795, in which year he was employed on the Staff in Ireland as A.D.C. to General Dalrymple, witnessing the surrender of the French in Bantry Bay in 1796, and was subsequently employed as A.A.G. in the Northern District. Served with the regiment in San Domingo, Jamaica, and North America. Promoted Major 9th November 1797.

In March 1799 commanded the regiment until early in the following year, when he was appointed Military Secretary to H.R.H. the Duke of Kent, then Commander-in-Chief in British North America; and returned with H.R.H. to England in 1800. Appointed on 21st May 1801 Lieutenant-Colonel of the 85th Foot and commanded the 1st Battalion at the first British occupation of Madeira 24th July that year. In 1802 was appointed as A.Q.M.G. in the Southern District, headquarters Chatham. On 9th March 1803 was made Deputy Adjutant-General, Jamaica; 26th May 1803, Permanent Assistant Quartermaster-General and employed under General Sir David Dundas in the Southern Command, and Deputy Barrackmaster-General to the Forces on 31st December 1803.

On 4th August 1804 he was brought into the 92nd as Lieutenant-Colonel, being appointed, on 1st July, Military Secretary to the Duke of York, then Commander-in-Chief; as such he appeared in 1809 as an important witness before the Parliamentary Committee of Inquiry into military expenditure, and also before the Wardle Inquiry, and thus stated his services: " I have served His Majesty very nearly twenty-six years, for the last twenty-four of which I have been employed in every part of the world (the East Indies excepted) where His Majesty's troops have been stationed. I have been four times to the West Indies, and have been there nearly six years; twice to America; and all over the Mediterranean. It has been my fortune, very undeservedly perhaps, to have a sword voted for my services, and to have been repeatedly thanked by General Officers under whom I have been placed. It is perhaps a singular part of my service that I not only served in every situation in the Army, from an Ensign up to my present rank, but I have also served in every situation upon the Staff of the Army, without one single exception."

Appointed Lieutenant-Colonel Commandant, Royal African Corps, on 13th June 1808; in March 1809 Military Secretary to Sir David Dundas, the Commander-in-Chief; in October 1809 Commissary-in-Chief; and Colonel, brevet, 25th July 1810. In 1811 Colonel Gordon was appointed Quartermaster-General of the Army in the Peninsula, with which he served till he resigned the following year through ill-health, being present at the capture of Madrid and Burgos. On his return to England in 1812 was appointed Quartermaster-General at the Horse Guards.

On 4th June 1813 he was promoted Major-General, and was appointed Colonel of the 85th Light Infantry on 27th November 1815. He was created a Baronet in 1818; and on the 23rd April 1823 was transferred to the Colonelcy of the 23rd Regiment, on the death of General Richard Grenville.

On 27th May 1825 promoted Lieutenant-General, and created a G.C.H., sworn in as a Privy Councillor in 1830; G.C.B. in 1831; and General 23rd November 1841.

He was a F.R.S. and also a Fellow of the Royal Geographical Society from its formation; also a member of the Consolidated Board of General Officers, one of the Commissioners of the Royal Military College, and of the Royal Military Asylum.

He died at Chelsea on 4th January 1851.

He married in 1805 Julia Lavinia, daughter of Richard Henry Alexander Bennet of Beckenham, Kent, and had by her a son and daughter.

He was the author of *Military Transactions of the British Empire*, 1803-7 (London, 1809, 4to) and a supplementary volume thereto.

SIR GEORGE CHARLES D'AGUILAR, K.C.B.

Appointed 31st *January* 1851.

Second son of Captain Joseph D'Aguilar, 2nd Dragoon Guards. Born at Winchester in January 1784; entered the Army as Ensign in the 86th Regiment on 24th September 1799, serving with it in the East Indies till the end of 1808; promoted Lieutenant on 1st December 1802, acted as Adjutant to the 86th from June 1803 to 1806, and as Brigade-Major on the General Staff from 1806 to 1808 (comprising nearly the whole of the Marquess of Wellesley's administration). During this period his principal service was against the Marathas; present at the reduction of Broach in Guzerat in August 1803, of Powerghar in Malwa in 1804, and the capture and occupation of Oogein, the capital of Scindia, in 1805. Served in 1806 at the siege of Bhurtpore by Lord Lake; severely wounded in the last unsuccessful assault.

Left India in 1808 on being appointed to a company on 31st March in the 81st Regiment, which he joined in England in May 1809; embarked in June for Walcheren, accompanying Brigadier-General the Hon. Stephen Mahon, afterwards Lord Hartland, commanding the 2nd Cavalry Brigade, as aide-de-camp; on return to England with the Brigade was sent to Sicily as Assistant Adjutant-General. There Captain D'Aguilar attracted the favourable notice of Lord William Bentinck, the general commanding in the Mediterranean, and was sent on a special military mission to Ali Pasha at Yanina and Constantinople.

Selected by Major-General Sir William Clinton to accompany him to the east coast of Spain as Military Secretary, and acted in the same capacity to Sir John Murray when he superseded Clinton. Present in 1813 at the action of Biar, and the defeat of Marshal Suchet at Castalla. Sent home with the dispatches announcing the victory of Castalla on 13th April 1813, and having been promoted Major on 1st April 1813, received the additional step to the rank of Lieutenant-Colonel for his news 20th May 1813.

Became a substantive Major in the Greek Light Infantry, raised by Richard Church, and remained with that corps till its reduction in 1815.

Joined the Duke of Wellington, but was not present at the Battle of Waterloo, having arrived immediately after the action. Gazetted Major in the Rifle Brigade on 6th March 1817; Major half-pay Rifle Brigade 25th December 1818; Major 3rd Foot 22nd June 1820. Joined the Staff again in 1821 as Assistant Adjutant-General at the Horse Guards, and was Deputy Adjutant-General at Dublin for eleven years from 22nd July 1830 to 22nd November 1841. While there Major D'Aguilar published his well-known *Practice and Forms of District and Regimental Courts-Martial*, which passed through many editions, and remained the official authority on the subject until 1878. He also published, in 1831, a little book called *The Officers' Manual*, being a translation of the *Military Maxims of Napoleon*, which has passed through three editions. Appointed a C.B. in 1834, and Major-General on 23rd November 1841. On leaving Dublin was appointed to the command of the Northern District in Ireland at Belfast on 1st April 1842, till 6th July 1843.

Selected for the command of the troops in China 12th January 1844, and proceeded to Hong-Kong to take command of the division left in that island on its annexation at the close of the first Chinese war, and also of the troops at Chusan and Amoy. On 1st April 1847, having been informed by Sir John Davis, the English Commissioner, that in consequence of the ill-treatment of the English residents of Canton an expedition must be sent out to punish that city, General D'Aguilar started the next day with the 18th Regiment and the 42nd Madras Native Infantry. Proceeding to Bocca Tigris, in two days he had captured all the forts and batteries on the Canton River, spiking no fewer than 879 guns, and had prepared to attack Canton itself, but the assault was prevented by the prompt submission of the Chinese authorities.

Returned to England in 1848; and was appointed to the Colonelcy of the 58th Regiment on 5th February 1848, and transferred to the Colonelcy of the 23rd Regiment on the death of General Sir James Willoughby Gordon, Bart., in January 1851. On the 11th November of the same year promoted Lieutenant-General and made a K.C.B. Lieutenant-General Sir George D'Aguilar held the command of the Southern District at Portsmouth from 4th November 1851 to 31st March 1852; and died in Lower Brook Street, London, on 21st May 1855, aged 70.

Sir George married in 1809 Eliza, second daughter of Peter Drinkwater of Irwell

House, co. Lancaster, by whom he had issue, including General Sir Charles Lawrence D'Aguilar, K.C.B., a distinguished officer who served in the Crimean War and Indian Mutiny.

HENRY RAINEY, C.B., K.H.
Appointed 22nd May 1855.

Appointed 2nd Lieutenant in the 21st Foot on 24th August 1804, being placed on the half-pay of the 4th Foot on 1st November; from that he reverted to full pay as a Lieutenant in the 31st Foot on 8th November, exchanging into the 82nd Foot on 23rd November; served with that regiment at the siege and capture of Copenhagen in 1807, with Sir Brent Spencer's expedition off the coast of Spain, and at Cadiz on the surrender of the French Fleet. From there he joined Sir Arthur Wellesley's army at Mondego Bay, and was afterwards present at the battles of Roleia, Vimiera, 1808, and Corunna, 1809.

Promoted Captain on 13th April 1809, accompanied the regiment to Walcheren in 1809, and was present at the surrender of Middelburg, and siege and capture of Flushing; joined the army in the Peninsula in May 1812, and served as aide-de-camp to Sir Thomas Bradford during the siege of the forts of Salamanca, battle of Salamanca (July 1812), capture of Madrid, siege of Burgos, and retreat therefrom.

Served afterwards in the Portuguese army in advance through the Tras-os-Montes in 1813, at the battle of Vittoria, actions of Villa Franca and Tolosa; exchanged on 10th June 1813 into the 55th Foot; was present at the storm of the fortified convent in front of San Sebastian, at both sieges—wounded—and storm of San Sebastian, passage of the Bidassoa, battle of the Nivelle, battles of the Nive on the 9th and 10th of December—severely wounded; received the war medal with 8 clasps.

Served in France with the army of occupation from the capitulation of Paris in 1815 to the end of 1818. Captain, half-pay, 55th Foot, 13th December 1821. Captain, Royal African Corps, 15th September 1825. Major, brevet, 21st June 1817. Major, unattached, 4th May 1826. Lieutenant-Colonel, brevet, 15th August 1822. Was appointed Military Secretary to the General Commanding at Gibraltar 8th January 1834 to 18th May 1835. Colonel, brevet, 10th January 1837. Lieutenant-Colonel, unattached, 24th June 1842. Major-General 9th November 1846. Lieutenant-General 20th June 1854. Colonel of the 23rd Foot 22nd May 1855, on the death of Lieutenant-General Sir George Charles D'Aguilar. He died at Brighton 26th December 1860, aged 71.

SIR WILLIAM JOHN CODRINGTON, G.C.B.
Appointed 27th December 1860.

Second son of Admiral Sir Edward Codrington, the victor of Navarino, was born on 26th November 1804; joined the 88th Foot as Ensign 22nd February 1821; going on half-pay on the 25th October; was appointed to the 43rd Foot on 24th October 1822, transferred to the Coldstream Guards as Ensign and Lieutenant 24th April 1823; Lieutenant and Captain 20th July 1826; Captain and Lieutenant-Colonel 8th July 1836. The 2nd battalion of the Coldstream Guards having been sent to Canada in

January 1839, to assist in quelling disturbances, Lieutenant-Colonel Codrington was allowed to find his own way out there as unattached, being posted to No. 6 Company in March 1841, and returning home with the battalion in October 1842. Colonel, brevet, 9th November 1846.

On 22nd February 1854 he embarked with the 1st battalion Coldstream Guards for Malta, leaving there on 21st April, landed at Scutari on the 29th, moving to Varna on 13th June, where he received information of his appointment as Major-General on June 20th. Was given the command on 1st September of the 1st Brigade of the Light Division, consisting of the 7th, 23rd, and 33rd Regiments. As a General commanding a brigade, General Codrington went into action in his first battle, the battle of the Alma, 20th September. His bravery in this battle showed that he deserved his command, and he again proved his courage at the Victoria Ridge at the battle of Inkerman. On Sir George Brown being severely wounded he assumed command of the whole division as senior Brigadier; and throughout the winter of 1854-5 he remained in command of the division: and on 5th July 1855 was made a K.C.B., being promoted Lieutenant-General (local rank, Crimea) 30th July 1855, and on 22nd October General (local rank, Crimea and Turkey), succeeding Sir James Simpson on 11th November as Commander-in-Chief of the Eastern Army instead of Sir Colin Campbell.

On return to England was promoted Lieutenant-General, dated 6th June 1854, and appointed Colonel of the 54th Regiment 11th August 1856; and in 1857 was elected M.P. for Greenwich in the Liberal interest. From 13th May 1859 to 9th November 1865 he was Governor of Gibraltar, being transferred to the Colonelcy of the 23rd Foot on 27th December 1860, on the death of Lieutenant-General H. Rainey. Promoted General on 27th July 1863, and G.C.B. in 1865, and transferred to the Colonelcy of the Coldstream Guards 16th March 1875.

He remained an active politician to the end of his life, and contested Westminster in 1874 and Lewes in 1880. Though he saw no active service except in 1854 and 1855, he was twice offered the rank of Field-Marshal, but declined the offer. He held a medal and four clasps for the Crimea, was mentioned in dispatches, was a Commander of the Legion of Honour, Knight Grand Cross of the Military Order of Savoy, 1st class of the Medjidie, and Turkish medal. General Codrington died on 6th August 1884 in his 80th year, at Danmore Cottage, Heckfield, Winchfield, being buried at Woking on the 9th with military honours.

CHARLES CRUTCHLEY.

Appointed 16th March 1875.

Son of Lieutenant-Colonel E. H. Crutchley of Sunninghill Park, born 1810. His first commission, dated 8th April 1826, was in the 23rd Foot as 2nd Lieutenant; was promoted to 1st Lieutenant 22nd July 1830, Captain 11th December 1835, Major 22nd October 1844, and Lieutenant-Colonel 24th July 1849. In August 1853 the 1st Battalion and the Reserve Battalion were amalgamated when in the Isle of Wight, and Lieutenant-Colonel Crutchley was placed in command; in 1854, on the departure of the regiment for the Crimea, was permitted to retire from the command on account of ill-health, going on half-pay from the 1st April; on 15th September was appointed to the Depôt Battalion, and on 28th November was made Colonel by brevet, going on the half-pay of the 21st Regiment on 1st January 1859, and being made Commandant Royal Military Asylum, Chelsea, the same date, which post he held till the 31st March 1864. Promoted Major-General 31st January 1864, and from 25th June 1864 to 31st July 1869 commanded the Brigade at Gibraltar; promoted Lieutenant-General 23rd April 1872, and appointed Colonel of the 80th Foot 26th January 1874; on the 16th March 1875 being transferred to the Colonelcy of the 23rd Regiment on General Sir W. J. Codrington being transferred to the Coldstream Guards, and promoted General 1st October 1877. He married in 1851 Eliza Bayfield, daughter of J. Harris, R.N., was a J.P. for Berkshire, and died at Sunninghill Park on the 30th March 1898 in his 88th year.

SIR EDWARD EARLE GASCOIGNE BULWER, G.C.B.

Appointed 31st March 1898.

Second son of William Earle Lytton Bulwer of Heydon, Norwich, born 22nd December 1829, and a nephew of Lord Lytton, the novelist. He received his commission as 2nd Lieutenant 11th August 1849, by purchase in the 23rd; became Lieutenant 13th December 1850 by purchase, Captain 21st September 1854 without purchase, Major 26th January 1858, Brevet Lieutenant-Colonel 26th April 1859. Served in the Crimean Campaign 1854-5, was present at the battle of the Alma and siege of Sevastopol: received medal and two clasps and the Turkish medal; after the war was appointed Private Secretary to Sir Henry Lytton Bulwer, 1856-7. Served in the Indian Mutiny 1857-9, was present at the siege and capture of Lucknow, commanded a column in Oudh 1858, including capture of the fort of Selimpore; and actions at Jubrowlee and Poorwah, and commanded the left wing of the 23rd Foot at the action at Buxar Ghat, where Benee Madho was defeated by Lord Clyde. Mentioned in dispatches, medal with clasp, brevet Lieutenant-Colonel and C.B.

Served in the Royal Welch Fusiliers until 9th May 1865, when he was promoted to an unattached Lieutenant-Colonelcy. Appointed October 1866 an Assistant Inspector of Reserve Forces. Becoming a brevet Colonel 23rd May 1866, was posted to the Staff of the Northern District on 1st April 1870 as Assistant Adjutant-General. Here his abilities obtained full play, and he established his reputation so thoroughly that his next move was to the Army Headquarters, which he joined 1st January 1873 as Assistant Adjutant-General for Auxiliary Forces. Obtained the rank of Major-General 1st October 1877. A period of non-employment followed, and on 10th March 1879 took over command of the Chatham District. Holding that command till the end of December, he rejoined the Staff at the War Office on 1st January 1880 as Inspector-General of Recruiting, an office he filled with great advantage to the Service for five years—five very eventful years too, in the history of the Army, as they included the Egyptian and Sudan War periods, 1882-5, and the far-reaching reforms inaugurated by the late Mr. Childers.

In 1886, being unemployed, he was chosen to sit on the Commission appointed by the Government to inquire into the cause of the Belfast Riots, was created a K.C.B. in the same year, and became a Lieutenant-General 21st January 1887. From 1889

SUCCESSION OF COLONELS

to 1894 he filled the office of Lieutenant-Governor of Jersey, became a General 1st April 1893, and was appointed Colonel of the Royal Welch Fusiliers 31st March 1898, and G.C.B. in 1905. After his retirement he was for many years a Commissioner of the Duke of York's Royal Military School, Chelsea; he was also President of the Royal Norfolk Veterans' Association.

He was educated privately and at Trinity College, Cambridge. Sir Edward married, in July 1863, Isabella Anne, daughter of Sir J. Jacob Buxton, 2nd Baronet, of Shadwell Court.

He died at 45 Hans Place, London, S.W., on 8th December 1910, in his 81st year, and was buried on 14th December at Heydon, Norwich, a memorial service being held at Holy Trinity Church, Sloane Street, S.W.

THE HON. SIR SAVAGE LLOYD MOSTYN, K.C.B.

Appointed 9th December 1910.

Major-General the Hon. Sir Savage Lloyd Mostyn, K.C.B., third son of Edward, second Lord Mostyn, born 27th March 1835, received his commission as 2nd Lieutenant in the 23rd Royal Welch Fusiliers on 13th May 1853, being promoted Lieutenant 21st September 1854, Captain 8th June 1855. Served during the Crimean Campaign 1854–5. Took part in the siege of Sevastopol, including the attack on the Redan on the 18th June, received medal with clasp, and the Turkish medal. Served during the Indian Mutiny 1857–8. Took part in the relief of Lucknow, defeat of the Gwalior contingent at Cawnpore, and fall of Lucknow; received medal with two clasps. Promoted Major 29th March 1864, and Lieutenant-Colonel 1st September 1869. Served in the Ashanti War 1873–4, was present at the battles of Borborassie, Amoaful, Becquah, and Ordahsu, and taking of Coomassie. Mentioned in dispatches three times, medal with clasp, and C.B., being promoted Colonel, 1st September 1874. From 1880 to 1885 he commanded the 23rd Regimental District, being promoted Major-General 11th July 1885, retiring on 11th July 1890; in 1904 he was appointed Colonel of the Devonshire Regiment, promoted K.C.B. on 28th June 1907, and was transferred to the Colonelcy of the 23rd Royal Welch Fusiliers 9th December 1910. Married, 22nd April 1891, Emily, daughter of the Rev. George Earle-Welby, of Barrowby. Died on 2nd June 1914, aged 78, being buried on 5th June at Marchwiel, Denbighshire, with military honours.

SIR LUKE O'CONNOR, V.C., K.C.B.

Appointed 3rd June 1914.

Major-General Sir Luke O'Connor, V.C., K.C.B., born at Elphin, co. Roscommon, on 21st February 1831; enlisted into Royal Welch Fusiliers 1849, at the age of 17.

Sergeant 1850, Ensign in the R.W.F. 5th November 1854, Lieutenant 9th February 1855, Captain 24th August 1858, Brevet Major 5th July 1872, Major 19th August 1874, Brevet Lieutenant-Colonel 1st April 1874, Lieutenant-Colonel 21st June 1880, Brevet Colonel 19th August 1879, Major-General 9th March 1887.

Served in the Crimean Campaign 1854–5. Took part in the Battles of the Alma (seriously wounded); 1st and 2nd attack on the Redan (dangerously wounded) and attack on the Quarries, siege and fall of Sevastopol. V.C., medal with two clasps, Sardinian and Turkish medals. 5th Class of the Medjidie. Promoted Ensign in the Royal Welch Fusiliers. Was awarded the Victoria Cross under the following circumstances: " Was one of the centre Sergeants at the Battle of the Alma, and advanced between the Officers carrying the colours. When near the Redoubt, Lieutenant Anstruther, who was carrying a colour, was mortally wounded, and he was shot in the breast at the same time and fell, but, recovering himself, snatched up the colour from the ground, and continued to carry it till the end of the action, although urged by Captain Granville to relinquish it, and go to the rear on account of his wound: was recommended for and received his commission for his services at the Alma. Also behaved with great gallantry at the assault at the Redan, 8th September 1855, where he was shot through both thighs." He also received the thanks of Sir G. Brown and General Codrington on the field. The Cross was pinned on his breast by Queen Victoria at the great military parade in Hyde Park in June 1857. Served during the Indian Mutiny 1857–8, was present at the relief and capture of Lucknow; defeat of the Gwalior contingents at Cawnpore. Medal with two clasps: the operations across the Gomtee under Outram and several minor affairs.

After several uneventful years he accompanied the 2nd Battalion Royal Welch Fusiliers to the Gold Coast for Sir Garnet Wolseley's expedition to Kumassi at the end of 1873; for this service he received a brevet Lieutenant-Colonelcy and the medal with clasp.

On 21st June 1880 he succeeded to the command of the 2nd battalion of the regiment in which he had enlisted, and in 1886 went on half-pay with the rank of Colonel. He was granted a Distinguished Service reward and retired on 2nd March 1887, with the rank of Major-General.

He was made a C.B. in 1906 and K.C.B. in 1913, and on 3rd June 1914 was appointed to the Colonelcy of the Royal Welch Fusiliers.

He died in London on 1st February 1915, being succeeded in the Colonelcy of the 23rd by Lieutenant-General Sir Francis Lloyd, G.C.V.O., K.C.B.

APPENDIX II

REGIMENTAL COSTUME AND EQUIPMENT

The earliest authoritative information as to the uniform of the regiment is to be found in what is known as the Thorpe Collection, now in the possession of the National Library, in Dublin.

In a Broadside dated Saturday, 20th July 1689, Chester, occurs the following:

" . . . the general encampment is a little above the South side of the River Dee, eastward of the bridge, where there were last Wednesday but two regiments encampt, viz. a battalion of the King's Guards, and since then three more are encampt, i.e. The Lord Lisborn's Regiment, Blew & yellow which came in last Wednesday, the Lord Herbert's, Blew and white came in the day following . . . "

In another Broadside, dated 5th August 1689, Chester, occurs the following :

" . . . The Regiments that are shipped off here are :

  Duke of Schomberg's Dutchmen. Blew.
  Lord Herbert Welshmen. Blew & white. . . ."

Judging from military pictures of the period it is probable that the coat was a long, somewhat tight-fitting, single-breasted garment, coming down to the knees; buttoning all the way down, without a collar; and with deep turned-up cuffs, showing the white sleeve-lining. Blue breeches would be worn with it, and white stockings; and garters with bows on them.

The coat was generally worn open top and bottom, fastening at the waist, thus exposing the long white neck-cloth; and had a cross-pocket on each side, with buttons below the flap. For how long the blue uniform was worn it is impossible to say.

The hat would be of black felt, with a low crown and a broad brim turned up in front, edged with white braid, and with a white hatband tied in a bow on the left side.

Black shoes, with bows, were worn, and the accoutrements included a buff leather belt worn diagonally over the left shoulder, supporting a bullet-bag on the right hip. A number of wooden powder-plugs were suspended by cords from the shoulder-belt. The arms were a musket, and a sword suspended from a wide buff leather waistbelt.

There are certain desultory references to the uniform of this period, such as that in 1680 Infantry officers wore gloves, that the men were ordered to wear waistcoats in 1686, and that in the same year grey undress, or fatigue-coats, were instituted, and that the coats were ordered to be looped back in 1696; but they do not throw much light upon what was then, and is now, a very obscure subject.

APPENDIX II

The following interesting document is to be found in the Irish Record Office, Dublin :

"Warrant dated August 3rd, 1699. Directed to His Majesty's Vice-Treasurer of this Kingdom (Ireland).

"Whereas the Commissioned Officers of the Regiment of Foot commanded by Brigadier Ingoldesby have agreed with the Undertakers for Clothing the said regiment, to furnish Clothes at the rate of £18 for each Captain, including the Field Officers : £12 for each Lieutenant, and Ensign : £12 for the Adjutant : which amounts in the whole to £474, to be paid within twelve months. We require you to pay to the Agent of the said Regiment £39 10s. monthly from the first instant, for six months, till the said sum is paid : same to be placed to the account of arrears of pay due to said regiment from the time of their landing to June 30th, 1699."

The few papers that can be consulted on old uniform give little, or no, information as to details ; and one is met with the further difficulty that Colonels were allowed a very free hand in the way in which they clothed their regiments, and very few details of their ideas on the subject exist.

Indeed, to such an extent had the custom grown, that on September 14th, 1743, it was deemed necessary to issue an order forbidding "*any Colonel for the future putting his Arms, Device, or Livery on any part of the appointments of his regiment.*" As this prohibition is repeated in the Clothing Warrant of December 19th, 1768, it would lead one to infer that the previous Order had not been very closely observed.

Until the Army Dress Regulations in their present form were first issued in 1822, it was the custom for the Board of General Officers, appointed in 1708 to regulate the clothing of the Army, to decide upon a uniform ; and having done so, to have the patterns sealed, and deposited at their office in Tooley Street. The Colonel of the regiment concerned was then informed of what had taken place, and he was requested to call as soon as possible at the office to inspect the uniform selected, and to see that it was taken into wear by his regiment without delay. The selection of the uniform only applied in a general way, the Colonel, as before mentioned, being allowed considerable latitude. Hence the reason why so few documents exist describing with any exactitude the uniforms of the period.

Letters exist stating that the Colonels were occasionally ordered to show the uniforms "*on the men's backs,*" before the Board of General Officers above mentioned. This was no doubt done with a view to uniformity, and possibly also to see that the large sum of money with which the Colonel was provided for equipping his regiment was properly laid out—more especially as the amount of his emoluments largely depended upon what he could save out of it. Probably also the variety of uniform displayed on these occasions gave rise to the order of 1743 quoted above.

The men were clothed out of the "*Off-reckonings,*" which were derived as follows : A certain portion (6d.) of the daily pay of the soldier (8d.) was set aside for subsistence, and the remainder was termed the "Gross off-reckonings." After deducting one day's pay per annum for the Chelsea Hospital Fund and other purposes, the net amount was handed to the Colonel, out of which he had to clothe his regiment. It was possible to make considerable savings, between the amount received and that spent on the uni-

REGIMENTAL COSTUME AND EQUIPMENT

forms, which was a perquisite of the Colonel. In one regiment in 1743 it amounted to £621, though the average was from £400 to £500. This system continued until 1855.

"*Half-mountings*," another term frequently come across in old documents relating to uniform, are described in Gross's *Military Antiquities* as follows : " The Black Stock and roller (neck-cloth) shirt, shoes and stockings are called the 'half-mounting.' The following order was issued on April 23rd. 1801 : In every regiment of Infantry of the Line, or Fencibles, serving in Europe, North America : or the Cape of Good Hope (Highland Corps excepted) each Sergeant, Drummer and Private man, to have annually for clothing, a coat : a waistcoat : or waistcoat front : a pair of breeches, unlined : a cap made of felt and leather, with a brass-plate, conformable to an approved pattern : the felt crown of the cap, cockade, and tuft to be supplied annually : the leather part and brass-plate every two years. And in lieu of the former articles of clothing, called '*Half-mountings,*' two pair of good shoes to the value of five shillings and six pence each pair. Should the price of good shoes at any time exceed the price of five shillings and six pence each pair, the difference, which is to be declared by the Clothing Board on, or after, the 25th of April each year, is to be charged to the respective accounts of the N.C.O. or soldier receiving them. . . . When His Majesty approves of the measure, the following sums, being the estimated amount of what the Colonels would have paid to their clothiers, after a reasonable deduction for incidental charges to which they are liable, are to be given to the men.

" To each Sergeant :
Clothing	. . . . . .	£2 18 0
Half-Mountings .	. . . . .	0 14 0
		£3 12 0

To each Corporal : Drummer and Private :
Clothing	. . . . . .	£1 5 6
Half-Mountings .	. . . . .	0 11 0
		£1 16 6 "

Half-mountings, as such, were done away with before 1805. In 1871 the clothing of regiments was transferred to the Royal Army Clothing Department in Pimlico, and the allowances to Commanding Officers withdrawn.

1742.—The earliest reliable reference to the uniform of the regiment that has been found is in a MS. book in the War Office Library showing a drawing of a private soldier in every regiment existing in the Army in 1742. That of the 23rd shows a man in a long red coat, with wide and voluminous skirts lined and turned back with blue. The coat is collarless, and has blue lapels coming down to the waist. On each lapel are six pointed loops of regimental lace, and pewter buttons, close together, and a button at the top corner. The lapels and neck are edged with regimental lace, as are also the cross-pockets. The cuffs are blue, and are wide and deep. They are slit on the outer side, and bound with regimental lace. A line of similar lace is traced round the cuff, a short distance from the edge. On the sleeve, above the cuff, is an oblong figure of regimental lace, with four cross-bars, and pewter buttons at the outer ends. The coat is fastened at the waist, and worn open above, thus showing the waistcoat and the long white neck-cloth. The waistcoat is red, and comes down to within a few inches of the knees, and is bound with regimental lace.

The breeches are blue; and long white gaiters are worn, coming well up the thigh, with black garters, and shoes.

The cap is of mitre-shape, with a blue cloth front, embroidered with the Prince of Wales' plumes in white, with a yellow coronet and motto. This is surmounted by a crown in proper colours, with long yellow scrolls down each side of the front of the cap. On a blue flap below is the white horse of Hanover embroidered in white. Edging three sides of the flap is a white label, inscribed in black letters, "*Nec aspera terrent*"; and above it another, charged "*Royal Welch Fusiliers*," with a red line between them. The front of the cap is edged with white cord, with a white woollen tuft on top. The back of the cap is of red cloth, divided into three panels with white piping, and with a blue turn-up round the bottom; with the number of the regiment in the middle. The cap, exclusive of the tuft on top, was 12 inches high; and the little flap $4\frac{1}{2}$ inches wide at the top and $7\frac{1}{2}$ inches at the bottom. The front of the cap was $9\frac{1}{2}$ inches wide across the bottom, and the tuft was $1\frac{1}{2}$ inches deep.

The accoutrements consist of a broad buff leather belt with a brass buckle worn over the right shoulder, and supporting a large pouch of the same material on the right side. A similar waistbelt is worn, supporting the bayonet; and a short curved brass-hilted sword.

The regimental lace was white, with yellow and blue stripes and a red "worm" stripe, and about $\frac{5}{8}$ inch wide.

1743.—The following orders were issued this year:

The drummers to wear red coats, lined, faced, and lapelled with blue, and laced with Royal lace (blue and yellow).

The officers to wear crimson silk sashes over the right shoulder. Their sword-knots to be of crimson and gold in stripes, and their gorgets gilt.

Sergeants to wear red worsted sashes round their waists, with a blue central stripe.

The skirts of the officers' coats were not turned back, and were laced with gold.

1751.—The front of the drums to be painted blue; with the King's cipher and crown, and "**23**" under it.

The following particulars are taken from the David Morier series of pictures in Windsor Castle, which includes the uniform of a grenadier of the regiment in 1751. It closely conforms to that of 1742, but the regimental lace is altered to white with red, blue, and yellow stripes. The coat is less voluminous in the skirts and is worn open down the front, showing the much shorter red waistcoat, bound with regimental lace. Blue breeches are still worn, and the little flap on the mitre-cap is now red. A black pouch is worn in front on the waistbelt, which still supports the sword and bayonet. The back of the coat is quite plain, except for three bars of lace on each side of the slit between the turnbacks. At each side of the waist is a button from which to the bottom of the skirts runs a bar of lace with branching arms arranged in the same manner as the lace on the sleeves. Brown gaiters were worn in marching order; when the officers wore boots.

REGIMENTAL COSTUME AND EQUIPMENT

1757.—The Inspection Returns from Chatham, dated September 24th, state: "The officers' uniforms only frocks, faced with blue, and bound with narrow gold lace. Men's uniform: red, lapelled and faced with blue, with a red, blue, yellow, and white worsted lace."

The uniform of the 2nd battalion, which was also at Chatham at that time, is stated to be the same as the above.

1766.—The officers' cap was of blue velvet, back and front bordered all round with broad gold lace, showing a blue light outside. On the front the Prince of Wales' plumes, embroidered in silver, with the motto "*Ich Dien*" in gold letters on a threefold crimson velvet, gilt-edged scroll, and surmounted by a crown embroidered in proper colours. A large gold tassel at each side in front, the end of the fringe not coming below the bottom band of the cap. The little flap at the bottom was blue, with the white horse of Hanover embroidered in silver. The flap was edged on the sides and top by two rows of gold lace, about a quarter of an inch apart, and showing a light of blue velvet between them. The centre of the lower band bore the word "Royal." The back, which was bordered with gold lace like the front, had "G.R." embroidered in gold in the middle; and below it a semicircular turn-up, with the white Dragon embroidered in gold and silver thereon, and edged all round with gold lace. There was a gold and crimson tuft on the top of the cap.

1768.—We now come to the MS. book in the Prince Consort's Library at Aldershot, which also gives details of the uniform of a grenadier of the 23rd Regiment. Considerable changes are shown in the uniform. The embroidered cap is abolished, and is replaced by a mitre-shaped black bearskin cap, twelve inches high, exclusive of the fur; with a black japanned metal plate with a curved top, at the bottom of the cap. On the plate, all in white metal, is the lion of England in the centre, standing on a helmet with lambrequins, with "*G*" on one side and "*R*" on the other. A curved label runs along the top of the plate charged with the motto "*Nec aspera terrent.*" On the back of the cap was a red cloth circle, with the Prince of Wales' feathers in white embroidery (silver for the officers) in the centre. A grenade on the lower part, with the number of the regiment on it.

The coat is much closer fitting, less voluminous, and more cut away in the skirts with a blue turned-down collar, and small round blue cuffs. It is lapelled from the neck to the waist with blue cloth three inches wide, and ornamented with ten square-ended loops of regimental braid with pewter buttons at the outer ends. A similar loop is at each end of the collar, which buttons down to the top loop on the lapel, and partially obscures it. The collar could be turned up in bad weather. Four similar loops and buttons are shown on each cuff. The shoulders are ornamented with wings having six loops of regimental lace, and a line of it across the bottom. The lace is white, about $\frac{5}{8}$ inch wide: with red, blue, and yellow stripes close together. The coat skirts are lined with white, and are buttoned back to show the lining. A plain white waistcoat, much shorter than that hitherto worn, is shown; with white breeches, and stockings coming well up the thigh. Black linen gaiters, with white buttons, come over the knee; and black shoes are worn. A white leather belt, worn diagonally over the left shoulder, carries the black ammunition pouch behind; and on the middle of the belt the brass match-case and chain are fitted.

A white leather belt with a brass buckle is worn round the waist, carrying the bayonet and a short steel-hilted sword. The belt is worn under the coat, and the left skirt comes over the sword. The coat is worn open, and shows the black neck-cloth.

The battalion men were similarly dressed, but had no wings on their shoulders, nor the match-case on their cross-belt, nor did they carry swords.

The drummers and fifers were dressed like the men ; but in addition to the King's crest, their cap-plate was ornamented with trophies of colours and drums. They were armed with short, curved, brass-hilted swords. A goatskin pack was carried over the shoulder by all ranks in marching order.

The officers wore long-tailed scarlet coats with blue lapels to the waist, collar, and round cuffs, and with cross-pockets. The lapels were three inches wide from top to bottom, and were buttoned back to ten gilt buttons, with the regimental number thereon ; and with a corresponding number of gold lace loops, placed at equal distances. The skirts were well cut away, and turned back, showing the white lining.

Officers of the Grenadier Company wore a gold lace epaulette, with bullions, on each shoulder : the battalion officers having one on the right shoulder only.

All wore waistcoats and breeches of white kerseymere with gilt buttons, and black linen gaiters with black buttons, and small stiff tops with shoes. The waistcoats were plain, without either embroidery or lace, and with cross-pockets without flaps.

They wore similar cap-plates to those of the men and gold cords with tassels across their bearskin caps.

Officers and sergeants wore crimson sashes round their waists, those of the officers being of silk, and of the sergeants' worsted, with a blue stripe down the centre.

The officers' swords had gilt hilts, with gold and crimson striped sword-knots. Grenadier officers carried fusils ; and the battalion officers espontoons. The Grenadier officers' shoulder-belts were 2 inches wide, and were fitted with pouches.

Corporals were distinguished by a silk epaulette on the right shoulder ; and the waistbelts of all ranks were of white leather, two inches wide. The Pioneers wore a distinctive cap, and arms. The former had a leather crown and a black bearskin front. The metal cap-plate was enamelled red : with the King's crest, and an axe and saw on it in white enamel. They also wore white leather aprons, and each carried an axe and saw.

1769.—The Inspection Return from Fort George, dated June 14th, states : " The officers' coats trimmed with a narrow gold lace ; and they have plain white waistcoats and breeches."

1770.—The Inspection Return for this year records that the rank and file were still wearing " caps of the old pattern," and that the officers were " in hatts." This shows that the regiment had not yet received from its clothier the " Black Bearskin cap " authorised to be worn by the Royal Warrant of December 19th, 1768.

1771.—By a General Order of December 25th, 1770, a Light Company was added to the regiment this year. The officers were clothed in scarlet, and the men in red ; but their coats were very much shorter in the skirts than those of the Grenadier Company, and of the battalion men.

They wore wings on the shoulder like the grenadiers, white breeches and stockings, and black half-gaiters coming up to the calf. Their caps were of black leather, very similar to those worn by light dragoons at that period, with a red turned-up peak in front; a black silk turban, and a black fur crest with white side-plume. They wore red waistcoats, and white leather crossed-belts, and had two frogs on the waistbelt, one for the hatchet and the other for the bayonet. When on the march the hatchet was tied on to the goatskin pack.

1776-1783.—The buttons on the men's coats were of pewter: flat, with the Prince of Wales' plumes in the centre, and "**23**" below, with a floreated edge.

1784.—On June 15th the powder-horns and bullet-bags of the Light Infantry Company were ordered to be laid aside: also the matches, match-cases, and swords of the Grenadier Company. A small priming-horn holding about two ounces of powder was provided instead. The pouch and bayonet belts were ordered to be two inches wide; the flap of the pouch to be plain, and to carry fifty-six rounds of ammunition; and the bayonet carriage arranged to slip on and off the waistbelt with two loops. It was now to be worn over the right shoulder by way of a cross-belt instead of round the waist as heretofore. It is a curious fact that in some of Morier's 1751 paintings in Windsor Castle some of the regiments are shown as having anticipated this order by about 33 years! The cloth straps on the men's shoulders were changed from red to blue.

The Inspection Returns for this year, dated from Doncaster, 14th May, state:

"The officers' uniforms with 'Royal' lappels (i.e. Blue) and gold-laced button-holes. Neither officers nor men had their fuzileer caps, as the cap-maker had disappointed them. They all therefore appeared in plain hats, i.e. three-cornered, with feathers in the form of H.R.H. The Prince of Wales' crest: which had a very pretty effect."

The officers' button worn about this time was gilt, with the Prince of Wales' plumes and motto in the centre with "**23**" below, with a ring of oak leaves at intervals round the edge.

1786.—In April this year the officers were ordered to lay aside the espontoon, and to provide themselves "with a strong, substantial uniform sword," with a straight cut-and-thrust blade 32 inches long, instead of the light one hitherto worn. The hilt to be gilt, to match the buttons and lace on the uniform. The sword-knot was of gold lace, with crimson silk stripes. When on duty, and with their sashes on, officers wore their swords slung over their uniform; and when off duty, and without their sashes, they wore them over their waistcoats, i.e. under their coats. The officers were still without their fuzileer caps, as is shown by the Inspection Return for July, which states that they "appear in plain hats."

1788.—The Inspection Returns sent this year from Chatham Barracks, dated May 22nd, state that "the men's accoutrement breast-plates are unique, with the three feathers engraved. The three feathers of Wales worn in the hats of the battalion appear showy; and give height to the battalion men in their undress." From this it would appear that the custom initiated at Doncaster in 1784 was continued.

1789.—Halberds for sergeants were abolished by a G.O. of 27th March, and swords were substituted. At the same time brass drums replaced wooden ones.

The gold lace loop on the officers' uniform at this period showed no light down the centre. The button was gilt, with the plumes, motto, and regimental number in the middle, and had a flat edge.

1791.—Towards the end of this year it was ordered that all field officers of infantry were to wear two epaulettes. Grenadier and Light Company officers, who for some time previously had worn two, were to be distinguished in future by wearing a grenade, or bugle, respectively, on the epaulette.

On October 6th pikes replaced the halberds for sergeants abolished in 1789. They were first of all issued on trial, and were finally adopted in April 1792. They were of much the same shape and size, as the espontoon previously carried by the officers.

1795.—In July of this year an officers' gilt gorget of universal pattern was ordered, which in most regiments continued until they were done away with in 1831. It was to be engraved with the King's cipher below a crown, in the centre; and suspended by a blue ribbon from the top buttons of the lapels, with a blue rosette at each end. It is doubtful whether this was at first adopted by the 23rd, as other designs have been found which are described later on.

1796.—During this year sundry changes in the uniform took place.

On February 1st it was ordered that the coat lapels were to be continued, as then worn, to the waist; but were to be made to button over occasionally, or to clasp close with hooks and eyes all the way down to the bottom, i.e. when the lapels were "buttoned-back." The collar was to be upstanding instead of lying down as heretofore, and an opening to be left at the flap, on the outside of the pocket, so as to admit the hand into it when the lapels were buttoned over. The pocket-flaps of the Light Company to be made oblique, or slashed. The collar was wide in the neck so as to admit of the large black neck-cloth.

The coats of the rank and file had ten loops of white braid, with yellow, blue, and red lines square-ended, across the lapels, arranged at equal distances with a white metal button about ⅝ inch diameter bearing the regimental number at the outer ends. There were four similar loops on the round blue cuffs, and one on each end of the collar. White leather crossed belts were worn, with a white waistcoat and breeches, and with black gaiters coming up to the knee, and shoes. The white shirt frill was allowed to appear from below the black stock to the middle of the chest.

1797.—At this period the Light Company officers wore a curved sword suspended by two slings from the shoulder-belt. In October of this year the coat lapels were ordered to be done away with; but the arrangement of the lace and buttons on the men's coats was to be preserved, but to be sewn on the coats, instead of on the lapels as heretofore.

The officers when on duty were ordered to wear short coats with epaulettes, like those of the N.C.O.s and men, except that they were to be quite plain, and without lace. When "off duty," or in "Dress," the existing uniform, i.e. the long-tailed, lapelled, and braided coat, was to continue in wear. Contemporary prints show a scarlet bag, with a gold tassel at the end, behind the officers' bearskin caps; but no official confirmation of this has been found.

1798.—The Inspection Returns from Guernsey, of October 4th, report that "the officers and men wear helmets. No great-coats as yet come." What the pattern of this helmet was, or why it was temporarily taken into use, there is nothing to show.

The Inspecting General further adds: "The helmets not being the dress of the infantry in general, give an appearance to the corps of singularity, which is the only unfavourable circumstance which I remarked in that sort of dress."

The officers' gorget at this period was of gilt metal, with the Royal Arms engraved in front, with "*G.R.*" on either side, and "**23** *R.W.F.*" in a dotted circle above. In the two top corners were engraved trophies of mediæval arms.

1800.—The head-dress of the Light Company was altered this year. It was now a cylindrical cap, seven inches deep, with a peak set on at an angle, and made of lacquered felt. On the front was a large rectangular plate, six by four inches, with rounded corners. It was decorated with trophies of arms, etc.: with the King's crest, cipher and Garter in the centre. Above it was a small black cockade, with a bugle-horn in the centre. A small green plume was worn in front of the cap, which had neither chain nor chin-strap. Colonels were allowed to have their regimental number engraved on the plate on either side of the lion.

At this period the privates wore a short red jacket, or coatee, with blue collar and cuffs; on each side of the breast, ten loops of regimental lace, four inches long with bastion ends, and white metal buttons. Their shoulder-straps were blue, and the battalion men wore small white woollen tufts on the points of the shoulders. The collar was laced all round, and cut away in front, showing the black stock and shirt frill.

Sergeants of the flank companies carried swords, and fusils on full-dress parades.

Sergeants of the battalion companies had silver-mounted malacca-canes, which could be fastened on occasion by a buff-leather thong to a button on the left breast of the coatee. White crossed-belts were worn by the men; also white breeches, and black gaiters coming up to the knee. A black leather ammunition pouch was carried behind.

The white waistcoat was now completely hidden, and was shortly afterwards abolished as an article of full dress; but it reappeared with sleeves, as a fatigue-jacket, and was so worn until 1830, when it finally disappeared from the Infantry of the Line.

1801.—Great-coats were this year provided for the N.C.O.s and private men.

1802.—Epaulettes and shoulder-knots for N.C.O.s were abolished in July, and chevrons on the right arm substituted. Sergeant-majors wore four, of silver lace; sergeants, three; and corporals, two. The first chevron was of silver lace, the second of plain white braid, and the third of white braid with red, blue, and yellow stripes; the japanned metal plate hitherto worn on the front of the Grenadier and Fusilier cap was altered to brass.

The button on the men's coats was pewter, with the plumes over "**23**" in the centre, flat, and with a corded edge.

1805.—This year a universal-pattern black-canvas knapsack replaced the goatskin pack, which had been used since 1750, or thereabouts. The officers' gorget now worn was of gilt metal with the monogram "*G.R.*" in front, with a laurel branch on either side surmounted by a crown. Above it "**23** *R.W.F.*" with a dotted circle. The holes for suspension in the top points were surrounded by dotted circles.

1806.—The Inspection Returns from Colchester on September 13th state that "there are fifty men only 5' 3" to 5' 4" high: and the caps disfigure these short men very much," i.e. the bearskin caps, no doubt.

The officers' dress-coat at this period had a blue collar, blue round cuffs, and blue lapels from neck to waist, wider at the top than at the bottom. On the lapels were ten loops of gold lace set on at equal distances with buttons on the outer ends, four similar loops on each cuff, and one at each end of the collar. The pocket flaps were horizontal, with four gold loops on, and four buttons under, the flap. At the waist were two horizontal loops and buttons, with two loops without buttons below them. The loops on the lapels, collar, and cuffs showed a blue light in the middle; those on the pocket flap and waist, a red light. The buttons were gilt, having in the centre the Prince of Wales' feathers, and motto; and "**23**" below.

The skirts were gradually cut away in front, and were turned back before and behind with white kerseymere.

A white leather sword-belt, with frog, was worn, diagonally, over the right shoulder, under the gold epaulette; white breeches; and black Hessian boots, with black tassels at the V in front. A crimson silk sash was worn round the waist, and tied on the right side. White gloves, a brass-hilted sword, with black leather scabbard, and a gold sword-knot. The lapels were sometimes worn buttoned over, but with the upper portion turned back, thus showing the blue facing. A sketch of this period shows the men wearing a red jacket, with the skirts, cut quite away in front, with eight bastion-shaped loops of lace on each side of the breast, a blue collar laced round the top and front, blue cuffs with four bastion loops on each, red wings with six bars of lace on them and woollen edges outside, white crossed-belts with a brass plate, and white breeches. The bearskin cap has a peak, brass plate, and white cords, tassels, and plume.

1810.—A G.O. was issued on 19th February regarding officers' epaulettes, the King having approved of the respective ranks of the officers of infantry being distinguished by them.

Field officers were ordered to wear two epaulettes: those of a colonel to have a crown and a star on the strap, a lieutenant-colonel's a crown, and a major's a star. Captains of flank companies who had the brevet-rank of field-officer wore wings in addition to their epaulettes; the epaulettes of the Grenadiers having a grenade on the strap, and those of the Light Company a bugle-horn below the badges of rank. Company officers and subalterns wore one epaulette, and that on the right shoulder, excepting those belonging to the flank companies. They wore a wing on each shoulder, with a grenade, or bugle-horn, on the strap, according as they belonged to the Grenadier or the Light Company.

Adjutants and quartermasters wore epaulettes like those of the subaltern officers, but in addition the Adjutant wore an epaulette strap on the left shoulder.

The Paymaster, Surgeon, and Assistant Surgeon wore neither epaulettes, wings, nor sash: and a waistbelt was now substituted for their shoulder-belt hitherto worn.

At the inspection of the 1st battalion this year at Halifax, Nova Scotia, the Inspecting General took exception to the officers not wearing epaulettes according to the new regulation. The Commanding Officer explained that as they were not procurable locally he had "directed a supply to be furnished from England."

The officers' cross-belt plate worn at this period was a bright gilt rectangular plate with silver Prince of Wales' plumes and motto in the middle, surrounded by a gilt garter inscribed "*Royal Welch Fusiliers*" and surmounted by a gilt crown. Below in gilt numerals "*XXIII.*" It continued in wear until 1816.

1811.—The Light Infantry Company's cap was altered this year. It was made of felt; beaver, for the officers, with a gilt oval-shaped plate in front, with the monogram "*G.R.*" reversed, and the regimental number "*XXIII*" below. In the middle were the Prince of Wales' plumes, and a Sphinx above "*Egypt*" (both in silver on the officers' plate), a crown surmounting the plate. The front of the cap, representing an up-turned peak, was three inches higher than the crown, which was 6¾ inches deep, and was bound with black braid, with a drooping black leather peak, two inches deep, in front. Across the front of the cap was a plaited cord, with tassels on the right side. The cords, tassels, and side-plume were green. The plume was worn on the left side, rising from a small black cockade with a small regimental button in the centre. A chin-strap was now worn with the cap. This cap was worn during the later years of the Peninsula War, and until after Waterloo, being abolished in August 1815. Special "bugler's lace" was introduced towards the latter part of this year, and their clothing was, otherwise, to be the same as the rest of the regiment.

1812.—At the Inspection of the 2nd battalion which took place at Haverfordwest in July by Major-General R. Browne he remarked on an article provided for the men but not included in the regulations, namely, a vice. Lieutenant-Colonel Wyatt wrote as follows in explanation: "I beg leave to state to you that prior to my having a Lock Drill established for sergeants and rank and file at every field day, I found at least 15 to 20 firelocks that were useless: and upon examination I ascertained that scarcely one out of 20 required repair from the armourer, but that the soldier could with very little instruction remedy the defects if he had the means. Ramrods and bayonets were generally made use of for the purpose of taking off the main and feather springs, which not only injured them very materially, but being very awkward instruments for such purposes some other parts of the lock were often injured by the use of them. Since the adoption of this vice, and no recruit being dismissed the drill until he is perfectly acquainted with the use of it, and is able to take his lock to pieces and put it together again, I find very few arms that require repair: and no useless firelock in the field excepting that the hammer occasionally may want hardening, or that the lock may be wood bound."

1813.—The rank of Colour-Sergeant was introduced on 27th July this year.

1814.—The brass shake-plate for the Light Company was done away with this year; and a bugle-horn substituted, with the number of the regiment below it.

The privates wore single-breasted red cloth jackets laced across the front with "bastion"-shaped loops of regimental lace, four inches long, set on at equal distance. The jackets were laced round the collar, which was worn open to show the shirt frill and black stock. The shoulder-straps were laced up the sides, and had white woollen shoulder-tufts. In the flank companies they terminated in red cloth wings trimmed with six bars of regimental lace, and edged with an overhanging white worsted fringe. The Inspecting General comments as follows upon the lace worn by the 1st battalion: "the jackets of the officers are not uniform, the lace in several of them being put on in different manner." He also refers to the fact that the lace on the wings of the non-commissioned officers and privates differs from the pattern jacket. In what year the shape of the loops was changed from "square-ended" to "bastion" has not been ascertained, but probably it was about 1798.

The sergeants were dressed like the privates, but in a finer quality of cloth, having the chevrons of their rank on the arm, which, together with their coat-lace, was of fine white tape. Their sashes were of crimson worsted with a blue central stripe. They carried a straight sword in a white-leather belt with a frog, and brass central plate, suspended diagonally over the right shoulder. Their other weapon was a pike, a plain steel spear-head with a cross-bar below, not unlike the espontoon formerly carried by officers. The earlier type was a battle-axe headed weapon (halberd), which was abandoned in 1792.

1815.—In August this year a new pattern cap for infantry was introduced, which affected the Light Company; and also the Grenadier Company when the full-dress bearskin caps were not worn. It was made of black beaver for the officers (black felt for the rank and file), $7\frac{1}{2}$ inches deep and 11 inches in diameter at the top; bell-shaped, with gilt cheek-scales, which could be tied up in front below the black cockade, in the centre of which was a regimental button. A green upright plume, 12 inches high, rising from a brass socket was fixed in front. On the man's caps, below the cockade, was a bugle-horn, with the number of the regiment on the cockade. The officers wore a band of gold lace round the top of the cap, $2\frac{1}{2}$ inches wide; and another half an inch wide round the bottom. Green looped cap-lines were worn.

The following is the description of a coatee made for General Grenville (who was Colonel of the regiment from 1786 to 1823) and is taken from a tailor's notebook of the period: "Blue facings, holes regular; eleven twist holes in lappels: four gold holes in slash flap (i.e. the pocket), five in cuff: one in collar: four holes across back (i.e. at the waist). Skirts laced: turnbacks laced and a blue edging. Gold-laced holes: triangle on back" (i.e. at the waist). "Undress: no lace on the lappels, or down. The gold braid of undress trousers to be traced on each side with eyes."

"Twist holes" were made of double bars of narrow blue silk cord, and no doubt there were eleven corresponding gilt regimental buttons on each lapel. This may be taken as a full description of the officers' coat of the 1800-20 period.

1816.—One of "Cremer's" sketches shows the officers' uniform at this period to consist of a scarlet coatee, with the skirts cut away much like those of a modern civilian dress-coat, turned back with white. Blue collar and cuffs, with two gold loops and buttons on the former, four on the latter; the lapels buttoned over, and showing ten gold loops arranged in pairs on the under-side; gold and scarlet wings; and a white leather cross-belt over the right shoulder, with a brass plate. A crimson sash and tassels round the waist. The bearskin cap has a leather peak, brass front plate; gold cords and tassels on the right side and a white plume on the left. In the centre of the back is a circular scarlet-cloth patch, with the Prince of Wales' plumes embroidered in silver in the middle.

The cocked hat which had been retained by infantry officers since 1806, for full dress when at Court, was abolished on 20th June, and it was ordered to be replaced on these occasions by the regimental cap.

1820.—This year short coats were discontinued for all ranks, except the Light Company, and long-tailed coats for officers were universal throughout the infantry. The button worn by the officers at this period was gilt, ⅝ inch diameter, with the Prince of Wales' plumes in the middle surrounded by a circle inscribed "*Royal Welch Fusiliers,*" with a crown above and "*XXIII*" below. The lapels on their dress-coat had a curved edge, and were wider at the top than at the bottom; with ten loops of gold lace arranged in five pairs, with buttons on the outer edge. Two similar loops on the collar, and four (two pairs) on the cuff.

The officers' cross-belt plate worn about this period, and until 1855, was a frosted gilt rectangular plate with bright bevelled edges. On it was a large flaming gilt grenade; and mounted on the ball were the Prince of Wales' plumes, coronet, and motto in silver, with "*XXIII*" in gilt-metal numerals below; inside a circle inscribed "*Royal Welch Fusiliers*" surmounted by a silver crown.

1822.—The following are the regulations laid down this year for the dress of the officers:

Full Dress: Scarlet coats: blue cloth Prussian collar: full 3 inches deep, with two gold-laced loops, and small buttons at each end; blue cloth straight lapels, buttoned back to ten large buttons, and gold-laced loops, occupying two-thirds of the space across the chest, from outward edge to the front seam of the arm-hole, tapering to 2½ inches at the bottom, and closing in front with hooks and eyes; blue cuffs 4 inches deep, with four gold-laced loops and buttons on each; coatee skirts with cross-flaps, four laced loops and buttons on each; four short-laced holes on the back; tommy back; back skirts and white kerseymere turnbacks laced, an embroidered grenade, on blue cloth, on each skirt. All the loops by pairs. The front and top of the collar, the top of the cuff, the lower edge and sides of the pocket flap, and the outside edges of the lapels were all piped with white cloth. The turnbacks of the skirts were edged with blue outside the gold lace.

Wings: Gold; gilt scaled straps 2 inches wide; two rows of gold bullion, 1½ inches long.

Epaulettes: Gilt scaled straps, two rows of bright gold bullion, 3 inches long, worn only by field officers. Field officers wear both epaulettes and wings.

Bearskin: black, about 16 inches deep; gilt plate with King's arms and regimental devices in front. Gold-plated cord-lines and bullion tassels, gilt scales and roses. A black patent-leather peak in front, and a white feather at the side.

Breeches: White kerseymere, with regimental buttons and gilt buckles, white silk stockings, and shoes with gilt buckles; or white pantaloons, with black Hessian boots.

Sabre: Gilt half basket hilt, with "*G.R. IV.*" inserted in the outward bars, and lined with black patent leather. The gripe of black fish-skin, bound with three gilt wires: the blade 32½ inches in length, 1⅛ inches wide at the shoulder, with round back, terminating off to a shampre within 9 inches of the point, and very little curved. Black leather scabbard, with gilt mountings. Crimson and gold sword-knot, with bullion tassel.

Belt: White buffalo leather, 3 inches wide, with a frog, worn under the coat, diagonally over the right shoulder. A black silt cravat, and white leather gloves.

Dress: The coatee, wings, epaulettes, bearskin, sabre and scabbard, sword-knot, gloves, and cravat all as in "*Full Dress.*"

Breeches (white) and black leggings were worn when on duty and white pantaloons and Hessian boots on ordinary occasions. The white leather shoulder-belt was worn over the coat in "*Dress*"; and a crimson silk net sash going twice round the waist, and tied with cords and tassels.

In "*Undress*" the same coatee was worn, but with the lapels buttoned over; the bearskin "cased"; blue-grey trousers and black ankle-boots. All other articles of dress and appointments as in "*Dress*."

A cloak of blue cloth, of walking length, lined with scarlet shalloon, was also worn. The great-coat (or undress frock-coat) was of blue cloth, single-breasted, with a Prussian collar, and regimental buttons.

The field officers' horse furniture consisted of a blue cloth saddle-cloth 2 feet 10 inches in length, and 1 foot 10 inches in depth, with an edging of gold lace $\frac{5}{8}$ inch wide, with a scarlet cloth edging. The bridle was of black leather, with a bent branch-bit with gilt bosses, having a rose, thistle, and shamrock in the centre, encircled by the words "*Infantry Mounted Officers*," and a crown above. The forehead band and roses of blue leather. A white collar, and holsters covered with black bearskin.

1823.—The establishment of the Band was ordered to consist of a sergeant (master) and fourteen musicians.

Breeches, leggings, and shoes were discontinued for full-dress parades, and blue-grey trousers and half-boots substituted. N.C.O.s, drummers, and privates of infantry regiments at home and abroad were ordered to have a pair of white linen trousers for full-dress parades for summer wear, i.e. between the 1st May and the 14th October.

On 30th August a sword-belt was instituted for officers to be worn outside the blue frock-coat. It was of black leather without other ornament than the usual brass rings and buckles. The clasp bore the regimental number.

1824.—Instructions were given this year that when the knapsack was not carried the great-coat was to be folded rectangularly 17 inches by 11 inches. In Light Marching Order it was to be carried in the knapsack, and in Heavy Marching Order it was to be rolled lengthways, and placed over the top of the knapsack, horse-collar fashion, round the mess-tin. The shoulder-belts were now increased to $2\frac{3}{4}$ inches in width.

1826.—The Dress Regulations published this year made no great alterations in the officers' uniform. The cuffs were reduced to $3\frac{1}{2}$ inches in depth, and two gold loops and small regimental buttons were to be worn at each end of the collar. The skirt ornaments to be embroidered grenade wings, and epaulettes of regimental pattern were authorised. A shako was permitted to be worn when serving in warm climates, instead of the bearskin cap. A blue cloth forage cap, with a leather top $12\frac{1}{2}$ inches diameter, a gold band round the bottom $2\frac{1}{4}$ inches wide, and a patent-leather peak were authorised for undress. The feather on the bearskin cap was to be 12 inches long, with a gilt screw-socket.

The officers' Levee Dress consisted of the shako, with cap-plate and coloured plume as laid down for officers of the different companies, a scarlet coatee with wide blue lapels, gold-laced; blue collar and cuffs; white turnbacked skirts laced all round with gold, and edged with blue, and gold badges of rank on the epaulettes of the battalion officers, and on the wings of the Grenadier and Light Company officers. White breeches, with silk stockings, and black shoes with gilt buckles. Neither belt nor sash was worn, and the sword was carried in a black scabbard with gilt mounts.

On 10th April the officers of the Light Company were ordered to wear coatees like those of the rest of the regiment: their only distinction being wings, bugle ornaments, and the green cap-feather. Whistles and chains were added to their cross-belts.

New sergeants' sashes were adopted. Instead of as heretofore having a single blue central line, they had a series of three crimson and two blue lines. The short jackets of the N.C.O.s and men of the Light Company were abolished, and alterations were made in the coats of the men, now all alike throughout the regiment. The lace round the front and top of the collar was removed, and a single loop of it worn at each end. The lace loops upon the breast varied in length, tapering from $5\frac{1}{2}$ inches at the top to $2\frac{1}{4}$ inches at the bottom. The lace was removed from the skirts, except the loops on the slashed pockets. The curious proviso is made, that the shoulder-straps shall not touch the lace on the bottom of the collar, " in order to make the men appear as broad as possible." Great care was also to be taken that the skirts did not open behind.

1827.—A new knapsack, smaller, lighter, and easier of access, was introduced this year.

1828.—The infantry shako was altered in December this year. It was bell-shaped as before, but was reduced in height to 6 inches; and was without lace. It had gilt chin-scales, and a large gilt star-plate in front. Above this was a rich gold festoon, with cap-lines and tassels, of gold for the officers. Those of the men were white, except in the case of the Light Company, when they were green. They were only to be worn on parade; and were fastened to the right side of the shako, and came down well below the chest, where they were looped with tassels on the left side. They were abolished in 1830. A white feather plume (green in the Light Company) 12 inches high was worn in front, on top of the cap. Fusiliers when serving in warm climates were ordered to wear this shako instead of the bearskin cap, but it is doubtful if the 23rd ever wore it, except at Court.

1829.—On 10th February of this year the officers' coatees were ordered to be without lapels, with the buttons in two rows down the front. The width between the rows to be 3 inches at the top and $2\frac{1}{2}$ inches at the bottom. Every officer to wear two epaulettes of universal design. The distinction in rank to be by the progressive size of the bullions and devices. Captains and subalterns to have a blue stripe on the epaulette strap, while field officers had no stripes. The Lieutenant-Colonel and Major to have devices on the strap; the Colonel to have them united.

Blue-grey trousers were discontinued, and those of " Oxford mixture " adopted for both officers and men. A blue forage cap, with a large stiffened top, and peak, and a red band round the bottom, was worn with the frock-coat; the bearskin cap only with regimentals, or the shako in warm climates.

On 20th March the then General Officer Commanding in Chief (Lord Hill), after having received reports from every regiment in the service on the articles of clothing, and equipment of officers, " distinguishing such as are fixed by the King's Regulations and such as have been introduced without authority," issued a confidential circular to General Officers on the Staff, expressing his great surprise at the state of affairs disclosed, " and the absolute necessity which exists for a decided check being given to the latitude many commanding officers have assumed and the inordinate expenses they have thereby imposed upon the officers of their respective corps."

Gold-laced trousers seem to have been a serious cause of offence; but in this circular the 23rd is not reported as transgressing in this respect.

With a view to the reduction of expenses, quotations were obtained from a number of military tailors for each article of uniform, stating a "ready-money" price. These were sent to commanding officers of regiments, as a check to extravagance. The observance of the Regulations was to be enforced by frequent inspections, and very close inquiry; and "Lord Hill confidently expects that every means will be adopted by General Officers and Commanding Officers of Regiments to give full and complete effect to His Majesty's orders." The gross cost of the equipment of an officer of the 23rd had been found to be £105 1s., while that of the 21st was only £61 12s. 6d. The attention of the General Officers was specially drawn to this excessive cost, and to preventing its continuance. The cost of a Fusilier officer's outfit, including the bearskin cap, was fixed at £60.

Epaulettes were not to be worn in future with wings, and braided frock-coats were forbidden. A plain blue frock-coat with regimental buttons and a small gold shoulder-cord to be worn, with a sash and cross-belt. The black undress waistbelt introduced in 1823 was abolished in April this year and a white patent-leather cross-belt was ordered to be worn, with the frock-coat only. The brass chin-scales were removed from the bearskin caps and were replaced by a black leather strap.

In June another type of knapsack was adopted. With it, in Light Marching Order, the men's great-coats were carried inside the pack. In Heavy Marching Order they were folded square, and carried on the outside, while on the Line of March they were rolled, and carried on the top of the pack. The knapsack was carried by two shoulder-straps united by a strap across the lower part of the chest. White leather crossed belts were worn: one for carrying the bayonet and the other for the ammunition pouch.

1830.—This year the regimental lace was slightly changed. While still being white the sequence of the coloured lines was altered: now being red, yellow, and blue. The sergeants' pikes were abolished, and in future they were ordered to carry fusils (light rifles) and bayonets.

The cap-lines and tassels on the shako were done away with, and the upright feather was reduced to 8 inches in height and a green worsted ball was substituted for it on the Light Company's shakos.

The men's white undress jacket was replaced by one of red cloth, of similar shape; and the band was ordered to wear white coatees, with blue collars and cuffs. This is the first order concerning band uniforms that has been found. Hitherto they were dressed according to the fancy of the Colonel—sometimes in the most fantastic fashion.

The officers' gorgets were finally abolished, and their shako-plume was ordered to be hackle feathers. Their crimson silk sash was ordered to go twice round the waist and to be tied on the left hip, the pendant being 12 inches long from the tie.

The stars on the epaulettes to be those of the Order of the Garter. Shoes and buckles were abolished in Levee Dress, and officers were ordered to appear in trousers on such occasions.

The chevrons on the waistcoats of the sergeants and corporals were in future to be scarlet throughout the infantry of the Army, and the waistcoat was to correspond in all particulars with the newly sealed pattern.

The button on the men's coats from now until 1855 was of the same design as that of 1820, but was domed instead of being flat.

The officers' wing at this period was of scarlet cloth with two gilt chains down the centre edged all round with gold braid, and with gold bullions on the outer edge. In the centre the plumes in silver on a gilt burnished centre, surrounded by a crescent. The strap was of gilt metal scales, with a silver grenade in the centre. The outside of the strap and the inner side of the wing were edged with blue cloth.

On 30th April field officers were ordered to provide themselves with a buff leather waistbelt, with a gilt plate in front, instead of the shoulder-belt with sword-slings hitherto worn; and a brass scabbard replaced the black leather one. Adjutants were ordered to wear steel scabbards; and mounted officers' spurs to be of brass, with necks $2\frac{1}{2}$ inches long, including the rowels. The bearskin cap to be 14 inches deep, peak $1\frac{1}{4}$ inches wide, and to fasten under the chin with a leather strap.

1833.—The narrow red cloth welt, as worn to the present day, was ordered to be worn down the outer seams of the trousers.

1834.—Apparently "*Full Dress*" was abandoned this year, as no mention is made of it in the Dress Regulations issued on 1st August. The coatee remains much the same as before, but the collar is now ordered to have two gold lace loops and buttons at each end. The cuff of blue cloth is to be round, and $2\frac{3}{4}$ inches deep, with a scarlet slashed flap on the sleeve, with four gold lace loops and small buttons on it; another on the skirt with four loops, and large buttons. Two large buttons and four short twist loops at the waist; white turnbacks, and skirt linings; and gold embroidered grenades mounted on blue cloth as skirt ornaments.

A new forage cap for officers was authorised on 10th July made of blue cloth with a band of red cloth round the head, and with the regimental number embroidered in gold in the centre of a gold embroidered grenade in front, and fitted with a peak.

The shoulder-straps on the blue single-breasted undress frock-coat were ordered to be edged with gold regimental lace all round, and to have gilt metal crescents at the point of the shoulders.

White worsted balls replaced the plumes of the shakos, those of the Light Company being green as heretofore.

The mounted officers' holster-caps were ordered to be covered with black leather when serving in tropical climates.

1835.—This year the peak and brass plate on the bearskin cap were abolished.

1836.—" Regimental lace " was abolished in all regiments of infantry this year, and was replaced by plain white braid without any coloured worm; each regiment was permitted to retain its peculiar mode of wearing the lace; but the loops across the chest on the men's coatees were continued. The sergeants, however, wore a double-breasted coatee without any loops on the breast; those of the Fusilier, Light Infantry Regiments, and Flank Companies were to have wings instead of epaulettes. Good conduct stripes, now first introduced by Royal Warrant of 18th August, were to be worn on the right arm, point uppermost.

The drummers' lace, namely white, with blue conventional figures representing the

Prince of Wales' plumes, was continued on their uniforms. The men's coatees were to be altered so that when looking at a man in his front, at two yards' distance, the turn-backs of the skirts were not seen.

The skirts were to be cut across instead of being made in one piece with the body. The flap on the skirt was to be 1½ inches below the seam of that cut. The bottom of each skirt to be 5 inches in breadth. The skirts to be rounded off over the hips, and not cut angularly. The cuff to be 2¾ inches deep, its upper edge being even with the centre-point of the slashed flap on the sleeve.

1837.—The undress jackets of the Band to be white. Attention again drawn against wearing long hair and whiskers. Side-arms to be worn on duty only—this on account of a drunken soldier having killed a civilian in the street with his bayonet. The coroner's jury petitioned the Ministry to order the wearing of side-arms, when off duty in the streets, to be discontinued.

1840.—The general supply of percussion-caps to be carried in a tin magazine containing 80–100 caps. Those for immediate use to be carried in a small patent-leather pouch attached to the coat, on the right side, by a ring, and clear of the belts.

1842.—When the Reserve Battalion was inspected at Kingston, Canada, on the 26th of September the Inspecting General in his report called attention to the fact that " the men's shako peaks have been taken off, diminished, and differently replaced, and on inquiry I found it was under the orders of Lieutenant-Colonel Torrens ; he has defrayed the expense, and regrets being betrayed into this error from a notion of improvement : he is full of zeal and anxiety regarding the welfare and appearance of the battalion."

1844.—The " Albert Shako " was introduced (for description see under 1846) and the bearskin cap was abolished for all ranks and all companies. It was henceforth ordered to be the prerogative of the Guards. The cap-plate was a large gilt flaming grenade, and on the ball the Prince of Wales' plumes, coronet, and motto in silver.

1845.—A plain crimson woollen sash was introduced for sergeants, described as " of the national crimson colour," the breadth being reduced to 2½ inches ; lavender-coloured trousers replaced the white ones.

1846.—The Dress Regulations of this year make no alterations in the officers' coatee, except to state that the entire gold-laced loop shall not exceed 1¼ inches in breadth, and to be square-ended.

The epaulettes of field officers to have a plain gold-lace strap, solid crescent, and an embroidered badge of the Queen's cipher. The fringe of a colonel and lieutenant-colonel to be 3½ inches deep, and that of a major, 3 inches. Captains to wear a gold-laced strap with narrow blue silk stripes, metal crescent, and fringe 2½ inches deep. Subalterns' to be the same as those of captains, but with smaller fringe. Officers of flank companies to wear wings, the straps having three rows of gold chain, and a gilt centre-plate bearing a bugle in silver (the Grenadiers having a grenade instead), a row of bullion 1¼ inches deep at the centre, diminishing gradually towards the point. The subalterns distinguished from captains by smaller-sized bullions.

The cap was of black beaver, 6¾ inches deep, and ¼ inch less in diameter at top than at the bottom (6¼ inches to 6½ inches) ; patent-leather top, turned over at the edge to the breadth of ⅝ inch, and stitched round; a band of the same, double-stitched, encircled the bottom of the cap; a peak of patent leather 2⅜ inches deep in front, and another 1¼ inches deep behind. The cap-plate was the same as that described for 1844, namely a large grenade. A gilt chain fastened at the sides with rose-pattern ornaments on the officers' caps. A worsted ball tuft with a gilt socket was worn in front on top: two-thirds white, and one-third red at the bottom, by the Battalion Companies; that of the Grenadiers being all white, and of the Light Company all green.

This shako was designed by the Prince Consort, and was known as "*the Albert shako.*" When it was first introduced in 1844 it was 7 inches high. It is surely the ugliest head-dress ever worn in the British Army. It was so unpopular when first issued that, I have heard it stated, the men, when "walking out," made a practice of taking it off directly they were outside the barrack gates and carrying it under their arms. The men's shako was made of felt, and had a leather chin-strap; and their small brass plate of 1845 was retained on the front.

Trousers of Oxford-mixture cloth, with a red welt down the outer seam, were worn from 15th October to 30th April; grey tweed from 1st May to 14th October. White linen trousers to be worn in hot climates.

Ankle boots were worn; and mounted officers had yellow metal spurs, with necks 2 inches long.

Their sword had a gilt half-basket hilt, with the Queen's cipher inserted in the outward bars, and lined with black patent leather. The grip, of black fish-skin, was bound with a spiral of three gilt wires. Length of blade 32½ inches, width at the shoulder 1⅛ inches, and at 12 inches from the shoulder, 1 inch. Thickness of back at shoulder ⅜ inch, and at 18 inches from the hilt ¼ inch. Solid flat shoulder 1½ inches deep, and the blade hollowed from the flat to within 9 inches of the point, which was spear-shaped. Weight not less than 1 lb. 15 oz. without the scabbard.

Regimental field officers wore brass scabbards; other officers on all occasions, and field officers at Levees, Drawing-Rooms, and in evening dress, black leather, with gilt mountings. The sword-knot was crimson and gold, with a bullion tassel. The Adjutant wore the sword suspended by slings from the shoulder-belt, and in the field a steel scabbard.

The sword-belt of field officers was of buff leather worn round the waist, 1½ inches wide, with slings 1 inch wide. The plate consisted of a rectangular bright gilt plate with "*V.R.*" surmounted by a crown in the centre, and "**23**" below: all in silver. Other officers wore a buff shoulder-belt, 3 inches wide, with a frog. The cross-belt plate was the same as that previously described for 1820. The badge in the centre of the wing was a burnished gilt domed circular plate, with a gilt laurel wreath surrounding the Prince of Wales' plumes in silver.

The crimson silk sash, going twice round the waist, and tied in front of the left hip, was worn as before, with a black silk stock and white leather gloves.

In undress, a scarlet shell-jacket was worn, with a Prussian collar and pointed cuffs of blue cloth. A row of small regimental buttons down the front and two on each sleeve to fasten down the front with hooks and eyes. The shoulder-straps formed of gold basket cord, twisted double, with a small figure at the bottom and a small regimental button at the top.

The frock-coat was of blue cloth ; single-breasted, with a plain Prussian collar, and eight regimental buttons down the front and two small ones on the cuff. Blue cloth shoulder-straps edged all round with regimental gold lace, with a metal crescent at the point of the shoulder, the different ranks of field officers distinguished by the crown and star. Officers of Grenadiers to have a silver grenade and those of the Light Company a silver bugle, inside the crescent. A black patent-leather waistbelt, with a frog, and a snake-clasp was worn with the frock-coat, mounted officers wearing slings, instead of the frog.

The " flash " was sanctioned for the officers in the Dress Regulations for this year, for the first time. It was authorised for wear by the officers and staff sergeants on 28th November 1834.

1848.—A General Order of 30th June abolished the lace loops and buttons on the skirts of the officers' coatees, the gold grenade being their only ornament.

The blue frock-coat was discontinued, and was replaced by the scarlet shell-jacket, with blue collar and cuffs, but with no gold lace or other ornament. The field officers' badges of rank to be worn on the collar.

A grey cloth overcoat was introduced for officers, instead of the blue cloth cloak previously worn ; and a black leather sling waistbelt, with a gilt snake-clasp for undress. The white leather shoulder-belt to be invariably worn in full dress.

The Band uniform at this period consisted of a bearskin cap, with a gilt grenade in front, and a gilt chin-chain. A white coatee with blue collar and cuffs, with a white slash on them ; four regimental buttons on the slash of white metal, and blue turnbacks to the skirts. Black trousers, with a narrow red welt down the outside seams. The " flash " was worn at the back of the collar. The Bandmaster wore wings of blue cloth edged with white lace. The musicians wore wings of blue cloth with six bars of white braid, edged with the same at the top, and with white woollen tufts at the shoulder-points. They also wore white leather waistbelts. The Master wore a sword in a brass scabbard ; and the bandsmen were armed with a bandsman's sword, with a brass hilt, in a black scabbard with brass mounts, in a frog from the waistbelt.

1850.—The officers' wing at this time was of blue cloth, the strap edged with scarlet cloth, and cut away at the corners at the top. The strap and wing were edged with gold braid, with tapering gold bullions at the shoulder point. They were ornamented with three gilt chains ; and in the centre, on a raised blue cloth oval pad, were the Prince of Wales' plumes in silver, surrounded by an ornamental oval gold border, with a silver grenade on top.

The men's shoulder-belt, with brass plate, which had hitherto carried the bayonet, was done away with ; and a plain belt to carry the pouch was authorised, the bayonet being henceforth carried in a frog on the waistbelt.

1851.—The epaulette ornament was the same as that worn on the wings in 1847, previously described.

1852.—The officers of the Grenadier Company wore the crimson cords and tassels from their waist-sash looped on the chest, and fastened to the upper buttons on the left side of the coatee.

The blue frock-coat, discarded in 1848, was reintroduced for undress. It was

REGIMENTAL COSTUME AND EQUIPMENT

ordered to be double-breasted, quite plain, and with covered buttons. These were later on replaced by gilt ones.

Sergeants received sword-bayonets instead of the swords and triangular bayonets previously worn.

The officers and men still wore the "Albert shako" with a white ball tuft in front, and a gilt grenade as cap-plate.

1853.—The N.C.O.s and men were ordered to wear full-dress uniform when in the streets, on all occasions between the hours of morning parade and that of evening roll-call. The shell or undress-jacket to be worn within barracks.

1854.—In August the rank of second lieutenant was abolished, that of ensign being substituted for it.

1855.—This year considerable alterations were made in the uniform. The long-tailed coatee, so long worn, was abolished on the 1st of April; and the officers took into wear a long double-breasted tunic, with lapels, which folded back at the top to show the blue facing. They were, however, buttoned over on parade or duty. The collar, which was rounded off in front, was, like the cuffs, of blue cloth. The cuff was round, and $2\frac{3}{4}$ inches deep, with a blue slashed flap 6 inches long by $2\frac{1}{4}$ inches wide with three bastion-shaped loops of half-inch gold lace and regimental buttons on it. Two rows of nine gilt regimental buttons down the front at equal distances, the rows being 8 inches apart at the top and 4 inches at the bottom. The skirt to be 14 inches deep for an officer 5 feet 9 inches in height; with a variation of half an inch, longer or shorter for every inch of difference in the height of the wearer. A scarlet slashed flap on the skirt behind, 10 inches deep; two buttons on the slash, and one on each side of the waist, and 3 inches apart, with three loops of half-inch gold lace on the flap. The coat, collar, cuffs, and slashes edged with white cloth $\frac{1}{4}$ inch wide. On the left shoulder a crimson silk cord to retain the sash, with a small regimental button at the top.

Field officers were distinguished by gold lace round the top and bottom of the collar, down the edge of the skirts behind, also on the edge of the sleeve flaps; two rows of lace round the top of the cuffs, and the following badges, embroidered in silver, at each end of the collar, viz. Colonel, a crown and star; Lieutenant-Colonel, a crown; Major, a star: the other officers had lace on the top of the collar only, one row round the top of the cuffs, and none on the edge of the skirts. Loops only on the skirt flaps and sleeve-flaps; and the following badges of rank at each end of the collar: Captain, a crown and star; Lieutenant, a crown; Ensign, a star. The buttons were gilt, with "23" surmounted by the Prince's plumes, etc., in the middle, surrounded by a circle of small dots between them and the raised rim, and the gold lace was not to exceed half an inch in width.

A lighter, and modified, form of "Albert shako" was introduced. It was of black beaver for the officers, felt for the men, $5\frac{1}{4}$ inches deep in front, $7\frac{1}{8}$ inches deep behind, and one inch less in diameter at the top than at the bottom. A black patent-leather sunk top, turned over at the edge, to the breadth of $\frac{3}{8}$ inch, and stitched round a band of the same, double-stitched, and $\frac{5}{8}$ inch wide, round the bottom of the cap. A patent-leather peak, $2\frac{3}{8}$ inches wide in front, and another $1\frac{3}{8}$ inches behind. A black leather chin-strap $\frac{3}{4}$ inch wide fastened inside to the top of the cap. The cap-plate was a gilt grenade with the Prince of Wales' plumes in silver on the ball; a bronze Gorgon's head was fitted behind as a ventilator. Two rows of gold lace were worn round the top of the cap by lieutenant-colonels, and one row by majors. The ball tuft was white for battalion officers and men and also for the Grenadiers.

A white-enamelled leather waistbelt was introduced, $1\frac{1}{2}$ inches wide, to be worn over the coat on all occasions, with a gilt hook. When the sword was hooked-up, the edge was to be to the rear. The belt was fastened with a round gilt clasp, having on the centre-piece the Prince of Wales' plumes, etc., with "**23**" below, surrounded by "*Royal Welch Fusiliers*" on the outer circle, in silver letters on a frosted gilt grenade.

The officers' crimson silk sash, with fringe ends, united by a crimson runner, was now to be worn diagonally over the left shoulder, instead of round the waist as heretofore ; the ends of the fringe not to hang below the bottom of the coat. The sergeants wore their crimson woollen sashes diagonally over the right shoulder.

The blue undress frock-coat was still worn. It was now, however, to be double-breasted, with a stand-up collar rounded off in front. Round cuffs $2\frac{3}{4}$ inches deep ; slash flap in sleeve $5\frac{1}{4}$ inches long and $1\frac{1}{2}$ inches wide, with three small regimental buttons. Two rows of regimental buttons down the front, nine in each row at equal distances ; the distance between the rows, 8 inches at top and 4 inches at the bottom. Slashed flaps on skirts behind, 10 inches deep, with two buttons on, and one each side of the waist. The skirt to be 17 inches long for an officer 5 feet 9 inches in height, with a variation of half an inch longer or shorter for each inch of difference in the height of the wearer. On the left shoulder a crimson silk cord to retain the sash, with a small regimental button. The field officers to have their badges of rank embroidered in gold at each end of the collar ; the collars of the other officers to be plain.

Epaulettes were abolished for all ranks, but other details of uniform remained as previously given.

The men wore a red double-breasted tunic, with blue collars and cuffs, and a slashed sleeve, piped with white ; and three buttons instead of four on the flap. Brass buttons replaced those of pewter.

Their belt-buckle was a round brass plate with the number of the regiment, surmounted by the plumes in the centre.

The officers' forage cap was of blue cloth and had a horizontal peak and chin-strap. It had a red cloth band round the bottom with a gold embroidered grenade in front, with the Red Dragon on the centre of the ball.

The drummers' lace was white with a figure, somewhat resembling the Prince of Wales' plumes.

The mounted officers' saddle-cloth was of blue cloth, was trimmed with one row of half-inch gold regimental lace, the same as that worn on the tunics, edged with a small vandyke of scarlet cloth, and the badge of rank embroidered in silver on the corner. That of the Adjutant was trimmed with a gold cord, edged with a small vandyke of scarlet cloth. Other details of the horse furniture remained as heretofore.

1856.—Pioneers discarded the musket, and carried instead a saw-backed sword, and in addition a shovel, pickaxe, and a bill-hook. They also wore gauntlets, and the black leather aprons hitherto worn were abolished, and white buckskin substituted, which are worn to the present day.

1857.—The double-breasted tunic was comparatively short-lived, and this year a single-breasted garment replaced it. There were eight buttons in front, set on at equal distances, blue collar and cuffs, the collar rounded off in front; the cuff $10\frac{1}{2}$ inches round and $2\frac{3}{4}$ inches deep. A blue slashed flap on the sleeve, 6 inches long by $2\frac{1}{4}$ inches wide, with three loops of half-inch gold lace and three regimental buttons. The skirt to be $10\frac{1}{2}$ inches deep for an officer 5 feet 9 inches in height, with a variation of half an inch either way for every inch of difference in the height of the wearer. Scarlet flaps at the plaits behind, 10 inches deep; two buttons on the flap and one on the waist, the two waist-buttons being three inches apart, with three loops of half-inch gold lace. The front of the coat, collar, cuffs, and flaps edged with white cloth, $\frac{1}{4}$ inch wide; and the skirts lined with white. On the left shoulder a crimson silk cord to retain the sash, with a regimental button. The trimming on the collar, and the badges of rank, remain as before.

In other respects the uniform remained practically the same as that worn in 1855; except that Wellingtons replaced ankle-boots for all officers, and a crimson-and-gold acorn replaced the bullion-tassel on the sword-knot.

The buglers wore a white double-breasted tunic, edged with red, and with two rows of brass buttons down the front. It had a blue collar and cuffs, the latter with a blue slash with three brass buttons on it, and the cuff was edged red round the top. The coat was braided with white lace with a blue figure on it, like the Prince of Wales' plumes. The shoulder-straps and wings were of blue cloth edged with red, and with blue-and-white fringe at the shoulder-points. They wore black trousers with a red welt, and the Albert shako with a white ball. They had white leather waist-belts, and carried brass-hilted bandsman's sword in a frog. The Pioneers wore white gauntlets and white buckskin aprons.

1858.—Flank Companies were abolished this year, and the whole regiment was henceforth clothed alike. The Band wore white tunics, with red collars, cuffs, and slash; red and white wings, and black trousers.

1859.—The pattern of the drummers' lace sealed on 19th February this year was white with the Prince of Wales' plumes in blue down the centre. Their fringe was blue and white, $1\frac{3}{4}$ inches long, with half an inch of blue and the same width of white.

A white horsehair plume drooping from a stem 5 inches high, with a gilt grenade socket, replaced the white ball tuft on the shako.

The scarlet shell-jacket was allowed to be worn by officers at mess instead of the coatee hitherto worn.

The number of the regiment in gold embroidery was added to the officers' forage cap below the grenade previously described.

Mounted officers were ordered to have brown leather bridles of cavalry pattern, and steel chain-reins.

Sergeants' sashes were ordered to be doubled longitudinally and passed over the right shoulder and under the shoulder-strap; the runner to be level with the waist-belt; the ends of the tassels to be level with, and not to hang below, the skirt of the tunic.

1860.—The peaks on the men's forage caps were done away with this year.

1861.—The Dress Regulations for this year thus describe the new shako introduced:

Blue cloth, with a horizontal peak of patent leather, and chin-strap. Colonels and lieutenant-colonels to be distinguished by two rows of regimental lace (showing a light of a quarter of an inch between) round the top of the shako; majors to wear one row. Brevet-rank to be similarly distinguished. The cap was 4 inches high in front, and 6½ inches deep behind, with a black patent-leather band round the bottom. The crown was 5½ inches wide, by 6 inches long, with a bronze Gorgon's head ventilator behind and ventilating buttons on each side. The cap-plate was a gilt grenade with the plumes in silver, in the centre of the ball. The body was stitched all round, resembling diagonal pleats. A white horsehair drooping plume was worn with it. It had a very handsome appearance, but the weight on the forehead was very great.

Officers were ordered to wear black leather leggings, 9 inches deep, with a variation of one inch either way according to the height of the wearer above or below 5 feet 9 inches.

The privates wore a small white pouch on the cross-belt for carrying the percussion caps; and a black leather ammunition pouch on the waistbelt. The knapsack was carried by a strap round each shoulder. The lower one across the chest was done away with, as it was found to be detrimental to the men's hearts.

1864.—At this period the blue cloth cuffs on the men's tunics were edged with a narrow white cloth welt along the pointed top, and inside the welt a white tape chevron, showing a light of blue cloth between it and the welts.

1865.—The Handbook of Equipment published this year gives the following badges and distinctions of rank:

Sergeant-major, quartermaster-sergeant, sergeant-instructor of musketry, drum or bugle-major, and band-sergeant, chevron on tunic composed of four bars of double half-inch gold lace.

The chevron of the sergeant-major is surmounted by a crown, that of the sergeant-instructor of musketry by a pair of muskets crossed, and that of the drum- or bugle-major by a drum, or bugle, respectively. The bandmaster-sergeant has no chevrons, but shoulder-knots of gold cords; paymaster-sergeants, and orderly-room clerks who have attained the rank and privileges of colour-sergeants, have three-bar chevrons of double gold lace.

Colour-sergeants: colour badge on tunic consisting of one bar of double gold lace surmounted by a device representing a Union flag, embroidered in silk, and cross-swords in silver. On serge frocks and shell-jackets three bars of single gold lace surmounted by a gold crown to be worn.

Second-class staff sergeants, or sergeants, and lance-sergeants, have three bars of half-inch white worsted lace.

Corporals have a chevron of two bars of the same; lance-corporals have one bar. All these are of double-lace for tunics, serge frocks, and jackets.

The pouch for the percussion caps was removed from the cross-belt and attached to the front of the ammunition pouch, and covered by the flap.

During this year a lambskin cap was authorised to be worn in lieu of the cloth shako.

1867.—On the 1st of April this year steel scabbards were ordered to replace those of black leather, field officers, however, retaining their brass ones.

In March the double-breasted blue frock-coat was abolished, and a blue patrol-jacket substituted. It was 28 inches long, measured from the bottom of the collar, for an officer 5 feet 9 inches in height, with a variation of half an inch either way for each inch of difference in the height of the wearer. It was rounded off in front, with one-inch-wide mohair braid all round and up the open slits at the sides. Four double drop loops with eyes in the centre, of ¼ inch flat plait up the front ; top loops 5½ inches, and bottom loops 6 inches long. One row of knitted olivets. An Austrian knot on the sleeve, seven inches from bottom of cuff to top of knot. Crows'-feet of flat plait at top and bottom of curved side-seams, with two eyes at equal distances ; lower eyes one inch apart. Hooks and eyes up front to neck. Stand-up collar, with braid on top edge only. Pockets jetted, with flap in and out. Field officers to have their distinctive badges embroidered in gold on the collar. No sash was worn with the jacket, and the sword-belt was worn under it.

Colonel Mainwaring's History of the 23rd mentions that in December of this year the lambskin cap previously worn was replaced by a black sealskin cap with a gilt brass grenade with the Prince of Wales' plumes in silver in front, but no details of it have been found. The sealskin cap was shortly changed for one of otter-skin, with a white plume on the left side.

1868.—The Band wore a shako with a white horsehair plume, a white single-breasted tunic with a blue collar and blue slashed cuff, edged with red round the collar, cuff, slash, and shoulder-strap. The tunic buttons were gilt, and the trousers black. The wings were blue and white, and the belts of white leather.

Alterations were made in the tunic this year, which is thus described in the Dress Regulations subsequently issued in November 1874 :

Tunic of scarlet cloth (for officers) with collar and cuffs of blue cloth. The collar ornamented with half-inch gold lace along the top, and with gold Russia-braid at the bottom, with the badges of rank embroidered in silver at each end. The cuffs pointed instead of slashed as heretofore, with half-inch lace round the top, and a tracing of gold Russia-braid a quarter of an inch above and below the lace ; the lower braid having a crow's-foot and eye, and the upper an Austrian knot at the top. Eight buttons in front, and two at the waist behind, and a gold square cord loop with a small button on each shoulder. The skirt closed behind, with a plait at each side, and lined with white. The front, collar, and skirt plaits edged with white cloth, a quarter of an inch wide.

Field officers had a row of braided eyes below the lace on the collar, two bars of lace along the top of the cuff, showing a quarter of an inch of blue cloth between the bars ; and the braiding on the sleeve in the form of eyes, above and below the lace for colonels and lieutenant-colonels, and above the lace only for majors. The lace on the sleeves extended to 8, and the Austrian knot to 10, inches from the bottom of the cuff.

Captains had no braided eyes on the collar. The lace and braiding on the sleeves were the same as those of field officers, except that the tracing was plain, without eyes.

Lieutenants had one bar of lace only on the cuff: the lace extending to 7½, and the Austrian knot to 9½, inches from the bottom of the cuff.

The Band wore the blue shako, with brass plate and green horsehair plume ; a white single-breasted tunic, with blue collar, rounded in front, and cuffs, with a blue sash on the sleeve. These parts, as well as the front edge of the tunic, being edged with red cloth, and having gilt buttons. Blue and white wings, and blue shoulder-straps. Dark blue trousers with a red welt completed the uniform.

The drummers wore a red single-breasted tunic, edged white, with blue collar and cuffs and brass buttons. Their shako and trousers were the same as those worn by the band. Their lace was white with blue chevrons, and a line of it was sewn down the front seam of each sleeve, and also up the back seams. They wore a white-edged blue slash on the cuff, and blue-and-white shoulder-straps.

A levee dress for officers was approved, consisting of gold-laced trousers, the lace 1⅛ inches wide, with a crimson silk stripe down the centre of the lace ⅛ inch wide; a gold and crimson net sash, 2½ inches wide, in half-inch stripes of gold and crimson alternately, gold and crimson runners and tassels; and a gold sword belt of the same pattern as the lace on the trousers, with slings of similar pattern, ¾ inch wide.

Sergeants were ordered to wear chevrons of half-inch gold lace on their tunics and shell-jackets: and regimental staff sergeants, ranking with colour-sergeants, to be distinguished by a crown over the three-bar chevron. In other respects the lace and braiding were the same as those of captains.

1870.—The rank of ensign was abolished this year, and was replaced by that of second lieutenant.

In November 1870 the plume on the cap was discontinued, and a racoon-skin cap replaced that of otter-skin previously worn.

1871.—The Band-sergeant wore a black bearskin cap with a gilt grenade in front, and a gilt chin-chain. A white tunic with a blue collar with a grenade on it, and blue-pointed cuff edged with gold lace and edged with red outside the gold. The tunic was piped with red down the front, and the wings were gold and blue. A crimson silk sash was worn diagonally over the shoulder, with three gold chevrons on blue cloth on each arm. The sword-belt was of white leather with slings, and a brass-hilted sword was carried in a black leather scabbard with gilt mounts. A black pouch with a gilt grenade in the centre.

1872.—Radical alterations were made in uniform this year: the men's tunics were altered in colour from red, as hitherto worn, to scarlet like those of the officers. Thus for the first time the same colour was worn by officers and men alike. The blue cuff was pointed, and was edged with white braid forming a crow's-foot at the top.

The round forage cap with the regimental number in front previously worn by the N.C.O.s and men was replaced by a Glengarry cap; the old knapsack was withdrawn, and what was known as the "*Wallace Equipment*" substituted.

The white tunics of the Band were abolished, and they now wore scarlet, being distinguished by a badge of crossed trumpets on the right arm.

The regimental drummers' lace was done away with, and was replaced by one of universal pattern, viz. white, with red crowns and red-and-white fringe.

Buttons with numbers on the men's tunics were abolished, and one of universal pattern bearing the Royal Arms was substituted. On the 1st of April blue tweed trousers were issued in place of black cloth trousers for winter wear.

On the 15th of July a plain scarlet serge frock took the place of the red-cloth shell-jacket for undress, with a line of white lace round the cuff, making a loop in the middle.

A universal pattern of infantry mess-jacket was introduced for the officers for the first time; and is thus described in the subsequent Dress Regulations: scarlet-cloth shell-jacket, with collar and pointed cuffs of the regimental facings (blue for the 23rd).

Gold braid edging all round, including the top and bottom of the collar. A loop of gold braid at the bottom of the collar to fasten across the neck. Shoulder-cords as on the tunic, i.e. a square gold cord loop, with a small button. A row of gilt studs, and hooks and eyes down the front, and scarlet silk lining.

Field officers had a row of braided eyes on the collar below the upper line of braid, and the badges of rank embroidered in silver at each end. Colonels and lieutenant-colonels had two chevrons of braid on each sleeve, three-quarters of an inch apart: the upper forming an Austrian knot extending to 10 inches from the bottom of the cuff, and the lower braid a crow's-foot and eye; a row of braided eyes above and below the chevrons, as on the tunic. Majors had the same braiding on the sleeve, omitting the lower row of braided eyes. Captains had similar braiding, but without the braided eyes, the Austrian knot extending to 9 inches only. Lieutenants had a single chevron of braid forming an Austrian knot 8 inches high, and a crow's-foot and eye below it.

The mess waistcoat was of blue cloth with gold braid edging round the top, down the front, and along the bottom of the side seams. The pockets edged with gold braid forming crow's-foot and eyes. A row of gilt studs, and hooks and eyes down the front.

The shell-jacket of the rank and file was abolished this year, and a scarlet kersey frock substituted, with blue collar and a plain braided cuff. Brass numerals were added to the shoulder-straps instead of worsted ones.

The officers were ordered to wear a black racoon-skin cap, 9 inches high in front. A gilt grenade in front with the Prince of Wales' plumes on the ball, and a gilt burnished chin-chain lined with black velvet.

The full-dress sword-belt clasp had a similar badge in silver on the centre-piece.

The levee-dress sword-belt clasp had the Prince of Wales' plumes, coronet, and motto in silver in the centre, surrounded by a gilt burnished laurel wreath.

1874.—In the Dress Regulations for this year two sizes of swords were authorised for infantry officers. The full-size had a blade 35 inches long and 1⅛ inches wide at the shoulder; extreme length, including the hilt, 41 inches; weight without the scabbard, 2 lb. The blade of the second size was 33 inches long, and one in width at the shoulder; extreme length, including the hilt, 38½ inches; weight, without the scabbard, 1 lb. 12 oz. In other respects the details were the same as of that previously described.

Slight alterations were made in the mounted officers' horse furniture. The blue saddle-cloth was ordered to be 3 feet long at the bottom, and 2 feet deep; and brown leather holster-caps were to be worn in tropical climates.

The skirts of the officers' tunic were altered to 10 inches in length; those of the frock-coat to 17 inches. Badges of rank to be worn on the collars: Captains, a crown and star; Lieutenants, a crown; Second-Lieutenants, a star. The gold lace on the officers' uniform was of the "oak-leaf" pattern; and the ends of the sash were to come just down to the bottom of the skirts of the tunic.

Mounted officers were ordered to wear knee boots, and black leather sabretaches. The central ornament was a gilt grenade with a silver dragon on the ball, and a large gilt cipher "*R.W.F.*" below in ornamental letters.

The forage cap was 2⅝ inches high with a horizontal peak; with a band and ornaments as previously described.

The regimental badge was worn at each end of the collar of the tunic by the N.C.O.s and men.

The men's forage cap hitherto worn was continued. It was customary with the men to reduce the depth of the cap, so as to make it look smarter, until this practice was stopped by a General Order.

1878.—The valise equipment consisted of an ammunition bag, a waistbelt, a set of braces, two ammunition pouches, each containing twenty rounds ; a pair of great-coat straps, a pair of mess-tin straps, a pair of straps for supporting the valise, and a valise of black leather to hold the service kit. All the straps were of buff leather, pipe-clayed. Only one pouch was carried on ordinary occasions in peace, and that on the right side ; and the ammunition bag only during rifle practice, or when required for blank ammunition. The braces were attached to the waistbelt when full ammunition was carried, as the weight was then too great for the waistbelt alone.

The great-coat was folded about eight inches high, by sixteen inches in width. It was carried behind the shoulders, and the valise at the waist, with the mess-tin between it and the great-coat. The haversack was carried on the left side, suspended from a white canvas belt over the right shoulder ; and the water-bottle on the right side, by a narrow white leather strap over the left shoulder. The regimental number was painted in white, on the flap of the valise.

With a view to facilitating exchanges between " linked " battalions, the facings on the collars and cuffs of the men's tunics from now until 1881 were a blue patch, somewhat like the present-day Staff pattern. The back of the collars and cuffs was of the same colour as that of the rest of the coat ; and the latter had white braid round them, with a crow's-foot at the top.

1880.—This year the badges of rank worn by the officers were removed from the collar, and placed on the shoulder-cords of the tunic and mess-jacket. Cloth straps were added to the shoulders of the patrol-jacket, which also bore the rank badges.

The waist-plate of the sword-belt worn on State occasions, and at balls, was altered to a round gilt clasp ; and in silver, on a frosted gilt centre, the Royal crest ; a wreath of laurel forming the outer circle.

A new forage cap of blue cloth was instituted for undress. It was straight up, 3 inches high, with a black patent-leather drooping peak, and chin-strap. The peak ornamented with half-inch full gold embroidery. A band of scarlet cloth, $1\frac{1}{2}$ inches wide, round the bottom of the cap. Field officers had a gold French-braid welt, round the top of the cap. The badge worn in front was a grenade in gold embroidery with the Red Dragon in silver on the ball. There was a black netted button, and a braided figure in the centre of the crown of the cap.

A blue Glengarry forage cap, of a similar pattern to that worn by the N.C.O.s and men, but not so deep, was introduced for active service and peace manœuvres. It was bound an inch wide with black silk riband, with riband ends $1\frac{3}{8}$ inches wide, with a red tuft on the top. A black silk cockade on the left side, on which was worn, on scarlet cloth, the same badge as described above for the round forage cap.

The buttons of the officers' uniforms were of gilt metal, with the Prince of Wales' plume within the designation " *The Royal Welch Fusiliers.*"

On the collar of the tunic a grenade in silver embroidery was worn.

The men's tunics had plain blue cuffs and collars.

1882.—The saddle-cloths hitherto worn in review order by the mounted officers were abolished.

1883.—Alterations were made in the badges of rank still worn on the shoulder straps: colonels wore a crown, and two stars below; lieutenant-colonels, a crown, and star above; majors, a crown; captains, two stars; and lieutenants, one star.

White metal whistles, of the same pattern as those used by sergeants, were authorised for all officers.

The new valise equipment, 1882 type, was adopted.

1890.—Brown leather gloves to be worn by officers, in other than review order, when white ones are to be worn as heretofore. White buff leather sword-belts to replace those of white enamelled leather.

A scarlet serge patrol-jacket was authorised; cut full in the chest, with blue collar, cuffs, and shoulder-straps. A small regimental button at the top of the strap, with the badges of rank on it, in gold, the collar rounded in front. Five small regimental buttons down the front; and a patch-pocket, with pointed flap, and a small button, on each breast. The cuffs pointed 5 inches deep in front and 2 inches behind. No badges on the collar. The men's serge frock was issued with the shoulder-straps only of the regimental facings.

A forage cap for active service and peace manœuvres of a new type was introduced. It was of blue cloth "Austrian" pattern, similar in shape to that worn by the N.C.O.s and men. The same badge was worn with it as that previously used with the Glengarry.

The steel chains of the mounted officers' furniture were replaced by head-ropes.

A glit embroidered grenade with the Dragon in silver on ball was worn on the round forage cap and that for active service and peace manœuvres.

1891.—Second lieutenants were ordered to wear no badges of rank, but otherwise to be dressed as lieutenants.

The skirts of the tunic were shortened from 10 to 9 inches for a man of average height; and brown leather gloves are noted in the Dress Regulations for this year.

1894.—Second lieutenants to wear shoulder-straps, but no badges of rank.

Swords to be $32\frac{1}{2}$ inches long, and 1 inch wide at the shoulder; to weigh, without the scabbard, from 1 lb. 12 oz. to 1 lb. 15 oz.

1896.—The cloth tunic for N.C.O.s and men was abolished, and a new pattern red serge frock took its place. The blue collar, shoulder-straps, and cuffs were edged with white braid. The sergeants' frocks had in addition a white piping round the edge.

1900.—The mounted officers' sabretache and bearskin wallet-covers were abolished; and also the levee dress.

The field-cap is thus described in the Dress Regulations for this year: folding, blue cloth, about $4\frac{1}{2}$ inches high and not less than $3\frac{3}{4}$ inches across the top; crown shaped similar to the Glengarry, folding peak in front; flaps at the side to let down, lower flaps to fasten under the chin when unfolded. When folded they fasten in the front of the cap with two gorget buttons. Crown, buttons, and piping of regimental pattern. The cap-badge was of gilt, or gilding metal; a grenade; on the ball a silver frosted circle inscribed "*Royal Welch Fusiliers.*" Within the circle the plumes, with a gilt coronet. Mounted officers might wear a chin-strap.

The N.C.O.s and men wore a similar cap.

The officers' silk lanyard was also ordered to be scarlet.

A new type of sword was adopted, with a straight blade $32\frac{9}{16}$ inches long from shoulder to point, and fullered on both sides; and with a steel hilt pierced with an ornamental device, so arranged as not to permit of a sword-point passing through so as to injure the hand; with "V.R." and crown near the top. A fish-skin grip bound with silver wire; the length of the grip 5 to $5\frac{3}{4}$ inches. The weight of the sword was 2 lb., and of the steel scabbard and lining $16\frac{3}{4}$ oz.

Slight alterations were made in the scarlet frock: the pointed cuffs were 6 inches deep in front and $2\frac{1}{2}$ inches behind; and metal badges of rank were worn on the collar. The collars of the tunics, frock-coats, and jackets were ordered to be cut square at the top in front, fastening with two hooks and eyes; and not to exceed 2 inches in height.

A new mess dress was authorised, consisting of a scarlet cloth jacket, edged all round with white piping, and a rolled collar. Pointed cuffs, 6 inches deep at the point and $2\frac{3}{4}$ inches behind; cloth shoulder-straps. The collar, cuffs, and shoulder-straps of blue cloth. Badges of rank in gilt metal to be worn on the shoulder-straps. Small buttons and buttonholed down the front. A blue cloth waistcoat; edges and pockets trimmed with gold cord, and three buttons.

A universal pattern brown leather "Sam Browne" belt, with two braces, revolver case, ammunition pouch, frog, and brown leather scabbard to be worn by all officers, with yellow metal fittings. When the sword-belt was worn under the tunic a web-belt was carried over the right shoulder.

A blue serge frock, with collar and cuffs of the same material, in other respects resembling the scarlet frock, was worn. It was abolished in 1902.

The cap was ordered to be of bearskin, or black racoon-skin, varying according to the height of the wearer from 8 inches to $9\frac{1}{2}$ inches, with a gilt burnished chin-chain, lined with black velvet and leather. A white cut feather plume $6\frac{1}{2}$ inches high on the right side, with a gilt flame socket.

1902.—In January this year a new service dress was introduced, for wear at home and abroad. It was first supplied to units returning from the South African War.

The following is the official description of that of the men: *Great-coat:* made of rain-proofed drab-mixture cloth, weighing about twenty-seven ounces per yard. Detachable capes are not worn, being replaced by a short cape with shoulder-flaps attached to the coat, and the armholes are made large to facilitate the garment being put on and taken off; an adjustable waist-strap at the back. *Head-dress:* A hat of thick felt with wide brim; the side perforated, about three-quarters of an inch from the top, with two rows of ventilating holes. Ventilation is also provided at the head-band, and clips are provided for fastening up the brim. *Jackets:* made of a drab-mixture serge, weighing from eighteen to twenty ounces per yard. It has a turned-down roll-collar, shoulder rifle patches, two patch breast-pockets with pleats, two strong side-pockets with flaps, and is pleated slightly at the waist. It has a wide false pleat down the centre of the back; and the shoulder-straps are removable. Five regimental buttons down the front. *Trousers:* of drab-mixture tartan, weighing about twenty-two ounces per yard. They are cut narrow as they approach the ankle, and are made short, just reaching the top of the ankle-boot. They are not to be worn in public without leggings or puttees.

Titles embroidered in white letters on a red ground, on a curved strip, on the upper arms of jackets and great-coats. The battalion number embroidered in similar colours on a separate patch close under the title.

Chevrons and badges of rank of special colour and material to be worn on both arms.

Crowns to be worn by colour-sergeants in place of colours. No collar badges to be worn. Buttons of gilding metal, which when not polished for some time assumes a dull colour matching the material.

For the present, forage, field, or Glengarry caps to be worn at home with the service dress.

For the officers the following rules were laid down: *Home Service:* cap, forage, Staff pattern; of material to match the Service Dress, but of cotton water-proofed; wide peak set at an angle of about sixty degrees, and carried well back to protect the temples; brown leather chin-strap.

Abroad: Felt hat, Army pattern.

Jacket: Special-mixture serge, to be of the same colour as that issued to the men; single-breasted, cut as a lounge-coat to the waist; very loose at the chest and shoulders, but fitted at the waist; a $2\frac{1}{4}$ inch expanding pleat down the centre of the back, sewn down below the waistband; and a waist seam and band $2\frac{1}{4}$ inches wide; military skirt to bottom edge. Cut low in front of neck; turn down (Prussian) collar to fasten with one hook and eye. Two cross-patch pockets, with flap and central pleat. Two expanding pockets below the waist, with flaps and buttons. Five large buttons down the front, the bottom one on the lower edge of the waistband. Shoulder-straps of Melton cloth, the same colour as the garment, edged all round, except at the shoulder seam, with a quarter-inch scarlet cloth; the top of the strap triangular, with a small button on it. Cuffs, pointed; $5\frac{1}{2}$ inches deep at the point and $2\frac{1}{2}$ inches deep behind.

Buttons of " gilding metal " ungilt; die struck of regimental pattern.

Rank was shown by braiding on the sleeves, with drab braid $\frac{3}{16}$ inch wide. *Second Lieutenants:* cuffs edged all round; a crow's-foot at the point. *Lieutenants:* as above, with double lines of braid added midway between the point and the seams of the sleeves; the line to be 3 inches long, starting from the braid round the top of the cuff; with crow's-foot at the top. *Captains:* as for lieutenants, with additional double-lines 3 inches long from the crow's-foot at the point of the cuff; a crow's-foot at the top. *Majors:* as for captains, with additional double lines added midway between the two outer and central lines, $6\frac{1}{2}$ inches long, beginning at the braid at the cuffs; a crow's-foot at the top. *Lieutenant-Colonels:* as for majors, with double lines added to the captains' loop, 5 inches long from the top of the crow's-foot; an Austrian knot $2\frac{1}{2}$ inches in length at the top.

Khaki knickerbocker breeches, and puttees; or Bedford cord breeches, brown leather leggings, and brown leather ankle-boots; with steel spurs for mounted officers.

The badges were: on the felt hat a grenade in gilt or gilding metal, on the ball a silver frosted circle inscribed "*Royal Welch Fusiliers.*" Within the circle the plumes with a gilt coronet, and a grenade in dull metal with dragon on ball on the collar of the jacket. The forage cap has a grenade in dull metal with plume on the ball.

On the 1st of February the following alterations were made in the officers' full dress uniform.

The skirts of the tunic to be made with a three-pointed slash edged with white piping as on the collar; three buttons at the points. The collar badges same as hitherto. A red silk web waist sash, 2¼ inches wide, with round ends, and to be worn with the tassels over the left hip, and coming four inches below the bottom of the tunic.

The web sword-belt to be worn under the tunic, with gold lace sword-slings, seven-eighths of an inch wide.

No piping, gold lace, or braiding to be worn on the mess-jacket, or waistcoat; and no buttons on any part of the jacket. The shoulder-straps to be of red cloth, and sewn down. On the collar a grenade in gold embroidery, with a dragon in silver on the ball, with badges of rank in embroidery on the shoulder-strap. The buttons on the mess waistcoat were gilt-lined with burnished edge; and "*R.W.F.*" in old English letters below the plume.

All tunics to be laced as laid down for lieutenants; distinctive rank lacing done away with; and also in all ranks the crow's-foot and eye below the lace on the cuffs.

The following items of dress were abolished: The crimson silk shoulder-sash; the full-dress sash, sword-belt, and gold and crimson trouser lace; the buff sword-belt and slings; the buff sword-knot; sabretaches and brass spurs for mounted officers, and "undress" clothing and equipment.

A universal pattern great-coat, frock-coat, and forage cap were introduced, replacing these previously worn.

The great-coat was made of drab-mixture cloth, double-breasted, to reach within a foot of the ground; stand-and-fall collar 5 inches deep; an expanding pleat down the back terminating under the back-strap; loose turn-back cuffs 6 inches deep; two rows of buttons down the front; four in each row, about 6½ inches apart; the rows 8 inches apart at top and 4 inches at the bottom. A two-inch cloth back-strap fastened with three buttons; and shoulder-straps as for service dress.

A forage cap of the Staff (or Naval) pattern was adopted with a plain peak for officers below field rank. To be of blue cloth with a band of scarlet cloth, and with a scarlet welt round the crown.

The badge in front was of gilt, or gilding metal, a grenade with the plumes in silver within a silver circle inscribed "*Royal Welch Fusiliers.*"

The frock-coat was of blue cloth, double-breasted, with a stand-up collar; plain sleeves, with two small buttons at the bottom; two rows of regimental buttons down the front, six in each row, at equal distances; the distance between the rows being 6 inches at the top and 4½ inches at the bottom. Flaps behind, 10 inches deep, with two buttons on each flap, and one on each side of the waist; the skirt to reach to the knees. Shoulder-straps of the same material as the coat; with pointed tops, and small buttons, and embroidered badges of rank. On the collar a grenade in silver embroidery was worn.

The crimson silk waistbelt was worn with the frock-coat; and when the sword was carried the web waistbelt with gold slings was worn under it.

The skirts of the men's tunics were made with a similar slash to that of the officers.

1903.—A new forage cap was instituted for the men. It was of blue cloth, similar in shape to that worn by sailors, and with a semicircular patch of the regimental colour in front with the regimental badge. It was very unpopular, and was nicknamed the "Brodrick" by the men, after the then Secretary of State for War.

1904.—The Dress Regulations for this year make certain alterations in the officers' service jackets. The cuffs to be round, with a three-pointed flap edged with half-inch chevron lace. Badges of rank, in worsted embroidery, to be worn on the flaps. Rings of worsted chevron lace and tracing braid to be worn round the cuff, according to rank: second lieutenants and lieutenants, one row of chevron lace; captains, two rows of chevron lace; majors, three rows, with tracing braid between them; lieutenant-colonels, three rows of chevron lace and four rows of tracing braid; colonels, four rows of lace and five of braid. The badge worn on the collar, above the stop, was the same as that previously described.

Badges of rank were restored to second lieutenants, who were ordered to wear one star; lieutenants, two; and captains, three stars, on the tunic, frock-coat, mess and service jackets.

The forage cap was of blue cloth, with blue welts, and a top $9\frac{1}{4}$ inches diameter. It was $3\frac{1}{4}$ inches deep, with a patent leather peak $1\frac{3}{4}$ inches deep set on at an angle of 45 degrees, with half an inch full gold embroidery round the edge for field officers. A black patent-leather chin-strap $\frac{3}{8}$ inch wide with a $\frac{1}{2}$ inch diameter button at each end, close behind the peak.

The badge worn in front was the same as that previously described.

1905.—The men were provided with brown leather bandoliers and ammunition pouches. A forage cap of blue cloth similar in shape to that introduced for officers in 1902 was instituted for the men.

1908.—Web equipment replaced leather for the men.

1911.—In the Dress Regulations issued this year second lieutenants on probation were ordered to wear no badges of rank.

White covers were authorised for wear on the forage cap in hot weather. The cap to be worn evenly on the head, and not with service dress, unless specially ordered as a distinguishing mark between opposing forces.

White linen collars worn with service dress jacket, and with mess dress, but not to show more than $\frac{1}{8}$ inch above the uniform.

Tunic collars to be square in front, and not more than 2 inches high. The skirts to be 10 inches long for a man 5 feet 9 inches high. The same badges as hitherto were worn on the collar.

1913.—Drab flannel shirts to be worn with service dress, with turn-down collars and khaki ties. A single-breasted blue serge frock instituted, with four outside pockets and pointed cuffs, straps, and collar of the same material as the coat. Four small regimental buttons down the front.

Certain minor alterations were made in the service dress jacket: a stop-collar was adopted, with four regimental buttons down the front; and the false pleat on the back was left off. Brown leather leggings fastening up the front with laces, and six studs were authorised for wear with the drab service dress, for mounted officers, other than those wearing the brown field boot.

1914.—The flash was ordered to be worn by officers only on the service dress jacket.

The men's service jacket was made with a plain back, with a slit at the bottom of each side-seam. There was no demarkation of a cuff, and the shoulder-straps and rolled collar were retained.

APPENDIX III

ARMS

The following is a brief summary of some of the firearms used by the regiment from time to time.

When raised in 1689 and till 1702 it was armed with a flint-lock smooth-bore musket; length, 5 feet 2 inches; bore, 0·75; length of barrel, 3 feet 10 inches; dog lock, safety catch, wooden ramrod, and a plug bayonet (a representation of the latter is shown at p. 124 of Vol. I).

1700: The bayonet was altered to a socket bayonet (also illustrated as above).

1750: The length of the musket was reduced to 4 feet 11 inches and that of the barrel to 3 feet 6 inches. An iron ramrod was now introduced.

1768–1791: The sergeants' halbert (as at p. 124 in Vol. I) was a battleaxe-headed weapon, with a spear point $9\frac{1}{2}$ inches long, by $2\frac{1}{4}$ inches wide at the rounded bottom, and $1\frac{3}{4}$ inches wide in the middle. Below the spear-head, in front, was a concave rounded axe-face, $5\frac{1}{4}$ inches long from the central axis, with a downward curving point of the same length behind. The length of the head from the point of the spear-head to where it fitted on to the staff was $11\frac{1}{2}$ inches, and a strap $14\frac{1}{2}$ inches long was provided on each side for attachment to the staff. The staff was made of ash, tapering from $1\frac{1}{4}$ inches diameter at the top to $1\frac{1}{2}$ inches at the bottom, where it was shod with a pointed steel shoe. The over-all length of the weapon was 8 feet 6 inches.

1771–1786: The officers' espontoon (an illustration at p. 124, Vol. I) was 9 feet long over-all; and had a blade 12 inches long and $1\frac{3}{4}$ inches wide at the bottom, rounded off below, and capable of revolving above the crossbar. The latter was 5 inches wide, and was fixed $12\frac{1}{2}$ inches below the point. The total length of the steel head was 17 inches, with a strap 9 inches long on each side for attachment to the shaft. The shaft tapered from $1\frac{1}{4}$ inches diameter at the top to $1\frac{1}{2}$ inches at the bottom. The lower end was fitted with a steel shoe.

1791–1830: The sergeants' pike did not materially differ from the espontoon formerly carried by officers, and was probably the same weapon renamed.

Peninsula Period: " Brown Bess " weighed with bayonet 12 lb. 3 oz.; bayonet was triangular, 18 inches long; weight of ball, 1 oz. Maximum range, 400 to 500 yards; effective, about 150 yards; flint lock; smooth bore; ·750 calibre.

1839: " Brown Bess " was converted to a percussion rifle.

1840: *Brunswick Rifle*, percussion, sword-bayonet.

1842: Percussion muzzle-loader, smooth-bore; weight, 9 lb. 14 oz. without the bayonet.

ARMS

1851: *Minie Rifle*, smaller calibre than "*Brown Bess*," triangular bayonet. The barrel was 39 inches long, with 4 grooves, and one turn in 78 inches. Bore, 0·702; charge of powder, 68½ grains; sighted to 1,000 yards.

It is interesting to note that the then Commander-in-Chief, who was always irascible with inventors and their inventions, is reported to have stated that " we should not be in a hurry to adopt these new-fangled inventions. It was ridiculous to suppose that two armies would fight at a distance of 500–600 yards " !

1853: *Enfield Rifle*, percussion, muzzle-loader, triangular bayonet; sixteen bullets to the pound; sixty rounds carried on the person; sighted to 1,000 yards; length, 54 inches; weight, 8 lb. 14¼ oz. Bayonet, slightly curved, 20¾ inches over all; blade, 17½ inches; weight, 13¼ oz. Arm complete with bayonet, 71½ inches long; weight, 9 lb. 12 oz. Barrel, 39 inches long; bore, 0·577. Three rifled progressive grooves, making one spiral turn in 78 inches. Bullet, 530 grains; length, 1·095 inches; charge of powder, 2½ drams.

1867: *Snider-Enfield*: breech-loader (converted to M. L. Enfield), triangular bayonet as above.

1871: *Martini-Henry*, breech-loader, 0·45 bore, 7 grooves, triangular bayonet. Weight, 8¾ lb.; the barrel 33 inches long; the bullet a little over 1¼ inches long, weighing 480 grains; 85 grains of powder; sighted to 1,400 yards.

1887: *Martini-Enfield*, weight, 9 lb. 2 oz.; bore, 0·402; length of barrel, 33 $\frac{1}{16}$ inches. Seven grooves, making one complete turn per 15 inches of barrel; the bullet rotated to the right. Sighted to 2,000 yards. Bullet, 1·288 inches long; weight, 384 grains; powder, 85 grains. Sword-bayonet, 18½ inches long; weight, 23½ oz.

1891: *Lee-Metford*, breech-loader, 0·303 bore, 7 grooves. Sword-bayonet. Magazine for eight rounds; later increased to ten. Smokeless powder (cordite) was brought into use with it in 1892.

1896: *Lee-Enfield*, breech-loader, magazine rifle; very short; sword-bayonet, 21¼ inches entire length; blade, 17 inches long; sword-hilt; double-edged, with a rib down the middle, gradually vanishing towards the point.

1903: *Lee-Enfield*, Mark III, short, breech-loading, magazine rifle. Extreme range, 3,500 yards, or two miles (see above note of 1851); length, 3 feet 8¼ inches; weight, 8 lb. 10½ oz.; sword-bayonet, 1 foot 5 inches long; weight, 1 lb. 0½ oz.; 150 rounds of ammunition carried in the man's bandolier and waistbelt.

Revolvers: The pattern of officers' revolver was governed only by the order that it must take Government 0·455 ammunition. N.C.O.s and men who carried revolvers were armed with the short 0·455 six-chambered Webley pistol.

APPENDIX IV

MEDALS

When the retrospective Military General Service Medal was authorised in 1848, 32 officers and 284 men of the Regiment were alive to receive it. The regiment was in thirteen actions commemorated by bars, or clasps, and twelve was the highest number of bars awarded on one medal. This occurred in two cases to privates, ten being the highest number awarded to an officer, and that in one instance only.

The regiment has received, in addition, from time to time the following medals:
The Waterloo Medal.
The Crimean Medal, with bars for "*Alma,*" "*Inkermann,*" and "*Sebastopol.*"
The Indian Mutiny Medal, with bar for "*Lucknow.*"
The Ashantee Medal, 1874, with bar for "*Coomassie.*"
The Indian General Service Medal, 1857, with bar for "*Burma, 1885-87*" and "*Hazara.*"
The Queen's South Africa Medal, with 5 bars: "*Relief of Mafeking,*" "*Tugela Heights,*" "*Relief of Ladysmith,*" "*Transvaal,*" "*Orange Free State.*"
The King's South Africa Medal, with 2 bars: "*S. Africa 1901,*" "*S. Africa 1902.*"
The China Medal, with bar "*Pekin 1900.*"
The Turkish Medal for the Crimea.
The French Medal for "Valeur et Discipline," to ten N.C.O.s and men in the Crimea.
The Sardinian Medal for Valour, to four officers and two Corporals in the Crimea.
Besides individual awards for gallantry, good conduct, etc.

Twelve Victoria Crosses have, so far, been gained by the combined battalions of the regiment.

The following "Regimental" medals are known to collectors:

(1) A silver engraved medal $1\frac{1}{2}$ inches diameter awarded to deserving N.C.O.s and men by the Colonel and officers on the return of the regiment from the Peninsula. The obverse bears in the centre the Prince of Wales' plumes, coronet, and motto, surrounded by olive branches. Above, "*Wellington,*" and below, "*Peninsula.*"

The reverse is inscribed with the names of the battles in which the recipient took part, within a laurel wreath.

(2) The Prince of Wales' plumes in relief, "*23 R.W.F.*" below on the obverse. The reverse engraved "*Badajoz*": "*Salamanca*": "*Vittoria*": "*Pampaluna*". "*Nivelle*": "*Orthos*": "*Sylvatara*": "*Toulouse*": Patrick McNulty.

(3) A silver medal $1\frac{1}{4}$ inches diameter, with the plumes and motto engraved on

the obverse, surrounded by a raised wreath of oak and laurel. Above, "R.L."; below, "W.F."

Reverse, engraved "*XXIII*": "*Orthes*": "*Badajos*": "*Vittoria*": "*Salamanca*": "*Martinique*": "*Pyrenees*": "*Toulouse*": "*Nivelle*": *Alexr. Mackie.* He also received the Military General Service medal with eight bars.

These medals were given by the officers of the regiment at their own expense; and were discontinued when the Long Service and Good Conduct Medal was instituted in 1830.

APPENDIX V

MUSIC

It was customary in remote times to enter battle with war songs, or cries, that of England being " Saint George," that of France " Saint Denis," that of Scotland " Albanach." Sir J. G. Ouseley says " probably no race of men has preserved so much unaltered, from the great storehouses of the past, as the Cambro-Britons (Welsh), and it is therefore not unreasonable to conclude that in the oldest lines we may have the remains of what was anciently the music of this country long before the Roman invasion under Julius Cæsar."

Dr. Crotch in his *Specimens of Various Styles of Music* says of the marches " The Men of Harlech," " Captain Morgan's March," and " Come to Battle," that the military music of the Welsh was " superior to that of any other nation "; and in the case of the Royal Welch Fusiliers, from the first mention of any form of music, viz. the regimental drums and fifes, it is evident that the regimental band was above the average, and looked upon with special care and pride by the regiment.

The idea of a military band was originally copied from the Saracens; drums were probably introduced into Europe from the east by the Crusaders, or by the Moors into Spain.

In the reign of Queen Mary the foot regiments answered to the drum calls of " March," " Alarm," " Approach," " Assault," " Battle," " Retreat," and " Skirmish," two drummers being allowed to each company of 100 men; the beats were afterwards termed the " General," " Reveille," " Assembly," or " Troop," " Taptoo " (since abbreviated to " Tattoo," a Dutch word signifying " no more drink to be tapped or sold "), and " Chamade " (parley).

Lieutenant-Colonel Elton (1668) mentions a Drum-major as part of the establishment of every regiment, and that his duties were to superintend the drummers and to know sufficient of languages to be able to summon hostile garrisons, and at a later date his duties included that of executioner at all corporal punishments.

Drummers were frequently employed to carry messages between the rival armies, and in consequence were expected to be of superior education and intelligence.

On the formation of the Royal Welch Fusiliers in 1689, two drummers were allowed for each of the thirteen companies, at a cost of 1s. a day each; they were described in the muster at Dundalk on 18th October 1689 as " Tambours." In November 1697 the number was reduced to one to each company; the Grenadier Company, however, still retained its two. The number was again altered to the original two shortly afterwards.

In documents known as "Custom House Records," preserved at the Public Record Office in Dublin, occurs the first mention in the regiment of the Drum-major, viz.:

"Due by Coll Herbert's Regiment of Foot in and about Ballinahinch
   in the County of Downe (1689)
    Roger Mote, Drom Mager to John Jordon .. .. .. £0 14 6"

And again on another page:

"Drome Major for meat and drink to D. Martin .. .. £0 1 6"

The rank of Drum-major was dropped during the Commonwealth period; and afterwards only the Foot Guards, and then the Royal Artillery, were permitted to bear a Drum-major officially on their establishments; the "Marching Regiments" were not allowed a Drum-major by the Regulations until 1810, though rarely without one.

In 1789 brass drums replaced the old wooden ones.

The fife is said to have been introduced by the Swiss; it is called "Tibia Helvetica" by Mersenne, a French philosopher, in his *Harmonie Universelle*, 1636. The fife was laid aside during the Commonwealth period in England owing to its being considered "profane," and seems to have been discarded from our military bands for a long time afterwards, not being restored till about 1745, when it was again introduced by the Duke of Cumberland, being adopted by the "marching regiments" in 1747—two fifers being posted to the Grenadier Company of the Royal Welch Fusiliers, as is shown by the returns for 1760, 1771, 1780, 1790.

The modern military band had its beginning in the reign of Charles II, who introduced from the French the "hautboy," "hoboy," or "oboe" into the bands of the Foot Guards and "marching regiments" by a warrant 1684-5; in the *Abridgment of the English Military Discipline*, 1686, "the Hoboys are to be on the right of the drummers."

During the first half of the eighteenth century the "Bands of Music" of the Guards did not number more than six performers, the bands of the "marching regiments" probably the same, or even fewer; as the authorities made no allowance for them, the entire cost fell on the officers, the drums and fifes only being on the establishment.

The following curious extract is taken from the *British Army and Navy Review* for 1864, but it has not been possible to corroborate it in any way: "with us the cheer has superseded the song . . . our Welshmen, too, so late as the middle of the last century, still adhered to the same practice. They abandoned it under very remarkable circumstances. In the summer of 1758, while a company of the 23rd Fusiliers formed a part of that unfortunate army which the Government dispatched to the coast of Brittany under command of General Bligh, and which was repulsed with great slaughter before the town of St. Cast, the Welshmen advanced to the attack singing one of their national songs:

    "In the night as we slept,
    We heard the war-horn's note;
    The sound of the war-horn in the wood,
    Hark, 'tis the Saxon! the Saxon! the Saxon!"

WELSH

Pan y cysgwn un noswaith arall,
E glywais swn udgorn;
Swn yr udgorn yn y coed,
Ho Saeson. Saeson. Saeson y fall.

BRETON

Pa oann kousketeun nosvez all,
E klevez son ar c'horn-buhal;
Son a c'horn-buhal, ekoat-sal,
Ho Saozon Saozon Saozon fall.

Among other regiments drawn up to receive them was one from Trequier and St. Pol de Leon, wholly composed of Bretons, who heard with amazement one of their own most popular airs sung by their enemies, and accompanied by words which sounded equally familiar to their ears. "When they had listened for a few moments," relates the historian of the scene, "they gave themselves up to natural feelings of patriotism. The Welsh, equally astonished, also remained immovable. The officers on either side gave the word to fire; but the order being spoken in the same language, the troops stood still as if they had been trees. This hesitation did not last long; their arms fell from their hand, and the two companies united, thus again joining the descendants of the Britons."

The statement that this happened to "a company of the 23rd Regiment" is not correct, as the 23rd did not take part in the third expedition to France in 1758; the writer must refer to the 2nd battalion of the 23rd formed on 25th August 1756, and regimented on 25th June 1758 as the 68th Regiment, as this regiment did form part of the third expedition which was repulsed at St. Cast on 11th September of that year.

The next instruments to be added to the bands were the bassoon, horn, and clarionet; the two former were in use before 1760.

From Inspection Returns of the Royal Welch Fusiliers, when reviewed by Major-General Oughton in Edinburgh on 27th May 1768, the following is extracted:

"The drummers and fifers play extremely well. The band of Music very fine."

The following are extracts from other Inspection Reports:

1769. "The band of Music and drums and fifes play extremely well, and are well appointed and cloathed."
1770. "The band of Music very good."
1784. "A very good band of Music. Drums and fifes very good."
1786. "Drums and fifes, beat and play well."
1818. "The regimental Band is a very excellent one. The Drummers appear to be very attentive, and to understand the different beats."
1823. "The band is composed of good musicians; the drums are well chosen, and the Drum Major is in possession of a printed copy of the 'Regulations for the Calls and Beats of the Drum.'"
1824. "The musicians play marches in correct time."

MUSIC

The following "Quick March of the 23rd Regiment" is to be found printed in Walker's *Hibernian Magazine* for February 1788:

The term "Band of Musick" or "Band" was not generally adopted until the nineteenth century. As late as 1834–5 the Army Estimates allow for "hautboys."

In the Regulations of the Army, 1811, general officers were ordered to report half-yearly whether the bands "play in correct time," the drum-major having to use "the plummet" to practise his musicians by; and on the march, to ensure a regular pace, he was to use his staff, or baton, "with an easy air one round, so as to keep time, and plant it every fourth pace." The leopard or tiger-skin still used by the big drummer and the flourishes which the drummers make with their sticks are survivals of the gorgeous tunics and the contortions used by the "black men," who previously to the accession of Queen Victoria were employed as cymbal, triangle, or Jingling Johnnie players.

By a general order dated 5.8.1803 it is directed that the number in the bands should "not be more than one private soldier to each Troop or Company to act as Musicians" and "that one non-commissioned officer shall be allowed to act as Master of the Band"; the men to be drilled and to fall in with their companies completely armed and accoutred.

On 8.11.1821, in consequence of the numbers of the band having been greatly increased in many regiments, contrary to the King's Regulations, the Commander-in-

Chief ordered that " this practice must cease," but at the same time permitted the band to consist as before of a sergeant and ten musicians, although the numbers of companies in the regiments had been reduced ; this did not include " black men " or boys. On 28.8.1823 a general order was issued allowing an increase in the band to " a sergeant (Master) and fourteen musicians."

The payment to the Band Fund by officers on appointment of not more than twenty days' pay, and an annual subscription of not more than twelve days' pay, was fixed by a circular memorandum of 16.2.1829 ; anything above these amounts was to be optional.

The following is an extract from the general order dated 2.8.1830: " The Bands of Infantry Regiments to be dressed in white Clothing with the Regimental facings " ; also, " The trowsers and caps for the Band are also to be conformable in every respect to the pattern for the Regiment at large."

In consequence of reports received a circular dated 18.2.1835 was issued from the Horse Guards to officers commanding depôts stating that bands were not allowed on their establishments, only four drummers being allowed, and the acting drummers were not to exceed six ; the latter to be clothed as privates without any additional lace or ornament, and not to be exempt from guards, picquets, fatigues, etc.

The following memorandum was issued on 19.8.1835 : " All Grenadier and Fusilier Regiments (including the 5th Foot now dressed as Grenadiers) are, when marching in quick time upon occasions of Guard Mounting Parade, or Review, to march by to the Grenadiers March, and no regiment whatever is on any of these occasions to march to a foreign tune." The undress jacket for bands was ordered to be white by a circular memorandum dated 4.1.1837.

It had been customary for an allowance of a quart of ale and also wine to be made in addition to a substantial supper to each of the members of the band who were in evening attendance at any of Her Majesty's Palaces, but, by an order dated 12.12.1838, the wine allowance was withdrawn with the exception of a pint of wine for the master of the band.

The subject of bands at the depôts was again dealt with by a circular memorandum dated 12.2.1845, wherein it is laid down that " there can be but one band in a regiment, and that must as a matter of course accompany the Service Companies whithersoever they go " ; the numbers of drummers at " depôts " having been increased to six, only four lads or boys are to be permitted to act as drummers, fifers, or buglers, and they were only to be allowed as long as they were not of an age or stature to bear arms.

On 2.4.1846 the number of the band was increased to a sergeant and twenty privates, and on 4.12.1856 a circular memorandum was issued stating that a Military School for Music, Kneller Hall, Hounslow, was to be formed ; and to meet expenses commanding officers were " to cause the sum of £5 to form a fund for the purchase of instruments, etc., and the annual subscription of £8 for the support of the Institution to be paid into the hands of Messrs. Cox & Co." The regiments at home were to send to the Adjutant-General " the names of two men, or one man and one enlisted boy or lad, for instruction as Musicians, Bugle majors, or Trumpet majors." Kneller Hall was self-supporting and received no assistance from the Government, but an increase in the establishment, etc., caused an increase in the annual subscription to £10 in October 1857.

MUSIC

In a confidential letter from the Adjutant-General, dated 24.2.1858, it was suggested that in future, instead of instruments being obtained by the bandmasters from one instrument-maker, whether they were brass, reed, or wooden, the commanding officers should make their requisition to the Adjutant-General; this would make sure of a reduction of 25 per cent. on the prices hitherto charged. Also " that instead of employing musical instrument-makers as their agents for the hiring of Bandmaster, they would do better to advertise in the public papers, and require testimonials and certificates."

A brass drum of improved construction having been settled on was, on 12.3.1858, ordered to be issued as the older form became unserviceable. They were to be lighter (3 lb. less than those then in use), more portable, and easier tuned; and the allowance to commanding officers in lieu of drums and bugles was to cease. They were to be issued in future in kind, and of one universal pattern; at this time a uniform pitch was decided on, that of " the Ancient Philharmonic Concerts " being selected.

On 30th September of the same year a circular memorandum stated that an issue would be made " of one bugle of a superior quality, and of one fife to each company, in lieu of a second drum ; and the distribution of drums and fifes in a regiment consisting of 12 companies will be as follows, or 1 drum, 1 bugle, and 1 fife to each company:

"12 Brass Drums with sticks.
12 Field Bugles with strings.
8 B Flutes.
2 F ,, with cases.
1 F Picolo.
1 E Flat do."

On account of the difference in elevation of the new drum from that of the old one a very great number of sticks were broken when the new drums were taken into use.

On 3rd May 1859 a drum and fife were ordered to be attached to each recruiting party, and the band of the regiment and the drums were to attend the nearest town on all market days.

On 29th August 1862 it was ordered that " the key to be used in playing the National Anthem of ' God Save the Queen ' shall invariably be that of B flat."

It was decided on 21st February 1863 to supply one Azemar silent drum to every two companies of a regiment for the training of the drummers; they were to last twelve years. In 1865, in consequence of the care and economy exercised by Lieutenant-Colonel Whitmore at Kneller Hall, it was found possible to reduce the annual subscription of regiments to that Institution to £8 per annum.

The following extract is taken from a general order dated 24th November 1874: " an objectionable practice has also of late been allowed in some regiments, viz. the use of stringed instruments by the Band, a proceeding at once expensive and inconsistent with the object for which Bands are maintained in all times, i.e. the performance of Martial rather than operatic music."

In a circular letter dated 20th December 1876 it is stated that there were nearly 100 military bandmasters who had qualified at Kneller Hall, and only 35 of the old class of civilian bandmasters left; also that there existed 36 regiments with stringed bands.

APPENDIX V

The following are the airs used by the Royal Welch Fusiliers:

March Past (in column)	"British Grenadiers."
(in quarter column)	"Men of Harlech."
On entering or leaving barracks or camp	"Men of Harlech."
Church Parade: Church Call and Hymn	"Aberystwyth."
	"Christ Church Bells."
On finishing a musical programme	"Land of our Fathers."
	"Men of Harlech."
	"God bless the Prince of Wales."
	National Anthem.

Of the thirty or so toasts used in connection with the St. David's Day Dinner, the following are usually now drunk with their appropriate airs:

Toast.	Air.
The King	National Anthem.
The Prince of Wales	"God bless the Prince of Wales."
St. David	"St. David."
Toby Purcell and his spurs	"Jenny Jones."
Shenkin ap Morgan	"Ap Shenkin."
The other Battalion	"British Grenadiers."
Our Guests	"For they are jolly good fellows."

APPENDIX VI

SPORT

1st BATTALION

CAPTAIN ROBERT BARCLAY, who joined the 23rd as Second Lieutenant on 10th September 1803, Lieutenant 19th November 1804, performed one of the most remarkable feats ever recorded in the annals of pedestrianism, having walked one thousand miles in one thousand successive hours at the rate of one mile in each hour.

This extraordinary performance commenced on Wednesday the 31st of May 1809 at 12 midnight. Captain Barclay walked half a mile from the "Horse and Jockey," across the Norwich Road up the Heath at Newmarket, and returned; the wager was for one thousand guineas a side, and there were often thousands of spectators present.

His signature appears in the mess minutes of the 1st battalion.

When at Chakrata in 1881 it became known that the battalion was to move in the cold weather of 1882-3 to Dum Dum, near Calcutta, by route march, it was decided to start a pack of hounds, and hunt jackals.

Those of the officers who knew M.F.H.s in England begged for draft hounds, and in this way some ten couple reached Chakrata early in 1882, and thus had time to become acclimatised prior to the departure of the battalion on the 31st of October.

Major R. F. Williamson was elected master, Lieutenants Lyle and Bright-Smith whips, and Lieutenant Dunn kennel huntsman.

The battalion used to finish its daily march by 9 a.m., and this left the afternoons and evenings free for sport and amusement, consequently very good fun with plenty of jumping was enjoyed two or three days a week with the pack. Hunting commenced about 3 p.m., and went on till dark, it being found that the scent improved as the sun declined. One of the most successful of these hunts took place at Dinapore, the officers of the R.F.A. and East Surrey Regiment, who were stationed there, joining in the sport.

From Dinapore the remainder of the distance was done by rail. Dum Dum was not a very good country for hunting, being mostly paddy fields and bamboo jungle, but the hounds were kept up, and were left with the depôt on the battalion's departure for Burma. We find the pack being hunted by Lieutenant-Colonel E. S. Creeke at Lucknow in 1887, but they were sold the following year.

While at Dum Dum, 1883-5, the battalion organised a race meeting which was attended by H.R.H. the Duke of Connaught, and at a race meeting at Barrackpore the Open Hurdle Race was won by Sir R. Colleton's Herringbone, ridden by Major R. F. Williamson.

Whilst the battalion was stationed in Burma in 1885-7 it was split up into numerous small detachments, and the question of fresh-meat rations was a difficult one, the officers being more or less dependent on their guns, small game abounding. The bullock and cow being sacred animals, the natives refused to kill them; but they had no objection, however, to selling the carcass of one shot " by accident," so the men did not do so badly.

From 1887 to 1890 the battalion was stationed at Lucknow, and weekly paper-chases were organised by Major H. T. Lyle, though why they were called " paper-chases " no one knows, as paper was conspicuous by its absence. They were really chases over some four miles of country with stiff made-up flagged jumps, the first two or three of which were made particularly stiff in order to thin out the field, which usually consisted of 40-50 riders.

During the cold weather of 1888-9 the battalion was the guest of the 8th King's Regiment (the only other British regiment in the Burmese Expeditionary Force, 1885-7) at Fyzabad, when the two battalions competed at cricket, polo, tennis, billiards, football, etc., etc. The following year the return matches were played at Lucknow, the Royal Welch Fusiliers being the hosts.

Lucknow was a popular station, and the battalion, both officers and men, left it with regret. Practically every officer played polo, there was good black-buck and wild-fowl shooting, and lots of cricket, rowing, racquets, etc., whilst the men were also well catered for. Whilst at Peshawar, 1891-3, good hunting was enjoyed with the Peshawar Vale Hounds. During the cold weather of 1892-3 the battalion played the 5th Fusiliers from Nowshera at everything—polo, cricket, tennis, shooting, billiards, racquets, football, etc.—and had rather the better of the encounter, in addition to a very pleasant week's amusement. The battalion moved during the cold weather of 1893-4 by route march to Jhansi, obtaining plenty of hunting, polo, shooting, pig-sticking, etc., *en route*, being entertained most hospitably by the regiments quartered in the various stations through which they passed. Jhansi as a station was spoilt by the battalion having to find a detachment of a wing (four companies) at Nowgong and one company at Sipri, and this interfered sadly with all forms of regimental and team sport.

During the battalion's tour of Indian service a very fair collection of heads was obtained by various officers during their hot-weather leave of absence, and these were added to by a fine collection shot by Captain J. B. Cockburn on the West Coast of Africa.

At Plymouth during 1897-9 the battalion took up football very keenly, and in the winter of 1898-9 won the Devon and Cornwall Association League Cup and the Devon and Cornwall Association Cup, amongst many other successes. The officers hunted with the Dartmoor Hounds, most of them keeping their horses at Ivybridge. The cricket eleven did well in their matches.

In 1899 they held their 1st Red Dragon Cup Meeting since the return of the battalion from foreign service. The officers took their guests out from Plymouth by special train to Buckfastleigh, and entertained them and others who came in from the surrounding country to lunch and tea on the course. There were three races on the card: (1) The Red Dragon Cup, which was won by Lieutenant Le Marchant's Teal, owner up; (2) a Red Dragon Farmers' Race; and (3) a race open to officers of the Plymouth garrison and members of the Dartmoor Hunt; the two latter events for cups presented by the

SPORT

officers of the battalion. There was a very large attendance, and the meeting was a thorough success.

Whilst stationed at Lichfield the officers hunted with the Atherstone and South Stafford hounds, and the Red Dragon Cup meeting was again held in 1904, having lapsed since 1899, owing to both battalions being abroad.

The meeting took place near Lichfield, and a card of four events was got together; two of these were open to the members of the neighbouring hunts and the third to farmers, cups being given by the officers. The fourth race, the Red Dragon Cup, was won by Captain Barnet Barker's Chance It, owner up, from a field of 17 starters. A large party was entertained by the officers to luncheon and tea, and a most successful afternoon's sport enjoyed.

Whilst at Aldershot, 1905-7, the battalion took up boxing very keenly, engaging professionals to teach the men, and several very successful boxing tournaments were held.

On moving to Cork at the latter end of 1907, and on to 1910, in addition to hunting with the United Hounds the battalion went in for hockey, boxing, and football, and among other successes won the Local Senior League Football Challenge Cup and the Munster League Football Cup; and when moved to Dublin in 1910 and on to 1912 the Irish Army Football Cup and Irish Army Boxing Cup.

Whilst stationed at Portland, 1912-13, they won the Weymouth Senior Football Challenge Cup, hunting chiefly with the South Dorset hounds.

2ND BATTALION

From a sporting point of view the "foreign service" of the 2nd battalion (July 1896 – March 1914) was highly satisfactory; and the battalion well upheld the regimental reputation in rifle-shooting, boxing, football, and polo.

During the period regimental teams won no fewer than 32 open competitions in rifle-shooting, football, and boxing. The following are some of the principal events won:

1896. Army and Navy Football Cup at Malta.
1898. Cretan Football Tournament, at Candia, five British battalions competing.
1902. North China Football Cup at Tientsin.
1907. Runners up in Durand Football Cup, India. Won the Bengal and Punjab Football Cup.

The Regimental Boxing Championship of All India was won by the battalion on three occasions, viz. 1909, 1911, and 1912; and the Patiala All India Boxing Cup in 1911 and 1912. The Quetta Boxing Challenge Shield was won the last two years the battalion was in India; and in Burma they carried everything before them in the boxing line. In 1914 Sergeant Spalding, while serving with the 1st battalion, won the Welter Weights in the Army and Navy Boxing Competition at Malta.

In polo during the first period of their service in India the team won the Cawnpore Cup in 1906.

There were over 100 polo ponies in the battalion, and at one time there were two regimental teams in the field at the same time, the 1st playing at Meerut in the Infantry and Inter-regimental Tournaments, and the 2nd at Delhi and Cawnpore. Two of the officers of the battalion were on "the Form List," a list consisting of about fifty of the best players in India.

In Hong-Kong the local tournament was won on every occasion the battalion was there. The team also went to Shanghai, and beat the team there; this had never been done before, and gave a great impetus to polo in the country.

In Burma the battalion teams won no fewer than nine out of the eleven tournaments for which they entered. They won the Burma Commission Tournament in 1908. In the same year they also won the Meiktila (Burma) Tournament and the Shwebo Tournament, and a subalterns' team won the Bhamo Polo Tournament. In 1909 the Regimental Team won the Maymyo Tournament, and the Regimental "A" Team won the B.P.A. Tournament at Mandalay.

In 1910 they won the Maymyo Open Tournament and the Shwebo Open Tournament.

On the return of the battalion in 1912 to India they were runners up for the Infantry Tournament at Bareilly, and they won the *Country Life* Tournament at Quetta in the same year, as well as the Infantry Tournament at Delhi. This Tournament is open to the Infantry of all India, and the success was a fitting conclusion to their stay in the country.

The race-course also provided many trophies for the officers' mess, races having been won at Hong-Kong, Amoy, Fou Chou, Shanghai, and other coast ports. The battalion also won the Hong-Kong Derby in 1901; and both in India and Burma many successes were obtained, and finally the Army Cup at Lucknow, the soldiers' Blue Ribbon of up-country racing, was carried off by Captain Johnson's drab Prince Charlie.

The Regimental Race Meeting was held at every station during their foreign service—the meeting in Crete being probably the first race meeting ever held in the island, and took the form of an International Meeting.

RED DRAGON CUP

The earliest record of the forerunners of the Red Dragon Cup is to be found in the year 1838; in the *United Service Gazette* for 10th March of that year occurs the following: "On St. David's Day a steeplechase by the officers of the Welch Fusiliers in Dublin came off, when 7 horses started, and Captain Powell's Mussulman was the winner, by a length before Lieutenant Torrens' horse Hector."

In the same magazine under date 18th September 1841 appears the following: "First Lieutenant Ferguson won the Queen's Plate of 50 guineas at St. Pierre races at Montreal on the 17th ult."

The Red Dragon Cup was apparently instituted to take the place of the St. David's Race mentioned on p. 133. Unfortunately the records of the earlier races are not available, but a race was run over the Abergavenny steeplechase course in 1869, and was won by Lieutenant W. F. Cowans' Limerick, owner up.

The next record that can be found is of a race run at the Curragh in 1873, and won by Captain Walwyn's Erin, owner up; this race appears to have been a flat race.

In 1875 the race was won by Lieutenant Thorold's Glutton, but no details are forthcoming.

SPORT

From 1876 to 1880 the 2nd battalion was abroad, but the race was run each year, though no details beyond the name of the winner can be traced.

    1876. Captain G. Hutton's The Shah.
    1877.   ,,   ,,   Bonito.
    1878.   ,,   Shepherd's Galgo.
    1879.   ,,   Luxford's Conejo.
    1880.   ,,   ,,   Conejo.

From 1881 the records are fairly complete, and the race as at present run in the British Isles consists of a point-to-point race of some 3–4 miles over a good hunting country, horses to be owned and ridden by officers of the regiment. As a rule two or three other races, such as a garrison race, a hunt race, and a farmers' race, are got up by the officers, and thus a pleasant afternoon's sport is provided.

The following is the list of winners as far as possible from 1881 to 1914:

Date.	Owner.	Horse.	Rider.	Place.
1881	Lieutenant H. Edward	Virago	Captain Shepherd	
1882	,, ,,	,,	Owner	
1883	No record			
1884	Lieutenant J. L. Lock	Rufus	Lieutenant Ethelston	Templemore
1885	Captain H. Edward	Snowball	Owner	Mallow
1886	Lieutenant Bright-Smith	Lord Cashel	Owner	Fermoy
1887	Lieutenant Ethelston	The Waif	Lieutenant Everitt	Fermoy
1888	Captain Phillips	Dorothy	Owner	
1889	Captain R. Gwynne	Anchorite	Owner	
1890	No record			
1891 {	Captain Ethelston	Wanderer	Owner	{ Dead
	Captain Bright-Smith	Fidget	Owner	{ heat
1892	Lieutenant Crosbie	Egan	Owner	
1893 to 1896	No record			
1897	No race, both battalions being abroad			
1898	No race, 1st battalion just home			
1899	Lieutenant Le Marchant	Teal	Owner	Buckfastleigh
1900 to 1902	No race, both battalions being abroad			
1903	No race, 1st battalion just home			
1904	Captain Barnet Barker	Chance It	Owner	Lichfield
1905	,, ,,	,,	Owner	Wokingham
1906	Lieutenant Skaife	Kilkenny	Owner	Hurst
1907	Major Dobell	Long Moor Lass	Owner	Sherborne St. John
1908	Lieutenant M. L. Mostyn	Twilight	Owner	Bartlemy
1909	Lieutenant E. S. Chance	Mayfield Lass	Owner	Carrignavar
1910	Lieutenant G. C. Blair	Eve	Owner	,,
1911	Lieutenant L. M. Mostyn	Golosh	Owner	Dublin
1912	Lieutenant E. S. Chance	Mayfield Lass	Owner	Glascairn
1913	Lieutenant Gambur Parry	The Mouse	Owner	Cattistock
1914	No race, 1st battalion abroad, 2nd battalion just home			

The races run from 1881 to 1892 refer to the 2nd battalion, then on Home Service, and those from 1904 to 1913 to the 1st battalion.

APPENDIX VI

In addition to the foregoing, the 2nd battalion abroad held races for the Cup, the winners being:

Date.	Owner.	Horse.	Rider.	Place.
1904	Captain F. Hayhurst	Eclipse	Lieutenant Crawshay	
1905	Captain H. Hill	Cinque Ports	Captain Johnson	
1906	,, ,,	Dale	Lieutenant Kearsley	
1907	,, ,,	Cinque Ports	Lieutenant Crawshay	
1908	Lieutenant J. P. Evans	Plover	Owner	
1909	Lieutenant G. O. Thomas	Perhaps	Owner	
1910	Lieutenant G. C. Blair	Lucky Devil	Owner	

APPENDIX VII

THE COLOURS

THE colours of a regiment have been aptly described as "its emblem and its rallying point." Those carried by infantry were originally one for each company, every company having its flag distinct in some particular from the other companies; the flag was posted in the centre, and was guarded by 10 halberdiers. During the reign of William III, however, the regiments were reduced to about 1,000 men, following the plan of the great Swedish commander, Gustavus II, and were composed of a central division of pikemen, flanked on either side by a division of musketeers: this led to the colours carried by a regiment being reduced to three in number.

The difficulty of tracing the fate of worn-out colours is due to the fact that from the outset they were regarded as the property of the head, or "proprietary" colonel; many also came into the possession of the colonel or lieutenant-colonel commanding the battalion, and, in consequence, it is as a rule impossible to locate them.

1743: The first reference to the colours of the 23rd which can be found is in a Clothing Warrant, the first of its kind, dated 14th September 1743, describing those then in use.

The number of colours carried was this year further reduced to two; the First, afterwards in 1757 called the "King's Colour," bore the "Union throughout" except in "all the Royal Regiments, the Fusilier and Marine Regiments . . . are distinguished by particular devices. . . ." The Second, or "Regimental Colour," was to be made of blue silk, with a small union in the upper corner, nearest the staff; the regimental device in the centre, and the number "XXIII" towards the upper corner, i.e. in the centre of the Union. The union above-mentioned consisted of the crosses of St. George (red) and St. Andrew (white) combined on a blue ground. Not for some sixty years after did St. Patrick's cross appear thereon.

1745: After the battle of Fontenoy on 11th May the losses of the regiment were so severe that it was sent to Ghent to perform garrison duty, and on 9th July the garrison was surprised by the enemy appearing in force, and was compelled to surrender. No trace can be found of what became of the colours, as no Inspection Returns for that period are in existence. It was customary for the colours to be given up when a regiment surrendered, but this was not always carried out.

1747: The following are the dimensions of infantry colours as laid down in the Regulations prepared by Colonel Napier, the Adjutant-General, in November of this year: 6 feet 6 inches flying; 6 feet 2 inches deep on the pole; length of pole, spear, and ferrule included, 9 feet 6 inches; length of cord and tassels, 3 feet, each tassel 4 inches;

length of spear head, 4 inches. These Regulations were delivered to the Clothing Board in 1749 and issued to the Army in 1751.

1751: The Clothing Warrant issued on 1st July this year thus describes the regimental colour of the 23rd: " In the centre of their colours, the device of the Prince of Wales, viz.: three feathers issuing out of the Prince's Coronet: in the three corners of the second colour the badges of Edward the Black Prince: viz. Rising Sun: Red Dragon: and the Three Feathers in the Coronet: motto ' ICH DIEN ' ": all on blue silk.

1756: At the capitulation of the garrison of Minorca on the 29th of June the troops are generally described as having marched out with the " Honours of War." This meant they evacuated their quarters, fortifications, etc., with arms and colours, but laid down both arms and colours at some appointed spot outside their lines of defence. The colours of this garrison are mentioned as being hung at the Invalides in Paris in 1814, and they perished there on the night of 30th March 1814, when some 1,800 Eagles (French) and colours and standards of other nations were burnt by the Governor and veterans of the Invalides to save them falling into the enemy's hands on the eve of the entry into Paris of the Allies (Russians, Austrians, and Germans).

It seems highly probable that the colours of the regiment did not fall into the enemy's hands at Minorca, since at the inspection which took place at Chatham on the 24th of September 1757 they are described as " bad," in which condition they could not possibly have been if new ones had been issued to take the place of those surrendered.

1768: The badges and devices are confirmed in the Clothing Warrant issued on 19th December 1768. The King's Colour was the Union, with the Prince of Wales' plume and coronet in the centre, and " XXIII " in the top left-hand corner. The Regimental Colour was blue, with a small union in the upper corner with the regimental number in roman characters in the middle; the Rising Sun on a blue ground in the right-hand top corner; the Dragon in blue on a red field in the lower left-hand corner; and the Prince of Wales' plumes on a white field in the lower right-hand corner, all surrounded by gold rings. The Prince of Wales' plumes and coronet in white and gold in the centre of the colour.

By the same Warrant the depth of the colour was reduced to 6 feet, the other measurements remaining as shown above.

1807: In 1807 Mr. George Naylor, the then Inspector of Regimental Colours, sent a circular to all Commanding Officers asking for descriptions of the colours carried by their regiments. The sketch, now in the Heralds' College, sent from Colchester on 10th May by Colonel Ellis, shows the colours then carried by the 23rd as follows:

The King's Colour, the Union, with " G.R." in the centre encircled by a gold ornamental border surmounted by a crown. The central device surrounded by a wreath of roses, shamrock, and thistles. Below the wreath a white sphinx, with " EGYPT " below in capital letters.

The Regimental Colour was of blue silk, with a small union in the upper corner, with the regimental number in roman numerals in the middle. In the centre of the colour the Prince of Wales' plumes, coronet, and motto, surrounded by the Union wreath in proper colours. Above, a curved gold scroll inscribed " MINDEN " in black letters. Below the wreath a sphinx. In the top right-hand corner the White Horse of Hanover facing to the left, on a red field (this took the place of the Prince of Wales plumes hitherto borne in the lower right-hand corner); in the lower left-hand corner a Red Dragon on white; and in the bottom right-hand corner the Rising Sun on white, each surrounded by an ornamental gold frame.

Many other sketches of the colours of the 23rd are to be found in the Heralds' College.

1820: Those for 1820 show the King's Colour as the Union throughout, with the Prince of Wales' plumes and motto in the centre, surrounded by the Union wreath in proper colours, with two gold curved scrolls on the lower part, one inscribed " 23RD REGT." and the other " I. BATTN." On three similar scrolls above are " MARTINIQUE," " MINDEN," and " ALBUHERA " (the first and third honours having been authorised on 17th November 1816); with three other scrolls below the wreath inscribed " PENINSULA," " EGYPT," and " WATERLOO." Between the scroll inscribed " EGYPT " and the wreath is one inscribed " ROYAL WELCH FUSILIERS," and below " EGYPT " is a sphinx, surrounded by laurel branches. The Regimental Colour is of blue silk with the Union in the upper corner, and with the plumes in the centre, inside the Union wreath, in proper colours. In the top right-hand corner is the Rising Sun, and in the right and left bottom corners the plumes, on a white ground, with blue motto; and the Red Dragon on a white field: each surrounded with an ornamental gold border. Above the wreath, on a curved scroll " MINDEN," and on the wreath, at the bottom, two curved scrolls, one inscribed " 23 REGT." and the other " 1ST BATT." Below the wreath a curved scroll with " ROYAL WELCH FUSILIERS " upon it; and beneath it another inscribed " EGYPT," with a sphinx, with green laurel branches on each side. On the right-hand side of the colour are two scrolls, one inscribed " ALBUHERA " and the other " WATERLOO "; and on the left two others inscribed " MARTINIQUE " and " PENINSULA " respectively. All the scrolls are gold, with black lettering.

1835: A petition was made to the King in February this year for permission to bear the distinctions (granted to the regiment on 1st July 1757 and 19th December 1768) of the Prince of Wales' plumes in the centre of the colours; in the second and third corners the Rising Sun and the Red Dragon; and in the fourth the White Horse. This was granted, and the bearing of the battle honour for " CORUNNA " was sanctioned at the same time. The sketch of the Regimental Colour, "*for His Majesty's approval,*" was as follows: blue silk, with the Union in the upper corner, and "*23rd*" in the middle of St. George's cross; the plume with a gold coronet in the centre, with a blue motto, surrounded by the Union wreath in proper colours, and tied with red ribbons with a curved scroll below it inscribed " ROYAL WELCH FUSILIERS," and with the Rising Sun on a white field, and green ground, in the upper right-hand corner. In the right- and left-hand corners are, respectively, the White Horse on a green ground, with a white label below it inscribed " NEC ASPERA TERRENT," and the Red Dragon on a white ground: each surrounded by a plain gold circle. Above the wreath on a curved and swallow-tailed scroll " WATERLOO," and underneath the scroll below the wreath two others, the upper one inscribed " PENINSULA " and the lower one " EGYPT." Beneath the latter a white sphinx with Egyptian characters on the base, surrounded by green laurel branches. On the right-hand side of the wreath were six scrolls, the upper one inscribed " MARTINIQUE " and the others in sequence, " BADAJOZ,"

"VITTORIA," "NIVELLE," "TOULOUSE," and "CORUNNA." On the left-hand side five scrolls inscribed in succession: "MINDEN," "ALBUHERA," "SALAMANCA," "PYRENEES," and "ORTHES." All the scrolls were gold, with black letters.

When withdrawn in July 1849 these colours were placed in St. Peter's Church, Carmarthen.

1844: A General Order was issued from the Horse Guards in January, discontinuing "the practice of placing any regimental record or device upon the Royal Colour, more than the number of the regiment surmounted by the imperial crown."

This important order very much altered things, and impoverished the appearance of new colours made after this date. When seen together an unequal effect was produced from the circumstance of one colour being so plain and the other so elaborately decorated. The crown being now placed over the numeral on the Royal Colour, necessitated the use of a corresponding crown above the wreath on the Regimental Colour, which from this time became universal. Further, it was considered wanting in respect to place anything over the crown, and consequently on all new colours the battle honours were ranged on each side with a few at the bottom. A crown over the wreath was not absolutely new—occasional instances had occurred—but speaking generally before this order crowns on infantry colours were unusual; even the 23rd, 35th, and 51st, all Royal regiments, had no crown on the central wreath before this period.

1849: The Regimental Colour presented by the Prince Consort at Winchester on 12th July 1849 was of blue silk with the Union in the upper corner, and with the same distinctions in the other three corners as described above. In the centre: the plumes, with "XXIII" below, inside a circle inscribed "ROYAL WELCH FUSILIERS" surrounded by the Union wreath, in proper colours, and surmounted by a crown. Below the wreath were two curved scrolls, the upper one inscribed "PENINSULA" and the lower one "EGYPT." Beneath the latter was a sphinx, surrounded by a palm, and laurel branch on either side. On the right-hand side of the wreath are six curved scrolls, inscribed "CORUNNA," "ALBUHERA," "SALAMANCA," "PYRENEES," "ORTHES," and "WATERLOO"; and on the left side six more, inscribed "MINDEN," "MARTINIQUE," "BADAJOZ," "VITTORIA," "NIVELLE," and "TOULOUSE." All the scrolls were gold, with black letters.

1855: On the 6th of November the dimensions of the colours, which had remained unchanged since 1768, were reduced in size to 6 feet flying, and 5 feet 6 inches deep on the pole.

1858: The size of the colours was further reduced in September to 4 feet flying and 4 feet 6 inches on the pole; the colours to be surrounded or edged with gold fringe, mixed with crimson for the First, or Queen's, and with silk the hue of the regimental facing for the Regimental Colour. The ancient spear-head (which had been a little altered in pattern about 1830) was now done away with altogether, and the pole surmounted by a gilt lion and a crown; cords and tassels of gold and crimson were made richer, the First or Queen's Colour still retaining the same plain roman numerals, with crown over.

In spite of this alteration in regulation the 2nd battalion which was raised this

THE COLOURS

year was presented at Malta on 1st December 1859 by General Le Marchant with colours of the old size with spear-head; these colours are still in use. The colours of these second battalions were precisely like those of the first battalions, generally differenced, however, by the words "*II. Batt.*" on a small scroll placed immediately under the wreath.

1865: A sketch sent to the War Office on 27th January shows the First Colour as the Union throughout, with " XXIII " in the middle surmounted by a crown and with "*II. Batt.*" on a curved label below.

The Regimental Colour is blue, with a small union in the upper corner; and the usual distinctions in the other corners. In the centre the plumes, with " XXIII " below, inside a circle inscribed " ROYAL WELCH FUSILIERS," surrounded by the Union wreath, and surmounted by a crown. At the point of juncture of the wreath a curved label inscribed "*II. Batt.*" and below it two others, the upper inscribed " LUCKNOW " and the lower " EGYPT." Below this a sphinx and laurel branches. On either side of the wreath the battle honours previously enumerated with the addition of " ALMA," " SEBASTOPOL," and " INKERMAN."

Both colours were edged with gold fringe, and had the lion and crown on the tops of the staves.

1880: The colours presented by the Prince of Wales (late King Edward VII) at Portsmouth on 16th August had " XXIII " surmounted by a crown in the centre of the First or Queen's Colour. The Regimental Colour was of blue silk, with a small union in the upper corner, and the usual devices in the other three corners. In the centre the same device, etc., as that described in the foregoing; and outside the wreath, curved gold and black-lettered scrolls: those of the left inscribed " CORUNNA," " ALBUHERA," "SALAMANCA," " PYRENEES," "ORTHES," " PENINSULA," " ALMA,"

Battalion.	Inspected at	Date.	Description in Inspection Returns.	Remarks.
1st Batt.	Chatham	24 Sept. 1757	Bad	Minorca colours.
Regt.	Plymouth	Spring of 1764	Good	
Regt.	Chatham	22nd May 1788	Bad	
Regt.	Windsor	2 June 1789	Good	
1st Batt.	Gosport	18 Oct. 1814	Bad; very old: new ones ordered	
Regt.	Neuilly	20 Oct. 1815	Good	
Regt.	Gibraltar	26 May 1826	Bad	
Regt.	Gibraltar	6 Dec. 1826	Good	Presented by Lieut.-Gen. Sir J. W. Gordon: handed to Regt. on 1 Dec. 1826 by Mrs. Pearson.
1st Batt.	Halifax	26 May 1848	Unserviceable	
1st Batt.	Windsor	16 Oct. 1849	Serviceable	Presented by H.R.H. the Prince Consort on 12 July 1849 at Winchester; the 1826 colours being placed in St. Peter's Church, Carmarthen.
2nd Batt.	Malta	21 Dec. 1859		Presented by General Le Marchant; still (1922) in use.
1st Batt.	Portsmouth	16 Aug. 1880		Presented by H.R.H. the Prince of Wales (late King Edward VII); still (1922) in use, those taken into use in 1849 being handed to H.R.H.

and "SEVASTOPOL"; and on the right "MALPLAQUET," "DETTINGEN," "MINDEN," "MARTINIQUE," "BADAJOZ," "VITTORIA," "NIVELLE," "TOULOUSE," "WATERLOO," and "INKERMAN." Above the crown were three similar scrolls, the upper one inscribed "BLENHEIM," and the lower ones "OUDENARDE" and "RAMILLIES." Below the wreath were four other scrolls, the top one inscribed "LUCKNOW," and of the other three in line one was inscribed "ASHANTEE," the central one "EGYPT," with the sphinx below, and the outer one left blank for symmetry. These colours are still carried by the 1st battalion, with the following honours added: "NAMUR 1698," "BURMA 1885–87," "RELIEF OF LADYSMITH," "SOUTH AFRICA 1899–1902," and "PEKIN 1900."

The table on p. 395 shows what is known of all the colours carried from about 1750 onwards.

APPENDIX VIII
OFFICERS COMMANDING, 1689–1914

Edwards, Sir Francis	Oct.	1689
Purcell, Tobias	20 June	1690
Montargier, J. de P. de	26 Oct.	1691
Sabine, Joseph	6 June	1695
Pennyfather, M.	1 April	1705
Patterson, J.	24 Dec.	1711
Brett, A.	1 June	1715
Wentworth, T.	10 Feb.	1718
Peers, Newsham	22 Dec.	1722
Ellison, C.	23 Nov.	1739
Waite, J.	11 April	1743
Hickman, W.	15 Feb.	1747
Pole, E. S.	9 Jan.	1756
Hemmington, C.	27 Jan.	1764
Bernard, B.	28 Aug.	1771
Balfour, N.	31 Jan.	1778
Ellis, J. J.	6 Dec.	1793
Peter, J.	1 Sept.	1795
Talbot, R.	15 March	1798
Hall, J.	12 June	1800

1st Battalion		2nd Battalion		
		(25 Dec. 1804 — 24 Oct. 1814)		
Losack, J.	14 Nov. 1804			
Jones, E. (from 2nd Batt.)	Feb. 1807	Jones, E.	23 Nov.	1804
Ellis, H. W.	23 April 1807	Wyatt, W. E.	18 Feb.	1808
		Sutton, C.	17 June	1813
Dalmer, T.			20 July	1815
Pearson, T.			24 July	1817
Harrison, J. C.			22 July	1830
Ross, W.			24 March	1837
Torrens, A. W.			15 Oct.	1841

1st Battalion		Reserve Battalion		
Torrens, A. W.	15 Oct. 1841	(14 April 1842 — 31 July 1853)		
Crutchley, C. (from Reserve Batt.)	May 1853	Holmes, R. P.	14 April	1842
		Crutchley, C.	24 July	1849
Chester, H. G.	March 1854	Chester, H. G.	May	1853
Lysons, D.			21 Sept.	1854
Wells, S.			16 Jan.	1857

APPENDIX VIII

1st Battalion

Pratt, R.	7 Dec. 1867
Prevost, G. P.	3 Sept. 1870
Elgee, C. (from 2nd Batt.)	June 1880
Tilly, J.	10 April 1885
Creek, E. S.	1 July 1887
Williamson, R. F. (from 2nd Batt.)	Jan. 1890
Norman, C.	2 April 1891
Griffith, H. W.	2 April 1895
Thorold, C. C. H.	4 Mar. 1896
Colleton, Sir R. A. W., Bt.	12 May 1900
Beresford-Ash, W. R. H.	12 May 1904
Iggulden, H. A.	12 May 1908
Cadogan, H. O. S.	12 May 1912

2nd Battalion
(3 Mar. 1858)

Bell, E. W. D., V.C.	30 Mar. 1858
Mostyn, Hon. S.	1 Sept. 1869
Elgee, C.	10 April 1880
O'Connor, L., V.C.	21 June 1880
Williamson, J.	21 June 1885
Williamson, R. F.	2 April 1887
Creek, E. S. (from 1st Batt.)	Jan. 1890
Blyth, S. B.	1 July 1891
Mainwaring, R. B.	1 July 1895
Bertie, Hon. R. H.	21 Aug. 1899
Lyle, H. T.	21 Aug. 1903
Mantell, P. R.	21 Aug. 1907
Delmé-Radcliffe, H	21 Aug. 1911

APPENDIX IX

THE "FLASH"

The "Flash" as now worn by all ranks of the Royal Welch Fusiliers consists of "a five-tailed flash of black silk ribbon" attached to the back of the collar of the tunic or

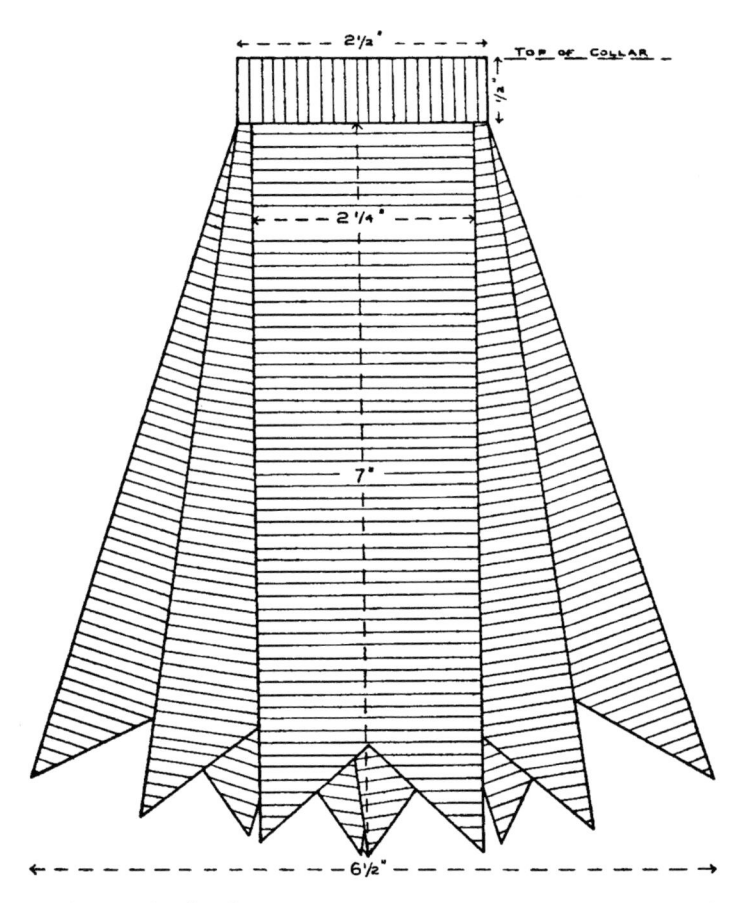

jacket; the regulation size is 2½ inches wide at the top, and 9 inches long for the officers and 7 inches long for the rank and file; the ribs of the silk are vertical in the band at the top, and horizontal in the ribbons

The derivation of the word is not clear; previous to 1700 it was used as a slang expression for a periwig: in a dictionary of 1760, a "flash" is stated to be a slang

400   APPENDIX IX

expression for a peruke, a "rum flash" is a "long full high prized wig," a "queer flash" is a "sorry weather beaten wig."

On the abolition of wigs, and the introduction of the fashion of tying the hair up in a queue, the name seems to have been applied to the bow of ribbon used to tie the queue, and eventually on the abolition of the queue to have been applied to the bow of ribbons, which the 23rd adhered to in spite of "regulations."

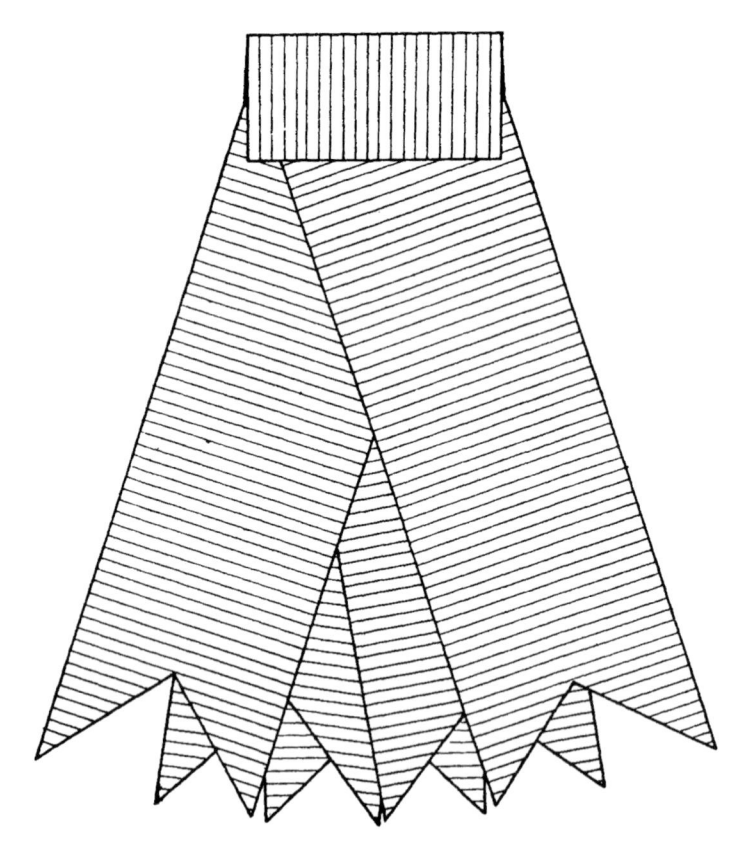

Reverse side of "Flash," showing position of Ribbon.

At the present day in Kent a "flash" is, in the local dialect, the ribbon used to tie up a horse's mane or tail, the tail being regularly "clubbed," when the horse is for sale, or on other special occasions.

To account for the wearing of the "flash" by the officers and men of the Royal Welch Fusiliers it is necessary to refer briefly to the custom of wearing wigs.

On the abolition of the periwig, which was in vogue approximately during the period 1600–1690, it was succeeded by the peruke, or campaign wig, a much less cumbersome article. Farquhar in his *Love and a Bottle*, published in 1698, says "it hath dildos

THE "FLASH"

or pole-locks," which hung from the centre of the back of the peruke as shown in the accompanying illustration. These are no doubt the originals of the pigtail. The

peruke remained in fashion until about 1714, when it gave way to the tie or bob-wig as shown below.

These bob-wigs were forbidden to be worn by officers in January 1754, and on 15th September 1756 all non-commissioned officers and men were ordered to wear

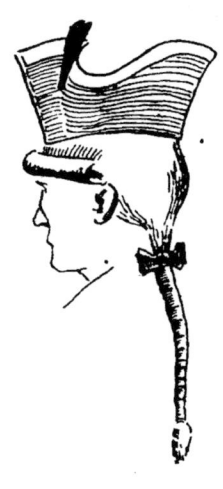

their hair clubbed, except those of the Grenadier Company, who were ordered to have theirs plaited.

"Clubbing" consisted of combing the hair into a long flat tail; and then folding it up into a long bunch, tying it round the middle with a black ribbon or leather strap.

The practice of powdering the natural hair probably dates from about 1755, then wigs (which were powdered) went out of fashion.

APPENDIX IX

In 1760 powder was, as a rule, only used by the men when on guard, or on Sundays, and was abolished for them on the 19th of July 1795, owing to the high price of flour, due to bad harvests. Colonels of regiments seemed loath to obey this order, which necessitated its repetition on the 8th of September 1797; though officers continued to use powder until 1808, when it was finally done away with. The hair powder was made from pulverised starch or flour.

On the 20th of April 1770 the following instructions were issued: "Hair to be plaited and turned up behind with a black ribbon or tape, three-quarters of a yard long, in a bow knot at the tye. Those men who have their hair so short that it will not plait must be provided as soon as possible with a false plat."

The following is an extract from Bennett Cuthbertson's *Management of a Battalion of Infantry*, 2nd edition, 1779:

"The hair of the Non-commission-officers, Drummers, and private Men, look tightest, when turned up behind, on a comb, and loosely platted, with a black ribband or tape (three quarters long) in a bow knot, at the tye, which must never be permitted to be made too close to the head, as such a practice cuts the hair, which should be encouraged, by every means, to be as thick and full as possible, in order to enlarge the appearance of the plat, which thereby looks more ornamental: to promote that end, no foretop must be allowed, and only as much short hair at the sides, as will make a little turn back, of about an inch and a half in length: when all these aids are not sufficient, from the natural thinness of the hair, a false plat must be added, which, if properly fixt on, can never be discovered: this method is also to be pursued, when a soldier's hair is but barely long enough to tye, as it will contribute much to the uniform appearance of a Battalion, particularly after having received any number of Recruits.

"A soldier must never be allowed to wear a wig, if it can possibly be avoided, but when there is an absolute necessity for so doing, it should be made to imitate the regimental form of dressing the hair, as much as can be: and it should be a rule to take off the wigs from Recruits, whenever the season of the year will admit it, although their hair be ever so short, as even that will look more military, than a peasant's wig.

"As nothing promotes the growth of hair, more than frequent combing, the soldiers should be enjoined to accustom themselves to do so, both morning and night, by which they will be under the necessity of undoing their plats, before they go to bed, and thereby prevent the hair from getting thin, which nothing sooner affects, than a neglect of this precaution: but as soldiers are not to be depended on in anything, let it be ever so much for their advantage, the Sergeants and Corporals must often examine into this particular, and insist on a compliance: and it will also be of infinite consequence to the improvement of their hair, to permit them, when not for duty, to appear at morning roll calling, with their hair only tyed, and hanging down the back: by which the Officers will be certain of their being combed in a proper manner, at least once a day, which cannot be the case if the hair be platted up.

"Pains must be taken to introduce a method of powdering the men's hair to advantage, that the powder may not be in cakes, on one part more than another, but rather have the appearance of being equally frosted over: for which purpose it will be right for each Company to appoint a soldier, who seems to have a taste for it, not only to powder all the men of the Company whenever necessary, but, likewise to keep their hair well cut at the sides, and their plats properly done up: for which, and to furnish powder, (and shave if required) he should be allowed a halfpenny per week, from each Non-commission-officer, Drummer, and private Man, with some little exemptions in point of duty: this will be a certain means of ensuring uniformity in the management of the hair of a Battalion, and will not be a greater expence to the soldiers, than if they had furnished powder for themselves."

The following is a description of the hair dressing in 1796, which must have been a serious business—" Each company had a barber, who found soap and hair powder, and was paid three pence a week by each man. The hair was well greased, combed out, powdered, and tied behind. The soldiers sat on a bench one behind the other, and tied each other's tails, taking it in turn to be powdered: so the junior had to be up betimes, the senior being left to the last. Hair was to be just long enough at the sides to frizzle a little, and behind an inch below the rosette. Both officers and men were clean shaved."

In 1798–9 it was customary for the battalion companies to wear their hair clubbed, while the flank companies wore theirs plaited.

In 1799 officers and men of the infantry were ordered to wear their hair queued: it was to be tied a little below the upper part of the collar of the coat, and to be 10 inches long, including 1 inch of hair to appear below the binding. The Grenadiers and Light Infantry were excepted, as by an order dated 6th June 1799; they were required to turn their hair up under their hats.

In 1804 the length of the queue was reduced to 7 inches: these were bound with ribbon, but without the bow at the top. In the Museum of the Royal United Service Institution there is a grenadier's cap with the queue sewn to the back, so that both could be donned at once!!

The following is a further description of hair dressing in January, 1808—" The hair 2 inches from the head queued within 1 inch of the end, of which 1 inch of hair is to be below the lace of the neck of the coat. The double knot of ribbon to be 1 inch in length, and the single ends to be 2 inches. It is also wished that the side locks be set back with a little pomatum, as well as that of the forehead, but in no case to be stiffened with soap."

In consequence of the authorities at last realizing that queues were of no practical use, but a positive hindrance during active service, the following General Order was issued:

"HORSE GUARDS,
20th July 1808.

" The Commander-in-Chief directs it to be notified that, in consequence of the state of preparation for immediate service in which the whole army is at the present moment to be held, His Majesty has been graciously pleased to dispense with the use of queues until further orders.

" His Royal Highness desires the commanding officers of regiments will take care that the men's hair is cut close in their necks in the neatest and most uniform manner, and that their heads are kept perfectly clean by combing, brushing, and frequently washing them. For the latter essential purpose it is His Majesty's pleasure that a small sponge shall hereafter be added to each man's regimental necessaries.

" By order of His Royal Highness the Commander-in-Chief,

"HARRY CALVERT, *Adjutant-General.*"

The Life Guards and Royal Horse Guards were excluded from this Order.

One of the modes in which this Order was carried into effect is thus related in Colonel Caddell's *History of the 28th Regiment* (which was then on board ship at Spithead):

"On the 24th of July, a general order arrived from the Horse Guards, which, droll as it may appear, gave universal delight: it was to cut off the men's queues.

"A signal was immediately made for all hair-cutters to repair to head-quarters.

"As soon as they had finished on board the headquarter ship, the adjutant, Lieutenant Russell, proceeded with them and a pattern man, to the other troop-ships. The tails were kept till all were docked, when, by a signal, the whole were hove overboard, with three cheers."

Another regiment made a bonfire of all the men's pigtails, whilst another buried them with all solemnity.

When the order discontinuing the use of the queue was promulgated, the 1st battalion of the regiment was then serving in Nova Scotia, and it is probable as claimed by Major Broughton-Mainwaring that it was " the last regiment in the army who wore the queue," although the actual date is not now ascertainable.

On the abolition of the queues on 20th July, 1808, it seems as if the officers of the 23rd Regiment were loath to part with everything that would remind them of the queue, consequently they continued to wear black ribbons attached to the back of the collar of the tunic reminiscent of the ribbon used for the purpose of tying the queue up.

At an inspection of the depôt companies at Portsmouth on the 6th of October 1834, by Major-General Sir Thomas McMahon, K.C.B., his attention was drawn by the "flash" then worn by the officers, and he remarked as follows in his report: "Officers' Clothing: I have noticed superfluous decoration on the collar of the coat." And in his "General Remarks" he observes: "I should have ordered the immediate abolition of the black canteen covers, knapsack, and greatcoat straps, as well as frills to the soldiers' shirts, and black ribbands attached to the collars of the officers' red coats, but that the Service Companies are now daily expected from Gibraltar."

The comments made by Sir Thomas McMahon at this Inspection caused Lieut.-Colonel Harrison to write immediately to Lieut.-General Sir J. W. Gordon, Colonel of the Regiment, and Quartermaster-General, who on the 7th of October wrote to the Adjutant-General, and received the following reply:

"HORSE GUARDS.
28th November 1834.

"SIR,

" By desire of the General Commanding-in-Chief I have the honour to notify to you that, in consequence of your letter and Lord Hill's recommendation, the King has been graciously pleased to approve of the ' Flashes ' now worn by the officers of the Twenty-Third Foot, or Royal Welch Fusiliers, being henceforth worn and established as a peculiarity whereby to mark the dress of that distinguished regiment. I have Lord Hill's command to request that you will be pleased to cause this mark of His Majesty's gracious favour to be duly registered in the records of the Royal Welch Fusiliers.

"I have the honour to be, Sir, your obedient servant,
(*Signed*)   JOHN MACDONALD, A.G.
"To Lieut.-General Sir J. W. Gordon, Bart., G.C.B.,
Colonel of the Royal Welch Fusiliers."

Lieut.-General Sir J. W. Gordon replied to Lieut.-Colonel Harrison in the following terms:

"HORSE GUARDS.
28*th November*, 1834.

"SIR,
"I have great pleasure in transmitting to you the accompanying letter from the Adjutant-General, conveying the King's gracious approval of the 'Flashes' now worn by the officers Royal Welch Fusiliers, being henceforth worn and established as a peculiarity whereby to mark the dress of that distinguished regiment.

"In thus making known to you this gracious mark of His Majesty's Royal favour, and in desiring that the enclosed letter may be duly registered in the records of the regiment, I have no doubt that it will be felt by the regiment, as it ought to be, both as an honourable proof of His Majesty's approbation, and as an inducement to use their best endeavours to merit a continuance of such gratifying distinctions.

"I have the honour to be, Sir, your obedient servant,
(*Signed*)   W. GORDON.
"To Lieut.-Colonel Harrison,
Commanding Royal Welch Fusiliers."

Since then it is needless to say that the "Flash"—

"Relic of many a fight, and siege, and sack,
It points a moral, and adorns 'the back'"—

has been fondly cherished and still remains, aye and ever will remain, a proud mark of distinction, whereby a Royal Welch Fusilier may be distinguished amongst all men. The following is an extract from Major Broughton-Mainwaring's Record:

"The 'Flash' became regulation in the Royal Welch: and though changed in all else, one bit of their costume remains the same, the same as when James and William fought for the Crown on the green banks of the Boyne Water: when shoulder to shoulder (each man having a green bough or sprig fastened in his hat to distinguish them from the Irish, who wore bits of white paper) the Welch Fusiliers breasted the swirl and flow of that rapid river: the same as when Marlborough won his laurels, and under his banner the Royal Welch Fusiliers fought at Schellenberg and Blenheim, Ramillies, Oudenarde, and Malplaquet: as when at Dettingen and Fontenoy British infantry again proved themselves the best in the world.

"This same 'Flash' fluttered in the van throughout the Peninsular, and afterwards at Waterloo, struggled up Alma's bloody hill, and later still relieved Lucknow's beleaguered and helpless garrison, and may now be seen setting off the slim figure of the officer of the guard as he visits his bearskinned sentries. Ornament assuredly: but has it not its use too?"

From 1834, onwards, the flash was worn by officers, warrant officers, and staff sergeants only until 2nd of June, 1900, when the right to wear it was extended to all ranks of the regiment.

This was the outcome of an Inspection of the 1st battalion at Raglan Barracks, Devonport, in the previous year, by Field-Marshal Viscount Wolseley, Commander-in-Chief, who recommended that it should be worn by all ranks.

The officers, warrant officers, and staff sergeants introduced the Flash on the service dress jacket, but exception was taken by the War Office to this practice while the 1st Battalion was at Aldershot in 1905-7; however, in 1914, the War Office withdrew its objection.

A LIST OF THE PRINCIPAL WORKS CONSULTED IN THE COMPILATION OF THIS VOLUME

BRACKENBURY, MAJOR-GENERAL H.: " The Ashanti War: a narrative prepared from official documents." Two vols.; London, 1874.

HAMLEY, GENERAL SIR E. B.: " The War in the Crimea." London, 1891.

KINGLAKE, A. W.: " Invasion of the Crimea." Eight vols.; London, 1863–1887.

LYSONS, GENERAL SIR DANIEL: " The Crimean War from First to Last." London, 1895.

LYSONS, GENERAL SIR DANIEL: " Early Reminiscences." London, 1896.

MAINWARING, MAJOR R. BROUGHTON: " Historical Record of the Royal Welch Fusiliers, late the 23rd Regiment." London, 1889.

MAURICE, MAJOR-GENERAL SIR F.: " History of the War in South Africa, 1899–1902." Compiled by direction of H.M.'s Government. Four vols. Maps in cases. London, 1906–1910.

NEVILL, CAPTAIN H. L., D.S.O.: " Campaigns on the North-West Frontier." Maps. London, 1912.

WOOD, GENERAL SIR EVELYN: " The Crimea in 1854 and 1894." London, 1895.

London Gazettes.

INDEX.

Abbotson, Private J., 102
Aberdare, 123, 226
Aberdeen, Earl of, 315
Abergele, 214
Accrofol, 145
Adams, Sergeant Elijah, wounded, 119
Aden, 222-3, 225
Adventure, H.M.S., 105-6
Afghanistan, Amir of, 307
Afghanistan, Maiwand disaster, 160
Aggemamu, 147
Aglish Camp, 309
Agra, 131-5, 305-8
Aherne, Private Michael, 95, 97
Ahkam Coomassie, 148
Airey, Brigadier-General, 70, 71
Aitken, Major W., R.A., 191
Aitkin, Private H., 103
Akazai Expedition, 206-9
Aladin, 71
Albany Barracks, Isle of Wight, 15, 16
"Albert Shako," 358-9, 361
Albion (transport), 38
Albuhera, centenary, 314-5
Alcock, Lieut., 26; Captain, 42
Alder, Surgeon-Major, 144, 148
Aldershot, 99, 104-5, 124-5, 130, 138-9, 140, 143, 145, 150, 153, 216, 218-9, 225, 305-7, 328, 345, 387, 406
Alexander II, 150
Alexandria, 138, 227
Alfred (transport), 8, 9
Alison, Brigadier-General Sir Archibald, 146-7
Allahabad, 106-7, 111, 135, 168
Allen, Police-Constable, 325
Allied Army in France, 7
Alma, battle of, anniversary, 318, 328
"Alma Day," 328
Alma Fund, 78
Alma Monument, 78, 198-9, 221
Alma River, 73
Almeida, Gibraltar, 17, 155
Aloung Pyah (river steamer), 173, 179, 180
Alphonso, King of Spain, 305
Alston, Lieut. L. A. A., 329
Alum Bagh, 111
Amesbury, 142
Amoaful, 147-8
Amoy, 388
Anderdon, Captain H. G., 48
Anderson, General D., 158
Andes (steamer), 71
Andrews, Private W., 102
Anglesey, 211, 214

Annapolis, 33
Anping, 266
Anstruther, 2nd Lieut. Henry, 69; killed, 75, 77, 78, 100, 102
Antigua, 44, 49
Anwyl, Lieut. M. I. H., 318
Apollo (troopship), 52
Appleford, Private J., 102
Applewhaite, Lieut. Augustus, 69; mortally wounded, 78, 100, 102
Aprons, white buckskin, worn by Pioneers, 195
Archdale, Captain H., 181, 186, 192, 194; Major H. J., 212, 218, 224-5, 228
Ardagh, Colonel John, R.E., 210
Armagh, 32
Arms, 374-5
Armstrong, Ensign, 57
Armstrong, Major-General Sir R., 41, 43, 46, 48
Army, changes in organisation, 1881, 166
Army and Navy Football Cup, Malta, 387
Arnott, Private J., 103
Arras, 3
Arrown, 112
Ascension, 106
Ashantee Campaign, 1873-4, 143; memorial, 150, 221
Ashanti, King of, 143
Ashby-de-la-Zouch, 332
Asirgurh, 137
Assheton-Smith, Mr., 213
Assistance, H.M.S., 157, 170
Aston, Quartermaster J., 69
Atholl (troopship), 48
Attiwell, Sergeant, 148
Attock, 206-7
Aubrey, Private J., 103
Auchinleck, Lieut., 145
Ava, fortress and town, 175-8
Ava Redoubt (Tsn Kyun), 176
Avoca (steamship), 227

Babington, Major-General, 256-7, 274-8, 280, 282, 301
"Babington's Foot Cavalry," 283
Badcock, Private C., 102
Badshah Bagh, 115-6
Bagot, Sir Charles, 39
Bailey, Captain, Royal Scots Fusiliers, 254
Baillie, 2nd Lieut. Thomas, 4, 5
Baker, Lieut., 41; Captain, 48
Baker, Lieut. H. E., 163
Baker, Private, wounded, 265
Baker, Private G., death, 148; memorial, 150, 221

Bakrai, 207-8
Bakshe-Serai, 79
Balaklava, 79, 80, 81, 85, 88, 97, 99
Balfour, N. (Officer Commanding), 397
Ball, Lieut., 291, 296
Ball-Acton, 2nd Lieut. C. A., 224; Lieut., 298
Ballard, Private F., 241
Ballyvonare, 312
Bamford, Lieut., 238, 255
Bampfield, Paymaster G., 163
Bancroft, Lieut. C. E., 212; Captain, 295
"Bandmaster" becomes Warrant Officer, 167
Bangor, 212, 317
Bank, 248, 288
Bantry, 153
Barbados, 42-5, 47, 50
Barchard, Lieut. D. M., 324
Barclay, Captain Robert, 385
Bareilly Infantry Tournament, 388
Barker, 2nd Lieut. V., 291
Barkly West, 240
Barnes, Private T., 102
Barnett, Private C., 102
Barnett, Private F., killed, 255
Barr, Lieut. and Quartermaster J. E. F., 224
Barrackpore, 171-2, 385
Barrett, Private J., 102
Barrow, General Sir E., 313
Barton, Major-General Sir Geoffrey, 228, 230, 233-6, 240, 243, 245-6, 248, 250, 252-6, 301
Barton, Lieut., 7th Fusiliers, 145
Barttelot, Lieut. G. F., 181, 186, 193-4, 197; Captain, 228, 234, 243-4; wounded, 245, 287, 292
Bass, Private C., 102
Bath, Private N., 102
Bathurst, Lieut. H., 69; wounded, 77, 101; Captain, 104
Battalion four company organisation, 328
Batten, Private J., 103
Battles, etc.:
Alma, 73-8
Ava Forts, 176
Borborassie, 146
Brakspruit, 281
Colenso, 230
Darbaurai, 208
Dwarsvlei, 246
Egginassai, 146
Frederikstad, 254
Hlangwani Hill, 234
Hussar Hill, 233

409

INDEX

Battles, etc. (*continued*):
   Inkerman, 83-5
   Ladysmith, Relief, 237
   Lucknow Residency, 111, 118
   Myngyan, 175
   Pekin, Relief, 267
   Redan, 94-6
   Rooidam, 240
   Seri, 207
   Simree Fort, 121
   Singboungweh, 174
   Tientsin, Relief, 259
   Tygersfontein, 244
   Yangtsun, 264
Bayly, 2nd Lieut. E. A. T., 228, 242, 244; wounded, 245; Lieut., 283, 306
Beauclerk, Captain G., 22
Beck, Lieut. C. H., dies of wounds, 95, 98, 100, 102
Becquah, 147
Bedford, Private J., 102
Beer, Quartermaster-Sergeant John, 201
Beggars Bush Barracks, Dublin, 31
Begum Kothi, 116
Beirne, J., Mayor of Wrexham, 156
Belbeck River, 79
Belem, 18
Belfast, 25, 26
Bell, Captain E. W. D., 69; captures Russian gun, and receives V.C., 75; commands 23rd, 75, 77; Brevet Major, 86, 91; Lieut.-Colonel, 105, 106, 112-4, 117, 123-6, 132, 134, 136; half-pay, 139; Brevet Colonel, 143; Major-General, death, 158, 398
Belleville, aid to Civil Power, 40
Belleville Park, 309
"Bell's Gun," 78, 198
Bells from "Incomparable Pagoda," 197
Benares, 107, 112, 168
Bengal, Enfield Rifle introduced into, 106
Bengal and Punjab Football Cup, 387
Bennet, Cuthbertson, 402
Bennet, Private J., 103
Berbice, 42
Beresford, Lieut. G. R., 79
Beresford, Lieut. W. R. H., 163, 173-4, 187-8, 191; Captain, 196
Beresford-Ash, Major, 275, 277, 279, 281; Lieut.-Colonel, commands 1st battalion, 304; half-pay, 308, 398
Bermudiana (brigantine), 45
Bernard, Lieut., 144
Bernard, B. (officer commanding), 397
Berners, Lieut. R. A., 224
Berrar, 114
Bertie, Major Hon. R. H., 223; commands 2nd battalion, 232, 261-2, 265, 268-9, 270-1, 273, 295; half-pay, 303, 398
Berwick-Copley, Brigadier-General R. C. A., 311
Best, Lieut., wounded, 255
Betagachin, 189

Bettws-y-Coed, 214
Bhamo, 180-6, 191-2, 195, 310-1
Bhamo Detachment, 183, 313-4, 318
Bhamo Polo Tournament, 388
Bhowsawal Junction, 137
Bibbings, Private, 192
Biddle, Private R., 102
Biddulph, Lieut.-Colonel G., killed, 108
Bigge, Colonel, 159
Bigge, Colonel Sir Arthur, 302, 312
Bigge, Captain T., 18, 19
Bigge, Lieut. T. S., 88; wounded, 96, 101; Captain, 113
Birkenhead, 38, 300
Birkenhead, H.M.S., 59
Birkett, Private R., killed, 237
"Black Battery," 75
Blackburn, 29
Black Mountain, 205-7, 209
Black Prince badges, adoption of, 205-6
Black River, 80
Blacktin, Lance-Corporal, 329
Blaenau Festiniog, 213-4
Blake, Private W., wounded, 197
Blakeney, Sir Edward, Colonel, 1, 5, 8; Major-General, 18, 23, 26; Lieut.-General, 31, 32, 37
Blanckley, Captain H. S., 2, 9
Blandford, 142
Blane, Ensign E. G., 98
Blauwbank, 235, 274
Blauw Krantz, 233
Blazer (transport), 46
Bligh, General, 379
Blizzard, Lieut., 215
Blockhouses, South Africa, 289
Bloemfontein, 288-9, 299
Bloy's Farm, 235
Blyth, Captain, 165; Lieut.-Colonel S. B., commands 2nd battalion, 210, 212, 214-6; half-pay, 220, 398
Boast, Private G., 204
Boh Hla-oo, 188-9, 191
Boiry Becquerelle, 1
Boiry St. Martin, 1
Boiry St. Rictrude, 1
Boisleux au Mont, 1
Boisleux St. Marc, 1
Bola Gate, 131
Bolton, 22
Bolton, Surgeon, 144
Bombay, 137-8, 163, 205
Bombay Presidency, 136
Bonner, Private, wounded, 260-1
Borborassie, 146
Bosphorus, 71
Botha, John, 294
Botha, Louis, 233, 235, 248
Bothaville, 292-3, 296-7
Botley, 27
Boucher, Captain, R.A., 109
Bouverie, Major-General Sir H., 29
Bovington Camp, Wool, 327
Box, Private T., 102
"Boxers," the, 257, 269
Boxing Championship, All India, 387
Boyelle, 1
Boyer, Private T., 102

Boyle, 12, 142
Boyle, Lieut. H. R., 144
Brackenbury, Captain Henry, 146
Bradbury, Private J., 102
Bradford, Surgeon E., 50
Brady, Sergeant W. M., wounded, 119
Braithwaite, Lieut. W. G., 212; Captain, 228; wounded, 241, 242, 251, 287
Brakspan, 282
Brakspruit, 281
Brand Drift, 298
Brandvlei, 248
Brecon, 16, 17, 20, 104, 124, 137-9, 140-1
Brelsford, Sergeant-Major (2nd Lieut. 60th Rifles), 18
Brett, Major (Paymaster), 198
Brett, A. (officer commanding), 397
"Brigade Depôt" System introduced, 155
Bright, Lieut.-General Sir R. O., 168
Bright-Smith, Captain S. B., 212, 385
Brisbane, Major-General Sir Thomas, 10
Britannia, H.M.S., 72
Brock, Messrs., illuminations at Carnarvon, 213
Brock, Captain F. T., 88
Brockville (Canada), 41
"Brodrick" Cap, 372
Bron Eifion, Criccieth, 213
Brooks, Private J., death, 148; memorial, 150, 221
Brooks, Private W., 330
Broomhall, Private, 329, 330
Brown, Captain E. M., 4
Brown, Lieut.-General Sir George, 70, 73, 76, 77, 82; wounded, 84, 85, 89, 93
Brown, Private G., 102
Brown, Private George, 324
Brown, Captain J., 26
Brown, Private J., 102
Brown, Private R., 102
Brown, Private W., 102
Brown, Private W., 103
Brown, Private Wm., 93
"Brown Bess," 374
Browne, Colonel C. H., 199; death, 201
Browne, Lieut. G. R., 79
Browne, Major-General R., 351
Bruce, Lieut., 54; Captain, 69, 98; Major, 107, 118
Brumwell, Private W., 103
Brunswick Rifle, 374
Bruxner-Randall, 2nd Lieut. J. G., 315; Lieut., 316, 317
Bryan, Private T., 103
Buckfastleigh, 386
Buckingham, Private E., 103
Buckingham Palace, 162
Buena Vista Barracks, Gibraltar, 134, 155, 157
Buffelsdoorn, 257
Buffelsdoorn Pass, 248-9
Bufflesvlei, 251, 283
Bulfin, Colonel E. S., 309, 327
Bulford Camp, 328
Bulganak River, 72, 73

INDEX

Bull, Private T., 103
Bullecourt, 1
Buller, Brigadier-General, 70
Buller, Sir Redvers, 229, 230, 233, 235, 237
Bull Point, 223
Buls Kop, 281
Bulwer, Lieut. E. G., 69; Captain, 105; Major, 119, 120-1; General Sir, 222; Colonel of Regiment, 225, 226-7, 307, 311; death, 313-4; career, 338-9
Bunbury, Major H. W., 69, 82, 84; Lieut.-Colonel, 96; commands 23rd, 97, 113
Bunnee Bridge, 119
Bunterah, 115
Bunyon, 2nd Lieut. C. S., 19
Burke, Lance-Corporal, wounded, 260
Burke, Surgeon, 68
Burke, Sergeant J., 102
Burma Commission Tournament, 388
Burmah Campaign, medals, 200
Burmah Expeditionary Force, 172
Burmah, King of, 172
Burnley, 29
Bussell, Lieut. G. W. H., wounded, 116, 119; Captain, 133
Butler, 2nd Lieut. Joseph Henry, 69, 71; killed, 74, 77, 78, 100, 102
Butterworth, Private J., 248
Buttevant Barracks, 9
Buxar Ghaut, 121

Caddell, Colonel (*History of 28th Regiment*), 404
Cadogan, Captain H. O. S., 271, 273-4; Major, 316; Lieut.-Colonel, commands 1st battalion, 324, 398
Caerynwch, 214
Cæsar's Camp, 233
Cahill, Private T., 287
Cairo, 226-7
Calais, 8
Calcutta, 106-7, 112, 169, 170, 172-3, 196-7, 299, 308, 385
Caldas, 18
Callan, 30
Callan, Private Thomas, 91
Callis, Corporal, 327
Cal Tolpes, 213
Cambrai, 3, 5, 7, 8
Cambridge, Duke of, 3, 99, 123, 150, 158; funeral, 304
Cambridge Barracks, Woolwich, 157
Camden Fort, 153
Cameron, Major-General Sir John, 22
Campbell, Lieut.-Colonel, 90th Regiment, 92
Campbell, Major-General Sir Colin, 32; Lieut.-General, 33, 34, 76; General, 107-8, 111-2, 114-7, 121
Campbell, Captain W. M., 2, 9
Campbell, Major-General W. Pitcairn, 315
Campbell, Captain W. P., 45, 47, 65,
69; wounded, 77; Brevet Major, 86; death, 91, 100, 102
Canada, 2nd battalion embarks for, 136
Canadian Eagle (transport), 35
Candia, 224-7, 387
Canea, 224-5
Canrobert, General, 71
Cantin, 8
Cap, bearskin, 346, 350, 356-8
Cape Breton, 50
Cape Coast Castle, 144-5, 148
Cape Colony, 238
Cape of Good Hope, 106
Cape Town, 229, 240, 243, 297-9
Capper, Brigadier-General T., 324-5
Cappoquin, 309
Capron, Lieut., 33
Cardiff, 104, 124, 137-8, 324
Carey, Ensign Annesley, 104
Carey, Lieut. O. de B., 161, 163, 165
Cargill, Lieut., R.E., 273
Carless, Private, 192
Carlisle, 40
Carlisle Barracks, 38
Carlisle Bay, Barbadoes, 42
Carlisle Fort, 153
Carlow, 26, 29
Carlyle, Mr. W., 328
Carmarthen, 88; Crimean monument, 101
Carmarthen St. Peter's Church, Old Colours lodged at, 56, 394
Carnarvon, 88, 123, 212, 214, 317
Carnarvon Castle, 213, 317
Carnegie, Lieut., 68
Carnegy, Lieut., 12th Madras Infantry, wounded, 188
Carr, Colonel, Royal Scots Fusiliers, 248-9
Carr, Sergeant Jabez, wounded, 119
Carr, Private W., 103
Carrick Island, 10
Carrick-on-Suir, 30
Carrington-Smith, Major, Roberts' Horse, 280
Carroll, Major-General Sir W. P., 33
Cartwright, Private, wounded, 260
Casemate Barracks, Gibraltar, 154-5
Casey, Sergeant T., 103
Cashel, 27, 28
Cashmere, 210
Castlebar, 33, 34, 37, 200
Castle Comer, 30
Castle Square, Carnarvon, 212
Castletown, Isle of Man, 65
Catalan Bay, 154
Cathcart (steamer), 60, 61
Cathcart, Earl, 64
Cawley, Sergeant, 298
Cawnpore, 107, 111-2, 114, 168, 388
Cawnpore Cup (Polo), 387
Cefnmawr, 216
Chadwick, Corporal, 77
Chadwick, Private James, 91
Chaka Khoti, 115, 117
Chakrata, N.W.P., 163, 166-9, 303-5, 385
Chalkley, Private R., 103
Chamberlain, Colour-Sergeant Daniel, 93
Chamberlain, 2nd Lieut. Sir Henry, 60
Chambley, Canada East, 48, 52
Chance, 2nd Lieut. G. O. de P., 324; Lieut., 328-9
Chang-chi-wan, 266
Chapman, Lieut. A. S., 163
Chatham, 113, 123, 125, 131, 140-1, 345
Chelsea Hospital Fund, 342
Chelsea Royal Hospital, Eagles at, 4, 329
Cheltenham, 34
Cherat, 210
Chermside, Colonel Sir Herbert, 224, 226
Chester, 29, 37, 38, 64, 65; Crimean memorial in St. Mary's Church, 103, 317
Chester, Captain H. G., 59; Major, 66; Lieut.-Colonel, 68; commands 23rd, 69; killed, 74, 77, 78, 100, 102, 397
Chichester, 40, 41, 306
Chieveley, 229, 231, 233, 235
China, 23rd leave England for, 105
Chingtu (steamship), 295
Chipping Camp, 220
Chobham Park, 67
Choung Dank, 185
Chowbepore, 112
Christiania, 242
Churchill, Private H., 102
Cingolo, 234
Citadel, Cairo, 226
Citadel, Plymouth, 59, 164, 165
Citadel Barracks, Dover, 4
Clack, Private M., 102
Clancy, Bandmaster W. J., 331
Claney, Private, 330
Clarence Barracks, Portsmouth, 68
Clark, Private M., 287
Clarke, Private, wounded, 237
Clarke, Private G., 102
Clarke, Private H., 103
Clarke, Private M., 102
Clarke, Private M., 102
Clayhills, Lieut. A., 4
Clayton, Corporal W., 103
Clayton & Bell, Messrs., 220
Cleeve, Lieut. and Quartermaster J. F., 262, 269, 271, 273
Clegg-Hill, Lieut. Hon. C. R., 229, 276-7, 287; Captain, 316
Cleland, John, 157
Clements, Major-General R. A. P., 248
Cleopatra (steamship), 105-6
Clerke, Lieut. W. C., 88
Clery, Major-General Sir Francis, 229
Clinton, Lieut.-General Sir Henry, 17
Clitheroe, Major-General, 38
Clonmel, 26, 27
Clough, Lieut., 144
Clough-Taylor, Lieut., 150
Clough-Taylor, Major E. H., 222
Clyde, Lord (*see* Campbell, Sir Colin)
Clyde Road, Dublin, 316
Coal Hill, Pekin, 269
Coal Mine Drift, 292-3, 297
Cockburn, Captain J. B., 277, 386

INDEX

Cocked Hat for Full Dress abolished, 352
Cockell, Captain, 23, 32, 33
Codrington, Major-General Sir W. J., 71, 74, 77, 82, 84, 85, 89, 94, 96; Lieut.-General, Colonel of 23rd, 130, 159; Colonel of Coldstream Guards, 151, 153; career, 336-7
Coed Helen, 317
Coimbra, 18
Coke, Major-General, 234
Colaba Barracks, Bombay, 137
Cole, Lieut. A. W. G. L., 173, 182-3, 186, 196, 198
Coleby, Sergeant William, 84
Coleman, Colour-Sergeant H., 201-2, 204
Coleman, Lance-Corporal J. G., killed, 187, 197
Colenso, 229, 233, 235
Colenso kopjes, 230, 235
College of Science, Dublin, opening of Royal, 316
Colleton, Lieut. Sir R. A. W., 162-3; Captain, 201-2, 207; Major, 218; Lieut.-Colonel, commands 1st battalion, 243, 246, 248-9, 250-2, 255, 275-9, 280-1, 283, 291-2, 297, 300-2; relinquishes command of 1st battalion, 304; Brigadier-General, 331, 398
Colleton's Column, 257-74
Collins, Drummer J., 102
Collins, Private M., 202, 204
Colonel Fytche (steamship), 182
Colours, the, 391-6
Colour-Sergeant, rank introduced, 351
Combermere, Field-Marshal Lord, 14
Commando Drift, 297
Commerce (steamer), run down by *Despatch*, 60-3; memorial service, 63-4
Commin, Private T., 148
Companies, "Grenadier" and "Light Infantry" abolished, 122
Companies, distinguished by letters instead of numbers, 122, 135
Companies, 1st battalion lettered W, X, Y, Z, 306
Companies, changed from eight to four per battalion, 328
Connaught, H.R.H. Duke of, 385
Connaught Shield, 305
Conolly, Captain John Charles, 69; killed, 74, 77, 78, 100, 102
Conroy, Private T., 102
Constable, Private C., 102
Constantinople, 86
Cook, Private, 265
Cook, Colonel J., 207
Cookson, Colonel, 281
Coolmorey Camp, 324
Coomassie, 147
Cooper, Captain A. F., 218
Cork, 8, 9, 15, 23, 26, 28, 32, 144, 153, 307-9, 310-12, 387
Cornwall, Canada, 41
Cornwallis West, Colonel, 215
Coronation, King Edward VII, 298

Coronation Durbar, 320
Coronation Durbar Polo Tournament, 320
Corris, Merioneth, 170
Corwen, 215
Cottonera district, 132
Cottrell, Sergeant, 286
Cottrill, Quartermaster-Sergeant, 316
Country Life Tournament, Quetta, 388
Courage, 2nd Lieut., 328
Courts Martial sentences, severity of, 15
Cowan, Lieut., 144
Cowan, Lieut. W. F. J., 158
Cowes, 46, 68
Cox, Brigadier-General, 192, 194, 196
Cox, Private, 154-5
Cox, Private G., killed, 237
Coyle, Sergeant Michael, wounded, 93
Craddock, Captain, 258
Craven, Rev. C. A. A., 161
Crawford, Lieut.-Colonel, R.A., 109
Crawley, Private H., dies of wounds, 197
Crawshay, Lieut. C. H. R., 317
Creek, Lieut.-Colonel E. S., 191, 193-6; commands 1st battalion, 198; to 2nd battalion, 203, 205; half-pay, 210, 213-4, 227, 385, 398
"Cremer's" Sketches, 352
Cretan Football Tournament, 387
Crete, 223-7, 232, 332, 388
Crew, Private, killed, 260-1
Crew, Private W., 295
Criccieth, 213
Crick, 139
Crimea, 71; first British troops to land, 72
Crimean War Memorials, Alma monument, 78; monument at Carmarthen, 101-3; original Alma tombstone at Wrexham, 198-9; re-erected in Memorial Chapel, 199, 221
Crocodile, H.M.S., 138
Crocodile River, 246
Crofts, Captain E., 88, 98
Croisilles, 1
Crosbie, Captain Sir William, 12, 15
Crosby, Lieut. J. D., 212
Cross, The, Carnarvon, 212
Crotch, Dr., 378
Cruize, Private W., 102
Crutcher, Private W., 102
Crutchley, Captain Charles, 32, 35, 40; Major, commands Depôt, 47, 52; Lieut.-Colonel, commands Reserve battalion, 59; commands 1st battalion, 65, 66, 67; commands regiment, 68; retires, 68; Lieut.-General, Colonel of 23rd, 151; General, 222; death, 225, 226; career, 337-8, 397
Cunningham, General, 275-6
Curragh, 143, 205, 211, 310, 312, 324
Curran, Private M., 102
Cush, Sergeant P., 201-2, 204

Custodian, the, 313
"Custom House Records," Dublin, 379

"Dacoits," 178
D'Aguilar, Major-General George Charles, Colonel of the 23rd, 64; death, 92; career, 334-6
Dalhousie, H.M.S., 195
Dalmer, Lieut.-Colonel F., 9, 10, 15
Dalmer, Lieut.-Colonel Thomas, half-pay, 5, 397
Danubian Principalities, 70
Darband, 206-7, 209
Darbaurai, 208-9
Darjeeling, 171
Dartmoor, 143
Davey, Private F., dies of wounds, 197
Davidson, Trooper, Brabant's Horse, 257
Davies, Lieut.-General, 218
Davies, Mr., Mayor of Carnarvon, 213
Davies, Private, 286
Davies, Private F., 102
Davies, Private G., wounded, 197
Davies, Private J., killed, 241
Davies, R., H.M. Lieut. for Anglesey, 211
Davies, Valentine, Esq., Mayor of Carmarthen, 57
Davies, Private W., 102
Davies, Private W., wounded, 197
Dawson, Corporal James, 81, 86, 91
Deakins, Lieut., 24
Deal, 4, 8, 131
Deane, Sergeant, wounded, 260
Deelkraal, 249
Defence (transport), 8, 9
Dehra Dun, 304
De Klipdrift, 242
Delamere Forest, 304
De la Rey, General, 247-8, 275-6
Delhi, 106, 114, 299, 319, 388
Delhi Infantry Tournament, 388
Delmé-Radcliffe, Lieut. F. P. R., 69; killed, 77, 78, 100, 102
Delmé-Radcliffe, Lieut. H., 195; Captain, 228; wounded, 253, 255, 279, 287-8, 296; Lieut.-Colonel, commanding 2nd battalion, 319, 322, 398
Demerara, 42-4
de Moleyns, Lieut. Hon. D., 144
Denain, 3
Denbigh, 215
Deolali, 163
Deptford, 38
Despatch (steamer) runs down *Commerce*, 60-3
Devna, 71
Devon and Cornwall Association Cup, 386
Devon and Cornwall League Cup, 386
Devonport, 138, 140, 223, 225-7
De Wet, 244-5, 248, 252-4, 297
Diamond Jubilee, Queen Victoria, 225
Dickens, Lieut., 68
Dickens, Charles, visits Montreal and takes part in theatricals, 38-9

INDEX

Dickson, Lieut. G. F. H., 224, 228, 237, 241; Captain, 242-3
Diepfontein, 296, 298
Dilkusha, 125
Dilkusha Palace, Lucknow, 115
Dilwara (steamship), 223
Dinapore, 168-9, 385
Dix, Private M., 103
Dobell, Lieut. C. M., 223-4; Major, 232, 243, 269, 271, 273-4, 287, 295; Brevet Colonel, 312, 315, 318; commands 2nd battalion Bedfordshire Regiment, 323
Dobson, Private G., 102
"Dockyard Ravine," 92
Dodd, Private W., killed, 241
Dolgelly, 213, 215
Dolwyddelan, 214
Dominica, 44, 49
Don, General Sir George, 15, 16, 19, 20, 22
Donald, Lieut.-Colonel, Royal Fusiliers, 238
Dongola (transport), 330-1
Donovan, Private J., 102
Dood's Drift, 293, 296
Doodson, Private, 261, 295
Doolystown Camp, 324
Dooner, Lieut. A. G. C. T., 328
Doornfontein, 281-2
Doornhoek, 277, 296
Doornkuil, 282
Dorchester, 325, 327, 332
Dorset Senior Cup, 326
Dorward, Brigadier-General, 262
Doughty, Lieut. C. H. M., wounded, 208; Captain, 224, 243, 273, 295
Douglas, Brigadier-General, 114, 118
Douglas, Major-General Sir J., 27, 30
Doundeakeara, 121
Dover, 4, 8, 131
Dover Heights Barracks, 8
Dowlat Khana, 118
Downer, Private G., 102
Doznin, Private, 154-5
Draper, Private S., 102
Drewe, Lieut. F. E., 69; Captain, 90, 91, 93; wounded, 95, 101; Major, 113
Drogheda, 22, 23
Dronfield Camp, 240
"Drum-Major," title becomes "Sergeant-Drummer," 167, 379
Drury, Lieut. J., 5
Dublin, 11, 13, 14, 23, 24, 29, 31, 32, 34, 154-5, 312, 315-9, 323-5, 341-2, 387
Dudley, 9
Duff, 2nd Lieut. J., 69; Lieut. 71, 82; prisoner, 84; Captain, 113, 118
Dufferin, Earl of, 170, 182
Dufferin, R.I.M.S., 318
Duglord, Private G., 248, 286
Dum Dum, 168-9, 170, 172-3, 194, 385
Duncan Carter, Major, R.F.A., 246
Dunkley, Sergeant Richard, 84, 103
Dunn, Lieut. G., 5, 34
Dunn, Lieut. R. H. W., 162-3, 173;

Captain, 196, 198, 203, 222, 385
Du Preez Drift, 275
Durand Football Cup, 387
Durban, 229, 240, 298
D'Urban, Sir Benjamin, 59
Durbar, the, 299, 319-22
Durkin, Private J., killed, 97, 103
du Toit, General, 240
Dwarsvlei, 246
Dwyer, Private E., 102
Dyneley, 2nd Lieut. D., 69; Lieut., dies of wounds, 95, 97, 100, 102
Dynevor, Lord, 97

Eagles of French Regiments, 4
"Eating the Leak," 159
Earl Roden (steamer), 29
Earl's Court, Army Pageant at, 312
Eastham, 37
East India Company, 114
East London, 228
Eaton, 216
Eaton Hall, 302
Edinburgh, Duke of, 145, 160, 163
Edmonds, Sergeant F., 102
Edward VII, H.M. King, 305; death, 311, 313
Edwards, Major (Mayor of Denbigh), 215
Edwards, Private, 330
Edwards, Lieut. C. A., 181; wounded, 192, 194-5
Edwards, 2nd Lieut. de Burgh, 286, 288
Edwards, Sir Fleetwood, 210
Edwards, Sir Francis (officer commanding), 397
Edwards, Private G., 103
Edwards, Sergeant J., 93
Edwards, Private J., killed, 255
Egerton, Colonel, 89, 91
Egerton, Major-General, 11
"Egerton's Rifle Pits," 91
Egginassie, 146-7
Egypt, 332
Eisteddfod Pavilion, Carnarvon, 213
Eitel Fritz, of Prussia, 305
Elema Gate, 131
Elgee, Lieut.-Colonel C., 137, 140-1; commands Depôt, 155-6; Brevet Colonel, commands 1st battalion, 159, 160-1, 163, 168-9; half-pay, 171, 398
Elgin, Lord, 58
Elles, Major-General W. K., 205-7
Elley, Sir John, 12
Elliott, Lieut., 17
Ellis, 2nd Lieut., 238
Ellis, Lieut. E. T., 15, 18
Ellis, Colonel Sir Henry W., 2, 33
Ellis, H. W., officer commanding 1st battalion, 397
Ellis, J. J. (officer commanding), 397
Ellis, Major R. G. G., 215
Ellison, C. (officer commanding), 397
Elmina, 143
Elms, Private H., 103
Elphick, Colour-Sergeant R., 148
Elton, Lieut.-Colonel, 378
Emerald Isle (transport), 32

Enfield rifle, 375
England, Major, 15
England and France, defensive alliance, 70
Engleheart, Captain E. L., 212
Ennis, 10
Enniskillen, 155-7
Enoch, Captain John, 34
"Ensign," rank substituted for "2nd Lieut.," 70, 361; "Sublieut." substituted for, 141, 366
Erie, Lake, 60
Erin (transport), 29
Escont St. Mein, 1
Estcourt, 229
Euphrates, H.M.S., 143
Euphrates (troopship), 54
Europa, 134-5
Europa Flats, 151
Eustace, Private J., 103
Evans, Private, wounded, 260
Evans, Sergeant, 192
Evans, Lieut.-General Sir De Lacy, 77
Evans, Private E., killed, 237
Evans, Lieut. E. R., 150, 161, 163; Major, 192, 195, 200; death, 209, 221
Evans, Captain Francis Edward, 50, 51, 52, 67, 69; killed, 77, 78, 100, 102
Evans, Private G., 102
Evans, Colour-Sergeant J., 201
Evans, Corporal J., killed, 237
Evans, Private J., 102
Evans, 2nd Lieut. J. M. J., 328
Evans, Private T., 103
Evans, Private T., 287
Evans, Private W., killed, 255
Evans, Private William, 75
Eveleigh, Colonel, 20th Regiment, 120-1
Everitt, Captain S. G., 224; Major, 273, 295
Ewart, Lieut.-Colonel, 110

Faegarrid, 309
Fame, H.M.S., 258
Fanny (transport), 15
Fantis, 144-5
Fareham, 27
Fatehgarh, 112, 114
Fatehpur, 107, 111
Fayal, 136
Featherweight Competition, Malta, 330
Fenwick, Major, Madras Pioneers, 182
Ferguson, Lieut., 42
Fermoy, 15, 26, 28, 181, 194, 199, 200
Fielding, Major-General, death, 22
Fielding, Private B., 102
Fiennes, Lieut. Hon. N., 98
"Fifteen Acres," Phœnix Park, 315-6, 323
Firman, Captain R. B., 196, 218
Firozabad, 114
Fisher, Sergeant, 284
FitzClarence, Major-General Lord F., 53, 54
Fitzgerald, Lieut.-Colonel, 26th Punjab Infantry, 186
FitzGibbon, Lieut. G., 5

INDEX

"Five Gun Battery," 82-4
Flaherty, Corporal J., wounded, 188, 197
Flash, the, 28, 245, 360, 373, 399-406
Fleetwood, 219
Fletcher, Rev. Canon, 222
Florentia (freightship), 49
Flower, Lieut. O. S., 224, 258, 260-3, 269, 271, 273
Foley, Private J., killed, 255
Foley, Private W., 103
Fontenoy, 315
Foord, Brigadier-General, 176
Ford, Gunner John, 109
Fort Cumberland, Portsmouth, 28, 68, 88
Fort Hubberstone, Milford Haven, 140-1
Fort Monckton, Gosport, 27, 105, 113
Fort Ricasoli, Malta, 125
Fort Tregantle, 223
Fort William, Calcutta, 106
Fort William Henry (or Sorel), 48
Fortune, Quartermaster-Sergeant Robert, appointed Quartermaster, 49, 68
Fou Chou, 388
Fourteen Streams, 241-2
Fowles, Private W., 102
Fox, Private C., 102
Fox, Lieut. L. D. A., 316
France, evacuation by British troops, 7
France and England, defensive alliance, 70
France and Prussia, war declared 1870, 140
France-Hayhurst, 2nd Lieut. F. C., 224
Frankhum, Private J., 102
Frederikstad, 249, 250, 252, 255, 283, 288
Freeman Murray, Major-General, 140
French 26th Regiment, Regimental Eagle, 4
French 82nd Regiment, Battalion Eagles, 4
French, General Sir John, 275, 305
Frere, 229
Frere, 2nd Lieut., 292
Fry, Private I., 102
Fry, Private J., 102
Fuller, Lieut., Oxfordshire and Buckinghamshire Light Infantry, 296
Futtiah, 112, 113
Fyzabad, 131, 386

Gabbett, Lieut. R. E. P., 212; Captain, 246; wounded, 247, 248, 298-9; Major, 304, 316-7
Gallagher, Private V., 103
Gallipoli, 69
Galway, 199, 202
Ganges, the, 111
Gardiner, Private J., 102
Garnett, 2nd Lieut. W. B., 294; Lieut., 311; Captain, 317
Gascoigne, Major-General, 271-2
Gaselee, General Sir A., 262, 295
Gatacre, Major-General Sir W., 228

Gatsrand, the, 248-9, 253, 288
Gauntlets worn by Pioneers of Royal Welch Fusiliers, 195
Geduld, 277, 282
Geiger, 2nd Lieut. G. J. P., 224; Lieut., 273; Captain, 331, 332
General Palmer (transport), 43
George IV, H.M. King, 16
George V, H.M. King, 311, 313; Coronation, 316
George Island, 32
George's Street Barracks, Dublin, 31
Gerard, Captain F., 135
Ghazikot, 207
Gibbs, Corporal R., 103
Gibraltar, 14, 15, 17, 19, 24, 26, 69, 133-5, 151, 153-4, 158-9, 160, 164
Gilbert, Lieut., 144, 146
Giles, Private T., 102
Gillogly, Colour-Sergeant J., 102
Glazebrook, Sergeant, 273
Gledstanes, Lieut. A., 5
Glegg, Mr. Harry, 212
Gleig, Rev. George, Chaplain-General, 54
Glengarry Cap, 366, 368
Glynn, Captain R. M. O., 228, 231; Major, 274
Goat brought from South Africa and presented to King Edward VII, 300
Goats, presentation to the Royal Herd of three Kashmir, 209, 210
Goddard, Private H., 102
Godden, Private, 86
Godfrey, Private A., dies of wounds, 208
Godfrey, Private J., killed, 251
Goff, Private J., 103
Gogra River, 122
Gold Coast, 143
Gomba Stream, 234
Gomba Valley, 233
Goodwin, Private A., wounded, 147
Goorsai Gunge, 114
Goorsaingunge, 119, 120
Gordon, Captain, R.E., 81
Gordon, General, 274
Gordon, Lieut.-Colonel, 122
Gordon, Major-General B., 110
Gordon, Major-General Sir James Willoughby, Colonel of 23rd, 12, 17, 50; deceased, 64; career, 333-4, 404
Gore, Major-General Hon. Charles, 52, 53, 65
Gort, 200
Gosport, 19, 27, 99
Gough, Lieut. A. P. G., 173, 186-7, 190-1, 196; Captain, 228, 238, 240, 242; Major, 243; wounded, 244, 245, 287
Gough, Lieut.-General Sir C., 202-3
Gould, Private S., dies of wounds, 197
Gould Weston, Captain, 117
Gourlay, 2nd Lieut. W., 5; Lieut., 18
Graham, Sergeant J. W., killed, 241
Grain, Isle of, 141
Grand Hotel, Llangollen, 215

Grant, Major-General Sir Colquhoun, 13
Grant, Sergeant-Major C., appointed Quartermaster, 45
Grantham, Assistant Surgeon, 60
Grant Smith, Mr. H., Shanghai Volunteer Corps, 263, 271
Grant Smith, Mr. John, 271
Granville, Lieut., 24; Captain, 45; relinquishes command of Depôt, 47, 98; Major, 125
Granville, 2nd Lieut. B., 69, 75
Graves, Lieut., 144, 146; Captain, 155
Gravesend, 140
Gray, Quartermaster W., 173, 198, 203
Great Imambara, 117
"Great Redoubt," Alma, 74
Great War, the, 1914-18, 331-2
Greaves, Mr., 212-3
Greaves, Private, 261
Greece, Cretan insurgents proclaim union with, 223
Green, Private John, 95, 97
Green Hill, 233-4
"Green Hill Battery," 80, 91
Gregorie, Ensign, 98
Gregory, Mr. F., 222
Gregory, Colour-Sergeant W., 287
Grenada, 44, 45, 48, 49
Grenadier Companies abolished, 122
Grenville, General Sir Richard, death, 12, 352
Grey, Earl, 45
Griffith, Major H. W., commands 1st battalion, 220; Lieut.-Colonel, 222, 398
Griffith, Private J., 202, 204
Griffith, Lieut. J. H. K., 163; Captain 4th Royal Welch Fusiliers, 212, 214; Major, 224
Griffiths, Lieut., 98, 144, 291
Griffiths, Brigadier-General R., 186
Griffiths, Captain Wynne, 212
Griffiths, Lieut. W. A., 22
Grobelaar Mountain, 236
Groom, Private J., 102
Guadeloupe, 4
Gubbins, Major, 123, 125
Guernsey, 17, 46
Guerrilla tactics of the Boers, 288
Gumti River, 115-7, 119, 120
Gun Club Hill, Kowloon, 232
Gun Hill, 252-4
Gwalior Contingent, 112
Gwynne, Lieut. J. H., 173, 187; wounded, 188, 191, 196; Captain, 224, 258-9, 261-2, 265, 268, 271, 273; Brevet Major, 295
Gwynne, Captain R., 194
Gwyther, Lieut., 273

Hackett, Ensign J. B., 98
Hackett, Lieut. T. B., awarded V.C., 109; Major, 141, 144
Hadden, Captain L. J. W., 163; Major, 168, 173, 186, 194, 196
Haifordunas Park (Llangerniew), 214
Haig, Captain A., 316
Hale, Lieut.-Colonel, 82nd Foot, 108-10

INDEX

Halifax, Nova Scotia, 32–5, 37, 50, 52
Halifax Morning Herald, extract from, 35
Hall, Private H., 102
Hall, J. (officer commanding), 397
Hall, Private J., 102
Hall, Dr. John, 92
Hall, Major-General Julian, 212, 216
Hall, Private T., 102
Hall Dare, Paymaster H., 69; wounded, 95, 98, 101
Hamelincourt, 1, 3, 4
Hamilton, 66
Hamilton, Major-General Sir Bruce, 306
Hamilton West, 65
Hammond, Sergeant-Major A. E., 198, 204
Hammond, Brigadier-General A. G., 206–8
Hanbury, Captain B. K., 224
Handrahan, Private J., 102
Hanmer, Corporal, wounded, 261
Hanny, Private J., 103
Hardinge, R.I.M.S., 314
Hare, Major, 280
Harlech Castle, 213
Harrington, Lieut., R.A., 109
Harrington, Purveyor's Clerk, 77
Harrington, Private J., 102
Harris, Lieut., 231, 234, 237, 243, 288
Harris, Private G., 103
Harris, Private J., 102
Harris, Private Thomas, 95
Harris, Lieut. W., 297
Harris St. John, Lieut., 297
Harrison, Captain J. C., 9, 12; Major, 17, 18; commands Depôt, 19; to Lieut.-Colonelcy of Regiment, 21, 24, 26, 27, 29; relinquishes command, 30–1, 397, 404
Hart, Major-General Fitzroy, 228–9, 235–6
Hartebeestfontein, 277, 281, 292
Hartebeestfontein Hills, 281
Hart's Hill, 236–7
Harvey, Captain, 51
Harvey, Lieut.-General Sir John, 50, 52
Harvey, Private T., 102
Hasanzai Expedition, 206–9
Hastings, Brigadier-General E. S., 309; Major-General, 314
Hatton, 2nd Lieut. G. F., 304
Haulbowline Island, 153
Hawarden Castle, 240
Hay, Lieut. A., 212, 223, 262; Captain, 269, 271, 273, 284; wounded, 286, 292, 298, 317; Major, 330, 331
Hayes, Private P., 102
Haynes, Private L., 103
Hazara Field Force, 207–9
Hazara Campaign Medals, 217
Hedge Hill, 236
Hedges, Private H., 103
Heigham, Captain G., 98, 119, 121; Brevet Major, death, 131
Hekpoort, 247
Hekpoort Valley, 247–8, 274
Helbert, Lieut. F. de C. Helbert, 194, 196

Hemmington, C. (officer commanding), 397
Henderson, Lieut. J. J., wounded, 108, 111, 125
Henin, 1
"Hen Wlad fy Nhadau," 331
Herbert, Brigadier-General, 143
Herbert, Major A. J., 88, 92, 93; Lieut.-Colonel, 113; Brigadier-General, 143
Hercules (transport), 32
Hereford, 9
Herefordshire (freightship), 50
Hetherington, Private J., 103
Heyworth Savage, Major, R.F., 243
Hickman, Colonel, 288
Hickman, Sergeant-Major, 224, 262, 269, 274
Hickman, W. (officer commanding), 397
Hicks, Colonel, 254
Higgon, Lieut. J. A., 224
Hildyard, General, 229, 235, 238
Hill, Captain, 321
Hill, Lieut.-Colonel, 11
Hill, Lord, 355–6
Hill, 2nd Lieut. H., 224; Lieut., 243
Hill, Lance-Sergeant W., 287
Hillen, Private P., 102
Himalaya, H.M.S., 137, 153
Himalayas, 168
Hine, Private H., 102
Hitchcock, Colour-Sergeant R., 102
Hlangwane, 230–1, 233–5
Hobbs, Private G., 102
Hokat, 184
Holden, Lieut. E. S., dies of wounds, 96, 98, 100, 102
Holland, Sergeant James, wounded, 116, 119
Hollister, Private R., 103
Holloway, Quartermaster-Sergeant, 273
Holmes, Captain R. P., 19; Major, commands Depôt, 22, 23, 26, 29, 32, 34, 37, 38, 40, 41, 48; Lieut.-Colonel, 49; death, 59, 397
Holmes, Private W., 103
Holroyd, Captain T. S., 138; Colonel, 227
Holyhead, 212, 317
Home, Lieut.-Colonel, 5th Bengal Light Infantry, 192
Hong-Kong, 227, 232, 243, 259, 261, 270–1, 273, 299, 332, 388
Hong-Kong Derby, 388
Hoopstadt, 297
Hope (transport), 19
Hope, Major-General Sir J. A., 40, 52
Hope Grant, Brigadier-General, 111
Hopton, Lieut. C. E., 52; Captain, 69, 71; wounded, 77, 101
Horne, Private R., 102
Horner, Private J., wounded, 231
Horning Spruit, 245
Horse Shoe Hill, 236
Horsford, Colonel, 114
Horsford, Lieut. F., death, 98, 100
Ho-Shi-Wo, 265
Hoskyns, Lieut. E. C. L., 328–9
Hotchkiss, Sergeant S., 287

Houghton, Private, 154–5
Houstoun, Lieut.-General Sir William, 22, 25–7
Howell, Lieut., R.F.A., 279
Howrah Station, Calcutta, 169
Htantabin, 190–1
Htigyaing, 182, 194–5
Huban, Private H., 102
Hudson, Private W., 102
Huffy, Sergeant W., 287
Hughes, Lieut. G. H., 69; Captain, death, 86, 100, 103
Hughes, Lance-Corporal John, 319
Hughes, 2nd Lieut. W. J. H., 228, 245, 283, 285
Hunt, Lieut., 275
Hunter, Major-General Sir Archibald, 238, 240, 242, 245, 309
Hurt, 2nd Lieut. F. C. A., 228
Hussar Hill, 233–5
Hutchinson, Captain A. R., 163
Hutchison, Captain, 144, 148
Hutton, Lieut. G. H., 144, 146; wounded, 147, 148
Hutton, Captain H. F., 144, 146; Brevet Major, 148

"Ich Dien," 345, 392
Iggulden, Lieut.-Colonel H. A., commands 1st battalion, 308, 315–7; half-pay, 324, 398
Illustrated London News, 89
Imogen (transport), 45
Imperatrix, 88
Imperial Carriage Park, Pekin, 268
"Incomparable Pagoda," 182, 197
India, 332
India, Northern, 105
Indian Trader (transport), 15
Indus, the, 205–8
Indus Valley, 206–7
Inglis, Brigadier, 112
Inkerman, 82
Innes, Private, wounded, 260
Inquabim, 146
Iola MSS., regarding Welsh achievements under Black Prince at Crécy, 205
Irish Army Boxing Cup, 387
Irish Army Football Cup, 323, 387
Irish Record Office, Dublin, 342
"Iron Bridge," Colenso, 229
Irrawaddy, H.M.I.M.S., 175, 308
Irrawaddy River, 173, 176, 184, 187, 189, 308
Isle of Man, 64, 65
Isle of Wight, 4, 15, 47
Ivybridge, 386

Jackalsfontein, 282, 293
Jackson, Colonel, 195
Jackson, Colour-Sergeant, 332
Jackson, Sir Richard, 39
Jackson, Private T., 264, 295
James, Lance-Corporal, 251
James, Mr. R., 214
Java (transport), 43, 52, 59
Jebbe, Ensign F. W., 88
Jellahabad, 114
Jelly, Private W., 102
Jelunga (transport), 226

INDEX

Jenkin, Assistant Surgeon E. A., 69; death, 71, 100, 103
Jenkins, Corporal T., 287
Jephcote, Private W., killed, 237
Jervis, Lieut. L. de R., 173, 185, 197
Jervoise, Lieut., 68; Captain, 98
Jhansi, 218-9, 220, 222-3, 386
Johannesburg, 243
John, Private D., 102
John, Lieut. G. T., 69, 82
John VI of Portugal, 16
Johnson, Captain, 3rd Punjab Cavalry, 261, 263
Johnson, Lieut., R.E., 292, 296
Johnson, Captain H. C., 9
Johnson, 2nd Lieut. R. B., 224; Lieut., 262, 269, 271; Captain, 319
Johnson, Private W., 102
Johnston, Lieut. W. A., 144; death, 148, 150, 221
Jones, Colonel, 6th Dragoon Guards, 122
Jones, Colour-Sergeant, wounded, 264
Jones, Sergeant, 319
Jones, Lieut. Atherley, 238, 255
Jones, Private David, wounded, 231
Jones, E. (officer commanding), 397
Jones, Private E., 102
Jones, Private E., 102
Jones, Colour-Sergeant F., 332
Jones, Sergeant-Major H., 102
Jones, Corporal J., 102
Jones, Private J., 102
Jones, Private J., killed, 251
Jones, Mrs. Jennie, 170
Jones, Corporal J. K., 319
Jones, Private J. M., 102
Jones, Private R., killed, 255
Jones, Private T. H., 103
Jones, Colour-Sergeant W., 287
Jones, Private W., 102
Jones, Lieut. W. G., 306
Jones, Colour-Sergeant W. W., 201-2, 204
Jonkers Kraal, 293
Jordon, Jeremiah, 157
Joseph Swan (transport), 15
Joyce, Private R., killed, 237
Jubbulpore, 135-6, 163, 166
Jubrowlee, 120
Junction Post, 297
Jupiter (troopship), 32

Kaalfontein, 284-5
Kaal Spruit, 278
Kachin Hills, 185-6
Kadu, 188
Kaffir Drift, 292
Kaffirs Kraal, 277
Kaiser Bagh, 110, 116, 117, 119
Kakrail, 115
Kalafat, 70
Kali Nadi, 114
Kalkspruit, 242
Kalsi, 168
Kamichla Lake, 71
Kamiesh, 99
Kanar, 207
Karachi, 318, 331
Karagoli, 71
Kasr-el-Nil Barracks, Cairo, 226

Katcha River, 79
Katha, 186, 191-3, 195, 198, 221
Katha Detachment, 191
Kathleen (steam launch), 174
Keen, 2nd Lieut. W., 218
Keene, Captain, 238, 255
Keightley, Lieut.-Colonel, 11
Kekewich, Colonel, 275
Kekewich Column, 257
Kellen, Private Thomas, 91
Kellock, Corporal, wounded, 260
Kells, 142
Kelly, Colour-Sergeant, 266
Kelly, Private, 324, 330
Kelly, Corporal J., 102
Kemish, Private G., 102
Kempt, Major-General Sir James, 4-8
Kennedy, Private Thomas, 95, 97
Kenny, Private, wounded, 261
Kent, Duke of, 3
Kerr, Lieut.-Colonel, R.E., 141
Kerr, Sergeant J., 102
Kerr, Lieut. Walter F., 4
Keys, Commander, 258
Khysabad, 205
Kiang Boassu, 146
Kilbride Camp, 323-4
Kildimo, 10
Kilkenny, 29, 31
Kill, 324
Killaloe, 11
Killarney, 170
Kilroy, Private J., 102
Kilworth Camp, 308-9, 310, 312
Kimberley, 240, 242, 298
King, Private, wounded, 260
King, Lieut. A. C., 173-4, 178, 186, 190-1, 195-6
King, Colour-Sergeant W. G., 241-2, 247-8, 287, 301
King of Prussia, 5
King's Corporals, 286
Kingscourt, 22, 23
Kingston, Canada West, 40-3
Kingston, Lieut. W. M., 228
Kingstown, 37, 142, 157
Kington, Lieut. W. M., 245, 252, 287-8, 293; Captain, 323
Kinnoo, 189
Kin-Wun Min Gye, 194
Kirby, Private, 154-5
Kitchener, Lord, 277, 286, 290, 297, 301
"Kitchener's" Field Test, 309
Klerksdorp, 255-6, 277, 281-2, 288, 291-2, 297-8
Klip Drift, 291-2
Klipkrans, 275
Knellor Hall, Hounslow, 382-3
Knight, 2nd Lieut., 165
Knight, Lieut. P. H., 97
Knightley, Colour-Sergeant, 112
Knightley, Private J., 102
Knobel, Mr., 267
Knox, Sir C., 254
Koffee Kalkalli, 143
Kole Kone Redoubt, 175
Koodoesdrai, the, 294
Koodoesdrai Drift, 296
Koppiesfontein, 277
Kotkai, 207
Kourgané Hill, 73-4
Kowloon, 232

Krantz Drift, 297
Kritzinger's Commando, 298
Kromdraai Drift, 291-2
Kroonstadt, 291-2, 296
Kruger, Paul, 228
Krugersdorp, 243, 245, 253, 274-5, 300
Kudjwa, 107
Kurjowlee, 120
Kyouk Myoung, 179, 187, 190
Kyouksai, 183
Kyoungs, the, 182
Kyrke, 2nd Lieut. H. V. V., 228, 240, 242-5; wounded, 247, 248, 279, 283, 287, 298, 300
Kyrke, W. A. V., 215
Kyundoung, 192

Lace Diamond Mines, 291
Lachine Rapids, 42
Ladwgan Voll, Captain, and origin of wearing the leek, 206
Ladysmith, 229, 233-5, 237, 238
La Martinière, 110-1
Lamb, Private J., 102
Langewacht Spruit, 236
Langley Mills, Major B., R.A.M.C., 229
Lansdowne, Lord, 210
Lapfontein, 281
Law, Lieut. A. M., 97, 125
Lawless, Private J., 102
Lawrence, Lieut., 98
Lawrence, Major-General, 124
Lawrence, John, of Crick, 139
Leadbetter, Private J., killed, 241
Leck, Surgeon-Major, G. D. N., 173
Led, 208
Ledbrook, Private F., killed, 241
Lee, Private, 327
Lee-Enfield Rifle, 375
Leek, origin of wearing, 205
Lee-Metford Rifle, 375
Lees, Captain, 125
Leet, Paymaster-Major, 144
Leeward Command, 49
Legation Guard, Pekin, 295
Legge, Pioneer-Sergeant H. A., 287
Leighton, Major C. A. B. K., 221
Leiria, 18
Le Marchant, Lieut. E. T., 225
Le Marchant, Sir John Gaspard, 125, 134
Le Mesurier, Archdeacon, 125
Le Mesurier, Colonel, 179
Lens, 8
Leominster, 34
Lester, Colour-Sergeant, wounded, 119
L'Estrange, Major-General, 31
Lewis, Lieut., 98
Lewis, Private W., wounded, 197
Lichfield, 153, 300, 302-5, 387
Lichtenburg, 242-3, 276-7
Liddell, Colonel R. S., commands 23rd Regimental District, 201, 211
Liddington, 218
Liebenburg, General, 240, 252, 279, 280, 293
Liebig Extract Company's Cup, 298
Lieut. (2nd), rank of "Ensign" substituted for, 70

INDEX

Light Company added to Regiment, 346
Light Division, 1854, 70
Light Infantry Companies abolished, 122
Lightweight Competition, 330
Lillie, Lieut. T., 5
Lilliers, 8
Limerick, 9, 34
Lindsay, 2nd Lieut., 19
Linen Hall Barracks, Dublin, 154
Lines, Private W., 102
Liptrott, Lieut., 145
Lisbon, 17, 18, 19
"Little Inkerman," 82
Liverpool, 29, 37, 64, 65, 304, 323
Llama Temple, Pekin, 268
Llanberis, 213
Llanfair, 211, 212
Llanfair Hall, 212
Llanfor, Merioneth, 134
Llangerniew, 214
Llangollen, 215
Llanrwst, 214
Llewellyn, Private, 329
Llewellyn, Bandsman Herbert, 322
Llewellyn, Captain Hoel, South African Constabulary, 296
Llewellyn, Private J., 204
Lloyd, Lieut.-General Sir Francis, Colonel of the 23rd, 340
Lloyd, Captain G. W. D. B., 300; Major, 310-1
Lloyd, Private John, died of wounds, 119
Lloyd, 2nd Lieut. W., 224
Lloyd, Lieut. W. R., 5
Lloyd Griffith, Mr., 212
Local Senior League Football Challenge Cup, 387
Lock, Lieut., 7th Rajputs, 267
Locke, Captain J. L., 222
Lockett, Captain, 23
Lockett, Private J., killed, 251
Lockhart, Brigadier-General Sir W. S. A., 206
Lohunga, 107
London, 326
London, Canada West, 43, 48, 60, 66, 68
London, H.M.S., 99
London, Lord Mayor of, 214
Londonderry, 11, 12, 155, 157
Long, Colonel, 230-1
Longman, Private R., 102
Longmoor, 307
Long Valley, 150
Losack, J. (officer commanding), 397
Louis Napoleon, French Emperor, 69
Love, Colonel, 56
Lovett, Captain R. G. B., 228; Captain, mortally wounded, 241-2
Lower St. Elmo Barracks, Valetta, 125, 130-2
Lowman, Private G., 102
Lowry, Corporal Richard, 91
Luby, Corporal Edward, 75, 77, 91, 113
Lucknow, 107, 111, 115, 118-9, 122, 124, 130-1, 172, 186, 194, 196-8, 200-1, 204-5, 210, 386

Lucknow Army Cup, 388
Lucknow Residency, 107-8, 110-1
Ludlow, 33
Lumley, Major, 124
Luxford, Captain G. B., 144
Lyle, Lieut. H. T., 163, 165, 173, 184; Captain, wounded, 185, 196; Major, 223, 245, 250, 254-5, 275; Brevet Lieut.-Colonel, 279, 281, 287-8, 293; commands 2nd battalion, 303; relinquishes command, 308, 385-6, 398
Lynch, Private T., 102
Lysons, Lieut. C., 163, 173-4, 182; death, 186, 196, 221
Lysons, Captain D., 44; *Early Reminiscences*, 45, 47; Major, 64, 65, 66, 67, 69; lands with first British troops in Crimea, 72, 77; Lieut.-Colonel, commands 23rd, 79, 84, 85, 87, 89, 90; Brevet Colonel, 93, 94; severely wounded, 95, 96; commands 2nd Brigade, 97, 99, 101; relinquishes command of regiment, 104, 113; Major-General, 139, 159; General, 222, 397
Lyttelton, Major - General, 230, 233-4, 236, 240; General Rt. Hon. Sir Neville, 315, 323

McCarthy, Surgeon E. T., death, 150, 221
McCorey, Private J., 103
McCormick, Quartermaster, 144, 163, 165
McCrum, Private R., 102
McCue, Private J., death, 148, 150, 221
Macdonald, Sir Claude, 268
Macdonald, Paymaster J., 19
McEvoy, Private T., 102
McFarlane, Sergeant, death, 105
McGuire, Private Thomas, 9
Machavie, 288, 291-2
McKenzie, Major, 83
Mackenzie's Farm, 80
M'Leod, Colonel, 42nd Highlanders, 146
McMahon, Captain, Royal Fusiliers, 242
McMahon, Lieut. H. W., 212; Brevet Major Sir, 232, 295
McMahon, Private J., 103
McMahon, Major - General Sir Thomas, 27, 28, 404
McPherson, Private G., death, 150, 221
Maddick, 2nd Lieut. H., 228
Madeira, 106
Madoc, Major, South African Constabulary, 296
Madocks, Captain, 243-4, 246; Major, 278-9
Madocks Kopje, 247
Mafeking, 240, 242-3, 274
Mafra, 18, 19
Magaliesberg, 275
Magherafelt, 26
Maguire, Mr. James, 157
Mahaica, 42
Mahon, Colonel, 240; General, 242

Maida Barracks, Aldershot, 305
Maidan, Calcutta, 170
Mainwaring, Colonel C., 1st V.B. R. W. Fusiliers, 214
Mainwaring, Lieut. R. B., 71, 144, 148; *Historical Records*, 160, 163; Captain, 171, 173-4, 181; Major, 184-5, 194, 208, 212; Lieut.-Colonel, commands 2nd battalion, 220, 222, 224; Brevet Colonel, 232; relinquishes command, 232, 302, 398
Maitland, Lieut.-General, 160
Maiwand disaster, 160
Makranai, 207
Malabar (troopship), 138, 160, 162-3; H.M.S., 181
Malacca (transport), 224
Malakoff, the, 81, 90, 92, 94
Mallow, 9
Malone, Corporal E., 102
Malone, Sergeant H., 273
Maloney, Private J., 102
Malta, 69, 86, 98, 99, 125, 130, 132, 223-5, 328-9, 330-2, 395
"Mamelon," the, 92
Mamlet, Police-Sergeant, 327
Manchester, 29, 40, 219, 220, 222-3, 318
Mandalay, 176, 178-9, 180, 182-3, 187-8, 190, 195, 197
Mandalay B.P.A. Tournament, 388
Mandalay Detachment, 182
Mandalay Hill, 182
Manleh, 193
Mann, Captain, 56
Manning, Private Michael, 91
Man-of-War, co. Dublin, 11
Mansfield, Private, killed, 260
Mansi, 185-6
Manteik, 193
Mantell, Lieut. P. R., 173, 186-7, 190-1; Captain, 218, 228; commands 1st battalion, 240; wounded, 241-3; Major, 275, 281, 283, 287, 292, 297-8; commands 2nd battalion, 308; half-pay, 319, 398
Marchi Bawan, 117
Marckwiel Hall, Wrexham, 216
Maribogo, 242
Marlborough House, 162
Marsa Muscetto, 130
Marsh, Private H., 102
Marshall, Private J., 287
Martin, Sir Theodore, 216
Martin, Private W., 102
Martin, Private W., 102
Martini-Enfield Rifle, 375
Martini-Henry Rifle, 375
"Martinique" on Colours and appointments, 4
Mary (transport), 26, 27
Maryboro', 30
Maskell, Private P., 103
Mason, Private W., 102
Matao, 266
Mathers, Private, 193
Matheson, Captain, 19; Major, 32, 37, 41, 42, 43
Matiana (steamship), 227
Maurice, Private M., killed, 241
Mawlu, 192
Mayhew, Captain C. G. A., 163

II—27

INDEX

Maymyo Open Tournament, 388
Maymyo Tournament, 388
Maynard, Private J., wounded, 147
Medals, 376-7; Sardinian War, 113; Burmah Campaign, 200; Hazara Campaign, 217; South Africa and China, 299, 301
Medjidie, Imperial Order, recipients, 113
Meek, Private W., wounded, 231
Meerut, 106, 168, 299, 303, 305, 387
Mee Taw Goung, 188
Meeton, Private G., 103
Meiktila (Burma) Tournament, 388
Mellor, Sergeant F. R., wounded, 248, 287
Mellor, Private John, 331
Melville, H.M.S., 19, 105-6
Memorial Fund, 221
Menai Bridge, 212
"Men of Harlech," 331
Menschikoff, Prince, 70
Meredith-Jones, Captain, 291
Merioneth, 214
Merriow, 124
Merthyr Tydvil, 123, 226
Merza River, 193
Metford, Lieut., 120
Methold, Lieut. E., 5
Methuen, Lord, 244-5, 282
Meyer, Lucas, 233
Middelburg, 296
Middelburg Drift, 296
Middlemore, Lieut.-General G., 45
"Middle Ravine," 85
Middleweight Competition, Malta, 330
Milden, Private W., 102
Miles, Private J., 102
Milford, Lieut. C. H., 169; Captain, 212
Milford Haven, 140
Millbay, 223
Millbay Barracks, Plymouth, 164-5
Miller, Private P., killed, 245
Millett, Lieut. S. C., 82; wounded, 95, 101; Captain, 113; Major, 140, 144, 148; Brevet Colonel, death, 158
Millington, Private T., 102
Mills, Private G., 287
Milne, Captain James, 3, 9
Milntown Camp, Isle of Man, 303
Minden, 315
Minffordd, 213
Minffordd Junction, 213
Minhla, Fort, 174-5
Minie Rifle, 375
Modah, 181
Modderfontein, 274, 297
Modder River, 299
Modder Spruit, 234, 237-8
Mogoung, 184
Moinsey, 146
Molyneux, Private Joseph, 91
Monastir, 71
Monger, Band Boy George, awarded V.C., 109
Mongol Market, Pekin, 267
Monklands, 53, 59
Monmouth, 88
Monroe Challenge Cup, 323
Monsell, Lieut., 110; Captain, 119, 121, 135

Montargier, J. de P. de (officer commanding), 397
Monte Cristo, 233-5
Montmartre, 1
Monto, Colonel, 80
Montreal, 35, 38, 40, 42, 52, 53, 59, 60, 68, 136-7
Moo River, 188, 191
Mooi Kraal, 233
Mooi Kraal Hill, 234
Mooi River, 229, 250, 253, 257, 274-5, 283, 291
Moore, Quartermaster-Sergeant Garrett, appointed Quartermaster, 18, 34
Moore Park, 308
Morar Mow, 120
Morgan, Captain, 144, 148
Morgan, Private, 330
Morgan Jones, 2nd Lieut., 291
Morier, David (series of pictures), 344, 347
Morris, Private, wounded, 285
Morris, Private A., killed, 255
Morris, Assistant Surgeon Charles F., death, 130
Morris, Private E., killed, 296
Morris, Lieut. F., 163; Captain, 173, 179, 180, 186, 188, 190-1, 204; Major, 219, 258; wounded, 259, 271
Morris, Private G., 103
Morris, Sergeant G., 154
Mortality of 23rd in West Indies, 44
Mory, 1, 2
Mostyn, Lieut. Hon. Savage Lloyd, 88, 98; Major, 137; commands 2nd battalion, 139, 140, 144, 146-8; Colonel, 151, 153; half-pay, 164, 165; Major-General, 222; Sir, Colonel of Royal Welch Fusiliers, 313, 314, 317, 325-6, 328; death, 331-2; career, 339, 398
Motto, "Nec Aspera terrent" on Colours, 28
Mountain Ash, 226
Mount Austin Barracks, Hong-Kong, 232
Moyenneville, 1
Muchee Bawn, 130
Mulders Drift, 246
Mullingar, 142-3
Munster League Football Cup, 387
Murphy, Colour-Sergeant, 266
Murphy, James, Mayor of Newport, 139
Murphy, Sergeant-Major M., 313, 319, 321-32
Murray, Major-General H., 60
Murray, Private J., 103
Murray Barracks, Hong-Kong, 232, 272
Murray Pier, Hong-Kong, 271
Murrin, Private J. D., 103
Musa Bagh, 117-8
Music, 378-84
Music, Military School for, 382
Musketry, 1st battalion, Bengal, 201
Musson, Private E., 317
Myena, 184
Myit Ngay River, 176
Myngyan, 175, 178, 182-3
Myngyan, Prince, 183

Naas, 26
Naauwpoort, 275, 283, 286, 288
Naauwpoort Hill, 274
Nagode, 135-6
Nagpore, 136-7
Nahakoung, 193
Naini Tal, 221
Nangle, 2nd Lieut. F. H., 228, 243; Lieut., 253; wounded, 255, 287, 299
Nanpara, 124
Nantclwyd Hall, 215
Napier, General Lord, of Magdala, 154
Napier, Major-General Sir, 37, 38
Nasmyth, Private J., 102
Natal, 229, 240
National Library, Dublin, 341
Naval Hill, 235-6
Navan, 142
Naylor Leyland, Mrs. 215
Neal, Private W., 102
"Nec aspera terrent," 344-5, 393
Nerbudda (transport), 172-3
Neville, Private T., 103
Newbridge, 37
Newcastle-under-Lyme, 29, 33
Newman, Sergeant J., 84
Newnes, Lance-Corporal, 257
Newport, 10, 22, 86, 104, 113, 123-4, 137-9, 140-1, 225-6
Newry, 25
New University, Carnarvon, opening, 317
Nicholas, Czar of Russia, 69
Nicholas Water, 277
Nichols, Private G., 102
Nile Expedition, 1898, 226
Nisbett, Colonel Parry, 210
Nixon, Private Frederic, 91
Nolan, Private J., killed, 247-8
Norman, Major C., 203, 205; commands 1st battalion, 208; relinquishes command, 220; Colonel, 227, 398
Norman, 2nd Lieut. C. C., 288; Lieut., wounded, 237, 280, 296
Norman, Brigadier-General F. B., 172, 174-5, 179, 185
Norris, Captain, 172
North, Private J., wounded, 147
North Barracks, Deal, 4
North Barracks, Limerick, 9
Northbrook, R.I.M.S., 308
North Camp, Aldershot, 143
North China Football Cup, 387
North Front, Gibraltar, 154
North Lines, Shwebo, 309
North Wall, Dublin, 317, 325
Norton, Captain C. G. C., 97, 107, 118, 120
Notmen, Sergeant C., 273
Nottingham, 29
Nova Scotia, 32, 404
Nowgong, 218-9, 220, 222, 386
Nowshera, 210, 218, 386
"No. 3 Company's Guns," 112
Nuggur, 121
Nunan, Private W., 102

Oakmere, 305
O'Beirne, Private John, 86, 91
O'Brien, Private T., 102
O'Brien's Bridge, 11

INDEX

Ocean, H.M.S., 19
O'Connor, Sergeant Luke, commissioned and awarded V.C., 75, 77, 91; wounded, 95, 101, 105-6, 113; Brevet Major, 144; Brevet Colonel, commands 2nd battalion, 164, 167; half-pay, 180; Major-General, 318, 327-9; Colonel of Regiment, 332; career, 339-40, 398
Odessa, 84
O'Donohue, Corporal Thomas, 91
Officers Commanding Royal Welch Fusiliers, 1689-1914, 397-8
O'Flaherty, Captain F., 9
Oghi, 206, 209
O'Gorman, Colonel, 271
Oldcastle, 142
Old Comrades Association, H.M. The King becomes Patron, 328
Old Gwalior, 218
"Old Redoubt," 84
Oliphant's Nek, 275
O'Loghlin, Major-General, 9
Olympia (steamship), 300
Omar Pacha, 71
O'Neil, Dr., 265
Ontario (transport), 164
Ontario, Lake, 60, 68
Ordah River, 147
Ordahsu, 147
Orford Barracks, Warrington, 318
Oriental (steamship), 228
Orinoco (transport), 69
Orontes, H.M.S., 134, 136, 138
Ortona (transport), 299
Osborne, Drummer, 319
Osborne House, 67, 162
Osborne (Royal yacht), 162-3
Osmond Williams, Mr. W., 213
Oswestry, 327
Oswestry Grammar School, 216
Ottawa, 88
Oughterard, 200
Ouseley, Sir J. G., 378
Outpost Hill, 249
Outram, Major-General Sir James, 111, 115-8
Owen, Lieut. C. S., 258, 262, 271, 273
Owen, Ensign W., 98
Owen, Lieut. W., mortally wounded, 93, 100, 102
Owens, Private, wounded, 260
Owens, Private F., 102
Owens, Private John, 91
Owens, Private T., 102
Oxford, 33, 34, 54, 88, 113, 123

Pack, Ensign G., 104
Pagan, 175
Painting, Private J., 102
Pakenham, Major-General Sir Hercules, 41
Palk, Lieut., 144
Pall Mall, 316
Palmietfontein, 277-8, 282, 297
Palosi, 207, 209
Palow, 180
Panji Gali, 209
Parady's Kop, 291-2
Parke, Major-General, 143
Parker, Sergeant-Major, wounded, 251, 287; Lieut. and Quartermaster, 316.

Parkhurst Barracks, Isle of Wight, 41, 47, 65, 67, 68
Parry, Lieut., 238
Parry, Lieut. G., 154
Parry, 2nd Lieut. M. D. G., 315, 317
Paterson, Private P., 102
Patiala All India Boxing Cup, 387
Patience, 277
Patrickson, Lieut.-Colonel, 8
Patterson, Quartermaster-Sergeant, 269
Patterson, J. (officer commanding), 397
Paulet, Major General Lord William, 99
Payne, Private C., 102
Payne, Sergeant Y., 273
Peace concluded at Vereeniging, 297
Pearce, Lance-Sergeant, wounded, 260-1
Pearce, Private, 86
Pearson, Captain, 77
Pearson, Mrs., 17
Pearson, Lieut.-Colonel Thomas, commands the 23rd, 5, 6, 8-15 18; Major-General, 20, 32, 397
Peel, Captain William, R.N., 107, 114
Peers, Newsham (officer commanding), 397
Peiho River, 262-6
Pei-Tsang, 263-4
Pei-Yang arsenal, 259
Pekin, 257, 259, 266-9, 270-2, 295
Pembroke Camp Barracks, 131, 133
Pembroke Dock, 141, 143, 167, 169, 170, 221, 227-8
Penally, 141
Peninsula, 8
Pennyfather, M. (officer commanding), 397
Penrhyndeudraeth, 213
Perkins, Major-General Æneas, R.E., 204
Perkins, Private C., 102
Perkins, Private H., 102
Perry-Knox-Gore, Lieut. W. H. C., 316-7
Perseverance, H.M.S., 125
Peshawar, 204-5, 209, 210, 386
Peter, J. (officer commanding), 397
Peyton, General, 321
Phaten, 184
Phibbs, Lieut. W., 144, 146; wounded, 147; Captain, 148
Philips, Captain B. H., 212, 218, 224
Phillips, 2nd Lieut. H. J., 292, 297, 299
Phillips, 2nd Lieut. J. Lort, 22
Phillips, Lieut. Peregrine, 47
Phillips, 2nd Lieut. R. N., 298
Phillips, Private W., death, 148, 150, 221
Phillott, Captain, 52, 53, 60-3
Phipps, Colonel, 66
Phœnix Park, Dublin, 315-6, 323-4
Picton, 35
Piet de la Rey, 247
Pietermaritzburg, 229
Pieter's Hill, 237
Pigeon House Fort, 11

Pigott, Lieut. G. E., 212
Pike, Private S., killed, 237
Pilcher, Brigadier-General T. O., 306
Pillgwenlly, 17
Pinden, 189
Pirbright, 324
Pishin Valley, Baluchistan, 171
Pitt, Private, wounded, 260
Plant, Private G., 102
Platt, Colonel, 317
Plenderleath, Private J., wounded, 197
Plymouth, 16, 19, 22, 59, 60, 64, 125, 138, 143, 164, 167, 386
Point Levis, 137
Pole, E. S. (officer commanding), 397
Polo Cristo, 131
Polo Tournament, Delhi Durbar, 320
Pont au Callière Barracks, Montreal, 35
Poole, Lieut. W. H., 82, 86, 88, 90; Captain, dies of wounds, 95, 100, 102
Poonah, 112, 114, 120-1, 137
Port Carlisle, 38
Porter, Private (No. 3644), killed, 260
Porter, Private (No. 4014), killed, 260
Portglenone, 25, 26
Portland, 325, 327, 329, 331-2, 387
Portmadoc, 213
Port Maitland, 60
Portobello Barracks, Dublin, 31
Portsmouth, 27, 28, 41, 52, 59, 68, 105, 113, 125, 137-8, 142-3, 148-9, 151, 160, 218, 395, 404
Portugal, 16
Potchefstroom, 243-4, 250, 255-7, 283-4, 288, 291, 298-9
Povey, Private D., 102
Powell, 2nd Lieut. D., 228; Lieut., 298
Powell, Private J., 102
Powell, Lieut. S., 18
Power, Private, killed, 259
Powis, Lord, 166-7
Prah River, 146
Pratt, Lieut.-Colonel R., 105-7, 116; commands 23rd, 118, 120; Colonel, 137-8; half-pay, 140, 398
Praya, the, Hong-Kong, 271
Prendergast, Major-General Sir H., 172, 176-7, 179
Prescott, Canada, 41
Presentation, silver kettle to 2nd battalion, 139; silver inkstand, 139; silver shield and chain to 1st battalion, 304
Presentation of Colours, Delhi Durbar, 320
Presentation of portraits, Delhi Durbar, 322
Pretoria, 246, 252, 256, 288-9, 298
Prevost, Lieut. G. P., wounded, 95, 98, 101; Captain, wounded, 116, 118-9, 125, 153; Lieut.-Colonelcy of 1st Battalion, 139, 140, 143; half-pay, 159, 160, 398

INDEX

Price, Lieut., 245, 248, 283
Price, Lieut. Sir F. Rose, 286, 288
Price, Private J., 287
Price, Private W., 102
Prime, Captain, 56
Prince Consort, 54, 99
Prince Consort's Library, Aldershot, 345
Prince Edward's Island, 50
Prince Ferdinand of Brunswick, 7
Prince Moung Hmat, 187-9
Prince of Orange (transport), 15
Prince of Wales, visits Malta, 132; Gibraltar, 154; presents new Colours, 160-3; Colonel-in-Chief of Royal Welch Fusiliers, 1901, 294, 295, 305-7; Investiture at Carnarvon, 317
Prince of Wales' Feathers, 28, 344-5, 347, 351-3, 358-9, 360-3, 365, 367-8
Princess Mary, 316
Princess Regent of Portugal, 16, 18
Prince The-Tang-Thit, 189
Prinsloo, 245
Pritchard, Lieut. T. L., 298
Probyn, General Sir Dighton, 162
Prome, 195
Prouvy, 5
Prussia and France, war declared 1870, 140
Pruth River, 70
Pulter, Abraham, 296
Pulu (steamship), 187, 194-5
Purcell, Tobias (officer commanding), 397
Purcell, Major Toby, 40
Purchas, Captain, South Wales Borderers, 284-6
Purnell, Brigadier, 122
Putfontein, 277-8
Pwllheli, 213

"Quarries," the, 92
Quebec, 35, 41, 42, 68, 136
Quebec (steamer), 136
Queen of the South (steamer), 88
Queen's Birthday, Review at Scutari, 70
Queen's Road Barracks, Hong-Kong, 232
Queenstown, 144, 153, 170, 181, 205
Queen Street, Cardiff, 324
Quetta, 318-9, 325-6, 331, 388
Quetta Boxing Challenge Shield, 387
Quisa, 146

Racquingham, 8
Radcliffe, 2nd Lieut., 60; Lieut., 79, 90, 93
Radcliffe, Lieut. H. D., 98; wounded, 101
Rademeyer, G., 296
Radford, Private, wounded, 261
Raglan, Lieut.-General Lord, 72, 73, 76, 79, 80, 84, 85, 88, 89, 92; death, 93
Raglan Barracks, Devonport, 138, 226, 406
Railway Hill, 237
Rainey, Lieut.-General Henry, Colonel of 23rd, 92, 122; death, 125; career, 336
Rait, Major, R.A., 147

Ramganga, 114
Rana Banee Madho, 121-2
Randall, Private C., 102
Ranfield, Private G., wounded, 197
Rangoon, 172-3, 178, 186, 195, 308, 313-4, 318
Rank, "Ensign" substituted for "2nd Lieut.," 70; "Sub-lieut." substituted for "Ensign," 141
Ransom, Quartermaster-Sergeant R. S., 201-2, 204; Lieut. and Quartermaster, 228, 287
Rawal Pindi, 205
Raynes, Captain R. T., 68, 88, 98, 104
Reading, 113
"Redan," the, Sevastopol, 81, 92, 94, 97, 102
"Redan Lysons," 96
Redding, Private J., 103
Red Dragon Cup, 388-90
Red Dragon Cup Meeting, 386-7
"Red Dragon" on the Colours, 28, 219
Redman, Lance-Corporal, 330
Red Sea, 163
Reed, Private S., 103
Rees, Private E., wounded, 197
Rees, Corporal Thomas, 91
Reese, Private T., 103
Regent's Park East, 316
Regimental Calendar, 326
Regimental Costume and Equipment, 341, 373
Regimental School, 6
"Regimental Sergeant-Major" becomes Warrant Officer, 167
Regiments, etc.

CAVALRY, YEOMANRY, ETC.

5th Dragoon Guards, 56
6th Dragoon Guards, 14, 114, 122
8th Hussars, 80
9th Lancers, 118
10th Light Dragoons, 17
11th Hussars, 80
12th Light Dragoons, 17
14th Hussars, 274
Denbighshire Hussars, 215
Dorsetshire Yeomanry, 284
Dundonald's Mounted Troops, 230, 233-4
Imperial Light Horse, 251, 253-4, 274, 284-5
Imperial Yeomanry, 19th Company, 249
Inniskilling Dragoons, 320
King's Dragoon Guards, 320
Kitchener's Horse, 278-9, 280
Lothian and Berwick Company, Scottish Imperial Yeomanry, 243
Marshall's Horse, 249, 250
Roberts' Horse, 280
South African Constabulary, 293, 296-7

ARTILLERY

"P" Battery, R.H.A., 278
7th Battery, R.F.A., 230
12th Battery, R.F.A., 263
16th Battery, R.F.A., 231
28th Battery, R.F.A., 240

Regiments (*continued*):

ARTILLERY (*continued*)

44th Battery, R.F.A., 231
61st Howitzer Battery, R.F.A., 234
78th Battery, R.F.A., 240, 243-4, 247-9, 250, 279, 281, 284
No. 1, Mountain Battery, R.A., 206
No. 4, Mountain Battery, R.A., 225
No. 9, Mountain Battery, R.A., 206-7, 209
Cheshire and Carnarvon Artillery Volunteers, 212
Cinque Ports Division, R.A., 2nd Brigade, 9th Battery, 174, 178-9, 190-1
Hong-Kong Artillery, 263

ENGINEERS

No. 7 Company, R.E., 291
"C" Pontoon Troop, R.E., 291

FOOT GUARDS

1st Foot Guards, 17
3rd Foot Guards, 17
Coldstream Guards, 151; 3rd battalion, 328
Grenadier Guards, 38
Scots Guards, 288

MOUNTED INFANTRY

2nd Mounted Infantry, 229, 276
7th Mounted Infantry, 298-9
8th Mounted Infantry, 278
Gloucester Mounted Infantry, 274
Thorneycroft's Mounted Infantry, 235

INFANTRY REGIMENTS

1st Royals, 5
3rd, 5
4th, 17, 18
5th, 5, 130
6th, 170
7th Fusiliers, 3, 8, 18, 69, 70, 71, 77, 78, 93, 99, 145
8th, 81, 144
10th, 17, 18
11th, 17
12th, 144
14th, 57, 114, 123
19th, 53, 70, 74
20th, 60, 117, 120
21st Royal North British Fusiliers, 140-2, 145
24th, 130
27th, 144
33rd Duke of Wellington's, 70, 93, 99
35th, 131, 144
37th, 130
38th, 112
42nd Highlanders, 144, 146-7
43rd Light Infantry, 3, 5, 8, 17
52nd Light Infantry, 5, 52
53rd, 108, 114
54th, 148
56th, 40

INDEX

Regiments (*continued*):
  INFANTRY (*continued*)
  57th, 144
  60th, 17, 18
  62nd, 92
  63rd, 17
  64th, 130
  66th, 40
  67th, 40
  68th, 40, 46
  70th, 40
  71st Light Infantry, 59
  73rd, 130
  77th, 53, 70, 91
  78th, 11
  79th, 114, 115, 117-8
  80th, 120-1, 151
  82nd, 108, 114
  85th Light Infantry, 5, 12
  88th, 70, 79, 92, 119
  89th, 50
  90th Light Infantry, 92, 99
  91st Highlanders, 5, 135
  93rd Highlanders, 108, 110
  95th, 74
  97th, 52, 93
  104th Fusiliers, 145
  108th, 137
  Anglesey Volunteers, 212
  Bedfordshire Regiment, 2nd battalion, 323
  Black Watch, 321
  Border Regiment, 2nd battalion, 298
  Buffs, The, 1st battalion, 314, 323
  Cheshire Regiment, 2nd battalion, 298
  1st Chinese Regiment, 263
  Derbyshire Regiment, 257
  Devon Regiment, 236
  Durham Light Infantry, 1st battalion, 218
  East Surrey Regiment, 236
  Essex Regiment, 318
  1st European Bengal Fusiliers (now Royal Munster Fusiliers), 114, 116-7
  Highland Light Infantry, 227
  Hong-Kong Regiment, 263
  King's Liverpool Regiment, 179, 386
  King's Own Light Infantry, 191
  King's Royal Rifles, 1st battalion, 206
  Loyal North Lancashire Regiment, 280, 284-5; 1st battalion, 327
  Middlesex Regiment, 2nd battalion, 330
  Monmouth Militia, 90
  Montgomeryshire Militia, 99
  Norfolk Regiment, 2nd battalion, 299
  Northumberland Fusiliers, 210, 276, 386
  Oxfordshire and Buckinghamshire Light Infantry, 288, 291, 296-7
  Queen's, The, 236
  Rifle Brigade, 2nd battalion, 70, 114, 144
  Royal Canadian Rifles, 68

Regiments (*continued*):
  INFANTRY (*continued*)
  Royal Fusiliers, 2nd battalion, 229, 230, 233, 235-6, 240-1; 1st battalion, 314, 320
  Royal Irish Fusiliers, 2nd battalion, 230-1, 235, 240-1, 318, 320
  Royal Marines, 162
  Royal Scots, 323
  Royal Scots Fusiliers, 195; 2nd battalion, 229, 230-1, 235, 240, 243-5, 248-9, 250, 253-5
  Royal Welch Fusiliers, 1st Volunteer Battalion, 214; 3rd battalion, 214; 2nd Volunteer Company, 291
  Royal West Kent Regiment, 323
  Ruthin Volunteers, 215
  Seaforth Highlanders, 2nd battalion, 206; 1st battalion, 225
  Somerset Light Infantry, 255, 276; 2nd battalion, 299
  South Down Militia, 99
  South Wales Borderers, 227
  West Yorkshire Regiment, 1st battalion, 218
  Wiltshire Regiment, 2nd battalion, 218, 317; 1st battalion, 218
  Wrexham Volunteer Companies, 216

  INDIAN CAVALRY
  1st Bengal Lancers, 262
  11th Bengal Lancers, 206
  Hodson's Horse, 120
  2nd Madras Cavalry, 188-9, 190-1

  INDIAN ARTILLERY
  No. 2 Derajat Mountain Battery, R.A., 206
  Hazara Mountain Battery, 175, 179, 184-5, 193

  INDIAN ENGINEERS
  Bengal Sappers and Miners, 183, 184-5, 193, 206, 209

  INDIAN INFANTRY
  2nd Bengal Infantry, 175
  5th Bengal Light Infantry, 190, 192-3
  7th Bengal Infantry, 262
  11th Bengal Infantry, 175, 206, 208-9
  19th Bengal Infantry, 206
  27th Bengal Infantry, 206
  28th Bengal Infantry, 209
  32rd Bengal Infantry, 206
  37th Dogras, 206
  Guides Infantry, 206-7
  1/1st Gurkhas, 209
  5th Gurkhas, 206-9
  Khyber Rifles, 206-9
  1st Madras Pioneers, 175
  12th Madras Infantry, 188-9, 190
  21st Madras Light Infantry, 191
  23rd Madras Infantry, 178-9
  25th Madras Infantry, 184
  2nd Native Infantry, 170

Regiments (*continued*):
  INDIAN INFANTRY (*continued*)
  12th Native Infantry, 170
  17th Native Infantry, 170
  32nd Pioneers, 207, 209
  2nd Punjaub Infantry, 116, 118
  4th Punjaub Infantry, 112
  19th Punjaub Infantry, 205
  24th Punjaub Infantry, 263
  26th Punjaub Infantry, 186, 193
  7th Rajputs, 263, 266
  1st Sikhs, 262, 267
  4th Sikhs, 206-7, 209
  36th Sikhs, 321
  Dinapore Regiment, 107
  Ferozepore Regiment of Sikhs, 117

  AMERICAN
  7th American Infantry, 261

  FRENCH
  26th, 4
  82nd, 4

  RUSSIAN
  Vladimir, 76

Reid, Captain D., 130
Reitzburg, 288
Remington, Captain, 108
Rensburg Drift, 254
Rentoul, Captain, 10
Resistance, H.M.S., 41, 42
Resolute, dashed to pieces in Balaklava Harbour, 85
Rewa (troopship), 329, 330
Reycroft, Private T., 103
Reynolds, Lieut., 288, 292, 293
Reynolds, 2nd Lieut. A. H., 228, 243
Rhenoster Kop, 292
Rhenoster River, 291-2
Rhenosterspruit, 282
Rice, Major, R.E., 289
Rice, Lieut. G. W., 33, 34
Richards, Mrs. (Caerynwch), 213
Richards, Ensign H. J., death, 119
Richards, Lieut. H. M., 212; Captain, 258, 262, 269, 271, 273
Richards, Private R., 103
Richardson, Private, wounded, 260
Richmond Barracks, Dublin, 13
Rickford, Captain, 50
Rickman, Lieut. G. E., 224-5; Captain, 229, 231, 234, 287-8
Ridge, the, Antigua, 49
Rifle, Snider, newly issued, 136
Rietfontein, 274, 278, 280
Rietfontein Spruit, 278, 285
Rietkuil, 281
Rietpan, 280
Ril, 207
Riley, Sergeant E., wounded, 248
Ripon, Lord, 170
"Rising Sun" on the Colours, 28, 219
Robert Clive, 95
Roberts, Corporal, wounded, 237
Roberts, Mr. (Mayor of Ruthin), 215
Roberts, Private D., wounded, 197
Roberts, Sir F. S., 182, 200; Field Marshal Lord, 240, 245, 248, 255, 286, 300-1